Stephanie Armentrout

# Western Civilization: A Brief History

ROBIN W. WINKS
*Yale University*

# Western Civilization: A Brief History

**COLLEGIATE PRESS**

Copyright © 1988 by Collegiate Publishing Company

All rights reserved under International and Pan-American Copyright Conventions. No part of this book may be reproduced in any form or by any means, electronic or mechanical, including photocopying, without permission in writing from the publisher. All inquiries should be addressed to Collegiate Press, 8840 Avalon Street, Alta Loma, CA 91701. Telephone: (619) 697-4182.

Library of Congress Catalog Card Number: 88-71785

ISBN 0-939693-05-4

Printed in the United States of America

Cover design: Paul Slick

# Contents

Introduction: The Relevance of History   1

## PART ONE
## Human Societies and Civilizations: Beginnings   9

An Overview: Beginnings   11

I. 1 Recoverable History Begins: People of River and Plain   16

*The Tool-Maker   17*
*The Beginnings of Agriculture   17*
*Primitive Trade   20*
*Priestly Castes   21*
*Tigris-Euphrates Dominance   22*
*The Nile   23*
*Continuity and Change: Climate   24*

I. 2 On the Edge of the Earliest Civilizations:
     The Spread of Influences   26

I. 3 Desert, Mountain, and Forest: Civilization and Barbarism in the
     Second Millenium B.C.   30

*Migrants and Invaders: Mycenae   31*
*The Hebrews   32*
*The Sea Peoples   33*

I. 4 An Age of Heroes:
     The Beginnings of Mediterranean Antiquity   35

*Legendary History of Israel   36*
*Zoroastrianism   39*
*Greece   40*

# PART TWO
# Mediterranean Antiquity: 500 B.C.–A.D. 750  *47*

An Overview: Our Greco-Roman World   49

II. 1 Greek Society and the Origins of Hellenistic Culture   53

*Sparta   54*
*Athens   55*

II. 2 Challenge and Response: The Golden Age of Greece   61

*The Persian Challenge   61*
*The Polis   63*
*Socrates, Plato, Aristotle   66*
*Decline of the Athenian Empire   68*
*Alexander the Great   70*

II. 3 From the *Polis* to the World: Hellenistic Civilization in the Mediterranean and Near East   72

*Interdependence   75*
*Ptolemaic Egypt   77*
*Palestine   78*

II. 4 A World Expands: The Rise of Rome   82

*Old Cultures, New Locus   82*
*The Origins of Rome   85*
*Intellectual Life   91*
*Toward a World State   93*
*The Beginnings of Christianity   100*

II. 5 The Crisis of Late Antiquity: Transformation of the Mediterranean World   103

*Diocletian and Constantine   105*
*The Decline of Rome   106*
*Barbarian Invasions   108*
*Byzantium   111*
*The Arab Peoples: At the Gates of the West   114*
*The Problem of Security   118*

# PART THREE
# Traditional Europe: A.D. 750–1789  *121*

An Overview: The Part We Call "the Middle"   123

III. 1  Regional Resources and Universal Ambitions: 750–950   127

*Constantinople and Cosmopolitanism  128*
*Islamic Culture  130*
*Germanic Europe and the Western Frontier  134*
*Growth of Christianity  135*
*Monasticism  136*
*Ascendency of the West  139*
*Charlemagne  143*
*New Invaders: On the Edge of Civilization  145*

III. 2  The Making of Europe: 950–1300   147

*The Idea of Europe  148*
*Security from Without: An End to non-European Invaders  150*
*An Agricultural Revolution  151*
*Warlord-Protectors: Territorial Principalities  153*
*The Dictates of Geography  155*
*Ecclesiastical Change  156*
*The Crusades: The West Strikes Back  159*

III. 3  Crisis and Recovery in Traditional Europe: 1300–1715   164

*From Village to Urban Life  164*
*Demographic Change  167*
*Rise of the Monarchies  169*
*The Papacy  172*
*Threats from New Invaders  174*
*The Renaissance  175*
*The Reformation  181*

III. 4  A New World in the Making: Modern Europe   190

*The Age of Discovery  191*
*The Bases of Expansion  194*
*Early Capitalism  196*
*Mercantilism  202*
*Scientific and Technological Developments  205*
*Political Organization  207*
*The Early Leadership: Portugal and Spain  208*
*France, Holland, and England  215*
*The Great War for Empire  219*
*The Modern State  221*

III. 5 The Modern Revolution in the West  228

    *The Enlightenment  228*
    *Changing Societies  232*
    *The Industrial Revolution  234*
    *The French Revolution: The Problem of Historiography  236*

III. 6 Restructuring Power and Society: 1715–1815  243

    *An Afterview: Transition and the French Revolution  243*

# PART FOUR
# No Break With the Past—The Nineteenth Century in Perspective  *251*

    An Overview: The Age of the Democratic Revolution  253

IV. 1 From Revolution to Revolution, 1789–1848  257

    *The Conservative Reaction  257*
    *The New Revolutions  260*

IV. 2 The Enduring Ideas: Finding Theoretical Bases for Security  264

IV. 3 The Surge of Nationalism: Postponement  268

IV. 4 Secular Attempts to Control Human Destiny  272

    *Socialism  272*
    *Marxism  276*
    *The Classical Economists  279*

IV. 5 Darwin and Darwinism: Salvation Through Science  282

    *Social Darwinism  284*

IV. 6 Europe's New Nations: Nationalism Triumphant, 1848–1914  288

    *Italy  288*
    *Germany  292*

## PART FIVE
## New Wine in Old Bottles: Today Enters the Front Door, 1848–1919  *301*

      An Overview: An Age of Insecurity   303

  V. 1  The Politics of Europe's Traditional Powers, 1848–1914   310

*Great Britain   315*
*Austria-Hungary   319*
*Russia   327*

  V. 2  A Century in Search of Security: Society and Growth   333

*The European Century   333*
*A Countercurrent: Decline of the West?   337*
*Expansion of the West: Imperialism   341*
*Nonrational Impulses to Empire   345*
*Did Colonies Pay?   350*
*Non-Western Responses to the West   353*
*The Balance Sheet   359*
*The British Empire   360*
*From Colony to Nation   364*
*American and Russian Expansionism   368*
*The New Imperialism   374*

  V. 3  The First World War: Causes, Conduct, Consequences   377

*The Window on the Sea   378*
*The Boer War   380*
*Secret Alliance Systems   381*
*The Art of Postponement   382*
*The Balkans: Tinderbox for War   384*
*Hurtling Toward War   387*
*The Balkan League   388*
*The War: Chance and History   392*
*Who's Responsible?   395*
*The Fronts   395*
*In Europe   397*
*The Home Front   402*
*Bringing America Into the War   403*
*The Collapse of the Powers   405*
*New Weapons, New Ways   408*
*The Peace   412*

# PART SIX
# The Years That Became Ours: 1919 to the 1980s  *415*

An Overview  417

VI. 1 The Hidden Political Collapse of Europe  419

*From Depression to War  419*
*The Soviet Union: Communism  422*
*The Rise of Fascism  426*

VI. 2 The Second World War: An Era of Continuous War for Continuous Peace  431

*Origins  431*
*The War  436*

VI. 3 The West Since 1945  443

*Pointing to the Future  443*
*The Cold War  446*
*International Organizations  452*
*The End of Empires  455*
*Time of Danger, Time of Challenge  460*
*Emerging Social Issues  462*

Epilogue  467

When You Want to Read More  473

Index  491

# Preface

All textbooks are unique, of course, for all bear the stamp of their individual author's approach to subject matter. This book differs from other textbooks on Western Civilization in several regards. It is my conviction that today's students read history largely to account to themselves for why they are as they are, and why the world in which they live is as they find it. To help readers toward these goals, I have placed particular emphasis on those developments which most directly explain the nature of the modern world: social diffusion, group and national consciousness, technological change, religious identities—those aspects of intellectual history that have contributed most (and most directly) to our current dilemmas. In turn this means that there is more in my textbook about nationalism, or imperialism, or ethnic identities than there is about monarchies, feudalism, or diplomacy. While I do not care for the word "relevant" because of the fashionable, not to say faddish, connotations thrust onto the word by those who do not see that history is a process, a growth, I do consider that the guiding principles behind this book have been designed to provide the reader with the information and argumentation most necessary (and in that sense most relevant) to an understanding of how History has led us from There to Here.

The result of the strategic and intellectual decisions made with respect to this textbook is that its proportions are not the customary ones. Particular emphasis is placed on the early origins of civilizations, on Greece and Rome, and on the period of the so-called barbarian invasions, because it is by studying these periods that students may best learn how societies are formed. Particular emphasis is also placed on the period from the French

Revolution, for it is the events of the last two hundred years that have most closely shaped our present condition. Throughout the text emphasis is placed on humankind's search for security, whether of a physical or a spiritual nature, and it is this theme of the struggle to achieve security that binds the diverse subject matter together. One end in mind is to lead the reader to think as the historian thinks, to be able to apply the historian's long view to today's headlines.

This book also was written to be read. This does not mean that it should not be studied. There is a distinction, however: some textbooks are constructed deliberately to invite careful underscoring of factual data and massive memorization. It is my conviction that, while the work of memory is essential to history, students often confuse memorization with understanding, and that many textbooks encourage this confusion by their construction and their style. I would hope this book can be read, straight through and in its entirety, as an interpretive statement about Western history written by a person who knows a good bit about non-Western history, and who can thus throw into perspective the unusual, the commonplace, and the comparable in that sector of history conventionally labeled "Western." While the book is to be used as a text as well, serving all the customary functions, I hope that it will help the student to see that history is not a body of data to be memorized; rather, history is a set of arguments to be debated. The book draws upon over thirty years of discovering, in the classroom, what students themselves wish to ask about the past rather than what a body of good and greying scholars may have concluded they should wish to ask.

To this end I have had much help, of course. I want in particular to thank Professors Edward Peters of the University of Pennsylvania and Joachim Remak of the University of California, Santa Barbara, for helping enormously with early drafts of the text; without them this book would not have been possible. For reading and reacting to sections relating to their own areas of special competence, I wish to thank my colleagues at Yale, Jeremy Y. deQ. Adams (now of Southern Methodist University), Raymond Kierstead (now at Reed College), Ramsay MacMullen, and Henry A. Turner, Jr. The world's worst handwriting was deciphered by Ms. Rose Esposito, who typed the manuscript. My wife, Avril, helped enormously with the proof-reading; my children, Honor Leigh and Eliot, kept me moving toward completion by reminding me of how many hours I was spending away from them, and by reacting to sections of the text. None of the above are in any way responsible for any errors that remain, of course—and no one can be a historian for long without learning that such errors will occur. This text was first published by Prentice-Hall, where I had much help from the editor, Robert Fenyo.

The book has been updated to appear in its new form, and I am grateful to the staff of Collegiate Press for making this possible.

When deciding what to record in history, one must always interrogate the material with three questions: Is it true? Is it interesting? Is it significant? All these people helped me to put these three questions to my text, as I now put them to my readers.

*Maps and illustrations.* The maps and illustrations in this text are to be studied in direct conjunction with it; the captions to the latter extend the argument of the text and cannot be omitted from the study. As historians know, one cannot grasp the flow of history without a clear mental image of the landscape across which the flow takes place. Most of these maps have been adapted from those originally created by Vincent Kotschar for *A History of Civilization,* by Crane Brinton, John B. Christopher, and Robert Lee Wolff (5th ed., Englewood Cliffs, N.J.: Prentice-Hall, Inc., 1976), and they are reprinted here by permission. Through them the reader may create his or her own mental maps. I have also been fortunate in being able to walk over the ground of much of the history described in the pages that follow; descriptions are informed by personal visits to the sites, and in some instances I have used my own photographs for the illustrations.

ROBIN W. WINKS<br>
June 1988

*Man Thinking; him Nature solicits with all her placid, all her monitory pictures; him the past instructs; him the future invites. Is not indeed every man a student, and do not all things exist for the student's behoof? And, finally, is not the true scholar the only true master? But the old oracle said, 'All things have two handles: beware of the wrong one.'*—Ralph Waldo Emerson, "The American Scholar" Phi Beta Kappa address, 1837

# Introduction: The Relevance of History

> *The past is but the beginning of a beginning, and all that is and has been is but the twilight of the dawn.*—H. G. Wells, *The Discovery of the Future*, 1901

Every year on the bathing beaches of France, some twenty people—usually children and teenagers—are killed by buried land mines and unexploded naval shells. Even though more than two generations have passed since World War II, and nearly four generations since World War I, fully half the deaths on those French beaches result from undiscovered ammunition left buried these many years. The young people killed may have thought such distant wars irrelevant to them, but events have a way of reminding us that they continue to work their effects on our lives—and deaths. These instruments of destruction are among the many visible reminders of our past.

Each day we live enveloped in history as we are enveloped in the air we breathe. Many survive the day, knowing nothing of either air or history. Others enjoy their days more because they know something of why they and their community or country are as they are. To this degree, one of the delights of history is that it satisfies simple curiosity. It adds to our sense of who we are and why we do what we do.

Every person, every field of knowledge, has a history. Medical science grows from the discoveries, inventions, and mistakes of yesterday. The desire to build the Panama Canal led to the discovery of the cause of yellow fever. Experiments with cough medicine produced Coca-Cola. Britain's desire to occupy strategic river mouths in West Africa led to the development of tropical medicine and to the discovery that fever is a symptom rather than a cause of disease, thus reversing a long-held set of assumptions about cause and effect in health.

Slowly, the conventional wisdom of one generation is displaced by new insights, which in turn become conventionally accepted themselves, only to be displaced yet again by further discoveries and additions to human knowledge. Those who do not understand how causes operate upon them cannot hope to be in any measure free of their effects. Those who think themselves free of the need to know history are in fact the victims, who can never be free. They will be trapped because they do not know what they are trapped by.

Yet much of the past *is* irrelevant to daily decisions. To balance your checking account, you don't need to know the history of double-entry bookkeeping or the reason for its introduction by Italian accountants five hundred years ago. Nor must you maintain a storehouse of trivia. History is more than antiquarianism (knowledge of details of the past, purely for themselves). It gives us a sense of why things happened as they did. History helps us come to some understanding of cause-and-effect sequences and priorities that may govern our lives. Ignorance does not free us from history, but knowledge gives us a chance to work to free ourselves if we wish.

Then why study history if the specific history that shapes our daily lives is derived more from personal experience than from books? The question answers itself, for the shape of our personal experience is, in part, governed by the knowledge we bring to those experiences. The price of plums in China *is* relevant to the price of wheat in Kansas, just as a Middle-Eastern conflict may impinge upon the most isolated and ill-informed Americans, however uninterested they may be in events in that quarter of the globe. Suddenly things thought not worth knowing may become very important.

It is important, too, that someone be a detective searching through the past, reconstructing past events, past feelings, past ways of life, creating some tolerance for the change and confusion about us. This search supplies tools for adjusting to that change and confusion. We gain a sense of morality by which we may judge ourselves and our society. History does not provide a means for predicting the future, but it does give us clues. History is the human story written large—complex, often exciting, on occasion dull, and always decisive, for those who do not remember their history *are* condemned to repeat it.

Of course, history changes as new material about the past is brought to light from recently discovered manuscripts or through the application of newly formulated techniques for research. Also our perception of the meaning of events changes, as those events recede further into our past. One generation asserted that the major cause of the American Civil War was slavery; a later generation (of the 1930s), preoccupied with economic problems, argued that the principle cause of the war was incompatible regional economies. Yet a later generation, taken up with the immediate problems of the civil rights movement, again saw slavery (now translated as racism) as the root cause of the war. All may be correct, though only one is wholly relevant to the moment.

Thus, historians are detectives, for they must reconstruct the act, the crime, the commission of the event, often from the flimsiest of evidence. Having done so, they must tell us what the event means in terms of our lives. To do this, historians must be concerned at once on two levels: interpretation and accumulation of factual data. The great British novelist and historian Dame Rebecca West wrote:

> The facts that, put together, are the face of the age . . . [are those that matter to us] for if people do not have the face of the age set clearly before them they begin to imagine it; and fantasy, if it is not disciplined by the intellect and kept in faith with reality by the instinct of art, dwells among the wishes and fears of childhood, and so sees life either as simply answering any prayer or as endlessly emitting nightmare monsters from a womb-like cave.

The face of our age must never be based on fantasy. In any nation, those who remain children—exposed to the simple solutions of tyrants, to the panaceas of childhood, to the nightmare monsters of the extreme Right and Left—do not understand how to think in historical terms. Yet the central task of life is to learn to decode the environment around us so that we may move safely within it, contribute to it, draw from it, and pass it on in altered form to the next generation. To decode an environment is difficult if one is ignorant of how that environment came to take the shape it has. To understand society, we must understand social history. History and its study provide a means, if not entirely sufficient perhaps the best means nonetheless, to understand our environment and hence ourselves.

In reading history, one must remember that the historian has been forced to select the facts as they have been recorded. In any decision to speak of subject $x$ and not of subject $y$, the historian places an interpretation upon the events. So, too, do newspapers. In reading history, one must remember that the historian chooses words—adjectives, adverbs—that color the acts described, perhaps choosing an emotive color which may be as powerful an influence on us as the facts themselves. So, too, does television. In reading history, one must remember that the historian is limited to the known, or to that which may reasonably be surmised from the evidence. In this he or she is less than scientific, but more than intuitive. The historian is humanist and social scientist, in search of objective reality; he or she must reconstruct the past on the basis of premises that may never be verified. The historian is, then, that most ambivalent of persons, one who must see all human action in the round, uncommitted to any final cause, any precise result.

To this end, as you read the material that follows, ask of any event, of any historical question, a series of subquestions. No event is without its economic aspects. None is without social meaning. None is bereft of intellectual significance. None is devoid of political purport. Ask of all events, then, what the economic, social, intellectual, and political aspects are that must be considered, remembered, argued, and ultimately placed into some pattern of priority. No reader who wishes to learn, to think, to grow through history will fail to interrogate every question put, every sentence laid out, every paragraph that follows. What if you were asked to comment on the following: "After its framers turned the United States Constitution into the first tragic compromise of American principles, was the Civil War inevitable?" You must know that you have been asked several questions at once and that you have already been led, perhaps intentionally, perhaps mistakenly, toward some implied answer. For this question, which the unsuspecting might simply translate into "What were the causes of the Civil War?" actually asks all of the following:

> If the Constitution of 1787 compromised American principles, what were these principles, and how had they come to be? Were those principles embedded in the Declaration of Independence, which declared all men to be created equal? Was the compromise contained in the constitutional clause that permitted judging men with black skins as being less than equal? Or if a Civil War did, in fact, erupt, can those principles be called "American" rather than merely "regional"?
> 
> Were the principles referred to uniquely American, or were they not shared by other peoples?
> 
> If one accepts the argument that American principles existed and were compromised, did the Constitution compromise them? Was it the first compromise, or were there earlier ones?
> 
> Was the inevitability a civil war, or merely a conflict between regions in some form?
> 
> Was this conflict inevitable only after the compromising of those principles, or was the conflict inevitable even before, for other reasons?
> 
> Was the Constitution, in fact, a compromise at all?
> 
> May one refer to events as inevitable or might not some human agency have intervened to prevent the outcome taking the form that it did?

Only after asking ourselves the questions above may we move on to the "simple" question, now seen not to be simple at all: What were the economic, social, intellectual, and political causes of the Civil War? In what way has your life today been influenced by that war? Now, having seen how complex such a question is, we must understand why history is not a body of data to be memorized so much as a series of arguments to be discussed.

The example here has been taken from American history; the text that follows is largely of Western European history. This choice is deliberate, for the questions remain the same, the problems similar, the relevance no less immediate: How did the world of which we are a part become the environment we must decode?

Until well into the nineteenth century, the United States was a fragment of European society. In many ways it remains aligned to that society today, even though it has developed a unique culture of its own. Thus, while we may feel that American history is in some way more relevant to our past than European history is, this is merely a relative judgment. The history of Africa and Asia are also of great significance to us in coming to an understanding, however imperfect, of why we are as we are. But by and large, through processes of acculturation, assimilation, and evolution, most of us bear a close relationship to the developments that arose in the world's first high-technology societies, those of Western Europe. Hence, our emphasis here on Western civilizations.

History must be read with care. One possible conclusion to a basic argument among historians already has been slipped to you in the paragraph above. It refers to Western civilizations, although many would argue that there is only one Western civilization.

That this book has an explicit thesis should, no doubt, be made clear at the outset, so that you need not beware of its words. A thesis does guide the selection of facts, of arguments, and of examples. The thesis is, quite simply, that history may best be seen as humankind's continuing search for security. This does not discount art or music or great literature, and it is not meant to embrace a materialistic view of history. The search for psychological and aesthetic security—for an environment of sights and ideas, of architecture, emotions, and feelings—in which one rests comfortably may be as important to individuals as the search for a purely physical or social security may be to animals (or was to early humans). We can best understand ourselves in relation to the growth of our own unique, individual definitions of security. We can best understand nations or social groups, tribes or religious movements in relation to collective thrusts toward mutually identifiable security systems.

To pursue such a thesis is to unite history in a way that may seem far too tidy to some. Yet history surely is something more than a series of random events (or the notion of cause and effect must be discarded from the social sciences and humanities), or a compound of "one damn thing after another." This does not mean that every event, every human action, must be interpreted in the light of a basic thesis, but only that the generality will be. Even if one believes that history has no meaning and man no ultimate purpose—a view rejected here—the cautionary observation of Sir Isaiah Berlin, an English historian, must be remembered: "The case against the notion of historical objectivity is like the case against international law, or international morality: that it does not exist." In short, even though daily headlines make it clear that international law does not exist, we do not cease attempting to make it so. And even though some memorizable "facts" of history may be found to be nothing more than a printer's error upon the page memorized, we continue to look for meaning in the progression of events—and thus in history.

Some among us believe that history misleads us in our emotions, either simply through a patent misrecording of the facts or complexly through denying to us the simple power of hating what we do not wish to understand (or perhaps love). To explain is to explain away, say some, when the historian analyzes events from the past in such a way as to suggest that no single party is responsible today for all the conditions leading to a particular modern confrontation. To explain is to understand and to understand is to sympathize, say others. Not so. One may fully comprehend the roots of a problem without losing the capacity for action, for moral indignation. There is preserved today at Mauthausen, in Austria, one of the infamous extermination camps employed by Nazi Germany to eliminate the enemies of the state, largely but not at all exclusively Jewish enemies. Each nation that lost lives at Mauthausen was asked after World War II to place a monument there in memory of its dead. Across the hillside that leads down to the great quarry face, over which so many human beings were pushed to their death by other human beings, straggle a number of monuments to hope, memory, and a few to forgiveness. At the very lip of the cliff stands a single stylized strand of barbed wire thirty feet tall, placed there by the Hungarians. On the plinth is engraved the words, in Hungarian, German, and English, "Forget? Forgive? Never!"

History does not cheat us. There are those who are offended when they discover that England's King Arthur and the Knights of the Round Table probably never existed. There are others who feel deceived when they learn in high school that George Washington did not throw any silver dollar across the Potomac and did not chop down any cherry tree later declaring that he could not tell a lie—tales told to nearly all grade-school children at one time. No one has been cheated. History is an ever-unfolding series of levels of truth in which meaning may on occasion best be conveyed by metaphor. Many historians feel that young children would not grasp the abstract argument that Washington was a man of integrity and that his first biographer understandably invented a story to illustrate the abstraction. The story is false, the abstraction is not, and only the unwary have been harmed by Parson Weems.

To pursue a thesis is, as we have said, to imply selectivity, and thus to omit what someone else considers important. Such is the case here. There are no lists of tariffs, no charts of dynasties, no compilations of treaties, and relatively few specific names and dates. This is not to say that these are not important. It does say that if Joan of Arc is mentioned, and the reader has no inkling of who she is, the reader must have the resourcefulness to look her up elsewhere; for the innumerable biographical sketches that could be recorded here would so crowd the stage that there could be no action. In a sense, then, this is a simplified history, meant to be read as a sweeping survey of Western peoples' development, or their desire for security. It attempts to provide the irreducible minimum of necessary knowledge on that development as well as a set of views over which we may argue at length. It can be used for general background prior to more detailed examinations of specific problems and periods, perhaps supplemented by the rich world of paperbacks. Or it can be read simply for its own point of view. But no one should be disappointed to discover that a favorite monarch is omitted, for the omission is intentional, defendable, and in this context, desirable. What follows should, in short, be capable of appealing to readers of widely varying degrees of sophistication and knowledge.

While there are subthemes here as well they have not been made consistently explicit, for the reader should not need to be hammered on the back of the neck with the obvious. One subtheme shows the conqueror conquered. Another reveals the inherently small beginnings of most things. Another relates to the assimilation of ideas preceding the assimilation of peoples. Still another recognizes the crucial significance of a new technological breakthrough. It is in these contexts that the quotations at the beginnings of each section are meant to be read. They are not windowdressing. They set the subtheme of the section, even if by intentional indirection and ambiguity. If a few quotations (and the text itself) send anyone to a dictionary, this is not a trick or failure to meet the readers on their own ground. It arises from the deliberate assumption that to read is to grow. To employ only words and concepts already familiar to the readers is to deny them that growth.

A final comment is necessary to understand what is meant here by the relevance of history, and why what is thought to be crucially relevant is organized as it is here. Obviously not all events, ideas, or persons are equally relevant to the present, just as all cannot be equally relevant to different people. Two elements, however, work most powerfully upon our understanding of an event, circumstance, or development. Those two elements are primacy and recency. That is, we must understand the early origins of our societies, and we must concentrate upon the ways those societies form roots for the modern world. The search for security, for example, becomes increasingly secular, even technological, in the twentieth century. But that does not lessen the importance of understanding just how deeply a spiritual search for security initially shaped people and still shapes humankind in many portions of the globe. Once we understand our origins, we can move quickly to the most recent 150 years, to the French Revolution and all that has happened since.

Ultimately, people are motivated by what they believe to be true. This fact is not diminished by historians who may prove strongly held ideas, systems, or models to be totally false. Religion, racism, imperialism, socialism, communism, capitalism—all may be proved to the satisfaction of some to be harmful, beneficial, false, or true. In this sense, all history is intellectual history, all "economic laws" merely conventionally satisfying responses to the mystery of life. The following material, while certainly not a history of ideas, rests upon the assumption that we must understand others as they see themselves if we are to know how to guide our relations to them—in the past, in the present, and even, one might suppose, in the future. Indeed, if we do not think about the past we will have no future.

# PART ONE

# Human Societies and Civilizations: Beginnings

*The beginnings and endings of all human undertakings are untidy....* John Galsworthy, 1933

## AN OVERVIEW: BEGINNINGS

One of the oldest, most enduring definitions of *self* identifies a human being in terms of family and region. Throughout most of human history, particularly since the time when relatively complex forms of self-identification became necessary, family associations have identified personal status, whether noble or slave. A person's roots in a region have reflected that inveterate sense of localism, the closed horizon, that has characterized the consciousness of self and the security of most humans. Self and security were one and the same: humankind locked in "the castle of my skin."

Both definitions remind us of the narrow roots of self-awareness. In the mid-twentieth century, with its infinitely more sophisticated and effective methods of leveling differences among local areas, we can still observe vigorous resistance to this equalizing process in many different areas of culture. In the past, sometimes in the very recent past and nearly always in remote antiquity, a sense of kin importance and local loyalty prevented societies from spreading. Yet, on many occasions, in many different parts of the world, the sense of self and the search for security provided by kin and land gave way to new forms of human association and different territorial loyalties. Enlarged civilizations emerged only when they offered, even to relatively small groups, opportunities for security that seemed preferable to earlier, more localized ones. In one sense, the history of civilization may be considered in terms of this continuous tension between local and more universal interests, between a distant security that might appear greater than a local one, between those who appeared to possess a superior technology, a more satisfying religion, or a grander view of the future, and those who found comfort in what they knew—the familiar, the well tried, the more immediately secure.

New forms of social organization and human relationships, developed through increased cultural contact, make people more alike as territorial, linguistic, religious, and economic boundaries expand. That likeness may not necessarily include all levels of society in the same way, nor all aspects of life; traditionally, it has not. Its principal identifying institutions may be religious, political, linguistic, or economic. The society's creation, spread, and survival may depend upon the dominance of a small elite living in isolated centers of large regions and ruling a much larger, and hostile, or indifferent population. On the other hand, the rulers may depend upon the active cooperation of large segments of the society. They may require wide distribution of different kinds of power and status throughout a participating population.

A society may close its circles on the basis of family, language, race, or religion. It may open them to talent, religious conversion, wealth, or prestige. It may vigorously assert a historical continuity stretching back into the remote mists of the legendary past, in order to explain itself to its members and to those, particularly the young, upon whom it depends for continuity. Its centers of power and influence may shift when economic or political change reduces their effectiveness. There is little in any civilization that has existed over a long period of time that has not been touched by human will. Conditions that give birth to a culture, and allow it to develop and spread, necessarily change in time. The character of a culture changes with those conditions. In this sense, the self-conscious traditions of a civilization exist in a state of tension with the forces of change. Visions of the past influence the perceptions of the present, and the needs of the present subtly transform past values. These tensions between localism and universalism and between continuity and change are two fundamental components of the history of all civilizations. A third is the relationship between any civilization and its near or remote neighbors. The essence of any civilization is the similarity of the lives and thoughts of its dominant groups. In defining themselves and their world, these groups also define noncivilization, barbarism, or—from the Greek *bar-bar,* meaning "not us"—those who speak another language. Throughout most of human history, civilizations have been bordered by peoples who existed at measurably different levels of social organization, had dissimilar material and cultural life styles and used other forms of defining themselves.

Anthropologists have suggested that a possible objective scale of these differences may be constituted by two distinct kinds of human achievement. The domestication of crops and animals separates *savage* from *barbaric* society. The establishment of literacy, however small its scale, separates barbaric from *civilized* society. In addition to such apparently objective standards, however, historians, anthropologists, and other social scientists have devised many other measurements. Still, part of the character of any civilization is rooted in its own standards of defining "others."

Two examples, fourteen hundred years apart yet similar in character, may clarify this argument. 1) Homer wrote the *Odyssey* around 700 B.C. In that poem, the poet described the values and institutions of a heroic society that existed long before his own time, a description influential in later Greek and Western culture. In one episode of the poem, the hero, Odysseus, is captured by the Cyclops Polyphemus and is subjected to brutal treatment before he escapes. However, in spite of his close call Odysseus is scornful of the monster because, in his eyes, Polyphemus is a savage. 2) Although they are children of a god, Odysseus and his kind know nothing of sedentary agriculture. They view herdspeople, who live apart from each other, as lacking the second essential feature of humanity, the social organization of the *agora* or meetingplace. Finally, they lack *themis*, the divine gift of the knowledge of proper conduct, a combination of manners, religious duties, and rules for social interchange that the Greeks of Homer's day regarded as the essence of civilized life that set them apart from the barbarous peoples surrounding them.

Fourteen centuries later, around A.D. 700, an English poet also wrote a heroic epic describing a past heroic age and its values. His audience, like Homer's, lived in a world very different from that of the poem, yet they shared a deep interest in the past. Later editors called the poem *Beowulf.* The hero, Beowulf, defends a primitive society from particularly dangerous nonhuman enemies. In one episode, Beowulf must fight the monster Grendel. Both on the poet's and the hero's terms, Grendel is a savage, for he hates the life, the lights, music, and song in the hall of King Hrothgar. He is a wanderer on the uninhabited heath. He kills men without paying the required compensation, the *wergeld,* to the dead man's kin or lord. Such payment is a sign of "civilization." Beowulf pursues Grendel fairly, without weapons, because Grendel does not understand their use.

To the Greeks after Homer, a barbarian was anyone who could not speak Greek and therefore could not think like a civilized person, regardless of how "technologically advanced" his society might be. At one time in Roman history, a *barbarism* came to mean an error in Latin grammar or syntax. (That meaning is still accepted today.) In tenth-century Christian Europe, *barbarian* meant either a non-Christian or a nominal Christian whose way of life was so strange that it put his or her status as a Christian in doubt. To the Chinese of the nineteenth century, all Westerners were barbarians. Whatever its explicit content, the sense of a sharp distinction between civilization and barbary has always been a marked component of a civilization's self-awareness, of its conviction of security from the eroding effects of conflicting values.

More complex than the relation between civilization and barbary has been the question of contact and relationship among the different civilizations. The first civilizations grew, largely independently of each other, in widely separated centers: the Yellow River, Indus, and Tigris-Euphrates Valley of Asia, the Nile Valley of northern Africa, and later in eastern and western Africa, and South America. The circumstances surrounding the origins of these different civilizations have caused considerable debate, as has the subject of mutual contacts and influences among some of them. Social scientists have postulated many bridges between civilizations, from the roles of vanished superior civilizations to the impetus provided by beings from outer space—views not accepted by the majority of scholars, although today romantically attractive and believed by some. Whatever evidence does exist suggests that most credibility should be given to theories that postulate purely human, terrestrial energies and efforts to make contact and to communicate.

In spite of the vast distances in space and time separating the earliest centers of civilization, human beings appear to have encountered one another either by accident or design from earliest times. Sailors from Sumer, Greek and Roman travelers, medieval Italian merchants and missionaries, South Pacific voyagers, and Spanish and Portuguese navigators —often looking for something entirely different than what they discovered—all reached distant lands and peoples. Although their encounters were only intermittent, they did occur before the late fifteenth century, when Europeans generated large-scale, regular contacts among different civilizations. Before the establishment of such regular contacts and apart from the discontinuous character of earlier encounters, the civilizations of Eurasia and Africa were connected by other kinds of bridges, those built and sometimes dominated or shattered by their barbarian neighbors. In terms of their own survival and contact with one another, the history of all civilizations must leave an important chapter open to the story of their barbarian neighbors—as debtors, transmitters, conquerors, often as receivers, and later as component elements of an expanding core civilization.

Civilization is often regarded as exclusively the achievement (and the processes) of the spirit and mind. The temple cities of Mesopotamia, the pyramids of Egypt, the Greek epic poems and tragedies, the sonorous language of Roman law and political theory, and the cathedrals of medieval Europe all appeal to those who are reluctant to be reminded that civilization is also a product of bone and muscle, or refined divisions of labor and status, and usually of appallingly marginal material conditions. The size and density of populations, food supplies, customs, economic systems, labor, military and political power—these are equally essential features of civilizations. High technology alone does not make a superior civilization, but neither does great poetry.

Material conditions must be taken into account; but we may not dismiss intellectual, artistic, or spiritual achievements. They are not merely offshoots of the "fundamental reality" explained in economic or political theories of humankind. Nor are they always to be understood through modern meanings of popular phrases. If the past is to be useful to us, we must be careful and explicit when we use modern meanings of terms such as *religion* and *secularism, freedom* and *servitude, bigotry* and *toleration, capital* and *labor,* and almost any abstraction at all that ends in *ism.*

An example of the attitude toward manual labor may suggest some of the complexity in analyzing past social notions and the origins of modern beliefs. Mesopotamians, Egyptians, Greeks, and Romans regarded manual labor as repulsive in varying degrees, suitable only for slaves or noncitizens or tolerable only insofar as it allowed one to lead a life without further labor. At best, in Greek and Roman society, work might ultimately produce the necessary leisure that anyone required to be considered fully "human." Leisure was spent in discussion, civic activity, or the development of the mind and spirit. Not until the sixth century, a period generally regarded as the beginning of the Dark Ages, did manual labor acquire a conceptual dignity as great as classical leisure. St. Benedict required labor of his monks, as did his successors, and the round of prayer and ceremony in monastic life came to be called the *Opus Dei,* labor for God, or God's Work.

Thereafter, monastic ideas on the legitimacy of work were extended into political and social spheres. Eventually these ideas combined with other new concepts of citizenship and the value of economic productivity.

In the nineteenth century, understanding the problems and uses of labor took on fresh importance and shaped social thought. Early in that century, most male clothing evolved into forms of workingman's dress identifiable with a trade. The revolution in the concept of the dignity of labor was affirmed in the novels of Charles Dickens, the writings of Karl Marx, and the social theories expounded by Pope Leo XIII. The connection between the modern status of labor and the attitudes of St. Benedict in the sixth century may not be immediately apparent; but that connection exists. It binds the present to the past in a seamless fabric. The revolution in social theory that this connection represents is one of the most striking hallmarks of Western civilization. It is remarkable enough to be set beside the artistic, intellectual, or spiritual triumphs that have been traditionally, though somewhat narrowly, regarded as the principal glories of that civilization. The fibers of civilization are far tougher and more intricate than the purely aesthetic or spiritual landmarks on the surface.

History then, is infinitely complex, demanding, confusing, and in the end persuasive. To understand history is to understand, to some degree, oneself; and to understand oneself is, to that degree, to know that for millennium upon millennium humankind sought security, in theory and in practice. It sought security through and outside the law—a law of both logic and experience—that was generated to provide a definition of security. The search took economic, political, social and religious forms, according to custom and in contempt for custom. The study of civilization, whether on an individual or comparative basis, is most fully and most effectively the study of humanity.

## I. 1 Recoverable History Begins: People of River and Plain

*Continuity with the past is a necessity, not a duty.*
—Oliver Wendell Holmes, Jr., 1921

Achievements of the earliest human beings—in Africa, Eurasia, and India—set humans on a track far different from that of any other creature. These achievements took place long before 8000 to 4000 B.C., the millennia when complex social structures and cultural bonds, part of the definition of civilization, appeared in the Tigris, Euphrates, and Nile valleys. These first structures developed far earlier, certainly, than the idea of a civilized world or the notion of qualities composing a civilization were conceived in the Greek East around 300 B.C. In role as well as in kind, humans were marked as distinct from other animals by the slow process of development of the human physique—from the erect posture to the intricate dexterity of the hand, the large brain, and the complex nervous system. His prolonged period of childhood helplessness and uselessness, his organic lack of strength, speed, or weapons rendered humans physically far more defenseless than other creatures. With apparent liabilities in relation to the environment, humans had the added disadvantage of being large-bodied predators. They had to find and to kill or otherwise gather food. Thus, as an individual and as a species, humans were tied intimately to a precarious food supply that demanded persistence, cunning, and originality. Species that live exclusively as predators can exist only in limited numbers; they survive only as long as their traditional prey survives but fails to evade them. In nature, when there are fewer deer than there are lions, soon there are no more lions.

## The Tool-Maker

The evolution of humans was long and uncertain, for the creature now designated "man" was not the only hominid variety to begin that ascent. Several hominid types existed in the remote past before *homo sapiens,* "intelligent man," arrived around 30,000 B.C.. Some of these types had developed the use of rough tools made of stone, bone, or horn. Some had gone on to shape stone tools by chipping and flaking. By 10,000 B.C., in fact, *homo sapiens* was chiefly distinguished by the role of "the toolmaker." Tools meant survival, for they allowed the possibility of altering the environment a very little bit in one's favor. The development of more sophisticated or compound tools such as hafted axes, and the use of tools to make yet other tools, lifted humans up one of the largest steps out of their "natural" role. They had developed the ability to use a combination of elements from the physical world, regularly, in a complex and learned way. From the necessary pooling of experience, knowledge, skill, and talent came a kind of life that may be described as social and an attitude toward nature (reflected in speculative cave paintings) that may be described as religious. Life was "solitary, poor, nasty, brutish, and short," yet at moments, it was also secure.

Still nature imposed limitations on all predators. The creation of tools was but the first giant step to a new world for their maker. Humans stepped out of their original ecological place when they began consciously to conserve, as well as prey upon, the food supply. As conservers, they took the first step in freeing themselves from their exclusive dependence upon the natural circumstances of a predator's life. They had to measure time (in seasons as game came and went, in days as food fell low). They had to form a society larger than the hunting party, for someone had to guard and deliver that food supply. They had to create weapons and a degree of cooperation so that they could kill bigger and more game. They had long gathered as well as hunted for food. The gathering of grains, as well as the "gathering" of game, became the threshold of the human's new function—the drastic reshaper of the environment. The environment needed to suit humans in their new roles as both conservator and predator. They had stepped out of their "ecological track" by discovering an alternative food supply that made them less dependent upon hunted food.

## The Beginnings of Agriculture

Sometime around 7000 B.C. we began to grow, rather than to find, grain. After the development of tool making, the domestication of crops —called the Neolithic agricultural revolution—marked another important stage in the transformation of both humans and their world. The earliest history of agriculture is that of the slow process of finding and selecting suitable wild grains, remaining long enough in one location to cultivate them, and finding areas with the proper physical conditions to make agriculture possible. The first rain-watered crops in the ancient Near East were probably planted by a society that still consisted largely of hunters. Yet the essentially different types of life constituted by hunting and agriculture must soon have come into conflict. The hunter is by nature a migrant, and the first hunters who also gathered grain lived no differently from hunters who did not. Areas especially productive of grain were found, however—particularly in the Near East—where hunters were not required to migrate very far with the game. They could protect and cultivate the new fields by weeding and reseeding. Thus began the first settled communities of farmers. In turn, the settled communities spawned the first of the many differences between the lives of hunters and farmers. A new variety of social functions turned up in farming communities. Newly found materials such as cloth and clay pottery were exploited. Permanent shelters were built, accompanied by a sense of territorial possession.

For perhaps the first time, an agricultural revolution made distinctly different kinds of human societies possible. First came the simple distinction between hunters and cultivators. Later, after groups of hunters had come into contact with sedentary agricultural communities a further distinction grew. Pastoral herdspeople migrated with their flocks and communicated with settled societies through simple trade or warfare. The agricultural communities settled into a cooperative life regulated by the recurring seasonal cycle. Such communities carefully divided labor and time. They required laws and enforcers of those laws to see that all met the demands and received the rewards of their labor and time. Migrating pastoralists, on the other hand, requiring little cooperation, fostered individualism and indifference to seasons and to places, offering few opportunities for technological and cohesive spiritual development. Behind the division of labor and function, there lies a division of mind and conceptions of life. The contrasts in the biblical story of Cain and Abel and the eternal rivalry between cattledrivers, sheepherders, and homesteaders in modern western films are echoes of the different attitudes toward life fostered by the first differentiated human societies.

The earliest agricultural communities were also limited in their possibilities for growth. Freed from total dependence upon game, they nevertheless found themselves restricted by other natural forces: rainfall, climate, crop blight, insect invasion, and exhaustion of the soil. Outside the Near East, the heavy clay soils of Europe and the sandy soils of the Mediterranean basin required far more care and effort than the earliest agricultural communities were able to give with the tools they had. There had to be a way to break the limits imposed by the earliest forms of agricultural life, to produce more than a sustenance crop that fed them precariously from season to season. For the security and trading advantages of a crop surplus, new techniques had to be developed. These included finding ways to propitiate the gods who brought or did not bring the rain.

By 5000 B.C. the creation of stone tools and domestication of crops were followed by the increasing use of metal tools and weapons—first, copper; and by the third millennium B.C., the harder alloy, bronze. The earlier inventions of the plow and the wheel meant that even before the establishment of large-scale agricultural communities, the farmer had already crossed a threshold that pastoralists and hunters had not yet found. The threshold was technology, the conscious study of tools to alter not only the way of life but the ecology of the world. The earliest plows drastically transformed the fertility of the soil. The first time a field was allowed to lie fallow in order to restore its fertility, the order of nature was rearranged. Imagine hunters without game or meat-eating herdsmen looking down from the hills and seeing for the first time a prosperous agricultural community somewhere in the ancient Near East, its grain stored in clay pots, its men and women performing functions that must have been barely comprehensible to the outsiders. From that moment, the divisions of labor and of life started rising to a level of consciousness far more acute than in any earlier human experience. The farmers, looking up at the outsiders, knew that they themselves would not go hungry, that their gods were properly propitiated and therefore generous, that within certain limits their settlement and their lives were secure. As more outsiders arrived, however, that security had to be strengthened by defensive measures, so that the security they had achieved internally, through worship and labor, might be augmented by a communal security established through defense.

In primitive Near Eastern society, as in primitive societies down to the present, specialized work functions might be conducted alongside everyday tasks of food production. The hunter or planter might be a spare-time blacksmith or weaver, priest or brewer. Primitive societies do not, as a rule, produce more than is required to satisfy their immediate needs. The sparse populations of the agricultural communities of the ancient Near East, the homogeneity of life in Late Stone Age agricultural villages, and the lack of a need for any social differentiation within these communities beyond divisions of the roles of women and priests marked the end of the achievements of the first agricultural revolution. Humans had found a food supply that was an alternative to game. Because of this, they were able to transform nature and to begin to exploit the physical world.

The different life styles of settlers and wanderers represented the beginnings of social differentiation within the whole human community. Yet there were still severe limitations imposed upon the growth and the character of human society. Isolated homogeneous agricultural villages could produce little in the way of surplus; also, the divisions of labor within agricultural communities—though greater than they were among hunters or pastoral herdsmen—were hardly specialties. The size and activity of these communities remained primitive.

## *Primitive Trade*

Primitive limits upon agricultural, pastoral, and hunting communities cracked when a number of these societies sprang up in the narrow lands bordering the lower reaches of the Tigris and Euphrates Valleys. Soil was fertile on these flood plains onto which different societies crowded in relatively small areas to exploit the discovery of irrigation, and opportunities for population growth and diversification of roles within a single society surpassed anything known earlier. By 4000 B.C., these new and larger societies dotted the lower part of the valleys; within the next thousand years they began to spread beyond the narrow confines of the flood plain. As the specialized knowledge required for irrigation and for placating the new gods became more complex, the role of priests became more prominent. By 3500 B.C., communities had begun to grow into cities, each with its raised temple. Priests directed the massed labor needed to fully exploit the riches of the flood plain and carry water into areas farther away. The need to regulate storage and redistribute grain and fodder during drought periods, as well as the need to resurvey the land following floods, was a major impetus to develop more complex social organization. Generally each temple-city was under the rule of a god, while the managerial class (priests, artisans, and others not directly involved in agricultural work) was supported by the agricultural surplus. This was the beginning of urban wealth.

By acquiring other goods and materials by trade, the temple-cities represented the first successful break with primitive agriculture. In these diversified societies, now being ruled and directed by priests with sacred knowledge and supporting a wide variety of occupations, the territorial authority of the temple slowly displaced the bonds of kinship and locality that had hitherto served to hold agricultural societies together. The spread of the temple-city's influence into individual lives suggests the importance of such priestly knowledge. The irregularity of the flood season in the Tigris and Euphrates Valleys, the danger of invaders, the fragility of irrigation systems eventually gave greater importance to the priestly caste than to the heads of kin groups. Security had moved from the household to the institutions of an enlarged society.

## *Priestly Castes*

It was among the Sumerians that expanded agricultural communities first rose to city status and elevated the rule of priest castes. Speaking a language different from the Semitic tongues to the north, the Sumerians completed the organization of temple-cities, massed the large labor forces (now numbering in the thousands) required for agricultural work, and established the social diversification that produced the first truly sophisticated human society.

A series of cause-and-effect relationships produced the most striking features of Sumerian civilization. Because they needed to keep records, the Sumerians made intricate carvings on cylinder seals, the first pictograph script for record keeping. Because they needed a building material for agricultural engineering (dams, silos, irrigation) they created brick. Because they wanted to explain the newer forms of life through theology, they embellished their temples and monuments. The massing of labor forces required for such temple architecture may be considered as a parallel to the massing of large agricultural labor forces to till the irrigated areas of these valleys.

As temple communities grew, aspects of their life styles spread northward up the Tigris and Euphrates Valleys. Such influence was, of course, selective, for the Sumerian experience could not be transmitted intact to peoples who lacked a history of organized agricultural society. Thus, Sumerian history offers the first known example of a recurring phenomenon among the history of civilizations. That phenomenon is the inevitable contact between civilized and noncivilized peoples and the selective internalization of some elements of civilization by the less developed borrowers. The borrowers accelerated their own development (or modernization) as a result of their borrowings. Slowly, a variety of civilized, semicivilized, and barbaric societies grew in close proximity. Patterns similar to this recurred again and again to the present time with peoples on the margins of civilization acting as both economic and cultural liaisons to less developed societies.

However, as productive and influential as Sumerian society was, it was also prey to both natural and artificial disasters. The complicated works of architecture and engineering would not survive a labor shortage. Spreading Sumerian institutions attracted the enmity of barbarian neighbors. Moreover, enlarging Sumerian temple-cities ultimately started competing with one another. The necessity to dominate rivers upstream in order to assure effective irrigation, and the relatively small supply of materials available to all of the temple-cities caused a growing rivalry among them until, by 3000 B.C., most had created military organizations. In time, the office of king as military commander challenged the priestly castes for prominence. Ambitious rulers attempted to combine several temple-cities under one rule, and by 2375 B.C. the largest of these kingdoms had taken shape. There were few institutions of direct rule, however, even under the relatively thorough domination of Sargon of Akkad around 2350 B.C. Successive governments were highly unstable. Still, the establishment of kingly government undermined the exclusive authority of the priests, and the strength of kings and warlords grew as the managerial roles were separated from the priestly castes. Later royal administrations added rulers, established codes of law, and attempted to raise efficient armies. As neighboring societies acquired levels of social development close to those of the great river valleys, a balance of power between them emerged in the Middle East, to be briefly disrupted by the domination of Hammurabi around 1700 B.C.. Hammurabi's code of law represented a thorough effort to spread governmental reforms on a secular rather than religious basis.

### Tigris-Euphrates Dominance

The dispersion of Sumerian Mesopotamian influences through political revolution, warfare, and trade had drawn neighboring societies into close relationship with those of the Tigris-Euphrates Valleys. From 2400 to 1700 B.C., the widespread use of trade and communication further transformed the world of the individual temple-cities and eroded the power of local gods and priestly castes. Sumerian civilization, modified by barbarian and semi-barbarian conquerors, reached a level of enormous productivity. Skills in architecture and mathematics stemmed from the development of temporal and spatial measurement and the 360° circle. Learning of various kinds had begun to be the preserve of different castes. Translations from one language to another had been worked out, which helped to free verbal and written language from the sacred aura they had once possessed. Because of several literary works, notably the epic poem *Gilgamesh*, of a hero who was two-thirds a god, human beings had begun to speculate upon the complex relationships between themselves and their gods. By 1700 B.C., the simple early differences among hunting, pastoral, and agricultural societies had given way before a wide variety of communications and influences. Civilized centers multiplied and influenced others. Barbarian communities on the fringes gained power. Fertile, irrigable river valleys constituted the hearths of civilizations until agricultural techniques spread sufficiently and could be adapted by peoples who lived in rain-watered lands.

## The Nile

Another great river valley, the Nile, had begun its own civilization by 3100 B.C. But the Egyptian experience proved to be far different than the Sumerian's and later Mesopotamian's. The fertile Nile Valley produced great annual floods of nearly predictable regularity. Therefore, within the narrow borders of the flood plain, agriculture could be carried out with more security. Furthermore, a bordering desert constituted a formidable defense against barbarian intruders. The Nile was easily navigable in both directions, and those who controlled the Nile traffic controlled Egypt itself. At the dawn of Egyptian history stands a legendary ruler from southern Egypt, Menes-Narmer. Menes united Upper and Lower Egypt and began a long line of divine rulers, the Pharaohs, whose households ruled the entire kingdom. Unlike Mesopotamia, Egypt had little need to propitiate her gods to produce fertility, so the divinity of the Pharaoh could loom over lesser Egyptian gods. The Pharaoh's gift of immortality to his loyal followers constituted the basis of his strength. His own immortality was recognized by elaborate funerary rituals: mummification, building stone tombs into pyramids by 2500 B.C., and decorative wall painting within these tombs. These constituted the first major expression of a native Egyptian culture.

However, the Pharaohs did not keep pace with the growth of Egyptian civilization. The royal household became less able to rule the enlarging kingdom efficiently. Local offices became hereditary, and local and divisive religious cults grew stronger. By 2200 B.C., the traditional date for the end of the Old Kingdom and the start of the time known as the First Intermediate Period, the authority of the Pharaoh was so weakened that many local authorities had risen to challenge him. This political and religious disintegration was paralleled by a marked decline in Egyptian art and by literature that suggests both widespread despair and a vigorous ethical consciousness. During the Middle Kingdom, customarily dated 2050 to 1800 B.C., central authority once more asserted itself, although local lords and religious shrines did not lose all their power, and the institutions of Egyptian civilization showed renewed vigor. The decline of the rulers during the Middle Kingdom once again reduced central authority, and the first major invasions by outsiders—by the Hyksos—destroyed the monarchy's remains.

The Hyksos came from the steppes-land of western Eurasia via Syria and Palestine. They introduced the light horse-drawn chariot and a new, powerful bow just as so many societies thereafter would introduce new weapons, means of communication, or applications of technology to change the old order. At first, this warrior elite seemed irresistible. In time, however, the Hyksos were expelled, leaving behind a linguistic inheritance still traceable among the Indo-European groups.

Egypt was reunited under the New Kingdom, and much of Syria and Palestine were, in turn, conquered by Egypt's King Thutmose I (1528–1510 B.C.), who was succeeded by his daughter, Hatshepsut. As Gilgamesh in Sumer had remarked, "Only the gods live forever under the sun." Although the Egyptians erected in Karnak the most extensive religious complex yet created in the West, there began a cycle of decay once again as priest and Pharaoh competed for the attention of the god, Amon.

The emergence of these two distinct civilizations based upon agriculture by irrigation suggests the vast differences that can arise from relatively similar geographical circumstances. The insecurity and instability of Mesopotamia, its lack of natural boundaries or defenses, and its openness to disaster created a highly deferential attitude toward the gods and their priests and a continuing practice of building more elaborate political structures. Constant communication with nearby people at different levels of social complexity extended throughout Mesopotamia. It also brought some elements of Mesopotamian culture to other peoples. Egypt, on the other hand, grew highly xenophobic, that is, fearful of foreigners. She was cut off during the period of the Old and the Middle Kingdoms from substantial, dangerous, yet sometimes culturally innovative invasions. The regularity of the Nile floods diminished the need for priests as rainmakers and raised the Pharaoh to a position of reverence and authority far greater than that achieved by the kings of Sumer Mesopotamia. Although the agricultural community lay at the core of economic production in both societies, civilization became secularized in Mesopotamia's urban communities more quickly than in Egypt's, tied as it was to the divinity of the royal household.

Other societies, particularly those bordering the civilized centers of Egypt and Mesopotamia and thus feeling less secure, possessed no such traditions. Hence they were able to respond to crises more flexibly, selectively borrowing detachable elements from the more developed civilizations, while not being committed to a traditional pattern of action. In time Mesopotamia and Egypt paid for their earlier security and precocious development with a commitment to cultural traditions that could not sustain them. In other early cultures as well, the price for early complexity of development often turned out to be rigidity in the face of new challenges and the creation of further internal crises.

### *Continuity and Change: Climate*

The developments described here took place across the sweep of hundreds, even thousands, of years. But their time span is dwarfed by another sequence of change that was absolutely fundamental to human life and yet virtually unobserved by human beings: the immense swings of climate conditions across human history. For food and, ultimately, shelter and life style are deeply influenced by climatic changes.

In climatology, as in history, the past explains the present. Three broad categories of climatic change have been described by earth scientists. The first type—tens of millions of years over which the earth slowly cooled and warmed—has in fact happened often. The most recent such cycle has taken place over the last fifty million years, with progressive cooling bringing in the Ice Age in which the great polar icecaps descended inexorably toward the earth's temperate zones. Human technology still lacks the capacity to influence such fundamental changes which are thought to arise from plate tectonics, or the drift of continents, which change the earth's land masses. The second category of climatic change has also proven to be beyond human influence: the repeated advance and retreat of the continental ice sheets over tens of thousands of years. The earth's relationship to the sun changes slightly over time, altering the distribution of solar radiation over the earth's surface. Over the last million years, or the span of human life, there have been no fewer than four and quite possibly as many as twenty such advances and contractions.

However, it is the third type of climatic change that is most important here—the changes that have occurred over a millennium or so down to perhaps the last hundred years. During the period known as the Climatic Optimum, which lasted from approximately 6,500 to 3,500 B.C., most of the earth was moister and warmer than it is today. Much of the Sahara Desert, as we call it, was grassland, hence the early identification of elephants with that area. Progressively these lands dried up, as did the great Indus Valley, effectively destroying the civilization that had arisen there. Europe cooled, the Mediterranean became more moist, and agricultural conditions thus improved in Greece and Italy, bringing about the conditions under which classical civilization would flourish. After 800 A.D., the northern hemisphere became warmer than it is now and northern Europe flourished, making possible Scandinavian growth, the spread of the Vikings from Russia to Ireland, and Norse settlements in Greenland. Cooling weather after 1500, and extending into the last century, destroyed the settlements in a land once called "Green," now virtually an icecap, and won for Iceland its modern name. During the Little Ice Age of 1550 to about 1850 grain growing was abandoned in the northern reaches of the world. Because of the slightly more temperate climate of the twentieth century grain grew once again in Iceland and the far north from about 1920 until the 1950s. Since that time the northern hemisphere has been cooling slightly once again.

Such cycles may one day be subject to truly substantial modification through the modern technologies of heat and air conditioning, but for most of human history, humankind has had to adjust not only to the capricious short-range cycles of wet and dry years but also, slowly, to the almost imperceptible cycles of the great climatic changes. Climate, then, has fashioned the environment in which human ingenuity developed. Climate has provided both security, in granting many generations predictable crops, and insecurity, in slowly undermining that very predictability that linked one agrarian generation to another. Over a very long climatic swing by which the Arctic icecap might shrink, the water level in the oceans would rise perhaps thirty feet, flooding such settlements as New York, Miami, New Orleans, Los Angeles, Seattle, London, Stockholm, Leningrad, Tokyo, Calcutta, and Sydney.

## I. 2 On the Edge of the Earliest Civilizations: The Spread of Influences

*Society is something in nature that precedes the individual.* —Aristotle, 384–322 B.C.

The early development of civilized life in the Nile and the Tigris-Euphrates Valleys did not leave the peoples around them untouched. Although some elements of technology were too complicated or inappropriate to spread easily, others moved outward very quickly. The plow, the practice of fallowing fields to increase yield, and the establishment of permanent settlements in naturally or rain-watered land created a potential for an agricultural surplus and an agrarian culture. However, greater vulnerability to outsiders made such village communities easy prey to casual marauders and to the flood plains' more mobile sectors: traders, soldiers, and self-styled kings. Rather than creating their own development, these exploited communities became part of a growing area in the Middle East that was influenced by the centers of civilization.

Island societies, protected hill communities, and neutral areas between contending major powers also constituted the edge of civilization. They, too, contributed both to the spread and the local, individualized development of civilization. The same processes of social differentiation, division of labor, rise of specialized occupations (such as mining, trading, and ruling), and the emergence of territorial rivalries with relatively long chains of dependence propelled larger numbers of people toward economic productivity. In other words, there followed the emergence of a market and the consequent social and artistic development characteristic of the earlier civilizations. Societies that bordered the Tigris-Euphrates all adopted elements of Mesopotamian civilization between 3000 and 1500 B.C. The Canaanites in Palestine, the Hittites and the Trojans in Asia

*The Rosetta Stone* By this stone, now in the British Museum in London, modern man has been helped in his understanding of ancient Egypt. The stone was found in 1799, and a French scholar, Jean-Jacques Champollion, unlocked the lessons of its three languages: Greek, hieroglyphics, and a post-hieroglyphic script. Ancient languages thus speak to us today. *Source: British Museum.*

Minor began social organizations during this period, benefiting from the needs and the creativity of neighboring Mesopotamia. Throughout the third millennium B.C., migrating peoples who had acquired the use of bronze for tools and weapons entered the borders of this growing region, influencing both its inner area and outer edges of civilization.

**Earliest Civilizations**
**3,000 B.C.**

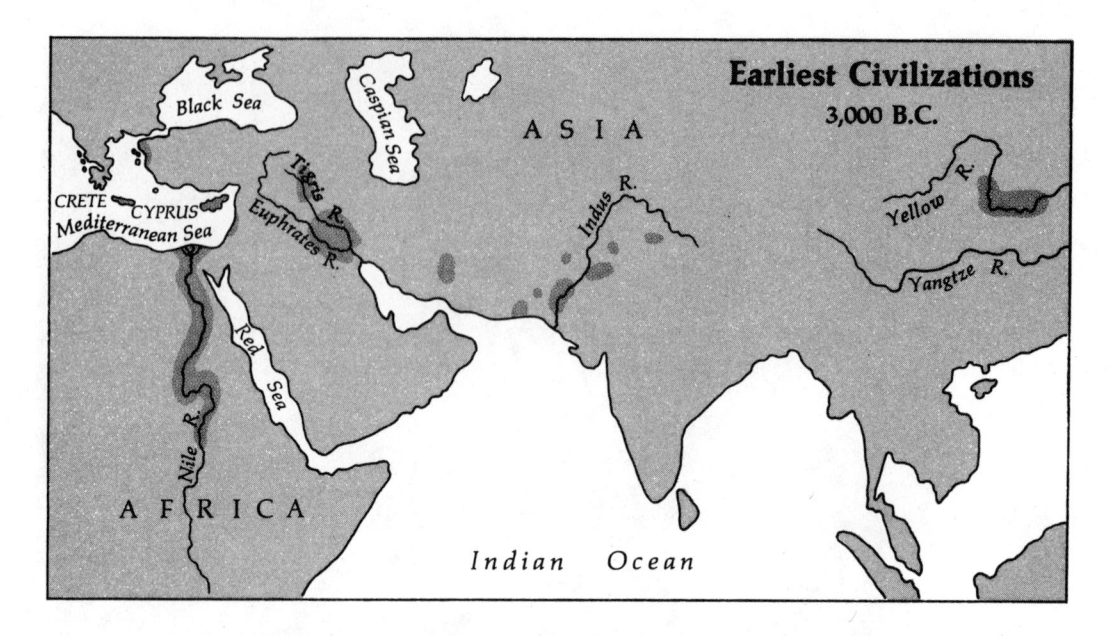

Opportunities for contact among different peoples abounded. Passes led through the mountains to the north of the Tigris-Euphrates Valleys. Iran and Anatolia offered vast upland plateaus. The Balkan plains provided easy access to the west, as did the area east of the Caspian Sea. The eastern Mediterranean lands grew more attractive to their neighbors. Once internal traditions became established as they had in Mesopotamia and Egypt by 1700 B.C., the most dynamic and novel developments increasingly took place "on the cutting edge" of civilization. Memories persisted strongly of the societies that emerged during this period such as literary legends of Troy and biblical references to Canaan and the Canaanites.

However, biblical references and literary legends omitted one of the most striking societies that emerged during this period. It flourished on the islands of the eastern Mediterranean, particularly Crete. Long before the Bronze Age, the Stone Age peoples—having discovered boats and the sea—made the first settlements on Crete. That was around 4000 B.C. Within a thousand years, these late Stone Age villages were engaged in sea trade, particularly with Egypt. Evidence of a much more developed society around 2000 B.C. has been discovered in the great palace complex of Knossos in central Crete. The hub of a trading society of great wealth, Crete was protected by its maritime location and made rich by its position as a liaison between barbarian Europe, the Levant and Egypt. The palace at Knossos (about the size of the Rose Bowl) included dozens of rooms and courts. Crete's hieroglyphic writing was developed, and a complex numerical system based upon the use of 10 was put into effect. Monument-

The many-storied palace of King Minos, at Knossos, in modern-day Crete, while largely in ruins, is a romantic reminder of an ancient civilization which appears to have been destroyed about 1400 B.C., perhaps in a sudden and still not fully explained cataclysm. The palace combined technical accomplishments with artistic refinements in a remarkable way. That it survives today is due in good measure to a British archaeologist, Sir Arthur Evans, who began excavations in 1900.

al stone architecture attested to the economic prosperity of the island. Cretan pottery found in Egypt and Egyptian statues and a cylinder seal from the reign of Hammurabi found on Crete give clues to the scope of trade. Extensive pictorial art of Minoan Crete (named after the Cretan King Minos) depicts a wealthy leisured civilization devoted to its gods and apparently thriving with considerably less state-induced compulsion to social cohesion than were other societies of the age. The isolated core civilizations of Mesopotamia and Egypt had bridged the spaces between and around them by 1700 B.C. and had helped to create a number of societies in an area that extended from India to Greece and from Upper Egypt to the Balkans and the Black Sea. Although fragile and ultimately undependable, the lines of communication and exchange, the complex linkages established by food and goods, and the migration of peoples had created a new base for human development in the Near East.

## I. 3 Desert, Mountain, and Forest: Civilization and Barbarism in the Second Millennium B.C.

> *[A] civilized society is exhibiting the five qualities of Truth, Beauty, Adventure, Art, Peace.* —Alfred North Whitehead, 1933

Early centers of social development in both Egypt and India reflect the influences of Sumerian civilization, probably brought by Sumerian sailors from the Persian Gulf. From 2500 B.C. on, maritime communities of the eastern Mediterranean also carried elements of Middle Eastern civilization to barbaric peoples along the western Mediterranean and the Atlantic coast of Europe (see section I.1). In the meantime, the Hyksos, before being driven from the Nile, had destroyed the early civilization of the Indus Valley and had penetrated present-day India. They laid the foundations for the Hittites from Asia Minor to dominate Anatolia and for the Kassites from Iran to dominate Mesopotamia. The first speakers of Greek, related Indo-European peoples, entered the southern Greek peninsula, the Peloponnesus. Centers of civilization had attracted these who seemed to dominate the scene at first; but there was a counter influence also. In many areas, with the notable exception of Egypt, the new conquerors became acculturated to the lands they had conquered.

From the wave of Indo-European barbarian conquerors of 1700 B.C. to the last major barbarian assault on Europe around A.D. 900, the pattern of contacts between civilized and uncivilized peoples suggests several recurring features. A powerful military organization had an enduring impact. After their conquest, the conquerors settled to become lords of the territories they had won. Their own culture, however, rarely prepared them to be leaders either as individuals or as a social elite. They were not trained to live under conditions other than those that had enabled them to mobilize their strength in the first place. The attractions and complex forces of conquered, yet civilized, centers overcame the initial advantage of military strength held by the conquerors. Bonds that held warbands together were weakened by new tensions among the warrior elites. Some, more than others, openly embraced the culture they had conquered and this led to a new stability. When the barbarians saw that it was better to share the fruits of civilization rather than destroy them, destruction was followed by reconstruction. Barbarian languages might be superimposed on local languages, and social reorganization might indeed take place under foreign rule; yet the more enduring strengths of local centers, as in Egypt by 1570 B.C., threw off barbarian rule entirely. Or, as in Mesopotamia, local strength generated change through the political instability of successive Kassite, Mitannian (northern Mesopotamian), and Hittite empires. Also, the influx of barbarian invaders around 1700–1500 B.C. tended to level out the differences among neighboring populations and spread a less advanced though influential civilization throughout a wider area.

The influence of the Hyksos invaders had driven Egypt out of the confines of the Nile Valley to secure ever more distant frontiers. Overthrown, enslaved, and ultimately expelled, the conquerors became the conquered. The new Egyptian Empire, reflecting the military influence of the former invaders, now consisted of ambitious Pharaohs at the head of mercenary armies of charioteers. But resources for social and economic mobilization on a large scale continued to lie in the civilized societies, and the balance of power tipped again and again against the newcomers. From 1700 B.C. to the second great wave of invasions—this time by barbarians armed with cheaper iron weapons—around 1200 B.C., Egypt and the Near East intensified communications and territorial overlordship. These vigorous Hittite and Egyptian empires created sophisticated codes of law and civil administrations. In Crete and on the Levantine coast (in Syria and Palestine), societies once again thrived, maintaining complex and political relationships with the core areas of Near Eastern civilization. However, not all barbarian invaders were so easily overcome, and some of the people whose migrations took place in the wake of the great invasions established smaller states between 1500 and 1100 B.C.

### *Migrants and Invaders: Mycenae*

Migrants and invaders speaking an archaic form of Greek began to migrate southward from the Balkans and penetrated the Greek peninsula around 2200 B.C. Although the first signs of their habitation indicate a level of social development less complex than that of the earlier inhabitants of the peninsula, the invaders soon developed a society and culture that began to rival the world of Minoan Crete, then at its height. The people of the Mycenaean civilization (named from the characteristic evidence found in the excavations at Mycenae) possessed a vigorous artistic creativity. They participated skillfully in the complex world of maritime trade in the eastern Mediterranean. The palace city of Mycenae reveals great architectural and artistic beauty as well as the resources of a prosperous culture. That pervasive culture was probably the first unifying force throughout what later came to be ancient Greece. In Mycenaean records we find the figures of gods from later Greek cultures (Zeus, Hermes, and Poseidon) as well as representations of the Mycenaean religion with its festivals and propitiatory offerings to the gods. Cults were closely associated with individual cities. The evidence suggests a formal public religion, rather than an extensively theological, personal form. This was a civic religion, one that sought the well-being of the community rather than the spiritual needs of the individual.

Although located on the edge of the civilized world, Mycenean Greece participated fully in that world. Egypt, the Aegean Islands, Syria, and Palestine all reveal Mycenean artifacts from as early as 1500 B.C., which were the remains of a flourishing trade. Similar evidence of Mycenean trade in Sicily and southern Italy reflects the first of many attempts by eastern Mediterranean peoples to penetrate the western Mediterranean. Their attempts finally resulted in permanent settlements by the eighth century B.C. The history of the rise and flowering of Mycenean society is that of an invading people who took over one of the borderlands of civilization and ultimately came to participate fully in the cultural and economic systems of that world.

By 1300 B.C., the Hittite Empire arose in Asia Minor and the Levant. Egypt's vast overseas empire was reduced, and Minoan civilization on Crete fell. These changes made Mycenean Greece a notable sea power in the east. Although the Myceneans played no political role in the struggles between the Hittites and Egyptians, they were recognized by both empires as a powerful neighbor. Other peoples, moving within the older confines of the civilized world, used the period during 1700–1000 B.C. to settle in new homes. Not strong enough to play a major role at the time, they nevertheless contributed to both the internal settlement of the Near East and to the development of new cultural institutions. The Hebrews were one of these people. Their history is especially complex, because the large collection of Jewish literature that composed the Old Testament is widely known and contains both historical and nonhistorical elements. The techniques of archaeology and comparative history must be applied with particular care to these sources.

## The Hebrews

The Hebrews, long before they had adopted that name, were originally part of the Semitic-speaking population of upper Mesopotamia. They moved into Canaan as part of the migrating populations of the second millennium B.C. Some of them, driven by famine or caught up in the turbulence of the eighteenth century, moved on into Egypt either with or in the wake of the Hyksos invasions of that century. The fall of the Hyksos and the resurgence of native Egyptian rule reduced the social status of the Hebrews who were viewed as Asiatic outsiders.

At the end of the thirteenth century a Hebrew leader with an Egyptian name, Moses (meaning son), asserted his authority over some of the

Hebrews in Egypt by claiming a spiritual authority based upon older Canaanite traditions of a single god, Yahweh (Jehovah). Moses declared that this god commanded the Hebrews to leave Egypt for Palestine. Around 1200 B.C., the exodus that gave the Old Testament its second Book took place bringing a number of Hebrew tribes from Egypt back into Palestine. There they found related peoples and the Canaanites, whose culture and society contrasted with that of the impoverished Hebrews. The Hebrew conquest of Palestine was therefore a slow process. Fusion of the populations brought a number of influences to bear upon the Mosaic traditions, illustrating again the close relationships between migrating pastoralists and settled societies. Hebrew tribes and clans were diverse; but by their use of common sanctuaries, they overcame some of their differences. Their potentially unifying force was the central Mosaic tradition of belief in one god, a belief that remained dormant between 1200 and 1100 B.C.

## The Sea Peoples

Around 1200 B.C., the Hebrews in Palestine, the Egyptian and Hittite empires, Mycenean Greece, and the other societies of the Near East underwent a second great wave of invasions, those of the so-called Sea Peoples. By the time of these invasions, the experiences of the Near East had made the people aware of the complexities of social life. They became curious about other peoples. Moreover, their creativity and artistic dynamism contained seeds of revolution. In an atmosphere of political instability, ruling aristocracies and kings communicated with each other beyond the boundaries of their territorial power. Trade and social interchange broadened. Literacy increased with the use of common languages such as the Semitic language called Aramaic.

In Egypt, Pharaoh Amenhotep IV had proclaimed (c. 1375 B.C.) the sun to be the only true god, and he renamed himself Ikhnaton, "pleasing to Aten," the sun. Social justice was an important concern in the cult of the sun, whose followers reasoned that because the sun shines down on everyone, it must be everyone's god. Although they did not end by preaching that all were brothers under the sun, their attitudes did strongly contribute to an ethical revolution that was fierce and complete. His reign ended seventeen years later, but his sun god heralded the monotheism of the later period.

Invasions of the Sea Peoples were not confined to Egypt. The Hittite Empire, southern Greece, the small society dominated by Troy in northwest Asia Minor, and the Levant all felt their blows. Their identity is difficult to establish, but the Sea Peoples probably consisted of mixed groups of migrants whose attacks not only threatened settled societies

*Pharaoh Ikhnaton* In 1978–79 thousands of Americans were excited by a travelling exhibition of the great treasures found in the tomb of the Egyptian boy king, Tutankhaman. So too did the Pharaoh Ikhnaton, who changed his name from Amenhotep to show that he honored but one god, leave the modern world a priceless heritage of art and of tablets by which we reconstruct the history of the fourteenth century B.C. *Source: The Bettman Archive, Inc.*

but also caused considerable migrations within the Aegean and eastern Mediterranean worlds. One of the most important consequences of the new invasions was the migration of displaced peoples throughout the eastern Mediterranean, for the dominance of Mycenean culture in Greece collapsed between 1200 and 1100 B.C. The vigorous trade relations declined, and some of the earlier civilized world centers were totally depopulated.

Mycenean Greece, Troy, and the Hittite Empire fell. Egypt was once again limited to the Nile Valley and Delta. All of this caused many changes in the civilization of the Near East between 1200 and 1000 B.C., which followed the great cultural vigor of the late second millennium. A complex economic system was enfeebled for several centuries. Communications were interrupted. Still, there was progress of another kind. Peoples who had formerly been in bondage or dominated by others suddenly became independent. The Hittites had long kept secret the technique of smelting iron ores; with their downfall, the method became available to others. By 1000 B.C., production of iron and steel implements spread into the turbulent societies of the eastern Mediterranean and Europe. Much wider distribution of iron ores and the low cost of the tools and weapons created from them propelled societies into the Iron Age.

Once again, the barbarian capacity to organize peoples for war proved superior and that threatened the fragile network of communications established by settled societies. Once again, new peoples had assimilated the remains of more developed societies. Aristocratic and hierarchical societies in which power had depended upon command of sophisticated military resources (such as chariots) found themselves challenged and occasionally defeated by less structured hordes—or massed infantry—wielding superior iron weapons. Smaller Iron Age states temporarily replaced the vast empires of the Bronze Age. But after 1200 B.C. the diminished centers of civilization began once more to extend their influence to surrounding regions. In the smaller societies that now emerged, tradition and need combined to create legends of the past and new social institutions for the future. That which we call prehistory moved into that which we know as history, which is less dependent on archaeological remains and more on written record.

## I. 4 An Age of Heroes:
## The Beginnings of Mediterranean Antiquity

> *[The historian] must be alive to the existence of many different pasts leading to the present in no pre-determinable succession....*
> *The points must make a line, but the line may be of any conceivable curve.* —William Scott Ferguson, 1913

From the twelfth to the sixth centuries B.C., the patterns of life in Greece, Egypt, and the Near East shifted between the restoration of older systems and the establishment of new ones. The destruction of the Hittite Empire around 1200 B.C. caused great turbulence in Asia Minor and Mesopotamia until the rise of a new empire under the Assyrians in the tenth and ninth centuries imposed a ferocious, thoroughgoing military control over most of the Mesopotamian, Anatolian, and Levantine areas. At the height of its power (745–612 B.C.), Assyria threatened to dominate the entire area of the former centers of civilization. Yet Assyria was also vulnerable to internal unrest and barbarian invasions. Although works of art portrayed military triumphs of Assyrian kings, their military strength was not infinite. Its increasing dependence upon mercenary forces and a weak administrative system contributed to Assyria's ultimate collapse around 610 B.C. The continuing power of invading barbarians once again overcame the movement toward large-scale political and social stability in the Tigris and Euphrates Valleys. It also reminded people of the dangers from the neighboring highlands in Persia (present-day Iran), Anatolia, and the open northeastern frontier, exposed as it was to the plateau and steppe barbarians. Barbarian military power, particularly as an initial strike force, met delayed, incomplete reactions from inhabitants of overrun territories. It was a recurring phenomenon and one of the most striking characteristics of the civilized centers between 1700 and 500 B.C. With the emergence of a Persian ruler, Cyrus the Great, around 550 B.C., a semibarbarous people from the fringes of the civilized world again established a single political power throughout the ancient Near East.

## Legendary History of Israel

The Hebrews, however, maintained their cultural dynamism. Following the exodus from Egypt and the slow settlement in Canaanite Palestine, linguistic, religious, and political unity developed rapidly. Like their contemporary Greek settlers, Hebrew tribes shared religious and political sanctuaries that linked otherwise independent clans. (Clans were separated by the lingering strength of the stronger centers of Canaanite urban life.) Between 1200 and 1000 B.C. the Hebrew tribes produced a series of remarkable leaders who first gained prominence as locally powerful citizens, military leaders, prophets, and legendary heroes. Of the heroes, Samson is a particularly striking example, while Samuel the prophet reflects the irregular combination of secular and religious authority that many of these figures claimed. Under several of these "Judges," the worship of Yahweh was invoked against the Canaanite deity Baal and other gods of the region. This religious authority established the beginnings of a tradition that claimed a continuous relationship between Yahweh and his people, from the first settlements in Canaan through the exodus from Egypt down to the twentieth century.

Stories of tribal leaders made up an important part of the legendary history of Israel. The Hebrews proved particularly resilient, and their god, Jehovah, slowly came to be regarded by non-Hebrews as an "international" god of justice—one of humanity's greatest needs in relation to its search for security. The Canaanites accepted him as theirs. By about 550 B.C., the Israelites—those tribes descended from the clans that had fled from Egypt under Moses' leadership—and others had merged their beliefs into a prophetic theology combined with an elaborate temple worship that came to be known as Judaism.

Long before, six of the ten tribes of Israel defeated the Canaanites in the Valley of Jezreel, but the pressure of the Philistines, against whom the legendary Samson fought so well, remained great. (The word philistine

Samson is both a real and a legendary figure of ancient Israel, whose remarkable strength, shown here in an old engraving, came from his long hair, which he would not cut. Using only the jaw of an ass as a club, he defeated the enemies of his people, the Philistines (a term which later came to mean "the uncultured"). In time Samson was betrayed by Delilah, and the Israelites retreated to the far north of Palestine. *Source: The Bettman Archive, Inc.*

came to mean barbarian, or uncultured.) A victory by Saul over the Ammonites led to his being made king (1028–1013 B.C.) of the Israelites. However, Saul's ambition and his introduction of new legal institutions that conflicted with the strong tradition of tribal and regional independence led to his downfall. His successor, King David (1000–961 B.C.)—a Philistine vassal who had been an effective mercenary soldier—restored the unified kindgom and chose the neutral city of Jerusalem as his capital. Solomon came next, entered into an alliance with the Egyptian Pharaoh and the King of Tyre, and began extensive trade. He introduced taxation and forced labor and turned Jerusalem into a showpiece of the Near East.

Upon Solomon's death, the northern tribes seceded. The remaining ones became the kingdom of Israel in 933 B.C. Thereafter followed a period of continuous warfare between tribes in and outside the kingdom and with other invaders. By 785 B.C., Jeroboam II reconquered the lost provinces and ruled over a powerful and prosperous kingdom, although Hebrew prophets were forecasting its ruin. In 744 B.C., the predictions of Hosea came true, and the new kings were forced to pay tribute to Assyria. When Samaria fell in 722 and thousands of Israelites were exiled, the kingdom no longer existed. In the meantime, Hebrew tribes outside Israel, drawn together as the kingdom of Judah, had unsuccessfully fought both Israel and the invaders. In time Judah passed to Babylonian rule through the victory of King Nebuchadnezzar whose anger at the continued resistance of the Jews led him to destroy Jerusalem in 586 B.C., bringing the kingdom of Judah to an end as well.

Although the rise of Assyria after the ninth century posed strong political threats for Israel, the worship of Jehovah had survived. Under the reign of Josiah in Judah in the seventh century B.C., a strong revival of the Yahweh cult, stripped of outside accretions, took place. The composition of the Book of Deuteronomy around 621 B.C. forged the powerful religious message of the earlier prophets into a legendary historical canon of laws. Those laws operated for the kingdom of Judah where restoration of the cult of Yahweh achieved deep and lasting roots before the rulers of Babylon destroyed its and Judah's independence. The Book of Jeremiah chronicles the end of the kingdom of Judah; the Book of Ezekiel describes the beginnings of Babylonian captivity.

Even in captivity, the earlier literature was preserved and compiled in the Old Testament, which was read aloud to the people in the synagogue. The writing of the so-called Second Isaiah developed the concept of universal obligation to worship Yahweh and the essentially spiritual character of Jewish religious institutions. During the rise of Persian dominance in the last years of the sixth century B.C., many Jews returned to Israel, the temple was rededicated, and the great prophets Nehemiah and Ezra began the process of restoring Jewish public life according to the principles of Old Testament canonical literature. Their vigorous work resulted in the emergence of the Torah, the first five books of the Old Testament, as the defining influence in the life of the Jew.

Thus the cult of Yahweh survived and slowly became the sole unifying force for the dispersed Jews. This cult emerged as a powerful social tradition and was enhanced by the further flowering of a great and enduring Hebrew literature. Transcending the local cult of a pastoral storm-and-war god, the cult of Yahweh underwent one of the most dramatic transformations in the history of ancient religion, and its power and majesty mark a stage both in the history of the conscience of civilized peoples and in the role of religion in societies threatened by political and economic disruption. The gods of Mesopotamia in Egypt had collapsed before the experience of these peoples and their religions. The god of the Jews emerged as the sole link holding together a people that might otherwise be blown to the winds and lost in the other populations of the Near East and Egypt, as so many other peoples of their period were. The code of law in the Torah and the visions of past and future in the historical and prophetic books of the Old Testament suggest an achievement as substantial and enduring as the domestication of grain and the elaboration of complex societies. That achievement was a concept of spiritual life that could survive otherwise formidable political and cultural threats. The heroic age of Judaism, from 1200 to 500 B.C., contributed a dimension to the human spirit that had enduring influence. Poets with the power of the Second Isaiah, Jeremiah, Ezekiel, and Amos embodied that spiritual awakening in a literary tradition whose influence has never declined.

The succession of Assyrian and Persian empires in the Middle East, the withdrawal of Egypt to the Nile Valley, and the emergence of distinctive, though often short-lived societies in the Levant—Israel, Phoenicia, and Damascus—occurred on a social base that remained surprisingly enduring. Peasant communities continued to live in symbiotic relationships with urban centers, and the spread of trading networks and the life of artisans continued. Widespread common languages, particularly Aramaic, opened up other avenues of communication after the sixth century B.C. Through commerce and social bonds, the entire Middle East gravitated toward a cosmopolitan cultural unity, politically dominated by Persia but containing many diverse strands. Between 1200 and 500 B.C., the experience of these peoples passed into heroic legend and religious history.

## Zoroastrianism

Alongside the articulation of Judaism, there emerged Zoroastrianism, a powerful set of religious beliefs that depicted the world as the scene of conflict between the forces of the God of Light, Ahura Mazda, and the God of Darkness, Ahriman. Ahura Mazda promised his followers immortality as a reward for their good actions, while evildoers were consigned to the House of Lies. Zoroastrianism emphasized a divine law applicable to all people. Once again, a religion had transcended local political and social traditions. During the middle of the first millennium B.C., the emergence of such universalist social institutions marked Iran as well. Thus, the Persians arrived to find that they could dominate a wider and more communicative world than that of their predecessors.

There existed other peoples on the edges of that world who were not at first directly involved in the cosmopolitan religious, economic, and political changes of the Middle East. Between 1500 and 500 B.C., for example, archaic Indian civilization took on its definitive shape. Between the tenth and the eighth centuries B.C., the nomadic pastoral peoples of the Eurasian steppe adopted the horse and developed light-armed mounted cavalry forces of great power. Northern and northeastern Persia, south Russia, and the western borders of China all felt the forces of these peoples, and frequently their power carried them to the heartlands of Chinese, Persian, and later European civilizations. By the eleventh century B.C., the characteristic elements of Chinese society also were becoming established.

## *Greece*

However, the most significant transformations for the history of the West and Near East, occurred in the northwest corner of the civilized Near East—on the Greek peninsula, in the islands of the Aegean Sea, and in the Greek speaking cities of the western coast of Asia Minor. The heroic age of Greece heralded a new center of civilization at the western edge of the old centers. At first developing largely apart from the political and religious turbulence of the Near East, the Greeks shaped a distinctive approach to civilization. Its earlier roots are revealed in the epic poems attributed to Homer and in the social and religious poetry of Hesiod of Boeotia in the ninth and eighth centuries B.C.

The destruction of Mycenean civilization by the migrant Achaeans and Dorians in the twelfth century B.C. reduced both the power and population of centers of wealth and trade that had characterized that civilization. The valleys and harbors that comprise much of the Greek peninsula with its inland plains and often dry mountain slopes became once more regionalized. Older urban life gave way to the life of the clan and the local shrine. Aristocratic warlords who ruled this society were only slowly drawn once again toward the sea and to the life of nearby societies. Like their chariot-riding predecessors of earlier centuries, an aristocratic cavalry dominated. Each warlord stood at the head of his household, the *oikos*. Attached to it were free and unfree laborers, servants, retainers, and slaves. The rest of the population consisted of free peasants, artisans, bards, and priests, but the *oikos,* actually a farm estate, stood at the center of life, and the form of one's attachment to an *oikos* determined social status. Loyalty to the household was paramount, and the family avenged the wrongs done to it. Even the armed retainers, dependents of these households, enjoyed a distinct prominence. In this society, as in many, trade and piracy were hardly distinguishable. The danger of a free person's being captured in a raid and reduced to slavery imparted a distinctive constraint to the relationships between slaves and slave owners, for what free person could be certain that he or she might not one day be a slave?

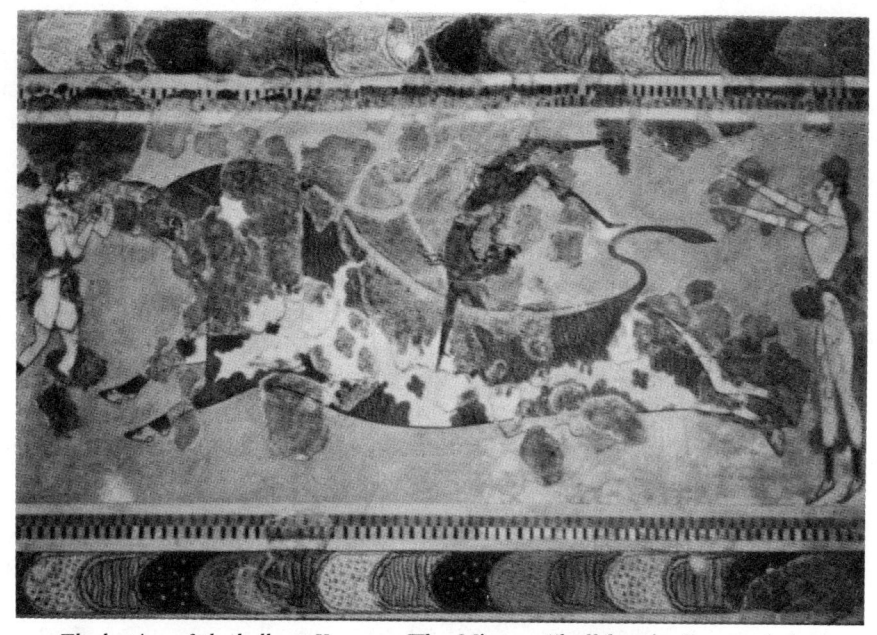

*The leaping of the bulls at Knossos* The Minoan "bull-leaping" sport is known to us through frescoes and designs that have survived to the present time. Acrobats somersaulted over a bull's back, using the bull's horns to begin their leap. The toreadors who assisted were women. The feat itself captured the sense of grace, of danger, and of sport so central to the Aegean civilization. *Source: Heraklion Museum.*

In this society, rulers with the title of king possessed little more power than did other great men who were allied to each other on the basis of friendship. They conducted their affairs—even when these sometimes involved an entire community—on the basis of individual status and honor, there being little significant concept of public welfare or integrated community needs. The values of this "heroic" society between the Iron Age and the spread of literacy may be illuminated by the work of recent anthropologists who study customs of societies still existing and who compare them with other past societies that had similar experiences. Thus, historians may draw an analogy between Greece from 1100 to 900 B.C. and the wandering Hebrew tribes between 1200 and 1050 B.C., as well as among similar societies in Ireland and continental Europe between A.D. 200 and 600.

Leaders of households and clans held values that were rural, militaristic, and local. They were loyal to regional deities. Glorious deeds of regional heroes and leading families were extolled in recitations of complex, if fictitious, genealogies which were all magnified to heroic proportions. With due care, we may consider some works to be literary idealizations of earlier societies: stories from the Book of Judges in the Old Testament, the Homeric poems, the Irish Ulster Cycle, and the later

Anglo-Saxon masterpiece *Beowulf*, first transcribed around A.D. 1000. Poets preserved what they chose to preserve of these earlier societies, neither completely understanding earlier social organization nor maintaining anything resembling historical objectivity. They wrote with emotion that was heightened by religious and cultural inspiration. Yet these literary works, their legitimacy supported by the results of archaeologists' investigations, reveal the image of that life and those values as seen by later generations. As with the Hebrews, the legendary periods were later reshaped into compelling historical visions that constituted the foundations of highly complex and influential religious movements. Much early Greek oral tradition received its fullest treatment and definitive shape by the writers of the Homeric epics. On the basis of this literature, religious and social values evolved which colored the later Greeks' impressions of their own period and their own civilization and created that which we still honor as the Greek way.

In spite of their scale, the Homeric poems deal with a society that was small in numbers, generally impoverished, and sharply divided—the *aristoi* (warlords) and household lords on one side, the *demos* (everybody else) on the other. The first word gave us "aristocracy," the second "democracy." Much of everyone's life was spent seeing to the essential requirements of security and survival: planting and harvesting crops, avenging domestic wrongs, defending the household, tending herds, importing specialists such as craftspeople, prophets, poets, and the *thes*, a poor, dismal, unattached laborer. Because of the relatively limited economic system, the life of a slave was not significantly different from that of the free householder, estate laborer, or peasant, nor in some cases from that of the lord of the household.

The enormous number of servants, the riches, and the vast armies of heroic legends are nearly always romanticized idealizations of a world in which a meager population and marginal poverty were always realities. Strangers who could not satisfactorily claim a recognizable stature in a community did not truly exist as a human in the eyes of this archaic people. Having a public identity was central to life. Personal relationships —loyalties, righting of wrongs, claims to power or protection—regulated social life, and the *aristoi* of one community probably felt closer to those of another, even when at war with that community, than they did to the lesser members of their own communities. Personal honor, an archaic value that is still found in street gangs today, degenerated into blind pride and undermined individual conduct. Everyone wanted to be a hero. In this society, the lives of certain men—not women, laborers, or slaves—received the most attention and had the highest status. The household community stopped at its leader; the life of the region depended upon the power of its warlord, whose life was ruled by a code far different from that which ruled the lives of others. Favoring individuals more by whim than by anything resembling spiritual merit, even the Homeric gods bestowed their favors and their wrath arbitrarily—always upon heroes. The *demos,* often the chief sufferers in this legendary world, shared nothing of the gods' or poets' concern.

The great literary classics of the Greeks were written during times that were very different from the turbulent period they claimed to depict. But the legendary past played a strong role in shaping new cultural conditions, as it still does. In the modern world, virtually every society, perhaps most notably pre-1945 Japan, uses the past to give purpose to the present. The heroic's world and the rural household were never as exclusive as Homer implies, of course. Cities survived, as did traces of Mycenean urban culture.

After 1200 B.C. Greek migrations to the Aegean islands and Asia Minor contributed to the restoration of older trading routes and to a renewing of the traditional Greek familiarity with the sea. Slow improvements in the cultivation of vines and olive groves made the limited agricultural lands of Greece and the islands commercially more productive; in addition traders brought their wares to the western Greek islands from the lands around the Black Sea. They came with metals, wool textiles, leather goods, dyes, and artifacts. They went back, especially after the seventh century, with blood-red wine, olive oil, and a distinctive pottery.

Homeric heroes were not interested in trade, but trade and piracy played important roles in their world as in the later, real world of Homer. Powerful Anatolian kingdoms, particularly those that succeeded the Assyrian Empire—the Phrygians, Lydians, and Persians—exerted both commercial and military pressure upon each other in self-defense. The spread of a language commonly revered by all Greeks added to a sense of shared "Greekness" throughout the post-Mycenean lands. As Greeks migrated eastward to Asia Minor and the Levant and eastward to Sicily and southern Italy, they noticed sharp linguistic and cultural differences between themselves and their non-Greek neighbors. Those observations have contributed to this homogenizing of Greek culture and a consciousness of being Greek, not *bar-bar,* that so strikingly characterize the world of the eighth through the sixth centuries B.C.

From Minoan and Mycenean days on, the limited topography and agricultural productivity had been overcome by exploitation of the sea, trade, and opportunities for migration. From Minoan and Mycenean Greece there survived cities with paved streets, multistoried houses, and sophisticated drainage systems. Public and religious structures were remarkable in their human scale and lacked the monumental impersonality so characteristic of Near Eastern and Egyptian structures. By Homer's day the Greek gods were considered powerful, remote and arbitrary, but they were not monsters, and their conduct could be understood, even if not regularly or predictably influenced through prayer or ritual. Where there was no room for an expanding population in Greece itself, the Greeks went elsewhere, taking their customs and culture with them as immigrants would continue to do forever.

The mobile Greeks after 1200 B.C. entered a world that was in constant movement—Mycenean and other Greek peoples moved to the islands, to Asia Minor, and to Sicily. Peoples from Asia Minor migrated to the Levant. Syrians, Phoenicians, Philistines, and the Etruscan migrants of Italy all found new places in which to settle. By 750 B.C., these new settlements began to expand by sending colonies of settlers westward into the little-known western Mediterranean Sea. Phoenicia sent colonists to Carthage and Utica in North Africa, to southern Spain, and to Italy. The growing Etruscan cities of north-central Italy exerted increased economic and political control over the northwest Mediterranean, while the cities of western Greece began to colonize southern Italy and southern Gaul.

The vigor of eighth- and seventh-century migration and trade began to overcome the imitation of the past that had been briefly restored by post-Mycenean Greek society. Homeric poets had seen social change occurring at what seemed an alarming rate, in an undesirable direction. Their heroic epics, like most historical preservation movements, were attempts to preserve certain traditional sets of values in the face of these changes. The values of a heroic world were not the only institutions under pressure during the period between the eighth and the sixth centuries B.C. A large-scale shift to wine and olive oil production transformed the nature of landholding and the economic life of the small farmer. The growth of trade created a new urban dynamism, altering the balance between the countryside and the city. Old divisions of families and tribes, with their local deities and *themistes,* or family laws, and their limited economic needs, gave way before the push of urban life and became the bases of urban social organization.

By the seventh century B.C., the heroic world of post-Mycenean Greece was already a legend of the living past. Its episodes, religious values, and ethics contributed powerfully to the emerging culture of the prosperous trading farms and cities. But by the late sixth century B.C., Greek cities in Asia Minor encountered the growing power of Persia. Two distinct centers of civilization in the Near East now veered toward conflict.

From 1200 to 500 B.C. the instability caused by barbarian or semibarbarian invasions into the older centers of civilization was countered somewhat by other conditions. Agricultural techniques spread. Complex forms of social organization and technology developed. Networks were formed by trade. There were widely-spoken languages and common tendencies to reconcile religious beliefs, including a distinctive spiritualizing of religious systems. The development of cursive forms of writing increased the possibilities—indeed, the inevitability—of cross-cultural communication. Most people in this network remained agricultural laborers, but agrarian life was never secure. Commercial crops, natural disasters, the insecurity of maintaining large holdings, and the growth of debt contracts made rural conditions precarious. Those who depended upon agricultural stability also suffered a loss of wealth and a threat to their status.

New wealthy groups emerged and took two courses. They either challenged older institutions and sets of values, or they assimilated the established values and imitated traditional status systems, as newly-rich groups (the *nouveau riche*) have continued to do. By 500 B.C. the agricultural, urban, and commercial systems of the Near East began to spread into the western Mediterranean, and the resulting wealth gave great impetus to the old western edge of civilization: the Greek peninsula, the Aegean islands, the Greek cities of Asia Minor, and the settlements of the Levant. The rising power of Persia, however, loomed threateningly large in this new world, as if the old centers of civilization were once more asserting a claim to dominance based upon a recovery of older traditions and military superiority. When Persia encountered the Greek cities in a new war later in the fifth century B.C., this claim to dominance acquired great importance for the future of the centers of civilization. The outcome of that Persian War contributed greatly to the increased westward drift of civilization and to the transformation of ancient Near Eastern culture through the youthful genius of the Greeks. From 500 to 200 B.C., the Greeks influenced both the ancient Near Eastern world and the new world of the western Mediterranean. In this period "western" civilization became distinctively "Western," and the culture that we designate Mediterranean Antiquity acquired its distinctive characteristics.

# PART TWO

Mediterranean Antiquity: 500 B.C. - A.D. 750

*Better beans and bacon in peace than cakes and ale in fear.*
—Aesop, *fl* 550 B.C.

## AN OVERVIEW: OUR GRAECO-ROMAN WORLD

Between 500 and 200 B.C., two particularly strong powers emerged on the frontiers of the Near Eastern civilized world. In the northwest, the city-states of Greece produced a culture and an economic and military force that marked a new dynamism in the eastern and central Mediterranean. In the southwest, the Persian monarchy restored new vigor to older imperial institutions and assumed rule over a productive, varied, and increasingly wealthy society. Between 494 and 445 B.C., many of the Greek city-states allied with each other to check the growth of Persian power, particularly among the Greek cities of Asia Minor. The effectiveness of the city of Athens in this war led to its rise to political and economic prominence among Greek cities. Athens turned exploitation of trade and military successes into commercial and political advantages for herself and she ascended with unprecedented speed. Athenian silver mines enabled the city to build, almost overnight, as large a navy as the rest of Greece had. Between 431 and 404 B.C., in the Peloponnesian War, an enemy league led by the city-state of Sparta warred with Athens and succeeded in reducing Athenian power to a shadow of its former self. The enormous toll in lives and resources taken by this war, the effects of a great plague in Athens in 430 B.C., and the bellicose attitudes of the city-states toward each other weakened victors and vanquished alike, and periodical Persian intervention further diminished the momentary stability established after the Persian War.

The political and economic weakness of the city-states opened the way for a new power to rise in Greece, that of the northern kingdom of Macedon, ruled by a talented dynasty, which admired much of Greek culture but remained militarily powerful and autocratic. Under Philip of Macedon (359–336 B.C.) and his son and successor Alexander (336–323 B.C.), the city-states were forced into leagues led by the Macedonian kings. Once again the ominous presence of Persia gave the Greeks a sense of unity and a military mission that required cooperation from all. The price of the disruptive political events between 445–338 B.C. had been high in terms of population loss, the transformation of culture, and the erosion of city independence. This century, however, had shaped Greek military forces into the most effective fighting organization the civilized world had yet seen. Throughout the late fifth and fourth centuries B.C., Greek mercenaries served under Persian, Egyptian, and Macedonian rulers. Harnessing these forces, Philip and Alexander advanced into Persia and destroyed not only the Persian Empire but the independence of all lands between the Nile in Egypt and the Jaxartes.

Alexander's sudden death in 323 B.C. resulted in his generals and their successors carving up parts of his empire. By the end of the fourth century B.C., the kingdoms of Macedonia, Epirus in Greece, Anatolia, Persia, and Egypt were ruled by Greek-speaking dynasties based upon Alexander's techniques and tempered by local traditions. Greece's fourth-century culture sustained these dynasties and their ruling elites; and the later stage of Greek culture, known as *Hellenism* (the imitation of Greek culture by Jewish, Roman, and other groups) permeated the older centers of the civilized world. Hellenism reached even the eastern and western frontiers. The emergence of Greece between the fifth and the third century and its triumph in the old centers of Near Eastern civilization caused a distinct westward shift to the centers of power in the civilized world. After Alexander's conquests, the temporary eclipse of Persia permitted the spread of Greek culture and the establishment of its role as an educational and artistic leader. Extensive territory controlled by the far-flung Hellenistic monarchies in the wake of Alexander offered a new cultural homogeneity to ruling elites of the Mediterranean and Near Eastern world.

Hellenistic monarchies survived from 300 to 100 B.C. (and to 31 B.C. in Egypt). During these two centuries the original city-state vitality of Greek culture took on great strength. A relatively small elite who ruled from Greece to India transformed its style of life. What it lost in original vigor it partially made up for by creating educational theories, dispensing lavish royal patronage, and accumulating treasures in libraries and museums. These were available to all. Historiography, drama, and lyric poetry now appeared in fixed academic forms; mathematics, astronomy, literary criticism, and religious thought grew. The schools of Athens remained a magnet for thinkers from the western Mediterranean as well as from the Tigris-Euphrates Valleys. A cultured Greek or Syrian could travel from Marseilles through the eastern Mediterranean and Syria all the way to Bactria, the last Hellenistic outpost on the frontier of India and the steppe, and find himself in a cultural continuum that was familiar. These remarkable political and cultural achievements laid down a firm, enduring basis for later developments. Indeed, the subsequent rise of Persia and Rome, the decline of the Hellenistic monarchies, the rise of Christianity, the settlement of Europe, and the spread of Islam all owed immeasurable debts to the exported form of Hellenistic culture that flourished in the fourth through the second centuries B.C.

But the Hellenistic monarchies of Greece, Egypt, and the Near East succumbed to other great powers in the second and first centuries B.C. In the east, the semi-independent Hellenistic provinces slowly declined under the twin pressures of the Parthian monarchy and invasions by Iranian nomads from the east. From the second century B.C. through the first century A.D. the Parthian Empire stretched from the Euphrates to India and drew considerable resources from the Hellenistic, Mesopotamian, and Jewish culture of the region. From the middle of the first century A.D., however, the influence of Hellenism was eclipsed by rapidly developing Iranian culture. Ardashir, a member of the Sasanid dynasty of south Persia, aided by warlords from the edge of the Parthian world, overthrew the Parthian Empire and signalled the rise of another vigorous Persian monarchy. That meant a further lessening of the influence of Hellenism from the Tigris-Euphrates Valley eastward to India. The eastern Iranian orientation of the Sasanid monarchy marked one significant break in the traditions of Mediterranean Hellenism that had grown between the fourth century B.C. and the third century A.D.

In the West, another power emerged on the ruins of the Hellenistic monarchies. That power was Rome. From the third century B.C., a vigorous force on the western frontier of the Hellenistic world once again acquired political dominance. But more importantly, the emergence of Rome was carried out under much stronger and more permeating Hellenistic influences than that of either Parthia or Sasanid Persia. The original eastern Mediterranean center of Hellenistic culture became the core of a political and economic empire that extended far to the west, into North Africa, Spain, and Celtic Europe and had reached the British Isles by the middle of the first century A.D. Hellenistic elements in the culture of the Roman world and their eclipse in Persia once again revealed the role of Mesopotamia as a fulcrum in the evolution of civilized societies in the West. When, in turn, the western parts of the Roman Empire succumbed to internal and external pressures in the fifth century A.D., a powerful Hellenistic civilization remained in the old Eastern part of the Roman Empire, centered upon the city of Constantinople (present-day Istanbul). There it survived until the middle of the fifteenth century. This civilization of Eastern Rome, or Byzantium, as it came to be called, influenced Germanic Europe, Arabic Africa, Persia, and the steppes of central Russia. It constituted one of the most visible and influential survivals of the old Hellenistic ideals.

Rome and Sasanid Persia dueled until the Sasanid Empire was virtually destroyed in A.D. 625. However, both Rome's weakness and the appearance of a renewed local dynamism in its various provinces cleared the way for the appearance of Islam, a political and religious movement that swept the Middle East in the last years of the seventh century A.D. Eventually, Islam absorbed both the less developed peoples of western North Africa and the sophisticated remains of the Persian Empire. Persia vied with Romanized Hellenism throughout the early eighth century, until the influences of Persia (and the Arabian tradition) triumphed in Islam after A.D. 750. From that date, the old homogeneity of the Mediterranean was broken. The Mediterranean itself became a frontier rather than a bridge separating the semibarbarian cultures of Christian Western Europe from the culture of Islam, while the Byzantine Empire, also Christian, served as a buffer between the two in the East.

From the middle of the eighth century A.D. on, Europe, Byzantium, and Islam developed in separate ways. The fall of Byzantium to Islamic Turks in 1453 changed the religious map of Europe affecting the Mediterranean, the Balkans, and Eastern Europe. Remains of Byzantine civilization continued to influence Western and Eastern Europe, however, and the period between 1500 and 1800 saw two major centers of civilization in the West—Western Europe and the Ottoman Turkish Empire—contending for supremacy.

From 500 B.C. to A.D. 750, then, Western civilization was centered in the Mediterranean Sea and the influence of Hellenistic culture in the lands surrounding it. After 750, Islamic Persia faced Christian Byzantium and a Christian and Latin Europe. Old Greek and Near Eastern centers of civilization had done their work, and the western part of Eurasia witnessed the emergence of two rival civilizations. Not until the nineteenth century, over a thousand years later, was it clear which would emerge the stronger, and even then the decision may have been a temporary one.

## II. 1 Greek Society and the Origins of Hellenistic Culture

> *A man may know everything else, but without ... knowledge [of Greek thought and life] he remains ignorant of the best intellectual and moral achievements. ...* Charles Eliot Norton, 1885

Agrarian and clan-oriented, the archaic Greek world of rural households, warlords, and tribal gods expressed its values in terms of identity, status, and security. Membership in an *oikos,* on whatever level, was a guarantee of security far greater than anything wandering craftspeople or homeless laborers could achieve. The *autarchy* (or self-sustenance) of these great households and the prestige of their leaders, recognized by gifts and wealth acquired by plunder, were expressed in terms that remained essential to Greek social thought long after the society giving rise to them had passed. A truly great man possessed *arete,* honor achieved through military prowess. He was *agathos;* that is, honorable or preeminent among his peers. A rough military sense of equality and limited resources instilled both a rigid formal code of honor and competitiveness among leaders, which never entirely disappeared from Greek civilization. The achievement of honorific status carried with it social preeminence in other areas of life as well, and the aristocrat's obligations to maintain personal honor and defend the code of aristocratic values were fundamental to the next stage of Greek society, the emergence of the city-state.

Town life had survived from the Mycenean period although on a much smaller scale, and commercial opportunities which were exploited by the settlements in the Aegean islands and the western parts of Asia Minor led to new economic influences in Greece itself. Grapes and olives were being grown commercially; and trade, rather than war, was producing fortunes. The local authority of the *aristoi* was threatened when some households were divided through inheritance and some were tempted to enter into a market relationship with the city or with others of their kind. Wider circulation of money and risks of market conditions made further inroads into the older, rural, aristocratic and autarchic way of life.

In early urban centers as well, aristocratic characteristics slowly faded as wealth was amassed through commerce and small industry. Although wealthy aristocratic leaders attempted to maintain their older values, their power increasingly depended upon economic success and landed wealth. Both those who continued to thrive and those admitted to the ranks of the urban patricians preserved the vocabulary of aristocratic values developed centuries earlier, even though the very terms themselves were taking on new meanings. However, those aristocrats who became impoverished and saw their status threatened by others bitterly denounced the new economic conditions.

For many older forms of Greek society, particularly in Athens but also for Greeks overseas in Syracuse, Smyrna, and Miletus, "the cake of custom" was broken. As circulation of capital increased, silver bullion became important. Debt and its attendant risks entered the lives of more people—people with widely different standards of living and control over wealth. For 90 percent of the Greek population, which still lived in centers of less than five thousand people, and notably for Spartans, Thessalians, Boeotians, and Macedonians, these changes were far slower in coming, creating a marked cultural imbalance.

Military changes as well contributed to the emergence of cities and the slow decline of rural household lords. A distinctive battle formation—heavily armored infantry massed to fight in unison—displaced the importance of the aristocratic cavalry in the seventh and sixth centuries B.C. New infantry armies trained for discipline, cooperation, and difficult maneuvers formed the backbone of the urban population. Thus there emerged a social ideal of working for the public good. Civic responsibility rivalled ideals of aristocratic competitiveness and individual distinction. It even slowed the drift toward polarizing class distinctions. Economic instability during the seventh and sixth centuries B.C. also worked against class distinctions because being rich or poor was not necessarily a lifelong condition. Poets such as Hesiod in the eighth century and Theognis in the sixth were bitterly aware of the disruptive influences of new wealth; as the latter noted, no one could take his wealth with him to Hades. But against that disorder there must be set the remarkable social innovations that softened the harsh consequences of a changing social order and the survival of an archaic social value system.

### *Sparta*

Two Greek city-states suggest the different ways in which communities responded to the new pressures after the sixth century B.C. Sparta in the Peloponnese, like other cities, retained the older social divisions based upon tribes and clans, shared cult centers, and as the most prominent city in its region, began to show concern over the economic and political changes taking place around it. Probably around 825 B.C. a legendary ruler, Lycurgus, instituted reforms that became the basis of later Spartan society. Under these reforms, citizens were sharply marked off from those who were not citizens, and they were organized with great thoroughness as a standing army. Supported by the government of the city, the Spartan citizen did not perform regular work. That was done by *helots,* who were not free, and by *perioeci*, who were free people in the hinterland but whose political affairs were controlled by Sparta. Nor did Spartan citizens live with their families on their own land. Rather, they lived with comrades-in-arms, in organized military clubs. First and foremost, the citizen of Sparta was a soldier. Male children at the age of seven were taken from their mothers and started on a strict course of training to be fighters. As adults, the assembly of citizen soldiers had a powerful voice in the government. This remarkable set of social reforms gave Sparta the most formidable army in the Greek world. However, as a result of its commitment to an exclusively military form of life, Spartan society was compelled to deny itself the variety of quasi-democratic reforms that put it out of step with Athens.

Nonetheless, it was typical of an important segment of the Greek world. Commerce, trade, and communication were in the hands of *perieoci* on a strictly regulated scale. Spartan citizens knew little of the world around them and avoided access to the new market relationships of the eastern Mediterranean in order to preserve their rigid social system and maintain both military and psychological defenses. Each citizen lived totally for the state; and although the demands of the state led to considerable security, this was at the price of cultural rigidity and harsh exploitation of the labor of the subordinate helot population. The personal lives of the Spartans depended more upon older forms of economic organization, particularly agriculture, than did the lives of citizens of other city-states. To a far greater degree than in any earlier society, the Spartan military ideal determined all aspects of the individual's life and thought. Sparta thus became the Military State par excellence.

### *Athens*

Emergence of the city-state as the focus of individual loyalty was a slow process in Sparta, as elsewhere. Even the successful stages of city-state growth after the sixth century B.C. retained many of the social structures and value systems of earlier periods. Yet the attraction of the cities was powerful, in spite of reappearing class consciousness and economic inequalities that city growth fostered. While Sparta responded to the prospects of change by transforming the citizen body into an army and thoroughly subordinating all other aspects of social cultured life to this single ideal, other cities responded differently. Sparta, located in the center of the Peloponnesus, depended upon land-based power and focused its concern upon its territorial security. Athens, on the other hand, close to the sea and to people of surrounding regions, had for centuries maintained contact with urban ideals and with the world. Although Athenian aristocracy ruled the city through elected magistrates, forces of social dislocation and economic change confronted the more democratic Athenians with the same problem that faced Sparta. However, cosmopolitan traditions of Athens and expanding economic opportunities produced a city-state far different.

Further, since 1200 B.C., the Greek world was one of migrants and wanderers, and nothing so changes an individual perspective as a change in environment. Their status in the archaic period of great rural households, small markets, and dependence upon family or peer relationships was uncertain, always insecure. As economic and social changes of the eighth through the sixth centuries B.C. opened these older closed societies to newcomers, many people with no connection in a region—mercenary soldiers (after the fourth century B.C.), traders, and laborers who had hitherto possessed no recognized status—found a place in the growing towns. They challenged the older power of aristocratic patricians. Political upheavals ensued during the seventh and sixth centuries B.C., and many city-states turned to forms of revolutionary government, whether tyrannies or oligarchies. Formation of the constitution of Sparta was one reaction to these changes; Athens's response was another, and by some thought to be the more progressive.

It was certainly smoother than most. The image of the *polis* (tri-state) as the focus of social life did not carry with it rigid stratification of society. Neither did it foment widespread social discontent and rebellion. Oppression of the poor and privileges for the aristocracy were curtailed under the leadership of the wise Solon, who became *archon* (or chief magistrate) in 594 B.C. Wealth and income were established as the criteria for citizenship and officeholding, and more people were allowed to participate in the affairs of the city. The broader scope of Athenian citizenship weakened the older exclusiveness of tribal and family authority, freeing individuals to act as they wished within the framework of a code of laws agreed upon by the citizen body. Throughout the sixth century B.C., Athenian civic reformers worked to restructure their society. Traditional forms of economic activity such as small landholdings were protected, and at the same time wealthy newcomers acquired access to power. The *polis,* as the primary area of change, attracted loyalties that had hitherto been reserved for the household and tribe. Popular assemblies and law courts gave a voice to poorer citizens, while for a time, aristocratic privilege was preserved in higher offices. Under the reforming tyrannies of Pisistratus (560–528 B.C.) and Cleisthenes (at the end of the sixth century B.C.), aristocratic privileges were further reduced. Tribal organizations weakened as residence rather than family bestowed citizenship, and common worship of the gods implanted similar religious loyalties among people who initially respected and depended upon one another on the basis of secular needs.

Athenian democracy thus created a flexible citizen body in which political power was widely distributed and the first loyalty of the citizen was to the *polis,* or city-state, itself. Institutional reforms had mitigated the worst effects of social and economic disruption; for example, the number of *hoplites* (infantry companies) was greatly increased both with the rapid development of the fleet in the sixth century and the necessity for all citizens to participate in the constant wars of the period. This wide participation in military affairs and the fluidity of the class structure within the body of citizens permitted Athens to build upon, rather than defend herself against, the economic opportunities of the fifth century.

Because they were in frequent contact, Greek city-states were conscious of their relatedness, of their speaking a language that was more and more the same, and of worshipping the same Olympian gods. Greek colonists shared values with the cities, the peninsula, and the islands; and Homer's nostalgic literature was popular with everyone. The Olympic games, according to legend celebrated every four years from 776 B.C., contributed to the common bond that outweighed different social structures among many of the city-states. Victors at the Olympic games brought glory not only to themselves but to their cities. Religious shrines, such as the oracle of Apollo at Delphi and Zeus at Dodona, were important because they were open to all Greeks. The city-state, rather than the family, became the mediator between the gods and the individual, further strengthening the sense of personal association with the *polis* and with fellow citizens. Homeric gods had been remote and arbitrary; but by the end of the sixth century B.C., many were transformed into gods that were concerned about human justice. Divine patrons of cities were increasingly expected to cooperate with human efforts, to be accessible to human reason, and to aid in attaining the ends of justice. The Olympian gods themselves became more accessible to all Greeks and were identified with particular cities. Now some thinkers looking beyond the anthropomorphic deities (gods having human attributes) toward more abstract and comprehensible principles that regulated the universe.

Nor was the sphere of the Greek gods so universal that it prevented wider speculation. Homer's gods had been appropriate to the heroic society in which they participated, but there was no universal priesthood on earth to guard the sacred lore. Homer's popular depiction of the gods limited their jurisdiction to the *polis,* leaving them little room for expansion. Other forms of religious activity survived, however, particularly mystery religions (secret cults with rites known only by the initiated); Greeks were not only aware of, but also curious about religious thought of other peoples. Thus, the way was free for independent thinkers to strike out along other lines without encountering substantial opposition. From the days of Thales of Miletus, who in 585 B.C. predicted an eclipse,

*The Discus Thrower* The Greeks thought of there being a "divine tension"—in art, in human relations, in statecraft—which shaped man's relations to himself and to his gods. This statue, dating from *c* 450 B.C. and now in the Museo Nazionale Romano, in Rome, reflects these concepts, as well as illustrating the Greek love of games. Throwing the discus is still part of track and field events in the modern Olympics. *Source: Alinari-Scala.*

and his successors, Ionian philosophers who sought to explain the workings of the universe in naturalistic, almost mechanistic terms, Greek thinkers struck out on a little-fettered track of speculation that remained well within the broad bounds of contemporary religious propriety.

This precocious Greek thrust toward investigating nature and humankind's place in the universe derived much from the political and cultural achievements of the sixth century. Human regulation of earthly affairs, the institution of enduring laws within the *polis,* and rewards for human efforts colored deeply the characteristics of Greek religious and philosophical thought. Achievements of soldiers, sailors, merchants, and neighbors in most city-states promoted an appreciation for success through human merit rather than by chance or the arbitrary intervention of a god. With an eloquence and profundity not surpassed to this day, Greek tragic drama probed the frontier between human freedom and responsibility. But even the terrible destruction of its heroes reinforced the security of the *polis* by distinguishing both the godlike and sinful qualities in men and women and by emphasizing a widely recognized sense of fully rational yet divine justice extended to humans. The citizen found security and human associations in the neighborhood and *polis*, rather than in the limited world of the *oikos*. These new experiences and responses were supported by a stronger, more cosmopolitan direction.

Yet these changes primarily affected only the citizen body of the Greek *polis*, which did not include all the human beings within a city. Even after the Spartan and Athenian reforms of the sixth century B.C., large bodies of people failed to acquire citizen status. Some were slaves, legally defined as living property, and their position probably worsened as the life of the city-state replaced the life of the *oikos*. In archaic society, there had been few differences between slaves and masters. But by the seventh century B.C., slave labor increased in the vineyards and olive groves, and a few centuries later slaves were pressed into performing the labor considered unfit for free men. The victims of warfare, kidnapping, and indebtedness were often turned into slaves. As the varied needs for slave labor increased, the lives of slaves generally worsened, even though domestic slaves might join their masters as they did in an *oikos*. For the helots in the kingdom of Sparta and the laborers in the Athenian silver mines, the worst aspects of slavery were particularly marked. Possessing no legal rights and considered as chattel, the slave population constituted the bottom and yet an important level of the fifth- and fourth-century labor force. The institution of slavery thus became an integral part of Greek, as well as Near Eastern, life.

Resident aliens, in Athens called *metics*, constituted another large part of the labor force. Technically free and usually employed in productive industries, the *metics* were nonetheless deprived of political rights. Their labor freed many citizens for full political participation in the affairs of the city. Slaves and *metics* were not the only nonparticipating elements in Greek urban culture. The position of women in Greek society was one of political and social disability. Traditional predominance of the male in the rural household was strengthened by the transition to urban life, and the woman—who had several responsibilities in an agricultural-based society—was relegated to the role of manager of household operations, not an insignificant social or even economic function, but one devoid of political significance nevertheless. Literary Greek lacked even the equivalent terms for the partners of a conjugal union, as if to imply that marital status was among the least important for a citizen. Post-Mycenean Greece was male-dominated, especially where military or political responsibilities were great. Male relationships, from formal friendships to homosexuality, played at least as important a role among the aristocracy and leading citizens as did male-female relationships. Ideas of the natural inferiority of women, common to other societies as well, reinforced a woman's legal position and kept her life largely confined to the house of her husband. Maintenance of the household economy and supervision of slaves constituted her chief obligations, and she was excluded from the normal social occasions. Male dominance of public affairs was echoed in male freedom in sexual matters. The wife was expected to remain chaste, while the husband, burdened by no such expectations, consorted with *hetaerae* (courtesans from the class of *metics*, hence women outside citizen-society) and female slaves. Although there is evidence of marital affection and much praise in Greek literature for the happy domestic household, marriage and domestic affairs played a small part in male life; and male life was the life of the town.

In a society dominated by male companionship and male social gatherings, pederasty played a wide and important role. Male meetingplaces, from the marketplace to the baths, provided far more numerous occasions for male contact than did the pure formalities involved in contracting a marriage or approaching a courtesan. Moreover, training the young included young boys but excluded girls, and mainly consisted of older men initiating younger ones into the responsibilities of citizenship. Thus, the broad spectrum of male affection ranged from civic responsibility to homosexual relations. In this complex interaction institutions such as education, apprenticeship, public training, and love all played respectable parts. In its ideal form, homosexuality (actually bisexuality) constituted an essential and recognized part of the training of upper-class Greek youths. Its character echoes both the older aristocratic concept of male affection and the male-dominated face of Athenian society. Only centuries later would changing sexual mores lead the conventions of society to view homosexuality with alarm. In time, civic life, limited to citizens, was increasingly common to all Greek city-states, as was a growing sense of a Hellenic community with common cultural values. The true vigor of Greek unity, however, did not emerge until the fifth century B.C., when its growing security was challenged from without. In its response to that challenge, the Hellenic community would be seen to exist precisely at the moment it fought most vigorously for its existence.

## II. 2 Challenge and Response: The Golden Age of Greece

> *For to famous men all the earth is a sepulchre: and their virtues shall be testified, not only by the inscription in stone at home, but by an unwritten record of the mind....* —Pericles' Funeral Oration, as constructed by Thucydides, c. 411 B.C.

### The Persian Challenge

The Persian monarchy had grown more powerful in Mesopotamia and the Iranian plateau from its foundation by Cyrus the Great around 550 B.C. to its height under Darius I, also the Great (521–486 B.C.). Military power was supported effectively by royal administrative institutions, a vigorous code of laws, and the suppression of centers of discontent, in particular the long-privileged priesthoods of the temple-cities of Mesopotamia. Under Darius's successor, Xerxes I (486–465 B.C.), improved communications throughout the empire and renewed vigor in the commercial economy expanded Persian power and continued the process of bringing much of the Near East into an economic and political sense of community. In the last years of the sixth century B.C., Persians conquered Egypt and extended their own borders beyond the Indus River. Persian monarchs successfully defended their eastern and northern frontiers against nomadic invaders. Even so, at the end of Darius's reign, rebellions arose in both Babylonia and Egypt.

Maintenance of so vast an empire had absorbed Cyrus's attention. Having destroyed Lydia, he now dominated the Greek cities of the Anatolian coast, but they posed a political problem. Although part of Asia Minor, these cities maintained contact with the islands and mainland of Greece. When Miletus and other cities revolted between 499 and 494 B.C., Persia adopted a policy of reinforcing its control not only over the Greek towns of Asia Minor, but also over the towns of mainland Greece and the islands. In 492 B.C., an expeditionary force penetrated northern Greece from Persia by sea as well as by land, put ashore at Marathon, and encountered the small citizen-infantry armies of Athens and Plataea. Under the command of Miltiades, a fervent anti-Persian who knew his enemy well, the Greek city-armies won a surprising victory. Not for ten years did a new Persian force return to the task of conquest.

In 480 B.C., a vast Persian fleet and army swept into Greece under the personal command of Xerxes, destroyed tenacious Greek resistance at the pass of Thermopylae, and again threatened the discordant and divided Greek cities. Under the command of Themistocles, the recently strengthened Athenian fleet defeated the Persian fleet at Salamis and

# Ancient Greece

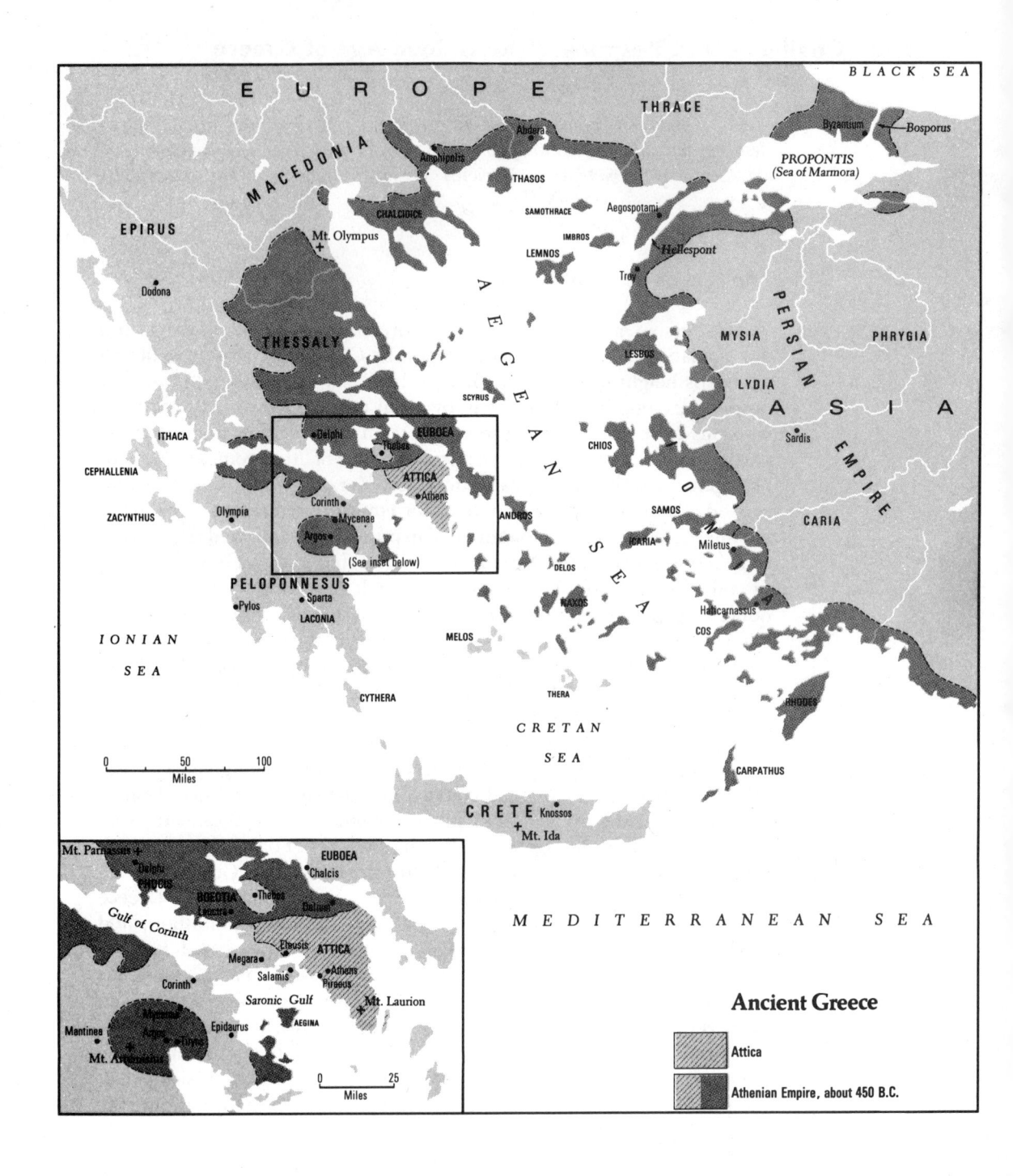

**Attica**

**Athenian Empire, about 450 B.C.**

once more set back the Persian plan of conquest, but not before Athens had been sacked. In 479 B.C., Athenian resources proved unequal to yet another Persian assault, and this time the Peloponnesians were strengthened by the disciplined Spartan soldiery, which defeated the Persians at Plataea while the Greek fleet successfully conquered the Persians at Mycale. Naval superiority in the eastern Mediterranean clearly passed to the Greek fleets led by Athenians, and the territorial ambition of the Persian Empire was checked in the West.

The experience of the Greek cities between 490 and 479 B.C. had revealed discord and rivalry, to be sure, but also a triumph in alliance, a vindication of what citizens came to consider the Greek way of life against the slave armies of the "barbarian" Persians. In the following decades, the prestige of Athens earned her the right to direct operations against Persia in the Aegean and Asia Minor, and her military leadership gave her an opportunity to increase the economic strength of her markets. Vigorous Athenian power and economic expansion reinforced the democratic character of the city-state and further weakened the traditional status of the aristocrats, many of whom, dismayed at the rising status of the lower commercial classes, openly sympathized with Athens's rivals, particularly Sparta. Although the growing Athenian empire originally was based upon a shared anti-Persian feeling, as Athens slowly came to control an enlarging regional commerce, she aroused the enmity of her rival Greek cities. From 431 to 404 B.C., a Spartan-led coalition of Greek cities thus locked in the inter-Peloponnesian War with Athens, which suffered considerable destruction of its overseas empire and market and of the lands around the city itself. The diminution of Athenian power prevented a single superstate from growing up in Greece. It threatened the basis of Athenian democracy and restored regional authority to individual cities.

### *The Polis*

From the Persian defeat in 479 to 404 B.C., then, the city of Athens had used its economic and political prosperity to make itself an image of the ideal *polis,* as well as the center of its expanding empire. But in spite of the glories of the Acropolis and the great temples with their beautiful sculptures and settings, much of the rest of Athens apparently consisted of extremely modest adobe houses crowded together in narrow streets filled with the teeming life of citizens, *metics,* and slaves. Although agricultural proprietorship still counted for much in this city-world, commerce and industry developed under the imperial expansion and were accelerated by the needs of the fleet as well as by the market of a trading empire. Athens became a great international commercial center. To enable even poor citizens to participate in the popular assembly and the law courts, state support of the citizenry came to include pensions, distribution of free food, and widespread state employment in many forms, all contributing to provide a modest scale of living for many.

Yet even during this remarkable commercial and urban revolution, the scale of Athenian life remained unpretentious. Much public money went to defense and display, and the limited productivity of artisan and industrial enterprises could not keep up with citizens' purchasing power. The ideal of life—that of endowed leisure—did not place value upon the labor that in itself might have changed city life. The ideal of leisured citizens, free to help their city or to improve their minds as they chose, conflicted with the necessity of work in a market economy and thus with the place that work held in the changing Greek system of values. Surviving aristocrats were, of course, steeped in the leisure ethic, but most Athenians liked the idea, too, transformed though it was by the attractions of public life in the *polis*. The competitive spirit was still there, from athletics to contests by tragic playwrights. Personal status remained important, and was considered exclusively in terms of individual shame and honor. The closed circle of citizenship and the limitation of outsiders also survived

*The Acropolis of Athens* Perhaps the most famous surviving structure from all antiquity, the Acropolis represents the serenity and grace, the tension and drama, of the best Greek art. This combination of temple, sanctuary, Parthenon, and fortification, at its height about 400 B.C., is without parallel in the Western world.

from an older value system to shape the contours of personal and public life in the Golden Age of fifth-century Athens. But the triumphs of Athenian culture in the tragedies of Aeschylus (525–456 B.C.) and Sophocles (496–405 B.C.) and of democracy under Pericles (460–429 B.C.) can best be understood in terms of the economic and cultural attitudes of the Athenians themselves.

The *polis* now constituted a new and productive social unit, which provided security, opportunity for survival, and occasions for social intercourse far greater than were available in the earlier *oikos* or the cumbersome empires of the East. In spite of the survival of aristocratic values, the *polis* constituted a new framework for the definition of self and offered both an increased degree of security in terms of material life and an unparalleled opportunity for intellectual exploration within the loose confines of *polis* religion. Disasters of the Peloponnesian Wars did not, therefore, destroy the results of the victory over Persia or the artistic and cultural triumphs of the early fifth century B.C. Although the growth of Athens was halted and internal rivalry among the city-states was renewed, memory of triumph over Persia colored the Greeks' view of their own civilization. Men sought a new framework for expressing the ideals that had grown up in the *polis,* a framework that thrust the values of Greek civilization to the edges of the civilized world (see section II.3).

Athenian pride did not reside in economic and military success exclusively. While the glories of fifth-century architecture and sculpture may have been possible only at a time of material prosperity, they also reflect an intelligent respect for the life of the mind and spirit. Athenians did not consider that political participation alone had created their society, and they had great respect and concern for the training of future citizens. Ideals of male beauty and health were reflected in the existence of centers for physical exercise and bathing where much of the male's life took place and out of which the process of becoming a citizen began. Athenian boys were compelled to undergo physical training, both for war and athletic competitions, as well as to study singing, mathematics, reading, writing, and the verbal monuments in which Athenians felt their culture was most embodied—the literary works of the eighth through the sixth centuries B.C. Public institutions, athletic competitions, religious observations, and the great dramatic festivals brought the citizen body together frequently, which contributed to a heightening of public awareness of ethical, religious, and social problems. Their complexities came to be seen in the forms of tragedy, burlesque, and comedy. Thus, in the course of the fifth century B.C., widespread concern was focused on solving increasingly tenacious problems—the preparation of citizens to deal effectively with the affairs of public responsibility.

*Socrates, Plato, Aristotle*

A group of men formed to teach or, rather, to investigate the best means of understanding the confusing life of the city. These men, called sophists, speculated upon the human problems behind citizenship and ethical conduct. Borrowing traditions of the sixth-century natural scientists, they developed a rigorous system of logical inquiry and a vocabulary of speculative terms that established criteria not only for investigating the best social institutions, but for considering larger questions of religion and society. The greatest of these figures was Socrates (469–399 B.C.), an heir of the earlier political and rational traditions of Greek thought.

The son of a stonecutter and a midwife, Socrates showed little interest in earning a living and so remained poor all his life. He preferred to exercise his citizen's right of open discussion and inquiry. Socrates was among the first to use the leisure expected of the Athenian citizen, however poor, more for intellectual explorations than civic affairs. One of the greatest by-products of the Athenian concept of citizenship was this encouragement to explore complex, abstract problems. By the fourth century these problems had ceased to be exclusively political and had moved on to general inquiries concerning the nature of people, truth, justice, good, and the application of such principles as these to political and social conduct. Thus, although the tradition that produced the Socratic method of persistent inquiry focused on people as citizens, Socrates now asked about people as thinkers.

The criteria for critical investigation developed in the intellectual circles of the Athenian citizenry were fertilized by the attraction Athens held for people from other parts of the Greek and Persian worlds. The practice of critical investigation became more important than training in civic affairs; the process of inquiry proposed the most complex questions humans had ever asked. In this process, which caused speculation about utopias (or ideal societies) and systems of ethical conduct that ignored the traditional gods, the *polis* and its citizens often came under heavy criticism. Socrates' life touched both these aspects of Athenian intellectual tradition with a particular and peculiar force, and so Socratic thought affected the life of Athens directly. Socrates stopped strangers and friends, the famous and the obscure, the learned and the ignorant, to probe their assumptions, their beliefs, their wisdom, and their values with a devastatingly rational critique. Conflicts between individual conduct and society's needs, on the one hand, and a desire to construct a society acceptable to unattainable Socratic criteria were never resolved; but they produced a dynamic, even "divine tension," which made Athens the father of much argumentation that we still pursue today. Socrates' own personality seems to have been an ambivalent blend of older religious

*The Death of Socrates* This painting, by Jacques Louis David, is the best known depiction of Socrates' death. David worked in the age of the French Revolution and of Napoleon, and he used classical themes to make political points about "heroism and civic virtue." What is David trying to say to his modern audience in this depiction of an ancient yet still relevant event? *Source: Courtesy of The Metropolitan Museum of Art, Wolfe Fund, 1931.*

and social values with a radically novel drive to find answers to problems that had never been sought so persistently nor included such speculative areas of thought.

Socrates' ideas are best known through the writings of his friend, pupil, and disciple Plato (c. 427–347 B.C.). Plato transformed some of his teacher's ideas and enshrined them in a series of prose dialogues. His literary skill owes much to Athenian literary culture, most particularly to the tragic poets. His form displays the shaping of thought in the poste and riposte of question and answer, criticism and response, and the application of a rigorously logical critique to even the most trivial or casual statements. Throughout these dialogues, human energies, passions, foibles, unseen personal weaknesses, physical features, and social conditions of the participants impart vividness to the dialectical movement of thought itself. They do this so forcefully that the term *dialectical* became basic to certain forms of reasoning (as in Hegel and Marx) in the nineteenth century, well over two thousand years later. Socrates led the life created by the opportunities of citizenship in fifth-century B.C. Athens. Plato, more withdrawn from the daily life of the *polis,* spoke to a more selective elite and established a center for such speculation. It was called the Academy, having been founded in a grove of the hero Academus, and it became the center of Hellenistic intellectual life until its abolition in A.D. 529. (From its name we take our modern terms for scholar and school.)

Plato's greatest pupil, Aristotle (384–322 B.C.), applied the rigorous intellectual traditions of the fifth century B.C. not to the immediate needs of the *polis* at all, which he considered with a dispassion unthinkable in Socrates or Plato, but to the problems of knowledge itself. He founded the Peripatetic (for "walking about") School known as the Lyceum, for the grove of the hero Lycus. By compiling an encyclopedic body of writings dealing with everything from natural sciences through sociology to constitutional analyses, he gave shape to human knowledge. Aristotle thus became the father of systematic analysis.

Separating these intellectual elites did not entirely destroy the vigor of *polis* life, of course. In fact, the strands of thought running from the sixth-century natural philosophers and editors of Homeric texts, through the tragic playwrights, philosophers, and teachers of the fifth century, grew stronger and wider as time passed. Images of human nature and the consequences of human action that were displayed in the tragedies of Aeschylus, Sophocles, and Euripides (c. 484–406 B.C.) reappeared in the work of Socrates, Plato, and Aristotle. Aristocratic values of the Homeric epics turned up in their works and in the story of the Persian wars as told by Herodotus (484–c.424 B.C.). The strands carried over to the scathing, brutally objective, and rigorously critical history and analysis of the Peloponnesian War recounted by Thucydides (471–c.400 B.C.). These values could also be found in the searching idealism and tension of Greek sculpture, and in the application of rationally analytical methods and a highly developed abstract vocabulary with which to express them. The intellectual vitality created and extended by the *polis* thus survived and transcended the historical circumstances of *polis* life itself. Although these developments meant less and less to the daily life of the citizen in the Athenian street, gymnasium, assembly, or lawcourt, they opened a dimension of human experience that easily commands the same awe as the domestication of crops, the use of metals, the growth of complex societies, and the shaping of religious consciousness.

### *Decline of the Athenian Empire*

Reduction of the Athenian Empire in 404 B.C. imposed severe economic restrictions upon Athens and constituted a victory for the forces of decentralization in Greece itself. Two major problems threatened the future even further: the divisiveness of individual city-states and the ominous power of Persia, defeated in Greece but triumphant elsewhere. Differences among the city-states increased throughout the fourth-century B.C. until any alliance similar to that of 479 B.C. was virtually unthinkable. A short-lived domination by Sparta and Thebes gave way to dissension and rivalry. Persia, having supported Sparta in the Peloponnesian War, once again controlled the Greek cities of Asia Minor and threatened what was left of the Greek maritime economy. Economic inequalities and differing social values turned individual cities toward political anarchy. Because of the criticism of philosophers and the economic and political pressures of the fourth century B.C., cities often resorted to desperate means, such as the execution of Socrates as an impious man. Disenchantment with public life and an increasing sense of insecurity followed as a result of political and economic instability. New and distant centers of production weakened the economies of many cities, and the disenchantment of the fourth century B.C., in spite of its remarkable intellectual and artistic achievements, undermined the superiority of the *polis* and marked the end of one of the most important stages of Western experience. By 350 B.C., the *polis* no longer seemed a sufficient framework for public and private life.

As the Athenian Empire broke up, opportunities abounded for political adventurers. Power was to be had by being in the right place at the right time. Declining effectiveness of the citizen-army caused a new resurgence of mercenary forces and a new separation between political and military life. People looked for programs that might lead to stability and long-range prosperity, rather than the earlier adherence to constitutional principles and plans to get rich quick. But even as the depolitization of the *polis* substituted economic security for civic participation, the *polis* gave birth to a way of thought and a body of social theory that ultimately touched upon problems that Western civilization has neither thoroughly solved nor completely forgotten.

Many of those living outside Greece had learned about Greek civilization through travel or, more commonly, by observing Greeks in action—perhaps as mercenary soldiers throughout the Near East. In fourth-century B.C. Persia and Egypt, Greek soldiers constituted the most effective forces on all sides. Ambitious provincial governors (satraps) in the Persian Empire hired Greek troops to serve their ends. Contenders for the throne of Persia paid handsomely for Greek soldiers to vindicate their cause and produce their fortunes. Rebellious Pharaohs of Egypt employed Greek armies to assert their independence from the Persian emperor, who employed Greek soldiers to suppress them. Once again, as in 479 B.C., Greek society witnessed a display of its military superiority over the forces of the adjacent world. The most striking demonstration of this superiority occurred in 400 B.C..

The same year that witnessed the humbling of Athens by Sparta (404

B.C.) brought the death of the Persian emperor, Darius II, and a struggle for succession between two claimants. One of them, Cyrus, hired Greek mercenary forces for his struggle. In the ensuing expedition, Cyrus was killed, native troops defeated, and his Greek forces abandoned deep in the heart of Persia. The Greek force, which was legendarily ten thousand strong, saw its original leaders murdered by Persian treachery and struck out due north in 401 B.C. After enduring great hardship on a grueling march, about half of the force reached the Greek coast of the Black Sea in March of 400 B.C. This exploit, recorded in the diary of one of the leaders, Xenophon, is known as the *Anabasis,* or *The March Up-Country.* It proudly signalled to the Greeks one enduring element of their strength, for the flow of Greeks into the Near Eastern world spread not only Greek mercenaries, but their culture as well.

A vigorous and powerful monarchy took charge in Macedonia, to the north of Greece. Philip of Macedon destroyed a coalition of city-state forces at Chaeronea in 338 B.C. and directed a new alliance of the city-states—the League of Corinth or the Hellenic League (which excluded Sparta). The stage was set for further exploitation of Greek military superiority and Greek social and cultural development. The kings of Macedon had long been admirers of several aspects of Greek culture; and although most of the city-states were relatively unenthusiastic, Philip now waged a Panhellenic campaign against Persian power in Asia Minor. Many Greeks had long appealed for a cause that would include individual city-states; and Isocrates (436–338 B.C.), an orator trained in the greatest tradition of the *polis,* even pictured a common campaign against the Persian territories of Asia Minor. He saw the campaign as a way to bring life back to anarchic Greece.

### Alexander the Great

It was as president of a league of Greek *poleis* as well as king of Macedon that Philip's son Alexander, who succeeded his assassinated father in 336 B.C., led Greek forces into Asia Minor two years later. There, in a little over a decade, Alexander destroyed the Persian monarchy, conquered all from Egypt to India, and swept the population of these lands into his armies, his court, and his system of administering the captured territories. Alexander, ruler of a backward if powerful monarchy on the edge of Greek civilization, was not so thoroughly committed to the values of Greek culture that he could not find ways to temper them with the institutions of the new world he had conquered.

Part Macedonian, part Greek (Aristotle had been his tutor for a time), open to the styles of life and the institutions of the Near East, Alexander proved to be an enigma not only to his contemporary biographers but to subsequent historians. His mercurial personality accepted all of the complex traditions to which he had been exposed, and his design to establish a capital at Babylon for his new Greek Near Eastern Empire could hardly have been comprehended by his Macedonian subjects and Greek allies. The "barbarians" seemed to be naturally inferior to Greeks, and when Alexander saw the value of Babylon and Mesopotamia as the center of a new empire, a choice that influenced subsequent rulers of Persia, he stirred resentment in the minds of Greeks and Macedonians as well. At his death in Babylon in 323 B.C., Alexander the Great left an empire without a name or a leader. His generals, preparing to carve that empire into separate satrapies, lacked his personal cultural adaptability, political vision, and intelligence.

Yet the world shaped by Alexander and his successors marked a distinctive and extraordinarily influential phase in the history of both the Near East and the West. Greek culture, detached in part from its origins in the *oikos* and the *polis,* was transmitted throughout the Near and Middle East. Greeks at all levels of the population left Greece itself, contributing to the decline of the city-state in the fourth century B.C. Settling in distant communities among strangers, they reconstructed as best they could the fourth-century *poleis.* Their broadening Greek vision of an *oikumene,* a civilized inhabited world, grew from its fourth-century roots and came to terms with local cultures. For five centuries the ensuing intellectual and cultural tone of the Mediterranean and Near East thus developed from the opening of the Greek vision of humanity to a larger and more diverse society. Men began to think in terms of the world rather than of the city. From the *oikos* and the *polis,* men looked on to the *oikumene.* Greek thought had moved from the farm to the world, from microcosm to macrocosm. It influenced local traditions in the old centers of civilization and the developing barbarian societies on the fringes of that world. The chief Greek contribution to Western civilization at last was seen not to be the flourishing of the *polis* culture of the fifth century B.C., but the export of that culture to an entire world in the fourth century B.C. and after.

## II. 3  From the Polis to the World:
## Hellenistic Civilization in the Mediterranean and Near East

*How much better it is to be envied than pitied.* —Herodotus, 484–424 B.C.

After Alexander the Great died, his generals and their successors carved a series of kingdoms out of the old Persian Empire and Egypt. New leagues of city-states formed in Greece. A renewed regionalism replaced the potential ecumenicism of a single empire ruling the known civilized world. Not until the expansion of Roman power during the second century B.C. did such an empire emerge again in the West. Yet the new regionalism was far more complex than the simple collapse of a short-lived military empire would indicate. Politically, the new Hellenistic monarchies of the Ptolemies in Egypt and the Seleucids in Persia and Anatolia asserted their independence of each other while exploiting local traditional institutions in places where they could work successfully. In spite of its political regionalism, this world of city-leagues and Hellenistic monarchies shared many cultural and economic institutions that had developed within the smaller world of the *polis*. Although the political role of the citizen diminished after 338 B.C., institutions which were once intended to train the citizen-soldier survived some aspects of the *polis* and spread throughout the Near East. Educational institutions of the *polis* had much to offer Syrians, Persians, Jews, and Egyptians. The gymnasium or *ephebeia* (by now a semimilitary social and aristocratic club for young people) and the private schools of individual teachers introduced linguistic studies, dress, manners, and lifestyle that had characterized the Greek military, commercial, and administrative elites throughout the Hellenized world.

Although the social process of Hellenization did not extend widely or deeply throughout Near Eastern society, it made the standards by which their world was ruled accessible to Greeks and non-Greeks alike. It also offered something new in terms of social and physical mobility. In earlier periods, even during the flowering of the *polis*, status in a community depended either upon citizenship or economic function, and there were few ways for a stranger to acquire that status. The great mobility within the world of the Hellenistic monarchies offered respectable status and even employment to anyone who could pass for a Hellenized gentleman. The wanderer throughout the world of the late fourth and early third centuries B.C. was less a rootless migrant than an individual whose cultural style offered him a home wherever he went, for he carried his sense of identity with him. Identity and a sense of self were not rooted to family, place or even *polis,* so much as to education, life style, and participation

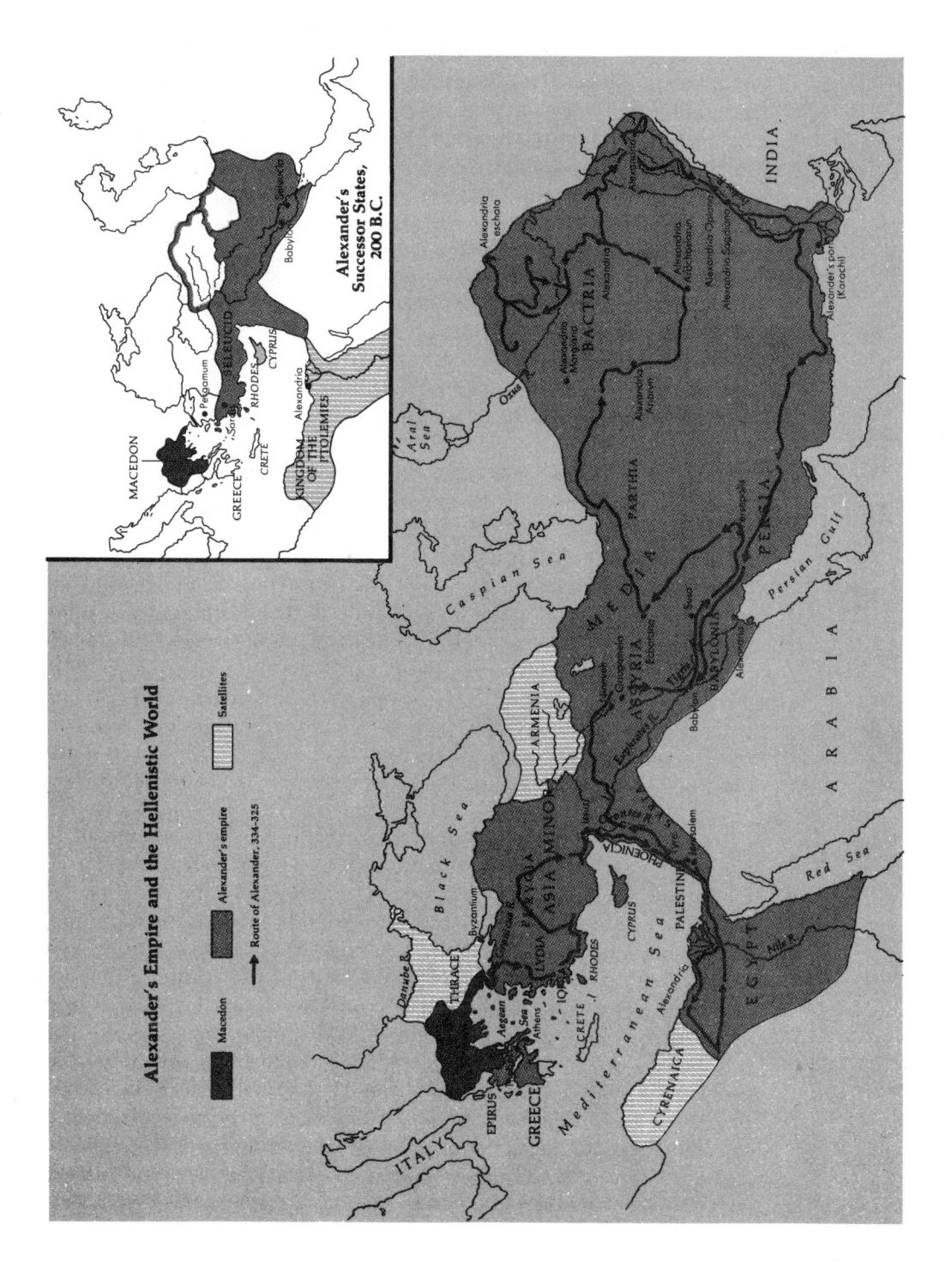

**Alexander's Empire and the Hellenistic World**

in an international Hellenized elite. This sense of cultural style reduced the differences between Greeks and Hellenized non-Greeks throughout the world of the third century B.C.

Alexander's conquests had ameliorated the economic crisis of the fourth century B.C., and for part of the late fourth and early third centuries, wealth from the known world once again flowed into Greece. Greek interests and needs spread, stimulating manufacturing and export, now not only from Athens but from the newly prominent cities of the Hellenistic world: Alexandria, Rhodes, Pergamum, Antioch. Growing numbers of consumers made great demands upon the means of production, and agriculture and industry struggled to increase in scope and rational management. Large cities depended upon extremely extended and fragile food chains, and Egypt again became their grain producer. Rapid expansion of the Greek market posed several threats that were never resolved, although it did cause different societies to come into close market relationships, which reduced the new regionalism. Dangers of inflation accompanied the new and increased flow of gold throughout this world, particularly in Greece itself. The sheer scale of economic interdependence and the availability of gold led toward severe price fluctuations and speculation. Limits upon production and export, difficulties of land transportation, and the emergence of new manufacturing centers made the life of the lower classes ever more precarious. In the cities, where most of the wealth was concentrated, a new commercial and entrepreneurial class emerged, which widened the gap between classes. Increasingly impoverished lower classes, possessing only citizens' rights, faced wealthy entrepreneurs whose economic power outweighed the diminished citizenship of the new *poleis*.

Trouble stirred not only within the cities but also between the Hellenized cities and the more traditional countryside. In spite of the decline of the independent *polis* and the rise of the kingdom and the league as political institutions, Greek-founded towns in the Hellenistic world took on the form and character of the *polis* and Greeks and Hellenized non-Greeks lived in these urban and rural islands of Hellenistic culture and economic power. In Egypt and the Near East, rulers looked out from cities such as Alexandria and Antioch, which appeared Greek to their Hellenistic managers and military and native to their distant and uncomprehending subjects. The *koine,* a simplified written and spoken Greek that slowly overcame the dialectical differences of the speech rooted in the different *poleis*, linked urban elites with the bustling world of industry, trade, and management. Its spread caused native languages and customs to retreat from the cities and become a bone of contention between them and the alien countryside.

## Interdependence

While the spread of the Greek koine and the process of individual Hellenization created cultural and social bonds throughout the remains of Alexander's empire, the Hellenized centers were never reconciled to the continuing existence of native languages and cultures. In some instances, notably in Egypt from the early second century B.C., champions of native languages and customs forced concessions from the Hellenized rulers. Among the Jews of Palestine, Hellenism was regarded with a religious abhorrence, although many Jews adopted Hellenistic manners. In other instances, local language and customs "went underground" in a sense and became the exclusive possession of the lower classes. The contrast between the attractions of Hellenism and the survival of local culture is one of the many complex aspects of the Hellenistic age, for the spread of any language carries with it forms of thought and expression that react powerfully upon those who adopt it. Even so, Aramaic—the first universal language of the civilized areas of the Near East—had not suggested such formidable cultural and social overtones as did Greek, its successor in much of the Near East and Africa and in much of the ancient world. When Greek was replaced by Arabic after the eighth century A.D., the religious focus on Islam and the cultural background of the Arabs were used as vehicles for spreading the older Near Eastern, particularly Persian, culture. The power of Hellenization lay precisely in the fact that it spread not only a language but an attitude toward humanity and society throughout the ruling elite of a wide area of the organized world. Yet its spread was only among an elite, and Hellenistic cultures reflected an economic and political distance between the ruling and wealthy classes and those without power or wealth. The citizen had become a subject.

Economic interdependence of the Hellenistic world spread the frontier of regular contacts well beyond the old Western fringes of the civilized core area. Greece and Persia, once remote frontiers themselves, were now parts of an expanded center of a cultural and political network of market relationships. Within that center, the organization of labor and the accumulation of wealth had become highly rationalized, efficient, even compartmentalized. By the third century B.C., agriculture and manufacturing units had grown in size, and the intensity of control exercised over them had likewise increased.

Deprived of much of its political freedom, the leisured elite of this world cultivated a style of life, an interest in literature and art, and a taste for public display that were served by an increasingly professionalized body of craftspeople and laborers. From the kings of Egypt and Persia to the wealthy landowners on the edge of India, patronage was extended to vast displays of cultural enterprise. The museum and library of the great city of Alexandria, the schools of Athens, and new, planned cities throughout the Near East reflected the cultural unity of the ruling elite. Scholars, actors, orators, and philosophers had become specialized servants of the political and economic elite, and vast sums went toward artistic and literary patronage.

Even the furthest frontiers of the Hellenized world reflected the vibrant life of the center. From the eighth century B.C. on, a Greek presence in southern Italy and Sicily had influenced the life of the Carthaginian civilization of North Africa and the Etruscan culture of northern Italy. On the Black Sea coast barbarian kingdoms were in contact with Greeks, and the separatist states in the eastern reaches of Persia took on a partially Hellenistic cast. From the end of the second century B.C., Chinese expansion westward linked Hellenistic civilization with that of eastern Asia. Trading routes over land and sea opened up this contact. Between 120 B.C. and A.D. 200 a sea route from Egypt to India connected to a sea route between India and the South China Sea, leading to direct contact across the Indian Ocean. From Ptolemaic Egypt, merchants and explorers moved south into east Africa; and in Italy and along the northern Mediterranean coast, Greek towns like Naples and Marseilles were in contact with the Iron Age peoples of Latium in central Italy and the Celts of the interior of continental Europe. Around the expanded center of Hellenistic influence, Celts, Iranians, steppe nomads, and Africans, as well as the more highly developed societies of India and China, felt the contacts of a complex world.

Almost always the Hellenistic experience was acquired at great cost. Technology and economic exploitation, pushed toward their upward limits in some parts of the Hellenized world but ignored in Athens, did not provide a comfortable standard of living for more than a small ruling elite. Even this was accomplished at the price of placing enormous demands upon the vast majority of the population, who were virtually deprived of any share in the results of their work. From the third to the first centuries B.C., the possibility of social revolution, from archaic Sparta to Egypt, loomed large, and the political instability of the Near Eastern world transformed the boundaries and the character of public power every decade. Because fortunes, both economic and political, were made and unmade with great and incomprehensible rapidity, people again became fascinated with the powers that seemed to rule the world invisibly. Fortune, personified by the Greeks as Tyche and by the Romans as Fortuna, became a deity to be worshipped. Philosophical schools as well as religious systems sought an explanation for flux, for the instability and insecurity of existence, as well as for a justification for prosperity.

The figures of the tax collector, estate manager, judge, and royal bureaucrat or privileged servant now appeared more frequently and more ominously than they ever had before. Ambitious kings, compelled to pay and give privileges to their Macedonian and Greek soldiery and court officials, exploited their kingdoms with a thoroughness and greed unmatched even in the earlier periods of the Pharaohs of Egypt and the Shahs of Mesopotamia. In many cases, these kings inserted a class of Greek merchants and officials into the existing social structure of their kingdoms. Military camps and their surrounding territories housed concentrated settlements of aliens, and new towns all experienced the imposition of some of the old institutions of the *polis*. However, their capacity for self-government was strictly limited, and actual *polis* status was given only to selected settlements.

## *Ptolemaic Egypt*

In the Egypt ruled by the Ptolemaic dynasty, great natural wealth in grain, papyrus, and olive oil was cultivated even more assiduously by Greek managers; these and other manufactured goods were sent into a market whose southern and southeastern trade routes were protected by the Pharaoh's wealth and military power. Ptolemaic Egypt gained footholds in the Aegean islands and Anatolia, and Egyptian diplomacy and money worked to create a stable and remunerative climate for Egyptian trade. New strains of grain, new tools, and closer management converted the natural wealth of Egypt into the economic power of the Hellenized Pharaoh and his managerial class. Egyptian wealth created the great city of Alexandria, a Hellenized outpost on a colossal scale in which the economic, political, and cultural nerve centers of the kingdom were centered.

Yet the differences between life in the imperial center of Alexandria and the rest of Egypt were marked, and the military necessities of the Ptolemies slowly weakened their absolute power. After the late third century B.C., native resentment forced the rulers to devote more and more energy to internal affairs and to neglect their essential foreign holdings. Warfare with the Seleucids to the east drained the treasuries, and the reduced numbers of immigrant Greeks during the century weakened the Greek cores of the managerial and ruling classes. By the middle of the second century B.C., Ptolemaic Egypt once again was close to withdrawing into xenophobic (hostile to strangers) native traditions. Alexandria survived the weakness of the Pharaohs, as an international center of trade, manufacture, and Hellenistic culture. Until its fall to Islam in the late seventh century A.D., it remained the cultural capital and economic center of the Hellenistic world—later, to a lesser extent, of the Roman world—for the complex economy of the Hellenistic world could not do without Egyptian products. When the Ptolemies grew helplessly weak during the late second and early first centuries B.C., other powers assumed control of Egypt, and Alexandria became—with Greece and the Near East—part of the growing empire of the Romans.

Egypt had been a wealthy, organized land long before Alexander's general, Ptolemy, took it over and passed it along to his successors. It had possessed a unity of government and culture. It had a language and a history that could not be overcome by the Hellenism of its ruling classes. Other parts of Alexander's empire also remained intractable or, at most, limitedly receptive to the new economic and political regionalism of the Hellenistic world. Macedonia remained a kingdom, as Egypt did, retaining its traditional frontier character. Macedonia exerted considerable force in Greece, where other kingdoms and weakened leagues of city-states fended off internal revolution and outside conquest ineffectively at best. In Anatolia and Syria-Persia, however, the existence of vast territories and polyglot populations posed different kinds of problems to their rulers.

The subject populations of Asia Minor and Mesopotamia regarded their Hellenistic rulers much as they had the earlier rulers of territorial states. Their system of government depended upon Greek and Macedonian soldiers, settled veterans, administrative officials, and provincial governors on the old Persian model. Nominally rulers of semibarbarian peoples developed privileged temple-cities within their territories (such as Jerusalem) and officially designated *poleis*. Yet the kingdoms of Anatolia and Persia covered vast distances. The eastern frontiers were populated with nomadic peoples who pressed closer during the second and first centuries B.C.; and the western frontiers drew their rulers not only into the vigorous and unstable market of the eastern Mediterranean but into the perennial and more unstable politics of the Greek and Macedonian worlds as well. Local rebellions and frequent declarations of independence, chiefly on the part of the eastern provinces, therefore fully occupied the Seleucid rulers' energies.

## *Palestine*

The history of Palestine illuminates some of the difficulties of rule. Once again, as during the imperial rivalry between Egypt and Mesopotamia, Palestine found itself caught between the two, now the Ptolemies and the Seleucids. From the 301 to 198 B.C., Egypt ruled Palestine. Large numbers of Jews, both voluntarily and involuntarity, migrated to Egypt to become part of the vast cosmopolitan population of Alexandria. Yet, although the most cosmopolitan of cities, Alexandria was not different in demographic profile from many others, particularly the new cities of the late fourth and early third centuries—Antioch, Seleucia, or Pergamum. Rhodes and Athens also shared a cosmopolitan character, and the rulers of the new kingdoms and cities were generally inclined to permit diverse elements of urban populations to live as closely to their own traditions and religions as public taste and conscience allowed.

Certainly never before in history, and only on a few occasions since, has the city been so open and so full of opportunities within a single society. The cities of the Hellenistic world were foundations for the power of post-Alexandrian rulers and influential centers of Hellenistic economy and culture. Old bases of *polis* life such as tribalism and individual political responsibility withered, permitting more generalized access to urban status, increased mobility, by removing the original ethnic prerequisites. By the second century B.C., those caught up in the cosmopolitan life of the Hellenistic world had long since left the security of *polis* life and tribe—and even, when they chose, ethnic origins—to find a new life and a new security in the turbulent, changing world of the eastern Mediterranean.

As soldiers, state officials, farmers, and later as bankers and business managers, Jews constituted a *politeuma* in Alexandria, a term that designated privileged ethnic groups either within a city or in a preparatory stage toward cityhood. Jewish life in Alexandria thrived, and the Jewish community of Alexandria became one of the centers of Judaism, as it later became one of the centers of Christianity. Judaism thus survived the conquest of Palestine by the Seleucid Antiochus II in 198 B.C.

Among the Jewish community of Alexandria sometime late in the third century B.C., the Torah—the first five books of the Old Testament—was translated into Greek, probably for the benefit of the non-Hebrew, non-Aramaic speaking Jewish population of the city. By the middle of the first century B.C., the entire Old Testament had been translated into Greek opening up Jewish traditional religion and thought to the rich and sophisticated echoes of Greek philosophy and ontological speculation. Although this Septuagint version remained exclusively for Jewish use until after the first century A.D., it circulated widely in the Hellenistic world. St. Paul used it in the first century A.D. To Jews who spoke koine Greek throughout the Mediterranean and Near Eastern worlds, it constituted a holy text written in a vulgate (a language) all could understand. During the second and first centuries B.C., when new schools and methods of interpreting the Old Testament became widespread, the vigor of Jewish interpretive thought spread equally swiftly throughout the Hellenistic world. For those literary works written after the translation of the Torah, such as the Books of Maccabees and Daniel, the works of the New Testament, and the Apocrypha, the Greek of the Septuagint offered principles of expression and translation that influenced the production of scriptural literature down to the first century B.C. Later, the Septuagint firmly shaped the translation of the Scriptures into Latin and the Hellenistic and Christian interpretations of them. At the same time, with the energy of

Hellenization and the wide circulation of the Greek koine, much Oriental material made its way West, first to Alexandria and Athens, later to Rome and the towns of the Roman provinces in Europe. The Greek-Jewish alliance of language and thought thus enjoyed wide circulation.

Transferring from Egyptian to Syrian rule probably did not change many aspects of Jewish life—other territories also changed hands frequently in the world of Hellenistic politics. But the conditions of the Seleucid monarchy soon instituted changes in Palestine that had far-reaching consequences in Jewish and Western history. In the reign of Antiochus IV (175–164 B.C.), the Seleucid monarchy, troubled by rebellions in the East, pressed by rival rulers in Anatolia, and less and less able to sustain its economic and political role, changed the status of a number of its territories. Jerusalem became a *polis* in 175 B.C.; that is, it received the status of a nearly self-governing city-state, in contrast to its earlier legal status as a temple community. The new authority given to Hellenized Jews—the right to confer citizenship, constitute a public assembly, and patronize institutions of education, particularly the gymnasia—sharpened already existing class feelings. Revolts in 168–167 B.C. brought Antiochus back into Jerusalem, where he reduced the opposition and supported the Hellenizers, to both the political and religious repugnance of much of the Jewish population. Thereafter, Jewish resentment increased along religious and class lines.

Local resentment against Antiochus and his Jewish supporters in Jerusalem may be read against the background of the Book of Daniel, composed around 160 B.C., and the Books of I and II Maccabees, written late in the second and early in the first centuries B.C. In these works, the powerful sentiments of the Old Testament are directed against Antiochus, who was depicted as one of various rulers throughout Jewish history who rose up against the Jews and their god and were destroyed for their impiety. These religious denunciations of the Seleucids masked what was in large part a political and economic war, conducted from 163 B.C. on. It resulted in the establishment of a dynasty of Jewish kings who ruled independently while becoming increasingly Hellenized and, in turn, stirred up pious resentment against themselves.

Development of Jewish religious thought and institutions under the Maccabees and their successor kings had powerful consequences. The Maccabean revolution engaged the sympathy of a group of rigorous supporters of traditional Judaism, the *Hasidim,* and the second and first centuries B.C. witnessed a new flowering of religious consciousness under the revolutionary fervor and slow Hellenization of the ruling groups that followed. Traditions of oral teachings outside of the scriptures were developed by a class of nonpriestly scribes; the growth of this tradition led directly to rabbinical schools and the Talmud of the early centuries A.D.

Two other groups also emerged. The Sadducees, rigorously accepting only the Torah, excluded both oral tradition and the teachings of the preceding centuries of Jewish experience. They generated a cultural separatism and a reactive sympathy for current forms of government and culture. The Pharisees, on the other hand, accepted the entire scriptural tradition, together with the oral teachings. To reconcile both, a program of education and study partially derived from Hellenistic theories of education emerged. Because of this religious competitiveness a number of other sectarian groups appeared, including the Essenes, an ascetic group that withdrew from Jerusalem to form its own liturgical community as others had done at Qumran. With the proliferation of sects, apocalyptic literature predicting a final resolution of the struggles among the Jews and between Jews and pagans increased in volume. By the end of the Hasmonaean kingdom in 63 B.C., the climate of Jewish religious thought had undergone momentous changes, most of them having been touched by Hellenism, and all of them affecting the Jewish communities scattered throughout the Hellenistic world.

Hellenistic culture and politics drew mixed reactions throughout the world of the second and first centuries B.C. Political consequences were greatest among the Jews in Palestine, but temporary stability in other post-Alexandrian kingdoms was also in jeopardy. Political ambitions surfaced in an environment of limited resources. Political independence or empire building paralleled resurgent localism (although often strongly tinged with Hellenistic traces). In northern Asia Minor along the southern shores of the Black Sea, other kingdoms shared this culture as did Armenia to the southeast, and to a lesser extent the growing Parthian Empire of eastern Iran. Upper Egypt (that portion further up the Nile, thus south on the map) resisted Ptolemaic rule, and the Greek towns in southern Italy and Sicily influenced and struggled with the Carthaginians in North Africa and the Etruscans in northern Italy. Greek cities also experienced increasingly frequent contacts with the Iron Age Celtic peoples of Europe. The spread of Greek migrants, institutions, and ideas before Alexander, the birth of Alexander's empire and its partial dissolution into separate kingdoms ruled by elites sharing the same culture and economically dependent upon one another, had greatly expanded a core area of civilization—eastward beyond the borders of India; south to east Africa and Arabia; west to the central Mediterranean, Carthage, and Italy; and north to the Balkans and the northern coasts of the Black Sea.

At these new frontiers of the Hellenistic world there emerged the power of Parthia in the east and Rome in the west. Within that world, native traditions and separatist tendencies grew stronger. Even at the frontiers, Parthia and Rome faced less developed, partially Hellenized peoples whose presence constituted a threat.

From the fourth to the early first centuries B.C., more people than ever before found themselves at home in a wider and wider world. For the ruling elites of the Hellenistic world, security and identity depended upon education, life style, exploitation of the frequent opportunities, and similarity to the culture of others in lands widely separated. The intellectual and economic elites of the Hellenistic world represented a very small percentage of the total population, and the social and technological conditions of these centuries prohibited their numbers from substantially increasing. Those conditions also comdemned the vast majority of people to a life of localism, oppression, and brutal exploitation. Meanwhile, the civilized elite rode upon a fluctuating base of wealth that had enormously increased since the days of Mesopotamian and Persian dominance. But this wealth was controlled by only rudimentary political and military methods. The complex culture and economy of the Hellenistic world found little stabiltiy in powers that ruled by such methods, and a reversion to localism occurred as soon as those powers grew too ambitious, too poor, or too weak. By the middle of the second century B.C., the Hellenistic world was an economic and cultural empire without political unity. Still, it prepared the ground for such unity far more than any earlier civilization had done, and the emergence of Parthia and Rome represented two powers with the strength and opportunity to reshape the Hellenistic world into a new unity.

## II. 4  A World Expands: The Rise of Rome

*To yield to the stronger is valor's second prize.—* Martial (A.D. 40–102)

### Old Cultures, New Locus

The centers of "Western" civilization seem to flow constantly in that direction: from Sumeria and Egypt to Greece, then to Rome, then out of the Mediterranean world into western Europe, and finally to the Atlantic and North America. Such a view, however, is highly simplified, for it neglects the continuing attraction of the eastern Mediterranean and the Near East, as well as their more complex economic and intellectual development through the thirteenth century A.D. Today's sharp differences among twentieth-century "Western," North African, and Middle Eastern societies heighten this westward view, as the roots of the differences between modern and less developed societies in these regions are often traced back to the seventh-century emergence of Islam and the spread of Arabic. Yet the history of "Western civilization" remained—for fourteen centuries after the rise of Rome—in important measure the history of the eastern Mediterranean. Two millennia of proximity and mutual influence created the cities and agricultural districts of the ancient Near East, the cosmopolitan cultures of the towns, and their attraction for the rural ruling elites. People of different racial, ethnic, linguistic, and religious backgrounds constantly moved about, changing and being changed. Intricate networks of trade—from the camel caravans in Africa, Arabia, and Asia to the sea routes of the Mediterranean, the Persian Gulf, and the Indian Ocean—helped to construct, in a few centuries, a society unequaled by most areas of the world. The enduring power, wealth, and internal dynamism of the ancient Near East underlie both the spread of Roman power and the later growth of Persia and rise of Islam.

Circumstances beyond the frontiers of the civilized Hellenistic world also contributed to the subsequent history of civilization. In the East, independent Persian principalities faced not only Hellenistic monarchies of the Seleucids but constant incursions of nomadic peoples from across the great open frontiers east of the Jaxartes and the Hindu Kush and northward between the Caspian and Aral seas. Great migrations of Eurasian steppe nomads made frequent alterations in the Middle East from modern Turkey to Persia and, in particular, introduced major political changes. The growing predominance of Iranian power and culture in the area from the Tigris-Euphrates Valleys eastward gave a progressively distinctive Iranian cast to the culture of Persia, and later, to Islam. Residual Hellenism had less influence here than in the Roman world to the west. South of the Black Sea, the Iranian culture of Sasanid, and later Islamic Persia, lay open to barbarian forces whose advance and pressure required vast energies.

To the west, however, both the frontier and the barbarian worlds beyond it were different. On the western edge of Hellenistic civilization lay several societies with close connections to the Near East. Carthage—the great economic empire then stretched from Egypt to Spain—had its thriving center in North Africa, in economic and cultural contact with the Hellenistic world. In Italy and Sicily, Greek colonial cities had Hellenized the lower part of the peninsula, had extended their influence among the Latin tribes of the center and ultimately to the highly developed Etruscan civilization to the north. A busy rivalry among Carthaginians, Greeks, Etruscans, and Romans on the western fringe reflected the frontier character of the central and western Mediterranean between the eighth and the third centuries B.C. There, Carthage and Etruria, both with roots in the westward expansion of the peoples of Asia Minor and the Levant between 1000 and 700 B.C., used their power in North Africa and northern Italy to keep barbarian neighbors at bay.

On this frontier the influence of Hellenistic civilization was strongest in the Greek cities of Italy, but it did not completely overcome the distinctive traditional cultures of Carthage and Etruria. Hence the persistent rivalry among Carthaginians, Etrurians, and Greeks offered opportunities to the initially undistinguished small city-state of Rome, in central Italy, to establish its own dominance—first within its immediate environment, later in other areas previously ruled by older cultures and powers. Etruria and later Rome successfully controlled the Celtic peoples to the north.

To the south, desert nomads of Africa had no power that could stand against the Carthaginian armies or the later Roman legions. After a serious challenge by barbarian invaders in the first century B.C., successfully resisted by the Roman general Marius, barbarian peoples penetrated yet did not shake Romanized Europe. In the tenth century, such invasions came to an end. Still, the barbarian threat loomed large on Persia's eastern frontier from the fourth century B.C. until the eighteenth century A.D. The far West thus faced a less enduring problem.

The West was now on the eve of the emergence of Rome as the greatest ruling power in the old Mediterranean world. Upon the back of the Roman Empire, Hellenism would spread to North Africa, Spain, and Europe. Even so, it is important to remember that even the most powerful political organization in Western history had inherent limitations. It could not, for example, duplicate the highly urbanized pattern of Near Eastern life. Provincial towns and city-states dotted the Roman Empire, and under Rome their number increased. But neither the population nor its economic complexity sustained a densely settled urban complex comparable to the Hellenistic Near East, at least until the end of the thirteenth century A.D. The resources of the West could match neither the vast agricultural enterprises nor the growing industry of the Near East. While Roman soldiers overseas numbered from a yearly average of 50,000 in the early second century B.C. to 125,000 in the first century A.D. (not counting veteran colonists and traders), Romans were soldiers and administrators far more often than they were entrepreneurs, colonists, or professional artists, teachers, or craftspeople. Much of the culture and trade of the Roman world continued to be built upon a Hellenized Near Eastern base.

After the ultimate passing of Roman imperial strength in the West, the core of the empire withdrew to the area where it had originated—in the Greek and Greek-speaking areas of Greece and Asia Minor. There Greek replaced Latin. Yet these subjects of the "Emperor of the Romans" referred to themselves as Romans and regarded their empire as a direct continuation of the great empire that had emerged in the second century B.C. In this sense, the Roman empire did not fall until A.D. 1453, just thirty-nine years before Columbus voyaged to the New World. During its time, far longer and far more beset by enemies than any earlier civilization had been, the later Roman Empire reembodied the dynamics and the power of Hellenistic civilization. As such, it became the teacher, the transmitter of customs of not only Rome and Europe, but Damascus, Baghdad, and Cairo. Thus its cultural descendents include Vienna, Paris, Moscow, and Washington. Roman-Hellenistic culture influenced youthful Christianity and Islam, as it had Judaism and other religions of the Near East.

The Hellenistic period, from the fourth to the first century B.C., thus represents the most dynamic stage of the ecumenical cultural, economic, and social development of the ancient Near East.

## The Origins of Rome

Rome, on the western side of the Italian peninsula, was settled by the Latin people of central Italy around 800 B.C. The powerful civilization of the Etruscans to the north strongly influenced early Roman society, and Rome's earliest kings were Etruscan, as were the urbanizing forces that linked several hilltop villages (mythologically put at seven) around 753 B.C., to form the earliest city itself. In spite of such forces, however, Romans maintained close links with the countryside and with rural religion, the archaic values of tribal society, and the power of clan leaders. In this respect, early Roman society did not differ much from early Greek society. Status depended upon family and clan membership, and outsiders or the poor became dependents of more powerful families and households. The earliest kings consulted leaders of the most powerful clans, although the growing wealth of these groups challenged the kings' strength. Again, as in early Greece, the increasing use of infantry tended somewhat to strengthen lower social ranks at the expense of the aristocracy and its cavalry. As citizenship came to be based increasingly on residence, the earlier tribal structures were further weakened. Around 510 B.C., an aristocratic revolt toppled the king and recreated a now altered aristocratic and privileged basis for society.

Royal powers were divided among aristocratic magistrates (consuls), and a class of *patricians* emerged as a ruling aristocratic elite over the majority of the population (*plebians*). It is traditionally held that the Roman Republic was founded around 509 B.C. The fifth century brought considerable caste rivalry, particularly with the revival of infantry tactics, the growing well-being of the patricians and plebians, and the more frequent contacts with the Hellenistc world. After the middle of the century, substantial reforms came into effect. The early law of Rome, hitherto unwritten and interpreted by patrician judges, was codified (c. 450 B.C.) as the *Twelve Tables*. Harsh and brutal though the laws of the Twelve Tables were, their existence in written form prevented arbitrary interpretation on the basis of a class interest, and made them accessible and generally consistent for all until the second century. Spokesmen for

*The Capitalino wolf with Romulus and Remus* Art provides for us visual images which reinforce the legendary. A superb example is this fifth century bronze wolf to which have been added the Renaissance figures of Romulus and Remus. Romulus is said to have built Rome in the 8th century B.C. and then killed Remus. In the first century A.D. the historian Livy would retell these legends, giving them the authenticity of History, in order to make his contemporaries proud of their presumed past. *Source: Capitoline Museum.*

the plebian assemblies (*tribunes*) were declared sacrosanct so that they might safely speak, and slowly the major burdens and signs of plebian status were erased. After 367 B.C., one of Rome's two consuls could be chosen from the plebian class.

Yet the admission of new members to the Roman elite on the basis of wealth spread the aristocratic values prominent in earlier Roman history to a new group. While social change often serves to open the ranks of a ruling elite to those hitherto excluded, the newly admitted ones often assume the value systems of their new status. In the rise of the Greek *polis*, the values of the early aristocratic period permeated civic consciousness throughout. In Rome, a distinctly aristocratic view of life came to dominate the ruling groups, whether patrician or plebian, and this view, with its emphasis on military success, helped to determine Rome's relations with neighboring states. From 400 B.C. on, Rome fought a series of wars with Etruria—the Latin peoples north of the Tiber—and with the Greek cities to the south, thereby bringing Roman military power to bear on one of the key areas of the Hellenistic world.

The strength of the Roman armies lay in the tough peasantry of central Italy and their cultural integration with the ruling elite. The numbers of remarkably disciplined soldiers that Rome could put into the field, and the relatively small difference in life styles of the highest and the lowest ranks of Roman society were unique in the fourth and third centuries B.C. Moreover, even Roman aristocrats at least paid lip service to the virtues of peasant rural life, or to *rus in urbe* (the country in town). Rome itself, a single city-state, attracted the undivided loyalties of larger numbers of people than could the numerous and rival Greek *poleis*. In the course of her conquests, Rome developed a scale of relationships, of indirect forms of rule, of imperialism between allied and conquered societies and herself that left self-government for the most part in local hands. Other cities "bent" to Rome according to both a complex scale of military support and, after the First Punic War (264–241 B.C.), by taxation of the conquered.

Such spreading of Roman influence soon brought the city into hostile contact with two other powers of the area—the empire of Carthage and the kingdom of Epirus in northwestern Greece. Rome's growing contact with the Greek cities of southern Italy also drew her into affairs in Greece itself, and the wars with King Pyrrhus of Epirus (305[?]–272 B.C.) set the stage for further Roman intervention in Greece. In North Africa, the vast empire of Carthage stretched from Libya to Spain and into the Mediterranean to Sicily. Roman activity in southern Italy brought it into conflict with Carthaginian interests, and the first of the wars between the two powers, that First Punic War, deprived Carthage of her Sicilian possessions, giving Rome her earliest provinces. Continued Carthaginian activity in Spain led to hostile contact with Roman allies there, and under a brilliant general, Hannibal, a new war with Rome began in 218 B.C. At the outset of the Second Punic War (218–201 B.C.), Hannibal dramatically invaded Italy from the north and inflicted a series of severe defeats upon the Romans. However, Roman military power coupled with control of the sea enabled the resistance against Hannibal in Italy to succeed. Rome then carried the war to Africa itself, ultimately defeating Carthage in 202 B.C. and bringing Spain into provincial status while reducing Carthage to a client state.

Client status meant that in diplomatic relations the client state was a poor nephew approaching a rich uncle, or an ambitious climber seeking favors from powerful, aristocratic patrons. Carthage and, after 201 B.C., many cities in Greece were assigned such status by Rome. Overlapping rebellions in Africa (the Third Punic War, 149–146 B.C.) and in Greece (148 B.C.) seriously tested the system, but Roman military power pushed on to a virtually unchallenged position in the central Mediterranean.

An unbroken series of Roman military successes between 264 and 146 B.C. propelled Roman power far faster than social or economic resources could follow. At the end of the fourth century B.C., Rome had been a vigorous, agricultural city-state with little sophistication or interest in the world beyond it. Social friction between the patricians and plebeians had been partially resolved within the emerging class structure of central Italy, and by the end of the third century B.C., a new aristocracy made up of both patricians and plebeians had risen to power. Now the string of military triumphs offered vast wealth and opportunities to this aristocracy on a scale beyond their capacity to absorb them. The aristocracy participated competitively in government and exploited, often brutally, the wealth opened to it in the new provinces. Not only did the aristocracy increase its wealth and power, but it used these resources in the internal political life of the city itself, a city whose population was swelled by a growing proletariat and whose armies, by now detached from their earlier peasant existence, further strengthened the power of aristocratic generals and provincial administrators. A new class, of knights, or equestrians, emerged between the increasingly wealthy and powerful aristocracy and the poorer and more easily displaced masses. Taking advantage of Rome's new economic opportunities, the knights consituted first a trading and industrial class and later a banking and tax-collecting one as well. Aristocrats, increasingly interested in building large and profitable agricultural estates, further weakened the peasant farmer-soldiers. Those who amassed vast sums of cash and booty sought outlets in capitalist farming at the expense of the poorest class of free men.

Roman government, more loosely managed by the aristocracy, came to be an arena where personal and factional interests contended viciously. Powerful aristocratic leaders packed the popular assemblies with clients and dependents; and after 125 B.C. two approaches to political power were taken: one by the Optimates, the other by the Populares. Each aroused its own support and played on different social tensions. Deepening distress of the lower classes, their abandonment or loss of rural farms, and urban unemployment attracted the attention of a number of political figures. In 133 B.C., the tribune Tiberius Gracchus proposed a program of restoring peasant farmholdings and reducing the size of large estates. Gracchus, bitterly opposed by the Optimates, was assassinated. His brother Gaius, tribune in 123–122 B.C., then proposed more far-reaching reforms, including a subsidized food supply in Rome. He also increased the power of the equestrian class. Nonetheless, he too was slain and his death resulted in class wars, standing armies, and the overthrow of the Republic.

In the ensuing decades, a series of political leaders whose control was broadened by emerging aristocratic functions, used social and military reforms to increase their own power. General Gaius Marius, after subduing Jugurtha—claimant to the throne of the Roman client kingdom Numidia (111–105 B.C.)—was elected to five continuous terms as consul

(104–100 B.C.). Marius transformed the composition of the army. By admitting landless citizens, ties developed between soldiers and their commanders, rather than between soldiers and the state. A younger military leader, Lucius Sulla, gained prominence during a savage war with Mithridates VI, ruler of the Hellenized kingdom of Pontus on the southern shores of the Black Sea. Sulla, an Optimate, restored the power of that group as he established his own dictatorship. Sulla's death in 78 B.C. was followed by pressure for popular reform, and two former associates, Gnaeus Pompeius (Pompey) and Marcus Licinius Crassus, emerged as the head of a populist reaction to Sulla's Optimate reformers. Pompey's powerful military enabled him both to control Rome's military affairs and drive his enemies out of the eastern Mediterranean by 66 B.C.

The growing power of both Pompey and Crassus and a half-century of threats to aristocratic privilege sharpened the senatorial aristocracy's resentment of political adventurers and heightened the consciousness of senatorial prestige. In their stand against senatorial resistance, however —best voiced by eloquent orators such as Cato and Cicero—Pompey and Crassus took on a new ally, Gaius Julius Caesar. Caesar had been active in politics as a young man, and he came from a patrician family. Siding with the poor, he worked with Pompey and Crassus, who made him consul when they took control of the popular assembly in 59 B.C. From this base, Caesar sought absolute power so that he might be a benevolent autocrat and therefore capable of forcing reforms upon Rome. The following year he became proconsul of Gaul, which sat astride the northern and southern sides of the Alps. For eight years there he fostered the spread of Roman culture and grew in power, prestige, and wealth and maintained a powerful and almost wholly personal army.

Recalled from Gaul by the Senators, he chose—contrary to law—to bring his army with him. Crossing the southern boundary of Gaul at the River Rubicon in 49 B.C., he cast his die against his senatorial opposition, defeated his former sponsor Pompey in battle at Pharsalus, which destroyed the forces of the Optimates, and took control of the major offices of the Roman Republic in 46 B.C., becoming dictator for life. His reforms were numerous: he resettled war veterans on farms, gave Roman citizenship to parts of Spain and Gaul, admitted provincials to the Senate, and sought to make the aristocratic Romans more aware of their responsibilities to the far-flung empire. His monuments were also numerous: he erected handsome public buildings and a superb system of Roman roads. But he also abused his powers by allowing a religious cult to grow up in his honor. This eroded the power of the old republic; he took on the purple garb of the ancient kings and packed the Senate with his friends. Caesar was struck down as a tyrant and was assassinated when he visited the Senate House in the Ides of March in 44 B.C., leaving behind a legacy of unceasing political struggle. Cassius and Brutus, leaders of the conspiracy against Caesar, saw themselves as liberators, while the army, which was inspired by Mark Antony, Caesar's fellow Consul, turned against them.

In time, Caesar's grandnephew, Gaius Julius Caesar Octavianus (Octavian), emerged as his political heir. By defeating Mark Antony's and Cleopatra's combined forces at Actium in 31 B.C., Octavian (also called Augustus) came to stand alone at the head of Rome's government. His political success constituted only the first of his remarkable achievements: he restored old and new temples, gave people renewed pride in the traditions of Rome, and reformed the Senate. Yet social and economic problems that had plagued the Roman Republic for the preceding two centuries remained, as did the social and political chaos of the period from the rise of Marius to the death of Caesar.

Roman society had been drastically influenced by the sudden rise of Roman power. For the stern agrarian morality of the aristocracy, skyrocketing wealth and new avenues to personal power were too much, too soon. Nor could they cope with the erosion of citizens' rights. Economic gaps between the very wealthy and the poor widened beyond anything Roman society had seen previously, and there were few real reforms. Instead, there were "bread and circuses"—public events or "spectacles," largely to provide entertainment. Even the lowest class of Romans technically had privileged status. Cities consumed but did not produce. Rome demanded an unceasing flow of wealth, purely for consumption. Provinces were methodically though not brutally exploited by their governors, or large areas were ruled directly by Octavian under a ficticious governorship. Administrative personnel obtained the collaboration of the richest classes in Italy for Octavian. The Equestrian order, the most mobile group in this society, pushed upward toward senatorial privileges.

From 31 B.C. on, Roman power held sway from Spain to the Tigris-Euphrates border with Parthia and from the Rhine to upper Egypt. Old Hellenistic kingdoms, city-states, and urban leagues existed as client states under Roman hegemony, and their wealth was directed toward the city of Rome. Egyptian, Sicilian, and African grain fed the city; the vast wealth of the Hellenistic Near East was exported to Rome *en masse*.

The once humble city-state of the fourth century now sprawled over central Italy with luxurious palaces, vast public buildings—the forum and temple—and teeming, many-storied slums. A program of road-building connected Rome to other key areas of Italy, and the busy, consuming life of the city drew ships to the port of Ostia and up the Tiber River. Much of life took place outdoors; pedestrian traffic crowded the narrow streets and broad courts. Business was transacted in public, and wares were displayed on the streets. Backing usually came from wealthy people, chiefly property owners.

Various means led to the upper ranks of public service, where former magistrates merged in the senatorial class. In the face of a vast population of the very poor, the senatorial class recognized its responsibility for enhancing the appearance and life of the town, while currying favor with large masses of the poor by entertaining everyone with gladiatorial and theatrical spectacles.

### *Intellectual Life*

When the culture and power of Hellenistic society began to spread in the fourth century B.C., the traditions of the *polis* and the bonds of culture were stabilizing influences. In a sense, Hellenistic society ideally developed to foster change and dislocation. However, Roman society was from the first reluctant to adopt Hellenism at face value, partly because of a simpler, sterner moral code that survived from earlier Roman history, and partly because of Roman contempt for values of people they had conquered. Thus, during the second and first centuries B.C., the literature of statecraft, popular art, educational institutions, and aristocratic and equestrian living styles all reflected the conflict between traditional Roman values and the attractions of the culture of the Hellenistic world. Rome was in the process of conquering the world, while the stresses within Roman society created an air of crass, ruthless practicality and an increasing gap between official moral pronouncements and the actual conditions of life.

By late in the first century B.C., Latin had become a literary language, and the intellectual character of Hellenistic civilization began to color the native intellectual traditions of Italy. Institutions of the Hellenistic city-state took selective, vigorous roots in Rome itself. Oratory—the discipline of persuasion according to the rules of literary and dramatic elocution—had developed in the *polis,* but there was little occasion for it when political activity declined in the Hellenistic kingdoms. Oratory made a great impact on Rome, particularly in the second and first centuries B.C. when political activity was heightened. Individual orators could sway large assemblies, and the constant round of political trials called for eloquent defenders and prosecutors. Public speaking combined the talents that today would be divided among the writer, the actor, the lawyer, and the politician, and it constituted perhaps the principal focus of the disciplines of Hellenistic education. Rhetoric—the study of proper forms of literary expression—was shaped as a discipline between the sixth and the third century B.C. Careful study of Homeric literature had generated a new attitude toward works of the past, and these became the standard "classics," a purely Hellenistic concept, with which all educated people were expected to be familiar.

Early philosophy separated into a series of schools, each with its own master. The study of philosophy and its history became the study of forms of transmitting knowledge. During this process, Socrates emerged as the father of philosophical thinking, and other "founders" of philosophical schools were elevated nearly as high. Building upon Greek models of oratorical and rhetorical technique, Romans in the first century B.C. nonetheless infused these techniques with a genuine Latin spirit. The verse of Catullus and Virgil in Latin equalled the best of Greek poetry. Cicero, Ovid, and Livy shaped a Latin prose style derived from Hellenistic ideas concerning the lives of political entities and human nature, and they elucidated Roman history and political problems. Cicero was also chiefly responsible for a Latin philosophical vocabulary. With it, Latin thought and Latin prose could express the complex shades of meaning that the Greek language of the fourth and third centuries B.C. had developed.

However, Roman writers and thinkers were not primarily literary figures whose work was separate from the daily life of the empire. Cicero, who was from central Italy, worked his way up as a brilliant attorney, held the consulship in 63 B.C., and struggled in the factionalism between Caesar, Pompey, and the Senate. He became a provincial governor in Cicilia but retired in political bitterness to his estates to take up the study of philosophy. Politics called him back once again to Rome, however, and to his death in 43 B.C. Such a career reflects both the thought and action that the Roman public career was expected to display at its best. Although a man like Cicero did not save the Roman Republic from its headlong plunge toward disintegration, he may have preserved some of its values by his philosophical exploration into the morality of governance. Caesar, who was one of the stormiest figures of first-century Rome, wrote a brilliant analysis of his campaigns in Gaul, revealing both the mind of the politician and the eye of the anthropologist. Earlier, the poet Lucretius (95–55 B.C.) directed his somber genius against what he considered to be superstition and religion, to produce a philosophical epic poem, *On the Nature of Things,* or *De Rerum Natura.*

The brilliance of the golden age of Latin literature reflected both the profundity of Hellenism's effect upon Roman thought and the vast amounts of income that could be expended for education and patronage by the ruling aristocracy. Cicero studied at Athens and Rhodes; other Roman youths flowed to Alexandria and Pergamum where they learned first the manners and dress and later the literary and philosophical traditions of the Hellenistic world. Romans found that the vast interdisciplinary studies of the Hellenistic schools linked scientific thought to literature as they linked history and religion to philosophical thought.

All of this high-pressure intellectual adventure created a distinctive intellectual culture. First, the mutual influence of different disciplines upon one another tended to develop a similar methodology in different kinds of mental activity. Second, the highly literary and rhetorical cast of thought tended to reinforce the Greek dislike of manipulative, experimental, and scientific investigation. It made science a purely intellectual activity, like philosophy. Even mathematics and astronomy, two of the greatest triumphs of Hellenistic culture, did not remain free of this antiscientific influence, and in time this produced serious consequences for Roman technology. Third, the decline of the political independence of the *polis* focused philosophy upon ethics and the individual and generally disregarded the political and social contexts in which the individual lived.

Accordingly, Epicurus (341–270 B.C.) attacked the religious beliefs of his day. He wanted to free individuals from forms of bondage created by superstition and help them avoid physical or mental pain. Although accused of hedonism (devotion to pleasure), Epicurus was far more interested in a theory that saw all things as material, all constructed of atoms. Everything and everyone depended upon the cohesion of atoms. When they separated, there was nothing—there was no soul after death. Epicurus placed his confidence in the reliability of the trained mind and senses. His disciple, Lucretius, was a good representative of the power of Epicurus's thought. He was also a sharp reflection of the weakness of religion in the first century B.C.

Stoicism, on the other hand, held that there was an inherent connection between human beings and the universe. Only by misunderstanding this relationship did humans perceive evil. Since all individuals shared the gift of reason, the *polis*-man was not an exclusive phenomenon. A cosmopolitan person, ideally, could live in a society with people from anywhere. Cicero later gave this concept the name *humanitas*. Stoicism's intellectual and moral justifications of a world community proved very attractive to Roman thinkers, just as the goal of a world community has proved attractive to the powerful ever since.

### Toward a World State

A world state was Octavian's goal. Renamed Augustus, he was a new kind of personal dictator who preserved outward signs at least of traditional republican values. He tried to draw the magistracies, or divisions, of the old republic into his own hands, while he pretended to preserve their separate character. Proconsul, *pontifex maximus,* Augustus was technically *princeps,* "first citizen," of a restored republic. In fact, he was an emperor, the individual ruler of a world-state. He reformed the government, acted as controlling partner with the increasingly powerful senate, and restored stability through the use of his vast personal fortune and the imposition of new taxes. He used the money to develop a civil service and strengthen the army, upon which his power ultimately depended. By his death in A.D. 14, Augustus had preserved the shell of the old republic—senatorial dignity. He had stabilized the vicious cycle of political civil wars that had nearly destroyed the Roman state, and he had preserved the vast provinces of the empire.

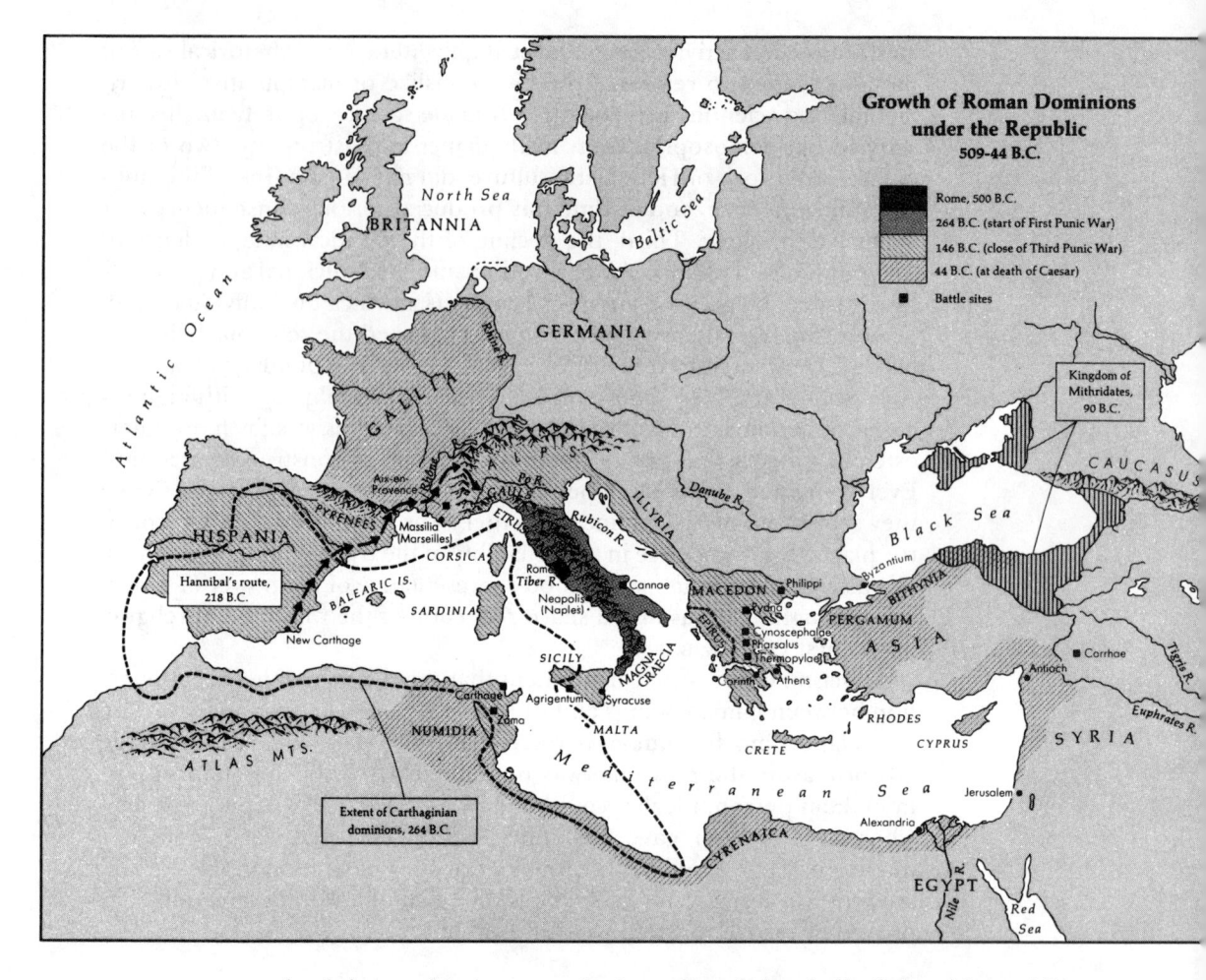

Augustus's powers were unique, however, and it was his genius as well as an altered constitution that sustained his program of reform. Succession proved difficult. A series of relatives from the Julio-Claudian house followed each other to the throne until A.D. 69, when the armies installed four emperors in succession. Another dynasty, the Flavian, exercised power from A.D. 69 to 96. Then another crisis produced a series of rulers whose high degree of cooperation with the senate and maintenance of peace throughout the empire gave them the name of the "good" emperors. Among these, Trajan (A.D. 98–117) and Marcus Aurelius (A.D. 160–181) were particularly revered by their contemporaries and later rulers.

Trajan represents the growing cosmopolitanism of the imperial office. He was from a family of Italians who settled in Spain, and during his reign the empire reached its greatest territorial extent.

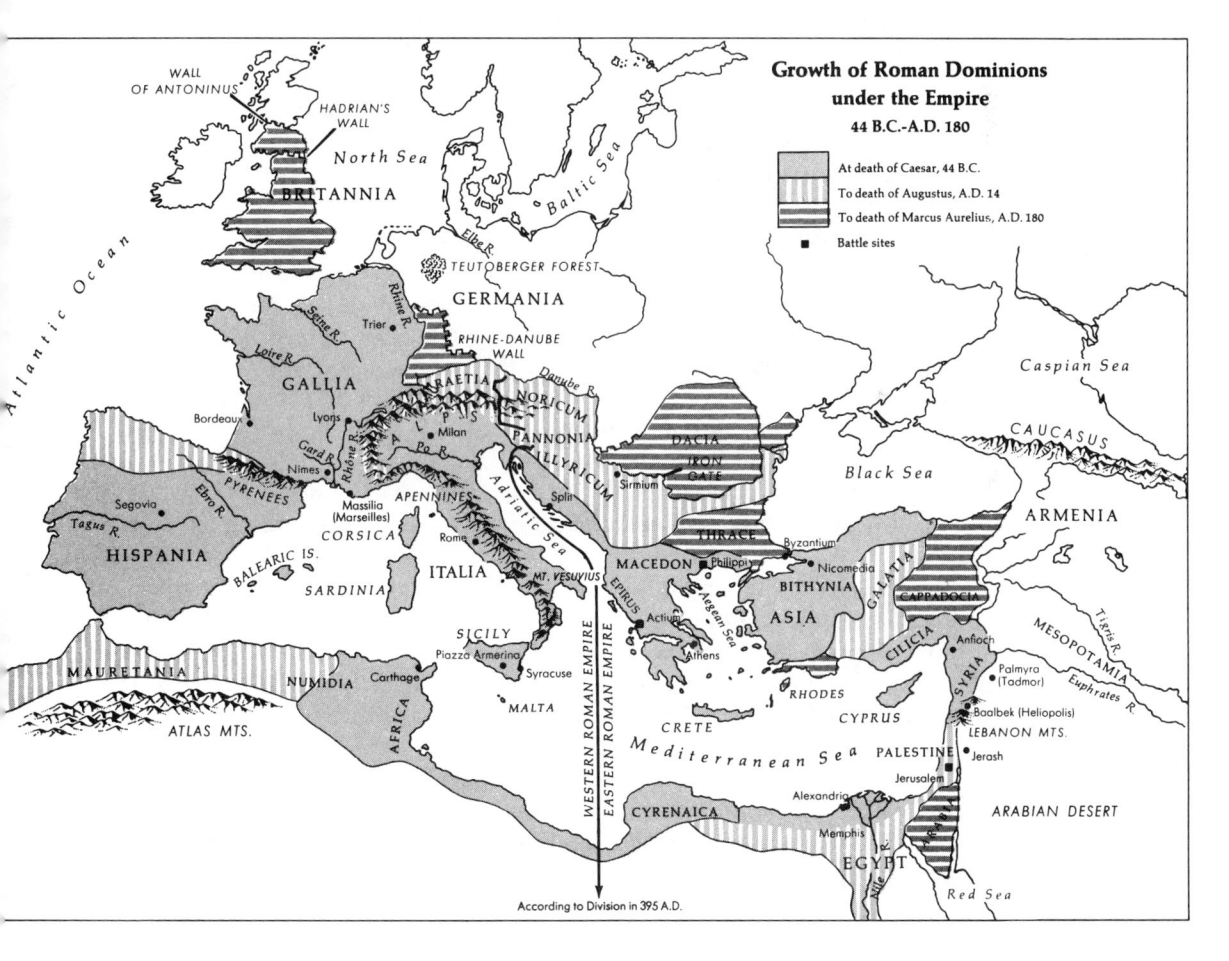

Rome expanded at the expense of its closest neighbors—the villages of Latium, Etruria, and the Greek cities of southern Italy. Intervention in the south, however, drew Rome into a suddenly wider political world, which included Carthage with her western Mediterranean land-and-sea empire, and the Greek kingdoms and city-states of the Hellenistic world of third-century B.C. The conquest of Carthage took Roman arms, officials, and colonists to northern Africa and Spain, and the dangers of being isolated in Spain made them establish contact with the Greek towns on the northern Mediterranean coast and with the Celtic hinterland. Celts, or Gauls, were a late Iron Age society speaking an Indo-European language. As descendents of the great wave of barbarian migrations of the twelfth century B.C., they had shaped a society in continental Europe based upon a warrior aristocracy, a rich culture of oral literary tradition, and a form of nature worship led by a priestly caste called druids. In the early fourth century B.C., Celtic warriors had sacked the city of Rome. In the third century, other Celts had broken across the Balkans to threaten Greece before they settled in Asia Minor. There, as the Galatians (Celts; in Greek, *Keltoi;* in Latin, *Galli*), they became effective mercenaries and were the recipients of St. Paul's famous epistle.

While Celtic society in the second century B.C. was no longer strong enough to threaten Rome, the presence of leagues of Celtic settlements north of the Mediterranean inspired the Romans to connect Spain and Italy by a land route. The founding of the city of Narbonne around 120 B.C. (now in southern France) and the construction of the Via Domitia, which connected it to northern Italy, had brought the Romans in force beyond the Alps to Europe. Allied with Greek cities on the coast, Romans pressed upon the Celtic Gauls until the proconsulate of Julius Caesar. Then, for political and military reasons, Caesar drove the Roman legions straight into the heart of Celtic Gaul and vastly expanded the province. Thus, the search for a new boundary to protect Mediterranean and Roman interests in Gaul led the Romans beyond the Rhine River, as the dangers to the north led them beyond the Danube in their search for secure boundaries. In time a Rhine-Danube frontier became the northern limit of Roman expansion in Europe. From Britain, the Romans traveled to the mouth of the Rhine, down to the Danube, then across the Black Sea through Asia Minor. From there they progressed to the Tigris-Euphrates Valleys and along the border with Parthia, then across Arabia, Egypt, and western North Africa. The Romans threw up frontier posts and filled the hinterland with colonists, officials, tax collectors, country estates and public monuments. Even Roman cities, in keeping with the old Hellenistic custom of creating *poleis* to help stabilize the countryside, appeared on these frontiers. The most remarkable of these, Timgad in North Africa, reflected not only the reach of Roman authority but also the vast investment in personnel and money that Rome was willing to make.

People of the empire were at enormously varying levels of social development, from the sophisticated cities of Athens and Alexandria to the teeming and busy Levantine coast. There were more subdued administrative centers like Bordeaux in the old Celtic settlements, and relatively untouched pockets of primitive agriculture and herding in the mountains of Asia Minor. Beyond the frontiers, barbarian societies came into increasingly frequent contact with Rome, often peaceably. Within the empire, a homogeneous style of life evolved, which slowly included many of the empire's new inhabitants. Romanized Celts from northern Italy and Gaul, Celt-Iberians from Spain, Hellenized Syrians, Arabs, and Jews could meet in the forae and baths in Bordeaux, Trier, Milan, Athens, or

Alexandria. The cultural cosmopolitanism of this Hellenistic world adapted and spread through the politically stable Roman Empire, as it vastly expanded between the second century B.C. and the fifth century A.D.

The new stability and freedom from invasion which was produced by the reforms of Augustus and his successors, revitalized trade and commerce throughout the empire and tempered the fearful insecurity that had plagued society during the late second and early first centuries B.C. The Pax Romana, or Roman Peace, was real, especially under Augustus. Provincial life thrived, frontiers were defended without vast expenses. Roman citizenship and administrative and legal institutions spread and combined with the easy bilingual Greco-Roman culture of the upper classes both in local and cosmopolitan society. The vast personal wealth of the emperor supplemented the yield of taxes, and the civic spirit that produced lavish public works and festivals continued to thrive till the end of the second century.

Ultimately, older divisions of society gave way in the early third century A.D. to two divisions: *honestiores* and *humiliores*. *Honestiores* included the now provincialized senatorial class, the equestrians, the higher ranks of the army, and the local urban gentry (*decurions*). Social mobility was possible among the *honestiores,* and military service helped to create a provincial gentry that slowly became Romanized. Military service was also a path upward to higher civil office, which in turn was another means of social improvement. *Humiliores* constituted the enormous mass of the population: rural free laborers whose status was constantly threatened with depression (as more slave laborers became free), artisans and laborers joined in religious and social fraternities in the towns, and unemployed citizens whose lives were partially sustained by civic philanthropy. *Humiliores* were a class with restricted rights and a clearly inferior status.

Agriculture constituted the economic base of Roman life, and the relatively small ruling elite largely supported itself locally, importing only luxury goods unobtainable in its region. Land transportation was so expensive that long-distance trade was simplified by largely dealing in luxuries. The only really complicated system of economic interchange was involved in supplying the cities which served the empire as administrative headquarters of regions. They did not have the economic dimension that characterizes modern urban life or, to a certain extent, characterized the urban life of the ancient Near East. Cities were not so much a source of wealth as a drain on the resources of the empire because industry tended to export itself, not its products. Local centers of production grew whether they made pottery, weapons, bricks, or mass-produced statues and imperial portraits and tended to localize everything except the most demanding and expensive trade and industry.

Roman military and administrative institutions permeated local life far more than trade or Hellenistic learning did. Army camps grew into frontier or provincial cities by drawing their recruits from the local region and discharging their soldiers to the camp towns of Gaul, Britain, the Balkans, or North Africa. As the army drew more and more upon outsiders—barbarians and remote provincials—to fill its ranks, Roman military life determined the kind of Romanization many of these people experienced. When the emperor Caracalla opened Roman citizenship to all free people in the empire in A.D. 212, Roman law was made universal in even local courts and remote societies. Roman legal thought made remarkable strides in the second and first centruies B.C., influenced as it was by the rush of economic change, the pressing demands of a new society, and by the work of lawyers like Cicero. A distinct legal profession was in the making with a rational approach to legal relationships. Citizens could hope for security in their relationships with one another and with the state. The homogeneity and sophistication of Roman law made it easily adaptable to most of the societies that comprised the empire and thus it became the vehicle for much Roman thought about human nature, governance, and security.

Yet perhaps Rome's greatest achievements were administration—and survival. After the economic and political explosions of the third through first centuries B.C., an imperial administration imparted security and stability to the Hellenistic world and to the less socially developed peoples that the new empire ruled. Romans may have regarded these as their finest triumphs because the greatest of Roman epic poems, Virgil's *Aeneid,* applauds the transformation of older Roman values by the Augustan reforms, and Livy's *History* of the founding of the City praises the stern patrician morality that expressed itself in political rule. Romans extolled humility, obedience, discipline, steadfastness, and piety, even at those moments when there seemed to be no political way out of the rampant crises and corruption. Regularity, clear authority, official toleration of nonpolitical controversy, and a focus upon the Stoic concepts of political morality constituted the Roman contribution to the organization of knowledge and to the social dynamism of the Hellenistic Near East. Without committing itself overmuch to local linguistic or cultural styles, Rome's rule tolerated local differences within an effective administrative framework. During the period from the late first century A.D. to the early third, few serious demands were made on the system, and it worked remarkably well. People were more than willing to repay Rome with allegiance and loyalty in return for the social stability and regularity it imparted to their lives. The empire meant personal security, and it delivered security more effectively than had any earlier state.

Even so, the conditions of life characteristic of the Hellenistic Near East did not change perceptibly under the empire. A small elite controlled the economic and political power, which was sustained by the labor of the many. Few technological developments affected the conditions of labor. Few agricultural discoveries relieved the burden of providing food to large cities and stricken rural areas. As better management improved life for some areas, the life of most people was marginal, their comforts few. Local rural religion and life styles remained little changed by the empire and the imperial religion of emperor worship. Urban life was rather the opposite. Newcomers, torn from their accustomed surroundings, preserved what they could of their former culture. They formed new religious and charitable associations in the melting pot of the city, but they had been cut loose from moral bonds and communities that might have strengthened or enforced these new associations.

If the cities offered much to choose from, they offered few criteria for choice. Religion, magic, astrology, exotic rituals, and strange philosophical traditions were taken up by populations who believed that slaves could be suddenly propelled to vast fortunes, become imperial favorites, and then just as suddenly be degraded. The personification of fortune itself—or, for linguistic reasons, herself—elevated *fortuna* to the status of a goddess. Roman state religion—a rather formal, unspiritual homage paid to the conventionally deified emperor—put few limitations on religious variations; consequently, many religious systems competed for the attention of a spiritually rootless urban population. Egyptian, Near Eastern, and native Roman cults openly attracted members, and membership in one of these rarely precluded membership in others. Even formal philosophy, with its long history of concentration upon ethics and metaphysics, slowly turned to a distinctively religious approach to reality.

Thus, the spiritual climate of the first centuries B.C. and A.D. was perhaps the least stable aspect of Roman life. In Palestine, where the first two centuries B.C. had witnessed a violent Jewish reaction against Hellenizing rulers, many people regarded Roman state religion as anathema. Bitter revolts in A.D. 69 and 135 brought the destruction of the Temple at Jerusalem and the final dissolution of the Jewish state. Turbulence within Judaism over security and faith gave rise to sectarian movements, from the traditionalist and tolerant Sadducees who were traditional by accepting only the five books of the Law and tolerant in rejecting resurrection and immortality, to the ascetic practices of the Essenes and Qumran communities. Fervent Jewish thought directed itself toward two themes: an apocalyptic literature that predicted the end of time, the finality of the impending divine judgment on the world, and the appearance of a Messiah as either a redeeming savior god or a messenger of Yahweh; and communities of sectarian believers.

### The Beginnings of Christianity

In one such small community lived the followers of Jesus of Nazareth, a preacher who not only continued many apocalyptic traditions of late Judaism but also proclaimed himself to be the Messiah, or rather a particular kind of Messiah. Jesus was captured, tried, convicted with Roman approval, and executed around A.D. 33. Disciples spread his teachings, which gradually separated them from their deep roots in Judaism. In the eyes of the disciples, Jesus was the Christ, the God-made-man, and his death and resurrection heralded a new era, a new covenant between God and his people, a new law.

The old law, the Mosaic law, was rejected by Jesus' most remarkable follower, Paul (*fl.* A.D. 50). Christian sects appeared in many Jewish communities of Palestine, the rest of the Near East, and by the middle of the first century A.D., in Rome itself. Christian communities slowly severed themselves from the Jewish communities out of which they had grown, opened their society to gentiles, and developed a literature centered on the life and teachings of Jesus. This literature is now represented in part by the *Epistles* of St. Paul and others, and the gospels (or as they were known, the "Good News," *euangelion* or *evangelium*). They were biographical and figurative accounts of Jesus's teachings, of which four became particularly prominent. The Gospel of Mark, probably produced in Rome, and perhaps another lost gospel, appeared between A.D. 64 and 70. Around A.D. 80 there appeared the Gospel of Matthew, thought to come from Syria; and near the same time the Gospel of Luke, whose second part, *The Acts of the Apostles,* demonstrated the continuing power of Jesus's message among his apostles after his death. The Gospel of John, the last, has been dated around A.D. 90–100 and was composed at Ephesus.

This literary tradition constituted the basis of Christian teaching. Written in the Greek koine and enhanced by the *Epistles* of Paul and others, it was verified by the authority of the Apostles and those taught by them. As traditional Jewish scholarship established a canonical or official body of Old Testament works in the first and second centuries A.D., so the Christians slowly established a list of canonical works of the New Testament. Gospels appeared in Coptic in Egypt, in Latin in North Africa, and in Syriac in the Near East, so that Christian teachings spread widely throughout the Hellenistic world and reached down to social levels that did not know Greek. Weekly meetings centered upon a communal meal and the reading of scripture. Charities were organized within the Christian communities. Jews, gentiles, and women gained admission as full participants. All of this added to the strength of the radical young churches; a common body of scripture and interpretation, a rigorous code of ethical conduct, and the promise of eternal salvation constituted

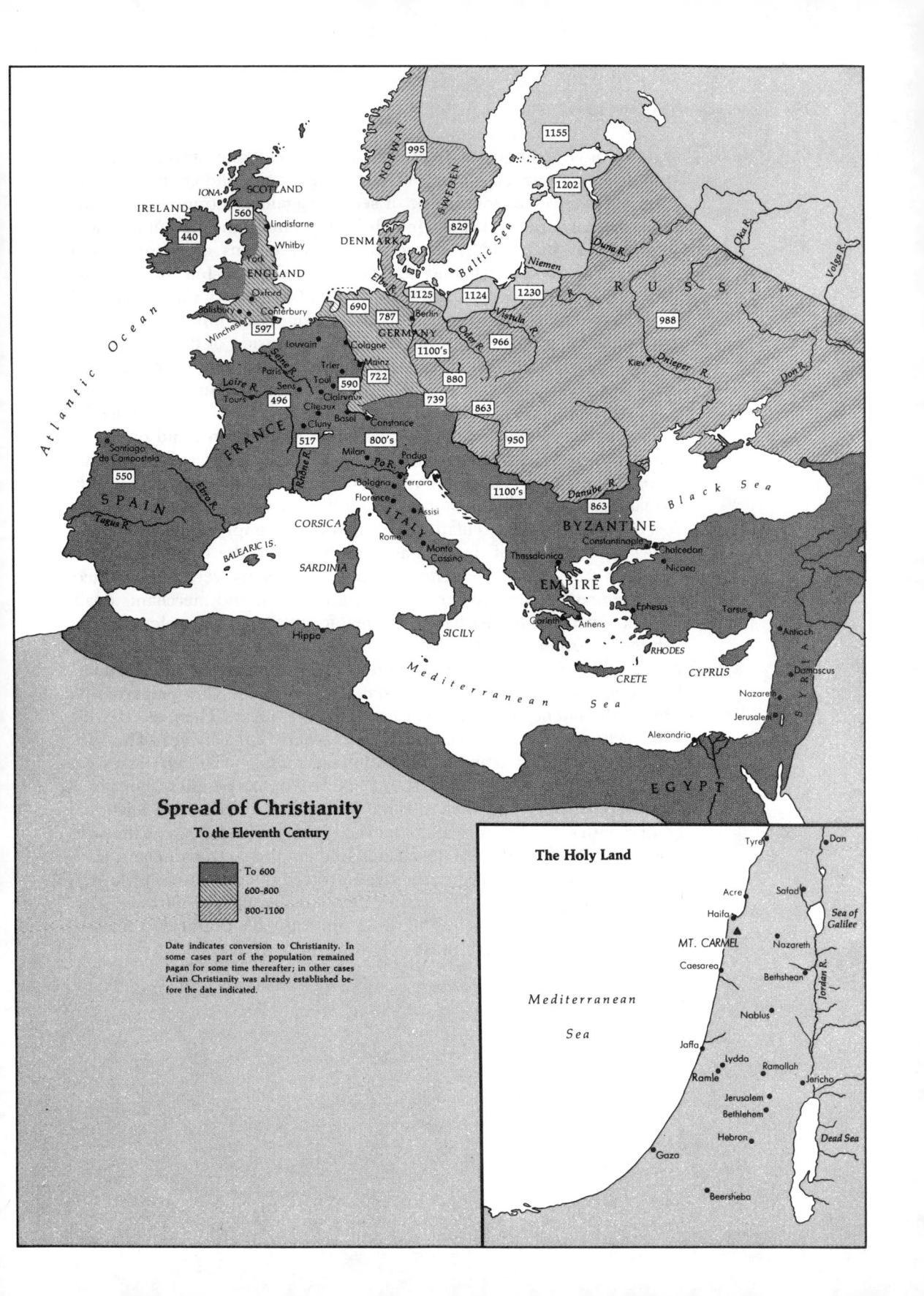

# Spread of Christianity
## To the Eleventh Century

**Legend:**
- To 600
- 600–800
- 800–1100

Date indicates conversion to Christianity. In some cases part of the population remained pagan for some time thereafter; in other cases Arian Christianity was already established before the date indicated.

## The Holy Land

their spiritual strength. No matter how vast a city one lived in nor how troubled a life one led, the promises of Christianity offered an attractive form of spiritual consolation or of security against outrageous fortune. Only partially attached to its Jewish background—and that attachment weakened by increasingly allegorical interpretations of scripture and Pauline theology—Christianity could open itself to non-Jews in a way that Judaism could not and did not wish to. Yet, Christianity's intolerance of other deities and cults gave its adherents a rigor and inner security that most other religions did not offer, and the extension of this intolerance to the imperial state cult forced the Christian communities to rely only on themselves, often in the face of imperial persecution.

The spread of Christianity throughout the Roman world was aided by the improved communications provided by Roman force and organization, by the development of the transportable *codex*—a series of papyrus leaves bound at the edges to form a book, rather than sewn at the ends to make a roll—and by the social and spiritual attractiveness of its beliefs. In a larger sense, the circulation of religions was simply one aspect of the growing prosperity of the Roman Empire during the first and second centuries A.D. The consequences of the Pax Romana were not confined to the empire alone. Roman soldiers, governors, and merchants dealt with the affairs of the barbarian Germanic and Iranian peoples who inhabited the other side of the Rhine-Danube as well as other frontiers. In Africa, Roman exploration pushed further south. Through the Parthian kingdom, economic contact was established with the Han emperors of China, who opened the Silk Road across southern Asia. Then, in A.D. 166, a small fleet sent by Marcus Aurelius reached China by sea. The vast empires of Han China and Rome had made contact. The two possessed many similarities: both were surrounded by barbarian peoples whom they influenced strongly; both were ruled by palace autocrats and a landed gentry; both looked back to a remote and highly stylized image of the past —Rome to the early days of the farmer-soldiers and stern patricians, Han China to the image of the gentleman portrayed in the writings of K'ung Ch'iu (Confucius) in the fifth century B.C. Finally, both empires experienced severe crises between the third and the sixth centuries A.D., and both emerged from these drastically transformed.

## II. 5 The Crisis of Late Antiquity: Transformation of the Mediterranean World

> *It is rare that a state can be securely established in lands inhabited by many tribes and bands.*— Ibn Khaldun of Tunis, Arab philosopher (1332–1406)

Rome's power had stemmed from the tough discipline of a large, well-led army of peasant soldiers from central Italy. When those soldiers turned conquerors of the Carthaginian, Celtic, and Hellenistic worlds, they had access to cultural institutions far different from their own, and frequently far more attractive. Wealth and power came to Rome very quickly, transforming its economic structure and placing unbearable strain upon traditional social and cultural institutions. Political and social chaos in the late second and early first centuries B.C. virtually tore apart the Roman state. The Augustan settlement, continued by successive emperors until the late second century, had brought extraordinary stability to the Mediterranean world, but it dealt only casually with deep-rooted economic and social problems. Expansion and administration of Roman power after Augustus worked satisfactorily until the institutions of empire became too expensive. Then these institutions could not be administered without transforming the finances of the state; and the delicate balance between compromise, military power, senatorial prerogatives, and the lower classes of society could not be maintained.

The enormous wealth of Rome in the first centuries B.C. and A.D. found its way into the hands of new entrepreneurs, the senatorial aristocracy, and the imperial treasury. Entrepreneurs and the senatorial aristocracy acquired land; the imperial treasury paid for buildings and beautification of the cities. Imperial taxes supported the army. Slowly and steadily money was drained from central Italy; by the late first century, Rome's gold and silver coinage was devalued and taxes were extended. Between A.D. 106 and 117, Emperor Trajan expanded Rome's frontiers in the East which weakened the kingdom of Parthia. Under Trajan's successor, Hadrian, the bitter Jewish revolt of A.D. 130 destroyed the Jewish community in Palestine; and in A.D. 165 during the eastern campaigns, the Roman army brought back a plague (probably smallpox) which spread throughout the whole empire. During the second century, new pressures were exerted upon the frontiers in the Balkans as well. Increasingly frequent military obligations of late second-century emperors, notably Marcus Aurelius, gave enormous power to the army, and a succession of crises following the assassination of Marcus's cruel son Commodus in 192 brought Septimus Severus to the throne. Severus, succeeded by his two sons, established a dynasty that generously rewarded the army, raised army pay, and continued the lavish scale of imperial patronage that had characterized its predecessors.

On Rome's eastern frontier, a revolt against the last of the weakened Parthian monarchs introduced new leadership and direction to the Parthian Empire. The revolt was led by Ardashir, Sasanid warlord from Persia. Native Iranian culture took the place of the Hellenized Parthian state. Centered on the court of the Shah, the Sasanid monarchy held itself together partly by a revived Zoroastrianism that survives today. The growing power of this vigorous Sasanid monarchy created a much more formidable enemy in the east than Parthia had ever been.

In the north and northeast, new migrations of peoples threatened the frontiers. Stabilization of the Rhine-Danube frontier in the first century A.D. had allowed much of Celtic Europe to become incorporated within the empire, but it blocked the age-old migration routes west from the Danube valley. During the second century, migrations were stepped up in western Eurasia, as Germanic peoples of northern Europe began to move south and east. They encountered Roman frontier posts and provincial towns in the area of the Rhine where many barbarians settled as farmers and soldiers, thus acquainting others beyond the frontier with the riches of the empire. Another group of Germanic peoples migrated to southern Russia. Known as Goths, they mingled with nomad barbarians from northern Persia and probed the defenses of the Balkans, penetrating Greece and Asia Minor and threatening yet one more frontier, a threat Rome at first ignored.

When the emperor needed money, his primary source of revenue was the managerial class of the cities, those who had emerged as the principle figures in commerce. Peasants paid some of the bill; but the masters and inhabitants of the vast senatorial estates were, by the fourth century, shielded from governmental demands. As a large and privileged landowning class of *potentiores,* "powerful men," they interposed themselves between the demands of the emperor and the lowest ranking labor force. In time the *potentiores* loomed large throughout the empire: as privileged and well-connected landowners, they would intervene in many processes of imperial administration, protect their inferiors by other than legal means, and, as patrons, offer to small, free farmers, a kind of security that the state could not give them. Both the former senatorial class and the peasants bore the brunt of the new military demands, and the financial demands of the emperors were backed up by a reinvigorated bureaucracy of tax collectors, accountants, police, and spies.

Assassination of the last Severan emperor in A.D. 235 opened the imperial office to a rapid succession of emperors enthroned by the armies, some of them victims of assassination plots in their own courts. Between 235 and 284, two vast areas of the empire operated as virtually independent territories: Gaul proclaimed a short-lived separatist kingdom, while the Arab caravan city of Palmyra emerged as a powerful separatist force. Palmyra even proclaimed its ruler, Zenobia, as empress in 270. Persian armies drove into the eastern provinces and twice sacked the great city of Antioch in Syria. Only the appearance of several able generals late in the century preserved what was left of the frontiers. Under Aurelian (270–275) in particular, Rome's military force began to counter attack.

### *Diocletian and Constantine*

The necessity of supporting the army was clear to the series of soldiers from Illyria (roughly, northern modern Albania) who succeeded each other as emperors at the end of the third century. The army, nearly doubling in size between 275 and 375, placed the soldier Diocletian on the throne in 284. The most far-reaching reforms since the age of Augustus were put into effect under Diocletian. Recognizing that the problems of an empire were too much and too dangerous for one man, Diocletian divided imperial power by creating two offices with the title *Augustus*. One ruled the *pars orientalis* (the eastern half of the empire), the other, the *pars occidentalis* (the western part). Each *Augustus* was aided by a Caesar who would be his successor. Each *pars* was divided into two great areas subdivided into dioceses, and each of these into provinces. He separated military command from civil authority and greatly enlarged the imperial bureaucracy to expedite the needs of the government. A new tax base was developed, and the most accessible source of taxes—the mercantile class of the cities, the craftspeople, and the peasants—were forced into hereditary continuation of their work. They and their descendents could not change their occupations. Although Diocletian's freezing of prices in 301 did not successfully curb the rising inflation, other rigorous attempts to control the economic life of the empire succeeded, at an enormous price. The government of the empire, originally designed to protect Roman privilege and to wield Roman power most effectively throughout the empire, now further debased the coinage and drained all imperial resources in a terrible struggle for survival. The citizen body now existed solely for the needs of the government. Security, once symbolized by the Pax Romana, could now be found only in illegal flight from governmental demands, in seeking refuge under the patronage of powerful men, or by entering government service.

In his attempts to give an air of tradition to his reform program, Diocletian participated in the revival of Roman antiquity and vigorously enforced both the Roman state religion and what he imagined to be an earlier Roman morality. In his eyes, Christianity in particular seemed a treasonous violation of Roman religion and state loyalty. Throughout the last years of his reign Diocletian launched the most severe persecutions the Christian church had yet witnessed.

Diocletian's plan of a divided imperial office lasted exactly one generation. After his abdication in 305, rivalry and civil war grew among his designated and undesignated successors for the next eight years. By 313, one of these, Constantine, emerged as the determining force in imperial rule, and under his guidance persecutions of Christians were ended. Christian communities were given legal status and, later, vast privileges. At his death, Constantine himself was baptized a Christian.

### The Decline of Rome

Both a converted emperor and the freedom to believe in and practice Christianity raised an entirely new set of problems in the history of both Rome and the Christian churches. Christianity had never anticipated a place for a Christianized Roman emperor in the series of communities governed by bishops, priests, and deacons. Christians found new security and new uncertainties in their fourth-century status. Oppressed members of the curial class—hereditarily bound to office and under increasing pressure from the imperial government to accept personal responsibility for tax revenues—could find few other places of refuge, while the loss of access to civil and military office resulted in the withdrawal of the senatorial landowners to their immense estates. There, they virtually ruled unchecked as *potentiores* and formed the basis for much of the agricultural economy of the next six hundred years. The army began to provide paths, not only to high military command but into the imperial civil service as well. Governmental dress began to resemble the military uniform, and men from the remotest backwaters of imperial provincial society, the lowest social ranks, and even from the barbarian hinterlands were increasingly used as officers of the state. Domination of the armies by countrified provincials, the lower orders, and barbarians provided the means for tapping vast pools of manpower and talent.

Economic and social reform, the unifying of military command, efficient restructuring of the armies, and the growing practice of substituting goods (often crops or minerals) for money in payment for government services and requisitions helped preserve the unity of the empire for a century after the death of Constantine in 337. Constantinople, founded in 330, gave the empire a permanent eastern capital, and Constantine's three-generation dynasty imparted a much needed central stability to the imperial office. It slowed the process of militarizing the throne. Valentinian's dynasty in the second half of the fourth century also began as a military regime which was civilianized after two generations. The succeeding Theodosian dynasty further reasserted the civilian character of the imperial office. Thus, the dramatic militarization of social and political life of the empire early in the fourth century was ended, having done its work. Military revolutionaries from the reigns of Diocletian and Constantine could now move into traditional roles of a ruling, civilized, Roman elite. By the third quarter of the fourth century, the government of the empire appeared to achieve a new stability at the cost of increased social and economic problems.

The price of survival had been high in many ways. In spite of enduring influences of Hellenistic culture, knowledge of Greek slowly declined in the West. Indeed, from the second century, Christian worship had been conducted in Latin. Western cities, never the centers of commerce that eastern cities had been, became impoverished and depopulated—except for those like Trier, Milan, and Ravenna, which were centers of imperial administration and residence in the West. Still, land values remained high and immense fortunes survived in the West, although only among a smaller group of aristocratic families, whose wealth did little to help the empire. Imperial patronage of public works declined after curial patronage of local public projects disappeared.

Behind the drastic and often ineffective internal reforms within the Roman state, there loomed the seemingly inexhaustible needs of the army. The strong Sasanid monarchy in Persia arose at the same time that renewed pressures were exerted by western Germanic peoples on the Rhine and by the Goths and their allies on the Danube. Armies loyal only to their generals moved quickly from one frontier to another, challenging imperial authority. The desert Bedouins of North Africa began to make inroads, not only into Roman North Africa and Egypt but into the new communities of withdrawn ascetics, the first monks, who had begun to live isolated lives of religion in the Egyptian deserts. If barbarian pressures did not cause the downfall of the empire—internal economic and social difficulties had begun that process in the third century—they certainly accelerated it.

By the end of the fourth century, more and more traditionally educated intellectuals had become Christians, and imperial patronage had made the Church a powerful presence in the empire. Although both ecclesiastical and civil service ranks grew, ecclesiastical institutions often were exempt from the more onerous burdens of public duties. The first buildings exclusively reserved to Christian worship appeared, designed along the lines of the late imperial basilicas or audience halls. Much of the imagery and symbolism of imperial Rome, from the costumes of civil service grades to the decoration of the basilicas, reflect this transfer of many of the themes of the late imperial state to the Church. With acceptance came diversity, causing many splinter groups among the Christian communities to carry their differences to the imperial court and its ecclesiastical advisers. Several doctrinal disputes—notably those focusing on the two natures of Christ, the character of the Trinity, and the sacramental powers of the clergy—divided these religious groups. Faced with these and other specific problems, a series of ecclesiastical councils shaped the beginnings of a body of dogma that became official imperial and ecclesiastical policy.

### Barbarian Invasions

During the fourth and fifth centuries, the eastern parts of the empire held firm. Barbarian invasions were defeated or bought off, commerce thrived, taxes were paid. Fiscal order was restored through greater economy of resources and the work force and through curbing dissidence. It was also helpful to have an emperor living at Constantinople, where he could be closely associated with the concerns of the East. The West, underpopulated, less urbanized, more frequently struck by invasion, and largely ruled by an independent and intractable senatorial aristocracy with antiquarian tastes and great power, succumbed during the fifth century to the barbarian invasions.

Of these invasions, the most successful was carried out by the Huns during the last quarter of the fourth century and the first half of the fifth. The effects of new developments and military innovations arose with equal frequency on both sides of the border between civilized and barbarian society. In the first century B.C., another military revolution had taken place, this time on the border between the horse-nomad warriors of the steppes and the Parthian Empire. Where it had the space to operate, the light cavalry of the steppe warriors was exceedingly effective until the development of the armored horse and rider. Stronger horses were bred to carry a rider in armor, and with that armor, the Parthian and Persian monarchies impeded nomadic invasions from the east and north for several centuries. The wealthy aristocracy of Persian warlords could pay for such new devices, and with their support the Shah stabilized Persia throughout the third and fourth centuries.

However, in central Asia nomadic warrior confederations had been taking shape since the sixth century B.C.; and in the fourth century A.D., the migrating Hun confederacy of steppe warriors emerged with such power that neighboring nomadic peoples were either drawn into it or forced to flee into China or the western part of Eurasia. The Han Empire in China sustained a series of Hun invasions in the late fourth and fifth centuries. Germanic and Iranian inhabitants of south Russia felt the shock in the middle of the fourth century. The Huns moved toward south Russia, destroyed the Gothic monarchy, and drove the Goths west and south toward the borders of the Roman Empire. The Goths were admitted to the area south of the Danube in 376, but imperial misadministra-

**Germanic Invasion Routes 375-568 A.D.**

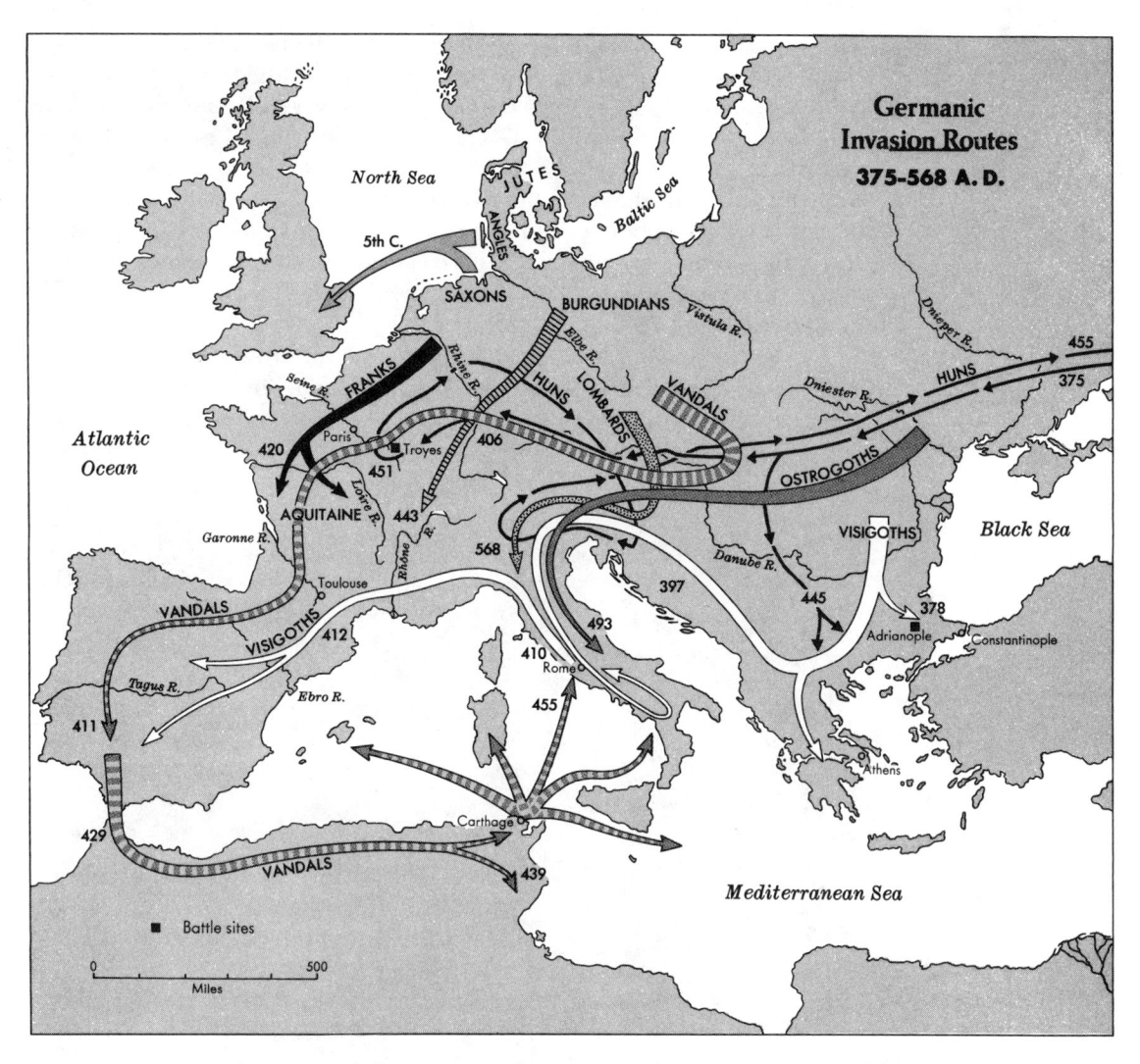

tion caused them to revolt two years later, destroying a Roman army at Adrianople and killing a Roman emperor. After 378 the Ostrogoths (east Goths) swept through Greece and northern Italy, moving onto southern Gaul and then to Spain, where they ultimately established a separate, partially Romanized kingdom that lasted until the first quarter of the eighth century. In 410, a confederation of western Germanic peoples pushed across the Rhine, leaving barbarian settlements within Gaul, storming through Spain into northern Africa, where the Vandal kingdom (source of our modern usage of the word) survived for a century.

Late in the fifth century, the Ostrogoths swept westward and occupied Italy, a country weakened by the final struggles with the Huns in 451–454.

The imperial structures in the West virtually collapsed. Only the East—richer and more populated, with a strong imperial line ruling in impregnable Constantinople—survived intact. The power of Rome withdrew to the old centers of Hellenism (Greece, Asia Minor, the Levantine coast, and Egypt), and it was at Constantinople that a Christianized Greco-Roman Hellenism shaped a taut, prosperous state, the last Roman empire, which would endure until 1453. In the course of the late fifth, sixth, and early seventh centuries, only this eastern Roman Empire and Sasanid Persia remained of the once vast ecumenical civilization sustained by Roman arms and Hellenistic culture.

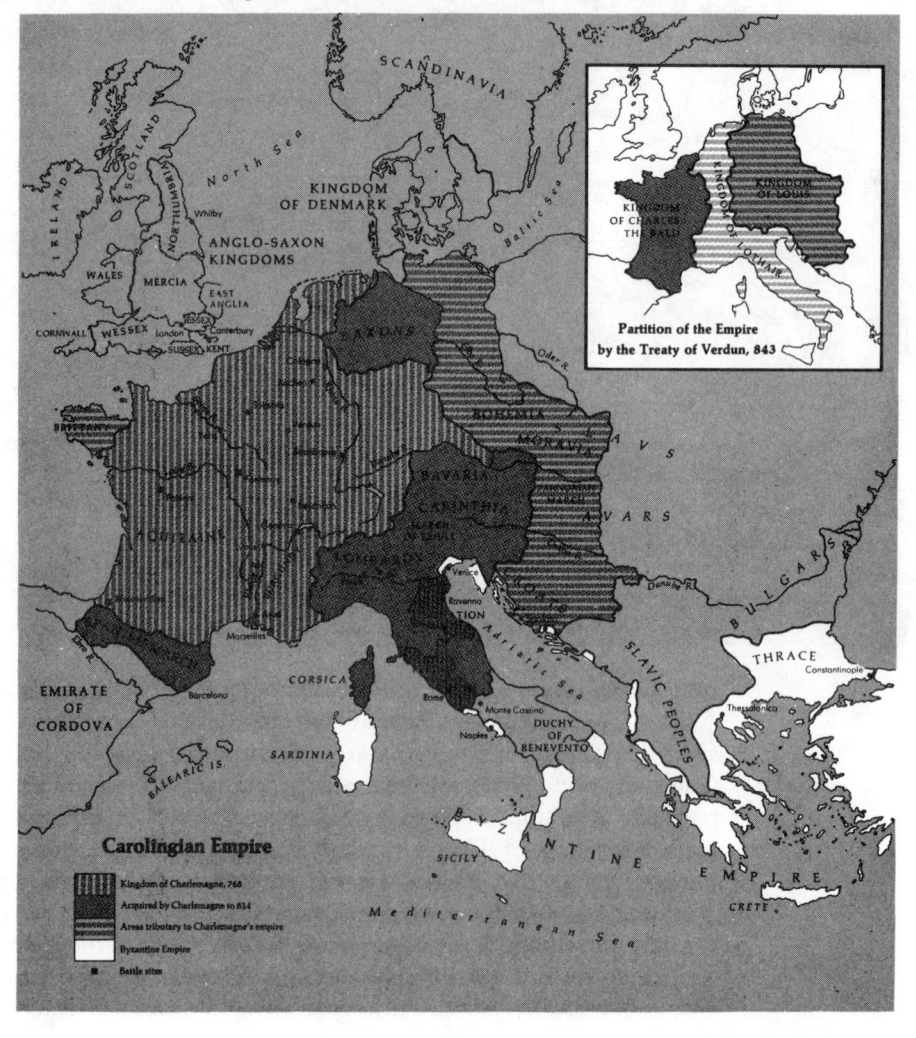

The barbarian kingdoms established in the old provinces of the western Roman Empire absorbed their Romanism and Christianity from impoverished provincials and dedicated clergy. Acculturation of Romans to barbarian ways and of barbarians to Roman ways occurred throughout the fifth and sixth centuries. Germanic societies slowly changed their character—barbarian war leaders became more like provincial Roman governors and generals and barbarian customs were written in Latin as were legal codes. This helped to regularize the former ways of barbarian life on a political basis.

## *Byzantium*

The enduring power of the Roman East, however, soon reached out to reclaim the western provinces. Under Justinian (527–565), a Latin-speaking descendent of Illyrian soldiers, the East Roman Empire reconquered North Africa, Italy, and parts of Spain from the barbarian rulers. Gaul remained in the hands of the Franks, a people who had shaped a strong kingdom under Clovis (481–511) and his successors. The Franks thrived upon the agricultural produce of Gaul and the Rhineland and upon booty from their conquests. Soon after Justinian's conquests, however, a new Eurasian nomadic people, the Avars, swept into the Hungarian plain. In their expansion, they hurled the Slavic peoples who settled there before them into Greece, drove the Lombards (another tribe of Germanic invaders) into an exhausted Italy, and opened the western coast of the Black Sea to new nomadic migrations. At the same time, Moslems were detaching North Africa from the Roman Empire.

Justinian's success in the West was only temporary, but he did strengthen the position of Byzantium. Drawing upon steadily flowing tax revenues, an increased work force in Asia Minor and the Balkans, local talent, and the support of Greece and Syria, Justinian reshaped Constantinople into a capital and a shrine. As a result of rebuilding the city after a dangerous riot in 532, he exercised firm political and religious authority, which was strengthened by the intelligence of his wife Theodora. His successful choice of administrators, from generals to legal advisors to architects, transformed Constantinople into the center of a powerful and resourceful state. It embodied the greatest energy of Christianized Hellenism and was sustained by the core of the Hellenistic East. Justinian transformed the Eastern Roman Empire into the Byzantine Empire, preserving Greek intellectual and religious heritages and Roman concepts of the universal state. The western provinces of the empire were divided among different Germanic kingdoms, Roman aristocrats, and new invaders. They were also separated politically, economically, and linguisticly from the surviving and strengthened Greek East. From the late fifth century when the last emperor in the West was deposed, the single Augustus reigning at Constantinople was the sole imperial power authority in the shrunken Roman Empire. His reduced needs and the productivity and security of this contracted world gave the Byzantine Empire both a resilience and a degree of loyalty and religious devotion virtually unsurpassed in Roman history.

Thus within the old cores of Hellenistic civilization two civilizations emerged, combining Hellenistic roots with new sources of internal strength. Sasanid Persia drew heavily upon the Iranian past, the warlord aristocracy, and the religious strength of Zoroastrianism. Byzantium drew upon the commerce and culture of the Greek Near East and the Roman tradition of universal political authority. In the far West, ecclesiastical culture not only Christianized the Germanic invaders but transmitted to them what survived of Hellenistic Roman culture, which laid the groundwork for the later blending of Germanic and Roman traditions. Influences form Byzantium also touched the West. At the center were two civilized cores: Byzantine military power and diplomacy, which held off barbarians and Persians; and Sasanid power, which cleared Persia's eastern frontier. These two societies could not have survived without the toughness and thoroughness of Hellenized Christian culture and Iranian nationalism, the economic and social achievements of three millennia, and the vigor of more recent Roman and Sasanid innovations.

One of the prices paid for Justinian's attempt to reconquer the lost western provinces was neglect of the Balkan and Tigris-Euphrates frontiers. Another cost was the alienation of African, Palestinian, and Syrian Christian sects, who resented the harsh policy of reimposing imperial institutions. Justinian and his successors appointed bishops and councils to further orthodox religious beliefs, and Justinian tolerated the Monophysites, who believed that Christ had a single rather than trinitarian nature. In these areas, religious and political resistance to imperial rules became inextricably mixed. On the military frontiers, the reduced forces of East Rome could not prevent the growth of an alliance between the Avars (a mounted nomadic people from the steppes of central Asia) and the Slavs of southern Russia and the Balkans, nor the expansion of Sasanid Persia into Asia Minor.

In the first quarter of the seventh century, the crisis peaked. Persian armies, in conjunction with Avars and Slavs, attacked Constantinople and in 619 virtually reduced the empire to the spaces within the walls of the city. A new emperor, Heraclius I, left the defense of the city in the hands of its inhabitants, raised a last compact army, and sailed east along the southern coast of the Black Sea. He struck deep into Persia at Nineveh in 627 and destroyed the power of the Sasanid rulers. The successful defense of the city of Constantinople in 626 not only drove back the Avars and Slavs but opened the way for the reassertion of East Roman influence among the new inhabitants of the Balkans. It gave the people of the

Byzantine Empire a new sense of divine protection under the power of orthodox Christianity.

The early seventh-century survival of the Byzantine Empire was followed by a vigorous renewal of ecclesiastical contacts between Greek and Latin Christian churches, partly because many Greek-speaking clergy had fled to Italy in the troubled period between 550 and 650. Contacts were also renewed because the city of Rome, a narrow belt across the center of Italy, and the seaport towns on the Adriatic coast still technically formed part of the empire. Imperial institutions and power had survived there. The Roman Church, after the troubled fifth and sixth centuries, developed contacts with the scattered Christian churches in the West, from Spain to the Rhineland. Under the energetic pontificate of Pope

*Ikon of St. Simeon Stylites* This ikon, or stylized representation of a saint, richly worked with gold and silver, is a Russian depiction of a Syrian hermit who in the 5th century lived for 35 years on a small platform atop a pillar. The ikon was found in Cyprus and was created in the 16th century, telling us much about the Eastern church. *Source: The Bettman Archive, Inc.*

Gregory I (590–604), missionaries went as far as Britain, which had been evacuated by Roman legions in 407, and quickly converted the barbarian Anglo-Saxon invaders of that lost province. Byzantine sea-power strengthened the seventh-century sea contacts between Constantinople and the Italian west, and the resurgence of Latin Christianity under Gregory was aided by the flow of Greek and Syriac clergy into the West.

One such clerical figure, Theodore, reflects the cosmopolitanism of the seventh-century church. Born at Tarsus, the city of St. Paul in Asia Minor, Theodore came to Italy in the seventh century, received papal approval, and with an African abbot, Hadrian, went to England. In 668 he became the seventh Archbishop of Canterbury, formed a brilliant school of ecclesiastical learning, and organized the English church. Such resourcefulness strengthened the Christian world of the West during the seventh century and opened the way for the expanded communications with Rome that marked the eighth century. Meanwhile, ecclesiastical diplomacy cleared the path for renewed contacts among different regional societies in Latin and Germanic Europe. If the power of the emperor was weak, that of the Roman bishops was strong—not as rulers, but as cultural influences among the young Germanic societies that divided the old western provinces.

Both the revived Byzantine Empire and the western Germanic kingdoms, however, faced an unsuspected new threat during the course of the late seventh century: the rise of Islam.

### The Arab Peoples: At the Gates of the West

In the long military duel between Rome and Persia, the Arab peoples had participated as mercenaries, allies, and commercial liaisons. The prosperous Arabic kingdom of Nabatea had been conquered by the Roman Emperor Trajan in the second century, and the wealthy caravan city of Palmyra had emerged, first as a powerful Roman ally, then as a contender for imperial power in the late third century. As other Arabic kingdoms came under the Persian orbit, only the traditions of the kingdom of Saba in the south of the Arabian peninsula were still remembered by the seventh century. Military and economic difficulties had reopened one of the key trade routes from the Levant to the Persian Gulf down the western side of the Arabian peninsula; and in cities such as Mecca and Medina, even former nomadic Bedouin Arabs had entered commerce and taken up the urban life that their fellow Arabs in the south and northeast had lived for several centuries.

Life styles in such societies widely differed. Hellenized Arabs of Palmyra and Nabatea had little in common with the merchants, commercial liaisons, and caravan managers of Mecca and Medina, who had not yet found a culture that eased the transition from nomadic tribal existence to early urban life. Nomads lived a still different life; they were divided into tribes, feuded and raided and possessed a chivalric code of honor and a tradition of heroic oral poetry not unlike the nomads of the steppes nor the Celtic society of early Europe.

In the second decade of the seventh century, a middle-aged caravan manager in Mecca, not from the highest ranks of Meccan society nor particularly distinguished in his earlier life, began to have visions of a divine revelation, and he proclaimed these visions to his people. Mohammed (570–632) spoke directly and categorically: the one god, Allah, demanded proper worship from humankind, for whom He had a great affection and whom He would judge when each person died. Allah was the great one God who had revealed Himself in earlier stages to both Jews and Christians. By perverting his truth, they had fallen away from true belief. Allah now spoke through Mohammed, his prophet, and described a way of life that required submission (the way of *Islam*) to His will in all things. In time Mohammed's utterances were collected in the "revealed book," the *Koran,* in which the life of the Moslem was clearly laid out. Driven out of Mecca in 622, Mohammed's flight—the Hegira—took him to Medina where he had been invited as a peacemaker in quarrels between townspeople and farmers. His success and the success of his followers in raiding caravans from Mecca soon rallied many to the new religion, and in 630 Mohammed returned to Mecca, having made converts in both cities and having formed alliances with the desert tribes.

Under Mohammed's successors the Arab townspeople and nomadic warriors were united by their adherence to the Koran and to the wars waged against the unbelievers to the north. The fire of a new faith fused hitherto dissimilar peoples, and the skill of the Arab generals led Moslem armies to sudden victories in Syria (635), Iran (641), and Egypt (642). This initial string of complete victories against formerly powerful neighbors sustained Islamic faith in its early decades, and the flow of tribute, tax, and plunder satisfied even the least Islamized tribal warriors. Arab power flowed steadily into the vacuum that followed the recession of the Roman conquest of Persia earlier in the century. Many North African and Levantine Christian communities, disaffected by religious and fiscal quarrels with imperial Constantinople, made the Arab conquest easier. Arab policy dictated leaving local institutions in local hands, allowing a broad toleration of the religious practices of Christians and Jews—of whatever sectarian character—and collecting a tax from non-Moslems. This policy encouraged submission to Arabic power, particularly because the Arab armies were generally reluctant to destroy the areas they conquered.

Arabs lived apart from the peoples they had conquered and settled in military camps organized along tribal lines near the cities. This preservation of tribal bonds strengthened the armies and prevented them from

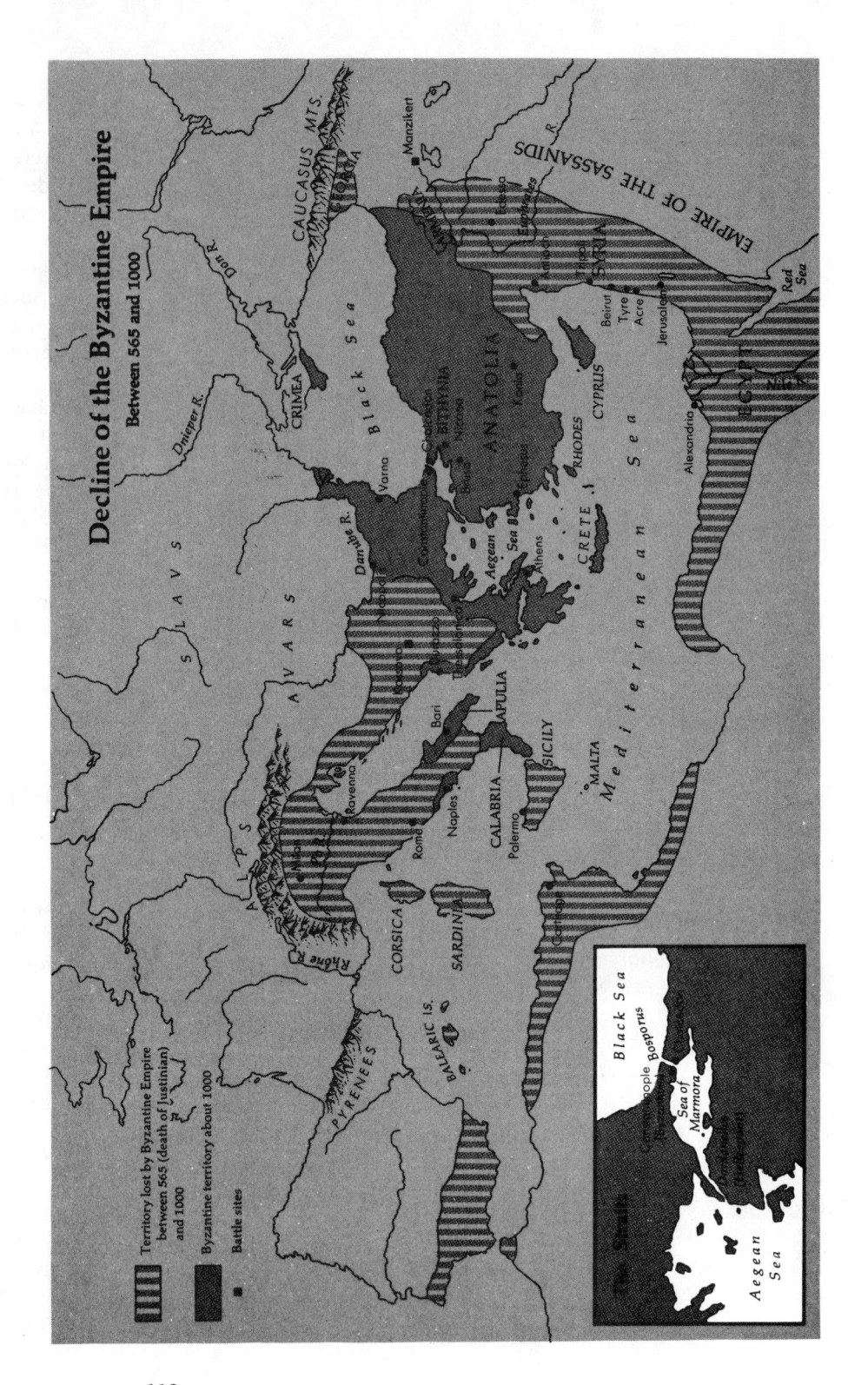

# Decline of the Byzantine Empire
## Between 565 and 1000

being absorbed into the conquered populations. It also slowed the full assimilation of non-Arab converts to Islam. The Umayyad family came to power, and under their prosperous caliphate (661–750) the center of Arab rule was moved to Damascus. There, strong Byzantine influences and a purely Arab ruling class developed the earliest characteristics of Moslem society and law.

However, the fierce pace of conquest slowed to a halt by the end of the seventh and beginning of the eighth century. After having spread west to Spain, which fell between 711 and 715, and east to India, Islamic expansion was checked. The African and Levantine provinces of the Byzantine Empire had been lopped off; Gothic Spain had fallen; the old Persian Empire had been absorbed whole; but Byzantium remained as well as the broad plains of southeastern Gaul. And it was on these eastern and western fronts that Islamic expansion was halted. From 673 to 678 and again from 717 to 718, Islamic fleets and armies besieged Constantinople, more effectively even than the Avars, Slavs, and Persians had done in 624. Yet on both occasions they were turned back by the tough defenses of the city and by the powerful Byzantine fleet. The defense of Constantinople prevented the expansion of Islam into Europe and stabilized the border in Syria.

In 732, an army of Franks defeated a Moslem expeditionary body at Poitiers, near Tours. Led by the warlord Charles Martel, and strengthened by the wealth of confiscated church property and a heavy cavalry force, they drove the Arabs back to the Pyrenees. Of the two victories, Constantinople was probably of greater strategic importance because it constituted the last significant resistance that Islam was likely to meet in Europe. (The eventual fall of Constantinople to the Ottoman Turks in 1453 suggests how much of Europe lay open to conquest if Constantinople had fallen. After 1453, Turkish Islamic power thrust deep into the Balkans and central Europe and threatened Austria and Poland. Then, Ottoman power was partially checked by the resources of sixteenth- and seventeenth-century European states, as well as by the Turks' own internal problems. In the eighth century there had existed no such states to prevent Islamic advance if Constantinople fell.) While Charles Martel's victory had many consequences within the kingdom of the Franks, it did not take place against the full thrust of Near Eastern Arabic military might but against the much more extended and less numerous Spanish Arabs. Nevertheless, the Spanish Arabs returned to harass southern France and virtually to dominate portions of the western Mediterranean until the eleventh century.

Failure at Constantinople, growing resentment of non-Arab Moslems, and internal dynastic conflicts brought down the Umayyads. Their last representative fled to Spain in 751. Successors to the Umayyads, the Abbasids moved the center of government to the new city of Baghdad in

*Shah Mosque in Isfahan* The impact of Arab thought on the Western world has been enormous, but the impact of the Muslim faith has been even greater. In Isfahan, in modern day Iran (ancient Persia), the city Persians once described as "half of the world," the mosaic splendor of the Masjed-e Shah, one of the finest monuments in the world, shows how Muslim architects used space and stone—as did the creators of the great European cathedrals—for mystical purposes.

762, close to Ctesiphon, the old capital of the Sasanid Empire. Baghdad was also closer to the now Islamicized Persian culture, and anti-Arabic, antitribal reactions set in. Islam was succeeding by virtue of its expanding, through conquest and the wealth it generated for the tribal elites. Islam now took deep root in the older Persian culture and opened itself to the influences of the ancient Near East. As a result, the Koran and the sacred law took over as arbiters of the diverse customs. No longer did only feuding desert tribes come under Islam's jurisdiction. Old centers of civilization, with their special influence on the court circles of the ruling class, opened themselves to Persian and Hellenistic traditions, literature, and culture. Such influences laid the groundwork for the breakup of the united caliphate of Baghdad in the ninth and tenth centuries and for the brilliant flowering of Arabic intellectual culture at the same period.

## The Problem of Security

By the middle of the eighth century, then, the face of the antique Mediterranean world had changed drastically. Gone was the unity imposed for seven centuries by a cultured Hellenistic ruling elite and for six centuries by Roman political power. In its place stood several societies at widely different levels of development. Moslem faced Christian; Greek East faced Latin and Germanic West; courtly Persian Moslems in Baghdad faced barely Islamicized North African Bedouins. The Mediterranean Sea saw many battles between Byzantine and Moslem naval forces. Precocious, secularized, intellectual traditions of the Hellenistic world now served as religious thought. In spite of the vastly different levels of society within Christian and Islamic culture, religious differences had replaced political differences. Yet religion also wove bonds.

Barriers still separated a small elite from the masses supporting them—neither Hellenistic intellectual culture nor the distribution of power in the Roman Empire had changed the old realities of class differences. Only twice had these two levels of society been brought closer. In the fourth century, the Roman army served as one dramatic connection. In the fifth and sixth centuries, lowering cultural levels in the Roman West had been another equalizer. Now religion in the Christian and old Islamic worlds offered another such connection by transmitting ideas through different levels of society. Religion could do this with greater efficiency than earlier cultural and political institutions had been able or willing to do. Holy men and monks in the countryside and intellectuals in the old cultural centers engaged in profound theological discussions that strengthened the psychological security offered by religion, on however primitive a level.

Much of the life of the ancient world went on as before, however. Peasants, townspeople, and rulers exploited the limited resources of material life and sought the material security that so often eluded ancient civilizations. But the price of religious development was high: the fabric of the Mediterranean world had been rent. Hellenistic tradition had gradually withdrawn to Constantinople and the hinterlands around it as the problems of assimilating barbarians—from the Berbers of North Africa to the Germanic, Slavic, and steppe peoples on the old Roman frontiers—grew greater. Three cultures, each with a different legacy, emerged from the Roman and Persian dominance of the Hellenistic world. In the mid-eighth century, the most powerful of these was Islam; the most traditional was Constantinople; and the most remote and fragmented was Christianized Latin and Germanic Europe.

# PART THREE

Traditional Europe:
A.D. 750–1789

*The first who was king was a fortunate soldier:*
*Who serves his country well has no need of ancestors.* —Voltaire, 1743

## AN OVERVIEW: THE PART WE CALL "THE MIDDLE"

Socrates once remarked that the Greeks "live around the sea as frogs around a pond." They communicated with relative ease, and their easily accessible culture penetrated westward along the Mediterranean coast. Early Roman imperial power had afforded enough security for the spread of their achievements, yet the lives of most people remained only marginally secure. Strenuous, prolonged physical labor of the many supported the wealth and achievements of the few. Forms of slavery became more widespread, as living conditions among the poorest and least mobile of the free population generally deteriorated. At times, slavery and freedom became indistinguishable, because many gladly relinquished the insecurity of a purely legal freedom for realistic protection by the wealthy and powerful.

First-century Rome, fifth-century Athens, and the generally tolerant Hellenistic monarchies had a genius for constitutional distribution of power; but that worked for only a small part of the population. When protection and the means to live could no longer be guaranteed by the formal public powers of the *polis* or the empire, people sought those informal power—influence, wealth, privilege—could offer them greater security. The patron emerged as a mediator between the citizens and the soldier, judge, and tax collector, just as, in Christianity, the patron saint emerged as a mediator between mortal and God.

Only in the most favorable periods and under the most favorable conditions did antique societies achieve economic stability. Economic fluctuations, vast inflation, and the debasement of coinage occurred from time to time, yet they affected certain classes only. Except for those engaged in commercial agriculture, most Mediterranean farmers were not largely affected by these changes. Depopulation of the countryside, new kinds of taxation, periodic extraordinary governmental requisitions, and underemployment in the cities, however, did constitute serious problems with economic dimensions.

Social mobility outside the military was limited. Political rights were restricted; "high culture" was narrow; economic systems were inflexible. There was more mobility within classes than between different classes, and one of the most profound results of the religious ferment between the second century B.C. and the fifth century A.D. was the creation of new bonds among different social ranks. Although these bonds were not strong and did not uniformly overcome traditional caste consciousness, they did disseminate important aspects of traditional thought to all be-

*St. Jerome* Jerome experienced a vision of Christ, who rebuked him for engaging in pagan studies, and he took refuge in the desert to study the scripture and for a time to live the life of a hermit. Ultimately his translations from the Hebrew into Latin of portions of the Scriptures became the basis for the Vulgate, the Bible available in the tongue of the people. Here Geraerd Dou, a 17th century Dutch artist, provides his own vision of the 4th century ascetic. *Source: The Bettman Archive, Inc.*

lievers. Traditions of Hellenistic intellectualism powerfully shaped both Christianity and Islam, as the aristocracy of the Roman world influenced the aristocracy of the Latin churches. The writings of Jerome (c. 347–419) and St. Augustine (354–430) influenced the learned clergy of Latin and Greek Christianity because they embodied the intellectual traditions of Hellenistic thought and letters. In addition, they influenced Pope Gregory (from 590) in his effort to create the medieval papacy and affected the monastic reformers of the sixth and seventh centuries, thereby popularizing traditional intellectual concerns within a religious framework.

Religion created new avenues of communication. Popular Egyptian piety strongly influenced both the image of the monk and the holy man, It also introduced new refinements to Christianity at large; namely the concern for the holy picture, or *icon,* and by the twelfth century, veneration of the Virgin. Such movements among the peasants and poor townspeople of Egypt spread through the Greek and Latin Christian worlds, through both Rome and Constantinople, until they influenced societies as different as Europe and Russia. When the spirit-filled universe of late Platonic metaphysics encountered Persian traditions, the results were "angelology" and the identification of evil with demons and ultimately with Satan himself. Traditions of individual mysticism clashed with codified orthodox belief in both the Christian and the Islamic worlds.

Limited technology and a shortage of workers could not sustain the vast expanses of the Roman and Persian empires. Nor could Roman and Persian military organization and technology alone overcome the barbarian invaders. The barbarians' success in penetrating both empires was due not so much to their overwhelming numbers as to their persistence and the scale of their invasions on all frontiers at the same time. Much of the security of the ancient Mediterranean world depended less on the defeat of the barbarians than upon their absence. climatic, political, and social changes in the Eurasian steppe, China, and India now propelled nomadic warriors outward. There were migrations from the Baltic and North Germany. Given new mobility through domestication of the Arabian camel in the first and second centuries A.D., desert peoples in North Africa increased their raids. These new pressures and the political instability of the third-century Roman and Parthian empires produced political revolutions. Still, the fourth- and fifth-century Roman Empire, ruthlessly reorganized for defense, survived for two centuries in the West and for another thousand years in the East. Revival of Iranian aristocratic traditions by the Sasanids preserved Persia for another two centuries, and the Sasanid culture of Persia again exerted powerful influences upon Islam after the middle of the eighth century.

Stirrings of a social transformation were evident as barbarian kingdoms began to organize politically. Laws were written and new kinds of complex social and economic relationships developed in the Roman provinces. Conversion to Christianity produced a new thrust toward literacy and a new spiritual consciousness for increasing numbers of people. Economic interdependence was one of the greatest, if most fragile, creations of the Hellenistic, Persian, and Roman worlds. As it lessened, a new localism developed. Smaller, more manageable societies reconciled their barbarian pasts with the radically different social relationships suggested by religious thinkers.

What was lost was the broad, easy, free interchanges that had once characterized the Mediterranean. But the hopelessly incompetent set of institutions that had attempted to sustain such interchanges also disappeared. What was gained after the middle of the eighth century was a new start: forest and desert peoples took up what they could of the dismantled traditions of earlier societies, while they absorbed much from the proximity of surviving ones. Religion made the triumphs of the Near Eastern and Greek minds available in a new form to new peoples. Islam and Christianity offered illiterate and socially undeveloped peoples new forms of social organization that satisfied both civilized and barbarian alike. The gradual disappearance of the judge, soldier, and tax collector was accompanied in many places by the disappearance of the slave, the gladiator, and the learned although narrow and restrictive elite that sat at the top of the Roman world for centuries without concerning itself with the bottom.

Dismemberment of the antique world into local areas of social intercourse, political power, and trade contrasted sharply with the universalist ideas of the religious forces of Christianity and Islam. "Pagans are wrong and Christians are right," said the eleventh-century old French poet who wrote the heroic epic poem *The Song of Roland,* and that view was a mirror-image of the one held by the anti-Christians. The limited experience and resources of the new inhabitants of Europe and the Near East forced grandiose visions of universal truths into an idealism that rarely found expression in daily life. The new bases for social intercourse that a common religion offered were much more practical to neighboring peoples in their dealings with each other.

In spite of the similar life styles of late Iron-Age, barbarian societies continuing tribal feuds, limited resources, and poverty often set Germanic peoples at each other's throats. The function of a common Christianity, although it was far from thorough, enabled new social links to grow, as did the Islamic religion. Half-barbarian Christian and Islamic societies could assimilate both conquered and conquering newcomers at many different levels. With Christianity and Islam came increased literacy; remnants of the great Hellenistic institutions of education changed in their moral outlook and content and shaped the earliest educational institutions of barbarian Europe.

After the mid-eighth century, the most striking feature of Islamic and Christian societies—and Chinese and Indian societies as well—was the process of rebuilding complex social organizations. These organizations were influenced by barbarian traditions and outlooks and by remnants of earlier complex societies, which were transformed and sometimes mutilated beyond recognition. Of course, those earlier societies were never reconstructed exactly. The geographical, environmental, and political realities of Europe were different from those of North Africa and the Near East. From the eighth to the fifteenth centuries, it was not at all clear that Western Europe would develop the social, economic, and technological resources that sent its voyagers around the world in the early sixteenth century and advance European forms of political and economic organization in the seventeenth and eighteenth centuries.

In the nineteenth century a crisis started that has continued to the present time. In trying to imitate Western technology and culture, other societies temporarily forget about their age-old desire to advance while preserving their own culture. Societies in Africa and Asia (as well as long-ignored more primitive societies in western countries) will no more easily assimilate Western culture intact than desert sheiks and barbarian warlords of the eighth century would have easily accepted or revived fifth-century Athens or first-century Rome. This Western power that has so influenced the world in the past two centuries has its roots both in antiquity and in the European experience between the eighth and the nineteenth centuries. During that long period, traditional Europe took root. The foundations of modern Western power started here.

## III. 1  Regional Resources and Universal Ambitions: 750–950

*History never embraces more than a small part of reality.* —La Rochefoucauld, 1665

Byzantine sea power and the growth of a new citizen-army preserved the governmental financial structures of the Byzantine Empire and saved Constantinople from destruction. Loss of the turbulent and religious provinces of Syria, the Levant, Egypt, and North Africa had taken a heavy toll. Grain supplies, the wealth of the African and Near Eastern commercial cities, a large work force, and the religious vigor of Alexandria and Antioch were gone. Yet the loss of these (and the western provinces) removed dangerous centers of religious opposition and instability from the empire. It removed political rivals of the recently founded city of Constantinople and ecclesiastical rivals of the Patriarch. Imperial attention turned back to Greece, the Balkans, the Black Sea coasts, and Asia Minor where vast reserves of workers now received their first heavy exposure to Hellenized Christian culture. A stalemate between Constantinople and Baghdad produced an uneasy but generally stable border in southern Asia Minor, while masterful Byzantine diplomats employed briefly rising tribes like the Jewish Khazars and others to secure the border with Islamic Persia between the Black and the Caspian seas. The slow process of re-Hellenizing Greece drew large Slavic populations into contact with Byzantium and Byzantine culture, and the importance of the Black Sea led to contacts with the Slavic peoples along the great rivers that flowed south into it. During the ninth century, political pressures in the Balkans—where the Avars had established a huge confederation—enabled steppe peoples, particularly the Bulgars, to settle south of the Danube. The Bulgars were slowly assimilated by the large Slavic populations over which they ruled, and rivalry between the Bulgars and the Byzantines ended in 1018 when Emperor Basil II destroyed the Bulgar Empire.

By the ninth century, Byzantine religion and diplomacy reached the western Slavs, Russia, and Asia Minor. During the same period, Byzantine naval strength declined, partly because of lax government policy and partly through the growth of land forces. Their armies—consisting of tough peasant infantry from Asia Minor and the Balkans and strengthened by armored cavalry—became one of the most successful fighting forces the world had ever seen. At the head of both army and state stood the emperor of the Romans, *Vasileus Rhomaion*, as his Greek title read. The descendent of Augustus, Trajan, and Constantine, the Byzantine emperor ruled much in the style of his predecessors, although with less absolute religious authority. Surrounded by a complex palace staff and a horde of lesser officials, he commanded a bureaucracy that wisely and effectively used public finances to defend the interests of the towns and the economy. In nearly four hundred years, only one certifiable maniac and a half-dozen incompetents stand out against a line of remarkably intelligent, able, and tough Byzantine emperors.

## *Constantinople and Cosmopolitanism*

In the eyes of Moslems as well as Slavic warlords Constantinople became "the Eye of the World." The extensive building program of Justinian was followed by those of his successors. Bordered on one side by the Sea of Marmara and on the other by a wide inlet called the Golden Horn, the great city of Constantinople commanded the strategic approach to the Bosporus and the Black Sea. Where the water borders joined, the great Hippodrome and Palace complex of the emperor stood among stately squares and upon broad avenues. Nearby, the architectural triumph of the Church of Holy Wisdom *(Hagia Sophia)* was the center of the Byzantine world. Its great dome and its base shining with a band of clear windows seemed to hover, supported only by great figures of angels. Here were glittering mosaics, bits of enamel, glass, or colored stone set into a shimmering depiction of the emperor, the apostles, Christ in Majesty, and a pictorial symbolic representation of the Church. "We do not know whether we were in Heaven or on Earth," reported a tenth-century Kievan Russian delegation to the city, "but we cannot forget such beauty." The power of Byzantine art and religious structures exerted a magnetic pull on Slavs, Bulgars, Serbs, Moslems, and Armenians for a thousand years.

So did Constantinople's trade. Busy docks on the Golden Horn were protected by a great chain stretched across the mouth of the inlet to Galata on the opposite shore. Roads from the Adriatic coast of Greece ran directly through the gates and down to the *Milion,* a great stone pillar from which all distances within the empire were officially measured. From the *Milion,* the road out of the city ran across Asia Minor and down to the Tigris-Euphrates Valley. The city itself was the world's most cosmopolitan. People of all races and religions, from Scandinavian pirates to Arabic sheiks, Roman ecclesiastics, and half-wild Isaurian mountaineers surged through its streets.

Constantinople had come to terms with much of the defining of Christian orthodoxy that had taken place in the fourth and fifth centuries, and even its perennial rivalry with the Bishop of Rome did not dim its ecclesiastical majesty. In the middle of the eighth century, the Emperor Leo III, influenced by diverse religious and political motives, prohibited the display of icons in an attack upon the Greek concept of pictorial religious art. For a century this prohibition rocked the Greek and Latin churches; but with the restoration of the icons in 842 came an impulse to build and decorate churches, and the architectural genius of Byzantium spread into the far corners of the empire. In the ninth century, St Cyril and his brother St. Methodius set out to convert the Slavs in the western reaches of the empire. In the process, Cyril created an alphabet for writing Byzantine liturgies, and this Cyrillic alphabet is still used by Russia, Bulgaria, and other Slavic countries. The literary language that emerged, Old Church Slavonic, helped bring literacy to Slavic Europe. Further conversion of the western Slavic peoples was hampered by an invasion of the Hungarians in the tenth century, so Byzantine missionary activity focused on the southern Slavs and Russia where powerful religious, political, and cultural bonds grew.

In the tenth century, declining maritime power and the growing aristocratic power of the leaders of the diverse land armies reduced Byzantine authority in the Mediterranean and threatened the empire's stability. Aristocratic landowners and warlords vied with the imperial bureaucracy and the power of the cities to assert their own candidates for the imperial throne. From the seventh to the eleventh century, however, Byzantine sea power and diplomacy still dominated the eastern Mediterranean and the

Black Sea, and the imperial government continued to forge religious as well as political bonds within Byzantine society. These bonds extended beyond Byzantium to the Slavic, Germanic, and Islamic worlds around it, and they helped to acculturate the last remaining barbarous areas of Asia Minor and the Baltic, in addition to providing an avenue to a new culture for the northern Slavs and the steppe nomads who infiltrated south Russia.

Asia Minor and Greece, now united in a single state, drew liberally upon the Hellenistic past as well as the Christian present. Although Emperor Justinian closed the Platonic Academy at Athens in 529, Hellenistic thought continued to flourish in Christian Byzantium. In the schools, noblemen memorized the poems of Homer. The emperor of the Romans, no longer a god so much as a vice-regent of God, lived in a style reminiscent of the later Roman emperors and the shahs of Persia. The clergy of the Byzantine Empire enjoyed a vigorous spiritual life, and—unlike in the Roman and Persian Empires—the life of small artisans, businesspeople, and peasants was on a relatively high level as well. Once again, a citizen-soldiery defended its own lands. Costs of military defense did not overstrain a public budget, and the budget itself did not overtax the thriving Byzantine economy. In the sixth century, when silkworms were smuggled out of China across western Asia to Byzantium, silk production vastly improved Byzantine economic life; and for approximately seven hundred years the Byzantine *solidus*—Constantine's great gold coin —remained the most stable monetary unit in the Christian and Islamic world.

A vigorous bilingual culture grew up on the Syrian frontier between the Byzantine Empire and the caliphate of Baghdad. People on both sides lived similar life styles, spoke Greek and Arabic, and developed a fruitful interchange of ideas and styles without constant warfare. Their language capability enabled Christian clergy to translate much Greek and Hellenistic thought from Syriac into Arabic. Trade moved across the frontier; so did adventurous, discontented warriors, who fought as mercenaries in each other's armies. The tenth-century Byzantine epic poem *Digenis Akritas* depicts the career of one such frontier soldier, who was in some ways similar to the eleventh-century Castilian warlord El Cid (The Master). The Byzantine epic, however, has features of romance and educational traditions that the Latin westerners would have found incomprehensible.

### *Islamic Culture*

Intellectual traditions of pagan and Christian Hellenism did not catch on at the same pace everywhere in the Islamic world. By the late eighth century, the protected courts of caliphs and aristocratic warlords, whether in Spain or Iran, encountered Plato's and Aristotle's philosophies and scientific thoughts. They turned the genius of Islam toward problems of metaphysics, mathematics, and medicine; and that genius flowered in the tenth to twelfth centuries, especially in the work of Averroës (ibn Rushd, c. 1126–1198), in Moslem Spain. Islamic thought took philosophical and scientific traditions from Hellenistic antiquity and developed them more quickly and more extensively than did either Byzantium or the Latin West. By the eleventh century, when the Latin West sought new intellectual masters, it turned to the Arabic continuation of classical philosophy, science, and mathematics that had grown up between the eighth and eleventh centuries. Arabic and Jewish thought therefore constituted the main bases of intellectual growth in Europe during and after the twelfth century.

Islamic culture and commercial influences also touched parts of the surrounding world that neither Hellenism nor Roman power had been able to reach. The Arabian peninsula was brought into contact with the Islamic world. In East and West Africa, growing black kingdoms entered into market and cultural relationships with Islamic cultures, while the far more primitive nomadic Berbers of North Africa, as well as the fierce Turkish tribespeople of eastern Iran, also entered the civilized world through Islamic doors.

Perhaps the greatest strengths of Islam were its concept of the jihad (holy war) and its essentially simple and compelling core of prescribed ritual prayers in which believers abased themselves before God five times a day. The necessity of alms-giving, fasting from dawn to dark during the holy month of Ramadan, and making a pilgrimage to Mecca were the core of seventh-century Islam, as they are the core of twentieth-century Islam. This is a remarkable record of intellectual tenacity shown by no other faith. Upon this core was built the sacred law (the *shari'a*), which was interpreted by specialized legal scholars, the *'Ulama* and the religious injunctions concerning abstinence, marriage, and spreading the worship of Allah. The *shari'a* reflects both the primitive imaginative world of the bedouin tribes before the seventh century and the compelling spiritual consciousness of Mohammed and his later interpreters. Islam is at the center of each Moslem's life. Its power is far more remarkable than the Koran that Westerners view as picturesque and simplistic. At the heart of Islam is the individual, standing before God. Neither tribe, priest, nor town supports him. The ideal godly community of Islamic society is an assembly of such individuals. No priesthood, no complex theology, and relatively little divisive sectarianism deflected the religious concentration of the Moslem. A slave might lead the Friday prayers at the mosque in Mecca, and the most ragged beggar in the streets of Samarkand might be a holy man.

All religious revolutions have a new religious spirit or doctrine at their heart, a new role that religion is to play in the life of the individual. Often it is a wider role than was previously a part of religious life. The sacred law of Islam succeeded in overcoming not only the tribal fragmentation of the bedouin and the growing secularization of the townsperson, but also the cultural differences between nomad and settler. A literate Persian courtier could find a religious community where he was welcome in the foothills of the Atlas mountains, in Spain, Sicily, Crete, or southern Asia. A bedouin Berber would not be excluded from a mosque in Baghdad. Such a community of believers was a powerful element in Islamic expansion and in the survival of Moslem culture.

Yet the set forms of ritual prayer and the reduction of theology to a bare core had other consequences. Power and wealth in Islamic society and the directions of patronage drifted away from the control of those who dominated spiritual affairs. No Moslem clergy comparable to the clergy of the Christian West existed to cross-fertilize ecclesiastical and lay circles. Even though conflict between religion and law was kept alive by the jurists, no religious authority remotely comparable to the papacy challenged temporal rulers' claims to greater authority, which would spur the development of complex political theories, as happened in the West. In a sense, the personal religious life of the Moslem was continuously threatened with becoming a smaller and smaller part of the individual's life, leaving secular affairs outside the pale of ritual obedience to the Sharia and verbatim prayers repeated time after time.

The size and diverse cultural traditions of the Islamic empire also weakened the central authority of the caliph of Baghdad. The golden age of Baghdad lasted almost exactly a century, from its founding in 762 until the beginning of the breakup of its central power in 861. Under Harun al-Rashid (786–809) and Al-Mamun (813–833), Baghdad became the most flourishing city in the Moslem world, the city of *Arabian Nights* legend. Under Al-Mamun the cultural inheritance of Hellenism and Near Eastern Christianity began to be translated into Arabic. From the end of the ninth century, however, political and religious authority of Baghdad was threatened and finally broken.

During the reign of Al-Mamun, strength of the caliphate came to depend more and more upon a household slave army owned by the caliph. These slave-soldiers, mostly Turks, slowly came to dominate the caliphs. Growing political disaffection was coupled with rivalry from the Fatimid dynasty in North Africa, which set up separate caliphates in Libya and Egypt. Both rulers claimed the title of caliph; and during the tenth century, the rulers of Cordoba in Spain also took that title. After 945, Syria and Iraq broke off into independent states. Islamic seapower in the Mediterranean and the Indian Ocean after the first quarter of the ninth century brought new wealth to western Mediterranean Arabic powers; and alongside the caliphs of Cordoba, Libya, Egypt, and Baghdad there

## Muslim Expansion

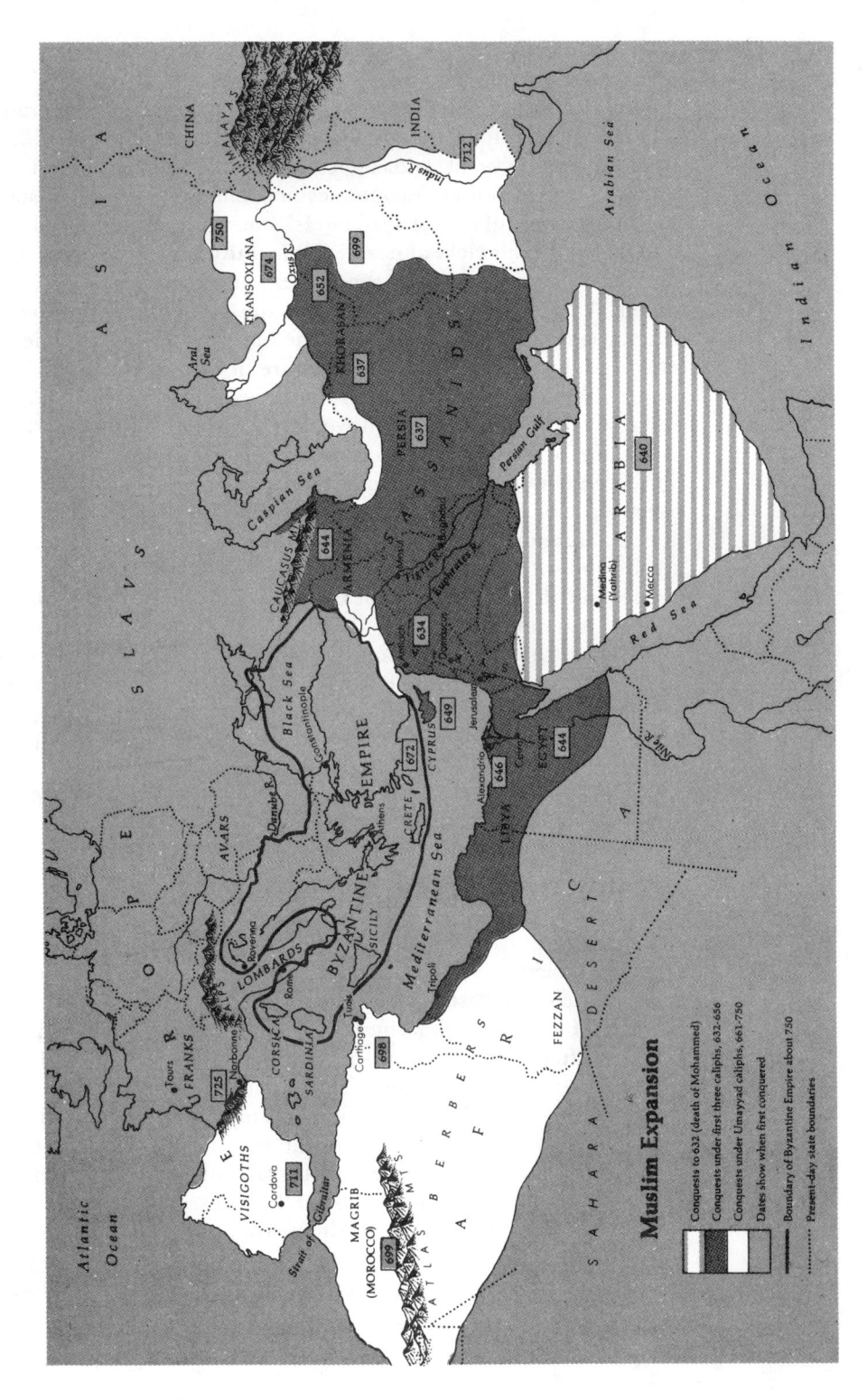

Conquests to 632 (death of Mohammed)
Conquests under first three caliphs, 632-656
Conquests under Umayyad caliphs, 661-750
Dates show when first conquered
Boundary of Byzantine Empire about 750
Present-day state boundaries

emerged a host of petty warlords, or *emirs,* whose courts operated virtually independently of the greater powers of the Islamic world.

However, the breakup of the caliphate of Baghdad did not signal the end of Moslem power. Economics and military strength sustained the multiple centers of authority in the Islamic world. Commercial enterprise and the enormous yield of Islamic agriculture kept some areas productive and secure—such as Sicily, the Levant, and the emirate of Cordoba in Spain. A desert people's respect for the garden and the town turned Islamic cities and hinterlands into the most productive commercial societies and the most advanced agriculture of the old core areas of civilization. Although rooted to their localities legal scholars, adventurers, merchants, or soldiers might travel freely through a wider world than the Byzantine or Latin Christian could. Their world was filled with greater variety and opportunities than any other, where old occupations could be taken up from Spain to China and from South India to the plains of Russia. Scandinavia, Russia, Constantinople, and Rome all knew Islamic wealth and witnessed the passage of the inveterate Arabic travelling gentlemen. Silver coins in parts of Christian Europe carried praise of Allah in their inscriptions to verify their value to people who knew no other signs of worth. One important indication of continuity between the Roman-Hellenistic and Islamic worlds was the history of the *denarius,* the Roman coin that gave its name to the *dinar* of Islam (still the term for the basic coin of Yugoslavia), which in turn gave its name to the *denier* of medieval France (even today a term for measuring worth and the quality of textiles). Its first letter, *d,* remains a symbol for the British pence.

### Germanic Europe and the Western Frontier

The Germanic inhabitants of Latin Europe inherited many institutions from the fallen western part of the Roman Empire, but they brought many of their own customs with them. The vast estates whose owners had mediated between weak farmers and the imperial government survived, but they often had new Germanic landlords who recognized little difference between the legal status of slaves and the oppressed free peasantry. In the European provinces, the elements of political organization that the Germanic peoples knew best were the provincial governor, the military commander, and the privileged aristocrat, not the shadowy emperors or the by now nonexistent curial class of the cities. While ruling over settled peoples of different races and cultural traditions, Germanic kings modelled their power upon the exceptional military authority of provincial field commanders, local and overly powerful governors, and on the images of Christian leadership they found in the Old Testament and in the correspondence of the aristocratic bishops of Gaul.

Even the impoverished western European provinces were strongly attracted to the new lords of the Roman west. The kings of the Franks after Clovis (d. 511), as well as the rival kings in Anglo-Saxon England, Burgundy, and Italy were hard pressed to establish a stable rule over a people uprooted from earlier barbarian life. But they offered the managing direction of what was left of Roman civilization in Gaul, Italy, and Britain. However, not only the weakness of barbarian political tradition but the rising prosperity of the free Germanic warriors contributed to this relative instability. The attractions of Roman provincial life, the independence of the free warrior, and new wealth all introduced Germans to Roman culture. Only the greater wealth of the Germanic kings, which was derived from their personal ownership of previously imperial lands, and the greater number of people directly dependent upon them gave kings even a slight superiority. In the course of the seventh century, it was not clear what the political constituents of the Germanic kingdoms would be, nor was the role of military power clearly delineated. Each German warrior was a free man, and social gradations among the new ruling groups of the old Roman west were just emerging. In southern Gaul and in central and southern Italy, surviving imperial institutions and culture were particularly powerful, and they were strengthened by the Church.

## Growth of Christianity

As we have seen, Christianity had grown out of the turbulent religious consciousness of Palestine during the first centuries B.C. and A.D. Its initial appeal was to Jews, and only slowly did Gentile Christianity emerge. From the provincials and the alienated artisan and merchant classes of the cities of the Roman world, Christianity then extended its influence toward the educated, wealthy, and powerful ruling elites. As it reached these groups, it tended to take on the intellectual colorings of late Hellenistic thought, just as Judaism in Alexandria had taken on a strong Hellenistic intellectual coloring. Serious studies compared Moses and Plato, or the literature of the Old Testament with Homeric poetry. By the age of Jerome (d. 420) and St. Augustine (d. 430) Christian orthodoxy had acquired the many-hued intellectual tones of the Greek and Syrian east, Athens, and the Latin west. Such figures as St. Ambrose (340–397) and Pope Leo I (or "the Great," pope from 440 to 461), brought the traditions of the Roman senatorial and governing class to Christian thought. Because of this, the early ferment of more provincial styles of religious life was remarkably ameliorated as those styles were adapted for far different publics by monastic leaders. Under the protection of the Islamic rulers of Damascus, the last great father of the early Church (St. John of

Damascus) shaped a theory of dogma and proper beliefs that influenced the Christian world until the seventeenth century.

In the Islamic and Byzantine worlds, such high traditions of religious thought continued to flourish. In the west, however, neither demography nor social conditions permitted its survival. As Greek and Latin Christianity drew further apart, the cause was increasingly the gap between the sophisticated metaphysical and philosophical vocabulary of Greek and the more limited dimensions of Latin. Moreover, Latin education and thinkers were severely affected by the events of the sixth and seventh centuries. The traditions of Latin education came under heavy attack because they included the pagan Latin literary classics, and only slowly were Christian literary works substituted for them. The purposes of education narrowed considerably in the sixth and seventh centuries—the Church had a monopoly on learned, literate people. Thus, the precocious complexities of Christian theology in the fourth and fifth centuries were hardly useful and barely comprehensible to the Christians of the sixth and seventh centuries.

### *Monasticism*

Two forces in particular popularized Christian thought during this period: the simplification of authority in the writings of such popes as Gregory I (590–604), and the traditions of monasticism. By the end of the sixth century, a momentary stability settled upon the Latin and Germanic West. Under Gregory and his successors, Roman churchmen made earnest attempts to contact the ecclesiastical leaders of the Christianized Germanic peoples. Their own writings reveal a new directness and simplicity because they used the moral fable and the simplified legal rules of the contemporary Roman church. Pagan shrines were used as Christian places of worship. Such appeal enhanced the bishops of Rome in the eyes of others; in his letters, biblical commentaries, and miracle stories Gregory exerted a far stronger influence upon Latin Christian society until the twelfth century than the more complex and learned Latin Fathers, Sts. Augustine, Ambrose, and Jerome (the last being the creator of the first Latin Bible, the Vulgate).

Gregorian Christianity with its intense practical concerns, its broad appeal, and its sense of ritual, became an effective spiritual institution in monasticism. The varieties of monastic life, from its beginnings in Christian society in third-century Egypt to its establishment in Italy and Gaul in the fourth century, had been a reflection of the religious variety of the late Empire. Isolated hermits, spectacular holy men, and groups of spiritually troubled townspeople and peasants had all fled what Christians had for centuries called "the world"—the temptations of unregenerative secular life. With the Christianizing of the Empire, however, a predictable lowering of standards in Christian communities continued to make many people suspicious of "the world" and to flee to ever remote places where they could practice a more nearly perfect spiritual life. (St. Augustine, on the other hand, held to a model that was urban-based.) Many of these communities followed individual compilations of rules, and several great figures in early monastic history—for example, St. Antony the Coenobite in Egypt (*c.* 285) and St. Basil of Caesarea in Asia Minor (330–379)—had established groups of rural communities devoted to living the same type of life. St. John Cassian of Marseilles (*c.* 400) brought much of this monastic influence to the West, and by the end of the fifth century there existed many communities of monks from southern Italy to Ireland. St. Benedict of Nursia founded his monastery at Monte Cassino in Italy (*c.* 529) and exerted particular influence upon Pope Gregory I. Gregorian enthusiasm for the Rule of St. Benedict gave that remarkable document a great theoretical, as well as practical significance in the West.

The Rule of St. Benedict laid out a carefully delineated scheme for each community's day, dividing the hours into prayer, labor, and common liturgical services, recommending dietary and clothing rules, and restricting some of the exceptionally severe asceticism that characterized many other monastic practices. The ennobling of manual labor as an element in the divine service was only one of the great achievements of the Rule. By tying the monastery to its material resources and making the community responsible for the support of itself and its dependents, St. Benedict laid the groundwork for an important new social core. This effectively linked religious activity with practical labor and related the intellectual ardors of applied monastic scholarship with the spiritual needs of the communities surrounding the monastery. Finally, the Rule may be regarded as a monument in the history of psychology by regulating activity and diet, by restricting spectacular displays of personal asceticism, and by focusing the monks' energies toward communal worship and work. The Rule may very well have helped create the most stable psychological personality types in early Europe. A modern reader is likely to object to early monasticism as excessively narrow and sexually and socially oppressive. However, the security of monastic life, both to the monks and to the lay communities in contact with them, lay precisely in offering stability and expression of self in ways that satisfied the needs of sixth- and seventh-century people. The extraordinarily powerful influence exerted by monastic institutions between the fourth and the thirteenth century—from the peasant villages of Egypt to the Hellenistic city of Constantinople to un-Romanized Ireland and the frontiers between Frankish and pagan Germanic societies—suggests something of the great social and cultural role these institutions played in the history of early

Europe. Monasteries sustained both the traditions of antique education and the practices of Christian spirituality. Out of them came many bishops, advisers to kings, and popes (including Gregory I); and the devotional exercises of monastic culture spread to the laity, and helped promote large-scale conversion of the Germanic aristocracy and the peasantry of the countryside to a common Christian belief.

Yet monastic culture did not affect society at an exclusively spiritual level. Monks' labor and freedom from secular obligations made monastic economic enterprises successful and farsighted. New techniques in agriculture, new technology (such as a much improved water wheel), and new ways of organizing labor made their way into lay society from monastic origins. Down to the thirteenth century, monasticism played an important role in the history of technology and economic management as well as in the religious and intellectual development of Europe.

The Germanic kingdoms and Roman bishoprics of Spain, Gaul, and Italy were linked with the newly Christianized cultures of Ireland and Britain in the fifth and sixth centuries. This brought, in the case of Ireland, both literacy and an antique influence to a province that had never been Romanized and that represented the last frontier of pagan Celtic Iron Age culture. In the case of Britain, Christianity and antique influences were brought again to a land from which both had been slowly driven between A.D. 450 and 550. This linkage had several channels, none of them particularly strong. The influence of the papacy upon the Latin Christian Churches was fitful and irregular. In spite of intense contacts in the pontificate of Gregory I, in which the pope communicated with Visigothic Spain, Britain, Gaul, Italy, Constantinople, Alexandria, and North Africa, subsequent popes could not reach or influence the particularistic churches of the Latin West. Only the idea, rather than the practice, of a common Christian norm set by Roman standards existed for much of the time between the seventh and the tenth centuries.

The relatively underdeveloped character of the Germanic Latin kingdoms make them appear homogeneous. In the eyes of Byzantium and Islam, Latin Europe was a poor and neglected segment of the old Mediterranean community. It assimilated only a few of the elements of an earlier cultural tradition, practiced an unsophisticated Christianity, was linked by fragile and nondynamic economic bonds, and existed upon warfare and the labor of a captive peasantry. Still, trade relations among the regionalized sections of western Europe became more regular, with Lombard Italy constituting a link with the Byzantine Empire in the south and Germanic merchants making contact with Scandinavian pagan merchants and pirates to the distant north. Across the frontier, now populated by Christianized Germanic communities and pagan Germanic peoples, travelled many goods including slaves. Such towns as Verdun became active centers for a slave trade that began in the pagan Germanic

*Carcassonne* A walled city, a citadel, Carcassonne represented two ages of European splendor: a medieval city restored in the nineteenth century by Viollet-le-Duc, and a "new city," founded in the thirteenth century as a trading and manufacturing center for clothes. *Source: Editorial Photocolor Archives, Inc.*

East and wound through western and southern Europe into North Africa. Papyrus from Egypt continued to appear in Gaul, and Arab gold coins have been found as far north as Russia, England, and Norway. Nonetheless, the excellent river systems of Europe—far superior to Mediterranean systems—could not increase traffic between areas separated by heavy forests, territories where dangerous local centers of power prevailed, and those that had little need for products made by restricted economies similar to their own. As a result, diplomatic relations among the rulers of the Germanic kingdoms of Visigothic Spain, Frankish Gaul, Anglo-Saxon England, and Lombard Italy were rudimentary at best and consisted of *ad hoc* legations, dynastic marriages, fitful alliances, and all the limitations of primitive, highly personal monarchies.

### Ascendency of the West

Between 700 and 950, however, these same underdeveloped, spiritually primitive Europeans laid the groundwork for a demographic, agricultural, religious, and political revolution that made them superior to their neighbors in nearly every respect by the sixteenth century. The causes of that revolution are numerous and complex. To understand them requires a review of the entire process that created settled agricultural communities. To consider the Germanic kingdoms of western Europe, we turn once again to the end of the Iron Age and to some of the conditions that prevailed in Greece after the eleventh century B.C., in Rome after the seventh century B.C. and in Celtic Romanized Gaul after the first century B.C.

Irrigation agriculture had sustained the first societies in the Tigris-Euphrates and Nile valleys. Agriculture was brought to the rain-watered lands around the Mediterranean on this scale only by independent development and technological imitation. The soil of Europe and Russia, however, posed new problems. The slight scratch plows of the Mediterranean sufficed for the light, sandy soils of that region but could make little headway against the wetter, heavier, more clay-filled soils of Europe. Nor were native northern Europeans sufficiently numerous or well-organized to undertake clearing forests and swamps to increase soil yield. The Germanic lords of southern Europe made a few changes in their agricultural techniques by living on the labor of a subject slave and peasant population. In the north, however, agricultural techniques developed by the Mediterraneans could not exploit the heavy soil sufficiently. In the fifth and sixth centuries the heavy plow appeared in Europe and revolutionized farming. This was an instrument with a deep wooden or metal share and a moldboard to turn the cut soil to ensure drainage. The introduction of the heavy plow produced a social as well as a technological change. The animal power required to pull the plow made it advantageous for a farming community to pool animals—before the tenth century, oxen—and the difficulties in turning the new plow required a longer rectangular field, rather than the square hatch-plowed Mediterranean field. The new plowing techniques were developed most quickly in areas where older boundaries and customs were weak, and where peasant shares in large, rectangular fields had replaced individually owned fields plowed by one person. In some areas large, open fields developed rapidly; in others, closely fenced individual fields remained. But in both cases the new plow brought about a true agricultural revolution; at last the heaviest, wettest, most heavily forested soils were opened before the plow, and although the village community remained poor, it grew socially stronger and more secure.

The weakness and insecurity that had prompted even free peasant farmers in the late Roman Empire to offer their land to wealthy powerful men in return for protection and tenancy had blurred the differences between free and slave agricultural labor long before the barbarian invasions of the fifth century. Wealthy Visigothic, Frankish, and Lombard landlords continued to rule their subject peasantry until economic circumstances began to develop social differences among the Germanic conquerors. Successful landowners exploited their lands, combined estates by marriage, and avoided the parcelling of the family estates among too many sons, as was the tendency under Germanic law. The emergence of powerful landowning families with strong royal connections dates from the seventh century, and in time these became particularly strong in the Rhineland territories of the Frankish kingdom. The army was composed of such families and their retainers, and their royal wars were financed by much of the property of the regal successors of Clovis throughout the sixth and seventh centuries. Bishops from these ranks slowly replaced the expiring Roman episcopal aristocracy.

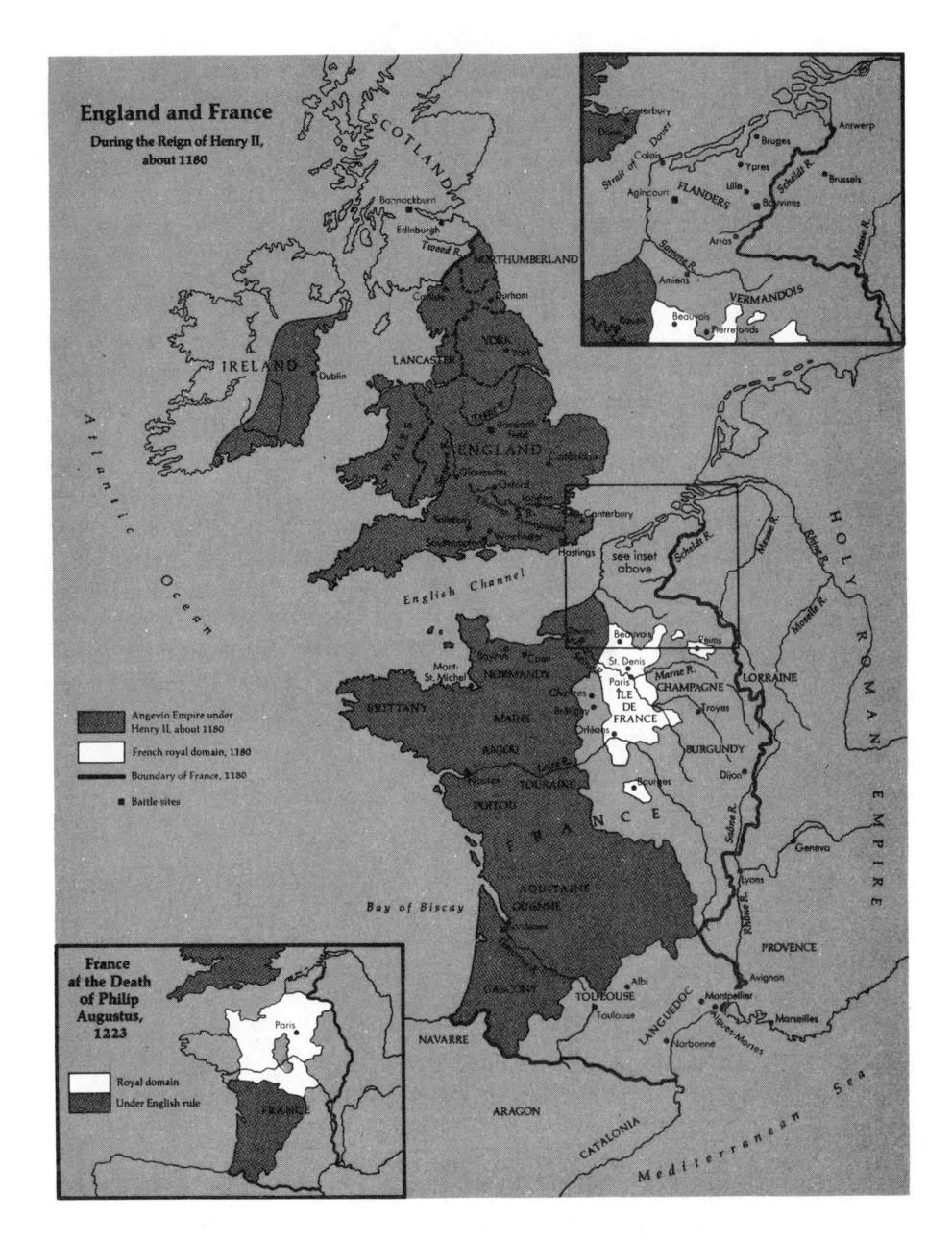

There were certain limitations that existed in fragmenting royal wealth and power and barbarizing the higher clergy. In the late seventh and early eighth centuries, a vigorous line of Lombards consolidated royal power among the separatist warlords of northern and central Italy. In Anglo-

Saxon England, a large number of petty monarchs and warlords slowly came under the control of a series of strong kings. In the seventh century, Northumbria became a powerful kingdom; in the eighth century the midlands kingdom of Mercia arose; in the tenth century the southern kingdom of Wessex won the loyalty of the majority of English people. The consolidation of political authority resulted in ecclesiastical patronage. Northumbria was Christianized in the seventh century, and the joint influence of Irish monks and Roman missionaries laid the ground for a fertile ecclesiastical culture, which was closely associated with royal authority and possessed the beginnings of strong ties to Rome.

Among the Visigoths of Spain, the precocious royal and ecclesiastical institutions that grew up in the late sixth and seventh centuries, including the first ruthless persecution of Jews, were destroyed during the Islamic invasions and conquests of the early eighth century. A small Spanish Christian society withdrew to the northern mountain areas of Asturias, while many Christians and Jews continued to worship under the political authority of the caliphs of Cordoba. The divisions among the royal inheritances weakened the monarchy of the Franks in Gaul, as did the emergence of several powerful families who controlled royal wealth and disposed of much royal authority. Beyond the eastern borders of this kingdom, pagan Germanic and Slavic peoples continued to exert pressure, as did Byzantine diplomacy and tribute.

In Italy the growing centralization of royal power over the warlords of northern Italy increased friction with Rome and the popes. By the middle of the eighth century the papacy was faced with two crises: the growing threat of the Lombard-supported Arian heresy (which held that Christ was of a different substance than God) and the hostility of the iconoclast emperors of Constantinople. Early in the eighth century the emperor Leo III had stripped the bishop of Rome of many ecclesiastical territories and much of the landed wealth of south Italy. Roman appeals to Constantinople against the Lombards went unheeded. In 754, when the Lombard threat increased, the people therefore turned to the Christian king of the Franks for help.

Frankish Gaul had exhausted the wealth that remained in the province without significantly improving economic conditions in towns and rural areas. The dynasty of Clovis grew weaker because royal wealth was expended for such nonproductive ends as gifts to supporters and luxury purchases from outside the kingdom. The rise of a family of eastern Franks to the high position of Mayors of the Palace, the new military incursions of Arabs in the south, and the need for a larger army led Charles Martel to confiscate much ecclesiastical property; the income supported his warriors while the ecclesiastics had possession of the property. In addition, the requirements of heavy cavalry—expensive breeding of horses, arms, and the training of soldiers—necessitated a leisured warrior class. As noted earlier, the powerful infantry and cavalry led by Martel, the Hammer, carried him to victory over the Arabs in 732 at Poitiers, and elevated his son Pepin to the throne.

### *Charlemagne*

The new dynasty was strengthened under Pepin's rule (751–768). This was because of the newly endowed and reinforced Frankish army, the intellectual and ecclesiastical reforms of Anglo-Saxon England and Rome, and Pepin's papal endorsement. In return, ecclesiastical life was reformed, monasteries and churches were endowed with new land and wealth, and the new east Frankish aristocracy was put to the service of the Carolingian kings. The personal ability and considerable military successes of Pepin's son and successor Charles the Great, or Charlemagne (768–814), expanded the Frankish kingdom at the expense of both pagan Germanic Saxons and Slavs and the Lombard rulers of Italy. Charlemagne continued the close association of his house with the papacy. The Carolingian dynasty exploited the political and military opportunities inherent in the instability of the time, as well as the loosening relations between the papacy and Constantinople. Charlemagne's destruction of the Avar kingdom in 795–796 brought vast amounts of liquid capital into the kingdom, and opened the way for Germanic colonization to the east—a recurrent theme in Germanic history. Ecclesiastical, artistic, and intellectual patronage flourished until Charlemagne's death.

Landholding underwent further changes. The late Roman Empire had witnessed the subordination of the free peasantry and the growth of the landlord's power. Under Charles Martel, ecclesiastical lands were supporting the increasingly expensive armored cavalry. In the course of the eighth century, these lands were granted on the condition of loyal service, with the provision that the land be returned to the king's power after the death or dismissal of the incumbent proprietor. In promising loyalty and aid, the recipient—although a free and often powerful man—became the subordinate of the man from whom he received the land, and the nature of his social status became more clearly defined. Pepin and Charlemagne also used nobles in their own households, as well as in the office of *count* (the manager of part of the kingdom on behalf of the king).

Next to the landed powerful aristocracy, there emerged another service aristocracy which soon began to mingle with the earlier group. Beneath this slowly differentiating society, there existed a group of minor officials and clergy, judges, stewards, and merchants; beneath them lived the peasantry. The proliferation of slavery had subsided toward the end of the sixth century because the predominantly agricultural character of Frankish society required a few slaves, and the original sources of slaves had dried up. Instead of slavery, there emerged serfdom, in which free individuals were bound to the land upon which they worked as were their children after them. Although serfs could not leave, they could not be exploited beyond the terms of custom, and they might rise to the rank of reeve or steward. Serf status was at times entered into voluntarily because the security of service to a powerful lord often was preferable to the insecurity of being a helplessly weak neighbor of powerful landholders and warlords. Analogously, local landlords might become the "men" of ones more powerful than they. There was a security offered by such dependence and the followers of a powerful lord possessed an enhanced status as well as a promise of wealth and land they might obtain in return. In this sense, the king with his retainers, his noble household servants, his clergy, and his serfs was similar in character and power to other great lords, and all were linked in a system of rough feudalism.

The power of Charlemagne became more and more essential to the stability of Europe. His power backed ecclesiastical reforms and softened the harshest conditions of life. The turbulent city of Rome and the Byzantine iconoclastic controversy prompted successive popes to turn to him; the unique personal circumstances of his reign (and the weakening position of the pope) are reflected in the pope's coronation of Charlemagne as Emperor of the Romans on Christmas Day, 800. The image of a king ruling in God's name had grown up in the Germanic West after the fifth century, partly enhanced by the powers of the Byzantine emperor and partly by the teachings of the *Books of Kings* in the Old Testament. As Emperor of the Romans, Charlemagne extracted a more sweeping oath of allegiance from his subjects, Frankish and otherwise. He probably considered his coronation a justification for him to spread Christianity among the pagan Germanic peoples of the east, by the sword if necessary. However, Charlemagne's rule was essentially one of personal triumph and its strength depended upon his own vast energies and the quality of his advisers and supporters. During his last years that control began to weaken, and at his death he may have left more of the trappings and ideology of a Christian Empire than an actual empire.

Under Charlemagne's son Louis the Pious (814–840) the disintegration of the recently assembled empire accelerated, and particularism emerged triumphant after Louis's division of the kingdom among his own sons. For a century the imperial title was much weakened. The ruling dynasties of the Carolingian family divided and redivided the old parts of the Empire among themselves. Their servants and the independently wealthy aristocracy obeyed them less and less, and the extremely successful army assembled by Martel and used with genius by Charlemagne was disintegrating as it came to be at the beck and call of pretenders, warlords, and weakened if legitimate kings. The relatively homogeneous economic character of much of Europe prevented any expansion of economic activities. But if there were few surviving centers of monastic learning those that did survive, with the aid of Carolingian patronage, were of the highest significance.

Yet the foundations of territorial lordship and agricultural productivity and management went deep. The improved technology of farming in monasteries and on many estates was slowly responsible for the clearing of more land and the harvesting of better crops. The intellectual drive of English, Frankish, and Italian monasticism never entirely died out, and a rough, irregular contact was maintained with the edges of this half-civilized world.

### *New Invaders: On the Edge of Civilization*

New invaders from those edges attacked the remnants of Charlemagne's empire from the late eighth to the early tenth century. Scandinavian merchants and pirates had long plied along the coasts of the Frankish and English kingdoms; they were mobile and swift because of their superior marine technology. In the ninth century they gave way to armed bands of plunderers, the Vikings, who assaulted the coasts and inland waterways and, in time, the very inland hearts of settlement. Only occasionally successful European resistance and the slow growth of stable political units in Scandinavia slowed and then halted the Viking raids but not before the end of the tenth century. By this time many Norwegians and Danes had permanently settled in England, Ireland, and Gaul; many Swedes had probed the river systems of the east to settle in Kiev and attack Constantinople; and Nordic settlers had, in all probability, set foot upon that land later called the New World.

From the east, another steppe people had migrated into the area vacated by the Avars. The Magyars, settlers of modern Hungary, were steppe nomads who had been driven from western Eurasia by the rise of new nomadic confederacies. They struck Europe with a force comparable to that of the Huns four centuries earlier. As the Magyar raids pushed into Germany, France, Switzerland, and Italy, only the slow resistance of the inhabitants and the effects of Magyar settlements in the Hungarian Plain slowed their attacks in the middle of the tenth century.

Vikings and Magyars attacked, burned, and looted freely. No place was secure, no area unvictimized. Yet within a century and a half after their first raids, these peoples had adopted the religion and much of the culture of their victims and had been drawn into the economic and cultural complex of Germanic and Mediterranean Europe. In turn, they opened both the northern seas and the great plains of central Europe to cultural influences from peoples not much further developed than they were. The tenth and eleventh centuries thus saw the acculturation of virtually the last of the European peoples to be drawn into the system. In 1016 the Danish kind Canute conquered portions of England; and in 1066 Danes and Norwegians attacked England again, as did the Normans. Under William the Conqueror, the Normans defeated King Harold in the Battle of Hastings, which was the last successful invasion of the British isles. But after the eleventh century there were no further large-scale, successful barbarian raids upon western Europe. The work of rebuilding was begun.

However, the third wave of invaders was not assimilated into the Germanic Latin Christian culture of tenth-century Europe. Renewed Arab raids into southern France, Switzerland, and Italy followed the decline of Byzantine sea power and the localizing of the areas of rule on the continent. The northern coast of the Mediterranean became a battleground between local Christian towns and warlords and Arab and Berber raiders. Rome itself was attacked. Germanic Europe had never been rooted securely along the northern Mediterranean coasts, and if the Arab raids had succeeded, the Frankish kingdoms might well have remained landlocked in the south and therefore isolated from the world of Islamic and Byzantine civilization. Yet successful small armies succeeded in keeping the Mediterranean coast open. Local small powers, strengthened from time to time by whatever help they could get, turned back raid after raid and finally sacked the major Arab fortresses. By the middle of the tenth century, Europe had developed its own version of the Germanic and Latin traditions its peoples had inherited. Scandinavia and Hungary and much of the lands of the western Slavic peoples shared a common Christianity and a common agricultural civilization, if little else. Yet the last traces of late Roman and early barbarian occupation had been destroyed. In their place was a society trying to recover with vast, empty lands to repeople.

## III. 2  The Making of Europe: 950–1300

> *Purity of race does not exist. Europe is a continent of energetic mongrels.* —H. A. L. Fisher, 1934

Neither the Byzantine nor the Islamic worlds experienced anything comparable to the devastating raids of the Scandinavian, Magyar, and Arab invaders of Europe between 850 and 950. Byzantium grew stronger and wealthier after the theological and social recovery following the end of the Iconoclastic controversy in 842, and under the new Macedonian dynasty, finally destroyed the dangerous First Bulgarian Empire that had arisen on the western shores of the Black Sea. From 850 on, Byzantine culture and diplomacy touched wider and wider areas, until at the death of Basil II in 1025, the Empire was more powerful and wealthy than it had been at any time since the reign of Justinian in the sixth century. The late ninth and early tenth centuries also witnessed a flowering of Islamic culture across European and Asian lands. The full impact of Greek and Hellenistic thought began to flower in Arabic thinkers; the wealth from the separated Arabic principalities in Baghdad, Cairo, and Cordoba, and the cultural levels of the ruling elites of the town and countryside overshadowed that of Europe, central Africa, and northern Eurasia. Such wealth, trade, and careful administration had created a world that would become the foundation for the *Arabian Nights*. These stories reflect the various roots and interests of Islamic culture.

Yet neither the Byzantine nor the Islamic worlds were free of problems. The rivalry in Byzantium between the court bureaucracy and the towns on the one hand and the landed military leaders of the countryside on the other threatened to tip the balance of Byzantine concentration away from the cosmopolitan maritime power of the seventh through the tenth centuries and toward the more narrow interests of the landed aristocracy. In the Islamic world, the particularized principalities that began to succeed the Abbasid caliphs of Baghdad in the late ninth century were individually too weak to sustain strong offenses against their enemies, and in some parts of the Arab world—particularly North Africa and Spain—the numbers of the ruling elite were too few to defend their way of life against the passionate, puritanical, religious convictions of the newly converted Berbers. In the east, the migration of Turkish-speaking peoples into eastern Persia produced a steady stream of half-barbarian converts to Islam whose presence soon proved to be disruptive. Linked to their new neighbors by a common religion, the Islamic inhabitants of Mesopotamia, the Levant, and Persia nevertheless lived in only an uneasy alliance with them. The rise of Turkish principalities, particularly those of the Seljuk Turks in the early eleventh century, became an important chapter in later Islamic history.

By the late eleventh century, the Byzantine and Islamic worlds had greatly disintegrated. The Seljuk Turks had stormed across the Byzantine frontier and virtually removed Anatolia, or modern Turkey, from the Byzantine Empire. At the battle of Manzikert in 1071, a Byzantine field army suffered its worst defeat at the hands of an invading force, losing the emperor and transforming the new Islamic frontier into a war zone. Turkish principalities also replaced older Islamic principalities throughout the Near East. In the West, the powerful religious movements of the Almoravids and the Almohads swept barbarian Berbers from North Africa into the Islamic principalities of both that region and Spain. In the case of both the Byzantine and the Islamic worlds, outside invaders and internal forces weakened both their positions at the beginning of the eleventh century. The elaborate, complex societies of these worlds, which were facing new challenges, responded slowly and with difficulty. When the crises of the late eleventh century were partially overcome, new crises awaited them, particularly from the new and emerging Latin Christian society in Europe.

## *The Idea of Europe*

The devastation caused by the invasions of the late ninth and early tenth centuries in Europe resulted in depopulation, demographic movements, the breaking of old lines of communication, and a shift to the interests of local groups. The resettlement of Europe between the fifth and the ninth centuries had worn away most of the differences between Roman and Germanic Europe which were replaced by regional varieties of a generally similar culture. That culture was neither particularly well-developed nor widespread. The conversion of Scandinavia, Hungary, and the Slavic lands to the east was carried out with far fewer resources than the conversion of barbarian Europe in the fifth through the seventh centuries. Even at the height of his power and influence, Charlemagne had wondered aloud "whether we are truly Christians." In the eyes of Byzantines, the question was appropriate and the answer negative. The lack of social resources turned the Latin churches of the early tenth century into isolated centers of life and learning. The papacy was virtually in the hands of powerful local nobles of central and northern Italy. The vigorous missionary efforts of the ninth century left little fruit, and the ecclesiastical leaders of Europe north of the Alps had to be warriors more than prelates. The reports of those who were concerned with the spiritual condition of Europe reflect the following conditions: improper and often sacrilegious practices passing under the name of Christianity, few or no priests, vacant and depopulated monasteries, and everywhere the control of ecclesiastical life by the laity.

The spiritual crisis of the early tenth century paralleled a social and economic crisis of equally great proportions. The invasions had emptied parts of Europe, introduced Scandinavian and Hungarian settlers into others, and reduced the size of many earlier centers of society. Paris had been besieged by land and water, great Carolingian monasteries had been broken, productive fields lay fallow and empty, and small awkward armies scuttered great distances to harass the invaders. The security of Carolingian Europe was tenuous, and peasants, clerics, and lords alike faced the task of reorganizing the society on a greater scale than was necessary at any time since the sixth century.

The results of that reorganization were profound. Within a century and a half, European armies and traders were present in the hearts of the Byzantine and Islamic worlds. By 1100 Latin Europe had begun to reform its own culture internally and in so doing borrowed from the Hellenistic traditions present in the Byzantine and Islamic cultures. By 1200 the economic balance had tipped in favor of Europe. By 1300 European diplomats, missionaries, and merchants crossed Eurasia into China. Between 1200 and 1450 European sailors linked the Mediterranean and the Atlantic with regular sailing routes and within a generation were beginning to circumnavigate Africa and cross the Atlantic westward. After 1600, European interests and affairs were played out across the world, and European political power was a presence to be reckoned with from Russia to Japan and from the Pacific Islands to North and South America. In time, Europe dominated 85 percent of the surface of the globe in the age of imperialism—the nineteenth and twentieth centuries.

During this same long period, both the Byzantine and the Islamic worlds as known to the early tenth century disappeared. Byzantium, weakened by internal dissent and Latin economic power, left its last and most enduring traces in the eastern Slavic lands after its fall to the Turks in 1453. Islam, partially restored and unified by Turkish political genius, never overcame its localism and adherence to little changed social and religious traditions that appeared after the twelfth century. For two centuries after 1453 the Ottoman Turkish Empire and the Christian states of Europe faced each other across a Balkan frontier; by the eighteenth century that frontier had become insignificant. Thus the reorganization of Europe had consequences which were not only internal but also affected crises in the Byzantine and Islamic worlds. In the fifteenth and sixteenth centuries, European thinkers proclaimed themselves the sole heirs and restorers of the culture of Greece and Rome, and they named their age the Greco-Roman Rebirth—the Renaissance. They ignored the intervening centuries from the fall of the western Roman provinces in the fifth century forgetting that these centuries had been the very ones that had shaped their present culture. They were now seeing themselves as Europeans. One of the main components of the European experience between the tenth and sixteenth centuries was the construction of powerful social and cultural institutions that laid the basis for later European expansion throughout the world. These institutions carried European imperial interests into a wider world that is still in the process of trying to deal with them. Just as the concept of one world lays ahead in the twentieth century, the concept of an enlarged entity known as Europe was the product of these laborious, groping six hundred years.

### Security from Without: An End to Non-European Invaders

The first requirement for civilization is sufficiently large numbers of people to create an economic base for its enterprises, and the second, principles of organization that ensure both security and the efficient development of its demographic and natural resources. The end of the most serious invasions by the eleventh century signalled the beginning of a period in European history that was virtually free from outside attack until the Mongolians stormed eastern Europe in the thirteenth century and the Ottoman Turks loomed in the fifteenth and sixteenth centuries. And even these events did not reach the heart of Europe. The freedom from outside invasions that marked much of the development of earlier civilizations increasingly became a characteristic feature of the European experience after the middle of the tenth century. On this level, Europe experienced after the tenth century a collective security unmatched in the world since the Roman and Han Chinese Empires before the fifth century and rivalled by no non-European society since.

The unmatched richness of European soils were exploited by Roman provincials in the first century B.C. and by better-equipped Germanic immigrants after the fifth century. Although the invasions had devastated and depopulated these agricultural lands, they did not eliminate the extensive exploitation of the heavy clays, forests, marshes, and plains that constituted much of the topography of Europe, which had begun to be opened up to cultivation between the fifth and the ninth centuries. The heavy plow and moldboard, the practice of continuous cultivation of larger fields, ensuing peasant cooperation, and careful exploitation of agricultural resources to support an expanding fighting force all survived the invasions and the insecurity of life between 850 and 950.

Moreover, from the tenth century on, new techniques appeared with startling rapidity. The appearance of the stirrup in the eighth century revolutionized European warfare. The heavy weight of a great horse and armored rider could be placed behind a lance, with the rider secured by the new stirrup. This innovation resulted in a charging cavalry force that could not be withstood except by another force similarly equipped. A technological innovation had again given superiority to a new society.

From the eighth century on, cavalry slowly became the primary striking arm of European armies, just as it had been in Iran in the third century B.C. In the tenth century equally striking technological improvements in agriculture appeared in Europe. The slow ox team—previously preferable to horses because of the limited weight that horses could pull—slowly gave way in many places to plough horses harnessed in a new way. The old Roman horse collar had encircled the horse's neck, thereby choking the horse after a certain pressure had been reached; now a new type of horse collar placed the weight of a load on the horse's shoulders instead of the neck. The new horse collar and the development of the horseshoe provided a significant increase in the amount of nonhuman power available to farmers of the tenth century and after. The watermill, known to the Romans but sparingly used in the erratic watercourses of the Mediterranean zone, spread widely in Europe after the tenth century; the windmill also appeared after the eleventh century.

## An Agricultural Revolution

Thus, European farmers and estate managers after the tenth century turned with surprising ease to technological improvements that vastly increased the output of European agriculture. Water- and windmills, of course, could turn other machines besides grindstones, and by the end of the twelfth century Europeans possessed the rudimentary capability of drawing upon considerably larger sources of nonhuman and nonanimal power than any society in history. Mills for the preparation of various stages of cloth production, sawmills, mining pumps, and wire-drawing machines all appeared within the next three centuries. From simple single-motion milling processes complicated transfers of motion quickly developed from linear to circular and—with the invention of the escapement mechanism in the thirteenth century—reciprocating motion. Although until the nineteenth century the numbers of people whose work was affected by these developments remained small in relation to the vast agricultural population, the period between 950 and 1350 witnessed the most remarkable increase in exploitation of nonanimal power sources since the Iron Age. The relatively extensive application of these processes to productive economic enterprises contrasts sharply with the technological reluctance of Byzantine, Islamic, and Asiatic societies in the face of proffered change. Stripped of much of its own cultural traditions, the European West was perhaps more easily influenced to develop technological innovation than other societies.

The invasions also cleared space in which to work. Many of the older patterns of settlement and cultivation disappeared forever in the wake of the invasions, and the erasing of old boundary lines and old conditions of servitude made it easier to adapt new techniques and distribute land in novel ways. The survival of the armies and of the clergy depended upon the peasant's production; and the growth of the peasant population after the tenth century meant that not only could old lands be brought back into cultivation more efficiently, but that new lands, often of marginal forest and swamp, could be opened up for surplus population.

From the tenth to the fourteenth centuries, crop productivity increased, new techniques were applied widely, and demographic growth took place in the old centers of Gaul and Italy. In addition, in England, Flanders, and Germany new lands were brought under cultivation, often on terms favorable to the peasants who were enticed to migrate and work them. Survival of monastic institutions ensured a continuity of rational management of large estates, and monastic agricultural techniques were often handed down to lay proprietors. In the twelfth and thirteenth centuries, the development of new forms of monasticism, particularly the Cistercian movement, led to placing monasteries in remote, uncultivated areas. The intelligent management of these areas further increased the knowledge and application of advancing agricultural methods. New degrees of cooperation and new technology led to the increasing spread of crop variation, the reduction of land that formerly had to lie fallow to recover from overuse, and to a marginal increase in both the security and the prosperity of the European peasant. The three-field system spread, in which large areas were divided into three sections, one of which was planted with a winter crop, one with a spring crop, and the third left to lie fallow. This reduced the fallow land from one half to one third of any given acreage, made it possible to cultivate more acreage, and allowed farmers to plant protein-rich leguminous vegetables like peas and beans as their spring crops, which improved the diet of the population while increasing agricultural efficiency. Once successfully tapped, the agricultural riches of transalpine Europe produced nutrition and wealth on a vast scale.

The agricultural boom continued until the end of the thirteenth century. By 1300 agricultural productivity in Europe had been stretched to its limits, marginal lands had been brought under cultivation, and chains of food dependency had stretched out over vast distances. A series of natural and manufactured disasters in the fourteenth century halted this productivity and constricted the amount of land under cultivation. However, in England after the Peasant Revolt of 1381, increased development of agricultural technology and, more important, new managerial techniques led to a renewed agrarian vigor and further loosening of the bonds restricting peasant society. Only in eastern (and to a lesser extent, central) Europe, where vast open fields offered their owners the opportunity to enrich themselves by selling vast quantities of grain to the west, did the status of the peasant decline into serfdom. On the other hand, in western Europe from the twelfth century on, the status of the agricultural proletariat generally leaned toward lifting the onerous burdens of servitude and the increasing economic prosperity. The demographic curve—an indication of agricultural productivity—picked up in the fifteenth century. This was so despite the fact that the feudal economy persisted in Germany into the time of the Peasants' War (1524–25). The growth of the agricultural population, the spread of cultivation, new techniques of land management, and the discovery and use of new sources of power all characterize the agricultural boom of the period between 950 and 1300. This agricultural vigor led to the adaptation of agricultural techniques from other cultures as well, particularly from Islam, and to the addition of a wide variety of foods in the European diet. These physical changes, together with the rise of the town constitute the base upon which the culture and social structures of traditional European and later Atlantic society were built.

### *Warlord Protectors: Territorial Principalities*

The society that these developments sustained grew more diversified after the tenth century. The power to protect the nascent agricultural life of the tenth and eleventh centuries lay in the hands of local lords; each defended the territory he claimed with whatever resources he could lay his hands on. Wandering mercenaries, strong-armed peasants, a small band of household retainers—these were the resources with which local strong-men protected their holdings. When these proved insufficient, such lords either succumbed to invaders or rivals, or offered their small resources to more powerful men in the locality who could provide the protection they could not provide for themselves.

Many, perhaps most, of these local lords had no more clear title to lordship than the mere fact of their personal power, although many of them also adopted titles from the older period of Carolingian government. Thus, many a "count," "duke," and "marquis" whose only claim to his title was his personal audacity and military strength constituted the principal line of defense against the invaders. Ruthless and ambitious, they nevertheless did their work well. When successful, they provided a physical security to the endangered peasantry and religious establishments which, in their turn, expressed a willingness to endure their dependence upon their new masters. Out of these relationships there emerged new patterns of community, and with increasing military success, a new social stability.

The tenth and early eleventh centuries are filled with great and small signs of this success. On the islands of Europe's western shores (in what is now England) stubborn resistance to Danish pressures by the harried kings of Wessex produced a precocious national and royal rule, which was manifest in the legends of King Alfred and in the growing strength of the Wessex monarchy. The king was responsible for resisting the invaders, and with the king's successes, his royal prestige and later practical royal authority extended almost to the borders of Wales and Scotland. In the old Germanic lands east of the Rhine, Carolingian administrative practices placed Frankish dukes at the head of old areas of tribal unity. By the tenth century, the descendents of these Dukes ruled the five great duchies of Saxony, Franconia, Bavaria, Lotharingia, and Swabia. With the extinction of Charlemagne's line in 911, one or another of these dukes became king of Germany, borrowing Frankish trappings while depending upon personal resources for real power. In 955, Otto, Duke of Saxony, defeated an army of Magyars at Lech in Austria. This launched him and his dynasty to particular prominence among the territories of Germany and began a powerful political push toward the restoration of Charlemagne's empire.

The spectacular triumphs in England and Germany engineered by politically able and militarily successful leaders of large territorial units were paralleled in miniature elsewhere. In 911, the king of the West Franks, in desperation over the vulnerability of the River Seine, gave a small territory guarding the river's mouth to a band of Scandinavian

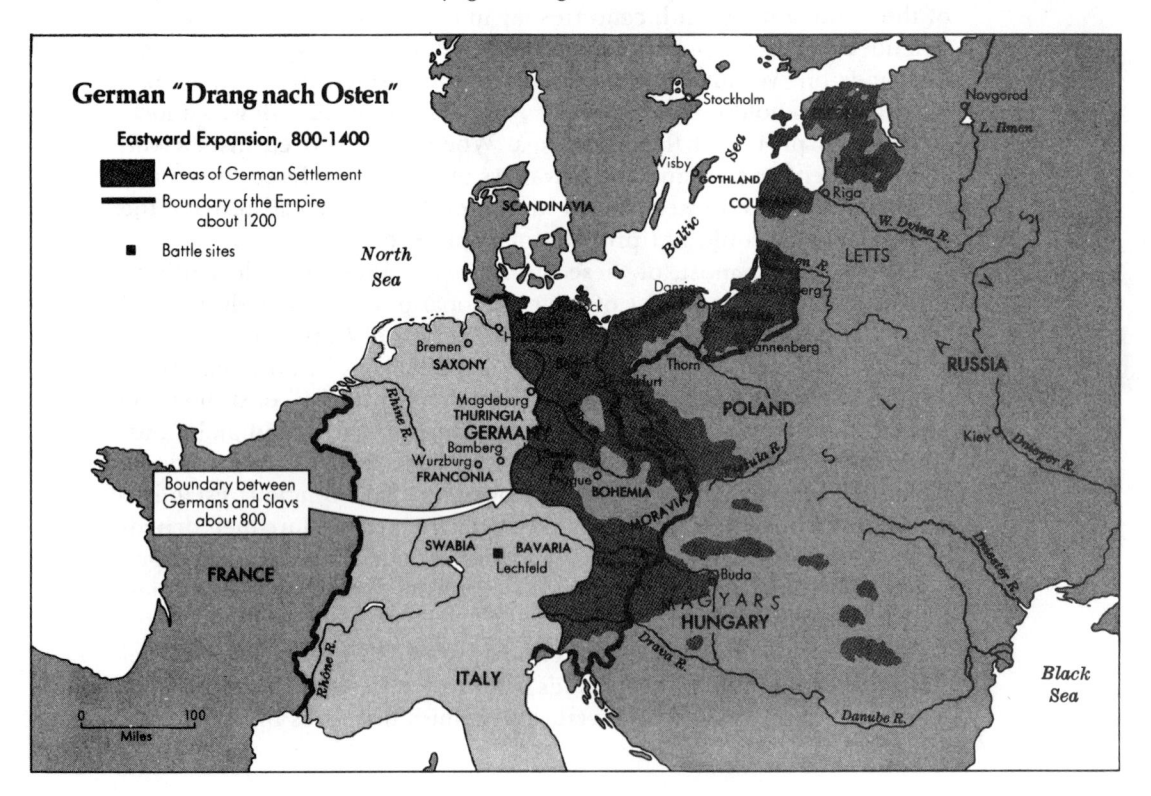

**German "Drang nach Osten"**

Eastward Expansion, 800-1400
- Areas of German Settlement
- Boundary of the Empire about 1200
- Battle sites

invaders led by a warlord, Rollo, count of Normandy. If this small Scandinavian colony was of dubious value in protecting the Seine and Paris, it became the core, under Rollo and his successors, of a political unit that became the duchy of Normandy—the first major foothold of the Northmen upon central continental soil and one of the strongest and most politically precocious territories of eleventh and twelfth-century Europe. In southern France, under a series of talented military leaders, the Islamic advance had been halted by the early tenth century. In Italy a song of the watchers survives in Latin on the walls of the small city of Modena urging the defenders to keep a sharp eye out for Magyar invaders and reminding them of the watchfulness of Rome and the vigilance of Hector at the walls of Troy. These and innumerable other occasions upon which small European forces staved off invasions constituted the central political reality of the late tenth century. At the end of the century, the Europeans had turned the tide and the local leaders who survived either began to consolidate their territories or saw them swallowed up in larger but truly European ones. The beginnings of agricultural prosperity increased their resources, and a vigorous search for spiritual security contributed to their psychological development.

The success of the warlord-protectors of the tenth and early eleventh century laid the foundations for the great territorial principalities of France and Germany, the counties and duchies whose names still echo in modern culture: Normandy, Anjou, Aquitaine, Bavaria, Champagne, Flanders. However, in the course of their creation conflicts among rivals became nearly as savage as conflicts with the old invaders. The rivalry and warfare among the new princes of Europe created innovations nearly as fruitful as the increased agricultural and technological changes between 950 and 1300. Politically adventurous and lacking in any but the most shadowy claims to legitimate authority, the warlords of eleventh-century Europe paid nominal homage to traditional ecclesiastical and royal authority, thereby permitting the tenuous survival of the claims of ecclesiastics and kings to authority in certain areas of social life. Their own patronage of ecclesiastical institutions, particularly monasteries, encouraged the development of reforms—especially those associated with Cluny. These reforms slowly but considerably influenced the daily lives of many. Throughout eleventh-century Europe, new political units arose from the aftermath of the invasions and the increasing regional agricultural productivity of a growing population.

### The Dictates of Geography

Several elements of European geography contributed to the changing patterns of social and economic life. Besides the natural fertility of European fields, once they were properly plowed and, less often, fertilized, there were significant changes in communication. The waterways created by the numerous long, navigable rivers, from the Douro in Portugal to the Vistula in Poland, were used more effectively as trading centers developed. The Scandinavians linked the North Atlantic with both southern Europe and the river systems of Russia. The Alpine passes were opened to greater traffic, enabling European communications to move with even greater speed. Road and bridge building and widening became almost a constant European effort, and the growth of large territorial powers protected movement on roads and rivers.

New resources were used more fully. The soil of Europe is particularly rich in minerals, especially iron; and the development of mining in what is now modern Germany, Austria, Hungary, and Poland accelerated in the ninth and tenth centuries, which provided Europeans with considerable resources in metals. The skill of the Baltic, North Sea, and North Atlantic fishers rivalled and surpassed that of their Mediterranean contemporaries, and the Christianizing of Scandinavia opened the great northern forests to the shipbuilding needs of all Europe. Previously, these resources could be tapped only partially, even by the organizational genius of Roman provincial administrators. The technological developments of tenth- and eleventh-century Europeans, however, brought these resources into common circulation. Freedom from invasions from outside Europe and increasing political stability inside permitted technology to be developed on a rising crest of general economic prosperity that peaked in the late thirteenth century.

### *Ecclesiastical Change*

Demographic expansion and agricultural prosperity created by the frequently heavy-handed political lordships of the tenth and eleventh centuries, also laid the foundations for the spiritual revival of those centuries. Destruction of monasteries had been extensive, bishops turned into warlords, and the spiritual considerations of the lowest social levels—never successful—had virtually vanished. The Carolingian rural clergy, themselves peasants, had vanished into the body of secular peasants who struggled for survival during the late ninth and early tenth centuries. In some places, however, ecclesiastical standards had survived, and from the early tenth century a new religious consciousness appeared in Europe. It took several different forms. Some monasteries, benefiting from the patronage of the new territorial princes, recruited vigorous and promising men and women who were able to create fresh liturgical and devotional exercises. These in turn were borrowed by the powerful laity for their own devotions. The bishoprics of Germany, under the control of the kings of Germany (who after 964 were Emperors of Rome) became vast administrative units of the Empire. Older monasteries, either depopulated or reduced in numbers because of invasions and neglect, were refilled with reform-minded monks, and the patronage of princely if primitive royal courts encouraged the renewal of interest in the spiritual life.

From the early tenth century to the mid-eleventh century, at such places as Cluny in France, these ecclesiastical changes appeared throughout Europe. Energetic missionary bishops and abbots penetrated Scandinavia and the pagan Slavic territories until native Christian rulers and prelates asserted their own Christianity against that of their ambitious neighbors. This linked Christianity with a new political awareness. New religious orders sprang up, among them the Cistercians, which fled from settled areas and opened up the marsh and forest frontiers that still remained. By the end of the eleventh century the reciprocal influence of laity and clergy upon each other had shaped something close to Charlemagne's concept of an imperially guaranteed and directed spiritual revival. The German successors of Charlemagne's title took a particular interest in the true Rome, for its spiritual and its political traditions. In working to restore the papacy to its old freedom from Roman noble factionalism, these emperors of the eleventh century, particularly Henry III (1039–1056), the Black, used imperial administrative control over the German church and the reformers of France and Italy. From 1049, with the election of Pope Leo IX, the energetic reformers of the scattered churches and monasteries of Europe focused on the papacy. Those bonds of the fragmented European societies that centered upon a common Christianity were emphasized, first by imperial and monastic enthusiasts, and later by papal supporters. The idea of Christendom, a unified Christian society, took new roots in the particularistic political world of the eleventh century. From the eleventh to the seventeenth century, in fact, the culture that is now called European called itself Christian.

The nature of eleventh-century Christianity varied greatly throughout Europe. Only a few centers and a few individual thinkers approached the earlier complexity of fourth-, fifth-, and sixth-century Christian thought. Education was limited and generally confined to the understanding of scriptural texts, and those who sought to learn more than was available locally were forced to travel great distances. In the late tenth century, some knowledge seekers had gone into Muslim Spain, and by the early twelfth century, the Muslim world was visited by Europeans in even greater numbers. The study of logic, hitherto a generally neglected part of the curriculum, grew; new approaches to analyzing religious and secular difficulties were shown, first in the monastic schools and later in the more open schools of the churches and towns, and in the service of ecclesiastical and secular courts. Reforms of the curriculum and the revival and extension of logic found a ready market in the service of both the new political units and the advocates of ecclesiastical reform.

The reform of the papacy on a Cluniac basis created a new focus for these diverse energies. One aspect of the reforms in 1059 was the creation of an electoral college of cardinals; another was increasing papal resentment against lay domination of the Church, regardless of how instrumental that domination had been in reforming the papacy itself. Under Pope Gregory VII (1073–1085), relations between papal and imperial factions broke down and the papacy established stringent rules against the interference of the laity, no matter how highly placed, in ecclesiastical affairs. Although the influence of the laity continued to remain strong, the papacy emerged from this contest as the strongest ecclesiastical power in the Latin West. Reasserting the claims of the earliest adherents of papal primacy, such as Pope Leo I and Gregory I, the succession of popes from 1100 to 1300 created an effective instrument in the papacy for the concrete expression of Christendom as a real society with collective goals.

To accomplish these aims, the papacy developed its own court and administrative machinery and sharpened the vague collections of ecclesiastical laws to assert the spiritual universal authority of the pope. The papacy provided definitions of orthodox belief in a series of ecclesiastical assemblies whose decisions formed the framework for the scholastic theology and philosophical speculation of the thirteenth and fourteenth centuries. The growth of an administrative bureaucracy, based on new legal and educational professions, strengthened the papacy and introduced a new rationalism to discussions of political authority and ecclesiastical problems. The curriculum reforms of the eleventh and twelfth centuries produced the schools where these professionals studied and generated an interest in philosophical and rhetorical adventures that gave the thought of these centuries a liveliness and daring that is remarkable. Greek, Arabic, and early Latin ecclesiastical and philosophical literature were studied intensively, new forms of logical and mathematical expression were developed, and the sophisticated, complex legal systems of Roman law were investigated and applied vigorously to the legal relationships of twelfth- and thirteenth-century society.

The weakness of the secular-religious principalities continued to lay in their local character. This was detrimental in a period when communications and trade opened up larger and larger networks of interdependence, and when a nearly universal papal authority made demands upon even the most localized clerical institutions. From the late eleventh century on, kingships began to benefit the most from these changes. The weak kings of the ninth and tenth centuries had retained a claim, at least in theory, to certain services and loyalties from even the most powerful princes. The vestiges of royal spiritual authority survived in some cases

*Mont St. Michel* Founded in the eighth century according to directions received from the Archangel Michael in a vision, this Benedictine abbey—set on an island in the English Channel—came to be one of the finest monuments to the Gothic style. Spires soar upwards to heaven as man's thought must do; yet all remains firmly, and symbolically, rooted in the hard rock of reality. An American historian, Henry Adams, later would write that such structures represented the most forceful dynamic of the early modern world, the Virgin, eventually to be replaced by the Dynamo. *Source: Editorial Photocolor Archives, Inc.*

even the ecclesiastical revolution against lay authority. The skill of the dynasties of England, France, Castile, Aragon, and the Scandinavian and Slavic Kingdoms in strengthening the small personal territories they ruled made many kings successful princes in their own right. Using their new practical power and the traditionally superior claims of their titles, the kings of twelfth century Europe became the focus of larger and larger areas of real political authority. The personal status and regionalism of the princes could not successfully compete with the claims of kings, and they often found it to their advantage to cooperate actively with royal power. The emergence of larger social units—villages, towns, and cities—contributed to the diversity of the areas that only kings might successfully rule. In some areas—notably Italy, Switzerland, and the Netherlands—individual city-states and affiliations of urban and rural districts became substantial political powers with only a nominal overlord.

### The Crusades: The West Strikes Back

The late eleventh and early twelfth centuries were thus used for rebuilding a new society with a growing range of options and only the more superficial of traditional restraints. The earliest and most impressive sign

160 TRADITIONAL EUROPE, A.D. 750–1789

of these changes was the rapid growth of a common Christianity among the different peoples of Europe, a bond that could be invoked to override local differences and customs. In 1095, at a church council called in Clermont in southern France, Pope Urban II (1088–1099) invoked the new spirit of Christian unity for two purposes: to use papal authority to pacify the warring factions of Europe and to direct the energies and resources of Christendom in a Western counter offensive against the Moslem enemy who held the Holy Land.

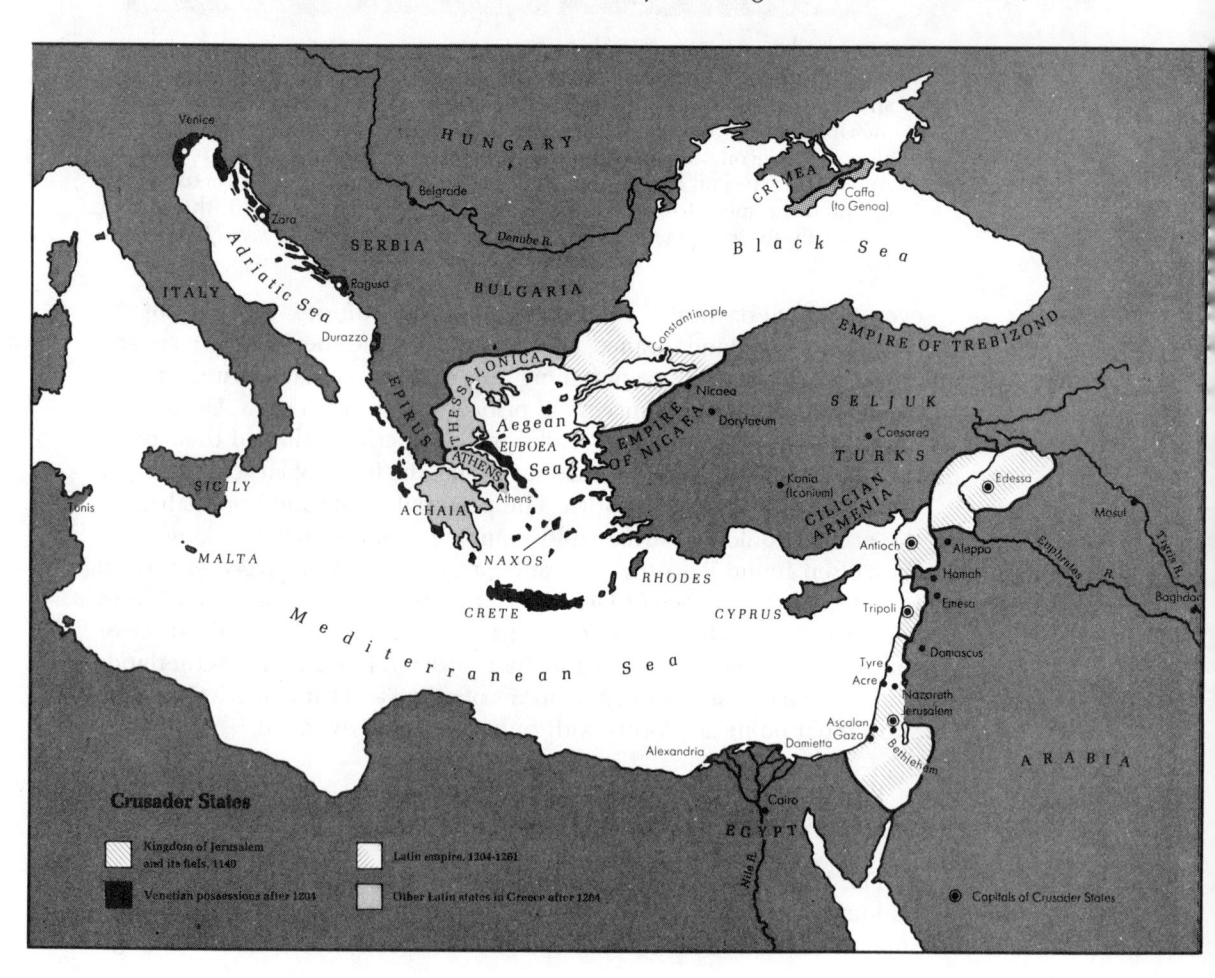

The whole of Western Christendom was busy with the "Great Crusades" against the Moslems to the East, whereas earlier the crusades aimed at the Slavs and the Moslems in Spain had only a regional support. The object of the Crusades was to recapture the birthplace of Christianity. For two centuries after Clermont all classes in Christian society were united, at least emotionally, in this goal. In these Crusades, Christian Byzantium was uncooperative, viewing Latin Christianity as expansive at the cost of the East. At the same time when Latin and German Christendom struck against the Moslems, they also turned their enmity against the Jews in their midst, denying them the right to hold land, serfs, or slaves, and pressing them into occupations that Christians wished to avoid. This external pressure augmented the Jewish tendency to congregate in their own quarters in the rising towns, in ghettos.

Despite the lack of sympathy between Western and Eastern Christendom, it was a call for help by the Eastern emperor, Alexius, that set the first Crusade in motion. The nomadic Turks, who had invaded Persia from the north in the ninth century where they had accepted conversion to Islam, had taken control of the Abbassid caliph at Baghdad. In the eleventh century a more aggressive dynasty, the Seljuks, took the title of Sultan and conquered westward to Palestine and Asia Minor (present-day Turkey). They then threatened Constantinople, and Alexius appealed to Urban, who reasoned that his assistance would force the Byzantine emperor to give official recognition to the supremacy of the western papacy over the whole of Christianity. As a Cluniac reformist, Urban also hoped that his triumph would assure the performance of Gregory VII's reforms.

Accordingly Urban ordered the rich and the poor of Western Europe into the field against the infidels. All who died on such a holy pilgrimage, he said, would be absolved of sin. The military class of knights and landholders, he hoped, would work for the expansion of Europe, which already was showing signs of being unable to support its growing population. The merchants of the Italian ports took a special interest in the opportunities offered by such a crusade because they would profit by providing the necessary shipping and supplies. Seldom have material and spiritual motivations been so well wed.

Four Christian-Latin armies set out for Constantinople. By 1099 they had pushed through the fragmented and totally surprised Byzantine and Moslem lands in the Near East, captured Jerusalem, and established a new state in the heart of the Levant. This Latin Kingdom of Jerusalem was placed under Godfrey of Lorraine, who transplanted the feudal system of western Europe to the Near East. Declining Byzantine naval power, political revolutions within the landed aristocracy, and the invasions of the Seljuk Turks had already weakened Byzantium, while the rise of the maritime power of the pirates and merchants of the Italian seacoast towns had reduced the strength of North African Islamic shipping. The uncoordinated political units of the Near East prevented the creation of Islamic alliances in substantial numbers against the puzzling armored riders from the West. Thus, European economic and military force was, in both the first and in some subsequent crusades, triumphant over Byzantine and Moslem weakness.

Even so, the Kingdom of Jerusalem soon encountered internal difficulties, and in 1187 Saladin, a daring Turkish leader, recaptured the city, which ever after remained outside Christian hands. Dozens of crusades followed. When the second Crusade failed in Asia Minor, its leaders were convinced that they were unsuccessful because the crusaders were sinful. This gave rise to the Children's Crusade in 1212, because children were presumed to have pure souls. This group never reached the Near East; the thousands of French and German youths were captured by slave dealers short of the Holy Land. Until 1270, despite these grotesque setbacks, Western Christendom continued to hurl crusading groups against Palestine. The end result was not the recapture of the birthplace of Christianity but the weakening of Europe by undermining the Christian Byzantine Empire that had protected its flank. Indeed, on the fourth Crusade in 1204, the French leaders who had intended to sail from Venice to Egypt agreed with the Venetians to go to Constantinople and pillage it. Constantinople and the European part of Byzantium were then reconstituted as the Latin Empire, and a patriarch for the Eastern Church was installed in a subservient role to the Pope in Rome. This new political entity soon collapsed as well, although not before the crusaders had been thoroughly discredited. A Byzantine emperor living in exile at Nicaea managed, in 1261, to regain Constantinople, but Byzantium was no longer a viable political power. When the Turks once again swept through Asia Minor in the fifteenth century, Constantinople passed permanently into their hands.

Stirred by some of the same crusading zeal that united Western Christendom from within, Europe sought to exclude Jewish access to the rising new states. Jews who refused conversion to Christianity were expelled from England in 1290, from portions of Germanic Christendom in 1298, and later from France in 1306 and Spain in 1492. Modern anti-Semitism may be traced from this period.

Despite the weakening effects of the Crusades, however, Europe continued to be growing stronger. The thriving commercial towns of northern Italy integrated the economic activity of their hinterlands and created compact, carefully governed states whose rivalry with each other spurred revolution, warfare, and the beginnings of the first formal diplomatic activity from which modern diplomatic services and protocol have grown. The Holy Roman Empire, deprived of its ecclesiastical support in Germany, found a brief dynastic base in Sicily and South Italy, where it continued to threaten both the papacy and Byzantium. The essentially personal and private character of the kingship led to the shaping of a large individual, yet dynastic, monarchy in England under Henry II (1154–1189), who also ruled, through personal acquisitions, much of France as well. Under a series of able and persistent kings, the Capetian dynasty of France increased the royal domain and the areas directly ruled by the Crown. The old, personal character of kingship was slowly transformed into public power, and the authority of kingship was enhanced. They were now responsible for guarding public welfare, upholding justice, and offering more available and cheaper institutions for carrying out the increasing volume of public business. Like the papacy, these monarchies surrounded themselves with royal officers to take up the increased legal, fiscal, and administrative affairs of the kingdoms, and the spread of royal government also drew the clergy toward the crown as well.

By the thirteenth century, security which in the eleventh century had lain in the hands of territorial princes and local warlords was increasingly guaranteed by the presence of royal officers. The virulent anti-Semitic and anti-Islamic feelings of the late eleventh century onward arose in part from a new military security while also reflecting the changing character of Christian thought and the insecurity of individual and collective religious consciousness. Indeed, the twelfth and thirteenth centuries witnessed the flowering of religious art and thought in works as varied as cathedrals, theological treatises, romantic literature, and heroic poems. A growing spirit of secularism was revealed in the loyalties demanded by secular authorities and in expressions of religious dissent by the laity. The increase in the number and variety of heretical groups in the West led the papacy, often reluctantly, to rely upon secular authorities to suppress them, as occurred in southern France during a crusade against Albigensian heretics in the first half of the thirteenth century. Papal dependence upon the cooperation of secular powers led to a primary papal weakness. In the course of the thirteenth century, those powers increasingly restricted the authority of the clergy in their own domains, claimed the right to tax the clergy for national emergencies, and began to assume some responsibility for affairs that hitherto had been reserved for the spiritual authorities alone. Because of this lines of conflict were more sharply drawn. In a spectacular conflict in 1286–1303, King Philip IV of France successfully opposed the claims of Pope Boniface VIII (1294–1303) to have total authority in secular as well as religious matters, approaching domination of secularism over ecclesiastical institutions.

## III. 3 Crisis and Recovery in Traditional Europe: 1300–1715

> *One of the difficulties with written history is that it describes events far more systematically than they were originally experienced. Often, it is only after the tide of history has swept out a government or changed old ways of thinking that we see any patterns in the events by which change was accomplished, and then we are apt to write as if that pattern has been evident from the beginning.* —Kai Erikson, 1976

### From Village to Urban Life

The birth of Europe that began in the tenth century rested upon the bonds of dependence that existed between different levels of society and between individuals. This provided support for both the soldier and the ambitious warlord at the same time that it offered security to the agricultural laborer and the ecclesiastic. However, the old farmlands could not easily sustain the growing population, and people went off into new lands —forests, marshes, and tidal plains—or to the expanding cities, where their work was also needed, and the conditions of life were not dependent upon the possession of a certain acreage of farm land. New routes of communication fostered both trade and the spread of ideas and artistic motifs, and the new urban centers served to link many different aspects of complex social activity. Universities drew students from distant places to Bologna, Paris, and Oxford. Towns swarmed with students and teachers, traders, artisans, entertainers, governing officials, the growing staffs of cathedrals, and more frequently after the twelfth century, the resident courts of rulers and their growing numbers of servants and courtiers. In the expanding urban atmosphere, ideas and opportunities abounded, and to many people the security of rural life proved less attractive than the opportunities offered by the cities.

However, the growth of urban centers not only produced economic benefits to the countryside and opportunities for migration, but new risks and new insecurities as well. Expected economic opportunities often failed to materialize, and the fluctuating economic life of the towns tended to generate a partially employed urban proletariat whose constant marginal poverty was accompanied by political restrictions and legal burdens. After the crises of the fourteenth and fifteenth centuries, towns in Italy and elsewhere were the first to institute large-scale social welfare programs, build hospitals, and initiate charitable enterprises. The biblical injunction, "If a man will not work, neither shall he eat," was slowly, significantly modified in the direction of improved welfare during the fifteenth century. Other consequences of the transition from village to urban life were equally unsettling. Detachment from family and local social and religious customs, lack of efficient pastoral care in towns, greater visibility of both wealth and poverty, and an influx of new, unorthodox, and infectious religious and social ideas into relatively dense population centers contributed to social unrest and religious fervor. The growth of heresy in the twelfth-century towns was one sign of this crisis, and the establishment of new religious orders—the Franciscans and Dominicans—in the first quarter of the thirteenth century reflected the ecclesiastical concern for the new urban collectives and their spiritual condition.

The detachment of large numbers of people from their places of origin often meant that traditional forms of law—customs and rights pertaining to villagers—did not extend to city dwellers. The density of population centers and the consequent increase in both violent crimes and public knowledge of them imperceptibly led to new definitions of crime and new forms of legal procedure and punishment. Older forms of justice often had depended upon the personal status of the accused, the status of the accuser (for there was no public accuser), and the community role of both. While peasants' lives were hard, the customs of manor and village restricted even the lord's powers against those beneath him. Around 1200, the old system came under heavy attack. The growing efficiency of royal and papal courts weakened the power of lords' courts, and theologians' objections to the forms of proof (notably the use of trial by ordeal) weakened traditional procedures. Early in the thirteenth century the first widespread use of legal torture began in the towns of northern Italy, at first exclusively in criminal cases. Later, heresy and treason (the secular equivalent of heresy) were also punished by torture. In 1350, a century later, England enacted the Statute of Treason for political offenses againt the state. No longer was judicial procedure determined by status, custom, and the social needs of small communities. An amalgamation of lawyers, magistrates, police, and executioners transformed the concept of legal violations from the limited character of traditional law to a more modern abstract justice that could be enforced against anyone, by torture if need be, and punished by increasingly severe institutions. These changes extended through the thirteenth century to heretics, and by the end of the century city-republics, monarchies, ecclesiastical courts, and principalities all possessed greatly strengthened legal institutions that reinforced the power of the state and subtly transformed the relationships within communities.

Throughout the thirteenth century vestiges of older cultures survived side by side with new institutions and values, much in the same way as they had in the growing city-states of Greece in the period between 800 and 500 B.C. The knight, sanctified and ennobled by his service in the Crusades on behalf of a lord, became an aristocratic ideal, which was emulated by lords and upwardly mobile merchants and administrators alike. The rules of knightly conduct, or chivalry, became the roots of later laws governing war and diplomacy. Tales of knightly adventure were popular and were read by a larger public, thus reflecting the psychological world of fourteenth- and fifteenth-century society. Far from being "escapist" literature they represent in their variety and interests concepts of personality, motivation, social values, and human emotions that are a valid reflection of late medieval Europe.

This adaptation of older values to reflect new social codes may also be seen in ecclesiastical life. In paintings, the figure of the solitary knight seeking a name and status in the service of a lord by encountering enemies on a symbolically littered landscape, may be paralleled by such figures as St. Francis of Assisi and St. Dominic who worked single-handedly to save the Church. Handbooks for the guidance of parish priests began in the thirteenth century in order to solve the problems of transforming the great theological discoveries of the twelfth and thirteenth centuries into practical guidelines for individual spiritual life. They showed particular concern for the nature of social collectives. The Inqui-

Western Europe—especially England and France—is dotted today with ruined abbeys. Symbols of the great age of the monasteries, when learning, the trades, and even commerce were focused on religious communities, these picturesque ruins became, by the late eighteenth and in the nineteenth centuries, symbols of modern man's yearning for the security he believed life in the past had represented. Here at *Whitby Abbey*, in England, the great poet Caedmon sang of Creation. Destroyed by Danes in 867, refounded by Benedictines in 1078, Whitby Abbey flourished until 1539. In 1914 it was shelled by the German fleet and in 1921 it became a national monument. *Source: Editorial Photocolor Archives.*

sition, as ferocious as it often was, also introduced new demands for pastoral care, and the heightened sense of clerical responsibility was sharpened by the rise of a much more vocal laity that criticized clerical shortcomings and social evils. The appearance in the fourteenth century of "saint-critics" like Catherine of Siena and Bridget of Sweden reflected the growing intensity of feelings about day-to-day religious life.

The recovery of the tenth through the thirteenth centuries was also accompanied by changes in social conditions, values, and institutions as well as by changes in popular and aristocratic sensibility, spiritual perception, and demands upon the Church. In Dante's *Divine Comedy,* written in the first two decades of the fourteenth century, a compelling picture of these changes may be seen. Dante, a layman and an exile from the great city of Florence, painted a vast canvas of religious ideas, minutely drawn individual figures, great heroes of the past, saints, the Virgin, and Heaven itself, with the fury and conviction of a secular prophet. There is no more eloquent introduction to the transformation of Europe between the tenth and the fourteenth centuries than a careful reading of the *Divine Comedy.*

Dante's lifetime (1265–1321) witnessed a series of crises. The character of these crises and their resolutions gave a shape to European civilization that remained well into the Industrial Revolution. The first tentative steps of the period between 750 and 950, followed by the vigorous changes between 950 and 1300, laid the foundation for an increasingly powerful Western culture.

## *Demographic Change*

Only within the last century has the majority of people in the western world ceased to be directly engaged in agricultural activity. The agricultural roots of civilization, which stretched back beyond the civilization of Sumer, also stretched well forward to the early nineteenth century. Egypt, Persia, Greece, Rome, and Europe—all produced elaborate and complex civilizations upon an agricultural base. Throughout world history, the frontier between the sown and the wild has directly affected the profile of the frontier between civilization and noncivilization, economic development and lesser development, power and weakness, prosperity and poverty. Sown areas, initially vulnerable to outside invasion, possess a resilience denied to pastoral lands. The history of agricultural production has a rhythm of its own that must be perceived if one is to understand the other rhythms of complex societies, trade, commerce, industry, and intellectual development. From Sumer to early modern Europe, fluctuations in agriculture had repercussions throughout the highest reaches of civilized societies from Sumer to early modern Europe. And after four centuries of prosperity, the European West faced its greatest crises in the fourteenth century.

The extension of agriculture to marginal areas, the increasing chains of food dependence by urban societies, the relatively stable ratio of seed to yield, and the delicate demographic balance of thirteenth-century Europe yielded great agricultural prosperity. They also created an extremely fragile structure for both field and market. From the late thirteenth century to the early fifteenth, this structure was shaken to its foundations. Bad harvests occurred with great frequency, which drove people off marginal lands and decimated the agricultural and urban populations. Political instability endangered the chains of food dependence, and increasingly frequent wars seriously affected both the natural rhythm of agricultural life and the capital investment and cooperation necessary to sustain mills, barns, and herds. In 1348, and for a century after, increasingly severe pestilence—originating in Asia and carried to Europe by the ubiquitous trading fleets of the Italian city-republics—raged among European populations. Between 1348 and 1361, the Black Death struck with a terrible fury, wholly depopulating some regions, scourging others, and causing social and intellectual crises for more than a century. Famine, war, and plague struck at the very heart of European society, and their consequences—economic instability, depopulation, rapid and unpredictable transfer of wealth and property, and the fitful movements of survivor groups—determined the economic and social configuration of Europe for four centuries.

One striking result of famine and plague was the reduction of population levels. Agricultural society rests upon a tenuous demographic balance which, when upset, shows serious consequences. Increased food production leads to increased numbers of people and more land being brought under cultivation. Growing numbers may entail less food per capita, and a decline sets in. This is the normal demographic mechanism of agricultural societies. Famine and plague, however, upset that balance and plunged the decline far lower. In the years between 1315 and 1317, local populations experienced a death rate as high as 400 per 1,000. Large areas of cultivation simply went vacant and some remain so to this day. A reduced population initially meant that labor was at a premium, and when wages went up, all prices except those for food went down, because of lessened demand. The improved conditions of laborers produced severely restrictive, if largely ineffective, measures against them.

More successful was the process by which services were converted into rents, and lords were forced to diversify their operations if they were to survive. Commercial agriculture—the converting of fields into vineyards; the production of industrial crops such as dye plants, hops, and flax for weaving; and the increase in dairy and stock farming—grew in the late fourteenth and fifteenth centuries. Urban populations increased faster than rural populations by migrations from poor lands into the towns, and the consequent supply of cheap, unskilled labor swelled the urban poor and unemployed. Partly as a result of the plague and the population drop, villages, towns and cities could be built along new communication routes; vanished villages became lakes and waste; and disused plow lands became the settings for new country houses and parks. By the end of the fifteenth century, a new physical profile of Europe had emerged out of the agricultural and demographic crises of the fourteenth and early fifteenth centuries.

The security of a prosperous agricultural and commercial society yielded to new social alignments and political forces during the fourteenth and fifteenth centuries. Yet the attitudes and values shaped between 950 and 1300 did not give way so easily. One of the most remarkable aspects of the European West after 750 was its capacity to absorb new peoples, ideas, intellectual and artistic motifs, and economic opportunities. Upon a rather limited theory of society biased in favor of a militarized aristocracy and a universally powerful church, the following emerged: a superstructure of theology, viable new social institutions, intellectual inquiry, and the beginnings of different ethnic cultures with vernacular languages, literatures, and local variations in artistic style. Against the crises of the fourteenth century, these old traditions stood out sharply, and they succumbed only slowly. The vestiges of a household government led by a king whose authority and affairs were personal and private contrasted sharply with the expansion of governmental institutions, new theories of public finance, taxation, and concepts of the state.

### Rise of the Monarchies

This inextricable intermingling of the private and public roles of the king was indicative of governmental forms until the nineteenth century. The personal claims of the king of England to be both king in England and duke in Aquitaine and Normandy by virtue of inheritance led to a conflict between the kings of England and France. This began with the conventional forms of a debate between a lord and a vassal and, as it progressed, it took on the proportions of a national war. The Hundred Years' War (conventionally 1337–1453) is a striking example of the new character of public governance and the residual traces of private royal affairs. Growing out of an old quarrel between the kings of England and France, the rivalry between the two kingdoms was heightened by a crisis of French succession between 1316 and 1327 and increasingly strong demands made by King Edward III of England (1327–1377) concerning his personal claim to the throne of France.

In addition to dynastic rivalry and the king's personal rights, however, there were more subtle forces at work. The vast English royal possessions in France dated from the Norman Conquest of England in 1066 and were augmented by the properties of King Henry II. The thirteenth century witnessed the loss of many of these territories, notably under the reign of King John (1199–1216). But those territories and others that remained were technically held by the king of England as a subordinate vassal to the king of France. However, by the early fourteenth century, these territories were administered by an increasingly sophisticated English governmental administration as part of the royal domains of England. Gascon wine, Breton salt, and public revenues had become important parts of the English economy, and the kings of England were less and less inclined to regard themselves as vassals of the kings of France.

These and other frictions set off the events leading to the hostilities in the Hundred Years' War. For the next century intermittent expeditions, a few pitched battles, periodic truces, and attempts by outside powers to mediate the conflict characterized the conduct of the war. Until 1435, England controlled the course of the war and occupied much of France, allying itself with the great duchy of Burgundy in the western part of France. The defection of Burgundy to the king of France in 1435 began to turn the tide against the English, and during the third quarter of the fifteenth century the English were expelled from virtually all holdings on the continent.

During the course of the war, however, the contending powers were subtly transformed. What began as a justification of English policy in Aquitaine and Gascony and a legitimate personal claim of the king of England grew in duration, scale and public feeling until it approached something like a modern national conflict. At the start of the fourteenth century, many English aristocrats held land in France and divided their time and their interests; French was the principal language spoken by the English aristocracy; aristocrats and kings in both kingdoms regarded themselves as similar; the elements of a modern idea of nationalism were present only in part. It was the traditional world of a universal church and a universal brotherhood of knightly aristocrats. For several centuries, however, European kings had been expanding their power by associating themselves with symbols of universal authority within their own domains. The images of crown and throne came to symbolize the nation as a whole, and the kings identified themselves personally with these increasingly recognized abstractions. In practice, kings had claimed that the royal oath to uphold justice and protect the realm gave them extraordinary authority that overrode local custom and even the powers of the Church. Royal administrators, courtiers, and lawyers spread through the kingdom until, by the fourteenth century in both England and France, the king had become much more than a private person ruling his private domains— he had become the symbol of the kingdom itself and claimed loyalties that were previously devoted elsewhere. The collection of these disparate powers into the king's hands and the shaping of the concept of an abstract state represented by the king, marks perhaps the most important development in the history of statism.

In the case of England and France, the needs of war, propaganda of the war parties in both kingdoms, and the economic and social changes that an intermittent state of war produced sharpened these developments and heightened the pitch of protonational feeling. At the end of the Hundred Years' War, the English aristocracy held no more lands in France; English became the primary language for all people in England; clerical personnel became more closely identified with the kingdoms in which they served; and the powers of the Church within the kingdoms were remarkably curtailed. Such ideas as a universal church survived, of course, but they were substantially checked by the growth of nationalism and by the new channels in which these ideas could operate most effectively: in establishing rules for military conduct, determining the status and privileges of diplomatic personnel, and opening channels of communication for powers that claimed independence from sovereigns while not having developed a mechanism for formal interchange. The economic problems involved in the mobilization of state resources, the increasing identification of the king's cause with that of the state's, and the national antipathy aroused by a century of conflict point toward the real significance of the Hundred Years' War. Its role as a crucible formed early nationalistic attitudes under extraordinary circumstances.

Other kingdoms in Europe were experiencing the same difficulties as France and England. There were internal struggles between royal dynasties and local aristocracies, privileged towns and ambitious rulers, and the Church's power was becoming increasingly restricted. These difficulties were set against a background of war, plague, famine, economic regression and organization, and the growth of crown authority. The fifteenth century witnessed, in short, a new beginning after the social and economic disasters of the fourteenth century. There were new political developments in which the old world of privilege and status slowly came to terms with the new world of state authority and relationships between kings and subjects. Only in the Italian city-republics was there such a status as citizenship, and here, as in ancient Athens and early Rome, citizenship was restricted to a small part of the population. The principal role for the unprivileged subject or the noncitizen was obedience—obedience to the judgment of those better fitted to rule. All else was sedition. The form of political protest by a politically unfranchised people took on the coloring of the culture in which it occurred. Religious polemic, eschatological prophecies, and secular criticism of the higher orders of society far outweighed the few instances of rational criticism and informed dissent. Constraints upon potential political structures were traditional and strong, and in spite of the often brilliant criticism of such thinkers as Marsiglio of Padua, William of Ockham, and John Wyclif, the traditional authority of crown and city-republic remained little touched.

The great weight of traditional forms of social organization thus survived the crises of the fourteenth and early fifteenth centuries. Personalized kingship, aristocratic and ecclesiastical privilege, and the divisions of society remained the foundations of the society of traditional Europe until the end of the eighteenth century. Within the framework of expanded royal governance, the privileges of the aristocracy and the Church were somewhat restricted, though never wholly eliminated. As one sign of some social mobility, newly successful members from the lower orders of society imitated the life styles of the aristocracy, turned themselves into rural landlords, and pointed their children either toward advantageous marriages or to careers in royal service or the professions. Education, formerly only useful for professional people, attracted more and more members of the aristocracy during the fifteenth and sixteenth centuries, and with the growth of town life and urban schools, literacy increased steadily. When printing with moveable type was developed after the first half of the fifteenth century, many inexpensive books became available.

### *The Papacy*

The religious tone of fourteenth- and fifteenth-century culture gave a distinctive cast to both social institutions and social dissent. Although many of the great organized heresies died out during the fourteenth century, lively kinds of protest took on strong religious coloring and were coupled with charges of ecclesiastical corruption. A long sojourn of the popes in Avignon between 1305 and 1377 created a brilliant papal court in southern France. Here, the papacy reorganized its ecclesiastical bureaucracy. This was necessary in order to handle the increased volume of business caused by public demand and a rising legal consciousness. Still, to many, the Avignon period seemed only to reaffirm the accusations of worldliness and greed that had long been leveled at the churchly hierarchy. After the return of the popes to Rome in 1377, conflicting papal elections produced first two, and after 1409, three claimants to the throne of St. Peter. The political authorities of Europe already having encroached upon traditional ecclesiastical powers, exploited the crisis of 1378–1415 to further curtail the Church's powers. From 1415 (when the Council of Constance overcame the divisions created by the great Schism) until the end of the fifteenth century, the papacy had to fight to restore papal primacy in central and northern Italy. For this reason, it was unable to deal with the large-scale crises in the rest of Europe. Papal legates attempted to make peace in the Hundred Years' War by being particularly prominent at royal courts and at such increasingly important international assemblies as the Congress of Arras in 1435. But the popes' energies for most of the century following 1415 were devoted to the

**The German and Italian Realms of Emperor Frederick II, 1212-1250**

restoration of papal authority inside the Church and in the old papal territories of central Italy.

Even though the problems of the papacy and the hierarchy of the Church were critical, there were greater crises brewing. The process of

Christianizing society, intermittently underway since the fourth century, had produced not only scores of ecclesiastical critics, but also a genuine return to interest in the body of Christian thought as more people demanded more intense spiritual guidance. Private devotion and private chapels, privately commissioned religious art and devotional literature, private patronage of religious services for individuals and families, and new religious societies and guilds reflected a fresh intensity and spread of religious feeling. The haunting quality and forthright immediacy of fifteenth-century religious art with its visual translation of literary imagery added to this intensity. The appearance of new religious movements, particularly the *Devotio Moderna* in fifteenth-century Holland, illustrates not only the spectacular side of this movement, but its profoundly pietistic side as well. Ironically, the growth of lay power, whether through royal agreements with Rome or by the town magistrate's promises to supervise the morals of the clergy, increased the criticism of the Church's failures and those of individual priests. (In the town courts of the sixteenth century, for example, the Protestant magistrates sometimes believed that they functioned as secular spiritual guides, who were responsible for the maintenance of justice, the preservation of law and order, and for the spiritual condition of those who stood accused before them.) Ill-prepared as magistrates were for this kind of effort, the spread of secular power constituted an effective vehicle for criticizing ecclesiastical personnel and institutions as well as an alternative means of distributing ecclesiastical authority. The State, although not yet completely formed, found itself stepping imperceptibly into the shoes of the Church.

Other crises hastened the process. The apparent failure of the Crusades, signalled most clearly by the loss of Acre—the last Christian possession in the Holy Land—in 1291, did not wholly denote the failure of the crusade idea, which survived to color later Christian relations with the Turks, the discovery of the New World, and the religious wars of the late sixteenth and seventeenth centuries. But it undermined European confidence. The spread of guides for pastoral activities placed clerical responsibility before both clergy and laity, and ecclesiastical failures as well as ecclesiastical obligations were now discussed in homes, by popular travelling preachers, and by quasi-religious groups of laypeople.

### Threats from New Invaders

Against this background of a pervading religious coloration to many aspects of daily life and a steady flow of religious criticism, the plague and famine of the fourteenth century provided stark examples of the precarious state of the western world. The continued assertiveness of the Ottomans, who had settled in Asia Minor and Syria during the fourteenth century, added to this insecurity. Successfully penetrating the Balkans and Greece, the Ottomans besieged Constantinople in the spring of 1453. The Byzantine Empire, already economically and politically weak, was further weakened by its emperor's formal acceptance of Latin Christianity. This was the price of Western aid in 1439, and it caused a schism in the Byzantine world from Russia to Constantinople. Under the heavy artillery of the Turks, Constantinople fell after a heroic defense. During the next decades the Turks consolidated their European and Asian conquests, and after 1519, the Ottoman Empire renewed its expansion into North Africa and central Europe. Internal dissensions that prevented combined Western resistance, the powerlessness of the papacy to call for a new crusade, and widespread rumors and fear of "the bloodie and cruell Turke" loomed over Europe between 1453 and 1683. Although Turkish power constituted little actual threat in the western Mediterranean, especially after they were driven out of Moslem Granada in Spain in 1492, the expansion of the Turks into the Balkans introduced chaos into the kingdoms of Central Europe, particularly Hungary, and caused the Hapsburg dynasty of Austria to focus its energies on southeastern Europe. Vienna, unsuccessfully besieged by the Turks in 1529 and again in 1683, now demarked a European frontier set against the Turks.

A second expanding power, in Russia, where the core of a strong Russian state took shape around the Duchy of Muscovy, at last expelled the Mongols and began the steady expansion of Muscovite influence westward into Lithuania. Thus, the concept of a universal Christendom, often little more than an ideal in preceding centuries, was severely shaken by the growth of vernacular languages, the adaptation of the liturgy into those languages, the growth of secular power, and the ravages of the fourteenth and fifteenth centuries. Only against such enemies as the Turks could the ideal be invoked. The idea of Christendom had given way in practice to the actuality of Europe, which was divided into independent states. But these states did share a common secularized culture, and offered on the local level a degree of security and identity that no ideal of a universal society could match.

### The Renaissance

Latin antiquity had always constituted a particularly strong influence upon later European societies. The memory of Imperial as well as Spiritual Rome, the works of such writers as Virgil, Cicero, and Sallust, and the physical presence of the remnants of Roman antiquity in much of Europe contributed to this survival. By the fourteenth century, Roman law had been revived in much of Europe. The study of classical literature and a more precise knowledge of classical Latin had made many people acutely aware of the differences between twelfth-century society and classical antiquity. Among many late thirteenth- and early fourteenth-century thinkers and writers there emerged a new and more accurate vision of the classical past. For some, this filled some of the gaps caused by the inefficiency of ecclesiastical and secular authorities. "People should take a pattern for their social and political conduct from the civic morality of the ancient Romans," thinkers argued, and this practical admiration was matched by the discovery and publication of new Latin texts. Contemporary thinkers considered their own age a rebirth, or as they called it, a Renaissance, of Latin antiquity. New linguistic and textual discoveries led also, although much more slowly, to the revival of Greek study and to the application of forgotten critical skills to contemporary problems, especially those touching ecclesiastical organization.

The people who wholeheartedly adopted this new image of ancient Rome did not become pagans, however. Their aim was to purify Christian belief by going back to the original thought of the early Church Fathers and to the customs of the earliest forms of Christianity. Such combinations of secular and religious criticism may be seen in the careers of the poet and social critic Petrarch (1309–1374), who is regarded as the father of Renaissance humanism; in the spirited writings of the storyteller Giovanni Boccaccio (1313–1375), one of the first "modern" men to study Greek; and in the textual critic Lorenzo Valla (1407–1457).

While the Italian origins of this movement are striking, a similar movement had begun in France in the fourteenth century, and by the late fifteenth century England, Germany, and Spain had felt its influence. With a new critical approach to the past, scholars undertook solving the difficulties of the present. At the same time they held up an attractive, wholly inaccurate model of a perfect Latin antique past and a barbarous, unthinking, brutal period between antiquity and the present. They gave the various uncomplimentary (and meaningless) names to this period: "middle time," "Dark" or "Iron Age," and finally, by the seventeenth century, the "Middle Ages." To the thinkers who considered Roman antiquity a perfect human society and to those who regarded early Christian practice as preferable to the vast superstructure of fifteenth-century ecclesiastical life, the centuries between the fifth and the fifteenth seemed to have been lost ones. The secret of success lay in the restoration of idealized conditions from the distant past.

The Renaissance was a time when people were rethinking their old assumptions. It heralded the Reformation, and both must be seen as a continuum. While some sought to return to antiquity, to the values they associated with Greek and Roman civilization, others sought consciously to promote the new, unusual, and experimental. Still others held even more strongly to the firm beliefs of the Middle Ages. In this contention of idea against idea, people experienced a liberation that stimulated innovation in many aspects of life. Particularly important was the literary movement labeled "humanism," to which Petrarch contributed so much in Renaissance Italy.

The humanists emphasized the importance of humanity as opposed to the significance of systems. Many of the humanists were lay writers, not members of the clergy, who wanted to turn back to the ancients—especially to Plato, Homer, Cicero, and Horace—for inspiration. These ancient writers were thought of as men of reason, secular men who did not quarrel over petty matters of church doctrine. They were master stylists who understood that the manner in which a thing was done was as important as the doing of it. Thus the humanists took books of etiquette, like Baldassare de Castiglione's *Book of the Courtier* (1527), seriously. To be a "gentleman" was to attain the highest virtue. In Italy, an elite studied the pre-Christian classics, but the Renaissance took on a different form to the north in Germany and the Low Countries. There the Christian humanists—of whom the most noted was Desiderius Erasmus of Rotterdam (1466–1536)—learned Greek and Hebrew to better reach the church fathers, and religion remained a powerful force. Erasmus was an enormously learned former monk who, although he remained within the Church, launched broadside attacks upon its abuses. He was reviled by

*Erasmus of Rotterdam*   Here the Flemish portrait painter Hans Holbein shows us his friend, in quiet contrast to his depiction of Henry VIII, a patron (see page 185). The one speaks of Intelligence, the other of Power. Both were characteristics of the sixteenth century. *Source: Oeffentliche Kunstsammlung, Basel, Hausaufnahme.*

both sides during the growing dispute concerning Martin Luther (see pages 181–85). His career perhaps shows most clearly the thin lines that divided orthodox dissent from true reforming thought. Both styles of virtue saw great merit in the pursuit of knowledge, in the *Homo Universale* or universal man. Both sought out adventures of mind and body. Both saw value in feats of statecraft as well, although many would not have embraced all of the arguments, often thought to be cynical, made by the Italian diplomat Nicolò Machiavelli in his Renaissance handbook of statecraft, *The Prince* (1513).

Renaissance thought also promoted science, not only in the practical sense of new discoveries and experiments or in terms of pure theory, but in finding ways for reconciling God and human. Although the Pope would not declare the thought of St. Thomas Aquinas to be the official basis for Catholic doctrine until 1879, Thomesian thought as presented in his *Summa Theologica* (1270) was widely accepted by the fourteenth century. It was Aquinas's feat to show that faith and reason need not be at war and that faith was under no challenge from reason. He assured that people would continue to seek wisdom in both spiritual and practical forms. Aquinas taught that a general idea or concept had greater reality than a particular example of it; that is, humankind was more real than a specific individual. A higher law of God was of greater force than the specific laws of humans. In that way, Aquinas made it possible for people to hold to the truth of the Church while attacking specific clergy members. Not only was Reason acceptable to the Church, but the Church was acceptable to Reason. Those who followed Machiavelli cast such reconciliations aside, and freed politics from theology or moral teachings. But there were people who longed for the world of Platonic idealism. Others wanted to give the Church first place in their lives. These people hoped for salvation through Christian humanism, science, and vigorous physical activity (as in the Crusades) on behalf of God.

As Aquinas's teachings became widely known, western Europeans thrust outward. At the same time, Arabic thought—once leading the world in mathematics, science, and philosophy—had come to rest on an agreed and stable doctrine, and further interpretation of the Koran ended. Until 1923, when Kemal Ataturk turned the Turkish Republic away from the Koran as the basis for law, Moslem thought, which was still brilliant and incisive, was nonetheless no longer innovative.

As we have seen, in 1453 Constantinople (now Istanbul) fell to the Turks. The world as known to Europeans was roughly divided into two great segments. Islam was contained in the West and able to expand only to the south into Africa and temporarily to the east. The West, stimulated in part by the long religious rivalry and cut off by Islam from traditional trade routes via the eastern Mediterranean to India, now looked to its little-known seas.

The Age of Discovery, therefore, often is said to have begun with the fall of Constantinople. The closing of the port to the merchants of the West and the consequent search for alternative trade routes led to new technological knowledge, especially in maritime architecture. New merchant classes were created in western Europe. The rise of nation-states and competition between them made it possible for explorers to receive support from monarchs of Europe. The Renaissance freed people from the old modes of thought, and the rise of Protestantism injected a competitive element into the search for new passages to the East.

Removing old constraints as it did, the spirit of the Renaissance redirected thought. While rooted in a reverence for past antiquity, it was forward-looking in encouraging experimentation. While this was evident in forms of statecraft, theology and philosophy, it was perhaps most obviously present in the flowering of art and literature. The visual arts grew particularly in Florence, the southern center of humanistic thought. For two centuries that Italian city was a cultural capital for Europe and produced painting, sculpture, and architecture so grand, so theoretically formidable that it rivalled the ancient seat of learning, Athens.

From these developments emerged the artistic movement of *naturalism*. Giotto di Bondone (1266–1337) began to paint an extensive series of New Testament frescoes in 1305; he turned away from the flat appearance of medieval art which, however beautiful in design or color, was largely meant to tell a story. Instead he used light and shadow in such a way as to create an illusion of depth or perspective. He also gave real emotion to the facial expression of his figures, which draws the viewer into the painting in a dramatic way. Rather than leaving his art to the world of anonymity, he signed his works and became the true person of virtue by fulfilling the humanist ideal. Many imitated him and developed perspective even further, as did Filippo Brunelleschi (1377–1446) and the Flemish painter, Jan van Eyck (1390–1441), whose works were especially detailed.

Such artists prepared the way for others. Donatello (1386–1466), a Florentine, studied Roman sculpture with care and then turned to live models, producing the first monumental equestrian statue since the days of the Romans. Sandro Botticelli (1446–1510) wished to go even further by not merely imitating reality with perfection but creating works of art that were beyond the beauty to be found in nature. Turning to classical mythology for inspiration, he helped bring the Greek myths into direct rivalry with the Christian stories in art. Sensuality, clearly not Christian, was even more present in the flesh tones of Titian, a Venetian painter (1477–1576), and the most embracing genius of the time, Leonardo da Vinci (1452–1519). This universal man, in creating the *Mona Lisa, The Last Supper,* and other works, was but one who represented the Renaissance at its height.

His rival was Michelangelo Buonarroti (1475–1564). The grandmaster at depicting human anatomy, Michelangelo was a sculptor, a painter, and a philosopher. Deeply influenced by the neo-Platonists, Michelangelo tried to merge their views with Christian conviction in the Sistine Chapel, which was created for Pope Sixtus IV. Michelangelo believed that humans were engaged in a hopeless struggle with their destinies; they wished to reach God but they were held back by their flesh. Only the soaring majesty of the great dome of a church could lift mortals above themselves. Later in life Michelangelo turned to architecture, and in 1547 began St. Peter's Basilica in Rome, the capital of Christendom.

The invention of printing, usually ascribed to John Gutenberg of Mainz, Germany, in 1447, ushered in a new age of literature. Books were increasingly available in the vernacular of the growing public. While Erasmus may have been the most widely read author at the time, three others were at least as important in capturing the diverse spirit of the age. François Rabelais (1494–1553) was widely censored for he wrote what were regarded as vulgar tales in colloquial French. These were clearly subversive to the teachings of the Church of which he had been an active member. In *Gargantua and Pantagruel* he spoke out against the doctrine of Original Sin, showing by example that free people could seek happy and productive lives. Rabelais was perhaps the foremost of the secular humanists. Another Frenchman, Michel de Montaigne (1533–1592), wrote sceptical *Essays* that provided deeply personal and quite tentative judgments on a variety of subjects. He showed that the educated who were steeped in classical and Biblical literature could and must think for themselves. Montaigne, Rabelais, and a Spanish writer, Miguel de Cervantes (1547–1616), who began his satire on chivalry, *Don Quixote,* in 1605, spoke for tolerance, secular wisdom, and the relativity of knowledge.

The crowning glory of Renaissance literature, however, were undoubtedly the writings of an Englishman, the acknowledged master dramatist of all time, William Shakespeare (1564–1616). Shakespeare's humanism was the voice of the Elizabethan age, of the Age of Discovery, and in his modernity, he was the voice of the present. "All the world's a stage," he wrote, and he ranged from tragedy to comedy to history, bringing a worldly sense of both power and patriotism to the Globe Theatre. Drawing much of his material from earlier manuscripts—*Hamlet,* for example, was inspired by a medieval chronicle—he reveled in conflict and high tension. Shakespeare fused all the great strands of Renaissance thought in his forty plays and his many poems. These comprised perhaps the finest literature (for while Shakespeare was meant to be performed, he could be read as well) in the English language. Over the next three and a half centuries English supplanted Italian and French as the *lingua franca* of the modern world. As Shakespeare's friend and fellow playwright, Ben Jonson (1573–1637), said, the great dramatist was "not for an age, but for all time." More than any other writer of the Renaissance, Shakespeare speaks to us today, alive to our concerns, to the shifting nuances of security, pride, revenge, and love.

With increasing fervor, ecclesiastical and secular critics attacked current values and beliefs by holding them up to the criticism of the early Church. Scholars produced better scriptural texts, and current customs and laws that were not covered by the Scriptures were condemned. Initially the most complex and scholarly aspects of such criticism were circulated among only a learned few. But soon popular criticism of ecclesiastical institutions and practices took up some of these topics and added them to the anticlericalism of earlier periods. A combination of learned, half-learned, and popular critical assaults upon ecclesiastical institutions, both from inside the Church and by neoclassical pagans, peaked in the first quarter of the sixteenth century and launched a widespread series of divisions among western Christians that are collectively known as the Reformation.

## The Reformation

It is not by chance that so many of the most influential reformers came from careers and areas where learned and popular culture met. The development of a personal, almost philosophical criticism of current ecclesiastical practices met a welcoming public. In turn the philosophical foundations of their criticism came to be institutionalized in new sectarian churches. Faced with such revolts, the Church reacted outwardly rather than reforming inwardly, and either offered more concessions to such already powerful rulers as the kings of France and Spain and the rulers of eastern Europe or remained intransigent and watched other old Christian kingdoms break away, as was the case with England.

The Reformation was not a new historical age; the problems it dealt with were old problems. The institutions and the new intensity of sectarian religious feeling that emerged simply underlined the transformation of European religious life that had begun in the thirteenth century. The scholar and monk, Martin Luther (1483–1546), began as a solitary individual with a personal religious crisis. It centered upon a person's complete inability, as he saw it, to act justly in the eyes of God. In his meditations upon a passage in St. Paul's Epistle to the Romans (1:17), "the just shall live by faith," Luther became convinced that faith and faith alone was that gift of God whereby mortals become righteous. What Luther referred to as "works," specifically a careful observance of established ecclesiastical practices, were useless in his eyes. What counted was one's own faith as an inward sign of God's mercy. One could be secure with God and in God's presence only if one truly believed without questioning the teachings of Christ. As a result of this momentous revelation, Luther was challenged to debates by other theologians and thereby embellished his own position. He condemned a number of ecclesiastical practices, including the primacy of papal authority, the sacramental powers of the priesthood, the efficacy of Mass, and all customs not vouched directly for in the New Testament. Other critics in England, France, and Switzerland undertook similar analyses of ecclesiastical authority and reached different opinions.

The Reformation was an attempt to cleanse the Roman Catholic Church of practices, and eventually of dogmas, that were considered illogical and even degrading departures from Christ's teachings. Protestantism was thus revolutionary in purpose. By the sixteenth century most Protestants had concluded that the Church of Rome could not be purged of its abuses and therefore must be destroyed. The Church had permitted so many "clarifications" of the Bible by the learned rather than the spiritual that it had departed utterly from the Bible itself. Thus, Protestants had in common an insistence that God could be found only in the Holy Scriptures, and they were determined to break the Church's monopoly on their access to salvation.

Luther was terrified of God, obsessed with his own salvation, and constantly searching the spiritual horizon for some new truth to make his suffering meaningful. He found peace from his spiritual anguish in St. Paul, upon whose teachings the Roman Church had been built. He then sought to remain peacefully in seclusion.

But as often happens, an obscure figure gave the world a major one. In 1517 a friar named Tetzel was distributing indulgences in Germany; the money went to aid the construction of the new St. Peter's in Rome. Indulgences were not actually sold, but they were highly desirable, because in 1300 Boniface VIII had declared that under the appropriate conditions an indulgence would relieve one of some of the punishments of purgatory, and the person receiving an indulgence was expected to make a donation to the Church. Tetzel put the "donation" before the indulgence. Luther, now a professor at Wittenberg, attacked such "sales" by posting ninety-five "theses" or arguments on the Wittenberg church and appealed to Pope Leo X to end the abuse of indulgences. The pope refused. Luther then asked for a general church council and declared in a public debate that even this council might make a mistake because no one had the authority to regulate Christian belief. Everyone could read the Bible and, through faith, reach one's own conclusions; therefore, there was no need for a priesthood or for the church.

Luther did not think of himself as a revolutionary, but his ideas fell upon fertile soil. Many Germans resented Rome for essentially political reasons, and Luther's religious arguments soon took on political overtones. In directing the laity to the Bible alone, he challenged the temporal authority of the church and of the Holy Roman Empire. He removed one of the anchors of the totally hierarchical life by casting away purgatory. In recognizing only two sacraments—baptism and the mass—which he called communion, he rejected transubstantiation. And in denouncing monasticism and celibacy, he made sex a legitimate part of the religious life. He focused attention upon the family and undercut the luxury of the monastic orders, many of which had departed from their traditional vows of poverty. Fundamentally, he asked the State to take control of religion and turned to the princes of the German principalities to achieve his reforms.

The German professor was now a heretic, excommunicated and summoned to Emperor Charles V's Diet, called at Worms in 1521. There Luther refused to recant, "since it is neither right nor safe to act against conscience," and he was banned from the Holy Roman Empire. Luther translated the Bible into German, and his ideas raced across Germany, increasingly feeding a political revolution.

Luther's career was supported by his prince, the Elector Frederick the Wise of Saxony, who was increasingly opposed by one of the most potentially powerful rulers in Europe, the Emperor Charles V. As a result, between 1521 and Luther's death in 1546, the Reformation began to take on its definitive shape. Charles V was the most prestigious ruler in Europe, the greatest territorial monarch since Charlemagne. He was the descendant of the great houses that had ruled the Duchy of Burgundy, the Hapsburg lands of Austria and southeastern Europe, and the kingdoms of Castile and Aragon in Spain. His grandparents, Maximilian of Austria and Mary of Burgundy, had joined by their marriage the fortunes of the imperial house of Hapsburg with part of the vast Burgundian inheritance, particularly the Netherlands. Maximilian's son, Philip, married the daughter of Ferdinand of Aragon and Isabella of Castile; through a series of dynastic accidents, Charles, the son of this union, inherited the Burgundian and Spanish possessions of his family; and in 1519 he was elected Holy Roman Emperor. Under this exceptional ruler, the vastly diversified possessions of the Hapsburgs were forged into a unified monarchy, which had to continually struggle with the local laws, customs, and traditions of its constituent parts. Supported by a superbly trained and staffed Spanish infantry, aided by both clerical and lay administrators—who saw Charles as the savior of the Church and of orthodox Catholicism—and funded for a time by Spanish dominance of European trade, the resources of wealthy banking families, and a flow of American gold and silver, Charles shaped the Holy Roman Empire into a weapon that could advance both Spanish policy and the Catholic cause. Initially successful against the Turks in the Mediterranean, the French in Italy, and the reforming movements in Spain and the Netherlands, Charles V initially shaped the Catholic response to Luther's and others' protests.

Luther now lent his support to the ducal and princely powers that would, he hoped, continue the reforms he had begun. Revolts by imperial knights in 1522 and peasant groups in 1525 strengthened his sense that only local princely authority could and ought to determine religious practices. This was the final settlement of the Reformation crisis. The princes of the many German states slowly took control over reforming movements in their own territories. With the Peace of Augsburg in 1555 between the Emperor and the Princes, princely control over local ecclesiastical life was asserted and all hopes of German unification were dashed.

Ultimately, Luther was appalled by what his followers did—they were violent and took extreme political and religious positions. He took a more conservative position by arguing that an established clergy still had functions to perform. Private conclusions about conscience might be antisocial in expression and therefore had to be controlled by the Church. Lutheranism now tended to recognize two worlds. One was the spirit, which only God knew, where there was internal, perfect freedom. In the other, perfect obedience to appropriate and pious authority was required for a stable society. Ironically, Lutheranism placed more emphasis on the state than Catholicism had done, which added yet another dynamic factor to those that had already promoted Western expansion. From 1555, the ruler of each German state of the old empire was free to choose between Lutheran or Catholic allegiance. That bound all of his subjects and created true state churches. Germany was divided roughly equally: the north was Lutheran and the south was Catholic except for Wittenberg. Scandinavia and the Baltic areas already were steadfastly Lutheran.

On a larger scale, similar principles were at work elsewhere. In England, complex forces that consisted of eager Lutheran reformers, humanist critics of the Church, and the policies of King Henry VIII (1509–1547) precipitated some ecclesiastical reform. But not until the problems surrounding Henry's divorce from Queen Catherine of Aragon (who was another daughter of Ferdinand and Isabella and the aunt of Charles V) did a genuine princely reform take root in England and extend Magna Carta. Henry employed royal authority in England in a novel, complex, and successful way to separate the English Church from the Church of Rome. Reluctant to remove the English Church too far, however, Henry's reforms did not satisfy either the Lutheran sympathizers or the more radical ecclesiastical critics. In spite of later attempts to push reform farther in England, the general conditions of Henry's changes became the basis of the separate Church of England.

The Reformation in the German princely states and free cities, in Switzerland, and in England may be regarded less as the beginning than as the end of a process. The Church's authority was challenged and restricted, and dogma and ritual were affected by new vernacular languages, evangelical criticism based upon the Bible, and subordination of pastoral clergy to public powers. In Germany among the Lutheran states,

*Henry VIII by Hans Holbein* Few monarchs have been so strong, and few paintings have captured such strength so well, as the Dutch artist Hans Holbein's representation of the English monarch, Henry VIII. The Flemish tradition of realism enhanced Holbein's portraiture, and his friend Erasmus of Rotterdam helped him to become a painter for the English court. *Source: Scala-Alinari.*

teams of "visitors" inspected each congregation; in England, a more intensive and thorough supervision of parish clergy and parish churches was undertaken; in the free cities, Switzerland, and in some of the reformed towns of eastern France, the town magistrates and a body of reformed clergy supervised the religious life of the townspeople. The urban theocracy, in fact, became perhaps the most characteristic form of Reformation society. Ulrich Zwingli (1484–1531) made the city of Zurich a prototype for reforms elsewhere in Switzerland, Scotland, and even in the early Massachusetts colonial towns of the seventeeth century. Under the French reformer, Jean Calvin (1509–1564), the Swiss city of Geneva became the most thoroughgoing example in Europe of the conversion of a town and its secular authorities.

Calvin was both priest and lawyer, and a Latin, Greek, and Hebrew scholar. He had converted to a form of Lutheranism when he was twenty-four and in 1536 he published *Institutes of the Christian Religion* in Latin.

Luther had written in the German vernacular for Germans. Calvin wote in the international language of the time with a view to universal applications of his learned and logical arguments. Further, he differed with Luther in two important respects: he found all people predestined to their fates, and he rejected the superiority of the state or of any form of government over the laws of religion. Calvinism was therefore more rigorous, more expansive, and more determined than Lutheranism, and it attracted the most uncompromising and militant followers. Luther had retained bishops. Calvinists rejected them in favor of presbyteries, or elected bodies drawn from the laity as well as the ministry. Lay control in the church both democratized and in time secularized religion, for laypeople were constantly faced with practical as well as doctrinal problems.

Geneva was meant to be the model Christian community. The logic of the *Institutes* was rigorously applied: ministers ruled the church and elders the town. Images of saints were forbidden, as were candles and incense, because they were supposedly emotionally distracting; they took the mind away from the intellectual content of the sermons. All aesthetic as well as emotional forms of worship were eliminated. Michael Servetus, a Spaniard who denied that Christ was divine, was burned at the stake as a heretic in 1553. Like-minded Calvinists converged from all over Europe upon Geneva, which became an international center of intellectual ferment within the confines allowed by Calvin. The arid, clear logic of the *Institutes* spread to Poland, parts of Germany and France, Belgium, Hungary, Bohemia, and Scotland, where John Knox (*c.* 1505–1572) took over. Ultimately it reached the New World through England, for the Puritans were Calvinists, the established Church of Scotland was Presbyterian, and the Congregational church in the United States would originally be the same. Still, for all its aridity, Calvinism often allowed considerable room for original thought and love of simple beauty. It also kept the state subordinate to the individual.

The Reformation, then, was not simply a reform of religious beliefs and practices. Political institutions everywhere in Europe were too closely tied to religion not to be affected, and religion was too inextricable a part of sixteenth-century culture for it to leave other aspects of life and thought untouched. The reforms of Luther and Calvin had attacked clerical privilege, status, and the effectiveness of the Church and its teachings. Calvin had argued that humankind was predestined to either salvation or damnation wholly apart from the merits of individual human efforts. Other reformers, the so-called "Left Wing of the Reformation," attempted to convert entire cities with proclamations of the imminent second coming of the Christ and the need for drastic and far-reaching social change. These doctrines had a wide appeal. High theology, particularly in its sixteenth-century forms, apparently meant little to many people of the middle and lower classes and remained excessively restricted to an intellectual elite. The forms of religious knowledge disseminated among lower, less learned groups often possessed no formidable intellectual persuasive power, and the institution responsible for this attracted little loyalty.

The great sixteenth-century enthusiasm for religious experiment is in one sense a continuation of the growth of private religious attitudes that emerged in the late thirteenth and early fourteenth centuries. In another sense, it is a result of the difficulties the Roman Catholic Church had in the early fifteenth century. The reforming theologians posited no doctrines that had not at least appeared once before in the history of Christianity. In this sense, the Reformation was less radically novel in its doctrinal content than it was in its success in continuing the processes of criticism and dissent that had been present in the Church for two centuries. The Reformation proved that a single Church could not contain either the religious sensibilities or the secular loyalties of the entire early modern European society.

The Church of Rome, however, did not fail to respond to the Reformation. New ecclesiastical orders sprang up, particularly the Jesuits. But those critics who remained in the Church, such as Erasmus, continued to urge much-needed reforms upon Rome. A new wave of pastoral energy occurred in the sixteenth century, and some of the great reforming Catholic bishops of northern Italy and France left an enduring impact upon subsequent Roman Catholic institutions and attitudes. The papacy, never fully convinced of the loyalty of Spanish policy toward the Church, often impeded the efforts of Charles V and his successor Philip II. Even those kingdoms that remained within the Catholic Church, particularly France, did not act in concert with the Spanish defenders of Catholicism.

The problem of Spanish power was only one that faced the sixteenth-century Church. Many high prelates recognized the validity of contemporary ecclesiastical criticism, but the critical years between 1517 and 1540 went by with little institutional response. When the great reforming Council of Trent (1545–1563) finally met, its energies were absorbed more in countering Reformation theology and ecclesiastical criticism than in continuing the remarkable internal reforms that began in the twelfth and thirteenth centuries. The Council did achieve significant nontheological reforms, however, and governmentally it produced the pope-centered Roman Catholic Church which has continued to our time. In this sense its work was parallel to the centralizing efforts of secular monarchs in the sixteenth century. Between the Peace of Augsburg in 1555 and the end of the Council of Trent, from which Protestants had been excluded, the lines between Catholic and Protestant Europe were set. In submitting to the secular control of lay authorities, the Church restricted itself to internal reforms while the reformed principalities permitted essential controls to slip into the hands of lay princes and magistrates.

In England and particularly in France, struggles between Protestants and Catholics were often related to royal authority. Between 1562 and 1610 France was torn by "The Wars of Religion," which were in fact wars among different political and religious factions for control of the throne. Under a short-lived series of kings and the domineering figure of their mother, Catherine de Medici, extreme Protestant and Catholic factions swirled around the throne, alternately exercising great influence, and frequently breaking out into armed opposition. France once again became secure only with the accession of Henry IV of Navarre (1589–1610) who, like his great contemporary Elizabeth I of England (1558–1603), was a conciliatory figure with enormous skill at persuasion and compromise.

One must ask, was the Reformation primarily a religious or a sociopolitical phenomenon? Certainly the new doctrines and the Catholic Counter-Reformation echoed controversies that were not new in Christian history. With equal certainty, in many respects the Reformation simply extended the growing power of secular authorities, and in both Catholic and Protestant states, ecclesiastical institutions became pillars of state authority. The revival of evangelical Christianity did not reproduce the ideas and institutions of the early Church. Rather, it explored a number of doctrinal and institutional views within the whole tradition of Christianity that had been expounded many times before but now were being studied within the unique confines of sixteenth-century Europe. The spiritual security (as well as the physical security) of most people was now in the hands of the state, and loyalties once extended absolutely to ecclesiastical institutions were being channeled into the newly sanctified secular powers of early modern Europe.

Thus the unity of the medieval Church was broken, and the inherent fragmentation embodied in the Reformation movements was unleashed. A scarcity of services and skills between the fifth and the end of the twelfth centuries made the small upper class responsible for providing the ecclesiastical structure for society. The Church in Rome functioned on an international level, so only it developed an international organization. But from the thirteenth century, Europe's new prosperity gave rise to regionally based subcultures capable of performing ecclesiastical roles with great sophistication. Political tension increased between the monarchies that vied for power and the papacy. As an international state challenged the local authority of the new monarchs, the question of control over the personnel of the Church—especially the local personnel opposed to the monarchs who saw themselves as reformers—became central. At the same time, the spread of printing presses made the Bible more freely available to the Christian laity and thereby undermined the Church's claim to being the sole intermediary between God and mortal. This contributed to people's desire to seek their own interpretations of the Bible. Despite the hope of the religious reformers who tried to impose their own universal dogma (in Geneva especially) the Reformation meant, almost by definition, that no new universalist Western Christendom would arise. While the Cluniac movement had captured the central Church whole in the eleventh century, there was now no central church, for all reformist thinkers, however much they might insist on close adherence to their own doctrines, were unleashing the possibility for freedom of individual thought in religious matters. True, the Reformation created religious and political opposition in many countries. This gave the Roman Catholic Counter-Reformation an opportunity to reorganize the Church in Rome and survive as an international church for half of Europe. For the other half, the church had been reduced to a partnership with the state, and the church in each state would take on increasingly different rituals and dogmas.

In the beginning of the seventeenth century there was expanded but not total state authority. Problems of public finance, defense, administration, and the nature and extent of royal power still remained to be defined over the following two centuries. In many kingdoms, regional customs and not central law codes defined legal relationships; and not until the late eighteenth and early nineteenth centuries did the state's absolute authority institute uniform codes of criminal and civil law that applied equally everywhere within the state's boundaries. Nor did the establishment of a permanent responsible civil service take root everywhere until the late seventeenth and eighteenth centuries. The aristocracy remained privileged until the end of the eighteenth century in France and even later elsewhere. The Churches were subordinate to the State, but they still echoed the controversies of the fifteenth and sixteenth centuries. The roots of traditional Europe went deep, and in spite of the great changes of the seventeenth century, the life of the majority of people changed little between 1400 and about 1800. Under a vigorous and deceptively distracting panorama of wars, revolutions, and economic shifts, the lives of peasants and proletarians continued on much in the same way during the seventeenth and eighteenth centuries as they had during the fourteenth and fifteenth. The dominance of secular authority in matters of religious practice and ecclesiastical organization extended to areas of economic enterprise into the late sixteenth and seventeenth centuries.

The pattern of shifting political, emotional, and religious alliances; the interaction of the new yet old ways of the Renaissance with the struggles for the old yet new ways of the Reformation; the expansion of Europeans overseas—these complex, overlapping developments make chronological history virtually useless. Cause and effect does not follow in direct sequences. Remote causes are utterly different from immediate causes. The "proximate cause"—that event or development which determines the point of no return in a sequence of events (when reconstructed with historical hindsight)—becomes more remote from the events it influences. The historical perspective of the antiquarian who unfolds fact after fact in clear chronological order is more rather than less confusing; and historical narrative turns increasingly toward fragmentation, overlap, and interpretation. To relate history less as a story and more as an interpretation of how we came to be as we are is also a feature of the time we call "modern." Seldom again would humankind enjoy the security of believing that it knew precisely who or what was to blame or to be praised for its condition.

## III. 4 A New World in the Making: Modern Europe

*There is nothing more difficult to take in hand, more perilous to conduct, or more uncertain in its success, than to take the lead in the introduction of a new order of things.* —Nicolò Machiavelli, *The Prince* (1513)

With the backing of powerful governments, economic activity as frequently achieved disaster as it did success. From the mid-sixteenth to the late seventeenth centuries, a great wave of inflation struck Europe and prices far surpassed most people's income. The inefficiency of many government controls diminished only slowly over this period as governments learned to exploit their vast power in more rational and productive ways. Indeed, from the fourteenth to the nineteenth centuries, one powerful reason for security and productive large-scale organization is that state governments learned to handle their growing new resources of power, finances, and spiritual loyalties in better coordinated and more productive ways. In doing so, they contributed to the rise of the economic system known as Capitalism; at the same time, Europe was making itself felt in hitherto largely unaffected parts of the globe.

Of course territorial expansion is not a phenomenon confined to the age of European exploration. The successive chapters of world history from earliest times have almost invariably begun with the story of an energetic and expanding people; the Assyrians, the Romans, the Arabs, the Mongols, and the Turks each flashed upon the stage of world history as explorers and conquerors. Yet it was the Europeans who ultimately reached out to establish contact with the East rather than the reverse.

Why might one think of the period beginning with such expansion as the start of the "modern world"? Partially because a condition of interconnectedness was so clearly in the making for the first time. Obviously "modernity" begins at no single point in time, because time is a continuum, a process of becoming. Equally obviously, the word is loaded. Most people like to think of themselves as modern, up-to-date, "with it"; each generation has marveled at how the preceding one could have survived without the wheel, gunpowder, the steam engine, television. To call oneself modern is a form of arrogance, for it implies arrival at a destination. The term was first widely used by the philosophers of the eighteenth-century Enlightenment in Europe, for they were convinced that they were at a special watershed in history. Yet every year has its watershed; the middle class is always rising; and each age thinks itself more rational and more able to cope with insecurity than the last. This is not utterly a delusion, for there are few historians who would not argue that life has greatly improved for the mass of humankind; that is, they would agree that there is something called "progress" and that, allowing for stops and starts, progress has taken place. Nonetheless, as we enter the early modern period of our history, we must beware of the arrogance of assuming that we are entering into a wiser period. It is more powerfully explanatory of the contemporary condition, yes; it is more visibly familiar to us, yes; and the connective tissue of cause and effect becomes clearer, yes. Thus we study it in greater detail than that which has gone before. But "modern" does not suggest the end of a journey or even its midpoint, because no one except the deeply committed ideologue and the religious fundamentalist can feel secure in declaring that the destination is in sight, not to speak of describing what that destination is. Let modern then simply stand for the interconnectedness of life, growing more so over the centuries until the command of the English writer, E. M. Forster, "Only connect!" (1910) becomes the cry for today.

## *The Age of Discovery*

Western European societies had long looked outward, even during the so-called Dark Ages; but they had limited their interests, even in the spiritual realm, to lands that could be reached without sailing on dangerous and uncharted open seas. However, from the latter part of the fifteenth century until the end of the eighteenth century, Europeans became aware of, explored, and in part conquered, a variety of new lands across the seas they had once feared. This resulted from the dynamic conjunction of a number of developments that concentrated unprecedented power, energy, and technology within Western Europe, that portion of the continent already oriented toward the sea.

Commonly, western historians refer to the period roughly between 1415 and 1799 as the Age of Discovery. Between these years the rough dimensions of the continents became known and incorporated into the

## Expansion of Europe, 1529

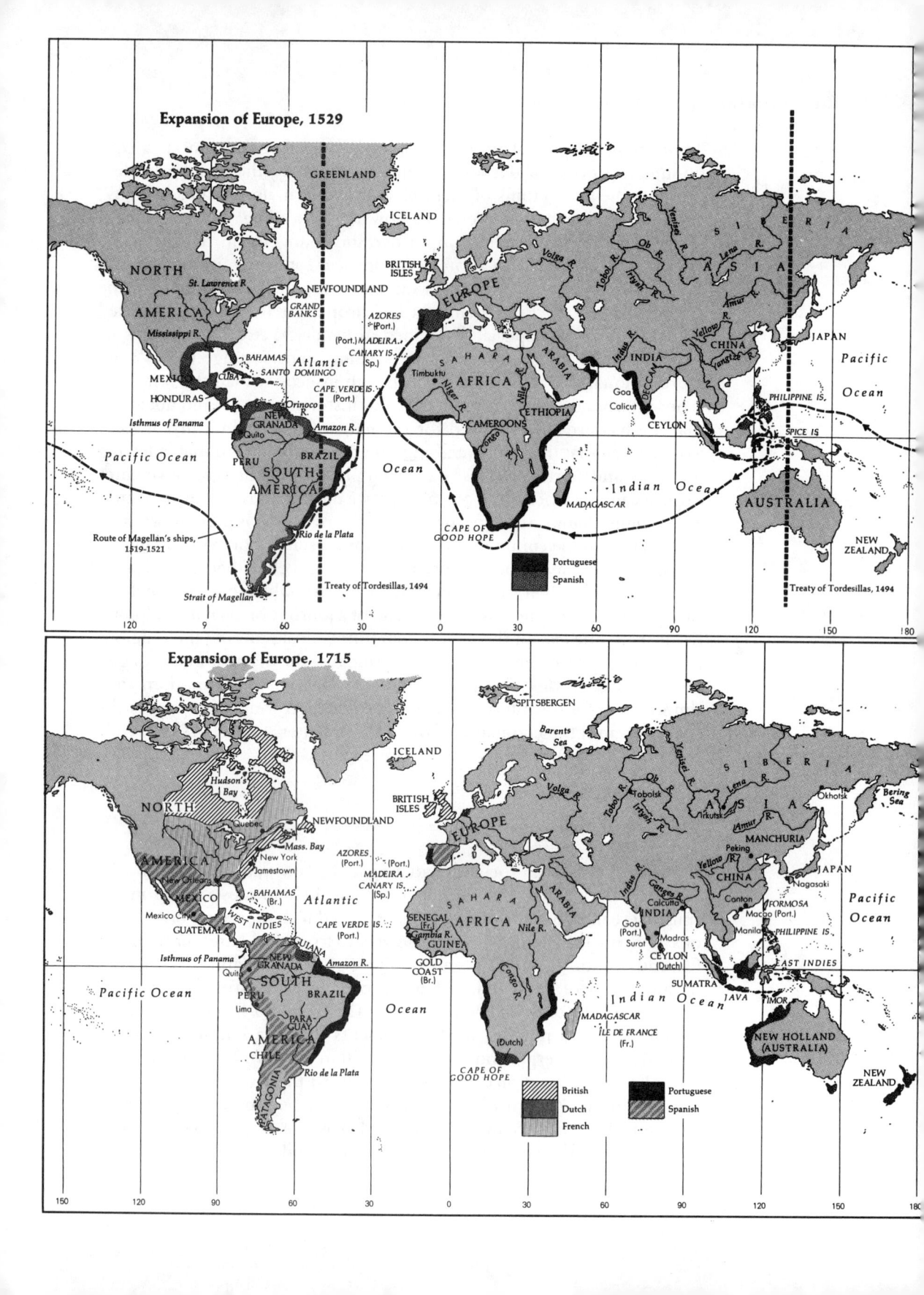

## Expansion of Europe, 1715

consciousness of the European mind. The Europeans and the historians who wrote of them betrayed a particular bias when they spoke of this as the Age of Discovery (a bias that remains with many of us today), for the millions of Asians and Africans were not waiting to be discovered. Long before the "discovered" began to play an important role upon the world's stage, their cultures flourished. Although history books may say that Jacques Cartier "discovered Canada," the Indians living there did not know that it had been lost.

An act of discovery is often one of perception, seeing something that has been present all along. At other times, "discovery" is a convenient word to use in describing the sudden thrust of a high-technology society upon one of low technology. We are dealing with two levels of reality: one is what the Europeans thought to be true; and other is the reality of the native peoples. The Age of Discovery, by its very title, betrays that it refers almost solely to the European view. It was the primary outward thrust of an explosive society and the motives that caused this thrust that inspired two later periods of major exploration. In the nineteenth century, Africa's interior in particular became known to Europeans. In the mid-twentieth century, outer space was the target.

The discoveries of the seventeenth and eighteenth centuries were the product of a remarkable expansionist drive. It produced the great empires acquired in succession by Spain and Portugal, by the Dutch, and by France and Britain. Later, as other nations gained colonies around the globe, they spread forms of government and culture predominantly European in origin. Everybody was colonizing: Belgians, Danes, Swedes, Germans, Italians, Russians, Americans, Australians, New Zealanders. There were non-European thrusts for empires, too. Arabs, Mongols, Chinese, and the Fulani enjoyed their own ages of expansion. Japan acquired an empire of its own in the twentieth century. Just as the Assyrian Empire both created and attracted satellite civilizations, so too did the new empires. Just as a Chinese imperial order made a *Pax Sinica* possible, so too was there a nineteenth century *Pax Brittanica.* Just as the medieval empires broke down, so too did the new European ones by the mid-twentieth century.

The Age of Discovery, then, was also an Age of European expansion. Southeast Asia, China, and Japan were not considered known, were hardly "real," until they were opened to European commerce, ideas, and people. The very geography of the world became European, with place names oriented strictly to the European map. The Near East, Middle East, and Far East were near, middle, and far with respect to points in Europe. This terminology is one of the persistent inheritances of the great age of cartography when the world emerged for the first time upon maps, *cartolani* (sea charts on a flattened perspective), and charts. It is a terminology employed at the deepest levels of the Western mind. Until recent years, even the settlers of Australia referred to Japan as Far Eastern, although it was neither far nor eastern from Australian shores (a fact now recognized in a new Australian phrase, Near North). Europeans gave entire peoples names the peoples did not know. They named the Maori of New Zealand, who had no collective name for their many tribal groupings. The Navajos of the American Southwest were so designated by the whites who infiltrated their lands. In a sense, the modern age began with the great explorations.

## *The Bases of Expansion*

The principle inheritance of the Age of Discovery was the complex, yet simply spoken medieval notion that all people were one under the same God so it was the Christian destiny to unite the world. This Christian doctrine emphasized the universality of humankind—that all lived in One World. Some aspects of Christian thought were translated almost directly into action in the eighteenth and nineteenth century empires. The British, for example, convinced themselves that in leading native peoples toward a distant goal of political independence, they were putting the doctrine of stewardship into practice or trusteeship (the idea that "advanced" people have a responsibility for the "less advanced"), which was argued by St. Thomas Aquinas. But with the Reformation, Christian thought worked to separate rather than unite humankind.

In practice, all people were clearly not one under God. Nor was Christendom united. Much earlier, by the middle of the eleventh century, Christendom—a series of independent states under the spiritual control of the papacy—had replaced the idea of a single Christian empire. Rome and Byzantium had polarized Christendom. In the East, no ecclesiastical authority had successfully contended against a politicized empire, while in the West the Pope had revived the ancient notion of a Roman Empire. A dual inheritance was handed to bustling, inquiring sixteenth-century Europe. In lands that were becoming England, Spain, France, Italy, and Germany, the tension between theory and reality helped propel people into the outer spaces of their world. Their acts of discovery helped define their national identities, shape their national rivalries, and change their national economies. From the Age of Discovery came, in part at least, the national state, and the state-supported exploration. In search of universality, which instead turned up diversity, Europeans were the first to open up the truly unknown and weakly defended lands. In the former category was the New World, a term invented by Europeans. The latter included the Pacific (judged peaceful by Europeans only), Southeast Asia, and Northern Africa.

Not all people responded to the idea of Christendom in the same way. For some, including many crusaders, the superiority of Christians to Pagans, Jews, and Moslems produced the anti-Semitic outbursts of late eleventh- and early twelfth-century Europe. It also caused the perverse indifference to Islamic culture that colored pre-twelfth century Christian-European attitudes. In the twelfth and thirteenth centuries heretical sects joined Jews and Moslems as enemies of the faith. And in the fourteenth century, new foes were added—witches.

Witchcraft and sorcery operated at the highest and lowest levels of European society and constituted a much more formidable threat to state security than either the dogmatic and political battles of the Reformation or the revival of Islam under Turkish leadership. To both the farmer and the ruler, the activities of the witches often served as explanatory devices for domestic and political disaster. In a world full of opportunities for natural disaster, the widespread acceptance of witchcraft and the phenomenon of witchcraft persecutions between 1450 and 1650 constituted a new strategy for attempting to achieve a form of psychological security in a troubled and unpredictable world. For the world held many new wonders requiring explanation.

The most singular new land discovered during the great age of exploration was one that existed only in the mind: Sir Thomas More's (1478–1535) island of Utopia. More's explorer, Raphael Hythlodaeus, who sought the perfect society, was "more anxious for travel than about the grave"; he was a man of infinite curiosity. More's *Utopia* was published in 1516. It captured perfectly the spirit of the Renaissance, which was embodied in the fictional Hythlodaeus and in many men of flesh and blood as well. Governments wanted to find bullion and spices to enhance their prestige and their power, but the common seamen and their captains who engaged in the voyages had mixed motives. Too often the Age of Discovery is seen as an age of Great Men. It was this. But it was an age of the Common Man as well.

The seamen were ignorant, superstitious, and tough. They too wanted riches, but they would gain little from their voyaging, and that little at great risk. The odds were against their ever returning—storm, disease, or war would take its constant toll. Their work on board ship was exhausting. One seaman complained that he was "tired of being always tired." Yet no voyage was forestalled for want of a crew. Governments paid for the explorations, and pay was therefore relatively certain. Life expectancy on land was 30 years; on sea, a bit less. In truth, the most important motive probably was one that has driven people on ever since: a desire for personal glory. Martin Frobisher, who in 1576 searched for a northwest passage to the Orient for England, called it "the only thing of the world that was left yet undone whereby a notable mind might be made famous and fortunate."

The courage of the explorers came partly from the new inquisitiveness and boldness of the Renaissance, when all things seemed possible. That attitude combined with the traditional fatalism of the earlier age of faith. Most seamen felt they were in God's special care. During a thunderstorm, if electricity glowed from a masthead, St. Elmo was riding with them. When a new land was discovered, it was given the name of a saint. Ludovico Varthema, who sailed from Venice in 1502 to Arabia, India, and Southeast Asia, was "determined to investigate some small portion of this our terrestrial globe." That sentiment was popularized by Shakespeare in *The Tempest* (1611–12). This, our terrestrial globe, was a physical encyclopedia in which people roamed for knowledge, for curiosity's sake, for excitement, and for the greater glory of God, as much as for gain. When governments or merchants added their sponsorship to such impulses, men would not only leave Europe but would try to plan well enough to return.

What voyagers saw and what they reported were not always the same. New worlds were expected to be strange and romantic, and sea travel was meant to be dangerous. When the printing press and the rise of vulgates (common speech expressed in writing) created reading publics, audiences expected new thrills to emerge from the unknown. When the first Europeans saw the Maori of New Zealand, they thought them to be 10-feet tall. When they found no gold, they readily listened to Indian tales of nearby cities where streets were paved with it. They went on searching, as Francisco Vásquez de Coronado did in North America in 1540 to 1542 for the Seven (lost) Cities of Cibola. When they found no remarkably new peoples, they persisted in seeking them out. They searched for decades for an island where the Amazons, a nation of warlike women who needed no men, were said to live. The conviction that something more strange, more rich, more challenging lay around the next corner, on the next island, in the next bay, drove Renaissance explorers onward in their incessant, prescientific curiosity. Myths were born, recorded in print and engravings, and preserved. Yet, the Age of Discovery forced people to make objective observations as well. It slowly eroded the medieval tendency to understand new objects only in terms of associations. ("This strange new animal, the elephant, reminds me of a rope, a tree trunk, a house.") People began to think in terms of the objects for their own sakes. Renaissance explorers thus also contributed to the scientific method emerging in the sixteenth century: to observe, hypothesize, and experiment.

### *Early Capitalism*

At this time European economies were changing, which quickened the commercial impulse and made people increasingly acquisitive, secular, and experimental. A new agricultural and commercial technology was growing out of the old forms of agrarian life and exerting itself upon the old medieval cities. Whether Portuguese, Spanish, Dutch, British, or French, explorers went abroad not for God or glory alone, but for gold as well.

Customarily one speaks of a commercial revolution. Perhaps there was no revolution as such, for the changes were gradual, rational, and individualized. Revolutions ordinarily are swift, violent, emotional, and expressed *en masse*. Yet the changes in economic thought and practice were so profound between 1350 and 1650 that they were fundamental to virtually everyone's life in western Europe. Further, the economic modes of society today may still clearly be traced to the commercial revolution, its attendant price revolution, and the eventual industrial revolution of the nineteenth century. During this period occurred both the rise of capitalism and the shift from town-centric to nation-centric economic systems.

In the Middle Ages, towns protected themselves against competitors with their own tariffs, which fragmented economic patterns in hundreds of ways. Many towns hoped for autarchy, the Greek notion of self-sufficiency, in which skilled craftspeople who were organized into guilds provided the shoes, benches, or other daily needs of the community. The outlying countryside would provide the necessary produce. Agriculture and manufacturing were linked and focused upon a single place—the market. Few ran the risk of great loss, and few realized great profit.

Some goods were limited by the availability of natural resources, of course. Not all towns could produce their own clay for pots, their own grazing land for animals that would provide cobblers with hides, or their own food supplies. Goods were traded across long distances—increasingly so, as modes of transport improved. But guild masters could not superintend local manufacturing with the precise care they once applied if the shoes that left their workbenches were destined for customers they did not know. In particular, they could not know what price their products would command under radically different circumstances in some distant country. They needed a liaison, and the larger operation demanded someone with capital who could afford to invest in quantities of unsold goods that would be stored in a warehouse for sale later. (In the East, storage was in a factory, which was originally a place where a factor, or agent, kept the stock, not a place of manufacture.) A person with money to spend on stocks that might remain dormant took the risk of selling them at lower instead of higher prices. This agent might know relatively little of the actual process of manufacture but had to be an expert in problems of international economies and knowledgeable in many currencies. The entrepreneur was such a person. The Medicis performed this function for Florence from the fourteenth century until the sixteenth century. The Fuggers filled the same office as merchant bankers, for Germany from the mid-fifteenth to the mid-sixteenth century.

Overseas trade, in particular, required new and imaginative entrepreneurship. The Fuggers helped underwrite Portuguese trade with Asia by providing credit advances for cargoes. But the Portuguese had little that Asians would buy, so the cargoes taken to the East were metals produced chiefly in Germany. Furthermore, for a time the Fuggers controlled the distribution of cargoes brought back from the East, because they had provided the outward cargoes. They could therefore dominate the economic life of cities well-removed from their traditional center of Augsburg. Because overseas exploration required even more willingness to take risks, and profits from the relatively stable trade with the East were large enough to make voyages into the unknown, which was unattractive to all save the most daring, most avaricious, or the most nationalistic, the Fuggers declined just as the Hapsburgs, to whom they had loaned overly great sums, had done. Other less spectacular if more enduring families filled the gap, often in specialized areas where knowledge of markets and trade routes could be more precise.

In the long run, England and France were the chief beneficiaries of the new changes. Until the fifteenth century, England exported raw wool and imported finished wool goods from Flanders. This mutual relationship helped industrialize the mainland in a primitive way, but it left England predominantly agrarian. Large enclosures were devoted almost solely to the sheep from which the wool clip was taken. The English wanted the profits from manufacturing as well as from primary production, so they began to develop their own spinning, weaving, and dyeing methods. To avoid the regulations of the guilds within the towns, entrepreneurs put the relatively simple work of spinning out into the homes of country people. This "putting out" system, or "domestic" manufacturing, spread quickly, for it promised large profits. It placed the workers at the mercy of the entrepreneur who owned the loom, and it broke the monopoly of the town, allowing "new money" to get a foothold within the economy. Individual weavers, paid by the piece, also worked with the merchants to develop new techniques for increasing productivity; and the cloth merchants of Rouen, in France, helped develop a simpler, cheaper, less bulky (thus less expensive to transport) woollen cloth. Because the guild rules of Rouen, which were designed to protect local workers, prohibited the introduction of the new cloth, French merchants carried it to the countryside in 1496, creating cottage industries throughout the region. This pattern of household industry remained representative until the late eighteenth century.

Capitalism was essentially European. While trading systems thrived in the Far East and Africa, and the Arab trader was a common figure in the European markets, a group of circumstances set European trading methods apart. The period between 1550 and 1650 was a particularly rich one for the merchant, the speculator, and the profiteer, especially in the northwestern countries. Capitalism was based upon the profit motive, and the Protestant Reformation made profit ethical; outward success was a sign of inward grace. Production was now for profit, not only for subsistence. The tools of production were owned neither by those working with them nor by the state but by people of means who acted as supervisors over production. Later, superintendents and managers were hired so that the investors could become long-range planners. Aggressive and well-organized, these businesspeople were vital to the nation's security. The state aided them with protective tariffs at home and trading privileges abroad. Having surplus money, they could experiment with new vessels, new routes, and new methods of manufacture. In an age when war was commonplace between states vying for dominance, they were able to meet the needs of the military. At first, they were the source of weapons; then as armies were organized along national lines, they provided uniforms, barracks, and fortifications. After the horse was replaced by mechanized mobility in the late nineteenth century, businesses supplied means of transportation. Early capitalism reached its height in the nineteenth century and gave new stimulus in 1856 with the creation of limited-liability companies. In those companies, risk of loss was limited to the actual amount an entrepreneur invested. In such a conjunction of circumstances, the European capitalist achieved an economic breakthrough. A revolution in the organization of trade and production thus became the dominant feature of economic life in the West until the twentieth century.

The domestic system was helping to create a new class system. Workers took wages for their work, worked as their employer wished, specialized in a specific job, and cared little about how that job fitted into a larger pattern. Because they could be laid off in times of economic depression, and because the birth rate appeared to assure an expanding work force, they represented low-risk labor to the capitalist. The owner was the only person with the total vision. He bought the raw materials and divided them among peasants who worked at looms that he owned. He paid exact wages that were calculated in advance. He coordinated all activities including the final sales of the finished product. He might even have a local monopoly over sales, which gave him a hedge against loss in an international market. While his risks continued to be considerable, they were more predictable than they were in a guild-and-liaison arrangement. Because woollen goods were not perishable, inventories could be built up and risks could be cut, although not quickly, by reducing the labor force, thus reducing dependence on unreliable workers. Within metropolitan centers such as London, great guilds of drapers arose. The wealth of their enterprising members placed them in positions of power within town politics. The original masters of the guilds, who controlled the knowledge of the craft but not of market conditions, virtually became wage employees, although of a higher status than the peasants.

Not all industries were organized around towns, of course, for many were international by their nature. Shipbuilding, the supply of weapons to armies, mining and other extractive industries, and printing—because presses were expensive and Latin was an international language—are examples. Growing trade with the East also increased the need for places to store and distribute bulky goods. At first tea, sugar, and rice were the principal commodities. Then, as shipping increased with international trade, naval stores were added to the list which held timber, resin, tar, and rope. These goods were originally drawn from the heavily forested lands of the Baltic states and Russia. Trade in heavy goods and staples requiring merchants who had much fluid capital at their disposal intensified the swing to capitalism.

Businesses needed to borrow money, and bankers expected to earn money by charging interest on their loans. The Catholic Church, however, discouraged bankers from charging interest, and this hampered both lending and the flow of capital. Certainly, early interest rates, which often approach thirty percent, were avaricious. Although Luther and Calvin, too, frowned upon interest taking because they considered it usury, their successors found that it was possible to define a "legitimate return" (and later a "just price") on loans. As borrowing developed into a custom, interest rates fell and bankers turned into respectable members of society. An emerging middle class could see the material benefits brought by the productive employment of capital.

Seventeenth-century Amsterdam served as the banking center of Europe. The merchant, now a distinct social type, flourished in the Italian and German states, in England, Scotland, France, the Lowlands, and in parts of Portugal and Spain. Buying and selling goods dominated many bustling towns. People came to them from the country, bringing their cottage handicrafts to store or distribute. Technology and political systems changed under the influence of people in search of profits.

Europe was fortunate at this time in experiencing what has been called a price revolution. Originally, precious metals were the medium of exchange. As Spanish ships brought unanticipated quantities of gold and silver back from the New World and elsewhere, the quantity of metals in circulation rose faster than the quantity of goods produced, so the value of the metals fell. This forced a rise in prices, because prices were directly related to the value of the metals, and more metal of higher quality was now put into given objects. Between 1550 and 1600, prices doubled. Those with fixed incomes suffered because their money would buy less. But those who had taken loans before the onset of rapid inflation gained because they paid in terms of the earlier amount rather than the current purchasing power. Also, as a result of this price revolution class differences increased.

Governments, in particular, were caught in the price squeeze. They needed larger armies and had to pay the mounting costs of more frequent wars. But Crown properties remained fixed in value. Many monarchs resorted to devaluation of their coinage. Others borrowed heavily. In France, government positions were sold. England sold monopolies over potential areas of development. "Merchant adventurers," entrepreneurs who could join together to take substantial risks, bought these monopolies in trade and in American settlement. The East India Company, chartered in 1600, was the most famous and productive example. The Royal Muscovy Company (1555), the Virginia Company (1606), Hudson's Bay Company (1670), and Royal African Company (1672) were similarly created.

Kings often attempted to solve the problem by requesting new powers of taxation. The increasing number of merchants in parliaments, however, wanted to keep costs down. They opposed those who accepted the king's powers as stemming from divine right. Tension heightened. The problems stemming from inflation lead parliaments to grant new taxes only in exchange for new political powers. This contributed to the final victory of parliamentary government in England. But only the absolute monarchies on the Continent seemed able to cope with inflation.

The social differences between western and eastern Europe were also intensified by the price revolution. In western Europe, the landed aristocracy suffered most. Peasants, selling their farm products from their own small lands, gained from rising prices, while those who owned the manorial estates were tied to fixed incomes. Often the nobility was forced to sell land to the rising merchant class. On the western part of the Continent the now dispossessed landed gentry often turned to the professional army as an occupation befitting the nobility. This further strengthened the sharp class barriers already present in the military. In England, however, many squires made the painful transition to "counter jumpers" (merchants) themselves. Others were able to hold on by using the new lands they had acquired from the monasteries for the production of wool.

To the contrary, the nobility grew in power in Poland, northeast Germany, the eastern Baltic, Russia, Bohemia, and Hungary. The peasantry there had not secured such carefully defined rights as in western Europe, and the gentry could force them into serfdom by exacting higher dues or unpaid labor. Typically, a peasant was able to retain land only by working three to four days each week for the lord of the manor. (Forced labor was called *robot* in Bohemia, hence our word for an automatic or unthinking machine.) Eastern peasantry remained illiterate and tied to the soil. Western peasantry slowly turned into farmers and were free of most forced labor. The West grew rapidly; the East stagnated, unable to take part in the most productive developments of the commercial revolution.

Of these developments, the one most closely related to Europe's expansion overseas was the emergence of an economic theory called mercantilism. By popularizing the concept of the "favorable balance of trade," this doctrine provided the final rationale for national competition in the exploitation of overseas resources. In mercantilism, the Age of Discovery and the commercial revolution merged and the price revolution found its solution.

### Mercantilism

As often happens, the word mercantilism—like Methodism, or Protestantism—was popularized by its enemies. Most notable among them was Adam Smith, the great free-trade advocate of the eighteenth century. In 1776 Smith wrote *Wealth of Nations,* which eventually became the Bible of the laissez-faire school of capitalism. It advocated free trade and competitive private enterprise. As Smith noted, mercantilism was an expression of an earlier phase of closed- rather than open-ended capitalist practice. Mercantilism (created by a group of economic theorists known as the physiocrats) was protectionist, nationalistic, and monopolistic. Mercantilist thought held that a nation was strong only when unemployment and begging had been eliminated, when regulations could be applied to a large rather than to a local area, and when a national market created a national labor supply.

Mercantilism identified wealth with money; accumulating gold and silver, or bullion, must be the chief objective of economic policy. A director of the East India Company wrote that because the flow of money is dictated by the balance of trade between nations, a ruler's primary economic goal should be a balance of trade favorable to his nation. This balance would prevent a scarcity of money and forestall inflation. Further, mercantilists maintained that there was a limited supply of bullion. By depriving another nation of gold and silver, therefore, one weakened a potential enemy while strengthening the domestic economy. Treasure was essential. Precious metals were easy to carry in relation to value; they would not perish but would retain their currency and could be divided into pieces. To achieve a balance of trade, nations designed regulations that fostered exports and discouraged imports. They paid bounties to merchants who developed export markets and imposed tariffs and other forms of taxation on those who sought to import goods. National manufacturers could then hope to achieve a monopoly within their home market.

Economic regulations actually were created to deal with specific situations, and the mercantilist theory later was used to justify earlier actions. Between the mid-sixteenth and mid-eighteenth centuries, England and France espoused mercantilism as a form of economic warfare upon each other. A growing awareness of the corporate nature of the new nation-state combined with fashionable, scientific notions about the necessity for equilibrium in all things. This led to a definition of economic warfare that was often beneficial to the merchant class alone. A strategy was required to aid in the acquisition of treasure, and in 1622 a Royal Commission set up in England provided one to deal with the trade depression that had arisen from inflation.

The findings of the commission were representative of much of imperial development. Britain was engaged in a continuing crisis that lasted until 1815. She fought a great war for her empire, at first with Spain, then with the Dutch, and finally with France. The strategy of 1622 was meant to deal with the Dutch which were then the richest nation in the world. Increasingly an enemy of Britain because of the prevailing economic theory, the Dutch amassed their wealth from shipping and herring fisheries that lay along the English coast. The Royal Commission determined that

1) Dutch herring fisheries must be taken over by British seamen.
2) English ships and merchants must stop supplying Dutch merchants with wool (for although the export of English wool was prohibited, English entrepreneurs had continued to feed Dutch industry by transshipment of Spanish and Turkish wool).
3) England must not export any raw materials connected with the cloth industry to Holland.
4) Britain must stimulate home manufactures especially in linen, hemp, and flax to reduce the need for imports and alleviate the drain on her treasury.
5) Foreign merchants who earned money in England as importers must spend that money on English goods.
6) All goods from abroad must come in English ships to promote the shipbuilding industry, or in ships belonging to the country producing the goods. In that way Britain would eliminate the Dutch liaisons.

The larger expressions of mercantilism emerged from these essentially defensive decisions, and they were executed under the pressures of the European economic crises in 1657 and 1662. England set out to remake herself. Wastelands were turned into productive land, which raised the value from six pence to ten shillings an acre. This added to the power of the gentry. The currently accepted principle of international law, that of Hugo Grotius's (1583–1645) *Mare Liberum* (open sea), was challenged by John Selden's *Mare Clausum* (1635). By 1663, the King and Parliament passed acts that made mercantilism the prevailing economic system. The new laws provided that no goods could be shipped to or from colonies except in English cargo ships. The captain and three quarters of the crew had to be English, which kept the profits of the carrying trade at home. The practice also developed a merchant marine and stimulated the navy. Certain colonial produce—called enumerated goods—could be shipped only to England or her colonies. European goods bound for the colonies had to go by way of England, and that turned London, Bristol, Southampton, and Liverpool into distribution centers. The stopover raised the price of foreign goods in the colonies, so that English goods were more likely to be purchased. Trade therefore moved in rough triangles with the West Indies as the pivot. Typically, high-grade fish, now caught by the English, was taken to Catholic Europe. (The Pope's desire to stimulate the fisheries resulted in moral good being attached to making a meal of fish one day a week.) The lowest grade in the fish catch was taken on to the West Indies by way of the new colonies of Massachusetts or Rhode Island. There, rum was picked up and later traded for slaves on the west African coast. The slaves were traded to the West Indies for sugar and molasses, which were taken again to Massachusetts and into rum. Rum was then exchanged along the southern North American mainland for additional slaves and barrel staves. The staves went to the West Indies to form casks for the sugar and the rum, which was again taken to Africa.

This pattern of trade was significant in the following three ways:

1) It was an extreme example of defensive capitalism. Competition was feared because services and other intangible exports were not valued as highly as treasure.

2) The colonies were kept inferior to the mother country, no matter how much intellectual or social flowering might be taking place within them. They existed primarily to supply raw materials and a guaranteed market for British manufacturers.

3) The system motivated the colonists to develop independent political institutions in order to control their economic futures. Ultimately, this led to the first of the great colonial wars for independence—the American Revolution of 1775–83.

Emphasis on a staple trade also determined the form that certain modern nations would take, even down to the present time. For example, New France (now Canada) developed around a succession of staple commodities dictated by mercantilist theory. At first Europe wanted only furs from the northern lands. Long before British settlers had left the new tidewater colonies, French explorers followed the migratory beaver into interior North America. The French became a Gallic Peril to the British that might encircle them. This fear, in fact, eventually erupted in a series of Anglo-French wars in North America. Because the southern, or British, colonists also trapped furs, there was no reason for residents of New France to trade along the North American coast, even if mercantile regulations had permitted. French trade therefore struck directly across the Atlantic to Europe. Later, when Britain acquired New France in the Peace of Paris in 1763, these east-west patterns of trade continued. Cod, wheat, timber, and minerals replaced fur as staples, but all were commodities in which the British seaboard colonies (and later the United States) were competitors. Indeed, competition was a principal reason why thirteen rather than fourteen colonies declared themselves independent of Great Britain in 1776. (Nova Scotia was viewed as part of the original group. Nova Scotia fishermen competed with Massachusetts fishermen for control of the valuable cod economy, and they hoped that by remaining loyal to the Crown, a grateful monarch would assure them a monopoly over the Newfoundland waters.) Patterns of political response, of social development, and of economic welfare—all products of mercantilist thought —continued to be shaped by the staple trades until the twentieth century.

Mercantilism also became the conventional wisdom on the Continent. The French monarchy, weakly financed, inefficient, and under Louis XIV highly expensive, sought to raise revenues through increased taxation and devalued currency. It sold government offices, commissions in the military, and town charters. Louis's chief minister, J. B. Colbert (1619–1683), applied mercantilist doctrine so extensively that Colbertism became a synonym for economic rationalization. He established a system of regulations on tariffs, taxes, subsidies, quality control, and exports. Colbert applied mercantilist principles even more rigidly than the English did, and until the end of the eighteenth century, France remained industrially abreast of Britain. Elsewhere, in Prussia and Russia, the effects of mercantilism were less far reaching. Although the governments fostered industry, there was much less privately owned capital for investment, and neither country could forge a clear link between state and trade by acquiring an overseas empire.

The most dramatic expressions of the merging of religious, nationalist, and economic thought were the companies created for trading with the East Indies: the English company formed in 1600; the Dutch, two years later; and the French, in 1664. Each had the support of the state, each was a monopoly, each was to acquire bullion and each led to empires that involved possession and administration of foreign lands. Merchants came to see the state as an ally rather than an enemy, and the flag began, sometimes reluctantly, to follow commerce. By the end of the seventeenth century it was legitimate for the state, rather than companies, to annex territories. Mercantilism vitalized the emerging industrial states of the West. It joined the new, worldly enthusiasm for gain and growth to the new scientific desire to spread modern technology around the world. It attempted to systematize the pursuit of material ends.

### Scientific and Technological Developments

The Age of Discovery benefited from and stimulated scientific discovery. Precise tools for measurement were devised. Architectural principles were applied to seacraft. New weapons and new industrial processes were invented. Such advances caused multiple effects that sparked other changes—unexpected and sometimes uncontrollable. This scientific revolution is often said to have begun with Nicholas Copernicus, Polish-born and Italian-educated, who wrote *On the Revolutions of the Heavenly Orbs*. Published after his death in 1543, this book used mathematical evidence to demonstrate that the earth moved around the sun (heliocentrism), rather than the sun around the earth (geocentrism), as was maintained at the time. John Kepler, a German, developed this heliocentric hypothesis further. He also used mathematics to show that the closer a planet was to the sun in an elliptical orbit, the faster it moved. When Galileo built a telescope in 1609, he was able to find visual evidence for the Copernican theory. Further, he concluded that the heavenly bodies were probably made of the same matter as earth, and he applied his findings to terrestrial problems. Such conclusions were terrifying, for they cast doubt upon the belief in Heaven as a real place and Earth as the center of the universe. The church condemned Galileo and forced him to recant. (Whether or not he really did so has been a subject of controversy.)

Pure but provable theory preceded practical demonstration of such findings. An Englishman, Isaac Newton, in his *Principia Mathematica* (1687), literally brought the heavens down to earth. He showed that all motion, whether on earth or in the solar system, was amenable to mathematical formulae. After inventing calculus to aid his studies, he concluded that the observable pull of the earth upon its objects was universal to the solar system. From his conclusions, mankind's perception of the law of gravitation and the laws of force remained unchanged until the twentieth century.

The practical effects of Newton's findings were enormous. Now we could predict tides by studying the interplay between earth, sun, and moon. Knowledge of the stars in their courses improved navigation and cartography. An improved calculus made it possible to work out exact curves and trajectories, adding to the effectiveness of artillery. Most important, by breaking the church's monopoly on the study of the heavens, the new theories freed people to speculate upon once routinely accepted canons of thought. No longer were humans the center of creation, but it was the human mind that had mastered the heavens' laws. People were not solely dependent upon God, and all things might be possible to human reason. A desire for hard evidence and for applied knowledge naturally arose.

The impact of the Newtonian discoveries was felt slowly but inexorably in a world already brought to the edge of religious questioning. The revolution in cosmology was as important in the diminishment of the church's power as the Reformation; and the intellectual revolution was as important in the general secularization of European culture as the economic revolution. Not until the nineteenth century did the German philosopher Friedrich Nietzsche declare that "God is dead," but God began to die for many in the seventeenth century. From that time thinkers ceased necessarily to be clergy, and abstract thought was not applied primarily to churchly or religious questions. One of the major intellectual battles of both the church and the "new science" was against the continuing practice of witchcraft in the countryside, against a form of counterculture in the Christian world. The commoner wanted reassuring explanations for natural events, and neither the church in its moral and ethical distance nor the new science in its complexity and abstractness seemed to provide satisfactory answers. A gap began to open with respect to knowledge as science grew in significance and difficulty, until even the learned might not any longer expect to understand the whole of it. How little, then, might the commoner comprehend of the intellectual revolution that was creating a new elite based upon learning of quite a different kind. And how natural that the church would oppose the new learning, fearing an approaching warfare between science and religion—a warfare that only became apparent in terms the commoner could readily comprehend in the nineteenth century.

The search for a means of applying pure knowledge as technology was especially evident in industry, transportation, and commerce. Discoveries in metallurgy and chemistry solved some of the problems. To increase production in an expanding world, however, French and British scientists knew they must find a better source of power. Thomas Newcomen, an English blacksmith, tapped that source when he produced a small steam engine in 1702. Fifty years later, a Glasgow technician, James Watt, developed it into a steam-driven engine that would geometrically increase the available power. Newcomen's engine was used to drive pumps in coal mines, and new methods of drawing raw materials from the earth were invented. When mining technology advanced sufficiently to produce the necessary coal and iron—especially in Britain and later in Germany—the industrial revolution began.

### *Political Organization*

Protestantism, mercantilism, and the new science had broken the old ways of the past. The effects of these changes might well have been diffuse and far less dramatic, however, had it not been for the rise of the new nation-state, and ultimately, of nationalism. A new system of political organization at the national level gave focus to all other changes. National bureaucracies emerged under the dual pressures of external threats and internal dissension.

The old monarchies had much in common, united as they were under a common Catholic faith. Taxation was generally unknown. The feudal tradition, lingering on in eastern far longer than in western Europe, depended upon customary fees and allotted workdays for the lord of the manor. The king was expected to act in concert with his vassals, and from these councils or talks came a variety of parliaments, which included members of the new town-based burgher class. In the thirteenth century such assemblies grew in Spain, Germany, France, and England. They were not representative bodies so much as speakers for the estates of the realm, that is, the collective interest groups within the country: chiefly the clergy, the nobility, and the burghers. The common people played no role in government. The nation was, in effect, its upper classes. In the fourteenth century, the Capetians in France, the reunited houses of Castile and Aragon in Spain, and the Lancastrians in England ruled firmly but with due respect to the estates and to the church.

By the middle of the fifteenth century, a group of new monarchs tried to lessen the power of their feudal nobility, and in so doing helped to determine the direction of the religious revolution then in progress. Enlisting the help of the new middle classes, these monarchs promised peace and stability in exchange for taxes. They sought to put an end to the nobles' private wars, and laid the foundations for territorily defined states. Henry VII (1509–47) led the New Monarchy in England with the Tudors, who wished to curb the growing power of parliament. In France, Louis XI (1461–83) had inaugurated the new statecraft. He built a royal army, applied new taxes, and asserted new powers over the clergy. In Spain, on the other hand, Ferdinand (1479–1516) and Isabella (1474–1504) worked through the church to create a religion-centered Iberian national sentiment, and there the Inquisition focused Spanish thought upon a counter crusade against all non-Roman Catholics. *Moriscos* (converted Moors) and *Merranos* (converted Jews) were suspect, and many of the country's most productive people were removed or fled until an unrelieved orthodoxy prevailed throughout Spain.

### The Early Leadership: Portugal and Spain

The first phase of European overseas expansion was dominated by the Iberian peoples. Geography favored Iberia, laved on three sides by water, only a long stride across a narrow strait from Africa. Four groups of islands stand downwind into the Atlantic Ocean: the Canaries, the Madeiras—later to be developed as a major wine center in the new trade—the Azores, and the Cape Verdes. Portugal and Castille could move toward uncharted waters on short tacks. Spain took the Canaries, Portugal the rest, and Europe was a quarter-way down the Atlantic while the Venetians were still trapped in the Mediterranean. The charts of the time assumed that other island groups lay further to the west, and voyagers did not realize that they were plunging into totally empty seas when they set out from the end of the line.

Portugal moved first, having a dominant position on the coast and a reservoir of navigational knowledge acquired from her Venetian and Genoan mariners. The government, in the person of Prince Henry, The Navigator, saw the need for overseas expansion if so small a land was to survive Europe's constant wars. From Ceuta (opposite Gibraltar), seized from Islam by Henry in 1415, the Portuguese learned of the rich trans-Saharan trade with the African kingdoms of the Sudan where gold, ivory, and slaves might be found. However, Henry sought this trade by sea, being superior in such equipment, rather than by land, and set about systematically opening up the coast of western Africa to European knowledge. Thus it was a Portuguese who first passed Cape Bojador in 1424, the first and most formidable bulge of northwest Africa.

The sea was not, as many had expected, boiling hot. No one of intelligence believed that the world was flat, and once it was seen that its equatorial regions could be tolerated by Europeans, the race was on. In 1487 the Portuguese established a factory on the coast of West Africa. In 1488 Bartholomeu Dias cleared the Cape of Good Hope, and the spice trade was open to anyone with the sea power to seize it. In 1498 Vasco da Gama reached India, and in 1499 Vespucci in all probability discovered Brazil. In 1501 he explored the eastern coast of South America, and the New World acquired his first name, Amerigo. In 1509 the Portuguese were in Malacca, the strategic port that dominated the chief approach to the Spice Islands—eventually the East Indies, which became a Dutch possession and is now part of Indonesia. The age of territorial exploration soon followed, as the Portuguese Christopher da Gama led an expedition to Ethiopia in 1541 and, despite his death converted successive rulers there to a form of Christianity.

And yet, advanced knowledge also hindered the Portuguese, for having a shrewd guess about the true circumference of the globe, they considered an ocean journey due west to the Indies to be impractical. Christopher Columbus, using bad maps, inaccurate knowledge, and poor mathematics proved the Portuguese right and in so doing discovered the New World. He concluded that Japan was only three thousand miles from Europe if one sailed due west, and that only minor islands lay between. After Portugal refused him, he won the ear of Isabella and on August 2, 1492, set sail in three small vessels, using the Canaries as the final point of departure. After a month of sailing, Columbus feared that his calculations were wrong, and on October 9th promised his nearly mutinous crew that he would turn back in three days if land were not sighted. On the third day a low-lying sandy waste within the Bahaman group was seen. Columbus named it San Salvador; we now call it Watlings Island. It was not Asia, although the stubborn Columbus continued to his death to insist that he had found an island offshore to Cipango, the Japan of which Marco Polo had written. Convinced that the unpromising islands they had found were the heralds of true riches, the Spaniards foraged. Only after Vasco Núñez de Balboa stood upon the heights of Darien and looked out upon the Pacific, in 1513, did they realize that they were making lands known to Europe for the first time that the old cosmography had never envisioned. (Leif Erickson had almost unquestionably made landfall on North America much earlier, around 1000, but he had left his knowledge undeveloped.) Between 1519 and 1522 Ferdinand Magellan attempted to complete his theory that ships could circumnavigate the globe; and although he was killed in the Philippines, his second in command brought the surviving vessel (of five) home safely.

The Spanish were rewarded for their persistence in 1518, when they began to develop the first overseas empire at the expense of another, that of the Aztecs. Spaniards had developed a mercenary skill as soldiers who hired themselves out to whomever would pay for them. When, in Mexico, they found that they could fuse their skills with their desire for riches and their wish to make converts of the heathen, they moved with murderous speed and ability. In 1504 a failed law student, Hernando Cortés, arrived in the Antilles, was active in the conquest of Cuba, and was chosen to lead an expedition to the Yucatan. With 600 men, 16 horses, and only 13 muskets (weaponry superior to anything the Aztecs had known), Cortés swept ruthlessly inland. His first act was typical of this ruthlessness: he scuttled his ships, so that his men could not hope to turn back from the dangers they faced. Seizing upon the divisions among the Aztecs, he accepted an invitation from Montezuma, their chief, to enter Tenochtitlan (now Mexico City) where Cortés took him prisoner. In a subsequent battle, Montezuma was killed, leaving the Aztecs leaderless. Nearly overrun by the Indians, who were forced into battle by their priests, Cortés fought his way from Tenochtitlan by night and laid siege to the city for four months. In August of 1521, it surrendered.

Cortés's victory arose from superior firepower, firmer leadership, an ability to play upon the superstition of the Aztecs, and implacable ruthlessness. Most of all it arose from his ability to exploit division within native ranks. During the siege of Tenochtitlan, Cortés used 800 Spanish troops and nearly 25,000 Indians. Thus began the pattern all empires followed for conquering thereafter: dividing to conquer, which created a new and intermediate class of people who were indigenous but for reasons of their own chose to cooperate with the invader. Such people were not necessarily traitors, for they often saw the conqueror as a liberator, having been poorly treated minorities within their own societies. Frequently, they intermarried or intermated with the conquerors, creating new racial classes of *mestizo* (half-breed) or *métis* (mixed-blood) who were often viewed as inferior by the Europeans and who saw themselves as superior to the native populations. Those who aided the conquerors were collaborators, and they were essential to the administration and stability of all empires. The *conquistadores* used them well.

An illiterate wastrel, Francisco Pizarro, repeated Spanish audacity in Peru and displaced yet another empire—the Incas. With his four brothers at his side, Pizarro crossed the Andes, captured the Inca ruler, Atahualpa, by treachery, and offered to release him upon payment of a ransom in gold and silver. When this was paid, Pizarro gave Atahualpa a choice of death at the stake by burning as a heathen, or baptism to be followed by strangulation as a Christian. Thus was Atahualpa converted to Christianity and to death. Pizarro then attacked Cuzco, the Incan capital. In 1535 he founded a new city, Lima, on the coast. Cortés and Pizarro proved that there were riches, established the principles for conquest, and realized the theories of the physiocrats.

In the meantime Portugal was concentrating on Henry's primary goal, Asia. When news of Columbus's assumed discovery of a route to the Indies reached Lisbon, the Portuguese redoubled their efforts. But technological knowledge in Portugal surpassed cultural knowledge. When da Gama reached Calicut, India, in 1498, he brought with him primitive gifts for primitive people, only to find the civilization of India and the sophistication of Arab traders as highly developed and as skillful as anything in Europe. The Portuguese made a mistake common to many mechanically advanced people. They assumed that those who were not as adept as they were at manipulating their environment were retarded in other respects. As a consequence, Portuguese trade was off to a slow start, for traders lacked goods that a sophisticated society wanted.

Still, profits are not necessarily a function of sophistication. The resourceful da Gama collected pepper and cinnamon, and when he returned to Portugal in 1499, he sold them at sixty times the cost of the expedition itself. With profits such as these, the Portuguese learned to adjust quickly to the new markets. They also sought to establish a monopoly in the Near East, denounced the *Mare Liberum,* which they had championed in European seas, as inapplicable to India, and terrorized their Moslem competitors. Finding that the East, for reasons of its own, was as eager as the West for bullion, Portuguese traders became the essential liaisons in East-West trade. They dominated the route around the Cape of Good Hope and the opening up of the Indian subcontinent, itself seriously divided between Mogul rulers in the north and disputatious Hindu rulers in the south. The Portuguese controlled the seas, having superior naval artillery and ships of great maneuverability. Because they wished to extract produce from the country rather than to administer it, they did not need to penetrate inland beyond the ports.

The chief obstacle was less the indigenous peoples than the Arab traders who were already present. The Portuguese governor general from 1509 to 1515, Alfonso de Albuquerque, therefore set out to remove the Arabs by taking control of strategic islands and headlands along the Arab route to the Indian Ocean. Socotra and Hormuz, which he captured, were islands that dominated the mouths of the Red Sea and the Persian Gulf respectively. Goa, on the Malabar coast of India, gave him a port, one that remained in Portuguese hands until 1961. Malacca put him in control over the principal Far Eastern trade route.

In 1513 a Portuguese ship reached Canton, the first vessel from Europe to do so. Soon the Portuguese had a factory and settlement down river from Canton, at Macao, which remains Portuguese to this day. An empire had been built, although it involved the possession of little land, few administrative responsibilities, no hinterlands to be pacified, and a minimum of disruptive contact with interior peoples. The costs of such an empire were low, and because of the strategic location of the islands and ports, the profits were enormous. With Mozambique and parts of Ceylon (now Sri Lanka) added to the network of trading and staging points, the Lords of the Sea truly seemed just that. They broke the Arab monopoly. Overland trade routes continued to be important, for the Turks still moved their goods through the Venetians, but Portuguese spices were Christian spices, and from Lisbon the Portuguese were well-placed to serve the more affluent western European markets.

The sixteenth century was the Golden Age for Iberia. Under the Treaty of Tordesillas of 1494, Spain and Portugal had divided the world outside Europe between themselves. All the lands west of a line running roughly thirteen hundred miles to the west of the Azores belonged to Spain. Lands to the east belonged to Portugal. The Portuguese sent out few colonists and were content to trade; the Spanish wanted more, and they sent settlers to the New World who Hispanized the Indian populations. Then, fearing that the conquistadores would become a new feudal aristocracy, Spain replaced them with administrative officials who imposed royal authority on New Spain.

The first colonial empire was administered by a Council of the Indies, located in Seville and supervised by the Crown. A viceroy in Mexico City and one in Lima had supreme authority in the field. New Spain (which included the Philippines, Venezuela, and the West Indies, as well as mainland lower North and Central America) was governed from Mexico City. The Lima viceroy controlled Peru (which included Panama). These two overextended units were divided into *audencias,* ten in all, which served as councils.

The principal issue of contention between colony and mother country was how to deal with the Indians. Settlers wanted a free hand, in order to enforce labor upon them. The church, however, held that Indians and settlers had equal rights, both being subjects of the Crown. The church

*El Greco's Toledo* El Greco, "the Greek," was born in Crete as Domenikos Theotocopoulos in 1541. His elongated renditions of the human form, of saints, countryside, and even clouds, capture a sense of suffering which is very modern. His combination of religious faith, mysticism, and realism result in an intensely emotional sense of spirituality. This is the Toledo which later would be savaged in the Spanish Civil War of the 1930's. *Source: El Greco Museum.*

also sought conversions and maintained that Christianized Indians had souls worthy of protection. A line of mission stations was built across Mexico, different religious orders being given responsibility for outlying areas. By the end of the seventeenth century, Father Eusebio Kino, a Jesuit, carried the church teachings into Pimeria Alta (Arizona), and in the next century a system of missions and *presidios* (for the accompanying soldiers) was extended into Texas and California. Franciscans were especially active. Church and the State were both perceptive enough to question the legitimacy of their practices in the New World, and both struggled to protect the Indians through a fairly administered system of justice, on the whole without success. Cortés and Pizarro had been brutal conquerors, but the Spanish bureaucrats who followed recognized that the colonial world posed sharp moral issues for a Catholic state.

Gold and silver weighed more heavily than conversions, however. The Spanish discovered silver in Mexico and Bolivia, where they forced native labor to work the mines. All precious metal was brought to royal offices and taxed at one-fifth its value. As a mercantilist nation, Spain exercised a monopoly over all trade through the merchant guild of Seville and a royal Casa de Contratación or House of Trading Contracts. The latter licensed ships, navigators, and immigrants. Licensing immigrants was a way to prevent emigration by Jews or heretics, and exports were strictly controlled to limit the traffic in firearms and slaves. As a valuable bargaining country, Spain could grant another European country *asiento* (permission to trade with one vessel once a year in New Spain).

For a time, Spanish monarchs prevailed in Europe through well-placed marriages. Ferdinand and Isabella sent their daughter to Philip of Hapsburg. Charles V, the child of that marriage, inherited the newly united Spanish kingdom, the Spanish New World, Spanish Italy (Naples, Sicily, and Sardinia), and the Hapsburg lands of central Europe, including Austria. Charles's grandmother also gave him her Burgundian lands, including Luxembourg and the Netherlands. In 1519 Charles was elected Holy Roman Emperor, a position Francis I of France and Henry VIII of England coveted. Only nineteen, Charles faced powerful, determined enemies as he tried to rule over an empire greater than any since that of Charlemagne. Further, he began his reign just as religion, economics, and technology were fragmenting loyalties along new lines. The result was a succession of Hapsburg wars, chiefly with the Valois of France, who forged an alliance with Suleiman the Magnificent of the Ottoman Empire. It was Charles who was forced to accept the Peace of Augsburg and give Germany freedom of choice between Catholicism and Lutheranism. In 1556 he abdicated and retired to a monastery, leaving his son Philip II the major portion of his lands.

Portugal followed a similar course toward ultimate decline. King Manual I's reign (1495–1521) brought Portugal to the height of its influence and sowed the seeds of its decay. He expelled Jews, established the Inquisition, and in 1578 the Portuguese were soundly defeated in battle by the Moors. Portuguese decline seemed to be symbolized in the death of their epic poet Luis Vaz de Camões in 1580. His *Lusiads* (*c.* 1571) was the world's greatest hymn to imperial power. The Spanish invaded Portugal, and from 1580 to 1598 Philip II (ruling as Philip I) united the countries. Portugal was dragged down as Spain disintegrated, and when Portugal regained its independence in 1640 it was much weakened.

Nor had Portugal's empire proved a blessing. Brazil, its largest possession, yielded little bullion and no labor force. By the seventeenth century, Brazil provided sugar and gold, but profits flowed to England, which furnished the manufactured imports the Portuguese economy demanded. Portugal's two million people did not include an unlimited source of effective leaders for its empire. In East Africa and India, human resources were further diminished by racism. Although the Portuguese were not as race conscious as other European nations (they readily intermarried in the New World and West Africa), the virus of racism was strong enough to reject much local talent. The conquerors thus deprived themselves of their only available source of new leadership.

## France, Holland, and England

Conditions were ripe for the new powers. France was prosperous and populous (sixteen million in 1600). England was busy developing manufacturing, a navy, and a sense of national pride. Her belatedly determined explorations had yielded a moving, inexhaustible resource not exposed to vagaries of economic theory, as gold and silver were. On the Newfoundland banks in 1496, John Cabot had found codfish. Grain for her new manufacturing workers was brought from eastern Europe by the Hanseatic League of the north, which also provided access to markets for their products. Timber for new ships came over the Baltic.

Monied classes of France, Holland, and England now regarded trade as a legitimate enterprise. Germany, the mining center of Europe, preferred them as trading partners because they were Protestants or at least citizens of anti-Roman nations. The price revolution was benefiting Northwestern Europe, class mobility was increasing, and forms of democratic government were emerging. Northwestern Europeans, who lived with bitter cold, were prepared to penetrate the Arctic regions, just as Iberians had sailed through the heat of the tropics.

England had become Protestant, although not principally for religious reasons. The king, Henry VIII, was not a Lutheran. He had written a *Defense of the Seven Sacraments,* and was called Defender of the Faith by the pope. But Henry VIII was more interested in his kingdom than in his church. Having no male heir by his queen, Catherine of Aragon, he asked the pope for an annulment, so that he might remarry and beget a lawful son. It was not an unusual request and it had been granted other kings. But Catherine was Charles V's aunt, and the pope feared that he would anger the Holy Roman emperor, so he procrastinated. Henry could not wait, so he installed his own bishop at Canterbury, the Primate of all England, and broke from Rome by declaring himself head of the Church in England. He then remarried, not once but five times, and gained the male heir he sought.

Henry did not wish to see any doctrinal changes in his English church, which he considered Catholic. In 1534 his Parliament declared the English monarch to be the head of the Church of England; and five years later Henry reaffirmed, in the Six Articles, the basic tenets of the Catholic faith. When Henry died (1547), his son Edward was only ten. As Edward VI, he lived only six years, to be succeeded by his older sister, Mary, daughter of the cast-off Catherine of Aragon. In her bitter desire to reassert the true Catholic nature of England, Mary drove away the new aristocracy Henry had created. She married Philip II, soon to be king of Spain, who theoretically would become king of England despite growing

English hatred for Spain. When Mary died in 1558, Catholics considered the succession of Elizabeth—Henry's daughter by his second wife—illegitimate because she was the child of an illegally annulled marriage.

Elizabeth I had no choice but to be Protestant. She was resourceful, tough-minded, apparently barren, and every inch her father's daughter. Faced with a possible Catholic heir to her throne (Mary Stuart), Elizabeth kept her imprisoned and ultimately agreed to her execution. Faced with possible rebellion from English Catholics if she openly helped the Netherlands achieve political independence, she secretly provided the revolutionary Dutch with aid. Because she was confronted with a still formless state church, she led it toward greater independence of doctrine. Latin fell before English as the language of the liturgy, clergy could marry, and in 1563 the Thirty-Nine Articles codified the creed of what was now the Anglican Church. A Church of Ireland was established as well, although most of the Irish remained Roman Catholic, partially as a political protest against their English overlords. Only an implanted ruling class in Ireland embraced Protestantism.

It was a Protestant England, then, which ultimately did battle with a Catholic Spain. In 1581 the northern provinces of the Netherlands declared themselves free of Spain and formed the Dutch Republic (or Holland, the name of the most important province). The southern provinces remained loyal to Philip II (and in time became Belgium). Using them, Spain hoped to reconquer the rebellious provinces. England would not permit this because Elizabeth wanted a divided Spain, and the Virgin Queen sent English troops into the Netherlands.

England was swept by a wave of nationalist fervor. The Dutch and the English were viewed as standing together against the greatest power in Europe and against the Catholic church as well. Their combined raiders attacked Spanish shipping off Europe and along the Spanish Main, on the northern coast of South America, and in the West Indies. Philip II launched a full-scale invasion of England, whereupon Sir Francis Drake darted into the Spanish port of Cádiz to burn the vessels assembling there to join in the invasion.

A great Catholic Armada of 132 ships sailed early in 1588. It was the largest massing of naval power the world had ever known or would know until the nineteenth century. Flying banners to the Holy Virgin, the Invincible Armada planned to sail through the English Channel to the Netherlands, there to pick up Spain's land forces and carry them across to England. From July 21–29, in the most intense sea battle the world had seen, 200 British ships under Drake met the Armada in the Channel. Attacking Spanish vessels individually, Drake's smaller but better-armed, faster craft methodically chopped the power of Spain to pieces. The Armada's crews were baffled by cumbersome commands in languages that not all understood. Fighting with technologically outmoded ships that could not contend with the heavier winds of the northern sea, they retreated toward Calais, only to be forced to sea again by marauding English fireboats. The final destruction was administered by a heavy storm, later called the Protestant Wind. It drove the foundering remnants northward into the icy waters of Scotland and Ireland, for which the Spanish were unprepared in clothing or charts. To this day the visitor may find Spanish coins along the west Irish coast. With these coins sank the Spanish empire, and a triumphant new English nation arose. Ten years later Philip died and his nation was caught in a price-wage squeeze, its industry lagged behind Europe, its people staggered under war-induced tax burdens. The English had gained access to the *asiento*. Spain was a sponge, unable to retain the wealth it gained from its colonies, unable to buy what it required to fight the wars it faced.

Freed of Spanish control, the Dutch proved to be a formidable rival to the English. If the sixteenth century was Iberian, the seventeenth century was Dutch. It was a time of fresh Dutch artists like Franz Hals (c. 1580–1666), Jan Vermeer (1632–75), Rembrandt van Rijn (1606–69); an age of Dutch science, law, and literature. Dutch society was urban, sophisticated, tolerant of new ideas. It was a time of "wood and steel, colour and ink, pluck and piety, fire and imagination." In a strategic location,

*The Syndics of the Clothmaker's Guild*  This painting, by the supreme artist, Rembrandt van Rijn (1606–1669), shows us the artist's sense of human psychology, his mastery over light, and his ability to capture action in a moment of interruption—for the businessmen of the new capitalism have just become aware that we have entered the room. *Source: The Bettman Archives, Inc.*

Holland made good use of maritime knowledge and skill in handling large herring and cod catches. A dense population-land ratio kept domestic transportation costs low. Their successful revolt against Spain turned Amsterdam into a leading European city, as the residents of Antwerp, repeatedly under Spanish attack, fled north. When Portugal and Spain were temporarily united in 1580, Dutch enmity turned toward Portugal. The Dutch were more systematic and careful than the Portuguese. With superior craft and tacit early support of the English, they took the lead over Portugal in the Spice Islands by 1602. It was a good time for merging private trading companies into a single national body. The United Netherlands Chartered East India Company (or V. O. C.) operated a Dutch monopoly in trade and shipping east of the Cape of Good Hope to the Magellan Straits. A second, lesser company was given the trade of the Americas and West Africa in 1621. Two years earlier a Dutch vessel had introduced the first cargo of slaves to mainland North America at the English settlement of Jamestown, Virginia. The companies could declare war, make peace, establish colonies, build forts, maintain armies, and coin money. They were virtually independent in the area of their operations.

When the Dutch ended their war with a declining Spain in 1609, they moved to eliminate the English and Portuguese from the East Indies. They already had forts on the Indonesian Archipelago, and they had a leader equal to Albuquerque. Between 1618 and 1629, Jan Pieterszoon Coen dislodged the Portuguese from the East Indies. In 1641 the Dutch drove them from Malacca and in 1658 from Ceylon, inheriting virtually all of the Portuguese empire east of Africa save for the tiny Indian ports of Goa and Diu, Timor in Indonesia, and Macao. Coen also established a factory on Formosa and pressed the English back to the Indian coasts.

The Dutch then, were the first to establish a territorial empire in the East. Unlike the Portuguese, they were not satisfied with tiny enclaves on island shores. To defend the forts that made it possible to control their monopoly, they entered into treaties with local potentates. Slowly, these treaties drew them into the administration of areas with which they were in alliance. Other nations did not diversify, but the Dutch did, introducing new commodities, especially coffee, which by the early eighteenth century became a major item in their carrying trade. For nearly two centuries thereafter the V. O. C. paid annual dividends of 18 percent. More than any other imperial nation, Holland depended on its empire for prosperity. This affluence was a direct product of the largest merchant marine in the world, the most efficient shipyards, and close links between captains, crews, and merchants, so that all shared in the profits.

The Dutch flag flew over New Amsterdam on Manhattan Island, from 1612 until 1664; over the Brazilian coast from Bahia to the Amazon; over Caracas and Surinam to the north on the South American mainland; over

Curacao in the Caribbean; and from 1652 over the Cape of Good Hope in southern Africa. Here the Dutch influence remains, translated into the Afrikaans culture of the Boers where the hand of Dutch mercantilism was at its heaviest. The Cape, administered from Batavia (Djakarta), in the East Indies, was a way station between Europe and the East, a strategic jewel coveted by the British and the French, and one eventual focus for a rising new empire of the British.

In the long run, Holland lost its mercantile war with Britain. Dutch vessels were the principal targets of the English mercantile acts, and the Dutch nation suffered heavy losses during wars with England between 1652 and 1674. She fared no better with France over the span of 1667 to 1713. Dutch ships had been designed for trade, with maximum space for cargo, and they were unsuitable for sea battle at close quarters. The Dutch decline was relative, and the empire remained largely intact; but no new additions were made, and Britain and France, both slow starters, began to overtake Dutch hegemony. Few ports changed hands, although Ceylon became British in 1815, as did Malacca in 1824. The fundamental imperial rivalry that spread European power across the globe thereafter was the competition between English and French.

### The Great War for Empire

English establishments in the New World followed the Spanish by a century. The Spanish brought the Renaissance; the English brought the Reformation. The Spanish annexed territories where advanced, complex societies produced a "native problem" from the outset. The English created "plantations" (settlements) along the tidewater seaboard of mid-North America. The Spanish were obsessed with conversion; the English, comparatively indifferent to it. English colonies soon had an air of permanence, for between 1620 and 1640 some sixty thousand people went to the New World. English settlements were highly diverse, with especially complex concentrations in New England and Virginia, while the Spanish had attempted a general uniformity of administration and control. Further, the New England colonies, particularly Massachusetts, began in opposition to the prevailing culture in the mother country, rather than as an extension of it. Massachusetts, an oligarchy (governed by a few) or a theocracy (governed by those who claimed to be directed by God), stood apart from the mainstream of development in Britain.

In other respects, English colonies were unusual. The educated class was larger than in the colonies of any other nation. In New England in 1646, when the population was 25,000, there were 130 university graduates, many coming from a single Cambridge college, Emmanuel. Puritans who came to America felt a sense of destiny. They were upon an errand into the wilderness, to set a city upon a hill, which they felt humankind would, in time, observe with envy and awe. Their sense of history sustained them in the face of incredible hardships and ultimately moved their imaginations and their indignation along a revolutionary path. The Spanish, Portuguese, Dutch, and to a lesser extent the French had, on the other hand, thought of themselves as visitors to the new lands. When they made their fortunes, they would return to Europe. The English sense of permanence, of place, and of purpose ultimately prevailed.

Newfoundland, and in Carolina, Roanoke, were the brief beginnings. The first permanent settlement was at Jamestown, in 1607. Plymouth became nearly as attractive a location and started in 1621. When the colony of Georgia was founded (1732), or when Halifax was set upon its rocky Nova Scotian hills (1749), the English dominated the entire eastern seaboard. The French, beginning in Acadia in 1605, in Quebec in 1608, and on Monte Real in 1642, penetrated much further inland, using the St. Lawrence River for communications and trade, but they did not control so diverse an agricultural area. Nonetheless, when the Sieur de La Salle journeyed down the Mississippi River from Canada to Louisiana in 1682, the French demonstrated that they could encircle the British colonies, and they claimed the entire Mississippi River basin for themselves.

After slow beginnings, the English colonies prospered. Initially mercantilism benefited them, for they enjoyed a guaranteed market for their raw materials, the protection of the British navy, and a supply of manufactured goods that were not cheap but of dependable quality. The great irony was revealed after the succession of Anglo-French wars reached their climax with British victory in 1763. With the Gallic Peril ended, followed by a relaxation in mercantilism, the colonists found more in common among themselves than with the mother country. The American Revolution may have begun, as John Adams, one of its leaders and the second president of the new nation, was to say later, when the first English plow cut the first American soil. It was rendered almost unavoidable by the removal of the French threat, a threat that took more than a century to eliminate.

The English colonies were of three types: those formed by chartered companies, those with royal charters to exist as political entities, and proprietary possessions of noble lords. Most were Anglican in outlook, although Massachusetts, New Haven, and Connecticut (and later Rhode Island) manifested various degrees of Puritanism. Maryland was Roman Catholic. New England colonists pursued fishing, lumbering, trapping, and local industry. The middle colonies produced raw materials: Virginia sent tobacco after it was introduced by John Rolfe into England; Maryland, Pennsylvania, and East and West New Jersey provided grain. The West Indies, together with the mainland south from Carolina, developed rice, indigo, unsuccessfully attempted silk, and above all relied upon the highly lucrative sugar trade. The northern colonies were settled by yeomen who wanted only small plots of land. They could not cope with larger areas of the rocky soil. In contrast, from Virginia and south and in the West Indies, plantations developed with gang labor, absentee owners, and aristocratic rule. Each colony had its own governor, a judiciary, and fractious executive council that evolved into a legislative council and later into an assembly.

The strength in the British sense of permanence in North America rested upon these small and expanding representative institutions. The chief bone of contention between royal and local officials was the price of merchandise in the colonies. Prices continued to rise under mercantile regulations, when non-British goods might be obtained more cheaply, if illegally. Economic issues thereby gave rise to political debate, and in the exercise of their political rights the colonists came to strengthen their local institutions. By the mid-eighteenth century, some felt capable of governing themselves in all except matters of foreign policy, defense, and perhaps currency. They also wanted to seize the western lands, but France had claimed these with La Salle's bold act. The colonies acting alone could not hope to gain this land. Only the might of the empire directed against the opposing center—Paris—could hope to do so. Nor were the French in possession of only the interior. They held strategically important islands in the West Indies, notably Guadeloupe and Martinique; and under Colbert's policy they were ready to make mercantile war upon Britain as the British had done upon the Dutch.

### The Modern State

The Peace of Augsburg brought a tenuous peace to Europe for half a century. During that time, the Roman Catholic states with the help of the Jesuit order had eliminated much of the remaining Protestant dissent within their borders. Fearing Catholic unity, the divisive Lutheran princes formed an armed league in 1608. As the two armed camps faced each other, revolt broke out in Bohemia, where John Hus (who had sought to bring religious reform to Prague) had been executed at the stake in the fifteenth century. Bohemia, a part of the Holy Roman Empire, had thereafter been a moderately tolerant land until a new Hapsburg king, Ferdinand of Styria, began enforcing anti-Protestant laws. As the Catholics crushed the resulting revolt, the king of Denmark intervened in Germany, and when Sweden and France also threw their weight against Ferdinand, Europe was caught up in a general conflict, known as the Thirty Years' War, which ran from 1618 to 1648. Germany (the principal battlefield) was devastated.

The war concluded with the Peace of Westphalia, and with it the period of religious wars (except, perhaps for the recurrent war in Northern Ireland in the 1960s and 1970s) was at an end. For Germany, the terms of Augsburg were restored and extended to Calvinists as well. Recognition of the German princes as virtually independent rulers reduced the Holy Roman Empire to a historical anomaly. The decline of the Habsburgs permitted the rise of the Bourbon dynasty in France, which ushered in the French Century. With the Peace of Westphalia, the modern state system began to emerge with greater clarity, for countervailing papal and imperial claims to power were now so weakened that genuinely independent states could rise. The state system thus legitimized endured until the Napoleonic Wars of the early nineteenth century.

Another result of the incredible rape and pillage that was common practice during the Thirty Years' War was an effort to create a body of international law. When the Dutch theoretician of the doctrine of open seas, Hugo Grotius, wrote *Law of War and Peace* in 1625, he defined legitimate states of war and argued on behalf of humane methods of making war. He wanted to eliminate indiscriminate terrorism, torturing of prisoners, killing of hostages, poisoning the civilian water supplies, and other "unjust" practices. Grotius's arguments became widely accepted by the "civilized" or European world and prevailed until the mid-twentieth century. At this time, bands of international terrorists, declaring that distinctions between just and unjust wars worked to benefit their enemies, threatened the traditional definitions of humanity and neutrality that had emerged from the Peace of Westphalia and its aftermath. In this sense the period from 1648 to *c.* 1960 constitutes a secular continuum in attitudes toward the legitimizing functions of the state. The peace also ended the Reformation and Counter Reformation, when wars had been at least as religious as they were dynastic in motivation.

The French Century began badly, with the assassination of Henry of Navarre. Louis XIII (1610–43), the new king, was nine years old, and the queen mother who served as regent was not politically competent, so that Catholic and Huguenot (Calvinist) nobility vied for power. The French Estates General, a representative body, met only once (in 1614) and became moribund until 1789. Only when the young king found a brilliant assistant, Cardinal Richelieu (1585–1642), did France recover her equilibrium. For the next eighteen years, Richelieu was the true ruler, and his goal was to apply the Reason of State to all matters, totally subordinating religious considerations. By the Edict of Nantes in 1598 the Huguenots had been granted many freedoms; in 1628, after defeating an armed league of Huguenots in southwestern France, Richelieu revoked the edict in all but its purely religious clauses. Richelieu also built the first French navy of significance, saw to it that France emerged from the Thirty Years' War strengthened, and promoted French culture.

Richelieu and Louis XIII died in successive years (1642–43), and another succession crisis loomed, only to be averted by the skill of Richelieu's handpicked successor, Cardinal Mazarin (1602–61). His methods were less subtle, however, and he openly enriched himself; resentment brought an uprising of the Fronde (named for the slingshot popular at the time) in 1648–53. Private armies roamed the countryside, and although Mazarin ultimately was victorious, the situation was for a time so precarious that the new young king, Louis XIV (1643–1715), faced a group of rebels who broke into his bedroom.

Louis XIV, although already king, did not begin to attend to matters of state until 1661, when Mazarin died. Thereafter he set out to make himself an absolute monarch, a spokesman for divine-right monarchy, and a creator for France of the truly Splendid Century. For half a century Louis XIV strove to "make the king supreme in France and France supreme in Europe." In both he was successful, working long hours to assure that Europe would imitate the French language, manners, and army. "I am the State," he declared, drawing ever greater power into his own hands. Under his minister of finance, Colbert, an energized French mercantilism rivaled British. Using the arguments of an advisor, Jacques Bossuet, who formulated the royalist propositions in terms of the Bible (justifying the Divine Right of Kings as being subject to no reservations on earth), Louis maintained that resistance to the commands of the king was resistance to God.

The absolutist argument also proved popular in Prussia, Russia, and England, although in the last the principal formulation of it was almost wholly secular. Thomas Hobbes wrote in support of the Stuart kings in 1651, but he used scientific rather than religious arguments to sustain the absolutist case. Politics could be a science, he thought; it was in essence the study of the human's search for security. No individual could be totally secure, thus—as he stated in his *Leviathan*, which was an analysis of the State—people sought to increase security through government, giving up their individually weaker strengths to the collectively greater strength of organized society. Because government was organized to enhance the greater security of all, all had an absolute moral obligation (as well as a rational duty) to obey it. Because he argued in favor of absolute monarchy as a means to supporting the individual's freedoms, however, he was not popular among monarchs, who far preferred the unchallengable arguments of Bossuet.

In 1688 the Glorious Revolution brought William III, Prince of Orange, a Dutch Protestant, to the throne of England. If the Stuarts had no quarrel with the Catholic King Louis XIV of France, William obviously did; in 1689 he began a series of Anglo-French wars which lasted until 1763. Each war carried a European name, for three of the four originated in Europe over European succession issues. Each also had a name popular in the colonies because each involved the empire extensively. The first, the War of the League of Augsburg, or King William's War, lasted until 1697; the second, the War of the Spanish Succession or Queen Anne's War, lasted from 1701 to 1713. The third, the War of the Austrian Succession, or King George's War, was from 1743 to 1748. In these wars the French forged an alliance with the Iroquois Confederacy in North America; the British gained Nova Scotia, Newfoundland, and Hudson Bay; and Frederick the Great made Prussia a power of the first order.

The fourth and final war was different. It began in the colonies in 1754 rather than in Europe, where war was not declared until 1756. At the end, the French Empire was at bay, the British at last victorious. This Seven Years' War, or the French and Indian War, culminated in the Peace of Paris in 1763, in which Britain gained the St. Lawrence Valley, all territory east of the Mississippi River, and predominant power in India. Spain, which had entered the war to help France, gave Florida to Britain. To compensate Spain, France gave her French land west of the Mississippi. France was humbled, retaining only her trading ports in India, a scattering of islands in the West Indies, Guiana, and two tiny islands off the Newfoundland coast. In the nineteenth century a new French empire grew largely in Africa, but it never posed the threat to British power that this first, great French empire had asserted. As the Spanish Empire had gone down with the Armada, so the French floundered in the snows of the Plains of Abraham, above Quebec, in 1759, where the youthful English general, James Wolfe, defeated the brilliant Marquis de Montcalm. They both died as a result of the battle, and the riches of Canada were forever lost to France.

The Anglo-French rivalry was expressed in Africa and India as well. Early in the eighteenth century the French placed themselves across the sea route to India by acquiring Gorée and the mouth of the Senegal River in Africa, and Madagascar in the Indian Ocean. In India, the French challenged the English for their holdings at Calcutta, Madras, Bombay, and Surat. After reorganization of their own East India Company in 1664, the French opened major ports of their own, strategically near their English competitors—Chandernagore below Calcutta, and Pondichéry south of Madras. Both cities could be reached by sailing vessels sailing north prior to reaching the English ports.

At first the Indian rivalry was not intense, for the subcontinent was in turmoil, and the Europeans wished to avoid embroilment. The great Mogul Empire (1526–1761) was disintegrating. Its emperor, Akbar the Great, died in 1605. Fifty years later, the last great Mogul emperor Shah Jahan, determined to impose Islam by force, created chaos and civil war throughout the essentially Hindu lands. Upon Aurangzeb's death in 1707, a dispute over succession displaced five emperors in six years at

Delhi. The traditional local governors regained their lost powers, especially under Maratha (or Hindu) leadership.

Collapse of central authority in India presented an opportunity and a challenge to the Europeans. Internal chaos would stifle trade, and English and French both saw the need to seize control over the warring rulers in order to stabilize the region. Disintegration also made a swift application of European power possible. While no one wished territory for its own sake, all wished profits, and profits required peace. French Governor Joseph Dupleix moved first in 1746, for he wanted wider areas to tax so that the resultant capital could be used to stabilize and stimulate commerce. Having few French troops, he trained Indians in the arts of European warfare and made many Indian rulers dependent upon his sepoys for their own protection. Two years after he was recalled, as Britain and France squared off in the Seven Years' War, the French were able to resist the first British advance because of his preparations. But ultimately the war was won at sea, for even at this distance British sea power told: Robert Clive, an official of the British East India Company, well supported from the sea, marched on Bengal, used Indian merchant collaborators to great advantage, and defeated the local Indian ruler living at Plassey in 1757. In 1761 the French surrendered Pondichéry.

The British victory in the Great War for Empire had been slow, decisive, and, in retrospect, clearly expected. The British had permanently settled in North America; the French had not. The French were divided among themselves, the British were not. The English had swarmed to the New World in search of new freedoms and new soil while the French had been content with their old freedoms (and absolutism) and their old soil, which was rich and extensive. By 1776 a third of the English-speaking world was living in North America. Never had there been so massive a movement of people from one place to another in so concentrated a period. Further, Britain had begun to catch up with France industrially, despite having only a third of the population, and the seventeenth century saw unprecedented growth in the woollen trade, in the use of coal as fuel, and in the harnessing of water power. English sea power—in numbers, skill, and construction—had become far superior to the French. The Seven Years' War was fought on the land, and many young colonists were first blooded by it within the backwoods of the continent (as George Washington was when defeated by the French at Fort Necessity in 1754); but the war was won upon the sea. Britain learned this lesson well, and until the twentieth century British politicians continued to conceive of the balance of power between nations in terms of sea power.

The Peace of Paris in 1763 ended the first great age of western European expansion, with Britain dominant. European ideas, goods, and people were firmly entrenched in all continents except Australia, where

*Washington Crossing the Delaware* The New World required new myths, and the Father of His Country was an excellent subject for their creation. Here Emanuel Gottlieb Leutze shows Washington being rowed across the Delaware River to attack the Hessians at Trenton on Christmas night, 1776. That the scene could not have been as shown here is not to the point, for a legend was in the making, one which would become part of History in the minds of most. *Source: The Metropolitan Museum of Art, gift of John Stewart Kerridy, 1897.*

the colony of New South Wales would be founded in 1788. There, in the Pacific, the age of maritime discovery also came to an end, marked by the voyages of the greatest explorer of all, Captain James Cook. In 1773–1774 Cook twice penetrated the Antarctic Circle and in 1778 passed through Bering Strait into the Arctic sea for England and science. By the time confused and frightened Sandwich Islanders, in what is now Hawaii, killed Cook in 1779, the great race was over. Until 1763 the power of the European states had emanated principally from within Europe; the colonies were appendages of increasing but not decisive importance. Now the empires were seen as decisive, and Britain's supremacy rested upon the fact that she dominated not one continent, but two. Colonialism was now imperialism, North America was now Europe, and Europe was, or saw herself to be, the World.

This World was showing most of the trends that today we call "modernization." Humans now believed that they might learn to master their universe, for the new science was unlocking the heavens. In 1690 an Englishman, John Locke, in his *Essay Concerning Human Understanding,* had shown how the combination of experience and reason produced a scientific method that freed people from the fear of innate ideas. The human mind was a blank page at birth, a *tabula rasa,* on which experience wrote its lessons and from which human reason read the meaning of those lessons. While some knowledge would forever be denied, humans could learn enough to lead rational lives by making choices and seeking security through means capable of being realized. Indeed, the old issues of theological inquiry were dropped, for as Francis Bacon and René Descartes had argued, repeated experimentation could produce general conclusions that led to descriptive truths upon which humans could live on an operational basis. Bacon (1561–1626) used inductive methods—repeated experimentation—and died for them by leaping from his carriage one winter day to stuff a dead chicken with snow to test the effects of cold upon it. He died from a chill he caught when doing so. Descartes emphasized deductive methods in his *Discourse on Method* in 1637, bringing geometry and mathematics to bear on logic and applying a rigorous methodology to reconstruct the picture of the universe. Between them, these thinkers molded the scientific method and prepared the way for Sir Isaac Newton's discoveries. More immediately to our point, they had eliminated the traditional concerns of religion from the field of intellectual battle.

The modernizing century also brought political changes so extensive as to represent that oft-mentioned, rarely real moment—a watershed in time. The slow emergence of parliamentary government in Britain set the stage for the Bill of Rights in 1688. Britain wanted assurance that there would be an alternative to the royal absolutism developed in France. All this took place during the short and intense period of civil war (1642–48) when Charles I was beheaded and the radical Puritan, Oliver Cromwell, established a nonmonarchical government. Holland, and briefly Poland, followed the British model; Prussia, Austria, Russia, and Spain followed the French, which created opposing sets of attitudes toward the state and the direction it should take. The functions, structures, and justifications of governments changed, especially as capitalism grew in importance.

The eighteenth century intensified these changes, brought unprecedented population growth, and ended with the Age of the Democratic Revolutions.

## III. 5 The Modern Revolution in the West

### *The Enlightenment*

There is no single point at which modernization began, but conventionally—and with good reason—historians have associated the beginning of modernization with the Enlightenment. A body of thinkers, largely in France, who came to be called the *philosophes,* applied scientific thought to society in a way that Kepler, Newton, Descartes, and others would have found amateur, but it could be more broadly understood by a larger segment of the population.

The Enlightenment is said to run from 1687, the date that Newton's *Principia* was published, to the outbreak of the French Revolution in 1789. This was, the *philosophes* thought, an age of light, of special wisdom about human nature. There was no longer any need for a God as the Creator of All Things; universal gravitation provided the First Cause. There no longer was either need or justification for miracles, for all so-called miracles should be capable of scientific explanation. The universe was governed by precise mechanical laws that were capable of mathematical proof; this universe could run for eternity without the intervention of God. The world was a machine.

God was not utterly without purpose, however, for while science could explain the operations of the machine, it could not yet account for the origins of the machinery. Increasingly, philosophers saw God as the Creator who then sat by to watch the creation at work, unmoved and unmoving in human events; the Bible introduced God "in the beginning" and this conception was still tenable. Some rationalists turned to Deism, which held that good conduct was still required, for there was a Supreme Being whom one worshipped through such conduct. By the end of the eighteenth century, even this compromise had lost its attraction, for many concluded that there was no evidence for a Creator of Divine Intelligence, and that accident and chance had created the universe, even though it might operate to laws that would endure for all time and that could be mathematically investigated.

The individual was therefore all important. Evil arose not from Original Sin but from bad institutions. Rational individuals should be capable of reforming their institutions to the point that the environment reinforced the good in people. Individuals might so improve so that one day they would realize perfection: perfectibility became central to many *philosophes,* and even to those who rejected it; the attractions of sending individuals in search of their inherent perfection were great. All social institutions should be remodeled in the light of Reason. History studied closely would reveal the mistakes of the past and guide the society of the

*Rodin's The Thinker* In 1900 Auguste Rodin (1840–1917) was the world's most famous sculptor. In 1880 he had created this figure, rugged and romantic, yet realistic, of Man Thinking, and many have taken it to epitomize the intellectual qualities of the Hellenistic civilization. In fact, the bronze figure originally was meant to be that of the great Renaissance poet, Dante. *Source: The Metropolitan Museum of Art, gift of Thomas F. Ryan, 1910.*

future. Nature and Reason would unlock the meaning of all experience. John Locke and Denis Diderot (1713–84) perhaps best represented this conviction, the former in his declaration that all human knowledge grew from experience, the latter in his thirst for knowledge and in his great Encyclopaedia or compendium of all knowledge. Nothing could stop the advance of knowledge.

Perhaps the most important of the *philosophes* was François Marie Arouet de Voltaire (1694–1778). Author of a hundred books, he was his

# Europe in 1715

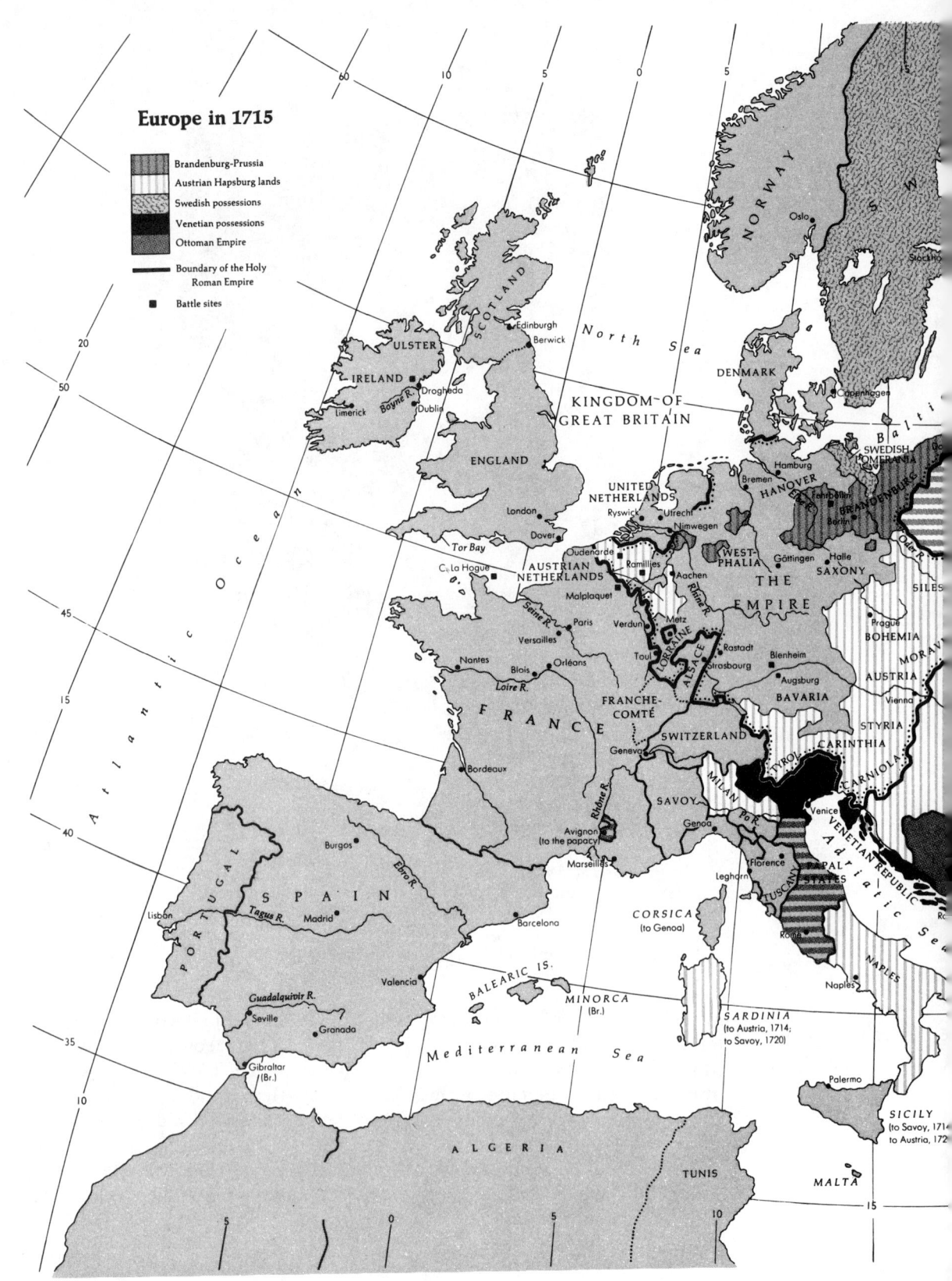

**Growth of France, 1559-1769**

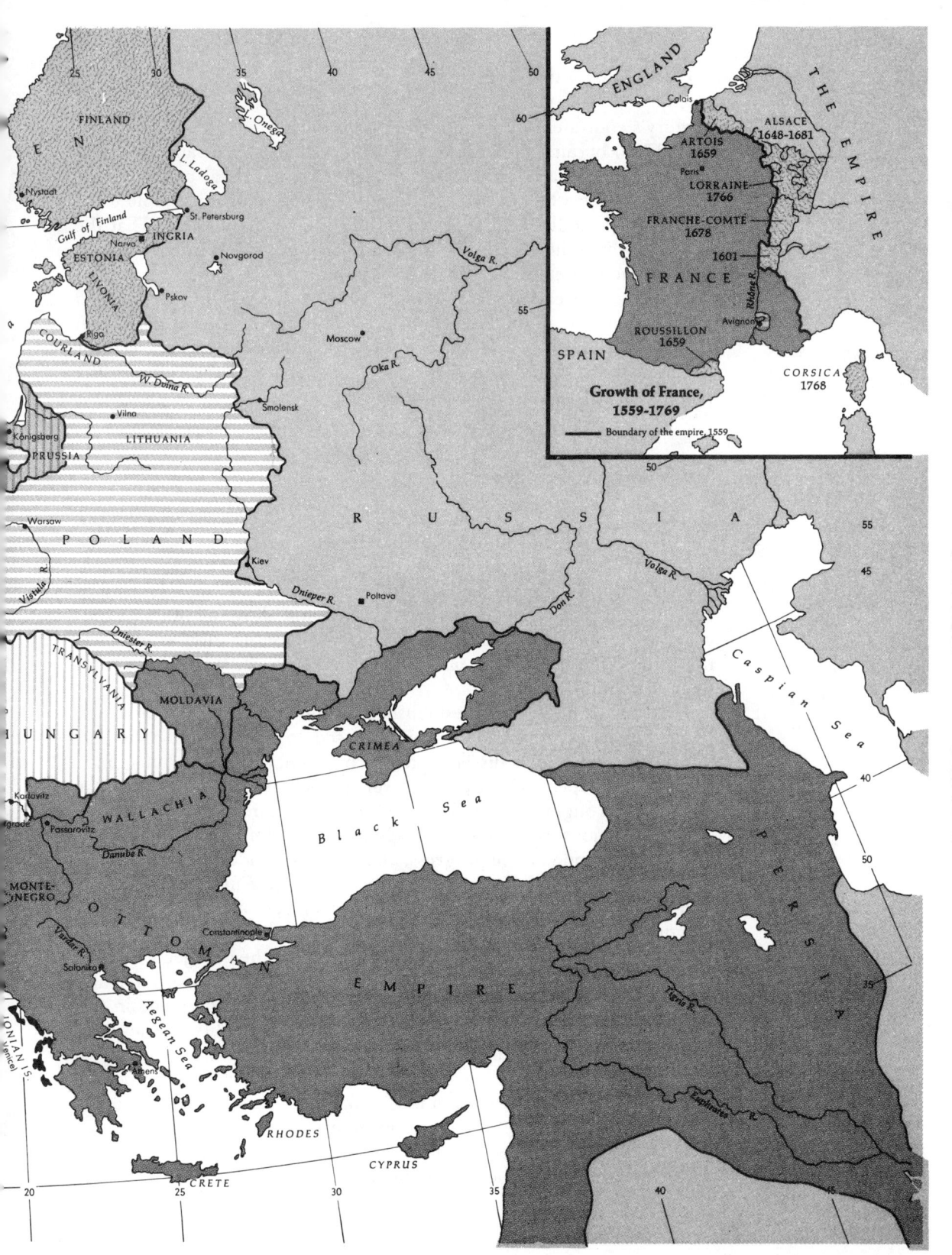

— Boundary of the empire, 1559

century's equivalent of the modern author of best sellers; of these, *Candide* (1759) became the best known. In it, Voltaire used satire to attack religion, war, the aristocracy, and all forms of sham. He also exposed the Cult of Reason when he felt it had gone too far, showing people to be moved by prejudice and superstition more than by intellect. That the world in which they lived was "the best of all possible worlds"—a view held by the contemporary English essayist and poet Alexander Pope—was clearly a falsehood. Yet, Voltaire believed that reason, science, and tolerance (above all the last) could provide progress—if not perfection then a vastly improved life. In so arguing, he helped prepare the way for the industrial revolution and new conceptions about the role of "the people" in the exercise of human wisdom.

### *Changing Societies*

The Enlightenment helped pave the way for the Industrial Revolution, but so too did the Industrial Revolution feed the idea of progress that was so essential to the Enlightenment. Indeed, a number of changes largely associated with the eighteenth century was basic to the modernizing of societies. Of these changes perhaps seven stand above all others, especially when one realizes that the process of modernization as we commonly describe it first took place in Western Europe. Why there rather than elsewhere?

First, the Enlightenment established an intellectual climate in which learned societies grew, knowledge was placed on an organized basis, and information was widely disseminated through encyclopaedias, dictionaries, and newspapers. The *philosophes* were preachers of a kind, urging that governments ought to be for the common good, ought to protect intellectual and religious freedoms, and ought to provide for equality before the law. Change tended to be progress, and progress tended to help humankind take control of the environment so as to increase material and social well-being. Such ideas were not limited to abstract thinkers, for a number of monarchs were enamored by at least portions of the arguments. These "enlightened despots" spoke of the well-being of their subjects, sought to reduce the power of the church, spread religious toleration, and make the State more efficient both in its governmental machinery and in the improvement of agriculture and commerce. The enlightened despots, while hoping to retain ultimate control, were modernizers.

Second, it was ironically not a despotism but an inchoate democracy where the Industrial Revolution first took root—Britain. Here the State actively encouraged the growth of an industrial business class, but the State lacked the power to be directly involved in the processes of industry, so it provided an impetus to individual initiative. Still, whether within a despotism or not, the State as an instrument of change was especially important at this time.

Third, during the eighteenth century there was an unprecedented growth in population. Most countries grew by at least fifty and many by a hundred percent, especially after 1730: the populations of Britain and Prussia doubled, while France increased by half. The century proved to be a warm one, so that crops grew in the far north as never before. Warm weather also reduced mortality and encouraged the transplantation of the new crops from America, which otherwise might not have taken root in European soil. One result was new foods, especially maize (American corn), beans of various kinds, and the potato. The last was central to the growth of several societies (especially Ireland's) for it provided more caloric value in relation to land and labor than any other starch known.

The great cycle of plagues fell to a low point, partially because the more efficient governments, such as that of the Hapsburgs who were able to block the old plague routes from the Middle East, and partially because of the change in diet and climate. In the past, deaths had balanced births; this was now not so. Perhaps 80 percent of the European population rise was a result of the declining death rate. The new populations provided more workers, more markets, and more family responsibilities.

Fourth, men and women began to marry earlier because now they might expect to cultivate a plot of land without waiting to inherit it. In the mid-eighteenth century birth rates rose, as did illegitimate births from perhaps 2 percent of the total to 11 percent. Parental and churchly restrictions on sexual practices, the growth of privacy, the rise of romantic love as opposed to arranged marriages, and the slow removal of the aura of sin around fornication, all helped to increase births. Further, a new conception cycle developed: in the past, births peaked in February and March. Children born in these months, and especially in rural societies, were stunted by the absence of food in these crucial months between planting and harvest. Now, for reasons that are not clear, births leveled out across the months, producing children of greater average size and, it would appear, of greater average intelligence.

Fifth, during this time the aristocracy performed very much as a dynamic minority. Worried about competition from the striving middle classes and in a position to seek new resources and explore applications for those resources, the aristocracy now invested in change, in part to prevent what they feared as greater changes. In a sense they turned to a controlled system of erosion, foregoing certain powers in order to retain the powers they considered to be more important over the long run. As their families also grew, they had to seek new outlets for their sons; while the eldest would inherit the estate, the next might typically enter the military, another the church, and yet another would follow up commercial possibilities.

Sixth, overlapping with this group was another, rising from the middle (and to a limited extent, even the peasant) class: the entrepreneur. Domestic manufacturing grew, especially in textiles. A new group of supervisors arose as intermediaries between the capitalists who provided the raw materials and took the profits from the finished products, and the village peasants who did the actual spinning. These supervisors increasingly became small capitalists, who slowly turned the village artisans into wage workers, reorganized the labor force and its mode of production and method of reward. In time these intermediaries became central to the functioning of the industrial revolution, for they understood the intricacies of actual production and the psychology of the worker far better than the capitalist, who turned more and more to finance and sales alone.

Finally, the changes in religious thought reemphasized the moral legitimacy of making money. Even Catholics now felt that riches were not in themselves sinful. As attitudes toward God changed, so too did attitudes toward death, work, the family, and of course material rewards in the present life. Conditions were right for the spread of the industrializing process that had begun in Britain.

### *The Industrial Revolution*

Only one earlier change in technology could rival the significance of the Industrial Revolution of the eighteenth and nineteenth centuries: the slow change from hunting societies to settled agricultural civilizations. For industrial technology changed virtually every aspect of human life, from perception of time to a need to cooperate with other workers. Now people worked to precise hours, and they had to appear at work at a specific time, for the growing complexity of the new machines meant that one key worker's absence could destroy the effectiveness of an entire team. Clocks and watches, "working hours" and holidays, time zones in large countries, "daylight saving" and other forms of time manipulation resulted from the need to predict the capacity of the work force.

Predictive capacity also required that labor and capital be concentrated in one place so that workers might be brought to the machinery rather than the machinery to them. One steam engine or one mill for iron ore could do the work of hundreds, and the hundreds had to be where the machine was. This concentration in turn led to rapid urbanization: in Britain, Liverpool grew from perhaps 40,000 in 1750 to 400,000 by 1850, the year in which Britain became more urban than rural in its population base. The city also concentrated protest movements more effectively in one place, increased the impact of education, and gave rise to the modern newspaper. In addition, it fed further stages of the Industrial Revolution by increasing urban transportation, building construction, and developing industrially based forms of entertainment.

Perhaps the most far-reaching effect of rapid industrialization (and the rise of the new commercial class that followed) was the shift from status-based to class-based societies. Until c. 1750, the most important possession a person had was birthright, together with the privileges the law conferred because of birth. Aristocracies passed on their status and their wealth through laws of entail and primogeniture, and while one might enter the aristocracy through marriage, the entry point was narrow and closely controlled. The Industrial Revolution (and the French Revolution) ushered in a time when class was more important, when people sought to make common cause with their neighbors on the bases of occupation, income, and expectations. Where status was based on money, there was always hope for the future because hard work could help one rise. The work ethic slowly took hold even in the countryside, although the gap between city and country was at least a hundred years wide. The middle class, in particular, was city based, "on the make," climbing for the top, "counter jumpers" who did not disdain to soil their hands, to take risks, or to accept change where it looked likely to produce more income and a better material life. The city became ever more secular, while the churches remained more deeply rooted in the country.

These changes were first visible in Britain. The growing empire and soaring internal population growth created ready markets for new goods. Successful commerce assured the presence of capital to invest in the new machinery as it was developed. The aristocracy was prepared to think in commercial rather than purely landed terms, while the artisan class had been more fully relieved of the old guild traditions than any other group of craftspeople in Europe. Britain also had the good fortune to have, for the time, an abundance of coal and iron—the staples of industry—and navigable rivers by which they could bring the iron ore to the coal. (France had too little coal, and Germany lacked the natural waterways to bring its coal to its mining centers.) Later Britain added a new thrust to her industrial might by tying her centers together with railroads.

Britain was first and for a time best at industrialization, but ultimately the British paid the price of being a leader: Germany overtook Britain after 1870 by copying and learning from her mistakes, just as the United States eventually overtook both. The industrialization of the United States began when Samuel Slater memorized the plans for cotton-spinning machines—which were illegal to take from Britain—and introduced them to Rhode Island in 1790. Britain was the magnet to which entrepreneurs and governments alike were attracted in the 1790s. Germany and other capital-poor countries relied on government effort to speed the industrializing process while Britain continued to be the center of private initiative. In time, competition between the industrializing nations led to great intercontinental rivalries.

In this complex process, one invention stood above all others: the steam engine, which made it possible to replace animal and human power with the power of machines. In about 1770, James Watt (1736–1819) invented the modern steam engine, which was soon applied to the textile industry, so that one worker could displace twenty. In 1814, when another Briton, George Stephenson (1781–1848), completed the adaptation of the steam engine to the railroad, the Industrial Revolution was turned into the Transportation Revolution, and within fifty years, Britain, Germany, Belgium, and France were transformed. These developments, together with new discoveries in metallurgy by which iron output was greatly increased, doubled and redoubled the impact of industrial change. In 1798 an American, Eli Whitney, engaged in arms production for the American government, developed a system of interchangeable parts, and as machine parts were standardized an international trade developed in yet another area of enterprise: machine building. As new breakthroughs in technology overtook each previous breakthrough, progress seemed limitless, and human life indeed appeared, at least in theory, capable of perfection.

### The French Revolution: The Problem of Historiography

If life was improving, what then gave rise to the most bitter revolution known to the modern world—the French Revolution—when the society that prided itself on its rationality systematically destroyed itself? Why was there a French Revolution at all? What were its causes?

In an important sense, these questions are more significant than the facts of the Revolution (outlined on pages 245–49) themselves. For the French Revolution is an admirable case study in the problem of historical interpretation, of ultimate meaning in any recital of the facts of the past. That the Revolution modernized France, that it was a blow on behalf of the liberty of the people, that it was in some small part stimulated by the American Revolution, that it was fed by the Enlightenment, that it could not have taken place were it not for certain changes in the French peasantry as well as the aristocracy, that it was in part the product of a grasping and aspiring monarchy, all are true. Yet the causes of the French Revolution remain a subject for debate to the present time. In examining the debate, we may see how contemporary concerns also influence the way in which we come to view the past.

The peasants of France attacked their seigneurs and the remnants of a feudal regime they found repressive in the summer of 1789. At the same time, the citizens of Paris were establishing a National Assembly. Both

*Liberty Guiding the People* Eugene Delacroix was inspired by David (see page 67) and sought to show exciting events in the manner conveyed by literature. His purpose was to stir people, to give them a sense of History, and here he has united Romanticism and revolution in an allegory painted in 1830. *Source: Alinari-Scala.*

groups had used violence to achieve their ends. The peasantry had been influenced particularly by the Great Fear, a wave of hysteria that followed the circulation of a rumor concerning an aristocratic conspiracy aimed at using hired hands to force the peasantry to observe all their seigneurial obligations, including duties that had been allowed to fall into abeyance. When the new National Assembly, meeting at Versailles, grasped the magnitude of rural anger, there were no troops available to quell the rebellion except for the king's, which might strike at the Assembly instead. The deputies therefore decided to legalize the situation and destroyed the feudal regime in France in a dramatic series of resolutions passed through the night of August 4.

But what had actually happened and why? The Assembly had acted as much from fear as from a sense of progress. Economic and political grievances had blended in one historic moment to fuel a genuine revolution that cut across birth to the class-based status groups. Yet precisely what were the facts about the economic and political condition of the French in the eighteenth century? In summary, several answers have been given to this question, and each answer has opened more doors to interpretation and debate than it has closed.

The first great history of the French Revolution, by Jules Michelet, followed only fifty years after the events it described. Michelet, eager to show that what happens is right, presented the traditional view: that the Revolution arose from the collective misery of oppressed peoples, urban as well as rural, who fought for freedom against tyranny, who saw that the seigneurs would exploit the peasant for all time unless toppled by violence, and who rightly saw the Old Regime of Louis XVI as purely oppressive, unable to change, and grinding the poor ever downward. This view was countered almost immediately by the appearance of a study of that Old Regime by Alexis de Tocqueville, who had recently examined democracy in America, and who was convinced that the peasant in pre-Revolutionary France was in better condition than any other farmer in Europe. The French peasant, he argued, was free, often a landowner, and enjoyed a rising tide of prosperity. In short, the Revolution had been needless. Although Tocqueville's views no doubt were colored by his displacement from the French government in 1851, his primary concern was with the tyranny of the majority, with the idea of a totalitarian democracy that might stamp out the rights of the minority, and he used the Revolution to argue his philosophical case.

The next stage in the interpretive battle came from Hippolyte Taine in 1875, some four years after Germany had defeated France in war (see page 294) and four years after the Commune of 1871 had shown many French people the risks of total revolution. Taine was determined to show the French that revolutions are always futile and evil, and he systematically sought to destroy what he regarded as the romantic myth of the revolution of 1789–94. Taine used historical manuscripts in great detail, and he proved to the satisfaction of his readers that the peasantry lived in conditions of utter misery. Thus he supported Michelet. But he also argued that the misery, however great, had not justified the Revolution, which brought disaster to the whole of France and destroyed the Age of Reason, as people turned increasingly to emotion and passion. Thus he supported Tocqueville.

By now in France another revolution had occurred, and the Third Republic had been established. Yet another historian, Alphonse Aulard, sought to defend his contemporary revolution by justifying the earlier revolution, whch he saw as ideologically linked. Rather than examining the condition of the peasant, he sought to show how little actual violence was used in 1789. Indeed, conditions had not been so bad as to lead to blind, emotional revolution; rather, the revolution was rational, progressive, and desirable.

The fifth stage of this great debate was begun by the Marxist historians of the early twentieth century. They now looked to the rising middle class, arguing that the Revolution had been the product of the confident bourgeoisie which, as capitalism transferred economic power to it, sought to win dominance in the political and social arenas as well. The middle class, the Marxists contended, felt frustrated by the grotesquely outmoded structure of the Old Regime, and as a class on the rise, they took the risk of revolution upon themselves in order to win a further rung on the ladder of class warfare. Thus, the earlier historians who had demonstrated that conditions were indeed improving had been correct, but they had drawn the wrong conclusions from the correct facts.

Of course, there also were promonarchical writers who felt that the revolutionaries had exaggerated the conditions of the Old Regime. These conservative historians found ironic allies among the Marxists, who argued from the same base to different conclusions. Some of the pro-Royalists turned to nostalgia as France approached the Armageddon of World War I and depicted the Old Regime as the last moment of a peaceful, prosperous French nation. Set against these, in turn, were other antirevolutionary historians of the twentieth century who, in their fear of modern Communism, condemned the Revolution as the forerunner of the modern movement. Because contemporary Communists claimed that Robespierre was the first person to found a socialist dictatorship, the anti-Communist historians appeared to have a sound basis for condemning the distant event on the basis of its present product. Arguing that economic conditions were favorable under the Old Regime, this modern group argued from the same historical data as those who had "proved" that the Old Regime was intolerably oppressive. Thus "the facts" supported a polarity of conclusions.

The debate goes on; understandably, one cry was for more facts, for ever deeper research into the social and economic realities of France at the most basic levels. Modern historians also were becoming more aware of how economic conditions were influenced by wages, prices, modes of production, rents, the nature of industrialization, and psychological perceptions of needs. One group argued that revolutions were caused by rising expectations—that precisely when the lower class was experiencing improvement, it was likely to rise in revolt, for at last it could sense both what it had been doing without and that the new goals were obtainable. The application of much quantitative data thus led historians to believe that they had arrived at an understanding, at last, of the causes of the French Revolution.

Yet, as another group of historians has argued, quantitative data are meaningful only when understood in terms of their human effect. What did people at the time perceive to be the truth? Studies that have examined the prevailing points of view have shown that the peasant and bourgeois views were diverging. The peasant masses felt an intense insecurity, arising from hostility toward the innovations associated with

# Napoleonic Europe, 1812

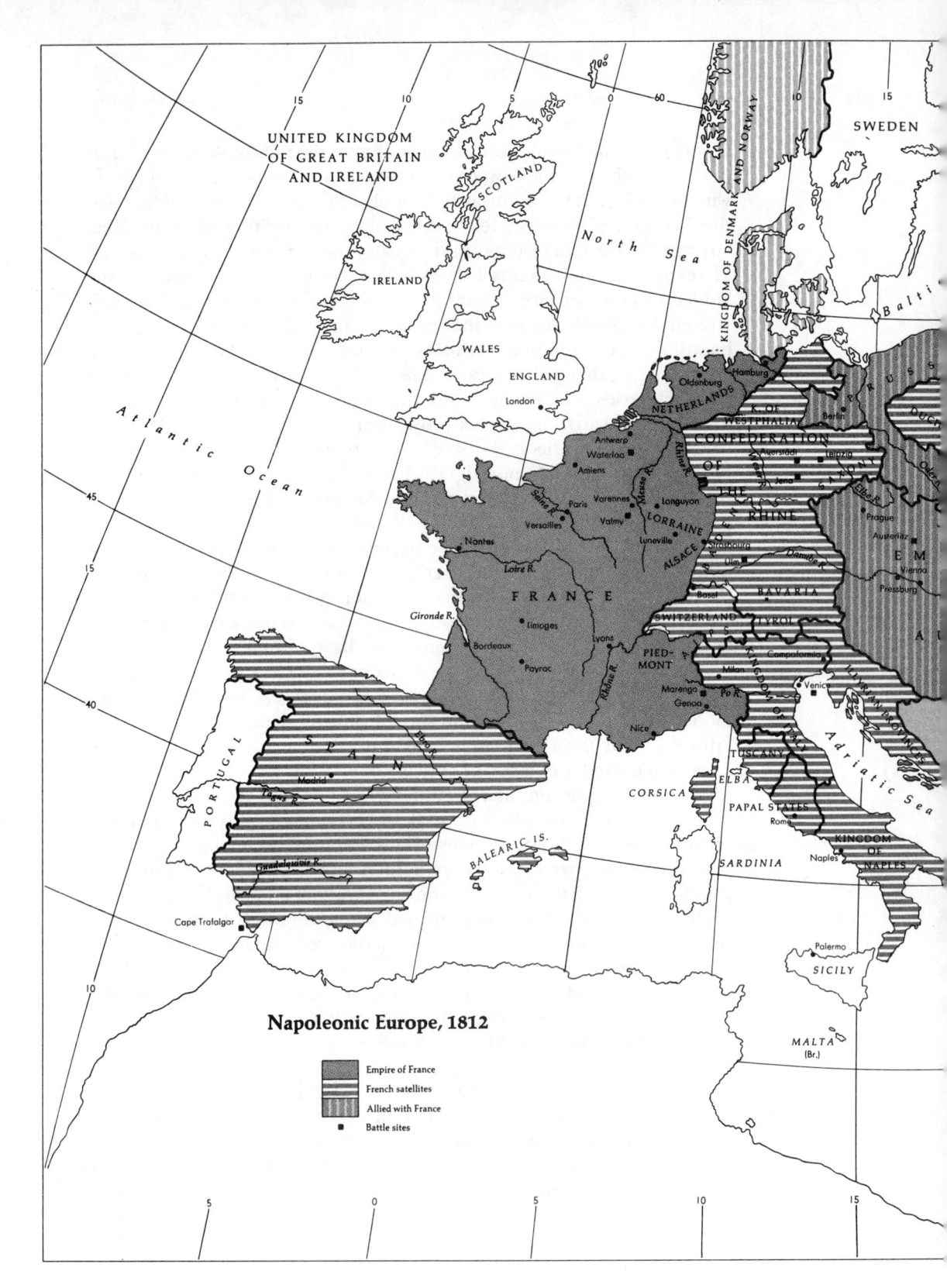

- Empire of France
- French satellites
- Allied with France
- ■ Battle sites

### Western Europe, 1798

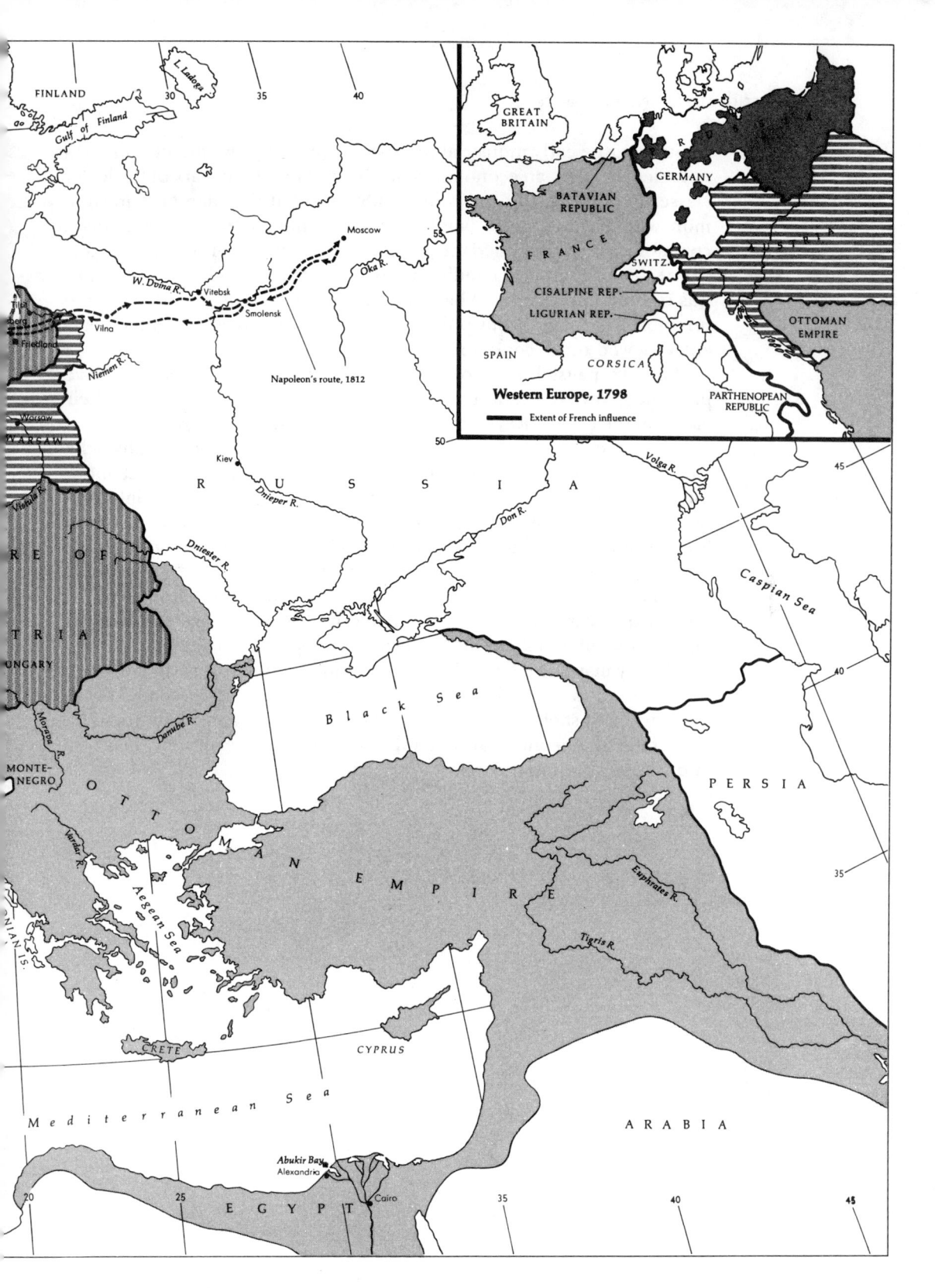

- Extent of French influence

*Napoleon's route, 1812*

capitalism, the early industrial revolution, and the new agricultural technologies. In 1789, an economic crisis that fed upon the fears of the lower classes in both the city and countryside (who felt they had little in common with the bourgeois landholder even though the seigneur was a common enemy) propelled the peasantry into revolution. Thus the objective reality of economic conditions, as reconstructed today by historians, was of little importance. What mattered, argued Georges Lefebvre, the foremost exponent of this point of view, was the way in which the peasantry viewed those conditions.

We have paused here to examine the way in which historians have presented, revised, counter-revised, and counter-counter-revised their views on the French Revolution in part because there is as yet no general agreement on those causes. But this exercise in historiography—the study of historical interpretation as it changes under differing contemporary social and other pressures, as well as in the light of "new information"—is also a fruitful bridge to modern times. For not only can we be less certain of the meaning of the events of the last two hundred years as they relate to us, but also the debate over the French Revolution is itself one sign of "modernity," of that process of modernization by which the world of learning admits more than one view of the past. Increasingly individuals will find themselves seeking for "operable truths"—truths by which they may live effectively—rather than absolute truths. In doing so, the lesson of the French Revolution is an especially telling one. For all the storm and shell of the Revolution and the even greater destructiveness of the Napoleonic Wars that followed, the ultimate meaning may rest in our view of it today.

# III. 6 Restructuring Power and Society: 1715–1815

*Revolutions are not made; they come. A revolution is as natural a growth as an oak. It comes out of the past. Its foundations are laid far back.* —Wendell Phillips, abolitionist, 1852

### An Afterview: Transition and the French Revolution

From the middle of the eighteenth century on, the economic and political interests of the European states began to turn the whole world into a market dominated by Europe, in which the western lands and colonies—North and South America and the Caribbean—were particularly important and hence received much attention. Trade with Asia usually meant the export of gold and silver in return for luxury goods, but trade with the Americas increasingly brought back advantageous agricultural and manufactured products, and thus, in the eyes of eighteenth-century economists, was more preferable. Although after 1760 trade with Asia—and particularly British exploitation of India—increased, it was in the west, with its large population of European colonists and its productivity, that European market interests were concerned. In politics as well, the extension of European military conflicts to the Americas, which had begun slowly by the English and Spanish rivalry in the sixteenth century, came to a head in the eighteenth over strategic concerns and the psychology of prestige. The drawing of North American and Caribbean colonies into English and French wars throughout the century and the increasing emigration to the west from many parts of Europe contributed to this Atlantic shift in European outlook. Not until the thirteenth century was commerce in the Mediterranean linked by regular sea routes to the Atlantic coasts of Europe. By the eighteenth century the North and South Atlantic seemed to be acquiring both a new economic and political status in European centers of power. The revolt of Britain's North American colonies below the St. Lawrence River in 1775–83 brought a new nation into the complex political affairs of Europe, one whose own self-image often seemed to be a deliberate rejection of eighteenth-century European colonialist policies and, by extension, an indictment of the structure of European society and power. However, the links between Europe and the western Atlantic coast remained strong and profitable. The eighteenth century witnessed the slow growth of an Atlantic civilization.

The expansion of the European market, diplomatic relationships in the seventeenth and eighteenth centuries, and the growing ambition and power of the state did not take place without severe social and economic difficulties. Most European states faced these difficulties throughout the century, and on the whole they were not successfully overcome. The affairs of these nations became the interest of larger and larger groups, and governmental intransigence, inefficiency, and lack of intelligent programs for reform only magnified their importance. Many eighteenth-century monarchies were conservative, as were aristocracies who lived by privileged legal status. But old forms of government and the privileged status of aristocrats were not sufficient instruments to avert the disastrous financial and political crises raised by public finance, the exclusion of reformists from governments, and the increasing lack of rational control over state resources that could have softened the effects of famine and fiscal incompetence. The growing voices of dissent insisted on being heard.

John Locke was one of several seventeenth-century philosophers who postulated a "state of nature"—the situation before humans devised government. In the state of nature individuals had equal rights to life, liberty, and property (a phrase that was changed by the revolutionary Americans in 1776 to life, liberty, and the pursuit of happiness, in which they included property). All people were governed by natural law which, being reasonable, they could discover and apply. Government could exist only by agreement among the people involved, through a social contract. While the contract gave the state power to govern, it reserved for all individuals their natural rights. Locke favored a separation of powers between legislative and executive branches to protect these natural rights against governmental excess. Citizens enjoyed a right to revolution if a government violated their natural rights.

Locke's ideas were elaborated during the Enlightenment of the eighteenth century. French theorists, in particular, praised the English system of separation of powers, defending freedom of speech and religion. Voltaire struck out at religious intolerance, demanding a government at once efficient and humane. He feared the idea of "government by the people," however, writing that no government could be effective unless it possessed ultimate power. Yet Voltaire helped prepare for the age of democratic revolution by making the ideas of the *philosophes* widely known, and by his hostility to aristocratic privilege.

The inherent contradiction was best seen in the work of Jean-Jacques Rousseau (1712–78). In *The Social Contract* in 1762, Rousseau maintained that when individuals contracted together to establish the state, they subjected themselves to the "general will." This general will was not the result of majority decision, for it comprised that which was in the true interest of all, whether the individual knew it or not. In Rousseau's society, true freedom lay in absolute obedience to this will; the state must "force man to be free"—ultimately an argument that could be used to justify a totalitarian state as well as a liberal one. Rousseau did not favor totalitarianism by the state any more than he favored the divine right of kings, but by challenging the traditional sources of government and suggesting some real or presumed contract among all people in the interests of government, he had broken the cake of custom and destroyed the old, grotesque, secure state, thus unleashing the revolutionaries.

In no state were these contradictory elements more critical than in France. The great age of Louis XIV had been followed by the rule of weak kings who were unable to exploit either the institutions of government or the talented ministers available to them. By the 1780s, the finances of France were a shambles. Enormous incomes had been spent upon ill-advised wars, often for empire; the extraordinarily heavy costs of effective state power had to be raised outside the privileged social orders, towns, guilds, universities, and the Church. The national assembly, the Estates General, had not met since 1614, and the interests of privileged groups alone were represented in the powerful *parlement* courts, the legal defenders of privilege. A series of reforming finance ministers tried throughout the century to break the grip of privilege and exemption upon the nation's crippled and now irrational finances; all failed. In 1778–87 the royal government collapsed, and in the same year a terrible food shortage struck France, whose population of twenty million was the backbone of its economic and military strength. The Estates General was assembled in May 1789, and the Third Estate, the unprivileged bourgeoisie and lower classes, became the focus of grievances. The revolutionary decisions following 1789 were less the result of democratic aspiration than the insistence that the idea of the state, now said to consist of the entire people, had to conform to certain obligations that could not be interrupted or suspended by privilege of a legal or fiscal kind.

The statements of grievance drawn up by the Third Estate, which embraced all who were not priests or nobles, were in accord with Enlightenment thought (although not necessarily caused by Enlightenment thinkers). In January of 1789 a priest, the Abbé Emanual-Joseph Siéyès, wrote in "What is the Third Estate?" that at last "the nation" as a whole should rule. He echoed the feelings of many peasants and, more importantly, of the business and professional people, who felt that their representatives ought to govern. Under pressure, Louis XVI gave the Third Estate twice as many representatives; he still hoped to follow the tradition by which each estate met separately and had one vote, so that the nobles and clergy together would prevail. The Third Estate refused to accept the traditional custom, and on June 17 it declared itself to be the "National Assembly." Thereupon the King closed their meeting hall, and the representatives met in a tennis court to sign the Tennis Court Oath, by which they affirmed that they were a legislative assembly with the power to prepare a constitution. In short, they claimed sovereign power for themselves.

Artisans and peasants completed the initiation of revolution. Riots in Paris forestalled the King's efforts to send troops to close the Assembly. On July 14 a mob attacked the Bastille, thought to hold political prisoners, and threw open the cells. The rioters took control of Paris and in October they forced the King to move from Versailles to the city so that he would be more under their control. Elsewhere peasants rose in rebellion, attacking their landlords and burning records. These lower classes were not moved primarily by Enlightenment arguments. They had suffered greatly under the economic slump that followed the poor harvests before 1789, and their march from Paris had begun quite simply as a bread riot. But many suffered from the pressures that resulted from the rising population on the land, and many others were disturbed by the new commercial activities of the local merchants. Artisans suffered from new competition in the cities and from the attempts by artisan masters to join the ranks of petty capitalists. Lower-class protest was a hostile reaction to the unsettling modernizing trends of the eighteenth century.

To meet the peasants' demands, the Assembly abolished aristocratic privileges: during August of 1789 manorial dues and work expectations, manorial courts, tax exemptions for the privileged, and church tithes were swept away. The peasants had won their demands; they could now work their plots of land without interference. And so they dropped out of the revolution, having no further ideological or political interests.

In August the Assembly also issued a Declaration of Rights of Man and the Citizen. It proclaimed the individual's inherent right to legal equality and freedom. The nation was sovereign; only the people (or their representatives) could make laws, which must bear equally on all citizens. The Assembly deprived the Church of its land and put the clergy under state control. In September, 1791, the Assembly produced a new constitution for the State, abolishing all former local units of government and substituting new *departement* which were given substantial powers of local government. The constitution created a single legislature, elected in a two-tier process by which the majority of adult males chose electors while a minority of the richer citizens selected the legislators.

So sweeping a revolution aroused great fear in France and abroad. Louis XVI and Europe's monarchs were dismayed at the challenge posed to the rights of kings. Aristocrats fled France, they and others to become *émigrés,* who were sources of hatred and fear for France wherever they settled. Roman Catholics abhorred the revolution. Domestic attempts to counteract it, further domestic insurrection, and a complex foreign war drove the revolutionary government to further, more extreme, measures. Increasingly the urban-based artisans pressured the assemblies, for little had been done to help them. The Assembly abolished the guilds and most forms of working-class associations, so that economic individualism could reign supreme—contrary to the desires of the artisans. The chaos of the revolution increased the economic crisis and prices rose to new heights.

During the most radical phase of the Revolution, 1792–93, the King was executed, and France became a republic. In theory, the republic was to be ruled by an elected Convention; in practice, it was governed by a Committee of Public Safety, ultimately under the dominance of Maximillien Robespierre (1758–94). The local governments were made powerless, with ever more power going to the central authority. Robespierre hoped to create a bond between citizen and State: citizens were to have a voice in government and receive benefits from it, and in turn they owed an active, intense loyalty to the State. The radical phase of the Revolution had turned to Nationalism.

In a Reign of Terror, Robespierre struck out against all enemies of the Revolution. Austrian and Prussian troops, who moved toward Paris in 1792, were pressed back; French armies entered Belgium (which was annexed) and western Germany. War was declared on Britain, Holland,

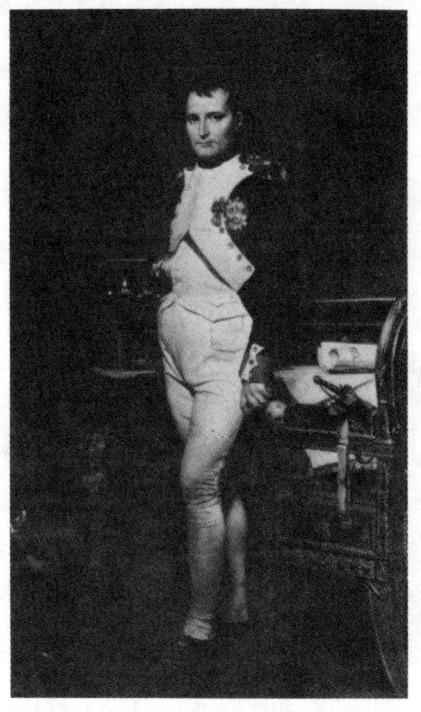

*Napoleon* Jacques Louis David was a court painter to Napoleon, and, although he saw himself as loyal to classical theory, his desire to "electrify the soul" led to paintings whose impact upon the viewer can best be described as emotional, romantic. At first glance this picture is of Napoleon; at the second, it is of Authority. *Source: National Gallery of Art, Washington—Jerry Palubniak/Scala.*

and Spain. At home, tribunals dealt severely with those who refused to give their loyalty to the State above all else; many were beheaded by the guillotine, a new device originally intended as a reform to assure a painless death. And when the threat of invasion lessened, Robespierre too was seized and beheaded. The following government, that of the Directory, revived property qualifications for voting and unsuccessfully tried to turn back to a less extreme position. It gave way, in 1799, to a virtual dictator. The factions for and against the Revolution in France had proved too much for anything less than autocratic rule to govern. The years of constant warfare, encouraged by the revolutionaries' desire to spread their principles and power by the sword, had given ever more power to the generals. Among them one, that virtual dictator, stood out.

The lifetime of Napoleon Bonaparte (1769–1821) included both the triumph of the principle of the State as a unit embracing all propertied citizens and the rearrangement of the major powers of Europe. Napoleon, an obscure lieutenant of artillery, moved up quickly in the revolu-

No one ever has shown us the horrors of war more starkly than the great Spanish painter Francisco Goya (1745–1828). His early style was vivacious and joyful, but the atrocities of the period of the Napoleonic Wars turned him to the brutality and darkness in mankind. Here he shows us *The Third of May, 1808,* when a French firing squad shoots down the citizens of Madrid. Source: Scala New York/Florence.

tionary army ranks between 1796, when he rose to prominence in the wars in Italy, and 1799, when the collapse of the republican government thrust upon him the powers of Consul, then Emperor. Under his reign, the bones of the Revolution—uniform law codes, reorganized public finance, the stabilization of the official orders of government and society, and the protection of property and power—took on their permanent flesh. Out of the myriad complaints, plans, alternatives, and secondary and tertiary revolutions of the period 1778–1804, the government of Napoleon strengthened and established those that appealed most strongly to the groups which supported him and whose complaints had effectively launched the Revolution—the middle classes, with their stability, wealth, and demands for opportunities open to talent, energy, and work.

The French Revolution plunged France into war with most of the major powers of Europe and constituted the furnace in which Napoleon's armies and the roots of nineteenth-century bourgeois European society and culture were forged. The eighteenth century talked about, but certainly did not institutionalize, democracy. Yet the breaking of the privileged orders of traditional European society and the opening of opportunity to the middle class constituted a sharp break with the world of traditional Europe (although not with the world of Mediterranean antiquity). It mobilized new kinds of state resources, particularly demographic ones, which presided over the transformation inaugurated by both the Industrial Revolution in the late eighteenth and nineteenth centuries and the conflicts between privilege and liberalism that dominated the early nineteenth century.

From the end of the dangers brought by steppe-nomads to the discovery of new principles of internal state operation, the eighteenth century marks a turning point in western and world history that is far more significant than the conventional divisions between Antiquity, the Middle Ages, the Renaissance, and the Reformation. For comparable western experiences, one must look to the opening of the European continent by Roman expansion in the first century B.C. and, further back, to the rise of Greece between 500 and 300 B.C. Although European and later Atlantic civilization are but two heirs of the centers of civilization that emerged between 4000 B.C. and 300 B.C., they are two that overcame certain enduring obstacles to the successful shaping of human societies everywhere. The changing concepts of self, flexible attitudes toward tradition, the physical and psychological security of western society, culture, religion, political institutions, and thought all mobilized Europeans and protected them, both from the risks they ran in experiencing change and from the dangers they habitually courted by their presumption, energy, and boundless curiosity.

# PART FOUR

No Break
with the Past:
The Nineteenth
Century
in Perspective

*We are not to expect to be translated from despotism to liberty in a featherbed.* —
Thomas Jefferson, 1790

## AN OVERVIEW: THE AGE OF THE DEMOCRATIC REVOLUTION

It is the beguiling custom of historians to say that "modern history" begins with the French Revolution and its immediate aftermath. This is a conventional statement, and neither true nor false, because it rests upon undisclosed definitions. But it is sound enough as a working truth, as an operative principle for interpreting our more immediate past. For the French Revolution was either the symptom, the cause, or the releaser of most of the forces now operating upon us, forces that we would unhesitatingly identify as modern. It was a phase of a broad, revolutionary trend that was democratic and reached its most dramatic moment in France. But between 1763 and 1811, it can rightly be seen as a World Revolution centered in the West. Not alone in America and France, but in Britain, the Hapsburg Empire, Ireland, Belgium, Holland, Poland, Sweden, Switzerland, and Greece, people who previously thought they had no right to express themselves politically began a process of transformation not complete to this day. The age of the democratic revolution grew from the problems and the society that preceded it and in this sense marked no sharp break with the past; the processes it so dramatically set in motion, while initially stymied in most societies, continued as an underground stream and surfaced again in 1848, in the 1870s, and for Africa and Asia, in the 1960s.

What set the French Revolution apart from the other revolutions of the time was the sweep of its initial successes, the extremity of its ultimate excesses, and the manner in which it represented an interweaving of diverse revolutionary intents and urgencies growing from aristocratic bourgeois, popular, and peasant societies. That the revolution was a bourgeois triumph did not lessen its impact on the rise of socialist and communist thought, or on the abstract ideology of human rights. While the American Revolution was fought over definable, finite issues within a common British politic—so much so that the American Revolution is perhaps best viewed as a civil war within the British Empire—the French Revolution took on so many extensions, vented so many hopes, raised so many expectations, and dashed so many aspirations, that it was virtually infinite in the ways in which it reverberated throughout that century—and the next. No simple statement can encompass it. Perhaps for that reason more than any other, it gave rise to an inordinate number of myths, interpretations, and counter-interpretations, all moved by the motivations of the moment.

But viewed in the context of the 1980s, the Revolution does have one significance that looms larger than others. This is the triumph of nationality based upon language and the impulse toward democracy defined in terms of leveling classes rather than in terms of constitutional growth. The effect of the period between 1789 and 1815 was the remaking of the map of Europe on a linguistic basis. This is not contradicted by the failure in central and eastern Europe to move toward self-government, for it was nationality that defeated liberty in the east, just as it hastened it in the west.

The French Revolution thus posed the major political problems of the nineteenth century. As Europeans moved from dynastic to national sovereignties and broadened the idea of the nation from the privileged classes to "the people," who were thought to have a "collective will," they unleashed the dynamic, harsh, unpredictable new force of nationalism. The tension between self-government (based on constitutionality) and self-determination (based upon language and, sometimes, religion) created and destroyed nations throughout the century. Self-government frequently meant rule by the landed class in the countryside, at the expense of the Crown, and rule by the rising upper middle class and by the intelligentsia in the urban sphere. As the lower classes found their own voice, often through a common language and religion, they demanded something more than such forms of self-government. Indeed, there are historians who argue that the Irish remained Roman Catholic precisely because the English did not. As conquest, plantation, and middle class dominance created the moral equivalent of modern-day Ulster in many corners of Europe, class, language, "race" (as spoken of in the nineteenth century), and religion became inextricably bound, and thus mutually reinforcing. The rule of some dynasty through divine right was easier to bear than rule by a garrison, by teachers sent to the countryside to teach the minority language of those who considered themselves superior, and by bureaucrats who saw themselves as official representatives of a master race in the land of a subject people.

In short, the age-old problem of conquest, accommodation, and assimilation—of the conqueror conquered, of the garrison merging with the culture of the subjects—was altered. The broad migratory stream, which had threatened to overwhelm Europe from east to west, had already been reversed, but now the reversal took the shape of linguistic groups, of nationhoods. There was a shift from west to east as entire populations found themselves moved, at first by the vagaries of war, and by the end of the century, by the calculation of the state. In 1815 the Italians and Germans (the most populous nations as defined by language) were hopelessly split by dynastic rivalries. By 1920 they were united, one victorious and the other defeated in a major war. But they were single nations at last based upon their languages, and no longer fragmented by increasingly irrelevant dynastic ambitions. (One of the reasons it is customary to devote far more space to the history of Germany and Italy than to, for example, the history of Poland or Sweden, is simply that their unification had far greater consequences for Europe—not some abstract notion that their peoples were more important.)

In the nineteenth century the problem of nationality arose first in relation to the most powerful of the nations. The issues of immediate importance were the aspirations of the Germans, Italians, Magyars, and Poles. The powerful nations wanted these issues resolved, for the continued ferment arising from them created an instability that made for insecurity. With respect to the Germans, Italians, and Magyars, the resolution lay less within themselves than within the Hapsburg monarchy. For this reason, the Austro-Hungarian problem tended to dominate the political sphere. Poland stood outside this problem because it was caught up in a competition between a consolidating Prussia and an expanding Russia. So long as the peasantry did not count in political matters the Roman Catholic and Polish landowners in White Russia and the western portion of the Ukraine saw to it that these lands were Polish; but serfs thought first in terms of religion, and the peasants of the region belonged to the Eastern Church and spoke forms of Russian. Hence, as religion and language came to identify loyalties, they gravitated increasingly toward the East.

Two great powers, Britain and Russia, were preoccupied with major shifts of their own in the nineteenth century. Both warily watched the Continent, intervening as they saw their changing national interests threatened. But Britain was expanding overseas; its center of gravity was moving toward the Second British Empire, while Russia symbolized its shift by moving its capital east from St. Petersburg to Moscow. Throughout the century neither power committed itself fully to Europe, unless the stability of the weakened Ottoman Empire—which could greatly influence the eastern end of the Mediterranean—were brought under challenge. More often than not the two powers took opposing postions on international issues, but in Europe's three greatest modern wars—the Napoleonic and World Wars I and II—they fought together. The United States, the inheritor of the First British Empire, fought against Britain in 1812–1815, and then with her during World Wars I and II. By the second occasion the Untied States took her place as the major European power west of Europe. (This was driven home by the Cold War of 1948 to 1971.)

As a result of the events of 1814–15, the Hapsburgs gave up Belgium and the Rhine, so they no longer posed a threat to Britain. Britain had always feared any occupation of the Low Countries by an enemy because they were the one pre-air age springboard for an invasion of England. Thereafter, it was Prussia that was expected to maintain a "watch on the Rhine"—a major shift, because Prussia previously had been a power only of Eastern Europe and the Baltic. Thereafter the battle between France and Austria shifted to Italy. In 1848, when a number of nationalities attempted to secure a separate nationhood by revolution, the Hapsburg Empire was most sorely tested. The subject peoples of the area saved the dynasty for fear that independent governments would mean domination by local groups who thought themselves to be the masters. Czechs could not favor the destruction of Austria, for this would mean that both would be engulfed by Germany—hence Czechs waited until 1919 to achieve a separate nation. Romanians or Yugoslavs could not favor the total destruction of the Hapsburgs, for a separate Hungary would dominate them; they too waited for independence. Thus, the most oppressed groups were also the least eager for the dismemberment of the Hapsburg Empire.

Ultimately, World War I brought the triumph of the small nations based on linguistic nationality. The implications of the French Revolution and the events of 1848 were played out. And thirty years later, in the blink of an historical eye, this too was wiped away, as those same nations either lost their independence (as along the Baltic) or were submerged under the ideological force of the greatest power on the European continent, the Soviet Union. By then an Atlantic civilization, with its power based more in New York and Washington than in Europe, became the western pole of tension and was set against Moscow, which became the eastern pole. And once again the ancient process of movement and exchange of populations and migrations of peoples began from eastern to central Europe and from the Old World to the New. In this way people sought better, more secure, lives.

Here our pace changes. More events with more immediate meaning in our lives today have impact upon us as we approach our own century. Density of detail is a reflection of proximity; so too is tentativeness of conclusion, for the larger meanings of the events of the nineteenth—and even more so of the twentieth-century are denied to us, as we wait to see what the future will bring. "Art is long, life short; judgment difficult, opportunity transient," wrote Johann Wolfgang von Goethe, the great German poet of the early nineteenth century. "Whatever you cannot understand, you cannot possess," he argued. To understand the more nearly immediate past is, as he knew, only a goal. The closer one comes to one's own times, the more the certitudes of one's own class, background, experiences—of one's own environment—work to prevent objective judgment. We strive for operable truths, then, for conclusions upon which we may act. With Goethe, in his last words, we seek "More light!"

## IV. 1 From Revolution to Revolution: 1789–1848

> *Would you realize what Revolution is,*
> *call it Progress; and would you realize what Progress is,*
> *call it Tomorrow.*
> —Victor Hugo, *Les Misérables,* 1862

### The Conservative Reaction

The mood of Europe's governments after 1815 was conservative. They wished to see no more change based on abstractions, no more wild threats to the established order, no more revolutionary tribunals, no more Napoleonic campaigns. A process of reconstruction had begun.

The case for conservatism was best put by an Englishman, Edmund Burke (1729–97), who had early diagnosed the French Revolution's potential for destruction. Humans, he had written in his *Reflections on the Revolution* in France, were not by nature good and corrupted only by organized society, as Rousseau and other philosophers of the Enlightenment had postulated. On the contrary, when left to their natural instincts, humans stole, maimed, raped, killed, and tortured. The force that kept them from behaving like wolves was the power of organized society. Thus society, far from corrupting, was protecting people from themselves. In other words, people were saved less by their innate virtue, which was a weak impulse at best, than by the state and its laws. Yet neither state nor laws would last very long if they were artificial creations, transparent conveniences designed by theoreticians. If they were to endure, they must be interwoven with traditions, conventions, and even prejudices going back over the centuries, backed by the whole complex structure of a society that grows organically and very slowly, as a large tree grows.

The Burkean conservatives pointed out that it would be easy, in theory, to project a faster growing, simpler, more symmetric, tree; in practice, that new tree was likely to die. Similarly, finer constitutions, or more rational laws, could be designed in the academy—and the eighteenth century had planned many—but they would result, as Burke predicted in the case of the French Revolution, in catastrophe. For as he wrote, "the nature of man is intricate," and "the objects of society are of the greatest possible complexity." Hence, there was the need to respect institutions that in their admittedly imperfect ways kept individuals from harming their neighbors, and in this way helped society survive. Hence, there was the need to respect authority. Otherwise, the law, and civic society, were in jeopardy.

Civil society might well be based, as eighteenth century political writers had suggested, on the contractual consent of the governed; yet this was a compact of a special kind. As Burke wrote in one of the most famous passages in the *Reflections:*

> Society is, indeed, a contract. Subordinate contracts for objects of mere occasional interest may be dissolved at pleasure, but the state ought not to be considered as nothing better than a partnership agreement in a trade of pepper and coffee, calico or tobacco, or some such other low concern, to be taken up for a little temporary interest, and to be dissolved by the fancy of the parties. It is to be looked on with other reverence, because it is not a partnership in things subservient only to the gross animal existence of a temporary and perishable nature. It is a partnership in all science; a partnership in all art; a partnership in every virtue, and in all perfection. As the ends of such a partnership cannot be obtained in many generations, it becomes a partnership not only between those who are living, but between those who are living, those who are dead, and those who are to be born.

Was any change possible at all then, in this sacred union between the generations, in this intense respect for the proliferating variety of humankind, according to either Burke or his followers in post-Napoleonic Europe? Of course change was possible, but it ought to be handled circumspectly, lest people, as they had done during the Revolution, "pull down more in half an hour than prudence, deliberation and foresight can build up in a hundred years." As the English Earl of Falkland had said a century or so earlier, "When it is not necessary to change, it is necessary not to change." Yet respect for institutions did not mean that these institutions were petrified. The same Burke who warned against precipitate change also wrote that "a state without the means of some change is without the means of its conservation." It was the question of means that was all-important. Change must be slow, cautious, and gradual. All reforms, thought Burke, should be introduced in such a way that "the useful parts of the old establishment" might be preserved.

To a world which could still remember the excesses of the French Revolution and the bloodletting of Napoleon, Burkean sentiments had a respectable amount of appeal. Thus an Austrian politician, Prince von Metternich (1773–1859), wrote:

> Men cannot make a constitution, properly speaking—that is made only by time.... Let people write as much as they like, and the less will always be the better, and yet you will have nothing in your hands but a piece of paper. England alone has a Constitution ... [and it] is the work of centuries.... Social order ever progresses this way; it cannot be otherwise, since it is the law of nature.

But history can be ironical as well as slow, and it turned out that conservative thought was fully as much subject to being distorted when put into practice as Enlightenment thought had been. Metternich was a writer in political philosophy in his spare time only; his principal occupation was serving the Emperor of Austria as foreign minister and chancellor, which he did for an unprecedented length of time, from 1809 to 1848. In that capacity, he felt he occasionally had to take the step from counseling caution—an attitude with which few disagreed—to sponsoring active repression. He knew the difference between arguing to a conclusion, as theoreticians did, and arguing to a decision, as people of action must. Thus, when faced with rebellious students and an open act of violence in 1819, Metternich prevailed upon a council of German ministers meeting at Carlsbad in Bohemia to pass a number of suppressive decrees. A desire for short-term security ransomed the security of the long run.

These Carlsbad Decrees tightened censorship of the press and restricted academic freedom, abolishing tenure for radical professors and dissolving the revolutionary student organizations, or fraternities, that had recently formed for the pursuit of political freedom. Burke's conservatism turned into reaction—an often crude reaction against any kind of change, against anything that seemed at all connected with the values and the ideas of the French Revolution, against anything that seemed modern.

Metternich, relatively speaking, was still a man of sense and moderation. The threats he saw to the state were not imaginary ones. Others, however, went considerably beyond the Austrian chancellor's police measures. Thus, in the papal states, Pius VII (1800–23) reestablished the Jesuit order (disestablished in the eighteenth century), put Jews once again into ghettos, and forbade vaccination against small pox. Thus the Bourbon ruler returning to Naples rescinded every piece of liberal legislation that passed under the French occupation. In Piedmont, King Victor

Emmanuel I (1802–21) not only revoked the constitution that had been granted under revolutionary pressure, but had the palace's French furniture thrown out of the window and the French botanical gardens uprooted.

These were extreme examples of Reaction. But Reaction not only created its own special absurdities; it also proved futile. For it did not, in the years from 1820 to 1848, produce undisturbed domestic tranquility. Instead, these years saw violence and revolution nearly everywhere in Europe.

## The New Revolutions

Trouble began in Spain where the restored monarch, Ferdinand VII (1814–33), suspended the constitution adopted during his exile, brought back the Jesuits, reintroduced ancient feudal ranks and privileges, and revived the Inquisition. He also announced his intention of regaining Spain's crumbling empire and assembled a fleet of ships at Cadiz to carry a small conquering army to South America. The fleet never sailed, for in January 1820, a mutiny broke out that spread to the rest of Spain, and then to Portugal and Naples. Ultimately, the Crown submitted to the demands of the revolutionaries—whose purpose was supported by liberal army officers—and granted constitutions that set clear limits to absolute rule.

These constitutions were very temporary, and by the mid-1820s they were again suspended, and the Crown reigned unchecked once more. Royal victories, however, were achieved only with the aid of foreign troops; in Naples, the French and the Austrians intervened and in Spain the French helped out of self-interest, hoping to contain the threat of revolution. Yet their successes in Spain and Italy did not stop the march of revolution. For profound forces of change were at work in that area of the continent largely bypassed by the French Revolution—Eastern Europe.

In Russia, a conspiracy of army officers in 1825 led to an attempted takeover of the government. While it was suppressed quickly and easily, revolutionary action in the Balkans had more lasting effects. The main issue was hatred of Turkish overlordship, which was expressed in a contest for national independence. The two most successful rebellions were waged in Serbia and Greece. In the former, a long and bitter struggle headed first by the Karageorge and then by the Obrenovic families resulted in Serbia's becoming an autonomous principality within the Turkish Empire by 1830. Following this example, the Greeks began to battle for their freedom as well in 1821. This conflict drew in some of the great European powers on Greece's side because philhellenism was a potent force, especially in France and Britain. It ended in 1829 with the establishment of a fully sovereign Greek state, with borders drawn less generously than some of the Greek patriots wished. The first nation had entirely broken away from the Turkish empire.

Then, in 1830, the sense of revolutionary change shifted to the West again. Again, France led the way. Originally the old order had been restored gracefully and peaceably. Louis XVIII (1815–24), brother of the executed Louis XVI, returned from exile in 1814 to reestablish "legitimate" rule. (The dauphin, who would have ruled as Louis XVII, vanished during the Revolution.) Louis XVIII ruled not by divine right, but under a charter he proclaimed in which he shared royal power with chambers of peers and deputies. And he confirmed religious tolerance and the equality of all French citizens before the law, managing to hold at bay those who wanted vengeance for the Revolution.

When the king died in 1824, however, he was followed by the Count of Artois, who ascended the throne as Charles X (1824–30). Louis XVIII had been a moderate in the style of the old regime, and even an eighteenth-century freethinker; Charles X was an émigré and a bigot. The direction of his policy was soon clear to all by the laws passed: allocation of one billion francs to compensate the nobility for part of the losses they suffered during the Revolution; subjection of antigovernment publications to censorship; institution of the death penalty for the theft of sacred vessels. The details were picturesque—the culprits were to have their right hands severed and their heads cut off. The facts were prosaic—like so many of the measures of Charles X, it was never enforced. After all, France was a civilized nation. Then, in 1829, the King appointed one of France's most reactionary politicians as his chief minister; the Prince of Polignac (1780–1847), whose decisions were guided by apparitions of the Virgin Mary. One of Polignac's initial acts was pushing a series of laws through parliament known as the Five Ordinances. These plainly violated the freedoms promised under the Charter of Louis XVIII and threatened to restore royal absolutism.

The reaction to the royal coup of 1830 was immediate and widespread popular resistance. Once more in France the barricades went up, and a militant crowd captured the Paris City Hall. Charles X went into exile, and a liberal monarch, Louis Philippe (1830–48), replaced him. A Bourbon, Louis had fought in the army of the Revolution; he knew his Rousseau, yet he had left France before the excesses of the Terror. He represented compromise, and he promised to govern France as a citizen-king. Acclaimed "King of the French by grace of the French people," he swore an oath to uphold the charter and made the tricolor of the Revolution, rather than the white of the Bourbons, the flag of France.

France set off the dominoes; there was no stopping of revolutions elsewhere in Europe now. In Belgium that year, rioters went into the streets. What they demanded was both a liberal, constitutional monarchy, and complete independence from Holland, because under the terms of the Vienna settlement, Belgium was then joined into a United Netherlands. Despite bitter Dutch opposition, the revolutionaries achieved both of their aims. Belgium became a fully sovereign state ruled by a constitutional monarch.

Belgium's success, however, was singular. In other areas, the revolutionaries fared worse. In Poland, a violent attempt to free the country from tsarist rule was initiated by a secret society of army cadets and suppressed brutally and easily by Russian troops. The rebellion lacked broad popular support because Poland's peasants had no more affection for the aristocratic cadets than they had for the Russians. In the words of one of her poets, Poland once more became "the land of graves and crosses." Nor did the revolutionaries do much better in the Italies. Despite some early successes in Parma, Modena, and the Papal States, the old regimes quickly reassumed their power. In the Germanies the monarchs of some states, notably Saxony and Hanover, prudently granted constitutions on their own initiative in 1830 so that, despite much ferment, there were no major revolutionary disturbances. Once the threat was over, censorship and a degree of police supervision returned. But it turned out that violence had merely been held in abeyance. For in 1848, there were a series of political upheavals in Europe of unprecedented scope.

Once more France was in the vanguard. For all his efforts and intelligence, Louis Philippe could not please either his right or his left wing opponents. By being too bland a king, he also failed to provide the excitement that appears to be a necessary ingredient of government. "France is bored," wrote one of his critics. While the conservatives merely grumbled, however, the liberals took action, scheduling a number of antigovernment banquets throughout France. When the government reluctantly prohibited a large banquet scheduled for Paris in February 1848, the barricades went up. A major riot erupted, troops sent to dispel the rioters refused to obey orders, and the next day Louis Philippe abdicated and was on his way, like Charles X before him, to London and exile.

But now events took an unexpected turn. This revolution became far more sweeping than the liberals had wished. In June, a group of radical workers occupied the National Assembly, and troops had to be called in to put down an uprising in Paris's working-class district. It was the first open outbreak of class warfare in Europe, of workers against the bourgeoisie, of have-nots against haves. It was of this moment that Karl Marx and Friedrick Engels wrote, "A specter is haunting Europe. The specter is Communism." Still, the specter remained faint. In the elections held at the end of 1848, the vote for president clearly indicated that the country's mood did not favor radical experiments. Instead, the overwhelming vote went to the candidate who, as Louis Philippe once had, seemed to represent the best compromise between progress and order—to Louis Napoleon, nephew of Napoleon Bonaparte.

Yet once more events in France started a chain reaction all over Europe. The one difference this time was that the chain had never been so long before. For in 1848 there were revolutions in nearly every major city in Europe. Calm prevailed in only two capitals—St. Petersburg and London. In St. Petersburg the apparatus of oppression was too efficient, and in London the situation was more complex. Public interest and discontent was channeled toward dissenting religious groups that did not favor violence, and a Reform Act passed in 1832 had obviated some of the need for revolutionary confrontation by enfranchising more members of the middle class. This Reform Act, however, did not mean that universal suffrage and democracy had come to Britain; before its passage, perhaps one English man out of a hundred could vote; now one in about thirty could. But coupled with the initial successes of the Chartists and the abolition of the Corn Laws in 1846, this was enough. Even so, the privileged few were still the shapers of public opinion in England.

Everywhere else in Europe, 1848 was the great revolutionary year. In Berlin, Dresden, Vienna, Budapest, Milan, Venice, Rome, Copenhagen, and Tipperary, the crowds were out, battling police and army. The aims of the revolutionaries had much in common—more liberal government and national independence. In the case of the German and the Italian states, this meant uniting under one central government, and in the case of the nationalities comprising the Habsburg Empire, such as the Czechs and the Hungarians, it meant seceding from the capital of Vienna. Because the aims were similar, so was the pattern of the various revolutions. After initial successes in which rulers either fled or granted constitutions

**Centers of Revolution**

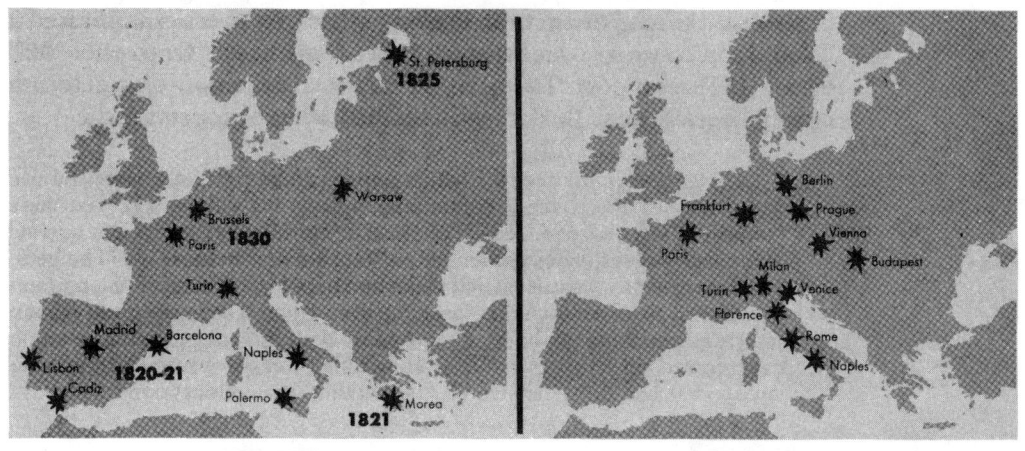

1820-1830        1848-1849

and agreed to national self-determination, in 1849 at the latest, the forces of the old order regrouped, reneged on promises given under pressure, and eliminated revolutionary leaders. Nearly everywhere, the results were the failure of revolutionary momentum, and frustration. The only exception was France; within three years after Louis Napoleon became president, he abolished the Republic and made himself Emperor, on the basis of a strong, emotionally charged, popular vote, carefully staged to achieve his ends.

So the French experience was still singular. The general pattern was failure. Enthusiasm and idealism were no match for the organized powers of government. But the ideas that had motivated the revolutionaries did not vanish and in their changing ways (for ideas, too, are subject to evolution) continued to affect the history of the nineteenth and twentieth centuries.

## IV. 2 The Enduring Ideas: Finding Theoretical Bases for Security

> *The sole end for which mankind are warranted, individually or collectively, in interfering with the liberty of action of any of their number is self-protection.* —John Stuart Mill, *On Liberty,* 1859

Paramount among the assumptions of nineteenth-century liberalism was what John Stuart Mill (1806–73), perhaps its most remarkable advocate, called "the belief in the individual." Individuals were to be left as free as possible—in speech as in actions—so that they could fully develop their potential. The only restraint that government might legitimately impose was keeping them from injuring others. As Americans phrased it, "Your right to swing your fist stops short of my nose." Or to quote Mill, whose 1859 essay, *On Liberty,* is as classic a definition of nineteenth-century liberalism as Burke's writings had been of conservatism:

> ... [the] only purpose for which power can be rightfully exercised over any member of a civilized community, against his will, is to prevent harm to others. His own good, either physical or moral, is not a sufficient warrant. He cannot rightfully be compelled to do or forbear because it will be better for him to do so, because it will make him happier, because, in the opinions of others, to do so would be wise, or even right. These are good reasons for remonstrating with him, or reasoning with him, or persuading him, or even entreating him, but not for compelling him, or visiting him with any evil in case he do otherwise. To justify that, the conduct from which it is

*The Houses of Parliament* The Mother of Parliaments, the British call their Parliamentary form of democracy, and from it has grown the governing form of a quarter of the globe. Actually the New Palace of Westminster, this late-Gothic complex was constructed on the River Thames between 1840 and 1888. *Source: Editorial Photocolor.*

> desired to deter him must be calculated to produce evil to someone else. The only part of the conduct for anyone, for which he is amenable to society, is that which concerns others. In the part which merely concerns himself, his independence is, of rights, absolute. Over himself, over his own body and mind, the individual is sovereign.

And it was Mill, too, who provided what became the classic defense of the sovereign individual's right to free expression:

> If all mankind minus one, were of one opinion, and only one person were of the contrary opinion, mankind would be no more justified in silencing that one person, than he, if he had the power, would be justified in silencing mankind.... [I]f that lone dissenter were perchance right, stifling his voice would deprive the majority of the opportunity to exchange error for truth.

Even should the minority be wrong, silencing it "would be an evil still," if for no other reason than that by listening to falsehood and distortion we gain a "clearer perception and livelier impression of truth, produced by its collision with error."

Were there no limits then, in the view of Mill and other liberals, to the exercise of free speech? Of course there were: they were the limits that the law imposed to prevent active harm to others. Thus, Mill suggested that individuals were free to express unflattering thoughts about what they considered the usurious or the objectionable habits of corn dealers, but were not free to do so before an angry crowd assembled in front of a corn dealer's house at a time of acute famine. In the words of Justice Oliver Wendell Holmes, Jr., a "clear and present danger" set the limits; the right of free speech did not include the privilege of falsely shouting "fire" in a crowded theater.

So much, then, for liberalism's basic assumptions. How were they translated into action? What, in nineteenth-century Europe, was the concrete liberal program? Perhaps *programs* would be the better term because there was no Liberal International. The emphasis and interests of French liberalism often varied substantially from those of British or German liberalism. Yet despite the variations, there were common denominators and a common mood.

Liberals tended to feel, in historian Peter Gay's phrase, that they were the Party of Mankind—the spokespeople for those who suffered and were without their own voice, whether Jews, or slaves, or workers. Nor were most liberals willing to accept the conservative argument that change must come slowly and circumspectly lest it destroy society; they thought that there was urgency in reforming prisons, in abolishing slavery, and in granting full civil rights to Jews. They also tended to favor parliamentary institutions with England as the model as the best means of implementing reforms, and of governing in general. Many also favored clear, written constitutions, with the United States and Switzerland as models. As far as the precise form of government was concerned, liberals tended to differ. English liberals were content to accept the monarchical structure, provided that a major share of power was reserved for parliament. Continental liberals, on the other hand, tended to be more radical, and advocated either a merely ornamental crown, or a republic. However, in the nineteenth century neither British nor Continental liberals thought that parliament should be elected by all. (John Stuart Mill favored universal suffrage, but he was the exception.) The preponderant feeling was that the right to vote should be reserved to those of property and education. In essence, liberalism was a middle-class movement. Few aristocrats, and fewer workers, embraced it.

There were two more specific common denominators of Liberalism. One was the liberals' tendency to be anticlerical, especially on the continent. Many liberals saw churches as institutions that had forced humankind to postpone a search for security in the here-and-now in favor of an unproved afterlife; they saw the churches as supporters of reaction, ancient privilege, and superstition. This was not true for all societies, however, as Alexis de Tocqueville wrote in 1831: "In France I have almost always seen the spirit of religion and the spirit of freedom marching in opposite directions. But in America, I found they were intimately united." Because Europe's liberals could never envisage such a union, they tended to be least tolerant of organized religions which they felt were basically intolerant and would deny freedom to those of other faiths.

Most liberals (especially in Britain) advocated a laisser faire or free enterprise system of economics. Their economic ideal was postulated by Adam Smith in his *Wealth of Nations* (1776). To achieve universal prosperity between nations, let there be the freest possible trade unhampered by tariffs. Let there be "freedom of contract." That is to say, let no union interpose itself between worker and owner. Let there be little legislation affecting prices, wages, or any other aspect of private enterprise. No artificial law was superior to the natural laws of supply and demand; hence let there be only the most minimal and unavoidable interference from the government in business affairs.

While voting rights did not go to all, basic freedoms were to be guaranteed to everyone regardless of social standing. The freedoms to read, to worship or not to worship, to be tried by jury, the freedom from arbitrary arrest and cruel and unusual punishments were to be shared by rich and poor alike. And the economic tenets of liberalism were in accord with its central theme: give the freest scope of action to the individual while reserving the smallest possible role to the state. In economics as elsewhere, the true function of the state was to permit the individual to develop talents and to follow desires. That, in fact, was the justification for the existence of government, and both the state and its citizens should perpetually bear this in mind. "That government is best which governs least," wrote Mill. Thus, in matters of society and politics, nineteenth-century liberals stood for the rights of the sovereign individual. This meant that they favored as little government as possible, opposed central planning, and wanted the state to be nothing more than a "passive policeman." Conservatives, on the other hand, ridiculed this concept of government as that of the "night watchman state." What they advocated was not unrestrained individualism, which struck them as coming dangerously close to anarchy, but strong governments that would help direct the lives of their citizens. For to the conservative, government was more than a convenience, having historic origins, rights and responsibilities. It inherited the old majesty that doth hedge a king.

Words like *liberal* and *conservative* have a life of their own, and they meant something different in the nineteenth century than they do in the twentieth. Nineteenth-century Liberalism stood squarely for free trade and for free enterprise; this meant that liberals tended to be antilabor. The typical nineteenth-century liberal was a person of means, clearly one class removed from the worker, and fearful that organized labor was a threat to wealth and position. The nineteenth-century conservative, on the other hand, was a person who favored government interference in the economy, particularly in the form of protective tariffs—the reverse of the conservative position today. Some of the most bitter nineteenth-century political battles were waged between liberal free traders and conservative protectionists. Also, conservatives took some notable prolabor positions, for neither Liberalism nor Conservatism were necessarily practiced in doctrinaire ways. It was the British conservatives rather than the liberals who voted for the first real factory legislation protecting the worker in the 1830s. It was Bismarck's conservative government in Germany which, fifty years later, inaugurated Europe's first modern social security legislation, including old-age insurance, medical care, and workmen's compensation. At the same time, it was Benjamin Disraeli's Conservative Party in Britain which pushed through better housing and health care for the poor. Yet in this age, this is scarcely what we have in mind when we say liberal or conservative. Instead, we often expect the present-day liberal to be suspicious of free enterprise, to be prolabor, and to favor legislative action affecting the economy, extending from minimum wage laws to increased social security benefits. In history, terms change just as facts do. One must not use yesterday's words to discuss today's events; the definitions prior to 1848 did not apply equally well after 1848.

## IV. 3  Surge of Nationalism: Postponement

*National honor is national property of the highest value.*
—James Monroe, 1817

The other great and universal force of nineteenth-century Europe, nationalism, is an idea that has changed in more subtle ways. The idea of national identity, and even of national superiority, is an old one in Europe, as we have seen. Even in the face of physical conquest, societies strove to retain their cultural identities. Consider:

> This royal throne of kings, this scepter'd isle,
> This earth of majesty, this seat of Mars,
> This other Eden, demi-paradise,
> The fortress built by Nature for herself
> Against infection and the hand of war,
> This happy breed of men, this little world,
> This precious stone set in the silver sea,
> Which serves it in the office of a wall
> Or as a moat defensive to a house

Against the envy of less happier lands,
This blessed plot, this earth, this realm, this England.

The lines, spoken by John of Gaunt, come from Shakespeare's *Richard II*, a play entered in the London Stationer's Register in 1597. A century and a half before, Joan of Arc (1412–31) had been very much aware of her Frenchness, and some time before that, foreign students at the Sorbonne were divided in their residences into what the university administration called "nations."

Three new elements made nationalism a rather different, and very much more powerful, force in the nineteenth century. The first was that it became more intense. Widespread reaction to being defeated and occupied by the French under Napoleon led to a heightened sense of separate identity, particularly in the German lands. Paradoxically, Napoleon stood for nationalism to many Italians and Eastern Europeans. Consider Heinrich von Kleist's *German Catechism*, written about 1810:

> *Question:* What do you think of Napoleon, the most famous Emperor of the French? . . .
> *Answer:* I think that he is a detestable person, the beginning of all that is evil and the end of all that is good. I think that he is a sinner, and that man has not enough words to accuse him of his crimes, and that even the angels, on Judgment Day, will run out of breath.
> *Question:* Did you ever see him?
> *Answer:* Never, my father.
> *Question:* How did you imagine him?
> *Answer:* As a parricide, risen from hell. . . .
> *Question:* How often did you repeat this sentence, quietly, to yourself?
> *Answer:* Last night, upon going to bed, and this morning, upon rising.
> *Question:* And when will you repeat it again?
> *Answer:* Tonight, when going to bed, and tomorrow morning, when rising.

The second new element was that nationalism increasingly rested on an emotional mass base. Medieval students, English dukes, and French patriotic saints had all been distinct minorities, but in the nineteenth century, national fervor captured the imagination of very large groups of people. Literary trends played a part in this, especially Romanticism with its concern for a nation's folkloristic past, its history, language, music, and native arts. So did the fact that the French Revolution's ideal of *fraternité* actually described the brotherhood of those who spoke the same language and shared the same history than the brotherhood of all humankind. The decline of traditional religion also played a part, for belief in the nation tended to become a substitute for religious belief. Thus days of national rejoicing or remembrance were now celebrated with the fervor formerly reserved for Christian holidays—in Switzerland, August 1 was the day when the representatives of the three original cantons swore an oath to oppose Hapsburg rule; on July 1, Canada commemorates the Confederation formed in 1867; July 14, in France; the Fourth of July in the United States: "America! America! God shed his grace on thee." The flag replaced the religious banner; the uniform replaced the clerical robe; the anthem, the chant; the national hero, the saint; and patriotic processions displaced religious ones.

Here was a meeting point between Nationalism and Conservatism, for both tended to see the state and the nation as the highest of all social organisms. European conservatives had little of their American counterparts' ingrained skepticism about government—indicated by the Americans' revolutionary experience. According to the German philosopher, G. W. F. Hegel (1770–1831), what was the state? It was nothing less, he said, than "the Divine idea as it exists on earth." Further, it was the end result of a long process of evolution, of a dialectic, which stipulated that a higher order of nationhood evolved from the clash of the old with the new, bringing humankind—in the name of the state—ever closer to perfection.

With so exalted a role ascribed to the state, and with nationalism a mass passion, the qualifications that individuals of greater sensibility made were often forgotten. In his *German Catechism* Kleist also wrote:

> *Question:* Do you feel then, that all things considered, the Germans already were at the summit of all virtue, of all salvation, and all glory?
> *Answer:* By no means, father.
> *Question:* Were they at least on the way of getting there?
> *Answer:* No, my father, not even that.

But the characteristic tendency was to assume that one's own nation did occupy precisely that summit of glory while others wallowed in the depths of infamy. Nationalism was also a clear program for action. The revolutions of the 1820s, 1830s, and of 1848 showed the desire for independence—of the Belgians from the Dutch, the Poles from the Russians, the Serbs and Greeks from the Turks, the Hungarians and Czechs and others from the Austrians—and overrode other considerations. In the case of Germans and Italians, nationalism meant a desire for union. There were no strong bonds between the host of German states; there was no true central government that united Prussia, Bavaria, Hesse, Württemberg, or Baden, any more than there were bonds between the many sovereign Italian states, from Piedmont in the north to Sicily in the south. Yet it was such bonds at the cost of local identities, it was a united nation state which many Germans and Italians wanted. It also was what they failed to achieve in 1848, just as the Poles failed to gain independence from Russia and the Hungarians from the Austrians. Thus a pent-up, frustrated Nationalism continued forcing change throughout the nineteenth century and well into the twentieth. The new religion had come to stay.

Yet all was not unrest and revolution from 1815 to 1848. The conservative mood of Europe's governments was inspired by more than self-serving bigotry. The French Revolution had been a very bloody event; the desire to prevent its repetition, in France as elsewhere, was rational. Hence it occurred to quite a few Europeans that "the old formal forces of order," as one writer put it, were still valuable, and that to give in to the revolutionaries' demands might "spell the beginning of the end." And even in those instances where conservatism ossified into reaction, the system was a bearable one. One banned books, but one did not yet hang authors.

The masses were largely unaffected by a consciousness of these political movements. Liberalism, in particular, appealed almost entirely to the increasingly well-educated and moneyed middle class, which in no country exceeded more than twenty percent of the population, and in many countries was smaller. At the beginning of the century, the great majority of Europe's people were still peasants, that group which scrabbled its living from the land. They were notably detached from politics because they were hampered by illiteracy in their appreciation of the issues and their ability to act on them.

There was, in a word, much "normalcy," a condition that the historian is likely to underplay, because history dwells on the extraordinary, the newsworthy event. Although the ferment of change was considerable as individuals and nations sought to achieve new environments for and definitions of security (emotional as well as physical), the Russian anarchist, Mikhail Bakunin (1814–1876), may have recorded the true mood of 1848. Visiting Berlin, he spied a sign in the window of a tailor's shop that showed a picture of the Prussian eagle. The words underneath it read:

Protected by the eagle's stance
I undisturbed can press my pants.

There were, between 1815 and 1848, more tailors than activists in Europe.

# IV. 4  Secular Attempts to Control Human Destiny

*We call that 'myth' which we do not believe, or which belongs to the culture of other peoples.* —Edmund Leach, anthropologist, 1969

After the failure of the 1848 revolutions, the mood of Europe became harsher and more extreme to many of those who had sympathized with the aims of the revolutions—with the ideas of democracy and national self-determination—it appeared that one clear lesson of 1848 was that pure enthusiasm was not enough, that right did not make might. A tough new realism seemed called for, and some historians have characterized the post-1848 period as that of *Realpolitik,* the politics of realism, as a time which valued practicalities over ideals.

The term is less than wholly illuminating, if only because it is redundant. Politics and politicians are usually realistic, for if they are not, they will not last. Yet there was a new determination to the movements and ideas of the second half of the nineteenth century. It can be seen in the new nationalism, which now availed itself of organized armies rather than of improvised street-fighting to achieve its aims. It can be seen in the new imperialism, which imposed European rule on Africa and Asia with great vigor and much ruthlessness. It can be seen in Darwinism, which became a fashionable explanation not only of the processes of nature but of society as well, where only the fit were seen to prosper and the meek fell by the wayside. It can be seen in the gradual replacement of Liberalism with Socialism as the great movement of the Left. And it can be seen even within Socialism itself, in a shift from theoretical Utopian Socialism of the pre-1848 period to a tightly organized, practical (and ideological) Marxist Socialism of the later years.

### Socialism

Socialism, like liberalism and conservatism, is not a static word. Webster's New Collegiate Dictionary defines socialism as "a political and economic theory of social organization and democratic management of the essential means for the production and distribution of goods; Also, a policy or practice based on this theory."

This is not only a concise and objective definition of Socialism, it is also one which manages to find the common denominators between its various forms—between Utopianism and Marxism, revisionism and communism. For despite all their differences, especially over what may be considered to be "democratic management," there has been in all of them the conviction that the distribution of wealth in modern industrial society was unjust, because the few were left with more than they could possibly need, while the many were left with barely enough for subsistence.

The proposed socialist solution consisted of the common rather than the private ownership of the means of production, as well as the common distribution of goods produced, so that each member of society might receive an equitable—though not necessarily an equal—share. Measures should be taken, in other words, that economic production be for the use of the many, not for the profit of the few. Most socialist movements also advocated basic political changes aimed at achieving what seemed to them a more just society; despite their emphasis on the material conditions of life, most socialists did not limit themselves to purely economic goals.

But beyond these common denominators, many differences in means and ends have existed between various socialist groups. These differences have been so strong that some arguments between socialists have even been more bitter than those between the advocates of socialism and those of free enterprise. This was true even in the early years of socialism when there were no Bolsheviks, Mensheviks, or revisionists. Then the argument was solely between Marxists and Utopians. (Marx was the first to use Utopian, which was taken from Thomas More's famous island. Marx was mocking what he considered to be that group's lack of common sense, and the name has stuck.)

Chronologically, Utopians came before Marxists. Two famous Utopians stand out, one French and the other English—Charles Fourier and Robert Owen. Fourier (1772–1837), like many socialist leaders, was not born into the working class. He was the son of a wealthy cloth merchant from Lyons, who devoted his life and small fortune to changing what he considered to be the wrongs of the prevailing economic system. He felt that the existing society was preventing the individual from giving true expression to his or her passions. Fourier's answer for remodeling society and creating a world in which humans could be free was the commune, or what he called the phalanx.

These phalanxes were to be self-contained communities of 1,620 people each. This would allow a potentially complete assortment of the 810 different types of male and female temperament that he believed existed. Like everything else in Fourier, the phalanx was a blend of practical genius and eccentric fantasy. It was to be composed of volunteers (none of the Utopians believed in even temporary coercion) and self-sustaining. All phalanxes were supposed to be rural and each surrounded by several thousand acres of green space. At the same time each was to be an efficient producer. There would be one spacious building only (the forerunner of the modern garden apartment), one central plant provided all the power, and one central kitchen was to relieve the drudgery of cooking. However, the financial profits Fourier foresaw were not to be distributed equally. Instead, they were to be divided three ways, with five-twelfths going to those doing the manual labor, four-twelfths to those managing it, and three-twelfths to those providing the capital. He wanted work to be made as agreeable as possible by using colorful and frequently changed decorations; by training animals to perform some of the heavier chores; and above all, by having each member of the phalanx change jobs several times a day. Fourier did not believe that enthusiasm could be maintained for more than an hour and a half at any given task. The more unpleasant or dangerous the job, the higher the pay would be. The dirtiest job of all, garbage collecting, was to be undertaken by small boys mounted on Shetland ponies and dressed in colorful costumes, so they would be free to indulge in children's fondness for dirt.

Here, then, was the great blueprint for the good society and the good life according to Fourier. Talent was finally to be fulfilled and passions satisfied, including the natural propensity to love freely; it was Fourier as much as anyone else who associated socialism with promiscuity in many people's minds. Under such conditions, thought Fourier, people would be happier, literally grow a foot or two taller, and live to be well over 140 years old. It struck him as logical that one day someone of wealth would appear to finance the scheme, and so that he might not by some chance miss this opportunity, he announced that he would be at his desk each day from noon to one o'clock to discuss the matter.

No sponsor ever appeared, but the phalanx idea was taken up by a Utopian across the channel, Robert Owen (1772–1858). A highly successful and self-made businessman, Owen was a saddler's son whose formal schooling had ended at the age of nine. He had then been apprenticed to a draper, and at nineteen he managed a textile mill employing five hundred workers. In his twenties he took over the management of another mill in New Lanark, Scotland. What he saw there horrified him; much of the work force consisted of children between the ages of six and eight, recruited from Scottish orphanages, and the adult workers were derelicts, "children in body and mind."

Owen resolved to change this state of affairs. He wanted to improve the lot of the worker, of course, but he also wanted to show that in so doing, he would increase the mill's profitability. A happier worker would be a better worker. He began to transform New Lanark into a model community. The minimum age of labor was raised to ten, and schools opened for children to attend after working hours. The worst of the slums were pulled down and replaced with decent, cheap housing. The pay scale went up and a maximum day of ten and half hours was established at a time when the average working day ran to twelve or thirteen hours. It was popularly thought that nothing could be done about shortening the working day because profits were supposedly derived solely from the last hour of operations, and to shorten the working day would eliminate profits and result in the closing of factories. The gin mills were shut down, for they had poisoned too many customers with their cheap liquor.

> Drunk for a penny
> Dead drunk for two pennies
> Clean straw for nothing

read a sign at such an establishment. But Owen also made clean liquor available at affordable prices while treating drunkards harshly who made a public nuisance.

The list of his reforms was impressive, and they worked. Working people who were treated decently produced more, and profits at New Lanark almost tripled. Yet in another way the experiment was a disappointment. Owen hoped that he was doing more than improving the workers' lot in a corner of Scotland. He felt that New Lanark was truly a model community, and that once its success was established other businesses would follow his lead. But while many distinguished visitors came to New Lanark and were duly impressed, few if any British set up anything resembling it.

Hence, in 1825 Owen's son, Robert Dale, embarked on a more radical experiment in the New World, establishing what he called a parallelogram at New Harmony, Indiana. Its organization closely resembled Fourier's phalanx. It was set in the country, yet was balanced between farming and industrial production. Its members were volunteers, its essence was that of cooperation and harmony, which in Owen's words was "to be woven out of the powerful yarn of interest and the silken thread of love."

But this experiment also failed. Owen was not the last of the Utopians. A good many others followed him, especially in France where Utopianism seemed to have a special appeal. After an exuberant start, the lazy felt reluctant to work and the industrious reluctant to share. A Utopian who had preceded both Fourier and Owen had been French—the Count of Saint-Simon (1760–1825), who taught that society should be organized "to strive towards the amelioration of the moral and physical existence of the most numerous and poorest class." There were others in this same tradition: Étienne Cabet (1788–1856), who preached about the classless society and peaceful cooperation; Fourier's follower, Victor Considérant (1809–93), who was twice elected a deputy to parliament; Louis Blanc (1811–82), who felt that national workshops—instituted by the government but independent soon after—should provide creative and decently paid employment for those who needed it.

None of them, however, succeeded in creating a true mass movement. This was left to Karl Marx (1818–83). His approach and theories were in many ways antithetical to the Utopians.

### Marxism

Born in the Prussian Rhineland, Marx was the son of a prosperous lawyer. His family was Jewish, but converted when the boy was six to Christianity; the reasons were civil rather than religious. The German poet Heinrich Heine, who knew Marx and was also a convert to Christianity, called the baptismal certificate "the ticket of admission to European civilization," and under the weight of discriminatory practices perhaps half of Germany's Jews turned Christian in this period.

The young Marx was a brilliant student, receiving his doctoral degree at the age of twenty-three. He then turned to journalism and edited a paper in the Rhineland, where he encountered trouble with the censor's office. This was during the period of Reaction, and he went into exile, first in Paris and Brussels, and finally in London. It was there that he lived from 1849 to his death in 1883, producing the bulk of the writing that supplied the theoretical structure of Marxian Socialism—essays, articles, and above all, the *Grundrisse* (the foundations) and the monumental *Das Kapital* (1867).

Even in this brief biographical sketch, two intriguing facts deserve mention because what Marx had to say about alienation—specifically of the worker from the things the machine produced, and more generally of individuals from society—has recently found such a receptive audience. One is that his family did not convert to Roman Catholicism, which was the predominant religion of the Rhineland, but to Lutheranism, which moved them from a minority of perhaps 2 percent in their town to one of about 4 percent. The other is that while Marx spent more than half of his life in England, he remained a German exile. Few of his friends were British; his German, to the end, was better than his English, and German was the language of *Das Kapital.* Hence there is an occasional suspicion that Marx either chose alienation for himself, or had it imposed on him. In either case it is thought that he declared his own condition to be the condition of humankind. As he noted, feeling a bit of tension toward one's environment makes one productive.

During much of his London period, Marx was poor. Three of his children died, in part at least, of malnutrition. It was a self-imposed poverty; he was a man utterly devoted to his writing and to his political mission. From time to time, he received financial help from his friend and closest intellectual companion, Friedrich Engels (1820–95), coauthor with Marx of *The Communist Manifesto* (1848) and sole author of some of the basic works of Marxism, such as *The Condition of the Working Class in England.* Engels, too, was a native German, who spent much of his life in England. But unlike Marx, he was no political exile. His father was a wealthy textile manufacturer, and Engels was acting as the Manchester

*Karl Marx,* German-born philosopher and political theoretician, was the father of modern-day Communism, as the author of both *Das Kapital* and the *Communist Manifesto.* Source: Wide World Photos.

agent of the family business. He thus was able to provide Marx with many direct observations of the lives of owners and workers which Marx could otherwise only obtain from books. Yet Engels remained content to let Marx dominate their relationship. "Marx," he said later, "was a genius. We others at best were talented."

Marx's theories are a complex web of thought in which five major concepts stand out. To understand them is to understand the movement's essence. They are: economic determinism, the materialist dialectic, the class struggle, the idea of surplus value, and the concept of socialist evolution.

*Economic Determinism.* What moves people and events? What has forever determined society's actions and institutions? What was the single greatest determinant of human history? Economic environment was Marx's answer. Marx was deeply influenced by a German materialist philosopher, Ludwig Feuerbach (1804–72), who at one time summed up his philosophy in a line, "You are what you eat"—that is, the material conditions of our existence determine our philosophy, our politics, our temper, our morality, our life style.

Marx added a more specific economic theory to this general Feuerbachian idea. Let there be, he said, a change in the method of producing and distributing goods from agriculture to industry, or from hand labor to the machine—both transformations were witnessed in Marx's lifetime —and before long everything else would change: philosophy, art, government, warfare, religion, morals. The basis of society and life was economic, the rest was little more than icing on a cake; the "superstructure," Marx called it. "The mode of production conditions the general character of the social, political, and intellectual processes of life."

*Dialectical Materialism.* This then was the answer to what moved history. To it, Marx added an explanation of how it moved. That explanation was the materialist dialectic.

If economic determinism was derived from Feuerbach, the dialectic owed much to another academic teacher who Marx greatly admired, the Prussian philosopher Hegel. History, said Hegel's followers proceeded by way of thesis, antithesis, and synthesis; that is, by conflicts and their temporary solutions. As a society or an institution—the thesis—developed, it was bound to engender its opposite—the antithesis. The old declining mores and the new practices would eventually clash, and out of that conflict would develop yet a third force—the synthesis—which would absorb qualities from both thesis and antithesis. In turn, the synthesis would harden to become the thesis, and the dialectical process would continue. (The idea of a dialectic appealed to many, including the most famous American interpreter, Frederick Jackson Turner.)

Once again, Marx did not simply appropriate another's idea. Rather, he added to it, and in the process, altered it. To Hegel, God was the controlling force of the dialectic; the rhythm of thesis-antithesis-synthesis was a revelation of the Divine Plan. As "scientific socialists" Marx and Engels rejected this idealism; they saw it as a dialectic that was "standing on its head and must be turned upright again." The true dialectic was a materialist dialectic, as in the great conflict between the medieval feudal economy—the thesis—and the modern capitalist one—the antithesis- which resulted in its synthesis—socialism.

*The Class Struggle.* Marx offered another specific explanation of how history moved, of what really went on underneath the deceptive superstructure. It was the class struggle. What had been taking place over the centuries hidden by such fine words as honor, ideals, culture, progress, or democracy was the merciless struggle of class against class. Thus in ancient Rome, it had been masters against slaves, patricians against plebians. In the Middle Ages what truly mattered was not tournaments, chivalry, or scholastic philosophy, but the conflict between master artisan and apprentice, merchant and peasant, squire and serf. The constant factor in all of recorded history had been the struggle between oppressor and oppressed.

Something happened in the modern industrial age, however, which was altering the quality of the process: The struggle was being simplified. It had been a complex, many-sided battle in the Middle Ages; there had been rich squires and poor squires, lords and vassals, yeomen and serfs, guild masters, plain guild members, skilled laborers, and apprentices. There had been, in other words, a variety of classes and subclasses. With the advent of the industrial revolution, the struggle was being reduced to two classes—capitalists and proletarians. True, there still existed a middle class, but its days were numbered. While few of its members might become wealthy capitalists, the vast majority would be "pauperized," and join the proletariat. And in the coming battle, it would be the workers who, by virtue of their numbers and being the dialectic's force of the future, would win—the workers, and not the capitalists, not "those eminent spinners, leading sausage makers, and influential shoe-polish dealers."

*Surplus Value.* Marx both despised and admired the bourgeois class for emotional reasons, but he also offered what, to his mind, was an objective theory to support his feelings. This was the theory of surplus value, and as so often, he drew less on the polemics of associate radicals than on the teachings of highly respected English economists. To "explain" the middle class he went back to the three great classical economists of the age, Adam Smith, Thomas Malthus, and David Ricardo.

### The Classical Economists

Adam Smith (1723–90) said in his *Wealth of Nations* that the source of wealth was not precious metals, as the mercantilists of the early North American colonial empire thought, nor was wealth even all of the nation's natural resources added together. Instead, the source of all wealth was labor; labor alone was creative. There would be no precious metals unless labor extracted them from the earth, no houses unless labor built them, no books unless labor wrote them, made the paper, set the type, bound the volumes, and distributed them. Smith, who was a subtle writer, added that a distinction should be made between management and labor (in the modern sense), that the skill with which labor was applied mattered as much as the act of physical labor itself. He also made a strong argument in favor of free enterprise. But these last points were of no use to Marx's labor theory of value.

Smith's writings were very optimistic. Malthus's (1766–1834) essay on the *Principles of Population* was not. In that essay, he made some very gloomy predictions about the prospects of feeding the world's population. For population, he argued after a close study of the statistics, was forever increasing more rapidly than the available food supply. As he put it, "The power of population is indefinitely greater than the power in earth to produce subsistence for man. Population, where unchecked, increases in a geometrical ratio. Subsistence only increases in an arithmetical ratio." Nor was there very much to be done about it because among nature's unalterable laws was "passion between the sexes" and hence, the production of more and more children. Wars, natural disasters, famine, and epidemics might slow the process but could not stop it. To do that, "moral restraint" on the part of the most numerous and poorest classes was needed, a check to their "immoderate sexual appetites."

David Ricardo (1772–1823) took the ideas of Smith and Malthus one logical step further. Smith said that supply and demand determined the price of the goods that labor produced. It was another of nature's immutable laws, and Ricardo fully accepted it, adding that supply and demand also determined the price of labor. This meant that when the supply of labor was greater than the demand for it, i.e. when labor was plentiful, wages would not go up. Yet with the constantly rising population that Malthus postulated, labor was seldom likely to be scarce. Hence labor, exceptions aside (such as the depletion of the working force by some catastrophe), was likely only to receive its "natural price," that is to say the wages "necessary to enable the laborer . . . to subsist and to perpetuate their race, without either increase or diminution." Subsist meant just that; nor could anything be done about it. For if, either by government action or by the initiative of some kindly employer, wages were raised above the subsistence level, the worker, deluded by temporary riches, would merely have more children, and hence increase the future labor force.

Very well, said Marx, here is Adam Smith demonstrating that labor is the source of all value, that labor alone creates wealth. And there are Malthus and Ricardo, proving that labor receives a mere subsistence wage, receiving only a fraction of the value it has created. What though, asked Marx, has been happening to something the classical economists have apparently overlooked—the difference between value created and wages received? What has happened to the difference between the market price of five shillings for a box of handkerchiefs, and the two shillings that all the labor involved in its production received? The answer, said Marx, was simple. The surplus value, that is, the value over and above the cost of an article's production, has been pocketed by the capitalist. The capitalist hence by definition was a thief and an exploiter, the person who robbed the worker of his true earnings.

Matters would not forever continue in this fashion. Exploitation became worse as the capitalists' acquisitive appetites grew. The condition of the proletariat became worse until it finally grew insufferable. At that point, the workers, made desperate by capitalism but enlightened by the Marxist analysis of their condition, rose and destroyed the old order and overthrew the regime of exploitation that they had tolerated for too long.

And that day of revolution came sooner rather than later because capitalism was incapable of running its own system and was hastening its destruction by its own internal contradictions, such as the industrial machine's capacity for producing immense amounts of goods which it kept out of people's hands by paying them mere subsistence wages.

*Socialist Evolution.* When that day of reckoning came, when "the expropriators are expropriated," society did not directly proceed to communism, however. It first had to pass through a less perfect socialist phase. In that phase, Marx postulated, the state and its coercive powers would still exist, because a "dictatorship of the proletariat" would have to be instituted to prevent any attempted revival of the old order. But that dictatorship would be a temporary expedient only. In due course, the state would "wither away" and socialism would evolve into communism. "This dictatorship," as he wrote to a friend, "only constitutes the transition to the abolition of all classes and to a classless society." In that truly classless, communist society, there would be no more oppression and injustice, no more private property and greed, no more exploitation of individual by individual. Instead, each person would contribute to society according to his or her abilities and receive according to his or her needs. And the rule of the few would be replaced by "an association in which the free development of each is the condition for the free development of all."

Marx was vague here, for he was providing a vision of the future that none had seen yet. But was he not also contradicting himself as some critics have alleged, in that he, the believer in the dialectic, now presented communist perfection as the end of the dialectic? He was not, for the communist vision he offered merely spelled the end of the *materialist* dialectic. This would enable the true dialectic, freed from its economic straitjacket, to determine events. As Lenin put it, "Marx did not say that history ends with Communism but that it begins with it."

All this was a new and more forceful socialism than the Utopians had offered. The Utopians believed in peaceful means to achieve peaceful ends. Marx advocated revolution. The Utopians relied on voluntary cooperation. Marx spoke of dictatorship. The Utopians were satisfied with building their individual communes. Marx wished to change the world. The Utopians were tentative in their conclusions and willing to experiment. Marx insisted that he was offering proven scientific laws. And the Utopians, finally, made few converts. Marx made many. He did so by building, in the First International, a still small yet more than local workers' organization. And he did so by providing the slogans that moved millions from "workers of the world unite, you have nothing to lose but your chains," to the state as "the executive committee of the bourgeoisie," to "a specter is haunting Europe—the specter is Communism."

## IV. 5 Darwin and Darwinism: Salvation Through Science

> *We will now discuss in a little more detail the Struggle for Existence.*
> —Charles Darwin, *The Origin of Species,* 1859

Marx intended to dedicate *Das Kapital* to one of the most celebrated British naturalists of the time, Charles Darwin (1809–1882). He apparently saw some clear parallels between Darwin's concepts and his own, between the struggle for survival in nature and the struggle for dominance in society. A cautious man, Darwin rejected the honor. He was regrettably ignorant of economics, he wrote to Marx, and did not think it appropriate that his name follow the title page. But he extended his best wishes to Marx in what he assumed was their common endeavor, the advancement of human knowledge. And in truth Malthus, Marx, and Darwin were part of the same environment: one of burgeoning, overcrowded cities, twelve-hour factory shifts for six-year-olds, of nations and nationalities attempting to find their "place in the sun," and of the repressive climate of the age of Metternich and the Concert of Europe.

In his own field, Darwin's findings revolutionized biology. They profoundly affected Europe's ways of thought in social and intellectual areas as well. Darwin's great work appeared in 1859, under the long and revealing title, *On the Origin of Species by Means of Natural Selection; or, The Preservation of Favored Races in the Struggle for Life.*

The problem of the struggle for life, or for existence, had done much to motivate the young Darwin's quest. Like most educated people of his time, he had read Malthus, and he was greatly intrigued by precisely why some organisms survived, in the constant struggle for the scarce food supply while others perished. Was it mere chance? Or was it simply an incomprehensible fate? Was it due to the intervention of some supernatural being? As a scientist, Darwin rejected such explanations. What he concluded instead, after his observations during the voyage of H.M.S. *Beagle* to the South Pacific, was that the individual organisms of any given species—whether squirrels, pigs, or humans—were not identical. Instead, variations appeared at birth, which in the perpetual battle for life's necessities, favored some and hindered others. In nature's eternal process of selection during the daily struggle for life, it was the fit who survived, and the less fit who fell by the wayside. What were the qualities that made for fitness and thus survival? Strength, speed, and intelligence might under some circumstances be outweighed by other attributes that mattered more. The one absolute was fitness, the possession of those qualities that allowed an organism to adjust to and withstand the conditions of the particular environment in which it existed. It was this ability to decode and adapt to a specific environment that was meant by survival of the fittest.

It was not merely that the fittest individuals—those endowed with the most favorable variations—survived in this fashion. It also followed that because only they were likely to live long enough to procreate their kind, very slowly there would evolve what amounted to a new species. Thus over the millennia, the pig had evolved from the boar, or the dog from the wolf. Nor had the process of evolution stopped short of the human race. Homo sapiens, too, was a product of evolution; it had evolved over countless generations from some ape-like creature. It was a point Darwin made very fleetingly only in the *Origin of Species*. He elaborated on it in the *Descent of Man* (1871); even before that, it became one of the most controversial of his theses.

Not that other aspects of his findings escaped controversy. The impact of the *Origin of Species* was enormous. All copies of the first edition were sold out on publication day. Few lay people read the book thoroughly, for there was little need. Other more easily read writers, notably Herbert Spencer (1820–1903) and Thomas Huxley (1825–95), were popularizing Darwin's discoveries. In 1901 a British newspaper asked a group of notables for a list of ten books, English or foreign, which struck them as having been the most influential in the preceding century; the list varied widely. Even *Das Kapital* was not a unanimous choice. The only book that all agreed on was Darwin's.

One reason was its impact on organized religion, giving rise to what the nineteenth century called the Warfare of Science and Theology. Darwin's explanation of life was clearly at variance with that of *Genesis*, which had stated that all forms of life had been brought into being by a single Creator in six days. It was true, of course, that many others before Darwin argued with this account of creation, and with its biblical sequel, which stated that all existing animals descended from those species that had found shelter on Noah's ark. But none of them offered any good alternative theories of how living organisms had come into being. Darwin did this. The shape of life arose through a steady process of variations and selections that had taken place over millions of years.

The fundamentalist Christian answer—Protestant and Catholic—condemned Darwin and his teachings. The Bible was right, the scientists were wrong. One comma of scripture contained a higher truth than all the work of natural science in the British Museum. We did not owe our existence to some "primordial ooze"; life was "not begun in a mudpack." God was the creator of all life. If Darwin could not agree with that, the fault was Darwin's. It was Darwin's words that should be reexamined, not those of the scriptures.

This view never entirely disappeared. It made the teaching of evolution a risky enterprise well into the twentieth century. Yet the fundamentalist position actually remained a minority position. By and large, the churches made their peace with Darwin on the issue of creation. They did so either by a studied, even wise, neutrality—that is, by disregarding Darwin—or by conceding that the Bible, though the word of God, was written by humans, and hence not free from the possibility of error, and that many of its accounts should be taken metaphorically rather than literally. Thus the six days of creation, while six days in the sight of God, might be six billion years in our limited human vision. This attitude pleased Darwin, who did not wish to attack Christianity. Along with his less rabid followers, he was ready to admit that science was without answers to ultimate questions, such as the nature of good and evil, death and eternity. Besides, as he wrote to a friend, it seemed to add to God's splendor that in the beginning, He had created just a few species, and endowed them with the capacity for self-development.

### *Social Darwinism*

But while the two accounts of creation might learn to coexist, it was infinitely harder to reconcile Christian values and ethics with those of a movement that Darwin's ideas inspired: Social Darwinism. Its earliest and clearest advocate was Spencer. He argued that all society and not just nature was dominated by the struggle for life. All was evolution and the survival of the fittest. We should be glad that this was so, for without it, there would be stagnation and disaster, while with it, there was the certainty of competition, improvement, and progress. As he wrote in *Social Statics* (1873):

> Pervading all nature we . . . see at work a stern discipline, which is a little cruel that it may be very kind. [Nature's] state of universal warfare . . . is at bottom the most merciful provision. . . . The poverty of the incapable, the distresses that come upon the imprudent, the starvation of the idle . . . are the decrees of a large, far-seeing benevolence. . . . It seems hard that a laborer incapacitated by sickness . . . should have to bear the resulting privations. It seems hard that widows and orphans should be left to struggle for life or death. Nevertheless, when regarded not separately, but in connection with the interests of universal humanity, these harsh fatalities are seen to be full of the highest beneficence—the same beneficence which brings to early graves the children of deceased parents, and singles out the low-spirited, the intemperate, and the debilitated as the victims of an epidemic.

Nature was harsh only to better bestow its blessings. For if one were to be kind—or, in other words, if one were to exercise Christian charity—and protect the lazy or inebriated workers from the consequences of their vices, the one predictable result would be to increase the number of lazy and drunken workers. And who would want to use the goods they produced? Were one to overlook the failures of the incompetent medical student, the one predictable result would be to provide the sick with an incompetent physician. "The ultimate result of shielding men from their folly is to fill the world with fools."

Darwin was not a Social Darwinist, himself. He expressly stated that it made little sense to him to apply his scientific findings to the nonscientific areas of morality and social conduct. Individuals in society, he wrote, were very different from beasts in the jungle. One needed sympathy and cooperation to achieve progress in society. "Selfish and contentious people will not cohere, and without coherence nothing can be effected." Nor was Spencer, as a quick reading of the quotation might indicate, a callous man. It was true that he was opposed to any sort of legislation or private action that would contribute to providing the world with more fools. But he looked with favor on whatever private aid was needed to keep people from utter privation. People should not passively watch their neighbors starve or freeze to death. And in the first book he wrote, his *Principles of Ethics* (1891), he went to some lengths to praise such non-Darwinian, Christian principles as charity, the condemnation of cruelty and compassion. Mutual extermination, if the law for tigers, was not the law for human beings, and the highest stage of evolution might well be altruism.

Few such fine distinctions, however, were made by Darwin's and Spencer's followers, and it was the followers rather than the originators who set the tone in subsequent years. In the economic sphere, for instance, Social Darwinians provided a rationale for some of capitalism's sharpest practices. Was there something objectionable about the accumulation of great wealth on the part of some if the price paid was the deprivation of the many? Not at all, said John D. Rockefeller, an American entrepreneur. All that was involved was "the survival of the fittest, . . . the working out of a law of nature and a law of God." Andrew Carnegie, the great Scottish-born steel-maker and contemporary of Rockefeller, admitted that this sort of economic contest "might be hard for the individual." But, he added, "it is best for the race because it insures the survival of the fittest in every department."

Was Social Darwinism entirely a matter of lay people misreading, or misapplying, an essentially scientific argument? Not quite, for there were biologists who now specialized in the new science of eugenics, in trying to improve the hereditary qualities of the race—of any race. One approach was an attempt to speed the natural by artificial selection. In practice, this meant mating the fit with the fit, and such an approach had obvious shortcomings. Improving plants and animals by means of artificial selection was one thing, but nineteenth-century liberals and conservatives still set definite limits to manipulating private human behavior. This left a negative approach; one might prevent the clearly unfit—the tragically deformed, the utterly insane—from having children. Thus some occasional laws passed calling for compulsory sterilization. Whenever eugenic legislation was proposed, it encountered vocal religious opposition; where it did in fact pass, it tended to contain the strictest of medical safeguards.

But eugenics did help popularize, and to some extent lend respectability to, a concept whose importance far transcended any legitimate eugenic concern. That was the transformation of Darwinian concepts from individual organisms to entire nations, or to races in a loose, nonscientific sense. Race-thinking became racism.

The historically significant struggle for life, said the second generation of Social Darwinians, took place not between individuals but rather between nations. What accounted for the rise and fall of civilizations? Fitness did. What accounted for the dominance of some nations, and the subservience of others? Again, fitness. Hence it was wise for both victor and defeated to accept this scheme of nature, to let the victors impose their rule, and for the defeated to bear such rule willingly.

One such advocate was English, Walter Bagehot (1826–77). He was a man of many talents: a successful banker, politician, scientist, journalist, and for many years the editor of the London *Economist.* In his *Physics and Politics,* which was subtitled *Thoughts on the Application of the Principles of Natural Selection and Inheritance to Political Science,* he wrote:

> The majority of the groups which win and conquer are better than the majority of those who fail and perish. . . . Conquest is the premium given by nature to those national characteristics which their national customs have made most fit to win in war, and in many material respects those winning characters are really the best characters.

These ideas were echoed by another advocate of British fitness and expansion, historian James Anthony Froude (1818–94). In *The English in Ireland in the Eighteenth Century* he wrote:

> In a world in which we are made to depend so largely for our well-being on the conduct of our neighbors, and yet are created infinitely unequal in ability and worthiness of character, the superior part has a natural right to govern; the inferior part has a natural right to be governed; and a rude but adequate test of superiority and inferiority is provided in the relative strength of the different orders of human beings.

This was pseudo-Darwinism, of course. Darwin had written about biological species, not nations, and his key terms had been fit and less fit, not superior and inferior. Still, this interpretation of Darwin pleased Froude, who did not think that there was anything objectionable about the order he stipulated. On the contrary:

> The better sort of men submit willingly to be governed by those who are nobler and wiser than themselves; organization creates superiority of force; and the ignorant and the selfish may be and are justly compelled for their own advantage to obey a rule which rescues them from their natural weakness.

Implicit in this, of course, was a new justification for the use of war and violence in the search for a sense of security. They were a nation's unmistakable way of proving its fitness. The one true test, wrote Froude, was strength: "And the right of a people to self-government consists and can consist in nothing but their power to defend themselves.... The heart of the nation is in its armies."

Nor was this an argument reserved for the English. It became a European fashion. War, wrote Ernest Renan (1823–92), a French historian famous mainly for his rationalist life of Jesus, was "one of the conditions of progress, the sting which prevents a country from going to sleep." Was not war detestable even so? By no means, said Heinrich von Treitschke (1834–96), one of Germany's most eminent historians of the time. "It is the perpetual conflict between nations which constitutes the grandeur of history." And such thoughts affected the American mood as well. In war alone, said Theodore Roosevelt (1858–1919), could individuals "acquire those virile qualities necessary to win in the stern strife of actual life."

We must take these quotations with a sense of the parodox that is inherent in humankind. Bagehot's points were largely debater's points. Andrew Carnegie actually was one of the foremost philanthropists of his age, endowing some 2,800 public libraries. Both Renan and Treitschke restricted their violence to words. Theodore Roosevelt received the Nobel Peace Prize for arranging an armistice between Russia and Japan. Yet theirs were ideas that made realism synonymous with force in many people's minds, with what one German chancellor called a policy of "blood and iron." And they were ideas that infused two older ideas with renewed vigor and violence in the second half of the century: nationalism and imperialism.

## IV. 6  Europe's New Nations: Nationalism Triumphant, 1848–1914

*Not with dreams, but with blood and with iron,*
*Shall a Nation be moulded to last.*
—Algernon Charles Swinburne, British poet, 1884

Nationalism had been a major force behind the revolutions of 1848, and it was sturdy enough to survive the revolutions' failure. In fact, in the decades that followed, nationalism celebrated its greatest victories in precisely those areas where the revolutionaries suffered their worst defeats: Italy and Germany. Nationalism's quality was changing, though. In both areas, leadership was passing from the amateurs and idealists to the professionals and realists. This was, people said at the time, the triumph of *Realpolitik*, the triumph of the tough-minded.

### *Italy*

There was still a mixture of the new realism and the old idealism in Italy. The events of 1848 left the country as divided as ever; Italy remained a "geographical expression," not a single sovereign state. But two leaders set about changing this. One was Cavour, a modern pragmatist; the other was Garibaldi, an old-fashioned romantic. They were not quite equals, however. The principal architect of unification turned out to be the realist.

Count Camillo di Cavour (1810–61) was an aristocrat by birth, and a liberal by conviction. He had travelled extensively in Europe and returned to his native Piedmont with a strong admiration for Western industrial achievements as well as for British and French parliamentary institutions. He was fortunate in having been born in the right Italian state; Piedmont was not only the largest and the strongest state in the north, for under King Victor Emmanuel II (1849–78) it was also the one Italian state that had not abrogated a democratic constitution granted in 1849.

After making a considerable fortune modernizing his family's large estates, having learned much about modern scientific agriculture during his travels, Cavour entered government service in 1850. He first served as minister of agriculture, then as head of various other ministries until 1852 when he became Piedmont's prime minister, a post which he held until his death a decade later. Under his leadership, Piedmont-Sardinia experienced a process of modernization that was without precedent. Cavour's administration was responsible for building an efficient army, for putting the economy on a healthy footing, for constructing roads, railways and canals, for founding a Genoa-New York steamship line, and for providing Italy's best civil service. Cavour even tackled the most sensitive problem of all, the Catholic Church, and curtailed much of the power it had inherited from earlier centuries by abolishing special clerical privileges, introducing civil marriage, and expelling the Jesuits. His aim here as elsewhere, however, was renewal and not destruction. What he wanted, he said, was "a free church in a free state." What he wanted, too, was an even greater aim: the creation of an Italian state, united and free.

The chief obstacle to an independent Italy was Austria, for the Hapsburgs still held Lombardy and Venetia in the north. To remove the Austrians, Italy needed allies; this was another lesson of 1848. One opportunity to gain allies seemed to present itself in 1854 when the Crimean War broke out between Britain and France on one side and Russia on the other. Even though Piedmont had not a single direct interest in the Crimea, Cavour dispatched a Piedmontese army to Russia to fight with the Western allies. Italy's indirect interests seemed compelling enough.

The immediate results of Cavour's action were disappointing. The British found themselves in sympathy with the Italian aims, but they were unwilling to offend the Austrians. A patient Cavour controlled his disappointment, and a few years later there came another and better opportunity: In the summer of 1858 he secretly met with the Emperor of the French, Napoleon III, at Plombières. This resulted in an equally secret agreement by which the French would aid Piedmont in expelling the Austrians, after which Piedmont would form a new and enlarged Kingdom of Upper Italy, while Italy in its entirety would be united in a looser federation. By way of compensation, Cavour agreed to cede Nice and Savoy, whose populations were partly French anyway, to France.

This marked a new departure in nineteenth-century international relations. Two powers had engaged in a deliberate plan of aggression to manipulate a war. The two powers also had engaged in a deliberate plan of deception—Austria, it was agreed at Plombières, must be made to appear the aggressor.

The rest of the story is quickly told. War there was, one year later, in 1859. Its two great battles at Magenta and Solferino were won by the French-Italian coalition. At this moment of triumph, however, Napoleon III had a change of heart. He signed a separate peace with the Austrians, providing for a compromise: Lombardy would go to Piedmont while Venetia remained Austrian. Napoleon had been shocked by the battle scenes; besides, he was under strong domestic pressure to stop a movement that, in uniting Italy, was threatening to engulf the Papal states. But the French desertion made little difference. The separate peace was unenforceable; the movement of unification was no longer to be stopped. A number of fairly unbloody revolutions broke out in various Italian states with the common aim of annexation to Piedmont.

The largest of these occurred in the south, and for a time its leader dominated events as Cavour had earlier. He was Giuseppe Garibaldi (1807–82). In some ways, he was Cavour's antithesis—a republican, a romantic, and an enthusiastic amateur. In May of 1860 he set out from Genoa with a band of a thousand red-shirted men—there was no ideological connotation in the color, the shirts were surplus issue—to liberate the "backward kingdom" of Naples. The expedition turned into a triumph—a little too much so for Cavour, who worried what the French reaction would be were Garibaldi's radicals to sweep on into the Papal states. Cavour's solution was to move the Piedmontese army into the Papal possessions first, though he left Rome unoccupied. After that, his troops moved further south, and it was near Naples, then, that the two groups met, Victor Emmanuel's organized army and Garibaldi's improvised troops. Garibaldi's patriotism proved stronger than both his republicanism and his personal ambition. "Hail, King of Italy," he greeted the surprised Victor Emmanuel. "Hail, best of my friends," replied the king.

And king of Italy he would be. In March 1861, the kingdom of Italy was proclaimed, with Victor Emmanuel as the monarch, and Florence—because Rome was still under papal control—as the capital. A month later, Cavour died, his work nearly complete.

His work was carried on by his successors, and luck was on their side. Venetia, the one major portion of Italy still held by Austria, became a part of the new kingdom as a reward for Italy's fighting on the victorious Prussian side in the Austro-Prussian War of 1866. This still left Rome—"the star of Italy," Cavour had called it—where a French garrison was protecting the Papal Court. But in the Franco-Prussian War of 1870 Napoleon III was forced to recall his troops, and after the French defeat was sealed in the summer of 1871, Victor Emmanuel entered Rome in triumph. Except for two small pieces of Italian territory, Trieste and the Trentino, which the Austrians still held, all of Italy was united with Rome as its capital.

It seemed like the happy ending to a centuries'-long struggle in Italian history. The hopes of Dante and Machiavelli, the longings of generations of Italian patriots, finally seemed fulfilled. Italy was one. Its citizens should have been able to live happily ever after.

Yet they did not. In the century that followed, Italy suffered rather more than a country's normal share of troubles. The major problem was an economic one. The new nation was poor. It was poor in natural resources such as coal and iron, and it was poor in skilled labor. While the statistics had been available long before 1871, few had paid attention to them. Unification had been an all-consuming passion. Now that it was achieved, there came the realization that Italy was a "have-not" nation, was behind—and was likely to remain behind—on the desired road to industrialization.

Another problem was the continuing division of Italy (despite a common administration, a common flag, and a common king) into north and south. Economically, for instance, the north was not doing badly; in productivity and prosperity, Milan compared with many Western European industrial centers. In the south, the economy was still close to medieval. There was next to no industry in Sicily, and farming methods had changed little since the early Middle Ages. All things historical are relative, of course. If one compares Sicily's development with that of Western Europe, Sicily will be in last place. If, on the other hand, one compares it with the rest of the Mediterranean region—with Tunisia or Morocco, for instance—Sicily emerges in first place.

Much besides unequal economic development separated north from south. The many northern Italian administrators who moved into the south after 1871 added a new divisive element. That they were often more efficient than Neapolitans or Sicilians did little to enhance their popularity, nor did their arrogance. There were times, wrote one historian, when Piedmontese officials "treated the kingdom of Naples almost as if it were an African colony."

Under these circumstances, enthusiasm for unification often evaporated rapidly. The old regionalism reasserted itself. Political union notwithstanding, there were many Italies still—the Italy of Ferrara and of Umbria, of Venice and of Milan, and a score of other regions, each with its own traditions, sympathies and antipathies, dialects, cooking.

Countries have been able to survive strong regional and ethnic differences, and even derive much cultural profit from them. Switzerland is one such example, and the United States another. Italy was short on what both these countries possessed, a tradition of government by compromise and a reasonable variety of resources. Political battles in the new Italy tended to be sharp, personal, and divisive. For a while there was no room at all for the legitimate participation of the mass of poorer Italians in the political process. Not until 1913 was there any real widening of the franchise.

Political sophistication can be acquired, and basically the nation of Cavour and Garibaldi was as capable as any of doing so. What deepened the division was the religious issue. There were few Protestants and fewer Jews in this overwhelmingly Catholic land; but there were nearly an equal number of faithful Catholics on one side and vociferous anticlericals on the other. It resembled the French situation, with their practicing Roman Catholics. In both nations they leaned toward conservatism in politics as the anticlericals leaned toward liberalism. What made Italy different from France was the existence of the "Roman Question." In 1871, the Papal states had been annexed over the pontiff's protest, and he and his successors continued their refusal to accept the legality of the new Italian state.

Until well into the twentieth century, the popes would not venture out of the Vatican Palace, claiming that they were the state's "prisoners." The Vatican told faithful Catholics to engage in what amounted to a boycott of the state by enjoining them not to take part in Italian politics.

The matter was finally resolved by Benito Mussolini's treaty with the Papacy in 1929, in which a small but sovereign Vatican state—the Citta del Vaticano—was established on Italian soil. Until then good Italian Catholics faced a dilemma, and they faced it in a country where the church and Papacy were much more visible than anywhere else, in the state that was the center of Petrine development. The dilemma was that as an Italian citizen, one owed national allegiance to a kingdom which was engaged in political warfare with an authority to which one owed spiritual obedience. At a time when one needed to constantly identify priorities, the individual could find little security.

It was true that Italy overcame some of these difficulties, or prospered in spite of them. The church issue did cease to exist after 1929, and long before that the north and south made much economic progress. After the turn of the century Italy even joined the great (and even some lesser) powers in their quests for expansion overseas and began to acquire colonies in Africa. Yet this pursuit of power benefited neither Europe nor Italy, for Italy had to maintain a military establishment that was too costly if one considered the country's resources. Italian troops moved into Tripoli (Libya) in 1911 and into Ethiopia (Abyssinia) two and a half decades later—and lost both colonies by the early 1940s. Italy changed sides, in some of the least subtle exhibits of *Realpolitik,* in the midst of the two World Wars—and gained little or nothing in the subsequent peace treaties.

Obviously some of this ambivalence was the doing of Cavour's successors. The fact remained that in this most civilized of nations, a barbaric lesson had been drawn; that the forty-eighters had been idle dreamers and that it was *Realpolitik* and war that had established the united Italy. This perception contributed to much bloodshed and to the excesses of fascism. It was the wrong perception, but then that is the frequent fate of lessons in history.

## *Germany*

Did the Germans fare any better? The great questions of the day, said Otto von Bismarck (1815–98) in a speech to Prussia's lower house in 1862, are decided not by speeches and parliamentary majorities—that was the great mistake of 1848—but "by blood and iron." Even so, Bismarck was a more complex man than "blood and iron" might suggest. It was Bismarck who coined the much quoted definition (often attributed to Theodore Roosevelt) of politics as "the art of the possible." It was Bismarck who said, apropos of Russian behavior in the 1860s, "Russia is not a government, it is a force of nature"; he also said "we can put our clocks forward, but time won't pass any more quickly for that—the ability to wait is a precondition of practical politics"; and when accused of being too lenient with the French after Prussia's victory in 1871, "It is not the task of politics to avenge what has happened; it is the task of politics to see that it does not happen again."

Born into the Prussian squirearchy, Otto von Bismarck survived terrible school grades and an early civil service rating that took note of his "deficiency in regular habits and discipline" to establish a brilliant professional career. He entered the Prussian bureaucracy as a young man, became Prussia's representative in the Diet of the German Confederation in 1851, then served as Prussia's minister first to St. Petersburg and after that to Paris. In 1862 he was recalled to Berlin and asked to assume the office of prime minister—in which he remained for the next twenty-eight years. The king was engaged in a constitutional battle with parliament, which had refused to vote a requested army budget. Only Bismarck was considered shrewd and strong enough to deal with the rebellious parliamentarians.

The way he dealt with the initial crisis was characteristic. He told the deputies that whether they liked it or not, the army reforms for which the extraordinary funds were needed would continue. That was the whip. But there was also the carrot. They must realize, he told the liberals in particular, that the united Germany they wished to see would come about not by Prussian rhetoric—that was the real mistake of 1848—but by Prussian power, and skillful diplomacy. And three wars later, he served both of his foremost aims—a strong Prussia and a united Germany.

The first of these wars was accidental. It took place in 1864 after the king of Denmark proposed to annex the largely German-speaking province of Holstein. Prussia and Austria joined forces to fight the Danes over the issue and won the war within a matter of weeks.

They also fell out among themselves with nearly equal speed. The fault was Prussia's more than Austria's. Bismarck was looking for a test of strength between these two politically dominant German states. If there was to be unification, there could be only one leader. As early as 1856 he had written, "Germany clearly is too small for both of us. . . . In the not too distant future, we shall have to fight for our existence against Austria. There is no other solution."

In 1866 he had his war, and as in the Danish case, the Prussian army acquitted itself brilliantly. Within seven weeks, the Austrians were suing for peace. The peace they received, at Bismarck's insistence (and it was an issue over which he had to battle the king) was a generous one. There was no triumphal Prussian entry into Vienna, no transfer of territory to

Prussia, nor were there any reparations. To Bismarck, the object of war was not the destruction of the opponent or the victory and triumph. Rather, it was the achievement of certain political objectives. Bismarck was the master of the limited war, and of the equally limited, clearly defined war aim. The war aim in this case was a free hand for Prussia in reorganizing Germany.

There remained, however, one more potential opponent to a Germany united by Prussia. That opponent was France. For centuries, under monarchy and republic, under Bourbons and Bonapartes, under revolutionaries and legitimists, France had pursued an unchanging goal—the prevention of a strong German state. Bismarck felt that only war would change the French attitude, and in the summer of 1870 he found a pretext. It involved the candidacy of a Hohenzollern, or German, prince of the Spanish throne. The French understandably but clumsily objected. In provoking war Bismarck received unintended assistance from Napoleon III, who hoped that either a diplomatic or a military victory would be his.

The desperate Napoleon was wrong. Six weeks after the war started, Prussian troops were deep in France, and the emperor was a prisoner. This did not mean the immediate surrender of all French forces. A revolutionary republican government took control of Paris and carried on resistance for several more months. But the military verdict could not be changed. In January 1871, Prussian troops entered Paris, and peace talks began. Partly because of the war's prolongation and partly because of Bismarck's inability to resist the annexationists, the result was a less generous peace than that offered to the Austrians. Alsace and much of Lorraine was ceded, and France was forced to pay an indemnity of five billion francs. And France was powerless to prevent the achievement of German unification. In fact, it was on French soil—at Versailles in the Hall of Mirrors—that on January 18, 1871, the German Empire was proclaimed. Its Emperor was the King of Prussia, William I; its Chancellor, Otto von Bismarck. All German states except Austria were finally united in a new Reich.

The architect of unification, Bismarck, directed the affairs of the new Reich for two decades, until his dismissal by William II in 1890. The German experience was a happier one than Italy's. Regional differences, while real, were not as divisive. Nor was there a comparable economic gap between those regions. At the time, disillusionment with unification was very much a minority attitude.

Yet some profound troubles afflicted and divided the Reich. During his chancellorship, Bismarck found that he had to engage in protracted political warfare against two major groups of Germany's citizenry, the Catholics and the socialists. The Catholics came first. The Papacy, in part as an overreaction to the political encroachments of the new Italian state, was reasserting and (so it seemed to some) exaggerating its spiritual powers. In 1864 the Holy See proclaimed a *Syllabus of Errors,* which denounced any sort of state interference in the affairs of the Church and condemned as erroneous such current ideas as the belief in the efficacy of science and rationalism. It was an error to assume, said the Syllabus, that the Pope "should reconcile and align himself with progress, liberalism, and modern civilization."

A proclamation of Papal infallibility followed in 1870. The first Ecumenical Council to meet since Trent, three centuries earlier, decided that in matters of faith and morals the Pope, speaking *ex cathedra*—that is, in the exercise of his office—could not err. To many a German, more was involved here than a spiritual claim. German Catholics had organized politically in a Center Party. This was a major party in the Reichstag, and it was ably led; its leader, Ludwig Windthorst (1812–91), was one of the few parliamentarians who could compare with Bismarck as a speaker. And while Germany as a whole was divided roughly equally between Protestants and Catholics, there was a disproportionate number of Catholics in those areas whose loyalty to the state was in some doubt—in the partly Polish eastern provinces and in the predominantly French Alsace-Lorraine.

To many it seemed essential to respond to the Pope's assertions. As a German professor of international law argued, "If the Pope is venerated as infallible in matters of faith and morals, he becomes the religious and moral leader of the world. If it is the duty of the people of the world to obey the infallible Pope in matters of faith and morals, then they must *not* obey any person or thing opposed to the Pope, or that the Pope is opposed to; neither science nor their own reason, neither the laws of the state nor the king's command." And Rudolf Virchow (1821–1902), a distinguished medical researcher and liberal member of the Reichstag, echoed the sentiment in a parliamentary speech in which he said that the contest between the progressive state and the archaic church was a *Kulturkampf,* "a struggle for modern civilization."

Quite possibly the threat from Rome was exaggerated. It was a weak and not a strong Pope who opposed modernism and asserted his infallibility. But Bismarck and many of his contemporaries did not see it that way. Thus, the 1870s in Germany became the period of *Kulturkampf.* With the support of the liberals, Bismarck's conservative government passed a series of anti-Catholic measures for Prussia. The Jesuits were expelled from Catholic Bavaria as well. The clergy was forbidden to criticize the government, some Catholic schools and seminaries were closed, and several nonconforming bishops were arrested or exiled. Prussia required civil marriages and suspended financial aid to the Catholic Church in

**Unification of Germany, 1866-1871**

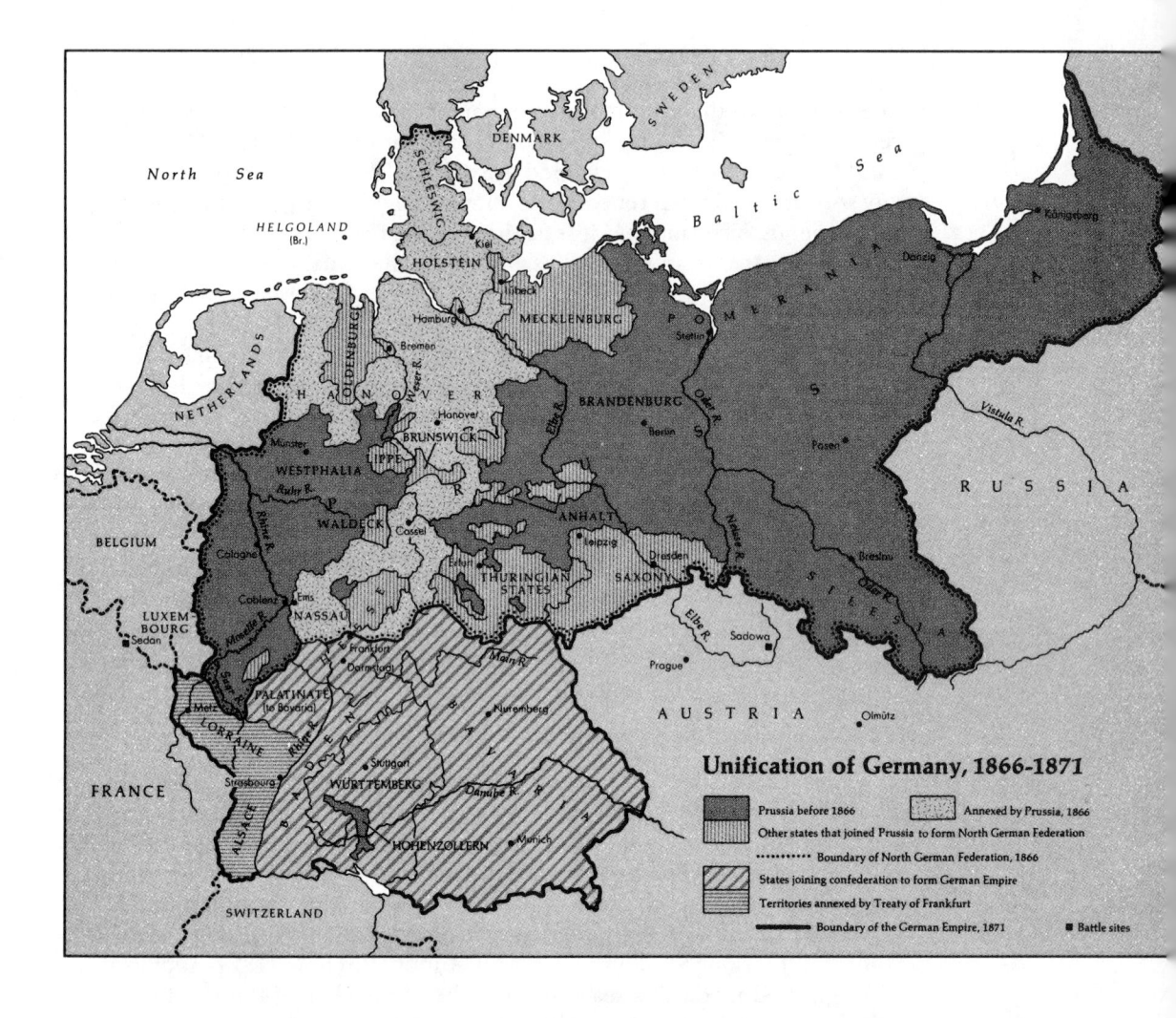

- Prussia before 1866
- Annexed by Prussia, 1866
- Other states that joined Prussia to form North German Federation
- Boundary of North German Federation, 1866
- States joining confederation to form German Empire
- Territories annexed by Treaty of Frankfurt
- Boundary of the German Empire, 1871
- ■ Battle sites

those areas where obedience to the new laws was refused. (The churches in Germany, as elsewhere on the continent, relied on tax money allotted by the state rather than on private contributions for their maintenance.)

These were sharp measures eliciting sharp responses. Rather than complying with the orders of the state, the Church fought back with great vigor. Pius IX (1846–78) declared Bismarck's laws "null and void," enjoining all German Catholics to disobey them. Catholic services stopped in many of the towns and villages of Germany in protest; there were no baptisms, no marriages, no final sacraments.

Bismarck's initial reaction was that he would not surrender to this pressure. But in the end he did, calling off the *Kulturkampf* at the close of the seventies. He had several reasons. He had come to realize that the church could thrive on persecution, that the old phrase about the blood of the martyrs being the seed of the church was more than rhetoric. Thus this looked like the one battle he could not win. He also felt that his liberal allies were beginning to ask too high a price for their aid, and that needlessly sharp national divisions were being created by the often ugly arguments against Catholicism. But there was something else now too. He saw a new enemy, and he needed the support of the Catholic Center Party of contain it. The new enemy was German Social Democracy.

The German Social Democratic Party, founded in 1869, was a Marxist party, and its literature and meetings abounded in revolutionary slogans. Nor was the party a handful of eccentrics: Eight years after its founding, in the Reichstag (or parliamentary) elections of 1877, the Party gained half a million votes, or ten percent of the total electorate. And a year later, there were two assassination attempts against the German emperor's life. Actually, the would-be assassins were anarchists rather than socialists, and the Party was far from being as revolutionary as its rhetoric proclaimed it to be. But these were distinctions that were too subtle for most contemporaries to appreciate. Ideological differences between socialists and anarchists seemed theoretical, and phrases such as "break your chains" or "dictatorship of the proletariat" seemed to mean pretty much what they said.

Hence, beginning in 1878, a number of bills were pushed through parliament that outlawed the German Social Democratic Party, forbade its meetings, suppressed its newspapers, and allowed the police to expel suspected Social Democrats from a particular region. Still, the ban was not total and had to be reconfirmed every two years, but while the Party as such was illegal, individual Social Democrats were free to run for the Reichstag. Bismarck's Germany was not a police state, was no rehearsal for Adolph Hitler. For Bismarck realized that suppression by itself was not enough. The ban of the Party was accompanied, to use Bismarck's words, "by a positive improvement in the welfare of the working classes." As he put it:

> Give the working man the right to work as long as he is healthy; assure him care when he is sick, assure him sustenance when he is old. If you do that, and do not fear the sacrifice, or shout 'State Socialism' as soon as the words 'provision for old age' are uttered—if the state will show a little more Christian solicitude for the working man, then I believe that the gentlemen of the [Social Democratic] program will sound their bird call in vain, and that the rush toward them will cease as soon as the working men see that the government and the legislature are earnestly concerned for their welfare.

In 1882, parliament voted for a general health insurance plan, with both employers and employees contributing the necessary funds. In 1884, compulsory accident insurance, or workmen's compensation, was added, with all costs being paid by the employer. In 1889, social security legislation followed, whose costs were divided between employer, employee, and the state.

These were exemplary laws in the full sense of the term. They often were sound laws, and they served as examples for similar legislation the world over. And the workers liked the legislation's benefits. Here Bismarck's calculation was right. But he was also wrong, for the workers' socialist sympathies did not stop. The Social Democrats remained the German workers' party. In this sense, the antisocialist fight had failed the way the *Kulturkampf* had.

In the end, Bismarck realized this. But in 1890 matters were taken out of his hands. In an ostensible disagreement over the socialist legislation, the new emperor, William II (1888–1918), removed him from office.

The old king of Prussia and emperor of the new Germany, William I (1861–88), had been a modest and sensible ruler, content to let Bismarck run the major affairs of state. The new emperor, William II, wished to be his own chancellor. Under the Constitution, he had every right to be just that—to appoint nonentities to the office of chancellor and to make the ultimate policy decisions himself. Yet, William II was neither a sensible nor a modest man, being given to grandiloquent speechmaking and to the pursuit of policies that, while lacking in any consistent direction, alarmed both his domestic opponents and Germany's neighbors. They did so especially because he was master over Europe's strongest and fastest-growing armed forces.

The "personal regime" of William II, as one German historian called it, has been the subject of much justified criticism. It may therefore be useful as well as fair to point out that despite the emperor's instability, despite his flights of fancy, his claims to rule "by the grace of God," and his tendency to consider opposition to his ideas nearly treasonous, there was much that was solid about his Germany. The nation was prosperous. Unification had ended the economic as well as the political fragmentation of the country, and production increased at a tremendous rate. As the Germans began to catch up with, and then to overtake, their competitors, the Ruhr became the industrial heartland of much of Europe. Between 1882 and 1907, German industry created some ten million new jobs, and in the decade before 1914, the nation's foreign trade doubled. If the emperor's arrogance was one German export, so was the soothing beer that Löwenbräu brewed and the pain-relieving aspirin that Bayer manufactured. This was also a Germany which offered a modest degree of social mobility. Access to education and wealth was easier than in Great Britain, and many new names appeared in German industrial and intellectual life. Germany led in the growth industries, in the new technology—in optics, in the development of the internal combustion engine, in electrical and chemical engineering. Zeiss, Siemens, and Benz were names that survived the empire. And for all the emperor's narrow artistic vision —modern art was "gutter art" to him—there was a great deal of intellectual ferment and achievement in the Germany of his time as there had been in Bismarck's. This was the age of the great historians, of Leopold von Ranke (1795–1886) and Theodore Mommsen (1817–1903). It was the time when a disproportionate number of Nobel Prizes in physics, chemistry, medicine, as well as in literature went to Germans. It was the time when Albert Einstein (1879–1955) first published his theory of relativity and Thomas Mann's (1875–1955) *Buddenbrooks* became a bestseller.

This society did not consider its opportunity for free artistic and intellectual expression compensation for political subjugation. The German press was free. The Reichstag did not hesitate to either criticize the government or vote its disapproval of imperial blunders. It was true that the Reichstag lacked one major power considered essential to parliamentary government: The cabinet was responsible to the emperor, not to parliament; the emperor had the sole right to appoint or dismiss ministers. Hence, parliament might find fault with the government and act as a strong pressure group, but it could not replace the government with another. Still, parliament did possess the power of the budget, and because it was elected on the basis of universal male suffrage, it represented the nation's will more clearly than did the state legislators, which often were not.

Besides, Germany under William II, as under Bismarck, was a *Rechtstaat*, a government of laws, not of individuals. The liberties of the citizen were assured—equality before the law, the inviolability of property, freedom of movement, secrecy of the mails, the right to assemble peaceably. Local self-government had been preserved. Given this plenitude of civil liberty, most Germans were content not to push political liberty to its limits, and as a result they enjoyed what was possibly Europe's best civil service. The state—from the internal revenue office to postal deliveries —was so well run that there seemed no occasion to worry. Germany, a critical Frenchman suggested, might be badly governed but it was very well administered.

Yet in retrospect it is clear that people should have worried more, that Bismarck's Germany suffered from birth defects that became fatal under William II. Too much had come too soon, the new state had simply grown fat too fast. Success had gone to some people's heads. As was the case with Italy, a false toughness and misapplied realism set the tone. One example may stand for many. Just before Bismarck began his war on Austria in 1866, a leading Prussian historian wrote, "Never, I think, has a war been engineered with such revolting shamelessness and alarming recklessness." A few weeks later, when the Prussians had won, the same historian wrote, "I bow to the genius of Bismarck.... For such a man, I would give a hundred men of impotent honor."

*Time Devours Us* The Spanish painter Francisco Goya became ever more pessimistic about mankind's follies, and as he himself became deaf, he turned to dark, horrific pictures. Here in "Saturn Devouring His Children" he captures the sense of insecurity in mankind: Saturn, or Time, will in a frenzy destroy us all. As he noted, "The dream of reason produces monsters." *Source: Editorial Photocolor Archives.*

However, behind the swagger there was much uncertainty, much lack of confidence. Had it been otherwise, the emperor would not have talked as loudly as he did. Twenty-eight years after "dropping the pilot," the Germany Bismarck founded was defeated by a coalition of Europe's powers. A Polish state was rising again, Alsace-Lorraine was lost to France, and the emperor was in exile. Twenty-seven years after that, in 1945, Bismarck's creation was wholly destroyed—parts of it annexed by Poland, parts by Russia, with the remainder forming the nucleus of one German state in the west and another in the east.

# PART FIVE

New Wine
in Old Bottles:
Today Enters
the Front Door,
1848-1919

*Justice . . . is the tolerable accommodation of the conflicting interests of society.*
—Judge Learned Hand, American Jurist, *c.* 1946

## AN OVERVIEW: AN AGE OF INSECURITY

The Enlightenment, the French Revolution, and the abortive revolutions of the following decades had secularized the old millennial beliefs of humankind. The vision of the Kingdom of God upon earth had become a dream of endless material progress, in which life had the prospect of becoming slowly more tolerable, even comfortable. Meliorism, which is the belief that the world may be improved by human effort, gave a special dynamism to nationalism, imperialism, socialism, and communism. At its extreme, meliorism could justify terrorism, for as Tocqueville wrote, "the politics of the impossible, the theory of madness, the worship of blind audacity," arose in the nineteenth century.

This new dynamic was felt abroad as well as in Europe. As the European powers expanded across the globe, they slowly created systems of governance that were much more disruptive to the mores of Asian and African societies than the rule of earlier conquerors had been. Less often now was the conqueror conquered; seldom did a European take on Asian or African ways; more often, it was the Asians or Africans who found themselves in mid-passage between the new, tempting, technologically exciting European culture, and their own seductive, comprehensible, psychologically secure culture. As the Europeans destroyed the traditional structures of their colonies, they produced deep insecurities that erupted against them in the twentieth century in India, China, east and west (and perhaps, southern) Africa, and the Near and Middle East. As people were separated from their cultural certainties, a new, secular certainty began to take the place of the old: nationalism was tempered by tribalism, race hatred, and by a great gulf between power and wealth. For where a people had wealth but no power, they lived in a vacuum of frustration; and where they had the power of a waning prestige but little wealth, they became a vacuum into which all the running dogs of communism and capitalism rushed. Increasingly the globe would be unified.

As mankind launched *missiles* into outer space, as men walked on the moon, man's curiosity opened up yet another New World—to conquer? *Source: NASA*

Increasingly a danger once felt only in a particular place would become generalized. Increasingly famine in Asia, riots in southern Arabia, falling cash crop prices in west Africa, and oil production in the Middle East would have their repercussions in Europe and North America. Technology would alter the world out of sight, so that in ten years a person might see more change than an earlier civilization had seen in a hundred.

The technological changes that occurred in the nineteenth century unified the globe, creating new sources of economic interdependence and spreading the idea of modernization into remote corners. New methods of communication and transportation meant that thoughts could be transmitted quickly from place to place, and that people and goods could follow. New developments in printing led to the rise of the mass newspaper, inexpensive books and lending libraries, and facts, skills, and ideas that could be called "common knowledge." This was especially so in the sciences, which could transcend language barriers because the language of science was quantitative, technical, and easy to translate. Increasingly, industrial forms of organization found in one nation became similar to those found in another. By 1914, a Belgian and an American scientist, while speaking different languages, could talk of the same subject with a similar technical vocabulary through instant telegraphic means.

Symptoms of modernization included urbanization, a decline in death and birth rates, the rise of political, social, and economic bureaucracies to communicate, administer (and sometimes control) the new knowledge, mass systems of education so that all might enjoy and contribute to the fruits of progress, the rise of a literate mass culture, and increased specialization. This was so not only in specific factory-related skills, but in dividing those who managed from those who worked at a machine, those who planned the innovations of the future and those who carried them out, those who speculated and those who did not. As the middle class broadened, blurring old class lines, industrialization and modernization created new, far more complex classes, based less upon what one owned than upon what one knew.

An invention and a process are different things. The former grows from the discovery of the latter; both of them first require the verification of scientific theory. The growth of science lay at the root of the magnificent flowering of industrial expertise in Europe after 1870. Since the turn of the last century, science has grown exponentially: there are more scientists alive today than have lived in the entire history of the world. This take-off started in the last decades of the nineteenth century, and while Arab and Chinese science were once of great importance, in those decades the acceleration of knowledge was largely Western. From the combustion engine to nuclear theory to modern day rocketry, each scientific breakthrough led to a profusion of patents that changed people's lives, from their bathrooms to their gardens, from the way they told time to the way they healed themselves. Ironically, the greatest spurs to practical applications of theory were times of international crises—of war, in particular—when national competition, national unity, and the desire to steal an edge on one's enemy spurred medical research, advances in means of communication, and industrial rationalization.

Among the inventions of the nineteenth century, one may single out six as especially significant: the telegraph, the application of steam to shipping, the rotary press, refrigeration, the camera, and the means of controlling births by limiting pregnancies. Inventions take place within a social and ideological setting, however, so that not all are accepted, applied, or improved upon with equal speed and skill. Although mechanical and scientific means of birth control may be dated from 1882, for example, the use of such technical knowledge is by no means accepted in all parts of the world today; conversely, from the moment in 1895 when an Italian, Guglielmo Marconi, invented wireless telegraphy, the world sought to transmit its messages with ever-greater speed and clarity. Basic to most of the inventions was the primacy of electrical power.

Between 1821 and 1831 an English scientist, Michael Faraday, developed the first electrical motor and generator. Initially electricity was not seen as a means of producing power so much as of sending messages. Samuel F. B. Morse, drawing upon studies of hundreds of experiments in electromagnetics over the previous century, developed the first practical electrical telegraph in 1832. Eight years later, William R. Grove invented the incandescent electric light. Now people could read, work, or travel after dark in greater safety and comfort than gas lights had permitted—the day was, in effect, extended. Thereafter, illumination and communication kept pace with each other. The first submarine cable was laid from Dover to Calais in 1851, after the problem of finding an insulator for underwater electrical transmissions was solved through the use of gutta-percha to protect cables. In the same year an electric locomotive was used on an American railway, although until the 1880s, batteries proved too costly for widespread application of electrical power to railroads. After William Thomson (who became Baron Kelvin) invented the mirror galvanometer, the first transatlantic cables were laid between Cornwall and Newfoundland in 1865–66.

Leadership in the commercial use of electricity thereafter shifted to the New World. In 1876 Alexander Graham Bell, a Scot working in North America, invented the telephone, transmitting the first of its ringing commands, "Come here, Watson, I want you," to his assistant. In the following year hydroelectric power was developed at Niagara Falls. A Romanian, Nikola Tesla, made long-distance transmission of electrical power possible through the discovery of the rotating magnetic field. Thomas A. Edison began his long series of major inventions with the phonograph, originally cranked by hand, to which he added electrical power in 1877, and two years later he improved upon the incandescent electric lamp. In 1879 in Germany, electricity was applied to the street car, in 1882 Edison designed a system for the central production of electrical power, and in 1885 a German scientist verified the existence of radio waves. In 1884 in the first commercial use of long-distance transmission, Boston and New York were linked by telephone. Then in 1895 Marconi's invention of the wireless freed people of the need to send voices across lines laboriously constructed from point to point. The age of instant communication had begun.

Each invention led to many others. When Edison invented the motion-picture machine, he was improving upon processes in photography that dated from the introduction of the wet collodian process in 1851. While at first the motion pictures of Edison and George Eastman depended upon manual power, they were soon linked to electricity and from 1894 the world came to know the movies as its most extensive form of mass entertainment. The cinema produced vast social changes in the ways families entertained, spent their evenings together, and learned about the world outside their own immediate environment. The inexpensive camera made forms of photo-duplication possible which assured accuracy and speed while eliminating hours of drudgery.

Each invention also led to an infinite variety of other changes, many of them nontechnical: the use of gutta-percha is an example. Gutta-percha is the milky liquid of the rubber tree after a lengthy processing; it is now used on golf balls and in dentistry as well. Because of the need for rubber, the British experimented with trees brought from Brazil to Kew Gardens near London, and then introduced the rubber tree to Malaya. The desire to control prime rubber-growing areas led, in turn, to further British expansion in Southeast Asia. The need for skilled rubber tappers forced the British to bring Indian and Singhalese laborers to Malaya in the 1920s, creating an ethnic problem that plagues Malaysia to this day. The need for rubber for automobile tires was among the reasons the Japanese conquered the Malayan Archipelago so quickly in 1941–1942.

The relationship between rubber and the automobile also illustrates how one process or invention fed upon another. People had sought safe, inexpensive, rapid means of land transportation for generations. The automobile was a result of the invention of the gasoline-powered internal combustion engine in 1887 by Gottlieb Daimler, a German inventor. In addition, the development in the United States of assembly-line means of manufacture by Henry Ford in 1909 meant that at last people could shrink distance on land as they had done on water and soon would do in the air. (This required rubber just as auto bodies stimulated the steel industry.)

The steamship was especially important to the creation of the "global village." It could carry great quantities of goods across rough seas throughout the year at speeds that would assure the transport of semiperishable cargoes to distant markets while demand for them remained high. James Watt invented the steam engine about 1770, using a separate condenser in order to conserve steam so that engines might be small and cheap enough to have a commercial application. Richard Trevithick and then George Stephenson (the latter in 1814) were the first to apply this invention to the railroad. Steam also was used for ships, Robert Fulton and Robert R. Livingston launching the first successful steamboat in 1807. As iron was introduced into shipbuilding, steam became more practicable: in 1826 the first vessel crossed the Atlantic under steam and in 1840 Samuel Cunard began the first successful transatlantic steamship run. When the Suez Canal opened in 1869, steam linked Europe and the East. What once had been a round-trip voyage of three years shrunk to three months; the New and Old Worlds were now two weeks apart; and as steam was applied to warships as well, the might of Europe stood just over the horizon. When refrigeration was added to transportation, first to railways in 1869 and then to oceangoing vessels in the 1880s, the perishable products of one part of the world began to flow to other parts, binding the world with cables of coins.

Yet, in the midst of this unprecedented technological progress, as labor-saving devices promised a broadening of individual dignity, there were weaknesses in the Western position. Heralded developments had negative as well as positive sides; for example, when the rise of the penny press made mass information possible, it also enhanced the power of those who wished to manipulate public opinion. In the years when technological, economic, and ideological threads seemed to have unified the Western world by extending the interdependency of peoples, nations drew further and further apart toward the ultimate destruction of war. Problems in the colonies—those areas meant to eliminate domestic problems—were in fact reflected in clashes at home: over Home Rule for Ireland, an issue which convulsed British politics between 1879 and 1916; over social unrest, the Paris Commune, and chronic political instability in France; over the unification of Italy, the Crimean War, and the partitions of Poland. Even contemporary observers were worried about Western decadence. The beginnings of a countercurrent to the optimism of the previous century was shown by those who predicted a decline in Western dominance. Social and political commentators like Anatole France (1844–1924) and Emile Zola (1840–1902) in France, Henrik Ibsen (1828–1906) in Norway, Karl Marx (1818–83) and Friedrich Nietzsche (1844–1900) in Germany, V.I. Lenin (1870–1924) in Russia, George Bernard Shaw (1856–1950) and the Fabian socialists in Britain, and Mark Twain (1835–1910) in the United States wrote of the dilemmas of mod-

By the 1970s two forces appeared to be contending for dominance in man's desire for security. Many were turning back to superstition, to the ancient beliefs of remote antiquity, to the expectation that creatures from outer space, other worlds, the spirit world, or the distant past would save man, as shown by the growing interest in the occult, well illustrated by the figure of the *Goat in the Thicket*, from the great Death-Pit at Ur, from $c$2750 B.C. Others felt that salvation and reason lay in science, in the complex laboratories of the physicists or the equally complex laboratory of the mind: in the computer, the research establishment, the university. Religion appeared to be less able to mediate between these positions than it had done, and so successfully, in the past. *Source: Reproduced by permission of The University Museum, University of Pennsylvania and Courtesy of FMC Corporation*

ernization: of nationalism and its excesses, of imperialism and its inhumanities, of industrialization and its social problems.

The trends were clear. The West changed through British trade unionism, and revisionist and revolutionary socialism on the continent especially after 1880, in the new physics and Darwinian emphasis upon struggle, in the waning of classical liberalism, in the decline of the church, and even by the extension of extreme specialization into the world of the arts where, by 1900, artists and composers increasingly directed their work to smaller and smaller groups. With the rise of socialism and racism in particular, critics—usually Westerners themselves—detected the beginnings of *The Decline of the West*, the title given in 1926 by Oswald Spengler, the German historian, to a sweeping indictment of European culture.

## V. 1 The Politics of Europe's Traditional Powers: 1848–1914

*"Ye sons of France, awake to glory!"*—The Marseillaise, French national anthem, 1792

In 1848 France ended that year's revolution by electing Louis Bonaparte (1808–1873), the great Napoleon's nephew, as president. This was a second attempt at a French Republic—the first had been established by the Revolution in 1792 and abolished by Napoleon Bonaparte a dozen years later—and this second was even more short-lived than the first. After three years the new president extended his powers by a bloodless coup, and in 1852 he received an overwhelming, if engineered, popular mandate to change the republic into an empire. But the empire remained an episode too.

Napoleon III, as Louis now called himself, tried to give France the kind of government that would combine authority with a sense of social responsibility. Under his reign there was much city planning and rebuilding in Paris and elsewhere, public health laws were passed and enforced, there was genuine concern for improved education, some public housing was provided, and a great railroad network was built. And when France tired of too much imperial authority in the sixties, Napoleon III began to liberalize his rule and delegated greater power to parliament and the cabinet.

Napoleon might even have created a lasting empire had it not been for his foreign policy. He was a restless and, in his later years, a sick man, and in his search for national greatness, he involved France in many a costly foreign adventure. In the fifties, without overwhelming need he took France into the Crimean War against Russia. He then aligned France with Cavour in his fight against the Austrians. He won these two affairs; the next two he did not. In the sixties he tried to establish a French-dominated empire in Mexico while the United States was preoccupied with its Civil War. The empire's open failure, and the execution of his imperial candidate, Maximilian, did much to weaken his regime at home as well. What ended his rule was a Franco-Prussian War, which he and Bismarck had helped to provoke.

While Napoleon was a prisoner of the Prussians in September 1870, a Paris crowd forced the few legislators remaining in the capital to decree the end of the empire, and proclaim a republic. The Third French Republic started under the worst possible auspices. It was born of war and defeat and was forced to accept Prussia's humiliating peace terms. It also faced a second revolution from the Left; from March to May 1871, much of Paris was in the hands of radicals who established a revolutionary council which, in emulation of the Jacobin-dominated assembly of 1792, they called the Commune. The Communards were patriots as well as radicals; many of them wished to reject Bismarck's peace and to go on fighting. Yet they clearly represented the lower strata of French society, and while there were relatively few doctrinaire socialists or anarchists among them, their tradition was that of Robespierre.

As soon as the new republican government could gather sufficient forces, it put down the Communards' rebellion ruthlessly. The Communards had shown little mercy to their opponents. They shot hostages, their victims including the archbishop of Paris. But the government's counter-terror was even more brutal. According to some estimates, well over ten thousand Communards were executed and twice that number were imprisoned or exiled. It was this terror that, according to one observer, caused "the secession of the proletariat" from the rest of the nation.

Thus matters had not begun well for the new government. While "secession" was too strong a term, neither the lost war nor the Paris Commune would be easily forgotten. France was a divided nation. In the beginning the Republic at best represented the center—to the right were the monarchists to the left the radicals, and these were irreconcilable. What saved the Republic was that the left was temporarily stunned, and the right was divided against itself. There were too many pretenders to the throne. France, in the preceding century, had known three dynasties. There was the old Bourbon line, there was Louis Philippe's Orleanist line, and there was the Bonapartist line. Yet as Adolphe Thiers (1797–1877), guiding spirit of the Third Republic and its first president, indelicately put it, "There isn't room on the throne for three backsides." A republic was, said Thiers, "the form of government that divides France the least."

The least was still a great deal. The constitution that passed in 1877 provided the new institutions on which the Third Republic was based, but it did little to stabilize conditions. The constitution called for a bicameral legislature—a Senate and a Chamber of Deputies, a president of the Republic, and a cabinet to head the executive branch. In the seventies, after one president made a disastrous try at enforcing his constitutional right to dissolve parliament, no successor repeated the attempt, and the president's office became largely ceremonial. The crucial issues for the rest of the Third Republic's life was the relationship between parliament and the cabinet. Its chief lesson was that if there was too little parliamentary responsibility in Imperial Germany, there was rather too much of it in France's Third Republic.

Under the constitution, the cabinet was responsible to parliament. And much as in the British case, parliament increasingly meant the lower house, or the Chamber of Deputies. As distinguished from the British case—where the government had the right to dissolve parliament and to call for new elections—power was weighed in favor of parliament in France. If government and parliament disagreed, the ministers had to resign while the deputies remained in office, facing no new elections. The result was that parliament made frequent use of its authority, and the average life expectancy of a government under the Third Republic was less than a year. This permanent governmental instability was perpetuated because France did not develop a two-party system. Instead, a dozen and a half parties were represented in parliament. Hence only coalitions could govern France. But because political alliances between so many divergent parties were bound to change from time to time, the first victim of such change was customarily the cabinet of the moment.

There also was the fact that parliament and cabinet played out their constant drama against a background of conspiracy and scandal. There was the Boulanger affair in the eighties. General Georges Boulanger (1837–1891), a former minister of war, and a handsome and popular figure, was seen as the one man who might avenge the French defeat of 1870–71 and also put an end to the Republic.

By 1889, the conspirators behind Boulanger were ready for the coup d'etat they had been preparing. They would overthrow the impotent Republic and let their strong man take the reins. But at the crucial moment, Boulanger found that he had no taste for revolution. Instead of moving against the government, he fled to Brussels. Here, two years later, he committed suicide at the grave of his mistress. One uncharitable French journalist summed up the whole affair by writing, "He began like Caesar, continued like Cataline, and ended like Romeo."

The Boulangist movement died with him, but many of his supporters were no more ready to make their peace with the Republic than they had been before. And they had many a scandal on which to feed their discontent with France. There was a much publicized affair in the nineties, for instance, in which the son-in-law of the president was caught selling posts in the Legion of Honor. There was the Panama scandal, which captured even more headlines, in which it turned out that the promoters of Ferdinand de Lessep's canal scheme had bribed cabinet ministers, parliamentary deputies, and journalists to obtain government backing of their financially shaky company. Then there was the affair that overshadowed all the others, that of Captain Alfred Dreyfus.

In 1894 Captain Dreyfus (1859–1935), a Jewish captain in the French general staff, was accused of treason in favor of the Germans, found guilty by a court-martial, deprived of his rank in a degrading ceremony, and sentenced to life imprisonment on Devil's Island. The charge against him, at first, was not entirely fanciful, although it is possible that the army might never had brought him to trial had it not been for the polemics of an anti-Jewish journalist who wrote that the authorities would never dare to proceed against an officer who could count on Jewish aid. Certain evidence did point to Dreyfus, and one of the foremost criminologists of the time, Alphonse Bertillon (later the inventor of the fingerprint identification system, and then an expert graphologist), thought that Dreyfus's handwriting matched that of the major incriminating document. When subsequent evidence appeared that cast grave doubts on Dreyfus's guilt, the army refused to reconsider the verdict. Facts pointing to his innocence were ignored, and when a colonel in intelligence, who felt that he was on the trail of the true culprit, insisted to his superiors that the trial be reopened, he abruptly found himself transferred to North Africa. But before leaving he informed some politicians of undoubted integrity of the basic facts. The Dreyfus case became a public issue that could not be suppressed.

France now was divided into two camps. On the one side were the Dreyfusards, those who were convinced of the captain's innocence, and also those who supported the Third Republic, the France of 1789, the liberals, socialists, and anticlericals—the new France. On the other side were the anti-Dreyfusards, those who, whether they believed in Dreyfus's guilt or not, opposed the Republic and the Revolution, were conservatives, monarchists, or militant Catholics—the old France. The division between the French became deep and obvious. Ultimately Dreyfus was fully vindicated. In 1906, a court set aside his original sentence, whereupon he was reinstated, promoted, and decorated on the same spot where he had been degraded twelve years before.

But Dreyfus was all but forgotten in the affair that bore his name. What could not be forgotten was that in effect, the French Revolution was not over yet, that in the words of a British historian, France was still divided into the believers in the God of Saint Louis and the God of Voltaire. And the consequences, too, transcended Dreyfus's personal fate. One was the creation of Zionism, for it was under the impact of the Dreyfus affair that Theodor Herzl (1860–1904) wrote his *Jewish State* and advocated a modern migration to Palestine; another, more French consequence, was a weakening of respect for the army, for many believed that the army had acted dishonorably in the affair. In the wake of the affair there were a number of concrete measures taken against the Church. Napoleon's Concordat of 1801 was ended, under whose terms the state had paid the salary of the clergy; several thousand Catholic schools were closed, and in 1905, under the ministry of Emile Combes (1835–1921), church and state were entirely separated, truly a radical step in a country that was overwhelmingly Catholic.

Weak institutions, corruption, and *affaires*—no wonder that to some writers, the Third Republic was an unhappy, even doomed period in French history. But the appearances on which they based their conclusions could be deceptive. In actuality, the Republic was a good deal more stable than it appeared.

If the constitutional apparatus was less than perfect, it suited the French mood. The French had no taste for a two-party system, preferring to be represented by clearly defined interest groups. They wanted whatever political deals and compromises were necessary made fairly openly after an election, not surreptitiously before as in the Anglo-Saxon countries. If that meant frequently changing coalitions and governments, so be it, especially because the cabinet changes were so much more apparent than real. Ministries changed, but the same ministers returned to office. Thus Aristide Briand (1862–1932), who completed Combe's separation of church and state and went on to become a great advocate of international peace, headed no fewer than ten different cabinets in seventeen years. Thus Thèophile Delcassé (1852–1923), architect of an alliance with Britain, served continuously as foreign minister in over half a dozen cabinets in seven years. The day to day operations of the government were carried on by an excellent, permanent civil service, which continued in office no matter what the mood of parliament. There was the appearance of perpetual change, which appealed to a certain French extremism; there was also the reality of government continuity and solid administration.

The country was rich enough to afford some questionable politics. Life could be sweet and luxurious indeed in nineteenth-century France. These were the days of experimentation and achievement in literature and the arts, an age in literature that spanned from Gustav Flaubert to Marcel Proust, in music from Jacques Offenbach to Maurice Ravel, in painting from Pierre-Auguste Renoir to Pablo Picasso. The Germans had a word for all this: the truly good life, they said, was to live like "God in France."

In less poetic more measurable terms, there was the matter of French industrial progress. In the period from 1871 to 1914, French production all but tripled while personal income doubled. The French growth rate was higher even than Germany's. French firms built the railroads for most of the countries of Europe. French engineers designed the harbors and dockworks of many of the continent's seaports. French inventors and manufacturers led in the development of the motorcar, as its nomenclature still reminds us—automobile, chassis, differential, carburetor, limousine, chauffeur.

A prosperous France was also an essentially conservative France. The backbone of the nation remained what it had been for a long time: Small, old-fashioned, and independent farmers, shopkeepers, and artisans were a group whose maxim was "think left, live right." There was much realism here, much distrust of big words, big promises, big institutions, whether in government or elsewhere. "My glass may be small, but I drink from my own."

## Great Britain

"English politics, exemplary but austere: French politics, deplorable, but entertaining," wrote a French political scientist. Did the judgment still hold, were the British still setting an example to the continent?

In some ways they were. There clearly was more governmental stability in Britain than in France. In the period from 1871 to 1914, for instance, there were only twelve cabinets in Great Britain, as compared to over forty in France. In fact, there were only seven prime ministers, and at least two of them, the conservative Benjamin Disraeli (1804–81) and his liberal opponent William Ewart Gladstone (1809–98), provided the kind of long-range leadership and influence that no French premier could match. A two-party system contributed to a sense of continuity and order, and so did the civilized manner in which political arguments were carried on. "The only progress in democracy since Athens," Albert Einstein once noted, "has been the establishment of His Majesty's loyal opposition in England."

There were other examples of progress. In the second half of the century there was a widening of the franchise, achieved without wild threats or riots. The Reform Act of 1867, passed under Disraeli's conservative ministry, gave the vote to nearly the entire urban male population, and a subsequent parliamentary reform act in 1884, passed under Gladstone's liberal ministry, widened this to take in the rural poor as well. Even more crucially, the Ballot Act of 1872 introduced the "Australian ballot" to England; now the vote would be secret. In sum, while at the beginning of the century perhaps one Englishman in a hundred had the right to vote, and was obliged to exercise that right in public, by 1918 just about every Englishman was entitled to vote in private.

Women were excluded, though the suffragettes were energetically fighting for what Queen Victoria (1837–1901) called "the mad, wicked folly of women's rights." Led by Emmeline Pankhurst (1858–1928) and her two daughters, the suffragettes resorted to violent and spectacular tactics in their pursuit of the vote and of women's rights, cutting telephone wires, smashing porcelain in the British Museum, pouring tar into mailboxes. "The broken windowpane," said Ms. Pankhurst, "is the most valuable argument in modern politics." In 1928 the suffragettes' initial goal was won, and the vote became truly universal.

Both conservatives and liberals acted to widen the franchise, and in other areas, too, there was a good deal of common ground between the two parties. The "Victorian Compromise" was more than a cliché. The two parties agreed on the broad outlines of foreign policy as well—of maintaining a balance of power in Europe, of keeping the world's markets open to British goods, of preferring diplomatic to military action. In essence, they even agreed more often than they disagreed on the issue of imperial expansion. Outwardly, this was not always quite true. In public debates, the conservatives were advocates of imperial greatness and of Britain's mission to bear "the white man's burden" of improving "lesser breeds," while the liberals tended to attack imperialism as immoral, inhumane, and unprofitable. Yet, when in office, the liberals did not reverse the policy of their conservative predecessors. As one historian wrote, "Gladstone regretted and no doubt neglected the empire, but he kept it."

Still, not everything was harmony and compromise. British politics were not all that amiable and exemplary. There was the deep, bitter, and long drawn out division over the tariff issue. The conservatives consistently argued for protective tariffs, or for a system of preferences for the members of the British Empire. The liberals, on the other hand, true to their traditions, just as consistently advocated free international trade. Then there was the battle over an even more basic economic and social issue, that of the coming welfare state. By the beginning of the twentieth century, the liberals were moving toward a program of extended social services, health insurance, better public transportation, sanitation, recreational facilities, and of more widely available free education. To raise the necessary financing, an energetic and radical liberal Chancellor of the Exchequer, David Lloyd George (1863–1945), offered a "people's budget" in 1909. For the first time a graduated income tax, a heavy inheritance tax, and other levies aimed at the rich were proposed; it was, a conservative opponent charged, "not a budget but a revolution." After a long parliamentary battle, in which the House of Lords opposed the vote of the Commons, the budget passed. But in 1911, the House of Lords was deprived of the power to interfere with future fiscal bills. The conservatives neither surrendered gracefully nor compromised. Instead, there remained a genuine division and a good deal of bitterness.

In part, Lloyd George had acted for reasons of compassion, mixed with a bit of contrariness. The conservatives, he wrote later, had "no sympathy for the people.... When I tried to do something for the workingman ... they denounced me as a Welsh thief." But in part, the liberals were advocating a prolabor program for much the same reasons that Bismarck had. They wished to halt the rise of a new political force, the Labour Party.

The Victorian Compromise was straining at its limits. Class divisions in Britain were ancient and sharp. The gulf between rich and poor, between the educated and the functionally illiterate, was immense. Disraeli, also a novelist, referred to the "two Englands" as those that had and those that had not. During most of the nineteenth century, the vast majority of England's lower classes had no vote; and where it did, the need to vote in public had inhibited any sweeping expression of radical sentiment. This now changed, and at the turn of the century a new socialist party emerged—the Labour Party. It was a relatively nonideological party; more practical trade-unionism than philosophical Marxism went into its make-up, and it tended to advocate gradual change rather than violent revolution. Yet the Party was not without its radical elements. It used the weapon of the strike and did have a majority among its leaders who believed in nationalization of Britain's basic industries. And the liberal strategy of preempting the Labourite program failed; the twentieth century witnessed a steady weakening of the Liberal Party and steady growth of the Labour Party, until after the end of World War I, the British two-party system was no longer Conservative and Liberal, but Conservative and Labour.

The problem that tested the Victorian Compromise more than any other was that of Irish Home Rule. The most venerable habits and traditions of British moderation were powerless against this issue. For the Irish problem went back for centuries; England and Ireland were divided by religion, culture, wealth, and social class. The Act of Union of 1800 had established a United Kingdom of Great Britain (which, of course, included Scotland and Wales) and Ireland, and had centered the legislature in London. The Irish aim was Home Rule, especially after a disasterous potato famine in the forties had increased the already strong antipathy to the English. Although Home Rule did not mean complete separation, it did mean autonomy—the establishment of a parliament in Dublin responsible for domestic legislation.

At first Irish demands were met with some concessions on London's part. Yet the English always offered too little, too late. When Gladstone assumed office in 1868, he said his mission was to pacify Ireland, which had been opposing the established church since the 1830s. Under his guidance, laws passed in parliament that put an end to two great Irish grievances. No longer did they have to pay a tithe to the Anglican Church in Roman Catholic Ireland, and the country's poor tenant farmers were protected somewhat from extravagantly high rents (although fair rents were not established until 1881). But the concessions did not appease the Irish. Partly as a result of the newly introduced secret ballot, partly as a result of possessing very able leadership, a large Irish contingent in the House of Commons now did battle for Home Rule. Charles Parnell (1846–91) organized these Irish members into a single voting block, which by virtue of its determination and size—it comprised between 80 and 90 members out of a total of 607 members of parliament—proved a highly effective force. By 1885, Gladstone was converted to the idea of Home Rule, and he introduced a bill to give Ireland its own parliament and government under the British crown.

The result was disastrous. A large group of liberals was unwilling to abandon union with Ireland and seceded from the Party. They formed a new "Liberal-Unionist" Party that later fused with the conservatives. In combination with the conservatives, this splinter group easily defeated Home Rule and voted Gladstone out of office in the process. In 1893 a second Home Rule bill was submitted in the House of Commons. This time it passed but was defeated in the House of Lords. In 1912, a third Home Rule bill followed. This time it passed because the previous year's Parliament Act had effectively limited the power of the Lords.

All should have ended happily here. There were two principal reasons that it did not. One was the matter of increased Irish expectations. There had been a great cultural renaissance in Ireland. There were writers such as William Butler Yeats and John Millington Synge, there was the Abbey Theatre, there was the revival of the Gaelic language. And this cultural energy supported, and in turn was supported by, a great surge of popular Irish nationalism, which on occasion became cultish. The British, under a liberal government, thought they had tried to meet the Irish demands; and under conservative governments they had tried to "kill Home Rule with kindness," by sponsoring reform legislation designed to transform Ireland into a country of independent peasant proprietors. Both methods failed, one because there were not enough votes for it; the other because the credit for improving conditions went less to Whitehall than to the Irish leaders, especially to Parnell. By the end of the century Home Rule was no longer enough for most of the Irish. What many wanted instead was full independence.

The other factor—nationality issues are never simple and clean-cut—was that Ulster, in northern Ireland, was strongly opposed to changing the existing arrangement. Ulster was predominantly Protestant, as well as economically more prosperous, and it refused to be governed by the Catholic south. Ulster's leadership decided to be just as militant and difficult as Parnell had been. Their slogan was that if Home Rule should pass, "Ulster will fight, and Ulster will be right."

When Home Rule did pass in the summer of 1914, the Orangemen of Ulster were as good as their word. They took to the streets, and Ireland was on the verge of civil war. As a result, Home Rule was suspended by Parliament. Even mighty Britain could not fight the Central Powers and two Irish factions at the same time—for war broke out on the continent almost simultaneously. The stage was thus set for an Irish rebellion on Easter, 1916, for two years of bloody civil war that followed the European armistice in 1918, and for the eventual establishment of an Irish Free State in 1921. Ireland finally had more than Home Rule—it had independence. But it did not have Ulster, and that problem has lasted as long as the century has, and finally Ireland erupted into civil war again in 1972.

Faced, then, with some profound differences between the parties on issues such as the welfare state, faced with the emergence of a Socialist Party, threatened with a general strike, with suffragettes, and, above all, with the untractable Irish issue, Britain was no longer quite the perfect example of a reasonable and harmonious government. Yet things were relative. And if one compared Britain's nationality problem with that of an equally venerable European state, the Hapsburg monarchy, it suddenly looked rather mild.

## Austria-Hungary

Austria did not have one Irish issue, it had a dozen. In this sense, the Hapsburg monarchy was unique among the countries of Europe, for this large state in the center of the continent—whose population in the second half of the nineteenth century numbered about 35 million—was not dominated by one nationality, as France, Britain, or Germany were. Instead, the Austro-Hungarian empire was a multinational multi-ethnic state. Among the major nationalities were Germans, Italians, Czechs, Slovaks, Poles, Ruthenians, Romanians, Magyars, Croats, Serbs, and Dalmatians. Among its major religious denominations were Roman Catholic, Greek Orthodox, Jewish, Protestant, and Moslem. Among its major languages were German, Italian, Czech, Hungarian, Serbo-Croatian, Polish, and Yiddish. No one nationality possessed a clear majority, no more than any one religion did. Two groups enjoyed a certain preeminence: the Germans in the west and the Hungarians in the east. This standing was based on their social and political position, not on numbers. Indeed, the Slavic peoples of the empire formed a theoretical majority. But because they were without cohesion—there were Poles, Serbs, Bosnians, differing customs, and ancient enmities—their majority remained a theoretical one.

At times, these local enmities were transferred to the empire itself. "A dungeon of nations," the Italian patriot Guiseppi Mazzini (1805-72) called it. Some less partisan observers echoed him. Austria, wrote an American historian, was "a howling chaos of conflicting demands . . . an incessant tumult of hostilities." The Austro-Hungarian empire represented a series of compromises struck between the many groups that had come to rest within its fragile boundaries through centuries of invasion, migration, and searching for security.

There were things to be said for this archaic state as well. Its lack of ethnic purity made it one of Europe's more tolerant states; it was relatively tolerant of different opinions, different races, different faiths, different ways of life, and absorbed parts from all of them. If it lacked ethnic unity, it also lacked that other attribute of nationalism, an unredeemable fanaticism. It was, as one of its greater writers, Hugo von Hofmannsthal (1874-1929) said, the one country in Europe where modern nationalism was "seen not merely as something limiting but as something positively immoral."

The old empire made both political and economic sense. It made economic sense to have a large free trading area in the Danubian region where wheat from the fields of Hungary, lumber from Slovakia, tropical fruit from the Dalmatian coast, industrial products from Vienna, Bohemia, and Moravia, oil from Galicia, and minerals from Bosnia could be exchanged without import quotas or customs barriers. It made sense to have labor and goods move as freely as they would in the European Common Market, which was formed more than a full generation after the monarchy's death. It was a prosperous empire. Nineteenth-century Vienna and Budapest were cities for which the term "conspicuous consumption" seemed to have been coined. Trieste was one of Europe's busiest ports, and the Skoda armaments works in Bohemia were serious competitors for Krupp and Vickers.

Of course, not all the areas of the empire were at an equal stage of economic development. This was one of the nearly insoluble problems of Austria. There were the prosperous industries of Bohemia and the backward farming methods of Galicia, the modern metropolitan Vienna and the still "Turkish" conditions of Bosnia. Still, it was argued, these regions would have been worse off had it not been for the common market that the empire provided. And the larger union which the empire offered could be justified on political grounds as well. Hardly one of its constituent nationalities was strong enough to stand by itself. Even Vienna's most bitter critics realized this. When, in 1848, the Czech patriot František Palacký (1798-1876) was invited to attend a Revolutionary Assembly in Frankfurt as a Czech delegate, he refused. Palacký favored

Czech autonomy as much as Parnell favored Home Rule for Ireland, and he spent a lifetime battling for it. Yet he did not, he told the Frankfurt Assembly, wish to be engaged in an enterprise that might "diminish Austria." For Palacký described the monarchy as:

> ... an empire whose preservation, integrity, and consolidation is, and must be, a great and important matter not only for my own nation but for the whole of Europe, indeed for mankind and civilization itself.... The true artery of this essential union of nations is the Danube; the focus of its power must therefore never be far removed from this river if the union is to be, and remain, at all effective. Truly, if the Austrian empire had not existed for ages, it would be necessary, in the interest of Europe, in the interest of mankind itself, to create it with all speed.

"Imagine if you will," he said, "Austria divided into a number of republics and miniature republics. What a welcome basis for a Russian universal monarchy!"

A man otherwise very different from Palacký by background, outlook, and aims saw matters in very much the same way. This was Bismarck who had argued so passionately for a "peace of understanding" with Austria after Prussia's victory in 1866. He challenged those who proposed Austria's destruction to define what different order they suggested for that part of Europe. He could not imagine any that would not induce intolerable instability in the region. For Austro-Hungary was so polyglot, had so many folkways, nurtured so many intellectual traditions within its borders, it was a state for which a cultural case could be made. For example, the arts flourished in Austria during this period. An astonishing number of writers, composers, artists, and scientists who are still received as innovators nearly a century later were citizens of the Habsburg monarchy: Hugo von Hofmannsthal, Franz Kafka, Rainer Maria Rilke, Arthur Schnitzler, Martin Buber, Gustav Klimt, Sigmund Freud, Alfred Adler, Gustav Mahler, and Arnold Schonberg. And there was a display of elegance, both in Vienna and in Budapest, that perhaps was rivalled only by Versailles under the Old Regime, and London and Paris.

To some writers, in retrospect, this all seemed a frenzied gaiety, an end-of-the-world frivolity. "The merry apocalypse of Vienna, *circa* 1880," one of them called it. But this was wrong. What was involved here was a quintessentially Austrian trait. "We are always playing," said Arthur Schnitzler (1862–1931), one of the most subtle writers of the period. "He who knows how to play a role is clever and satisfied." What was involved was an Austrian reluctance to become too serious; life, like art, was fragmentary. (Schubert's unfinished symphony remained that way not because it was his last but because he thought it too beautiful to continue —it might be less than perfect if he did.) Hofmannstal's one novel, *Andreas,* remained a fragment; "the simple act of putting something into

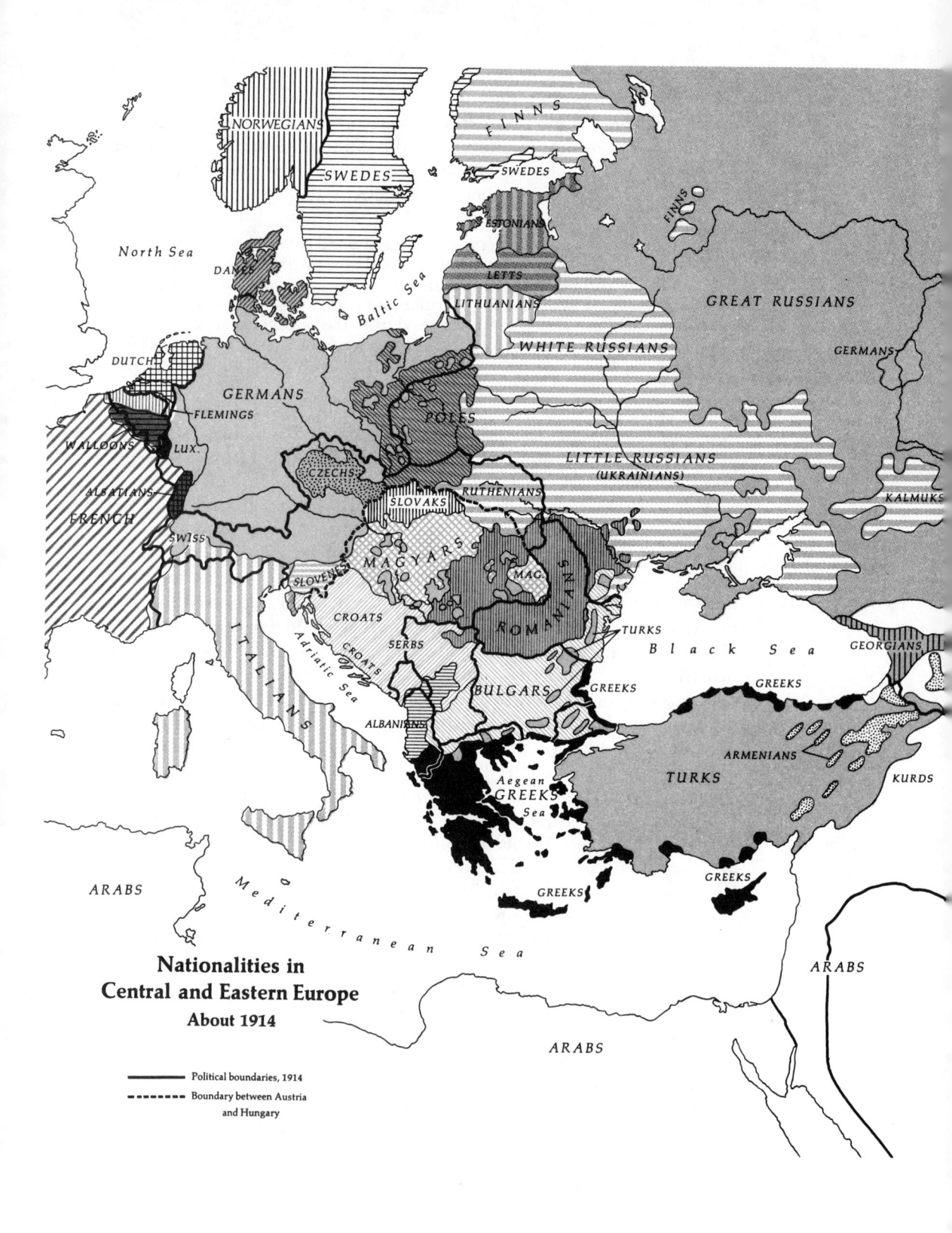

**Nationalities in Central and Eastern Europe About 1914**

——— Political boundaries, 1914
- - - - - Boundary between Austria and Hungary

words," one of his characters notes, "is indecent." The second spire of St. Stephen's Cathedral, Vienna's landmark, was started and intentionally never completed. A contemporary Austrian critic summed up this attitude as "the dislike of anything absolute or definite, improvisation instead of precise planning . . . leaving everything open instead of reaching conclusions."

Not every Austrian, of course, was busy playing, or intent on not finishing the day's work. One who definitely was an earnest Victorian was the Emperor, Franz Joseph (1848–1916). He had come to the throne during the revolutionary events of 1848, and he ruled until his death during the First World War. It was an unprecedented reign of sixty-eight years, which exceeded even that of Queen Victoria (1837–1901) in Britain. Franz Joseph was a prosaic man, and to his enemies "a demon of mediocrity," a ruler with "an almost touching weakness for untalented people." Yet it was he more than any other single individual who personified the empire and both held it together by his initial good sense and by the sheer amount of hard work he gave to governing the country, which he also helped destroy. He served by becoming a grandfather figure, achieving stability in the end by the length of his rule; even some revolutionaries found the concept of living in a country not presided over by Franz Joseph a difficult one to imagine. "His Majesty has died," went the final Viennese story told in 1916. "But no one dares tell him. It might frighten the old gentleman."

Even so, there had been a myriad of problems to frighten him in his lifetime, and none had been more vexing than the nationality issue—the constant struggle of the empire's various ethnic groups for what they considered their rightful place in the state. The initial reaction, after the frightening experience of 1848, was having a strongly centralized government in Vienna. When this proved unsuccessful in reestablishing peace, there followed some experimentation with federalism and negotiations with the more vocal dissident nationalities. In 1867, after losing the war against Prussia, there was a major constitutional restructuring of the empire. An *Ausgleich*—a Great Compromise—between the Germans and the Magyars resulted in the Dual Monarchy of Austria-Hungary. Hungary henceforth was an equal and independent state within the empire. It was tied to Austria by an emperor, who was crowned king of Hungary in a separate ceremony in Budapest; by the existence of three joint ministries (of foreign affairs, defense, and finance); and by a customs union, which was subject to renewal every ten years. Aside from those ties, each half of the monarchy was independent. Each had its own cabinet, its own parliament, its own civil service, its own official language.

The *Ausgleich*, while meeting most Magyar demands, did not end the nationality issue. Czechs, Serbs, Croats, Romanians, Poles, and Ruthenians wanted an *Ausgleich* of their own. Yet the areas they inhabited seemed too small for independent, or even fully autonomous, survival. Ethnic borders were nowhere very clear. Slovaks intermingled with Ruthenians, Tyrolians with Italians. There were German ethnic islands in Czech lands, and Romanian enclaves in Croatia. Here was a problem without any one fair and satisfactory solution.

On the whole, the arrangement in the Austrian half of the empire worked fairly well. Here, the provisions of the Constitution of 1867 that accompanied the *Ausgleich* were taken seriously—equal legal rights for all nationalities and considerable cultural freedom as well. Each region might use its language in official or in private life, and in the courts, schools, and army. But in the Magyar part these rights tended to be ignored and grievances were more pronounced. A consistent effort was made to Magyarize obviously non-Magyar citizens by threat and bribery. There was occasional protest in the streets, planned obstruction in parliament, and in the end the assassination of Franz Ferdinand which, as an international act, was intended to kill more than its direct victim.

Another issue existed that was related to the nationality problem: anti-Semitism. One reason for the rise of anti-Jewish feeling was that politicians thought that stressing the "Jewish issue" might take people's minds off other more intractable matters; that if Czech anger were directed at the Jews, they might have less energy to spare for Home Rule. Another was a certain amount of surviving religious bigotry; to some simple Catholic peasants, the Jew might still be presented as Christ's murderer. While both were very old motives—the search for the scapegoat, the fear and dislike of the religious outsider who threatened one's security—neither played a really major role in Austria. Ethnic demands were not to be deflected this easily, and too many religions coexisted within Austria's borders to stamp any one of them as wholly alien. What was rather more important was a different consideration. This was the locally abnormal social and professional structure of Austria's Jews.

In Austria, as just about anywhere else in Europe, Jews had been barred from a great number of professions until their emancipation during the Enlightenment. They could not own land or work it, could not be members of a craft or merchant guild, could not be teachers or serve the state in the army or the civil service. The chief ways of making a living left to them were money-lending and petty trade. The general change to industrialization bettered conditions for some Jews. The great banking fortunes—which in the United States were often a Protestant preserve—were almost always made by Jews in much of southern Europe. Yet this escape into very great wealth was only available to a few. The principal avenue besides trade after the bestowal of civic rights theoretically opened many careers, was by way of the arts and the professions.

This contributed to Austria's intellectual glory. Many of the artists representing Austrian culture were Jewish or partly Jewish: Schnitzler,

Hofmannsthal, Buber, Kafka, Freud, Adler. Between 1901, when the Nobel Prize was first awarded, and 1918, when the empire ceased to exist, three Austrians became Nobel Laureates; two of them were Jewish. Although Jews accounted for less than one percent of the total population, six out of seventeen German Nobel Prize winners during the same period were Jewish. This tendency made for an anomalous professional situation, for an overcrowding of certain fields. In the Magyar half of the monarchy 85 percent of all self-employed persons in finance and banking were Jewish at the turn of the century. Every second Magyar physician or lawyer was Jewish, all the better-known Budapest newspapers were Jewish-owned, and seventy percent of all journalists were Jews.

Such dominance was bound to cause resentment. Even so, had it not been for an additional factor, anti-Semites might have found the ground more barren. That additional factor was the mass migration of Jews into Vienna and Budapest from the more backward eastern regions of the empire, especially from the Bukovina and from Polish Galicia. They were people who for the most part were desperately poor and thus appeared to threaten the jobs of some of the more easygoing residents because the Jews were willing to work long, hard hours. Because the ghetto was a very recent experience in their case, they also appeared strange and clannish to some and seemed intolerant of Christians as Christians had been of Jews. It was this migration that greatly added to the professional imbalance and provided ammunition to anti-Semites. To be a Jew in the empire was to belong to an overprivileged upper class or to an underprivileged lower class.

Zionism was also an Austrian phenomenon. Theodor Herzl, its founder, was born in Budapest to a Westernized family. His original idea had been to solve the Jewish question by a mass conversion to Catholicism. After the Dreyfus affair, he outlined a new plan that called for a Jewish resettlement of Palestine. Yet Herzl lacked fanaticism; his Zionism was not meant to make all European Jews rediscover a lost identity and leave for Palestine. It was meant as an escape hatch for poorer Eastern Jews, and to give a clear nationality to those who remained behind, which the Jews alone in the monarchy appeared to lack.

Of the several anti-Semitic groups that came into existence at the time, two in particular outlasted their founders' lives. One was led by George von Schönerer (1842–1921), and the other by Karl Lueger (1844–1910). Schönerer, taking up a term popularized by the rise of social Darwinism, introduced a new element into anti-Semitism, that of race. Jews, he held, were by nature a race "arrogant, hard-hearted, profiteering and vicious," and to drop one's defenses against them merely because they had accepted baptism was foolish. Faith was skin-deep; race was permanent: "One cannot resign from one's race." Schönerer also propagated what he considered the old Teutonic virtues, attacked the Catholic Church and the Hapsburg dynasty, advocated union with Bismarck's Germany, and dated his letters by a non-Christian calender of his own invention.

A few years later, Karl Lueger, several times Lord Mayor of Vienna, showed that when properly exploited, anti-Semitism could be used as a vote-getter. He put the blame for the economic plight of Vienna's lower-middle class on the Jews, dramatically personalizing recent historical developments in a manner common to demagogues on all continents since. There were many small artisans and merchants in Austria who had fallen upon hard times by trying to compete with new machinery or with the more efficient merchandising methods that had come into existence in this stage of advancing industrialization. The Jewish-owned factory or department store was highly visible. Lueger directed his rhetoric against the Jews relying, to use the phrase of a historian of the monarchy, on "the habitual tendency of the untrained mind to leap from the particular to the general." Small shopkeepers liked to hear that their financial troubles were the fault of the Jewish banker, financier, competitor; the small farmer was glad to believe that the inability to make a decent living was the fault of the Jewish grain speculator. By the 1890s, Lueger and his new Christian Socialist Party achieved a mass following.

Were the old virtues of tolerance, compromise, and stability vanishing? Not quite, for much that was sound in the old monarchy survived. The Austrian workers voted for the Social Democratic Party, not for Lueger's people. Moreover, there was a Socialist Party that not only had no use for anti-Semitism—"the Socialism of the stupid," one of its German leaders called it—but that was strongly pragmatic and nonrevolutionary in character and given to gradualism as much as the British Labour Party was. Nor was Lueger even quite moved to fanaticism, for anti-Semitism was only a part of his program. He also happened to to be a determined advocate of social reform. "A state," he said, "that has no social security laws should be barred from intercourse with other nations." As mayor of Vienna after 1897, he carried out a program of municipal socialism, distributing free milk to school children and sponsoring city management of various utilities and services including parks, playgrounds, and funerals. (No one, he thought, should profit from the death of another.) There was also much new building under his administration, and a wide greenbelt constructed around the city made Vienna one of Europe's most livable capitals. Even Lueger's anti-Semitism was less than total. It never became racial; he was scrupulously fair in allocating municipal socialism, distributing funds to Jewish as well as Catholic charities. And it was Lueger who would make a comment that became famous, which showed that class rather than caste moved him. When someone accused him of hypocrisy (publicly he railed against the Jews while privately he numbered Jews among his good friends), he said: "Look, I decide who is a Jew."

If it were not for a coincidence, neither Schönerer nor Lueger might be mentioned at all in so short a history as this. That coincidence, of course, was that while living in Vienna an impressionable and unstable young man from the provinces became fascinated with Schönerer's ideology and with Lueger's appeal to the voters. His name is known to us as Adolf Hitler.

In the end, it was the issue of nationality, not anti-Semitism, that destroyed the monarchy. When war came in 1914, it initially unified the monarchy, as Germans and Croats, Catholics and Jews, Social Democrats and Christian Socialists fought together to defend the empire. But four years of terrible warfare, the certainty of defeat, accompanied toward the end by an Allied appeal for revolt, brought down the monarchy. Only then was a truly virulent strain of anti-Semitism unleashed upon Europe. The world of 1935 would differ greatly from the world of 1900.

## *Russia*

If Austria's great problem was the nationality issue, Russia's great twin problems were serfdom and a backward regime.

The greatest single issue that faced the tsars was serfdom. By the middle of the century a majority of Russians still lived in conditions of bondage. Of the world's powers, only the United States and Brazil had a form of institutionalized slavery to compare with it. In theory, a difference existed between slavery and serfdom that made serfdom somewhat less inhumane. Slaves were private property and as such could be freely bought and sold; serfs were tied to the land and could change hands only if the land did. But like a slave, a serf possessed neither freedom of movement nor any other civil right (including the right to choose an occupation). Like slaves, serfs were, in an overwhelming majority of cases, both illiterate and hopelessly poor.

The system was a cancer on the Russian body politic, and corrupting to master and serf alike. For years, Russia's intellectuals, and some of Russia's politicians, had advocated change. Their opportunity finally came in 1855 when the country lost the Crimean War against Britain and France. The defeat, in a war fought on Russia's homegrounds, clearly revealed that the system of Russian autocracy was oppressive, corrupt, and inefficient. The new tsar, Alexander II (1855–81) who came to power in the war's final days, was ready to institute basic constitutional changes. It was better, he said, to have them come from above than from below, better from reform than revolution. The death of an autocratic tsar and his replacement by a liberal one brought an end to serfdom.

In less than ten years, a great number of liberal reforms were enacted into law. A fairer legal system was instituted following Western precepts, which introduced public jury trials—trials had been secret and arbitrary before—and a degree of judicial independence. Some local government was organized. District assemblies, or *zemstvos*, came into being, and while they were not elected on the basis of universal suffrage, they did contain some peasant representatives, and on the whole worked so well that they seemed to justify the hope for a larger, national parliament. Censorship of the press and of literature, and restrictions on education, were relaxed. This did not mean the full freedom of the West, but it did mean a thaw.

The most momentous single piece of legislation under the rule of Alexander II, however, concerned the serfs. In 1861, by imperial edict, serfdom was ended in Russia. Under the new decree, some forty million formerly unfranchised Russians were allowed to own land and property, to travel and to change their place of residence and occupations, and to choose other than working the squire's land or waiting on his family. The serf had become a citizen.

Sweeping though the measure was, it left a major problem behind. What about the land? For years, while the abolition of serfdom was being prepared by the Tsar's advisors, the overriding question had been not whether to emancipate the serf or not. That decision was clear; the Tsar wished it. The question rather was whether to free the serfs with or without the land they had worked on. If they were to be freed without it, they were likely to starve or become the poorest of rural laborers, because as a rule they had neither property nor any appreciable skills that would enable them to survive in an urban setting. On the other hand, if one were to free them with some land, how was one to compensate the former owner? In the end, they reached a compromise. About half of the landed estates went to the newly liberated peasants while the other half remained in the landlord's possession. The landlord was compensated for this loss by the government, and the government, in turn, announced that it would collect the amount it had advanced from the peasants over a period of forty-nine years. To make sure that these redemption payments would be met, the government revived an old institution, the *mir* (the village commune), which was collectively responsible for meeting the payments and which no peasant could leave until these financial obligations had been met.

"The greatest legislative act in history," as the Russians called it, was less than perfect from the beginning and caused much criticism. The peasants felt that they had not received enough land, that the better, more fertile part of the estate usually remained in the landlord's possession. Also, they thought that emancipation was largely an illusion, because in a majority of cases the peasant had merely exchanged one master—the squire—for another—the *mir*—and hence was no freer than before.

There was much truth in both allegations. Yet it is difficult to see what other course had been open. Expropriating the landlords would have been both illegal and impractical in a system run by the aristocracy, which Russia quite legally was. Had the Tsar decreed such a sweeping change he would not have been Tsar much longer. On the other hand, compensating the landlord while excusing the peasant from redemption payments would have meant financial disaster for all. Farming in Russia was not a marginal activity—it was the basis of the economy. In all, then, this was an impressive reform measure (certainly superior to the American approach to emancipation, which freed the slaves without any property and without any apparent thought of how they were to make a livelihood at all). The Russian peasant was free in name. The landlord no longer had the right of private jurisdiction. No Russian, henceforth, could own another Russian. And the sober, hard-working peasant had a chance to give the next generation freedom in fact as well as in law.

For a number of Russians this was not enough. There existed in Russia, despite censorship and secret police, a vocal and violent underground opposition. Small in numbers, they possessed a sense of mission and a radicalism that had few counterparts in the West. The nihilists of the 1860s, the "believers in nothing," were women and men given to attacking all of society's values and institutions, going well beyond the position of the anarchists. They modeled themselves after a character in Ivan Turgenev's novel *Fathers and Sons* (1862), "a man who bows to no authority, who accepts not a single principle on faith." A second group, the Populists of the sixties and seventies, were more interested in direct action than the nihilists and went into the villages of Russia to politicize the peasants and help them as teachers, nurses, or simple laborers. Others went because they thought they would derive a new strength from their contact with Russia's masses. They were Slavophiles and represented a more extreme form of a Russian philosophy that was considerably older than they. For there had long been a great division among Russia's intellectuals, between Westerners and Slavophiles. The former felt that Russia essentially belonged to the rest of Europe and needed to catch up with Western institutions, whether political, social, or economic. The Slavophiles, on the other hand, felt that Russia's orientation was toward Byzantium and not Rome, toward the spiritual not the material, toward the peasants' village and not the modern city. They thought, in short, that Peter the Great (ruler between 1682 and 1725), had started Russia on a fool's errand when he had opened its doors to Westernization. "A pair of peasant boots," said one of the Populists, "matter more than all the plays of Shakespeare or the paintings of Raphael."

By the late 1870s, Populism was on the wane. Both police pressure and the confrontation with the realities of Russian village life made the original degree of enthusiasm difficult to maintain. It was replaced by an even more radical movement—the anarchism of Mikhail Bakunin (1814–76). His program called for nothing less than the abolition of all existing society—the state, the Orthodox Church, the family, private property. His tactics called for assassination and terror—by gun, bomb, poison. "Kill them in the squares, kill them in their homes," read one anarchist proclamation. Society, the anarchists felt, was so rotten that a few spectacular acts, performed by just a few devoted people, would bring it down. And traditional society had no right to define morality, said Bakunin, urging a friend's daughter to become a prostitute in order to bring in earnings for the cause. In the seventies, many a Russian duke, police chief, or provincial governor died at the anarchists' hands. And in 1881, after several unsuccessful attempts (the second of which blew eleven servants to pieces while leaving the intended victim unharmed), they assassinated Tsar Alexander II with two bombs thrown at his carriage.

Anarchism, after that, tended to become somewhat less addicted to the gun and bomb. (Still, a Spanish premier, an Austrian empress, an American president, and an Italian king were later assassinated by anarchists.) Some anarchists, especially Prince Kropotkin (1842–1921), now wanted to achieve the kinder society they envisioned by kinder means and argued that cooperation, not competition, was the natural instinct of humankind. Others joined a new movement, small at first, which believed not in individual terror but in disciplined, organized action. This was the Russian Social Democratic Party, founded in the eighties by George Plekhanov (1857–1918), who was convinced that with increasing industrialization, and with the conditions of exploitation that were the average worker's lot, Marxism could become a major force in Russia. In 1903, at a Congress held in London, the party split into majority and minority factions. The former advocated a more revolutionary, the latter a more moderate approach. Both are referred to by their Russian terms —the extremists as Bolsheviks, the reformists/revolutionaries as Mensheviks.

Both groups had an active competitor on the left, the Social Revolutionaries, who concentrated their efforts on Russia's peasants rather than on Russia's workers. They were anxious for immediate action, and unwilling—as good Marxists had to be—to delay the revolution until Russia had first passed through an industrial stage of development. They thought that effective organization coupled with terror in the anarchist tradition (until one of their chief terrorists was unmasked as a double agent) would rouse the country and destroy tsarism.

The irony of all this violence was that without it, those who governed Russia might have been more willing to institute progressive reforms. (Then, of course, they might not have. History offers few second chances.) As it was they were frightened. Thus two and a half decades of repression followed the murder of Alexander II. This, after all, had been the tsar who, however ambivalent, had freed the serfs, and who on the day of his death had signed a decree authorizing the preparation of new administrative reforms. If the wages of reform were death, a return to the police state seemed the better part of wisdom. Hence his immediate successor, Alexander III (1881–94), sponsored a program of "Orthodoxy, Autocracy, and Nationality." And Alexander III's successor, Nicholas II (1894–1917), said in his first proclamation from the throne that he was determined to uphold the principle of autocracy and that all plans for more representative government were "senseless dreams."

Yet reform would come to Russia, despite the eccentricities of the opposition and the impulse for repression on the Tsar's part. It would come because the Industrial Revolution was finding its way to Russia, and thus a move from the country to the city, and from old economic ways to new, was beginning. It would come because once again, Russia's rulers involved the country in a foreign war that exposed the regime's weakness.

This was the Russo-Japanese War of 1904–5. Its direct cause was a conflict between Russian and Japanese imperialism in Korea and Manchuria. Its indirect cause was the Russian leadership's desire to quiet the domestic opposition; all it would take to put an end to revolutionary agitation, said Russia's Minister of the Interior in 1904, was "a victorious little war."

The war turned out to be neither victorious nor little. Instead, it revealed once more how backward the Russian condition was. As a Russian historian wrote, "No more disastrous or badly conducted war could be found in the whole of Russian history." The result of defeat was domestic upheaval: strikes, demonstrations, and a naval mutiny. In October 1905, railroad workers and printers joined the strikers, so that Russia was without a newspaper or communication network. The prime minister, Sergei Witte (1849–1915), told Nicholas II that he had two alternatives; to establish a military dictatorship or to offer genuine reforms. The Tsar decided on a second course of action after asking his uncle, the grand duke Nicholas, to head the military, and receiving the answer "I'll shoot myself first." On October 17, 1905, he issued a manifesto proclaiming full and immediate civil liberties for all Russians—with freedom of the press, speech, and assembly—and promising the creation of a national legislative assembly, the *Duma*.

In theory, autocracy had come to an end in Russia. And in practice as well as in theory, tsardom had since gained another chance of surviving. But foolishly, as if trying to prove radical predictions, the Tsar tried to renege on some of the promises of the October Manifesto, dismissing Witte in favor of a more conservative prime minister and trying to make the new *Duma* into a largely consultative body without real power. At first there was much irresponsible and contentious behavior in the *Duma*, yet in time the *Duma* rid itself of its early excesses and did much useful parliamentary work.

Other conditions were arising in Russia that held the promise of modernization and change. The country's wealth was growing. Beginning in the late nineteenth century, an overwhelming agricultural country had started on the road to industrialization. Oil was being drilled at Baku, coal mined in the Donets Basin. A railroad network began to cover the country, and foreign capital was flowing into Russia. Witte's successor as prime minister, Peter Stolypin (1862–1911), brought modern methods of agriculture to Russia, and freed at least some of the peasants from the bonds of the *mir*. He allowed more enterprising peasants to consolidate the many small plots assigned to them by the commune, and to buy the land—and hence freedom, too—with the aid of government loans administered by a land bank. In a way, this was a ruthless program that produced a new inequality in the countryside, for many peasants lost their holdings and became agricultural laborers. The program was, in Stolypin's words, "a wager on the strong and the sober," and within a few years it freed one fourth of the peasant households of European Russia from the *mir*. In 1911 Russian left-wing revolutionaries assassinated Stolypin, in part because his measures had proved so successful that they were making it difficult to sustain revolutionary agitation among the masses.

As in the Austrian case, then, there was a sufficient degree of change and movement that would have enabled the regime to continue in power had it not been for the great clash of 1914. Tsardom would stumble into one more war, and once more, would destroy itself. The Crimean War had led to the emancipation edict, the Russo-Japanese War to the October Diploma. This time there would be no opportunity to respond to domestic pressure by offering reform. This war would mean the end of the Romanov dynasty.

# V. 2  A Century in Search of Security: Society and Growth

> ... *For the security of the future I would do everything.* —James A. Garfield, 1865 (on the assassination of Abraham Lincoln)

## The European Century

To think of bomb-throwers and mutinies, of battling suffragettes and rebellious Magyars, tends to falsify the past. For the overwhelming mood of the half-century or more that preceded 1914 was one of normalcy, progress, and hope. Progress, in particular, was the watchword, and Westerners still felt it attainable and desirable.

From 1914, one could look back on a century without a general war. Not that it had been a golden age of universal harmony and peace. The Prussians had fought their wars, and so had Piedmont. The Russians and the Japanese had clashed in the Far East. The Balkans had had their share of troubles. The United States had been rent by civil war. But all these conflicts had been "understandable," even rational in the eyes of participants and onlookers alike. Why shouldn't the Germans and the Italians seek by arms what had long eluded them by peaceful means; why shouldn't the Russians and the Japanese try to expand into Manchuria; why should the Balkan nations suddenly forget their ancient feuds? Why should an industrial free-soil north and an agrarian slave-holding south clash in North America? What was even more important was that these wars (except in the United States) had been brief, fairly unbloody, and limited both in their aims and in the number of active participants. They had also been somewhat exceptional, because in a vast majority of cases, disputes between nations were settled by negotiation—imposed, to be sure, by the achievement of the Concert of Europe, through diplomatic means—not by war.

And there was hope of even greater international cooperation to come. Economically and culturally, the world was becoming increasing interdependent, a condition that required the coordination of both governmental and private activities on a variety of matters, from the regulation of traffic by rail and sea, to postal services, to the protection of patents and copyright. During the century prior to 1914, there were some two dozen international organizations set up by the governments of Europe and over three hundred private ones. Among the most important were an International Labor Office, which was engaged in promoting both uniform and better standards of labor legislation; an International Institute of Public Health to deal with epidemic diseases, especially cholera; an International Patent Office, International Institute of Agriculture, and an International Association of Chambers of Commerce. As for the vital matter of war and peace, there existed since the turn of the century a permanent International Court of Arbitration at the Hague, to which disputes between nations could be submitted for judicial resolution.

In Europe people moved freely between one country and another without travel restrictions, visas, or currency difficulties. Lira, franc, pound, and mark were all based on gold and hence freely exchangeable. The citizen of an European country, wrote a British economist and exponent of deficit financing, John Maynard Keynes (1883–1946):

> ... could secure forthwith, if he wished it, cheap and comfortable means of transit to any country or climate without passport or other formality, could dispatch his servant to the neighboring office of a bank for such supplies of the precious metals as seemed convenient, and could then proceed abroad to foreign quarters without knowledge of their religion, language, or customs, bearing coined wealth upon his person, and would consider himself greatly aggrieved and much surprised at the least interference. But, most important of all, he regarded this state of affairs as normal, certain, and permanent, except in the direction of further improvements, and any deviation from it as aberrant, scandalous, and avoidable.

Not everyone, of course, had a servant to dispatch to the nearest bank for a satchel of gold. "The greater part of the population," said Keynes, "worked hard and lived at a low standard of comfort, yet were, to all appearances, reasonably contented with this lot." For "escape was possible, for any man of capacity or character at all exceeding the average, into the middle and upper classes, for whom life offered ... conveniences, comforts, and amenities beyond the compass of the richest and most powerful monarchs of other ages."

What had brought about this amazing change was the continuing, and accelerating, industrialization of Europe. Two momentous developments were taking place simultaneously, and no one could say with certainty which one had preceded the other. One was the increase in Europe's population. The other was the bounty of goods that Europe's factories were producing.

For centuries, the population of Europe had remained stable. Then between 1600 and 1789, it more than doubled. Between the time of the French Revolution and the Franco-Prussian War it nearly doubled again —from about 160 million in 1789 to about 300 million in 1870. And within another century, despite the two bloodiest wars in modern western history, it would double once more.

Because the land did not provide a sufficient living for so many people —and because farm life did not possess that much appeal in any case, provided a different choice was available—a vast exodus from the countryside took place. Life became increasingly city-centered. In the middle of the eighteenth century, well over three-fourths of the population of Great Britain still lived in the country, and only one-fourth in the towns. By 1914, the figures were reversed; some eighty percent lived in the towns and cities, and only twenty percent in the villages. The figures for the rest of Europe followed this trend, if more slowly in the east than in the west. While prior to 1800, not a single European city claimed as many as one million inhabitants; a century and a half later, more than fifty European cities exceeded that number.

Yet there was food and shelter enough for the millions. This was because of the application of machinery and other scientific innovations to agriculture. The introduction of artificial fertilizers alone in the middle of the nineteenth century freed agriculture from its dependence on animal manure, which had never been available in sufficient quantities. This doubled, and in some cases tripled, the yield per acre.

The breakthroughs in industry were equally spectacular. The decades prior to 1914 saw the discovery of electricity and its application to industry, of the development of the internal combustion engine, of the introduction of new steel-making processes that brought down the price of steel to ten percent of what it had been, of the founding of a great chemical industry, of the invention of photography. A majority of Europe's people lived with more of the material comforts of life than they had before, and they lived longer. The availability of food and of manufactured goods, and the immense number of discoveries and innovations in medicine, from aspirin to sterilizers, from anesthetics to modern surgery, added between ten and twenty years to the average European's lifespan in the century before 1914. These developments, first seen in England, Belgium, Germany, France, and the United States before long became nearly universal.

Not everyone, obviously, shared equally in the new prosperity. But toward the end of the century the majority of organized labor was turning away from revolutionary socialism. Even in Marx's own country, the Social Democratic Party favored a revisionist approach. Despite the compliments that the socialist leadership continued to pay to the genius of the founder, his teachings were revised in the light of changing developments. The poor had not become poorer, the middle class had not vanished, said the principal advocate of German revisionist Marxism, Eduard Bernstein (1850–1932). The class struggle had not become more desperate—it rather had become more peaceful. The state had not shown itself to be the executive committee of the bourgeoisie—on the contrary, it had taken an active role in improving social conditions. Hence there was little point in preparing for an inevitable dictatorship of the proletariat. What was called for, instead, was political action within the existing system to gain higher wages, better hours, and more generous social services. This did not mean the renunciation of the ultimate aims Marx had envisaged, of the just and good society in which people would no longer exploit each other. It did mean, however, that the worker, who now had both the vote and some minimal property, might achieve Marxism's peaceful aims by peaceful means. The road was clear, as Bernstein and his friends who ran the Social Democratic Party saw it, for "evolutionary socialism."

It was true that some radicals who formed communist parties opposed these revisionists as "bourgeois reformers" and "running dogs" of the imperialists. It was true, too, that not all the ills and distempers of society had been solved in 1914, and that new conditions brought new problems. Many workers still lived on the same subsistence wages that Ricardo had stipulated. Many Eastern European peasants had no prospect of ever owning enough land to free their families. Moreover, a certain cultural pessimism was having its vogue. Darwinism was not the most cheerful of philosophies, and at the turn of the century, the psychologist Sigmund Freud (1856–1939) showed that even a period of discovery and material progress had left some of people's darkest fears and instincts quite unaffected. Where people had found a new material security, they often remained insecure at their depths. Freud argued that humans were not the rational beings that the Enlightenment tried to prove them.

Yet at the turn of the century, the overwhelming mood was one of intense pride in Europe's unparalleled achievements and one of confidence and hope. When Hitler ruled over a frighteningly different Europe, Stefan Zweig (1881–1942) wrote in his autobiography, which he completed in 1942 while in exile:

> When I attempt to find a simple formula for the period in which I grew up, prior to the First World War, I hope that I convey its fullness by calling it the Golden Age of Security. Everything in our almost thousand-year-old Austrian monarchy seemed based on permanency, and the State itself was the chief guarantor of this stability. The rights which it granted to its citizens were duly confirmed by parliament, the freely elected representatives of the people, and every duty was exactly prescribed. Our currency, the Austrian crown, circulated in bright gold pieces, an assurance of its immutability. Everyone knew how much he possessed or what he was entitled to, what was permitted and what was forbidden. Everything had its norm, its definite measure and weight. He who had a fortune could accurately compute his annual interest. An official or an officer, for example, could confidently look up in the calendar the year when he would be advanced in grade, or when he would be pensioned. Each family had its fixed budget, and knew how much could be spent for rent and food, for vacations and entertainment; and what is more, invariably a small sum was carefully laid aside for sickness and the doctor's bills, for the unexpected. Whoever owned a house could look upon it as a secure domicile for his children and his grandchildren; estates and businesses were handed down from generation to generation.

... [E]verything stood firmly and immovably in its appointed place. ... No one thought of wars, of revolutions, or revolts. All that was radical, all violence, seemed impossible in an age of reason.

This feeling of security was the most eagerly sought-after possession of millions, the common ideal of life. ... At first, it was only the prosperous who enjoyed this advantage, but gradually the great masses forced their way toward it. The century of security became the golden age of insurance. One's house was insured against fire and theft, one's field against hail and storm, one's person against accident and illness. Annuities were purchased for one's old age, and a policy was laid in a girls' cradle for her future dowry. Finally even the workers organized, and won standard wages and workmen's compensation. Servants saved up for old-age insurance and paid in advance into a burial fund for their own interment. Only the man who could look into the future without worry could thoroughly enjoy the present.*

## *A Countercurrent: Decline of the West?*

This Western confidence of inevitable growth and a secure future contained potential seeds of decay. A rampant capitalism, which was not sufficiently attentive to either the dangers of excess, a persistent imperialism, or a clear racism, gave a cohesive strength to the Western thrust while generating a counterthrust from indigenous societies. Marx and Lenin (1870–1924), in particular, saw imperialism, "the highest stage of capitalism," as the final collapse of capitalism. Imperialism, according to Lenin, embraced five essential features.

1) Monopolies, created by concentration of production and capital, played a decisive role in a nation's economic life.
2) Bank capital merged with industrial capital to create finance capital.
3) Capital, instead of commodities and services, was exported.
4) International capitalistic monopolies, resulting from the export of capital, attempted to share the world's resources among themselves.
5) Territorial division of the world among capitalist powers followed. Powers struggling for hegemony trampled on lesser states.

Monopoly took four principal forms, Lenin argued: combines, cartels, syndicates, and trusts, which all arose from the concentration of production in an advanced stage of development. This occurred despite high tariffs (as applied by Germany) or a free trade policy (as pursued by Britain for much of the nineteenth century). Monopolies were responsible for capturing most of the important sources of raw materials. This was especially true of the coal and iron industries, which created an antagonism between cartelized and noncartelized industries and nations. Monopolies also sprang from banks, which resulted in an invisible empire of industrial and bank capital. Therefore, monopolies grew as an inevita-

---

*Stephan Zweig, *Die Welt von Gestern* (Stockholm, 1944), as quoted in the translation, *The World of Yesterday: An Autobiography* (Lincoln: University of Nebraska, 1964), pp. 1–2.

ble result of colonialism. Emerging from imperialism would be a bondholding, *rentier,* and usurer state in which the bourgeoisie lived on the proceeds of capital exports. The monopoly stage of capitalism was also the moribund stage, then, because it cut off rather than enhanced competition and growth.

Capitalism would be subject to chronic underconsumption because wages would be slow to rise, if they rose at all, and because investment opportunities would dry up as the rate of profit declined. The export of capital could counteract the decline in the rate of profit, however, by draining off excess savings. Thus, as Lenin noted, the high-profit pull of backward areas would combine ideally with the low-profit push of late-stage capitalism.

This is not the place to argue with the theory of Marxist-Leninism, but certain caveats are essential to the understanding of pre-1914 Europe. Marx and, at least initially, Lenin assumed that the surplus kept the same relationship to total income across time. Clearly it did not, for two reasons: the gross national product of a people included services and a variety of invisible exports. Economic statistics show that since 1870, the relative share of profits in national income indicate a downward, not an upward, trend, while the flow of savings over that period rose in the same proportion as income. Marx assumed that the working class would remain completely impoverished, and that the rate of profit would fall in the course of capital accumulation. Neither happened.

Many non-Marxists, among them the English economist, John Maynard Keynes, did admit in 1936 the possibility of investors' seeking foreign outlets when their savings exceeded domestic investment opportunities. To prevent imperialistic wars that might develop from these foreign investments, Keynes suggested public taxation to skim off the surplus. The tax money could then be used for public welfare programs. Thus a viable alternative to Marxism arose in a revitalized form of welfare socialism, especially in post-World War II Britain.

A second source of weakness in the nineteenth-century European position arose from racism. Most Europeans, probably not conscious racists, nevertheless accepted the easy and unexamined assumption that people of different racial origins diverged in fundamental ways that made it "against nature" to unite them. Some thought one race superior to another; some may have simply thought one race irredeemably different from another. Nearly all saw race as a highly significant index of culture, development, and physical and mental prowess.

Slavery had receded by the middle of the nineteenth century, having been abolished in the British Empire in 1833, in the United States in 1863, and in Portugal in 1876. However, the prejudice to which it helped give birth intensified. Spanish and Portuguese slavery may have left less of a prejudicial mark than British, American, and French did; but most black people, in particular, were seen as separate, distinct, and basically incapable of assimilation with white European norms. Color pointed a finger of "guilt" at nonwhites, and emotional race-thinking remained less open to revision than economic theory proved to be.

Racism exploited the developing scientific "objectivity" of observation, measurement, and cataloging, which arose from the time of the Renaissance. Racism claimed to be based not on prejudice, but upon science. During World War I the Society of Medicine in Paris seriously proposed urinalysis as a method of detecting German spies, because German urine was thought to contain 20 percent nonuric nitrogen, 5 percent more than that of other races. Measurement was a goal of "objectivity": measurement of cranial capacity, head shapes, lung size, genital area. Each new "objective" fact seemed to prove an irreconcilable difference between races.

Race-thinking became focused in the eighteenth century, when Comte de Boulainvilliers wrote of "the necessity of obedience [that is] always due to the strongest." By the end of the century, nationalism had led to a school of thought that used language as well as race to distinguish people, there being both pure and impure languages. Constant use of a pure language produced a flexible, luminous intelligence. Adulterated language produced a bastard people. Thus, German racial thought in the post-Napoleonic period created artificial divisions between peoples based less on class than on language. Another people were nothing so simple as merely another people. They were mysterious and romantically different, cut off by language and by the strange ways of thought a different language induced. Personality was given by birth, not acquired. In 1809 a German, Clemens Brentano, wrote in *Der Philister* that the philistine should be identified with the French and the Jew. Only a small step remained before insistence upon purity of descent became a test of nobility, to talk of "good blood" and "bad blood."

That step was taken in 1853 by Comte Joseph Arthur de Gobineau, in his *Essai sur l'Inégalité des Races Humaines.* Gobineau found decadence all about him, and he pessimistically set out to analyze the fall of civilizations. Such falls were caused by the mixture produced when the lower race conquered the upper through sheer animality. The best races, in the sense of the most intelligent and sensitive, could not hope to remain on top, for senseless violence would always prevail. The lower orders, being senseless, would use the ultimate weapon of irrationality to assert democratic—and destructive—excesses. When the French naturalist Leclerc Buffon (1707–1788) classified races upon the basis of European peoples, the geography of race, like that of place, was firmly wedded to a European mold.

The great organizing and energizing principle of the nineteenth century, the doctrine of progress, jusitifed competition, striving, hard work, and a sense of duty. It also held that some had moved farther toward the light than others. The Victorians saw time as an entity not to be wasted, given out in small quantities for self-improvement. Some people and races had failed to use it properly. Charles Dickens's Scrooge spoke of it as Past, Present, and Yet to Come. The White Rabbit in Lewis Carroll's *Alice in Wonderland* called time "him," not "it." William Hazlitt wrote a book on it, *The Spirit of the Age,* and the Germans coined a word for it: *Zeitgeist.* Each age differed from the previous one, and in each some races fell further behind. Progress could be scientifically measured, so that one could see that Hindus, Cherokees, and Bantus had not "progressed."

Darwinism met with such overwhelming success because it provided, on the basis of inheritance, ideological weapons for race as well as class rule. English writers in particular contributed influential books to the debate. In 1869 Francis Galton published a study of hereditary genius, which emphasized selected inheritance and argued that a comely lass always was more likely to have comely children than a drudge would. The dangerous aspect of such evolutionist doctrines was the way they combined inheritance with personal achievements and individual character, allowing them to be readily embraced by the upwardly striving middle class. A stream of books supported the relationship between hard work and an inherent nobility of character. Thomas Huxley, in *Struggle for Existence in Human Society* (1888), argued that the "higher societies" must control births if they want to remain superior to the more animalistic. Benjamin Kidd, in *Social Evolution* (1894), applied the biological ideas of Darwin to entire social systems; and in 1901, Karl Pearson, in *National Life,* argued for a national approach to eugenics. These ideas were echoed in Germany, France, and the United States by scientists, journalists, and popular writers, as in the fictional rags-to-riches dreams of the poor but hard-working and noble Horatio Alger in America.

Racism took on different forms of expression among different peoples, but these same people applied different racial arguments in different parts of the world. Chinese and Hindus tended to earn the respect of Germans and Britons for their antiquity, precisely because Germans and Britons were preoccupied with their own antiquity and used age as one index of civilization. Even within a single continent, different policies were pursued. Among the Portuguese on the west coast of Africa—especially in the Congo—black nobility was treated with respect; in Mozambique, in east Africa, they were not. An infinite variety of permutations clouded any clear understanding of the diversity of races. People were viewed less as individuals than *en masse* destined one day for some ultimate racial war.

## *Expansion of the West: Imperialism*

The rise of the national-industrial state created an unprecedented explosive new force. As new forms of power were developed and machinery became ever more productive, industrial states tripled and quadrupled their output within decades. Populations did not grow rapidly enough to absorb the new production, nor did wages rise quickly enough to create broadly based consumer economies. Industrialists sought other markets, other opportunities for investment, and other sources of raw materials as old ones were depleted or cut off.

Britain in particular became the workshop of the world by the mid-nineteenth century, producing two-thirds of the world's coal, half of its iron and commercial cotton cloth, nearly three-quarters of its still small supply of steel, and nearly half of its hardware. The United States, Germany, France, and Belgium were already becoming formidable rivals.

Although Britain was the first to become industrialized and therefore was in a dominant position at mid-century, its leaders saw that Britain would be by-passed if it were restricted to domestic sources of energy. Britain made about one-third of the world's steam power and had a limited agricultural base. By the 1880s its decline, relative to the other industrial nations, was apparent. By the 1890s both Germany and the United States had clearly passed Britain in production of the most important industrial commodity—steel.

Britain added another element to the steady thrust of industrialization —fear. It would have to maintain supremacy by practicing the balance of power in international politics; building a navy second to none; acquiring overseas colonies; and intensifying initial competitive advantages on the international market. Britain began with a monopoly on industrialization. Its close relations with the underdeveloped world dated back a hundred years when Britain took over French colonies between 1780 and 1815. Britain was therefore able to expand into a vacuum without competition at first, until the British economy as a whole relied too heavily on foreign trade. Only Belgium faced the same problem.

As other nations began to industrialize, they sought to protect their infant industries from the British by erecting tariff barriers around the home product. As Britain's industrial competitors grew, it had all the more reason to seek out foreign markets in the underdeveloped world. For about thirty years, the underdeveloped as well as the developed world had good reason to work with, rather than against, the British economy: 1) only Britain practiced free trade; 2) the major European nations adopted a gold standard for their currencies, making possible a simplified, multilateral system of world trade (and eventually banking) dominated by London.

Britain abolished the Corn Laws in 1846 and wholeheartedly espoused free-trade principles. From that time until the great depression of 1873, the advanced nations forced other countries to trade with them. Gunboats were used, if necessary, as they were in China and Japan. Then, the depression of 1873 turned most industrial nations toward the protection of their own products, a role that the United States had been taking for fifty years. Britain, however, alone among industrial leaders in having to import food as well as raw materials, held to the practices of free trade.

Further, British agriculture had not changed as rapidly as that of other countries. It was difficult to introduce technology to conservative farmers spread across the land; so that while Britain had manufactured goods to send abroad to meet the challenge of other nations, it needed cheap foodstuffs. Low cost was essential. If the price of food rose, the working class would find its wage increases wiped out. Social instability and less efficient production were bound to result. Caught in this bind, Britain had impelling reasons to secure firm control over underdeveloped areas of the world. Although after 1870 other nations found equal and other reasons for contesting her imperial leadership, Britain had much of the field to itself until then, becoming the first modern imperial nation.

At the time of the Congress of Vienna in 1815, Spain, Portugal, France, Holland, and Britain retained overseas empires. All but Britain were still very much as they had been in the previous century, or they had declined. Britain had changed as well as grown, both despite and because of the loss of the American colonies. Until 1763 the British Empire had been an American Empire. By 1815 it was without so clear a focus, for there were new beginnings in Southeast Asia and the South Pacific. By 1876, when Queen Victoria took the additional title of Empress of India, the new focus was on the subcontinent. Before the American Revolution, the British Empire (and most others) had been based upon mercantilism and settler peoples. In the nineteenth century, the trend was toward the annexation of African, Pacific, and Asian lands already in the possession of complex indigenous cultures, without the intention of creating European settlements abroad. The "first" (American) British Empire survived into the twentieth century in the Caribbean, and new French and British empires grew in Africa and Southeast Asia.

Rather than concluding from the American Revolution that they had governed from wrong principles, the British decided that they had governed badly and must not allow the same problem to reoccur. Britain therefore placed increased emphasis upon central control and authority and less upon liberty. This defensive reaction was strengthened by the complexities of dealing with a worldwide empire of highly diverse peoples, inherited from the inter-European wars during 1756 to 1815, which displaced the old single-culture empires. Although the Caribbean colonies and Canada retained the representative institutions of parliament, the Caribbean colonies were turned back to crown rule, and the North American provinces edged toward confederation. The Dutch maintained the navigation laws at first. American vessels were denied access to West Indian ports, and the Corn Law of 1815 excluded foreign grain from England unless home-grown grain reached a "famine price."

The old mercantilism soon came under attack. Indeed, in the world of economists, 1776 is as famous for the publication of Adam Smith's *Wealth of Nations* as it is for the American Revolution. As we have seen, Smith argued that restrictions on trade served only to benefit the landlord class while keeping workers' wages so low that they could not buy the product of their own labor. Any growth of markets was therefore limited. Smith compared domestic industry with international trade. Because people generally worked at the things they did best, why not apply this natural division of labor to colonies? Each colony should concentrate on developing its most successfully competitive commodity for unrestricted trade. Being then placed on a path of rising prosperity, it would not be a drag on the imperial treasury. In fact, mounting colonial incomes could buy more British goods. If trade were restricted, however, it would reduce rates of return on domestically invested capital and lead to domestic decay. This was an argument for decolonization as well, for those colonies that could perform a function within a system of free enterprise would be retained, and those that could not perform would be let go. As British Prime Minister Disraeli remarked (when not in office) the colonies were millstones around Britain's neck. Disraeli also applied the term *Manchester school* to a group of economists who favored free trade and laissez-faire in general. These economists and British merchants backed the Little Englanders, a group of politicians who prevailed for nearly half a century over those who advocated a Greater Britain.

Between 1815 and roughly 1870, then, European nations preferred not to acquire new territories, except from other European powers. When Britain won colonies from other continental nations, its decision to keep them depended increasingly on the need to protect sea routes to India and the Far East. Mauritius was taken from France because it had the best harbor in the south Indian Ocean. Ceylon, because of its port at Trincomalee, and Malacca, because it controlled the straits to the South China Sea, were acquired from the Dutch. Britain's continuing ascendency relied on sea power, and its concern for trade routes led to taking Singapore in 1819 and retaining Gilbraltar, Malta, and the Ionian Islands in the Mediterranean. Most of these colonies were without intrinsic importance, being pawns in a game of power. But they helped assure the safety of existing colonies, and they protected potential trade routes that might displace old ones. They also stabilized interior regions through which a rival power might attempt to move. France, having followed Britain into Africa and Southeast Asia, was the greatest rival.

The principles of free-trade imperialism were compromised toward the end of the century, as the relative positions of the industrial nations changed. On the whole, Britain held to a free-trade position from the abolition of the Corn Laws in 1846 until 1932. France moved toward protectionism after Jules Ferry became premier of the government in 1880–81 and again in 1883–85. In a year, high tariff walls protected home industries from direct colonial competition while they gave colonial produce a degree of protection as well. Germany and Belgium, despite moderate tariffs directed against Britain, held to free trade. The Dutch belatedly went over to it in the 1870s. Britain stood midway, manipulating imperial preferences to its benefit while espousing the general principles of free-trade competition.

Thus a modified form of mercantilist thought came to be applied to the colonies. They would 1) Supply raw materials for the industrial machine in Europe cheaply; labor in colonies cost a fraction of wages at home; 2) Purchase finished products; 3) Strategically protect trade routes by which the bulk of these products moved to other nations; 4) Become centers for investment and absorb surplus capital as well as produce; and 5) Help eliminate surplus production, which led to domestic cycles of unemployment, and thereby forestall the social revolution many predicted.

The new capitalist state would need new kinds of trading partners capable of sustaining a trend toward consolidation, large-scale marketing, and giant trading firms. It was a trend that made economies of scale possible (lower costs of large production). In turn, either profits increased or prices dropped, and markets broadened. Underconsumption at home was cited as the primary result of low wages. This was the view of John A. Hobson, the first analyst (and opponent) of imperialism as a phenomenon. In his book *Imperialism: A Study* (1902), Hobson wrote that underconsumption and low wages barred profitable usage of capital at home. Surplus capital sought outlets in the colonies. But Hobson felt that the problem could and must be remedied, for imperialism benefited only a few special interest groups.

At the Congress of Vienna, the European state system had been remolded around the concept of the balance of power. It was essentially a seventeenth-century doctrine projected into the nineteenth century. Louis XIV wished to create a "universal monarchy," a condition in which one state could command all others, and European leaders feared that he would—or that some other nation would do just that. To prevent the rise of such a superpower, they sought to assure at least a distribution of power among many states, so that no one state would be dominant. Each nation would have preferred to carry more weight than that of any other nation, so that in any coalition it would hold the balance of power. Each sought to manipulate its own policies, to preserve independent action, and to protect national sovereignty. Balance of power rested largely within Europe until the mid-nineteenth century. Then it began to shift toward colonial possessions as overseas trade gained importance and emotion and prestige became attached to having an imperial place in the sun. Balance of power no longer rested solely with the nation that had the most and largest ships, for prestige could not be measured in such terms.

## Nonrational Impulses to Empire

The search for national and personal glory surfaced as the most tangible of the emotional or psychological motivations for imperial expansion after mid century. Imperialism was closely allied to nationalism. To be without a colony at the end of the century, even if that colony was an economic liability, was to be weak. As late as 1936, when Italy overran Ethiopia, the primary goal was to achieve what Mussolini termed "manhood among nations." Colonies helped to assert the pride of the nation and give it security in a rapacious world where people, like Tennyson's description of nature, were "red in tooth and claw." It was basic to post-Darwinian thought that the quest for security depended on one's country being dearer than all others and therefore must at all costs be made safe in a competitive world. Even today this lies behind the foreign-policy objectives of the Soviet Union, the People's Republic of China, and the United States.

A related motive for expansion, then, was a strategic one. Islands, river mouths, peninsulas and other landmarks dominating trade routes or suitable as forts were coveted because they could make economic and political goals more accessible and the nation more secure. Colonies were often little more than adjuncts to some larger area of an empire. After the completion of the Suez Canal in 1869, Britain took Aden, Socotra, and Perim solely to protect the new route to India and the East. France annexed large portions of west and equatorial Africa as strategic hinterlands for the protection of travel routes to the coast or for protection of the coastal holdings themselves. Strategic considerations also altered as naval power and communication—in the form of the telegraph, the steamship, and the airplane—changed. An area once important could be traded for an area of greater importance, making indigenous populations pawns in larger, European-based strategic games. Even so, an area was of strategic importance only in relation to the prevailing economic and political theories of the powers.

Thus the strategic motive may generally be subsumed under the others. This was especially true in the acquisition of territories in east Africa after 1880 by Britain, France, Germany, and Italy. Britain wished to maintain control in Egypt, although without formal annexation. Conquest of the Nile to its headwaters seemed a strategic necessity. To stabilize the Nile holdings, the highlands and parts of Kenya and Tanganyika were taken by Britain and Germany, respectively. To maintain control over the Panama Canal route, the United States had to dominate —choosing dollar diplomacy rather than direct annexation—the Caribbean and Central American republics, and in particular, Cuba.

**Africa and the Middle East, 1910**

As strategic needs changed, the tenacity with which a nation held onto an area might have been expected to change if imperialism were a wholly rational system of world organization. To some extent, such changes did occur. Britain slowly lost interest in the West Indies after the abolition of slavery in 1833 and the subsequent accelerated decline in the sugar market. The United States' interventionist policies in the Caribbean receded gradually as air began to replace water transport. Yet for the most part, empires continued to grow in defiance of economic wisdom and strategic planning. Nonrational impulses to empire were clearly at work.

Foremost among these was the humanitarian desire to reform, to uplift. The "little brown brother" was felt to be in need of more efficient, liberal, or rational forms of government, economic organization, or worship. This humanitarian impulse had at least three aspects. Christian missionaries desired to save souls, to bring Christ to peoples whom they regarded as heathen and lost. The evangelists in particular sent missionaries into China, Africa, and India to educate non-Christians so that they might read the Bible for themselves. Some saw the machine as an instrument of God, and many embraced the new trinity of the imperialist—railroads, sanitation, and good government. Through them, less developed nations would be elevated so that they might grasp more vigorously at spiritual triumphs.

From the time of John and Charles Wesley, who preached to the colonists in Georgia in the 1730s, independent Methodist churches had grown among the middle and lower classes in Britain. This growth may have helped to prevent the spread of political radicalism then and in the first half of the nineteenth century. The Wesleyan Methodists were emotional, revivalistic, and conservative. They were also competitive, especially where Anglican or Roman Catholic missions were present. Catholics were active in Indo-China, for example, where they were conscious instruments of their nation's expansion. However, most of those missionaries who actively promoted imperialism, especially in Africa and the Pacific islands, did so for their church, not their nation. French missionaries opposed British because the French were Roman Catholic and the British were Protestant.

Humanitarianism also had its ethical, secular goals, as in the campaign to end slavery. This campaign was closely allied to the broad doctrine of progress. Many indigenous groups practiced slavery or, as in Malaya, a form of debt bondage. A Western nation was a powerful secular ally in the battle against nakedness, cannibalism, child marriage, sale of brides, and *suttee* (the Hindu custom of the widow's cremating herself on her husband's funeral pyre). Frequently, indeed, the central authority of the imperial power improved the life of the native population by intervening in local affairs to protect a minority group against exploitation by a majority. Dominant tribal or religious groups or white settlers attempting to press back indigenous populations in Australia, New Zealand, or southern Africa invariably thought of the imperial power as an interfering body, but the interference was often protection for the weak.

Britain slowed down the pace of self-government in Australia in the 1850s in order to speak out for the rights of the aboriginal population. She accepted a form of constitutional government for Canada in 1867 only after French-speaking rights were entrenched in the enabling acts. Rhodesia was refused independence in the 1960s because the blacks were not accorded a progressively equal political standing to whites in that colony's draft constitution. In the late nineteenth century, the United States' federal government sought to hold back the growth of statehood in certain western American territories because it feared that, once sovereign, they would create unrepresentative institutions.

Many were pleased to be called imperialists, determined to "take up the White Man's burden, . . . To seek another's profit,/ And work another's gain." In the words of the poet laureate of empire, Rudyard Kipling, in 1899, the United States too must

> Take up the White Man's burden—
>   And reap his old reward:
> The blame of those ye better,
>   The hate of those ye guard—
> The cry of hosts ye humor
>   (Ah, slowly!) toward the light—
> "Why brought ye us from bondage,
>   Our loved Egyptian night?"

In the final analysis, imperialism rested upon human acquisitive instinct, a desire to influence, control, dominate, own, or crush another people. Racism fed upon such a desire and also fed the desire. Racism usually was part and parcel of imperialism in the sense that imperialists held themselves to be superior to others. Some theorists of empire argued that racial differences were largely environmental; that is, if other races appeared inferior to the white, they were so only because of historical circumstance. Sufficient exposure to more advanced mores and technologies would, in time, make the "lesser breeds" functionally equal within the law. This position helped justify retention of land occupied by another race. Other theorists argued that some races were inherently inferior and always would need the protection of the stronger. That argument tended to present the native races as useful labor forces, while the environmental theory described them as societies in need of transformation. The nurture-nature debate showed a curious blend of the missionary, humanitarian, wealth-seeking, and power-hungry impulses of the West.

These motives were sustained in a cyclical fashion. The settlement colonies absorbed surplus population and drew the military-minded. Exploits of the French or British armies created tales of wartime glory, fostering more exploits and attracting youthful adventurers.

Imperialism thrived without the aid of annexation. Not only was annexation expensive, it was dangerous because it might bring a reaction from another power. It produced shock waves within the interior of an area, sometimes forcing further annexations to calm and control turbulent frontiers. It led administrators on the spot to intervene in intertribal, interethnic, or interpolitical affairs, until the moral involvement of the imperialist nation became too deep for the colonial people to accept.

Annexation could be avoided, however, by allowing informal empires to parallel formal ones. Informal empires were technically independent but their economies, communication systems, and often, politics and social life were inextricably bound up with an imperial power. Such power relations were new only in degree, for there have always been client states. The United States exercised informal control over portions of Latin America and the Pacific. Russia came to hold influence over vast, contiguous territories that eventually were absorbed into the Soviet Union. Germany, then France, sought to dominate much of the eastern end of the Mediterranean prior to World Wars I and II, respectively. In the nineteenth century, Britain thought of Argentina as virtually another dominion, because Argentine beef, rails, and minerals were so closely connected to the British Empire's needs. Strikingly, the economies of formal and informal portions of an empire might differ very little. In the late nineteenth century, the extractive economies of New Zealand, a British colony, and of Uruguay, an independent nation, bore remarkably similar relationships to Britain.

There were certain qualitative changes in expansion, then, turning points in the acquisition of empire that marked stages in the race for the sun. Initially an enclave was secured in order to establish a factory to benefit a single industry, especially for textiles. In time, the enclave became a wedge for more widespread investment, as in Chinese rails or Argentine beef. A place, a specific factory or warehouse can be protected with troops and a gunboat; investments can be protected only by exercising influence in a nation's seat of government and over its economy as a whole. So the factory system operating for a century or more before gave way to European competition for spheres of influence in China. A turning point in political and social relations between Europe and all her colonies was reached with the European decision to move into colonial interiors in order to make rural people more amenable to the needs of the city or the post. France's *mission civilitrice* in west Africa was just such a move.

In time, therefore, there grew what might be called ricochet empires: areas acquired by nations that were themselves former colonial dependencies. They hoped to play out the role formerly denied them. After World War II, the list began to grow: India's policy toward its Himalayan states and neighbors; Australia's policy in New Guinea and Papua; South Africa's efforts to create Bantustans; Malaysia's stance on Borneo; Ethiopia's attitude toward Eritrea; and Indonesia's activities in Irian Barat. Imperialism, in short, has taken many guises and has not been the monopoly of the West, even if—by virtue of the technological and industrial revolutions occurring in Europe first—it originated there.

### *Did Colonies Pay?*

Did colonies pay? In psychological terms, undoubtedly; in financial terms, generally no. In terms of security, they were a mixed blessing. At the time, however, many expected them to pay. Cecil Rhodes knew imperialism to be "a bread and butter question," and the neomercantilists of Britain and the continent agreed. Statistics are difficult to compare given competing systems of trade, inaccurate data, and the fact that different nations kept their statistics in different ways. Nonetheless, for the neomercantilist period, one may reach certain conclusions.

Some historians have asserted that the profits from the slave trade paid for nearly 20 percent of Britain's industrial revolution. Others have argued that Britain's mid-century industrial progress was financed largely from the cheap labor of India. Such judgments are at best guesses, although revenues from the colonies undoubtedly were drained to serve imperial interests. The Dutch drew 18 million guilders a year from Indonesia in the years from 1831 to 1877, a time when the entire Dutch budget was 60 million. Forty-two percent of Indian revenues in 1890 went to finance the Indian army under British officers, primarily serving imperial purposes. Britain's entire defense budget that year was 38 percent of its revenue. Still, the heavy costs of the colonies must be set against such financial gains from the empire. Ordinarily, they faced deficit budgets that the imperial power had to meet. Many small but expensive wars were fought over them, and administration was costly in terms of health. French expenses in Morocco more than wiped out any profits from trade. Italy's colonies cost 1,300 million lire, which was more than colonial trade produced between 1913 and 1932. Germany's external trade with its colonies was 972 million marks between 1894 and 1913, while the expenses of the colonies were 1,002 million marks. At the outbreak of World War I, Germany's empire was taking only 0.5 percent of her overseas trade. Even the Congo was always a small part of Belgium's total overseas trade, never contributing more than 7 percent. For Britain, the colonies were more important; but there, too, the balance was generally an unfavorable one. In 1850 the empire took 28 percent of

Britain's overseas trade (and 40 percent in 1934). Of the 1934 figure, however, well over half was with the dominions, the former colonies of settlement; only 7 percent was with India and 9 percent with the remainder of the empire. In short, for Britain the chief economic advantages lay in the older white settler colonies and in India, while the new African possessions were of little importance in economic terms.

Hobson and Lenin argued that the real economic gain from colonies lay in investments. But in Canada, Britain invested far less than the United States did. Leaving out the dominions, most capital exports flowed into Europe or to Latin America and the United States. At the outbreak of World War I, those areas were taking 53 percent of all British capital investment, while the dependent colonies took 6 percent (India and Ceylon took 22 percent). The figures for France were similar. Nor did the colonial investments pay meaningfully higher rates of return, as the Marxists argued, for most European investment was in government bonds or debentures with fixed interest. Their returns averaged 0.5 percent higher than returns from noncolonial stocks did.

Still, the nations of Europe—joined by the United States at the end of the Spanish-American War in 1898—continued to acquire colonial possessions until 84 percent of the land surface of the globe was under Western control in 1930. There obviously were powerful motivations toward empire. Clearly, in retrospect, they were not truly economic motivations. Yet one must remember that at the time many imperialists felt that the colonies would eventually pay. The search for a balance of power also made it seem valid to deny another nation a new acquisition. Moreover, it encouraged preventive annexations.

On balance, then, if there were profits to be won from annexation, they were specific to certain types of manufacturers rather than to the business community as a whole. Obviously, both munitions and mosquito netting were needed overseas. If a nation could control the source of supply of a high-cost, easily transportable, nonperishable commodity like rubber or ivory, it could realize large profits. King Leopold II of Belgium did so for a period of time in the Congo. Empires provided military and administrative employment overseas and for a burgeoning bureaucracy at home. They were a form of invisible income: One critic referred to them as vast systems of outdoor relief for the upper classes. Even so, profits and jobs were not peculiar to empires, nor were they greater there than in any other expanding sector of the economy. European powers did not partition Africa in order to develop markets, for they could do better elsewhere. They partitioned Africa out of political and psychological needs. French capital did not go to its colonies after the partition, but to Russia. Nor were the captains of industry particularly nationalistic, being quite willing to trade with potential enemies if profits were large enough. If the leaders of international capitalism had the power to dominate Europe,

## Asia and the Pacific, 1910

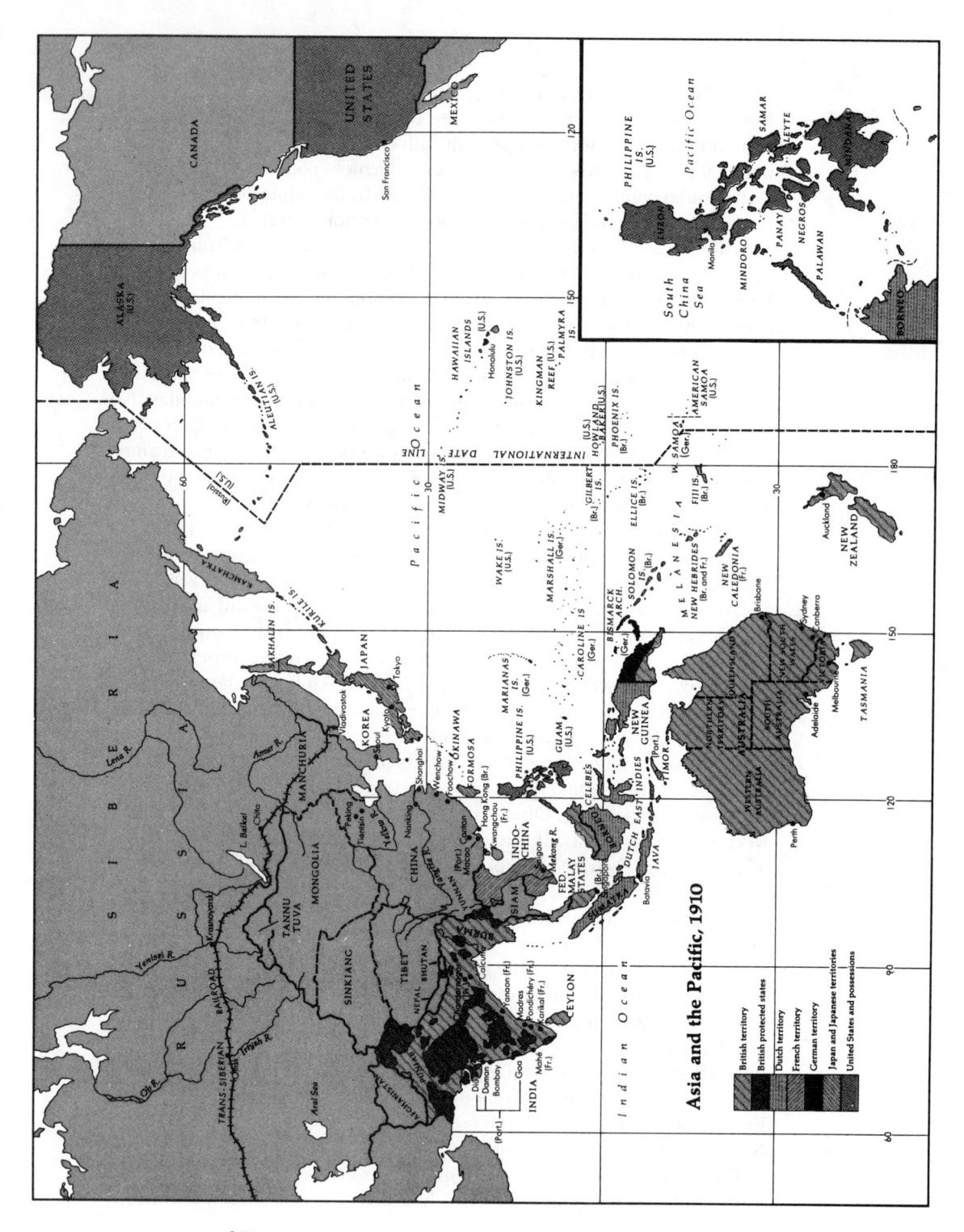

they would have prevented World War I, for it was clearly predictable that their best customers would be destroyed and their sources of supply severed. The dream of capitalist exploitation, not the reality, drove nations on. These dreams required advanced steps, for if one day empires were to pay, they must be secured. Those who willed the end willed the means: harbors for warships, depots for troops, frontiers based upon natural (i.e., defensible) lines, client states open to manipulation. Lord Salisbury, three times Britain's conservative prime minister between 1885 and 1902, remarked that the military would have wanted to garrison the moon had they seen the moon's potential. Salisbury was about sixty years ahead of his time.

## *Non-Western Responses to the West*

But what of the non-Western peoples themselves? In what ways did they respond to the presence of European administrators, soldiers, and merchants? In a variety of ways, of course. The variety was obscured, however, by the notion of a "Western impact" on non-Western societies. That notion contained three major judgments: 1) The West was a monolithic force, prevailing over other societies in basically similar ways and from a common base of a generalized Western culture; 2) Societies that absorbed the impact of the West were tradition-bound and subject to few changes except those induced by outside pressures; 3) The impact was almost wholly in one direction, of the West upon the non-West, inducing modernization. These judgments are open to challenge.

The West did not think of itself as a unit. Rather, it was a series of competing nations, each with goals of its own. Eastern societies were not so naive as to view all Europeans as the same, even though at times they were inclined toward this form of racism, an ironic inversion of the Western notion that all black, brown, or yellow people were alike.

The "traditional societies," while more conservative and slower to change than those of the industrializing West, were in different stages of transition, stability, disintegration, and unity. Some were ready to entertain innovations, especially technologically, when the West reached out to them. Indeed, the West often was the catalyst for a series of political and industrial developments that led, in time, to social and cultural changes in the receiving societies. But for every society that lost heart in the face of the Western thrust and fell into disarray, there was another society which stood firm, adapting the modes of the West to its own culture.

Comments on the third judgment must be prefaced by the fact that there was not a formal colonial system, as such. Rather, there was a series of systems with a common industrial base—the exploitation of other peoples to the presumed economic benefit of the metropolitan power—and the diffusion of Western ideals which stemmed from the Enlightenment and after. Because there was no common system of oppression, there were no narrow, common responses by the subject societies. In the complex interaction between imperial power and colonial peoples lies the functional definition of Western expansionism. In interpreting the diversity of responses, and in understanding the new nations that arose in the twentieth century out of the imperialism of the nineteenth, two theoretical structures may be kept in mind.

In the first structure, one may distinguish between three types of imperial nations. First, there are nations consciously thrusting toward specified national goals in a way that is attractive to other societies. Their means of expansion and the goals toward which they strive seem attractive enough to warrant imitation by other societies. Examples are the United States since the American Revolution, Great Britain in the nineteenth century, the Soviet Union in the twentieth, and—for some cultures—the People's Republic of China: dynamic, tension-inducing, goal-oriented, achieving societies that have been the object of ideological imitation.

There are also goal-sustaining rather than goal-seeking societies. Such nations, having achieved the relatively limited goals they initially set for themselves, find it difficult to define new national goals. They appear content to defend their achievements. These societies often are referred to as "garrison states," in the sense that their conservative purpose is to protect what they have. Examples include French Canada, white South Africa, and perhaps Australia. While such societies may be dynamic economically, on the whole they are not the object of other nations' envy. Nonetheless, they may be thrusting, acquisitive societies. One of the inheritances of the colonial period has been the tendency of some new nations, especially settler nations with basically European populations, to be imitative in their patterns of responses, to seek economic and ideological systems that are modified forms of those of the Great Powers.

A third type of society seeks few goals except the negative ones of separation from further contact with the former colonial powers. Examples include Burma and, in terms of external affairs, contemporary mainland China. Thus, another form of the colonial legacy is the sense of isolation produced in ancient, proud cultures. Once independent, then having passed through a period of colonial subservience, they renounce most of what they inherited from that period of subservience. Islamic and black Africa desire this pattern. There are those cultures so rich in their variety and antiquity that they remained largely untouched by the colonial experience. That period was for them a phase that may have induced numerous surface changes but few that are longlasting. Many historians argue that the dominant cultures of India, taken collectively, are such societies.

The second theoretical structure that is useful as one looks at the modern phase of Western expansion is best understood by posing four questions for each colonial experience. 1) What was the nature of the colonial power and of the settlers it sent into the colony at the time of primary authority? 2) What was the nature of the indigenous population at the time the colonial power sought to exert its authority? 3) How determined, and for what reasons, was the colonial power in its desire to seize or retain the area in question? 4) Over what kind of terrain—within what geographically defined compass—would the drama of challenge and response be played out?

In the material that follows, these questions may be asked of the nature of Western contact with Russia, the Middle East, India, Southeast Asia, China, Japan, and Africa, as well as of the fragments of Western society that come to constitute much of Latin America. For purposes of illustration, however, it is best to take a single, less obvious example as a case study: New Zealand.

New Zealand was discovered by a Dutch explorer, Abel Janszoon Tasman, in 1642. Another island well to the west, Tasmania, would in time bear his name. It was Captain Cook, however, who first made the Antipodes known to the world. The Maoris, a people of Polynesian origin who were conquerors, arrived there between 900 and 1400, having sailed in great boats from a semimythical Hawaiki elsewhere in the Pacific. New Zealand long remained unimportant to the European powers, despite some interest by whalers and sealers. A modest trade in timber and flax was carried on with the Australian settlements after their founding in 1791. In 1814 Samuel Marsden, chaplain to the British penal colony in New South Wales, established a Church of England mission station on the North Island. Missionary interest in the indigenous population preceded any serious commercial interest and generally opposed European settlement. But from 1826, when the first New Zealand Company was founded in England to promote immigration, the white (or *pakeha*) population grew. There was no massive influx, however, until after the founding of the New Zealand Association by Edward Gibbon Wakefield in 1837.

Wakefield had been instrumental in the colonization of South Australia. He taught the old economic doctrine of "just price" in terms of the land. According to his theory, a strictly controlled number of British middle-class farmers would be allowed to buy land. They would pay a price that would prevent speculation while it assured a progressive, steady, yet limited influx of settlers. Wakefield's theory was not adhered to in most of the areas of New Zealand opened to settlement, but organized bands of state-aided British colonists began to arrive. The British government, originally opposed to settlement in New Zealand, now worried about possible French annexation. Britain sent a governor who in 1840 concluded the Treaty of Waitangi, by which nearly five hundred Maori leaders conferred territorial sovereignty upon Britain in exchange for a guarantee of their ancestral lands.

In most colonies of European settlement, land proved to be the major bone of contention, and such was the case in New Zealand. English settlers in the North Island and Scottish settlers in the South soon established port facilities through which they hoped to export agricultural products to Britain. To create a market garden to the empire, settlers moved onto the soil where they clashed with the Maori tribes, who claimed collective ownership. In 1843 the first Maori War broke out; other wars followed until 1870. During this time (1846) the British government conferred a constitution on New Zealand, signifying that the settlers were to remain in the islands. Grazing-leases were issued from 1851, taking up increasingly large areas of land and initiating the wool-growing industry, which became the staple of the New Zealand economy. Responsible government was established in 1856. By 1870 steamship connections were opened to San Francisco, a transoceanic cable was laid to Australia six years later, and in 1882 the first refrigerated steamer left a New Zealand harbor with a load of meat for the British market. White agricultural New Zealand was firmly wed to the Industrial Revolution and its center, Britain. In 1907 New Zealand became a fully self-governing dominion. The nation had become a "fragment society," one in which an initial diffusion of Enlightenment, romantic, or industrial values from Europe led to goals that were imitative of, or dependent upon, a mother country.

Although there were spasmodic Maori-*pakeha* wars in the North Island, where the great majority of Maoris lived, the settlers and indigenous society accommodated to each other after 1870. While the aboriginal Tasmanians were driven to extinction by the white settlers there in a virtual policy of genocide, the Maoris began to find a role to play within the predominantly agricultural economy of the settler-dominated land. By the 1930s the Maoris began to recover a sense of pride in their culture. Their birth rate increased, and New Zealand became known to the world for its relative racial harmony. The challenge thrown out by Western expansion and the response shown by the Maoris was utterly different from that in Australia, for example, where the Central Australian aborigine was driven into the interior, given no place in society, and left to a Stone Age existence until the 1960s. Because the British government wished in both instances to protect the rights of the indigenous population against the white settlers, why was the pattern of response so different?

The truth lies in the answers to our four questions.

1) Many of the white settlers who went to New Zealand were middle class, often evangelical, relatively well educated, and at least marginally prosperous. Many of them accepted the notion of the *beau sauvage:* the ideal islander untainted by Western society—innocent, upright, and free. The white settlers of Australia were far less educated, often "marginal" people who experienced little early prosperity, remained under a form of military rule for many years, and brought few reformist sentiments with them (as did the Chartists who went to New Zealand).

2) The Maori were the most complex of Polynesian societies. They had art forms visibly worthy of respect. They lived within fortified villages, or *pa,* which showed a high degree of social organization. They fought according to European notions of chivalry and with tactics and courage that Europeans admired (because they seemed to reflect European modes). White settlers in Australia, on the other hand, confronted an unorganized, nomadic population that was, by European standards of the time, aesthetically unpleasing, incapable of sustained warfare, and easily demoralized.

3) While Britain was determined to retain New Zealand, it was equally determined to reduce the size of its overseas garrisons in the 1860s and 1870s when matters were tense within Europe. The white settlers saw that they would have to come to terms with the Maori or continue to do battle through their own militia, an unpalatable prospect in a frontier society where all able-bodied people could find ready employment and high wages in peaceful pursuits.

4) New Zealand was small, and the central area of encounter, the North Island, smaller yet. One could not drive the indigenous population into a distant interior, as in Australia or the United States, and then forget about it for a generation or more of seaboard consolidation. New Zealand was not large enough to have such an interior. Many of the settlers saw that they would either have to fight a war of extermination, as they did on Tasmania, or come to terms with the continuing presence of the Maoris. They chose the latter course, partially because there would be no British army to fight their war for them, partially because many had come begrudgingly to admire the Maoris, and partially because the Maoris, who had turned to guerilla warfare, were seen to be a most difficult foe. The pattern of response in New Zealand, then, differed radically from that in Australia (or Canada, or the United States, or South Africa).

The case study of New Zealand also shows the influence of many of the conditions at work within what is loosely called the colonial system. Distant military considerations and the reshaping of political systems played their parts. New technologies and an acquisitive capitalism reached out aggressively. In fact, the entire collection of intellectual baggage that nineteenth-century Europeans bore with them as they went overseas served to mold the nature of the imperial impact. Further, the Maoris' response also showed what became a classic pattern. At first they appeared to think of the early white settlers as an equal, perhaps even superior culture. Many professed to accept the teachings of the Christian missionaries. By the 1840s, however, a crisis of identity set in, some Maori tribes taking the collaborationist path, fighting with the *pakeha* against other Maoris, forestalling the development of any sense of *Maoritangi,* or common nationhood.

The old arts, especially carving and weaving, fell into decline. Many of the old songs—for which Maori culture was justly famous and through which Maori history, as genealogy, was transmitted—were forgotten. Yet, some Maori leaders sought to retain a collective sense of pride. Briefly, a group of Maoris sought solace in the past, reverting to cannibalism. In the Hau-Hau rebellion of 1865, believing themselves to be impervious to Western bullets and using prayer as their shield, Maoris marched into battle (as the Mahdists in the Sudan did later). Yet others sought a religious solution in a Ringatu church, which added to the Godhead of the Father, Son, and Holy Ghost a fourth, uniquely Maori figure, the glorious Nui, a special spirit of strength.

A third response was political. At first there was a movement to unite under a Maori king. Then, in the 1890s, increased participation in the rising Labour party was seen to be the path to survival. These responses were repeated in the Boxer Rebellion in China in 1900, the Maji-Maji uprising in Tanganyika against the Germans in 1905, and the Mau Mau terrorism in Kenya in 1952.

Such gestures of defiant despair within indigenous societies are commonly followed by attempts to copy the political organization of the encroaching European culture. Just as the Ceylon Civil Service became basically British in its organization, just as Ghanaian and Indian nationalism quoted Edmund Burke against the British, the Maori organized into political bodies that came to have a "national"—that is, all-Maori supratribal—appeal. Making their protests political was, in one sense, a final capitulation to the Europeans. They were meeting them on their own grounds. But it was also the most effective form of response, because it ultimately commanded the attention of the Europeans. Maoris met to rationalize their land ownership problems and sought to mechanize their farms. They asked for and received a voice in the New Zealand House of Assembly. They agitated for schools and their own college. Together, they fought as a particularly daring regiment in World War I. The path of *Maoritangi,* a positive response to *pakeha* pressures toward assimilation, led to a Maori capital at Ngaruawahia, just as Chaka and Dingaan had their southern African capitals or the Navajo based themselves upon Window Rock in Arizona.

The political response usually led to a desire for economic development, for political organization ordinarily must precede economic demands. New Zealand became a social laboratory for much of the world. It assisted immigration financially. Female suffrage became law. The state assumed ownership of land, and a progressive income tax was levied. Factory laws were stringent, and arbitration of labor disputes was compulsory. The eight-hour day, old-age pensions, and state insurance were other innovations. The Maoris participated in all this, but they often remained near the bottom of the economic scale. Economic equality was the most difficult goal to reach when the European controlled the means of production and distribution. In their pattern of response, then, the Maoris provided a microcosm of the larger story of "traditional" versus "Western" societies.

### *The Balance Sheet*

Was imperialism harmful? All forms of imperialism, while often bringing stability, sanitation, education, and improved communications to an area, forced one people to advance at another's pace. All imperialism, including that pointing toward ultimate independence of a colony, implied that only the superior power could name the stages by which the inferior must develop. Only the superior would judge the degree and speed of development. One may always find a test that another cannot pass. The most pervasive legacy of imperialism was the assumption that someone else had, by nature, the right to judge the progress of another people. For this reason, although many scholars favorably assess the short-run physical benefits of imperialism for both power and colony, others diagnose the psychological effects as ultimately harmful to both.

Assuredly imperialism was harmful because it created two special classes within colonial and postcolonial societies. Both classes became the object of special attention. One group consisted of the product of racial intermixture: half-breeds in the United States, *mestizos* in the Spanish colonies, and Eurasians throughout Asia. Often they were accepted by neither society from which they sprang. Some European societies and some churches showed less racial prejudice than others. Roman Catholics generally tried to ameliorate the condition of slaves and free nonwhites, although here too there were great differences between Orders. Jesuits practiced greater racial liberality than Franciscans, for example. The French often intermarried or intermated; and so long as a colonial people assimilated with French cultural norms and languages, the state did not support discrimination. The English and later the Americans, on the other hand, had far greater fears about race mixing.

A second halfway group created by imperialism was made up of those now referred to as the collaborators, those of the indigenous culture who felt that their future security lay with Europe, much in the same way the conquered of the first century worked with the conquerors. Some cooperated with the imperial powers for purely personal gain. They might see Europeans as peacemakers because they had the power to enforce peace when local chiefs could not. Other chose to work with the conquerors because they were impressed by European forms of representative government. Ironically, nationalist leaders in European colonies eventually used the words and techniques of the imperial power against them. India's Mohandas K. Gandhi (1869-1948) and Jawaharlal Nehru (1889-1964) adopted British parliamentary practices, among others, to achieve their goals of national independence. Uruguay had senators who were pleased to speak of themselves as British liberals. Africans took Western names, Maoris accepted knighthood, and an entire class of Anglo-Indians arose.

The patterns of Western influence were thus extensive at the surface. In many areas they did not touch the village level, and African and Asian societies remained essentially unchanged at the bottom. But the intellectual and political elites at the top were transmuted in fundamental ways, and even those who did not accept Western culture had to battle against it on Western terms. Military, technological, political, and intellectual patterns throughout the world were, at the top, often Westernized. Peoples faced crises of identity that spread into Asia and Africa. The nation-state, which was essentially a European concept, and the rampant nationalism of the twentieth century were both inherited from the imperialism of the nineteenth century. In this sense, the Western impact on traditional societies, if not by 1914 then by 1939, was so great that it constituted an imperial revolution no less pervasive than the scientific, industrial, or commercial revolutions. Imperialism became a state of mind, and Europe a place name on a mental map.

Did imperialism contribute to the modernization of new states? Modernization is a popular goal of new states, and that in itself indicates the influence of imperialism. In addition, the European period supplied and continues to supply norms for political thought and bureaucracy. It has shaped the economies of new states to fit the European economies. Nonetheless, it may be argued that in many portions of southern Asia and in Africa, in particular, life at the village level was little affected by the coming or the passing of the Europeans. Many Asian historians now argue that the imperial period of Indian, Burmese, or Javan history brought only superficial change.

### The British Empire

The best example of modern imperialism in the years before World War II is Britain's. The British Empire was the largest in the world, rivaling the relative power and sway of Rome centuries before. By 1914, common law, trial by jury, the King James Authorized Version of the Bible, the English language, and the British navy had been spread around the globe. At the heart of the British Empire lay the rule of law, and in administering the rule of law the British thought in terms of the dual principles of trusteeship and preparation. Belief in these principles united an otherwise dissimilar empire, for the notion of trusteeship and the doctrine of participation were rooted in a desire to justify the morality of exercising power over others. Both concepts were deeply in the conservative tradition. This tradition provided the thread of thought that linked the Western colonial dominance of the twentieth century with earlier overseas expansion.

The principle canons of conservative thought come through most clearly in the writings and speeches of Edmund Burke, a British political theorist and statesman. Burke opposed unfettered exercise of authority and spoke in favor of the colonists at the time of the American Revolution, mixing high-minded idealism with a pessimistic view of human nature. He held that a divine intent ruled in society, as well as in the individual conscience, creating an unbroken link between rights and responsibilities. Burke wished to protect the variety and color of traditional life styles. And he was convinced that to be civilized society required orders and classes and that the only true equality was moral. Thus, he argued, imperial administrators in India were responsible for protecting native people from exploitation by those who thought of progress purely in economic terms. Certain that people were governed more by emotion than by reason, Burke thought that laws created by mass minds were likely to be bad laws, because democratic assemblies act with emotion rather than reason. Reality was an unpredictable and mysterious growth; and government worked by trial and error, administration being an art rather than a science. Suspicious of abstractions and theory, Burke believed that an aristocracy should be disciplined in decision making, educated to rule. Having their own income and land, from which a sense of history might arise, they should act as a check on the power of the crown. The higher orders might slowly educate the lower to a sense of commitment to authority and trusteeship, to patronage and noblesse oblige (the noble behavior of the higher toward the lower classes).

This was not an ignoble philosophy, and it explained many of the realities of eighteenth-century Europe. In various ways, colonial powers showed they were not aware of philosophical problems raised by colonial rule. Translated overseas to the colonies, the canons of Burkean conservatism united with other principles to create a secular equivalent to the doctrine of stewardship—that the colony's rights were in trust to Britain for the benefit of those who were not yet ready to exercise the temporal rights that God might confer.

From stewardship in matters of morals to trusteeship in matters of politics was not a long step, and a succession of British administrators were the first to make that step. Most notable among them was Sir James Stephen, permanent undersecretary for the colonies from 1836 to 1847. Stephen was known as Mr. Mother Country because of his persistent advocacy of close ties between colony and metropolitan center. He felt a special responsibility for indigenous peoples and wanted to protect them from the most harmful effects of Western, especially settler contact. Contrary to those who believed that the ends of democracy were best served from local centers, Stephen relied on the distant and more objective power of parliament and the Colonial Office, operating through the doctrine of trusteeship. They gave the Bantu, the Central Australian aborigine, and the Hindu trader what little protection they enjoyed against the corrosive effects of daily economic and settler encroachment. An obvious extension of the notion that Britain held in trust the rights of indigenous peoples was the idea that one day, through a long rite of passage, these peoples once again would deserve to exercise those rights for themselves.

Trusteeship thus led to a more specific, programmatic doctrine of preparation. The doctrine held that there were a certain number of stages through which a people must pass before they were ready to again exercise the rights that they had placed—often unwillingly—under trust. Imperial powers defined these stages and decided whether they had been reached. In a sense, imperialism involved setting up an obstacle course for native populations. The course was by its nature European, and European tests were applied to performance. The justification for injecting an alien value system and creating foreign goals for native peoples was that the moral fiber of a people would be strengthened. Corrupt states would be made efficient, and modernization—although not yet so named—would help nonindustrial societies catch up to the West. Constitutional reforms would surely result in a steady movement upward, because, according to the West, political and social progress were the chief ends of humanity. Judged by the competitive and achieving standards of Western society, native institutions were inferior, even though they were the source of local pride and cohesiveness. Because the doctrine of preparation was defined largely in political terms, societies that strove to modernize often collaborated with imperial nations and suffered massive social dislocation.

Racism, however, did not arise specifically from this ill-formulated body of thought. Although the idea of preparation implied that the white man was better prepared, it did not deny that the black man could be equipped for rule in the future. Rather, preparation assumed an environmentalist approach to orders and classes. Many in Britain admired the complexity and subtlety of India culture: its diverse languages, fantastically mobile forms of art, and classical literature. They felt that Indians were not inherently inferior but had come to function that way because of a constrictive social and religious environment, the effects of which could be removed. In that attitude lay the contradiction between trusteeship and preparation. On the one hand, Europeans were holding in trust the rights of non-Western societies for some future resumption. On the other hand, Europeans must change the ways in which those non-Western rights traditionally were exercised, in order to prepare the society for its future role. The basically passive side of the policy did not want to intervene. The active, reforming side did.

Where European rule was direct, active reform tended to dominate. Where it was indirect and worked through native chiefs and local institutions, the more passive attitude took over. Britain used indirect rule in Uganda, northern Nigeria, Samoa, and the Malay States. Neither impulse clearly prevailed, so that one must look to individual colonies to understand the nature of the European empires. Both impulses were basically Darwinian (counting on the survival of the fittest). Both demanded that settler colonies and annexed territories achieve some efficiency in local government before they could pass the test of constitutional or cultural progress. As Tom Mboya, Kenyan trade union leader and politician of the 1960s, remarked, "efficiency" remained the last refuge of the imperialist. The doctrine of preparation thereby tied much of the imperial experience together.

In the British Empire, for example, four essential stages were involved in the process of preparation. 1) *Using the embryo of a two-house legislature:* A colony had to earn the right to have legislative and executive councils and to nominate local members for the legislature. 2) *Injecting the principle of representation:* At least a minority of unofficial members (non-British administrative officers) would be elected to the legislative council. 3) *Introducing the principle of responsible government:* In time, a majority of the members of the executive council would be drawn from the legislative council. 4) *Readying the colony for independence:* Nominated members (those put forward by the crown or the governor) would eventually disappear from the executive council. Both houses would then be elective and local in their membership. Britain might retain some residual authority over defense or foreign affairs even beyond this point. At any stage in the process, she could suspend the constitution or, in effect, instruct the colony to return to an earlier stage and begin again.

Ultimate British power was not, in fact, diminished as any of the first three stages were achieved. Preparation should not be thought of as two bodies compromising their positions as they moved more closely together. Rather, there was one society in which a minority set the goals for the majority. Further, because each stage was based on a transfer of skills through education and training, the imperial power could declare at any point that the skills had not been learned sufficiently well. The special presumptions of imperialism, then, were that the British or French form of government was necessarily the better; that tests could be set by outside forces to determine internal progress; and that tests were in themselves essential, even as they extended rather than shortened the period of preparation.

Ordinarily, colonies required several years to pass through these stages. Canada, although a direct inheritor of European models of governance, needed over thirty years to attain internal self-government. This was so despite its population of European stock who required relatively little "training." Ceylon required thirty-seven years. Yet, following World War II, as the European empires collapsed, colonies were pushed through these stages with unprecedented speed. The Gold Coast, which became Ghana, moved through the process in eleven years, for example. Not surprisingly, therefore, some recently independent societies have shown chronic instability or have adopted one-party systems of government. Having accepted a rationale, the British in particular sought to hold onto it. In doing so, they may have foreshortened the period of "training," making it meaningless and undermining the effectiveness of those who were to provide stability. Whether the stages were, in truth, necessary or the end product desirable were questions seldom asked.

### From Colony to Nation

Canada offers the most precise case study of the stages from colonial state to independent country. Between 1783 and 1931, Canada became England's first dominion. Most of the precedents by which the British Empire evolved into a commonwealth of self-governing nations arose because of the Canadian situation and because it was an area in which a rational solution to decolonization was more nearly possible.

Originally Canada had been French. Samuel de Champlain, royal geographer of Henry IV, founded a permanent colony at Quebec in 1608, laying claim to large areas of the interior. The society of New France was an extension of Louis XIV's empire at its height: centralized, traditional, and mercantilist. French Canada was a seigneurial society (one in which the estates were royal grants) based upon a modified form of feudal landholding along the St. Lawrence River. Her twin loyalties were to church and crown.

When the British added New France to their empire by the Treaty of Paris in 1763, Britain inherited a frontier society comprised of colonists who spoke the language of Britain's most dangerous enemy. Problems of internal security obviously would arise, and the new British administrators had the wisdom to recognize the need for tolerance. In 1774, therefore, in the Quebec Act, Britain assured French settlers that it would tolerate the Roman Catholic Church, protect their language, and retain French civil law while instituting English criminal law.

But an empire is much like an intricate Chinese puzzle: move one part, and all move. Once the Gallic Peril had been eliminated from the eastern seaboard, those colonies were no longer willing to be taxed to support the presence of British garrisons. The defeat of the British in the American Revolution propelled thousands of loyal Tories northward to Canada to start life anew as United Empire Loyalists. They sought protection from the French majority and security in their rights as English citizens, although not to the extent of rebellion against the crown they had just defended. They wished to set themselves clearly apart, morally and politically, from the upstart republic to the south.

The result was a history of constitutional changes that provided the pattern for preparation in other colonies. Some of these changes arose from Loyalist demands, some from the need to achieve a balance between French-language and English-language interests as the latter grew, and some progressively from the need for protection against an expansive United States. First was the Constitutional Act of 1791, establishing elective assemblies in both Upper and Lower Canada. These new provinces succeeded the single structure of Quebec—Upper was almost exclusively British and Lower mostly French. A constitutional struggle between the elective assemblies and the governors in council followed. As in prerevolutionary Virginia and Massachusetts, the central issues were the collecting of revenue, granting land for settlement, and the powers of the judiciary. Deadlock resulted in 1837.

Rebellion followed. In Upper Canada, William Lyon Mackenzie, "the Firebrand," who had read Tom Paine and lived in the United States, led a popular uprising. In Lower Canada, Louis-Joseph Papineau rallied the disgruntled in Montreal. But the mass of the population remained aloof. When the two rebel leaders were easily defeated, they fled to the United States and led raids into Canada. Their acts only caused further deterioration in relations between the two countries. These relations had already been strained for the quarter-century since the Anglo-American War of 1812–15. During the war, American militia burned York (now Toronto), the capital of Upper Canada, and the British burned the Capitol in Washington. Britain recognized the dangers of continued discontent within her North American provinces. This Achilles heel in the New World could not be allowed to result in persistent strife with the United States.

The solution was proposed in the most fundamental single document in the constitutional history of any empire: the Durham Report, written by Lord Durham, or "Radical Jack" Lambton, a Whig, who was sent to Canada by the British to investigate the causes of the rebellion. As governor-general with sweeping powers, he completed his inquiries in five months. Having worked himself out of a job, he was recalled by the home government, which felt he had dealt too leniently with the rebels. In February, 1839, *Durham's Report on the Affairs of British North America* proposed merging the two Canadas and granting full responsible government to the united colony. Britain retained control over foreign relations, regulation of trade, disposal of public lands, and the nature of the constitution. All other aspects of administration were surrendered to local authorities. Concluding that two cultures were "warring within the bosom of a single state," Durham was speaking to three problems at once: the lessons the British had slowly learned from the American Revolution, the dangers presented by the flourishing form of government to the south, and the competition between French and English traditions. While he predicted that in time French culture would be assimilated into the English, he saw that a number of practical measures were needed to assure continued French loyalty to the British Crown in North America.

Faced once again with a traditional contest between imperial authority and colonial self-government, the imperial authority must have the wisdom to appear to retreat in the face of self-government. Self-government on issues that mattered locally could be wed with imperial controls over issues that mattered imperially. The sense of Durham's report was embodied in the Union Act of 1840 and in the governorship of Lord Elgin (1847–1854). Elgin, by refusing to veto a bill that came to him from the assembly, was saying, in effect, that the assembly was capable of responsible government. The act on which Elgin exercised executive restraint was the Rebellion Losses Bill. Its purpose was to compensate people—many of them rebels—who had suffered losses in the uprisings of 1837.

In 1854, land that had been reserved for the clergy was secularized, and seigneurial tenure was ended. Yet, as Elgin remarked, the last hand in British North America to wave the Union Jack might well be French. Responsible government had assured the loyalty of the French-speaking residents, who feared annexation by the United States more than they feared Britain, which had shown itself progressively ready to concede self-government.

The next precedent that arose in Canada was economic. In 1858 New Brunswick and New South Wales sought tariff barriers to promote local industry, but their attempts were disallowed by the Privy Council in Britain. In 1859 Canada sought to do the same; and when an intimation of disallowance was heard from London, the Finance Minister, Alexander T. Galt, sent a stinging message. If Her Majesty's advisors were to recommend so clear a violation of the rights of Canadians, he wrote, they must be prepared to take over the administration of Canada itself. This was a direct hint that Canada must either move forward to another evolutionary stage or Britain would have to accept the consequences of a reversion to nonresponsible government. Galt received no reply, and the Canadian tariff of 1859 was put in force.

Between 1840 and the 1850s the French showed no inclination to assimilate British norms. The French birthrate increased, as the church promoted *revanche des berceaux* (revenge of the cradles) to offset the growing influx of English-speaking immigrants. Cut off from any further flow of immigrants from France, the French Canadians saw themselves as a garrison state, much as the Boers in South Africa did. Indeed, there had been little new French flow since the 1640s, so that the French Canadians of the mid-nineteenth century were unlike the French of France in many ways. Most were descendants of a rural, pious Breton and Norman culture, which had little in common with the secular, metropolitan society of Paris. The French Revolution had horrified the French Canadians, who clung to the church and wanted nothing of the Rite of Reason by which the Cathedral of Notre Dame had been desecrated. Many considered that France had betrayed them in 1759–1763, for they were convinced that France possessed the power to retain New France, had she chosen to do so. Although the English referred to the passage of New France into British hands as the Conquest, the French called it the Cession. Isolated from France, increasingly contained within a single province, and apprehensive of American designs upon the rich lands of the Canadian border regions, the French Canadians wanted some further political accommodation.

By now, Britain had turned to free-trade imperialism, abandoning the mercantilist principles by which furs and then codfish had moved the Canadian economy. These staples had enforced economic contact with Europe, the prime market, because the United States had an abundant supply of both. However, Canada's relatively uniform geography precluded widespread agricultural diversification, so trade with America was necessary. Britain therefore negotiated a reciprocal trading agreement with the United States on behalf of Canada in 1854, the first such treaty negotiated on behalf of a colony. The American Civil War, which broke out in April 1861, soon led to renewed Anglo-American tensions. Many European and Canadian observers predicted that the North would lose the war and then, with its vast standing army, attack Canada to seek compensation for the loss of the southern states. To this fear, two clear problems were added: no Canadian administration had been able to govern for a long time, because the parties were so evenly matched that each election ended in near deadlock; also, the mother country, preoccupied with problems in Europe and hoping to avoid embroilment in colonial wars, threatened to withdraw its troops. Britain counseled some form of regional union for the North American colonies so they might be less exposed to American annexation.

The result was a series of conferences, which by the end of 1865 led to an agreement on how the weak, separate, and threatened colonies might unite. In 1867 the united Canadas (now called Ontario and Quebec), Nova Scotia, and New Brunswick formed the Confederation of Canada. The new nation was called a dominion (from a passage in the Bible, in which God and mortal might achieve "dominion from sea to sea"). Canada was not yet, in fact, fully independent, but a giant stride toward the goal had been made, a stride that led the imperial authorities to associate progress of preparation with some form of federation between disparate colonies. (When Britain sought to decolonize other portions of the empire after World War II, it sought to do so through a succession of federations, all of which failed: the West Indies, Central Africa, Malaysia, Nigeria, and South Arabia.) This Canadian confederation did not fail and it continued to be the source or instigator of a succession of steps by which colony became dominion and dominion became independent in the interwar years between 1919 and 1939. Australia followed much the same path to the union of separate Australian colonies into a single commonwealth in 1901. Other dependencies and former dependencies of Britain—notably Ireland and South Africa—also contributed to the complex doctrine of preparation. After 1870, the doctrine of preparation was applied to dependencies that were the product of the "new imperialism."

### American and Russian Expansionism

But what of the other empires which, by 1914, were in competition with each other? For while the British Empire was the largest and set the pattern for imperialism, other nations also sought markets and sources of raw materials, thirsted after a place in the sun, and feared that their rivals might seize control of strategic positions. France, Germany, Portugal, Spain, the Netherlands, Belgium, Denmark, Sweden, Italy, and the United States had overseas possessions during the "age of imperialism." Russia, Argentina, Chile, Brazil, the United States, and later Japan expanded into contiguous territories at the expense of native peoples.

Americans did not regard their western movement as an exercise in imperialism but it showed many of the same characteristics. While the industrial powers of Europe were expanding overseas, the United States acquired by purchase and conquest the remainder of its Manifest Destiny, a dominion from sea to sea, that was "to bring the blessings of liberty to the entire continent." The United States had a moral obligation to expand against monarchical or dictatorial governments, in order "to extend the area of freedom." Americans, as a vital, progressive, and moral people were duty-bound to regenerate "lesser peoples." The whites, enjoying a highly productive physical environment and superior to all other races, were obliged "to uplift the less fortunate," or so the Americans felt.

The first American empire, then, was within the continent. By the end of the century the native American Indians had been swept aside off their ancestral lands into reservations. They were wards of the state. While the indigenous peoples of North America fared better than had those of Australia or southern Africa, they nonetheless fared badly. The last great Indian battle was at Wounded Knee, Dakota territory, in December 1890. When the Indian was "pacified," the frontier thought to be closed, and the main thrust of the westward movement over, Americans looked elsewhere for new worlds to conquer. In the meantime, the republic had established a system for administering its continental territories. The system was similar in many respects to that used by Britain. Those who wrote the Ordinance of 1787 foresaw the need to provide for the political organization of the then unpopulated lands to the west of the Atlantic seaboard states. As the territories were organized, they underwent transitional stages in which their residents were, in effect, living in a colony administered from Washington. A general formula was created for moving from territory to statehood. Between 1857 and 1867, six territories were admitted as states. In the next twenty years only one territory gained full equality, and thereafter the period of transition grew longer. Alaska, acquired from Russia in 1867, waited until 1912 before achieving even the status of territory and until 1958 before it became a state.

By the 1870s a national consensus was emerging. New frontiers should be sought overseas, especially in trade and particularly in the Caribbean and the Pacific. The Pacific Ocean had been the cutoff point for territorial goals of most American Presidents through James K. Polk at mid-century. Their primary aim was control of the harbors at San Diego, San Francisco, and within Juan de Fuca Strait in the northwest corner of the present state of Washington. Such essentially maritime considerations strengthened the desire of British and American leaders to find a peaceful solution to the Oregon controversy, and the acquisition of California was seen as essential to American progress. American traders already had been trafficking with China, chiefly out of Salem and Philadelphia. There were American whalers (as Herman Melville's *Moby Dick* [1851] attests) throughout the Pacific. In 1853 Commodore Matthew C. Perry had presented his American fleet in Japanese waters, despite the announced intention of the island nation not to trade with the West. His second visit, the following year, persuaded the Japanese to sign a treaty that opened two ports to American trade.

If this trade were to flourish, American vessels needed repair and refueling facilities elsewhere in the Pacific. The Hawaiian Islands proved especially desirable, for it had sandalwood for China, and sugar and foodstuffs for the mainland; this last was badly needed after the discovery of gold in California in 1848. In 1875, the sugar growers in Hawaii, largely Americans, obtained a reciprocal trading agreement with the United States. It stipulated that no part of Hawaii might be given by the

Hawaiian Kingdom to any other country. Sugar exports to Americans shot up until the islands were utterly dependent upon the continental market. When the agreement was renewed in 1884, the United States was granted exclusive use of Pearl Harbor as a naval base. In the meantime, the native population declined so rapidly from disease that planters, in need of labor, imported thousands of Chinese, Japanese, and Portuguese to fish.

The United States annexed Hawaii on July 7, 1898; it was the first land outside the North American continent to bear the American flag permanently. Although Hawaii had been within the American economic orbit for three-quarters of a century, annexation came only after three developments: 1) overthrowing the Hawaiian monarchy and creating a republic in which the American sugar producers counted heavily; 2) cutting off a portion of the American market for Hawaiian sugar. In 1890 a new tariff put sugar on the free list and thus made Cuban sugar, so much closer to the large eastern cities, competitive; 3) victory of American naval forces over the Spanish defenders at Manila Bay in the Philippines, nine weeks before annexation, accentuating the American need for a midway base between Asia and the west coast.

The events at Manila Bay would have been of little importance had it not been for a slow, corrosive series of quarrels with Spain in the Caribbean. America's quarrels with Europe over European colonial possessions in the New World seemed natural to many, for as early as 1823 the Monroe Doctrine made it clear that the United States thought it had to exercise a particular kind of influence in Latin America. The Monroe Doctrine took on a corollary in 1895, when President Grover Cleveland intervened in a boundary controversy between Venezuela and Britain. He asserted that America had an obligation to the mainland free nations of the Western Hemisphere—all of which had become independent of Spain and Portugal between 1810 and 1831—to protect them from abuse by European powers.

In the same year Cuba erupted in revolution against Spain. As the revolution spread, American owners of sugar, tobacco, and iron mines on the island complained of the destruction of their property. Outnumbered by Spanish troops in Cuba, the revolutionaries turned to guerrilla warfare, hoping to draw help from the United States. A new governor sought to limit the effects of guerrilla tactics by forcing large elements of the rural population, which was supporting the revolutionaries, into concentration camps. There thousands died. While American business opposed direct intervention in so unstable a situation, the popular, or "yellow," press—in the midst of intense campaigns to increase circulation—printed atrocity stories, which stirred public opinion to prorevolutionary sympathy. Then, on February 15, 1898, the U.S. battleship *Maine* exploded. At anchor in Havana harbor as an indication of America's intent to protect her nationals' property, the ship was destroyed, and 260 officers and civilians were killed. "Remember the *Maine!*" joined "Remember the Alamo!"—the war cry against Mexico in 1845—as a popular slogan, and Congress voted a defense appropriation of fifty million dollars.

Even so, had the United States wished to avoid war, it could have done so. President William McKinley sent an ultimatum to Spain, demanding an armistice in the revolution and an end to the concentration camps. Spain revoked the camp policy at once and sent the governor orders for an armistice. But the American people appeared to want war; they sought adventure. The nation was tense, worried over a five-year-old depression, and confused by an overheated political campaign that brought forth much rhetoric about America's future and its mission.

Without waiting to learn the details of the Spanish armistice offer, McKinley presented the Cuban crisis to Congress with the judgment that Spain's response had been "disappointing." After lengthy debate, Congress voted recognition of Cuban independence, authorized the use of troops to make recognition effective, and pledged "to leave the government and control of the island to its people." The scenario of escalation then played out its inevitable steps. McKinley signed the resolution, and the United States served an ultimatum upon Spain to grant Cuban independence. Spain broke diplomatic relations, the American navy blockaded Cuban ports, Spain declared war against the United States for an act of aggression, and the United States countered with a declaration of war against Spain on April 25, making the declaration retroactive to April 21.

The American Ambassador to Britain thought it "a splendid little war . . . begun with the highest motives, carried on with magnificent intelligence and spirit, favored by that fortune which loves the brave." *Little* it was, for it lasted 115 days, and the American forces swept all before them. The American army lost 5,462 soldiers, the great majority to disease in their camps rather than to enemy bullets. The Spanish Empire was broken, its army crushed, virtually all of its battle fleet sunk or driven onto the beaches. Admiral George Dewey reached Manila Bay only five days after war was declared and destroyed a Spanish fleet larger than his own. Important events quickly followed: Manila was occupied by American troops reinforced by Filipino guerrillas under General Emilia Aguinaldo; Hawaii was annexed; Puerto Rico fell; and Spain asked for peace.

When the Treaty of Paris (1898) was signed, the Philippines were ceded to the United States for $20 million. Spain surrendered all claim to Cuba but assumed the Cuban debt. She ceded Puerto Rico and the Pacific island of Guam to the United States as indemnity.

Americans quickly learned that they could enjoy the rewards of imperialism without annexing territory. American soldiers remained in control of Cuba until 1902. Before they could be withdrawn, Senator

Orville H. Platt proposed an amendment to an appropriation bill providing that Cuba could not enter into a treaty or assume any public debt without American permission. The United States might intervene in Cuba at any time "for the preservation of Cuban independence." The amendment was later made part of a treaty with Cuba and embedded in the Cuban constitution at American insistence. Although Cubans protested, acceptance was the price of quasi-independence in domestic matters, and in effect Cuba became an American protectorate. American troops landed in Cuba in 1906, 1912, and from 1917 until 1921. The United States acquired rights over two naval stations, and Cuba became the second largest recipient of American investments in the Western Hemisphere. Investment required stability in order to make dependable predictions concerning financial returns, and from 1917 until the Platt Amendment was abrogated in 1934, the American government made it clear that it would recognize no revolutionary regime in Cuba.

Nonetheless, it was the Pacific that continued to be the testing ground for the growth of an American empire. To maintain hegemony over Caribbean areas seemed natural, for Americans had long considered themselves to be the appropriate paramount power in the New World. To attempt the same in the remote Pacific invited new dangers. Filipinos showed that they felt betrayed by the continued presence of the American army, for when Aguinaldo learned that the Treaty of Paris had given the Philippines to the United States, he organized an armed revolt. It continued as guerrilla warfare until mid-1902. A special commission established by President McKinley recommended ultimate independence for the islands, with American rule to continue indefinitely until the Filipinos proved themselves ready for self-government. One condition of such proof was to terminate the rebellion and accept American rule. In 1916 partial home rule was extended to the Philippines; in 1935 the islands became a commonwealth; and in 1946 they were granted full independence. They proved to be a financial loss to the American people, and their strategic value was, in the long run, dubious. They provided the American navy with a valuable base for Far Eastern operations, and they also posed a constant challenge to the expanding Asian empire of the Japanese, especially in the 1930s.

On the whole, American expansion was nonterritorial in nature. This was best symbolized by the Open Door Policy. After the Sino-Japanese War and the disintegration of the Manchu Empire in the mid-1890s, China responded to the European nations' demands for political and economic concessions. Her trade was carved up into spheres of influence. The British suggested that the United States join in guaranteeing equality of commercial access to China for all European nations, fearing aggressive German designs in particular. The American government chose to act alone, although in such a manner that it promoted British ends. In a circular letter written on September 6, 1899, Secretary of State John Hay asked for assurances from Germany, Russia, and Britain (later from France, Italy, and Japan) that none would interfere with any treaty ports and that no power would discriminate in favor of its own subjects when collecting railroad charges and harbor dues. Although the replies Hay received were evasive, he unilaterally announced in March of 1900 that the principle of the open door was "final and definitive."

The American empire differed from other empires in three respects. For the most part, Americans sincerely believed that colonial status was purely transitional as was territorial status. Change might come slowly, but the new possessions were to be led toward independence. Other colonial powers thought that at least some areas would remain colonies. Nor did the United States establish a cabinet-level ministry for the administration of colonies, but left such responsibility to a variety of instruments: the departments of State, Interior, Navy, and War. Even in 1934 when a Division of Territories and Island Possessions was created within the Department of the Interior (the office responsible for Indian affairs), both Guam and Samoa were left to the Navy and the Panama Canal Zone to the Army.

The Canal Zone represented the third difference—the American attempt to compromise between economic advantage and political responsibility. The United States was now involved in a two-ocean foreign policy. It was also inextricably drawn into European balance-of-power politics and China's international relations. It was necessary that naval forces be able to move quickly from the Atlantic to the Pacific and that intervention in the Caribbean and Central America continue. Recognizing all this, President Theodore Roosevelt—who became president following McKinley's assassination—moved on two fronts. Desiring canal rights in Central America, he connived a Panamanian revolt against Colombia and immediately recognized Panama's independence. In November 1903, a treaty granted the United States perpetual rights of use and control of a canal zone across the Isthmus of Panama, in exchange for $10 million and an annual fee.

A year later Roosevelt added a further corollary to the Monroe Doctrine because he feared an armed European intervention in Venezuela after that nation had defaulted on its debts to Britain and Germany. Shaking a big stick at moral wrongdoers, Roosevelt stated that if Latin American nations could not clean their own houses and if they gave European nations cause for intervention, the United States might be forced to "exercise ... an international police power" in the western hemisphere. This was especially so in nations that could threaten access to the canal route. When the Panama Canal opened on August 15, 1914, the United States had further reason to protect its Caribbean approach paths. Santo Domingo became an American protectorate in 1907 under Roosevelt's corollary, as did Haiti in 1915. American marines were stationed in Nicaragua from 1912 until 1925; in 1916 the United States acquired the right to construct a canal across Nicaragua; and the Virgin Islands were purchased from Denmark in 1917. The Mexican revolution that began in 1913 led to American intervention at Vera Cruz (1914) and along the northern border (1916). Even this did not disturb the flow of commerce, investment, and vessels within the Caribbean, which had become an American lake.

The United States was not alone in expanding into contiguous territories. Most settler or industrializing peoples adjacent to underpopulated and weakly defended frontier lands did the same in the nineteenth century when the entire New World was virtually a frontier for the western part of the Old World. Argentina, for example, entertained territorial designs upon Uruguay until 1852. Under President Julio Roca (1880–1886), Argentina steadily encroached upon its Indian frontiers into the 1930s. Chile made the Araucanian Indian lands part of the national domain; and after 1889 Brazilians expanded into their own frontier lands at the expense of native populations.

The other major expansive continental power was Russia. Even though she sold Alaska to the United States, Russia began a concerted advance into Central Asia, taking Tashkent in 1865, conquering Kokand, Bokhara, and Khiva, and annexing the entire area east of the Caspian Sea in 1881. The British, fearing Russian designs on India, strengthened their northwest frontier forces, and a clash between Russian and Afghan troops in 1885 brought England to the verge of war. The crisis was temporarily resolved by diplomatic agreement. From the 1890s Russia also pursued a vigorous policy of expansion in the Far East, where its imperialism met Japan's in the Russo-Japanese War of 1904–1905.

Russia's continental drive continued even after the Bolshevik Revolution took place, although by different means, and the Russian Empire achieved its fixed frontiers in the 1920s. Within these frontiers the government started a program of Russification at the end of the nineteenth century. This policy assumed that Russians were superior to other subjects of the Tsar, that they would spread Russian bureaucracy and administrative norms, and that they would use distant areas as sources of raw materials. In short, many of the characteristics of overseas imperialism were contained within the expanding Russian frontiers. Russians pressured non-Russians to accept Russian culture, language, and religion, although they were generally disinclined to interfere with Moslem schools in Turkestan, Azerbaijan, and the lower Volga region.

### The New Imperialism

These continental imperialisms differed from the "new imperialism," however. The new form concerned itself more with taking territory for its own sake. It was more emotional and nationalistic, more intimately connected with industry, than earlier imperialisms were. By the 1870s, the Industrial Revolution had created a demand for goods from specific markets and appealing to national fashions. Higher quality goods for a critical market required local European control over the manufacturing process, over methods of planting and cultivation, over port facilities, storage depots, communications systems, and even local finance.

Some European states professed reluctance about adding new colonies because of their attendant administrative and defense costs. Nonetheless, they allowed and then encouraged their citizens to invest capital in underdeveloped areas: in mines, plantations, warehouses, wharves, railroads, steamships, banks, and land. To administer such expressions of European commerce as these required trained Europeans, who moved to the colonies in greater numbers each year. Because they were transient and their new environment strange, the Europeans created their own housing compounds, offices, hotels, recreational facilities, schools, and mountain and beach resorts. Few among the local population could afford to make use of such facilities, even if granted access to them, so that whites came to be physically separated from native populations.

Relations that were once friendly grew distant. Local inhabitants took jobs as wage employees of Europeans, but their true employers—the companies—were in distant European cities. The whites who supervised them were promoted by these companies largely because they kept costs low and production high, so that the welfare of local populations was not the primary priority. The labor situation was, by its nature, exploitative. Racial differences accelerated the obvious class problems. Where white colonial administrators attempted to meet their responsibilities to native populations, they often found themselves in conflict with the European business world.

Many areas in the tropics were thought to be unsuitable for whites to live for a long time. They preferred, therefore, to stay in their homelands and work through friendly, stable, and powerful local rulers: the Egyptian khedives, the Indian maharajahs, or the shahs of Persia. Such rulers often remained in power only through the money lent to them by Europeans, making them puppets on a string and their nations client states to the major powers. With massive investments at stake, Europeans sought to pressure their governments into direct intervention in the affairs of the client states if the pliant rulers appeared to be in danger. Often such intervention was entirely legal because of protective treaties signed by local rulers who sought outside support for their regimes. Where intervention was not legal, sheer force of arms made it possible. Equally often the European powers did not need to land troops, occupy territory, or rattle sabers, for threatening such force—gunboat diplomacy—was sufficient to secure concessions.

Gradually European governments were drawn deeper and deeper into the interior of Africa and Asia. Most governments preferred not to intervene, and time and again colonial secretaries warned against any "forward movement." And just as often the movement would take place. Theory and practice did not run parallel. The 1870s were years when no British colonial secretary favored the annexation of new territories, yet the decade began a series of giant steps toward vast new British administrative commitments. For example, in 1873 the British displaced the Dutch on Africa's Gold Coast; in 1874 the Fiji Islands were ceded by King Thakambau; in 1875 Britain left its island base in Southeast Asia (chiefly the Straits Settlements of Singapore, Malacca, Penang, and Labuan) to intervene directly in the Malayan mainland states of Perak and Selangor.

Native turbulence was common to these areas of expansion, and this threatened British trade. On the Malayan mainland, successive governors sought to avoid expansionism and yet expanded, for the Chinese-controlled tin trade was wracked by tong wars and rivalries, and the Malay sultanates—with whom stability within the peninsula rested—were subject to quarrels over succession to the thrones. Britain annexed Burma in 1885 because of a similar situation.

In southern Africa the British expanded north and east time and again despite an expressed desire not to. Being a mercantile community, the British wanted peace, stability, and dependable communications within the interior, so that raw materials might flow undisturbed into the ports that Europeans controlled. Thus circumstances led them to expand, for there were recurrent, if clandestine, raids upon native areas, and from the British point of view, successive Zulu chieftains constantly disrupted the stability of southern Africa.

Because a nation's prestige was in part measured by the extent of its colonial empire, threat of annexation by one nation brought a counter-threat from another. In this way, and for these reasons, France also assumed large-scale imperial commitments. Germany, late into the race, had a smaller share. Belgium held sway in the Congo, the Dutch in the East Indies. Portugal had significant possessions in Africa, India, and the Far East.

The new imperialism was thus far more widespread and far more pervasive than the old; and it often grew out of the barrel of a gun, as the old had grown upon the pages of a ledger. Although many colonies provided no economic gain for their possessors, the urge to expand was a psychological symptom of an economic problem: the intensely competitive nature of nineteenth-century capitalism. The industrial revolution in Europe had given the West an immense, worldwide advantage in weaponry, shipping, invention, and health. The guns did not actually have to be used against the colonies; once their power was demonstrated they exerted psychological authority far beyond their carrying range. Fewer than 100,000 British troops held millions of Indians within the Empire, as a single district officer held authority over a Hausa district in Nigeria larger than England. Within the Empire, such strength rested upon a sense of national and racial superiority backed by technological predominance and economic competition.

But within the West, no single nation held such superiority, even though several struggled to do so. The new imperialism appeared to consolidate the position of the major European powers, the United States, and Japan. The globe had shrunk, as competition and communications developed, until a crisis in Manchuria or an assassination in Serbia could plunge the whole technologically interdependent world into war. That the war beginning in 1914 was called a World War is not merely the bias of Western historians, even though vast regions of the globe were in no way directly involved. Its results changed the world, putting out lights that would never again be lit, starting fires that burn to this day within the empires as well as within the metropolitan powers.

## V. 3 The First World War: Causes, Conduct, Consequences

*No wars are unintended or "accidental." What is often unintended is the length and bloodiness of the war. Defeat too is unintended.* —Geoffrey Blainey, Australian historian, 1973

All wars have causes that are proximate and causes that are remote. All wars are open to interpretation by the victor, who writes the history, and the vanquished, who is unlikely to accept defeat on the printed page even after it has been met on the battlefield. All modern wars will be open to reinterpretation for many years to come as governments open previously closed archives. Nonetheless, certain facts will be clear and certain interpretations of those facts will be generally accepted by all parties.

The remote causes of World War I lay in the rise of European nationalism, of which imperialism was both symptom and cause, especially after 1871. In essence, the war of 1914–18 was a contest between allied France and Russia against the German and Austro-Hungarian empires. Other nations were drawn into the conflict through a complex system of alliances created to protect the national self-interest as it was then defined. Britain fought to maintain its might on the seas, its colonial hegemony in Africa, and its industrial position. Italy joined because of the crumbling Austro-Hungarian Empire. The United States had a persistent desire for freedom on the seas (which often meant freedom to trade) and was searching for neutrality.

Bismarck wanted a European equilibrium in which a Prussianized Germany would be secure. Germany stood at the crossroads of Europe, able to draw upon the East—Russia—and the West—France, as well as on its own physical and intellectual resources. After the French defeat at Sedan and the French humiliation in the Hall of Mirrors at Versailles in January of 1871 (see pages 290, 294), many declared that while Europe had lost a mistress—France—it had gained a master. The Treaty of Frankfurt, which followed, gave Alsace-Lorraine to Germany and forced a large war indemnity upon France. It assured that the two great nations of the continent would remain bitter enemies. As Germany's leading general, Helmuth von Moltke wrote at the time, "What we have gained by arms in half a year, we must protect by arms for half a century if it is not to be wrested from us."

Bismarck now chose a cautious path, for he was a moderate who recognized the dangers of an excessive nationalism and of too rapid growth. Internally he sought to assure the ascendency of political rather than military considerations, forcing a quasi-democratic constitution on Germany in 1891. Diplomatically he wanted to assure Germany's central position in the European balance of power. But he could not prevent the growth of a German sense of natural destiny, of cultural superiority, and of industrial necessity, which eventually carried German goods into a predominant position in world trade. By the 1890s German intellectuals, university teachers, and merchants saw their nation as the center of a *Weltpolitik,* which must take the shape they imposed.

### The Window on the Sea

The Iron Chancellor's great test came in 1878. For years Russia had been trying to secure a position in the Mediterranean. Its first goal was having an outlet from the Black Sea through the Bosphorus, which was controlled by a crumbling Ottoman Empire. That "sick man of Europe" was shored up by Britain and France, the three having united against Russia in the Crimean War. But in 1877–78, Russian troops swept aside the Turkish army and camped outside Constantinople. The Treaty of San Stefano, signed in March 1878, was a Russian attempt to create an enlarged Bulgarian puppet state, to assure a sphere of influence throughout the Balkans. Austria and Britain opposed this treaty, and Bismarck played the "honest broker," calling an international congress in Berlin. There, in July 1878, a treaty was signed, denying Russia the gains previously won by military and diplomatic means. Austria was given the authority to administer the former Turkish provinces of Bosnia and Hercegovina (now in Yugoslavia), blocking the Russian access to the sea; and despite the long and friendly relationship between Prussia and Russia since the days of Napoleon, Austria and Germany signed a defensive or Dual Alliance in 1879.

Even so, Bismarck sought to quiet the Austro-Russian contest. New negotiations with Russia resulted in the secret Three Emperors League, agreed to in 1881 by Germany, Russia, and Austria. In 1882 Italy was brought into the German-Austrian pact. The Triple Alliance, as it was now called, blocked Russian advances and protected each signatory from France. Bismarck initialed a Reinsurance Treaty with Russia in 1887, by which both nations agreed to respect each other. Three years later, Tsar Alexander III wished to renew the agreement, but Bismarck's successor, General Count Georg Leo von Caprivi, refused. Caprivi advised his kaiser that Germany's ties with Austria must come first. Bismarck had never been willing to face that priority, which is one of the reasons that young Kaiser Wilhelm II demanded Bismarck's resignation in 1890. Russia now sought a rapprochement with France, which feared the German surge. In January of 1894 the two nations agreed to a military convention by which both would resist any German aggression. Germany thus found itself faced with the prospect of a war on two fronts.

Neither France nor Russia wished a showdown, however, for both were preoccupied. Political scandals rocked France throughout the 1890s; and as it contested Britain for colonial power in Africa, France found itself in the Sudan at Fashoda in 1898. Russia was building a trans-Siberian railroad and seeking to establish its power on the Pacific coast. By wresting concessions from China, Russia acquired a naval base at Port Arthur in the same year. Germany, also expanding at the expense of China, received the port of Kiaochow in 1897. European rivalry was temporarily focused overseas and away from the central issues closer at hand in the Balkans, at the Bosphorus, and in north Africa. Indeed, France and Russia had cooperated with Germany in 1895 to force a victorious Japan to give up some of the gains it had made at the expense of China. Only after 1899, when Britain sought to reevaluate its international role in the light of a costly guerrilla war against the Boers in southern Africa, were the hounds of war to be heard once again.

They were heard most clearly by Joseph Chamberlain, the British colonial secretary between 1895 and 1903, who wanted to assure Britain's leadership in world trade, and thus in the colonies. Chamberlain believed that harmony between his country and Germany was essential to world peace, and in August 1898, the two nations agreed to spheres of influence in the Portuguese colonies of Africa and Asia. Despite obvious pro-Boer sympathies in the South African war, in which Britain was shortly embroiled, Germany maintained neutrality in the face of Boer cries for help.

### The Boer War

The Boer War arose from an old rivalry between the basically English Cape Colony and the Transvaal, the Boer colony. Earlier, the Cape had received responsible government in 1872, while the Boers in Natal were forced to wait until 1893. The Cape Colony saw itself as an outpost of the British Empire, while the Boer republics had become the homelands for Afrikaans-speaking settlers who seldom looked to Europe. Perhaps the different colonies could have coexisted in southern Africa had diamonds not been found in 1871 at Kimberley, which is north of the Orange River, the boundary between independent Boer Orange Free State and the Cape. A major gold strike in the Transvaal in 1886 also brought thousands of English-speaking miners into the Boer state, and these *uitlanders* wanted British protection. The Boers, while preferring their isolation, were willing to be wooed by the kaiser's Germany, for they wanted to balance the British arrivals. Germany, on the other hand, was happy to see southern Africa on fire.

The immediate cause of the war was not international rivalry, but British expansionism. Cecil Rhodes (1853–1902), a powerful entrepreneur, hoped to see the whole of eastern and southern Africa dominated by Britain. Rhodes saw that the Transvaal might become pro-British if the Boer government there would grant full political rights to the swarming British and continental settlers. Paul Kruger (1825–1904), the intransigent president of the Transvaal, was equally determined that the "outlanders" not receive political rights. In 1895 Rhodes turned his immense wealth to revolution in an ill-fated attempt to unseat Kruger. A raid into the Boer state was led by L. S. Jameson, Rhodes's personal physician. Rhodes was premier of the Cape Colony at this time; and when Jameson's raid failed, the charge of political interference directed against Rhodes led to his resignation. Britain steadily increased demands that Kruger give immigrants political representation; and in 1899, expecting to gain support from Germany, he felt strong enough to declare war.

Seldom had there been a war so unpopular in Britain. Expecting an early victory, the British found themselves defeated time and again by the guerrilla tactics of the Boers, who harried the British across the land. A simple, surgical operation became a long, sticky, and ultimately demoralizing war, as the British were forced to mobilize 300,000 troops to quell fewer than 75,000 Boers. In Britain, vocal anti-imperialists attacked the war as immoral. As the loss of life spiraled upward and London heard that British commanders in southern Africa were using internment and concentration camps, the public lost faith in the purpose behind the war. By 1902 the Boers were defeated and signed the Treaty of Vereeniging. But a public sense of guilt in Britain led to a desire to be magnanimous to the courageous enemy, and eventually the Boers won politically what they had failed to achieve militarily. The British Liberal Party, which took office in 1905, sought to conciliate Boer opinion, and two years later gave both the Transvaal and the Orange Free State full responsible government. In 1909 these two colonies united with the Cape and Natal to form the Union of South Africa.

Continental Europe had not intervened in the war. The kaiser had sent a personal telegram of congratulations to Kruger after the failure of the Jameson raid, but thereafter—partially because Germany did not wish to jeopardize the 1898 Anglo-German agreement over the Portuguese colonies—Germany maintained a strict neutrality. Nonetheless, the Boer War produced a fundamental shift in British policy, for throughout the war anti-British sentiment ran so high on the continent that Britain feared she would be isolated in a future conflict. Germany had not intervened in the war; but from 1900 forward, British leadership was convinced that Germany would attack Britain when able to do so. While Lord Lanstowne as Britain's foreign secretary considered an alliance with Germany in 1901, Prime Minister Lord Salisbury and the German leaders remained cool. The Germans were convinced that an Anglo-Russian war lay over the horizon, and they did not wish to be drawn into battle with Russia. Despite limited Anglo-German cooperation in China, therefore, Britain wanted a dependable ally in the Far East as well and in 1902 entered into a defensive alliance with Japan. Thus the world was divided into armed camps.

## Secret Alliance Systems

In 1902 the French foreign minister persuaded Italy into a secret agreement by which Italy would remain neutral in any Franco-German war. This effectively took Italy out of the Triple Alliance. The Far Eastern situation was developing to the embarrassment of France, however, for it was evident that at some time Japan would fight Russia and ask for French aid. France would then either be committed to a war against Britain or would have to renounce its treaty obligations to Russia. The French foreign minister therefore hoped to repeat his diplomatic realignment through an Anglo-French agreement that would break Britain's commitment to Japan.

Worried over the threat Russia posed to Britain in central Asia and China, and doubtful about the ability of the Japanese army and navy in the face of a Russian attack, the British chose to find a European way out of their Asian problem. In April 1904, an Anglo-French treaty was signed, giving France a free hand to expand in Morocco, and giving Britain the same privilege in Europe. This agreement did not come a moment too soon, for Japan and Russia were already at war; the Japanese had launched a surprise attack on the Russian fleet at Port Arthur in February.

By August it was apparent that British fears of Japanese incompetence were misplaced, for Japan was victorious in Manchuria. In March 1905, the Japanese army defeated the Russians at Mukden, and shortly after, the Japanese navy destroyed the Russian's Baltic fleet at Tsushima. Japan had not needed to call for British assistance. Britain had avoided war with Russia, and—given Japan's naval dominance in the east Asian sphere—Britain now controlled the naval balance of power, having far more battleships than any potential combination of enemies. The Anglo-French entente had lost its purpose.

The Germans seemed intent on giving the entente a renewed purpose, however. Germany had expanded its economy at an unprecedented rate. Coal production soared by 800 percent between 1871 and 1914. Steel production exceeded the combined capacity of Britain, France, and Russia, while electrical, chemical, optical, and textile industries placed Germany at the top of Europe's industrial competition. German population had also increased rapidly. With new docks and a substantial merchant navy, Germany was in a position to challenge Britain as an overseas, mercantile empire. Germany's *Weltpolitik* (foreign policy) required industrial expansion abroad, but both Britain and France wished to block such growth. Adding to British fears, the kaiser chose to expand his navy at the expense of the army. With many of its officers now from the middle class, the German army tried to influence foreign policy, but that policy remained an unclear and divisive reflection of the kaiser's own personality. His only undeviating concern was for sea power; and from 1898, with the assistance of his Secretary of the Navy, Admiral Alfred von Tirpitz, the kaiser won from the Reichstag repeated votes of support. In 1900 Count Bernhard von Bülow (1849–1928), who had served as the kaiser's foreign secretary, and who supported the Big Navy policy, became Chancellor. The British recognized the confusion and drift in German foreign policy and feared it more precisely for its lack of clear purpose.

### The Art of Postponement

The purpose seemed to take on a threatening clarity in the first Moroccan crisis of 1905–6. Worried by the Anglo-French entente and angered over Italy's deviation from the spirit of the Triple Alliance, German leaders feared the loss of prestige the nation would suffer if Germany did not continue to gain ground in the scramble for colonies. Certain that the French intended to make Morocco a dependency—as Tunis already was—Bülow persuaded the kaiser, who was sailing in the Mediterranean, to land at Tangier. There, in March of 1905, he declared that Germany would support the Sultan in retaining his independence. Germany was playing at brinkmanship. Few desired war, but Bülow hoped to separate Britain and France by showing that the British would not stand firm with the French. Bülow lost his gamble, however, and the Moroccan crisis drove France and Britain even closer together. Although Germany did succeed in bringing about the dismissal of the anti-German French foreign minister, Germany had aroused intensely anti-German reactions in Britain.

Bülow demanded an international conference on the Moroccan question, which convened at Algeciras, Spain, in January 1906. He had counted on support from Russia, Italy, and the United States. All fell away, and only Austria-Hungary and Morocco took the German position. The end result was French control over Moroccan finances and police and a humiliating diplomatic defeat for Germany, one which the pride of the German people could not be expected to accept for long.

A month earlier, a liberal government had taken office in Britain, and at the time of the Algeciras conference that government was confirming its power through the polls. The Liberal ministry preferred to emphasize social reform at home. It accepted the fashionable doctrine that only a nation healthy in mind and body could expect to sway world affairs. Foreign entanglements could only undermine the more important domestic programs. Nonetheless, Britain informed France that it would honor its commitment with respect to Morocco should Germany attack. British Foreign Secretary Sir Edward Grey (1862–1933) approved secret meetings between French and British military leaders with a view to coordinating military efforts, and Britain promised to provide France with 105,000 soldiers within 15 days, should France be forced to mobilize against Germany. Thus the Entente Cordiale secretly evolved into a military alliance. Even the British Cabinet was not informed of this foray into clandestine diplomacy until 1911.

At this time extraordinary power lay in the hands of British Foreign Secretary Grey, for successive British prime ministers, choosing to concentrate on domestic crises, seldom restrained their liberal imperialistic tendencies. Although Lib-Imps, as they were called, were of a variety of persuasions, they shared a geopolitical view of the world—shaped in part by the arguments of Sir Halford John Mackinder (1861–1947), the father of geopolitics. They tended to think of the state as a garrison in which social evils must be removed so that greater moral and physical authority on the world stage would prevail. Grey was personally anti-German, as were his principal advisers. He saw any attempts by Germany to become a world power, especially on the seas, as a direct threat to British hegemony.

Several paths lay open to averting war, however. One path, often chosen by strong states, was walking the delicate line between saber rattling (which would intensify resentments) and making it clear to potential enemies which boundaries they must not overstep (which would forestall war resulting from miscalculation). Had only two or three powers been involved, as would be the case in the post-1945 world, such a line might have been walked with success. But as the Entente Cordiale expanded into the Triple Entente, and as it was pitted against the Triple Alliance, the complexity of interactions among six nations jammed clear transmission of diplomatic intentions. Ultimately the overlapping, often secret obligations of Triple Alliance and Triple Entente virtually assured a war of some kind. The question was, therefore, not whether there would be a war, but rather, would it involve all six nations and if so, when, under what conditions, where, and for what immediate reasons?

Britain and Russia concluded an agreement in August 1907, which established spheres of influence in the Middle East, especially in Persia. Although not specifically anti-German in intent, this entente was seen by the Germans as having changed the balance of power in Europe against them. In the meantime the British had achieved momentary superiority in yet another race, for with the launching of the battleship *Dreadnought* early in 1906, both effective naval supremacy and clear technological superiority in armaments again rested with the Royal Navy. Germany responded to these threats slowly and after much internal debate, but in November of 1907 Tirpitz announced Germany's intention to build a High Seas Fleet that would match the British. The naval race was on, the stakes being the most sophisticated strategic weaponry of the time. The minimal essential goals were control of the Mediterranean (for Britain) and of the Baltic (for Germany). Britain wanted the Mediterranean route to the Suez Canal and India. Germany's steel industry needed the Baltic for importation of Swedish iron ore. Three major elements of instability were now at work: the shifting sands of multiple alliance systems, the inability to predict the race for technological superiority, and the personalities of the principal figures involved.

### *The Balkans: Tinderbox for War*

The Balkans also constituted an unstable situation at this time: the Balkans—proud, parochial, intensely nationalistic, and economically retarded. The chief political force in the area was the Austro-Hungarian monarchy, inheritor of the Hapsburg Empire. In 1867 the old Austrian Empire had become a dual monarchy: Austria and Bohemia united on the one hand, and the Magyars of Hungary on the other. The two were linked by joint ministries of foreign affairs, finance, war, and a common crown. Traditionally, an imperial power reserved foreign affairs, finance, and war for its central authority, however much delegation it may have allowed in other areas of human activity. In this instance, however, the central authority was too weak to properly exercise the powers it claimed. Further, with the capital in Vienna, German-speaking officials—especially in the military—tended to dominate, giving additional offense to the theoretically equal partner, Hungary. The Magyars also feared that Austria would liberalize voting, perhaps to the extent of universal male suffrage, which they found unacceptable. It would destroy Hungary because the Magyars would no longer be able to control their own subject peoples in Transylvania and elsewhere. Germans and Magyars together comprised just under 50 percent of the population of Austria-Hungary. They needed each other to maintain their tenuous dominance over aspiring nationalities, especially the Croats, Slovaks, Romanians, and Serbs, all of whom were becoming politically self-conscious.

While Magyars resented German-speaking officers, Croats resented even more that their own representatives to the Hungarian parliament were forced to speak Magyar. In 1907 Magyar was made the official language for the Hungarian railways, which further angered Serbs and Croats, who cast about for supporters for a growing Pan-Slav movement. The Serbs in particular were intent on maintaining their independence (won in 1878) as a separate state (and although the nation that they were officially a part of was defeated in World War I, the Serbs achieved precisely what they sought—Greater Serbia became the core of Yugoslavia in 1919). The realignment of the Balkan map was bought at the cost of the war that the Triple Alliance and Triple Entente had been constructed to postpone, limit, or even avoid.

Serbia was both the center of unrest and of the development of the most important stirrings of representative democracy. In 1903 a group of army officers assassinated King Alexander and Queen Draga, setting up a pro-Russian Karageorge monarch, Peter I (1844–1921), in their place. This threatened the Austro-Russian agreement of 1897 set up to maintain a balance of interest in the Balkans. Under Peter, a radical party was directed by Nikola Pašić (1845–1926), who later became Serbian prime minister. The party promoted local industry by entering into trade relations with other nations. Austria struck back harshly with a program of economic sanctions. These failed, especially because France was now providing the Serbs with the loans they needed.

Fearful that France would further insinuate itself into the Bulkan economy, worried that a Serbian independence movement would create similar movements elsewhere, and conscious that a Russian threat might emerge because of the growing overtures made by Belgrade to St. Petersburg, the Austrian foreign minister decided to come to terms with the Russians. He was aided by a revolution in Constantinople in July of 1908. The Young Turks, who came into power, wished to modernize the Ottoman Empire. They were prepared to consider new arrangements with their traditional enemy, Russia, as well as with their own subject peoples in the Balkans. Further, even though Russia had regularized relations with Britain, the Russian foreign minister was eager to counteract that clause of the Treaty of Berlin that prohibited the passage of Russian warships through the Bosphorus and Dardanelles into the Mediterranean.

The events that followed were confused and remain so, both because of their complexity and because, in the absence of full documentation, historians cannot agree on precisely what happened. The Austrian and Russian foreign ministers met in September. Russia allowed Austria to annex Bosnia and Hercegovina in order to stifle Serbian demands. In exchange, Austria would support Russia's overture toward the Dardanelles. Three weeks later, with Austrian consent, Ferdinand of Bulgaria declared his country's independence from the Ottomans, and the next day Austria announced formal annexation of Bosnia-Hercegovina.

Austria's fishing in already troubled waters landed several unexpected fish. Russia felt betrayed, and doubly so when its foreign minister discovered that the French were unlikely to accede to Russian access to the Dardanelles. Turkey boycotted Austrian goods and moved toward war with the Bulgarians. The Serbs assumed that an Austrian invasion would follow upon annexation and ordered a partial mobilization. Austria in turn sent additional troops into Bosnia. The Germans, who had been working toward closer economic ties with Turkey, were particularly incensed but were bound to assist Austria in case of an attack. Among these nations, Germany alone had the military power to play kingmaker; and when Austria insisted that Russia publicly recognize the Bosnia-Hercegovina annexation—in order to show the Turks, Serbs, and Bulgarians that they could expect no assistance from Russia—it was the German government that forced the necessary statement from the Russian foreign minister. The Germans, by shaking a mailed fist, had shown themselves willing to risk war, and that great war started in the Balkans.

Briefly, however, the pendulum of crisis swung back toward Morocco. Here there were elements more open to compromise; the issue was less one of nationalism than of economic interests. Compromise is more difficult when sentiments and emotions are involved than when there is something that can be measured. Further, the new German chancellor, Theobald von Bethmann-Hollweg (1856–1921), was a learned, ambitious, pro-British leader who was convinced that an agreement to limit the naval race might yet be reached. He turned to three fronts, therefore, and on two of them was relatively successful. When he met with the Russian foreign minister late in 1910, Bethmann-Hollweg persuaded Russia to allow Germany to move forward with its planned Constantinople-to-Baghdad railway. As late as June 1914, scarcely two months before Britain declared war on Germany, British financiers agreed to assist. Early in the previous year Germany and France had initiated an agreement on

Morocco, which guaranteed Germany economic equality there. Grey remained aloof, and the British navy set about constructing eight more dreadnoughts.

### *Hurtling Toward War*

The Agadir crisis of 1911 ended Bethmann-Hollweg's brief hopes. Although German business interests had moved into Morocco, there were few German residents there. Germany therefore recognized French hegemony in this area, in exchange for strengthened trading privileges in the Cameroons and the Congo. German imperialists dreamed of controlling a swath of land across central Africa from the Cameroons to Tanganyika, just as the British dreamed of the Cape-to-Cairo route. German financiers, especially those in mining, were convinced that Morocco held great promise, and only a genuinely important exchange could be permitted, such as the whole of the French and Belgian Congos. As tension over the unresolved realities of theoretical equality in Morocco mounted, an indigenous revolt in Fez in April of 1911 lit the fuse.

In the face of attacks on French residents, the French government informed the Germans that they must send a relief expedition to the city. Britain, too, was informed, and Grey was prepared to see France solidify its position in Morocco. Grey well understood that the relief expedition might serve dual purposes. In the midst of the crisis, the French government fell, and communications were temporarily severed. On June 28 a new French prime minister took office and turned at once to healing the breach with Germany. Two days earlier, however, Bethmann-Hollweg had persuaded Kaiser Wilhelm to send a gunboat, the *Panther,* to Agadir, in the mistaken notion that only a show of force would persuade the French to make concessions.

Britain remained aloof, although Grey was kept informed by the French. Now the British chose to make an extraordinary statement, spurred by the announcement of the *Panther*'s mission. Chancellor of the Exchequer, David Lloyd George (ultimately Britain's wartime prime minister), already was scheduled to deliver an address to an annual meeting of the bankers of London. Any warning from Lloyd George to Germany would be treated with respect, because he was known to oppose the anti-German members of the Cabinet. On July 21 he declared that Britain's position as humanitarian leader of the world would be endangered if Germany carried out its threats. If peace had to be purchased at the price of "the surrender of the great and beneficent position Britain has won by centuries of heroism and achievement," the cost would be too great, and Germany must step down. A wave of anger swept over Germany, and for the next six weeks, they were on the threshold of war.

For once, however, the restraining alliance system briefly worked for peace. The Russians warned that public opinion in their country would not accept a war over Morocco in which Russia had no interest, while the Germans realized that Austria was unlikely to provide more than token assistance, preoccupied as it was with the Balkans. Socialist leaders in both France and Germany declared that they would not fight over an imperialist venture. In November, therefore, Germany formally agreed to French preeminence in Morocco in exchange for a strategic transfer of territory in the Congo, which gave the German Cameroons access to the Congo River.

Germany had suffered a second major humiliation. Despite the transfer of territory, German public opinion regarded the conclusion of the Agadir crisis as a diplomatic defeat. Indeed, Germany's situation was much worsened, for the crisis contributed to the fall of the French government that was committed to reconciliation. Raymond Poincaré (1860–1934), a bitter, anti-German lawyer, became prime minister. The British and French renewed military conversations and in 1913 formally agreed upon measures for naval cooperation as well. In Germany, Tirpitz used the humiliation to ask for further naval armaments, destroying any hope for a pause in the naval race. Perhaps most important, the German army, convinced that it had been denied a proper voice in public affairs by civilian-minded leaders, now raised their voices. In particular, the General Staff wanted to conscript more soldiers; in proportion to its population, the German military effort was behind the French. When the news reached Paris that the Reichstag agreed to a substantial increase in the peacetime German army, France replied in kind, and a land army race was added to the naval race.

## The Balkan League

Now the attention of the world was drawn back to the eastern end of the Mediterranean and to the Balkans. The Italians, eager for their own place in the imperial sun, invaded Tripoli in north Africa and moved into the Dodecanese Islands in the Aegean Sea. The Italian navy forced the Turks to cede Tripoli late in 1912, leaving the crumbling Ottoman Empire open to Balkan attack. Ten days before the final transfer of Tripoli to the Italians, Montenegro declared war on Turkey. The day before the conclusion of the Turko-Italian war, Serbia, Bulgaria, and Greece, hoping to annex the Turkish territories they regarded as rightfully theirs, joined in a Balkan League offensive against the Ottomans. War, so long avoided in the Balkans, had come.

Russia began strengthening its army after Bismarck and his international congress (1878) had forced it to back down in the Balkans. The

German army had 700,000 soldiers; the French, 675,000; and the Austro-Hungarian, 450,000. Yet, the Russian army was now in excess of 1,500,000 and still recruiting. The Russian railway system, which could move mobilized troops to its western borders, had been much improved, and the iron and steel industry in the Ukraine was providing valuable diversity in that wheat-exporting region. Russia and Italy had secretly agreed to oppose any further changes in the Balkan area. Further, the Bulgarians and the Serbs secretly named the Russian tsar as arbitrator of any future dispute involving Austria or Turkey. Russia might now play kingmaker, too.

The Balkan League proved to be a formidable fighting force. Moving into Thrace, Bulgarian troops achieved an overwhelming victory, pushing the Turks back to within sight of their capital. On the same day a Serbian army routed the Turkish army in Macedonia. The Greeks, moving north to meet with the Serbian and Bulgarian thrusts southwards, closed upon Salonika. Within seven weeks the Turks, previously thought to be more than a match for the unassisted Balkan League, had been driven from Europe, except for Constantinople's defensive perimeter and three forts that lay under siege. As peace negotiators met, parted, and met again under the aegis of the major powers of Europe, two of the fortresses fell. On May 30, 1913, the Turks accepted defeat, giving up all of their European possessions except the portion that allowed them to maintain strategic control of the Bosphorus and the Dardanelles.

The Balkan states now found their victory blunted by the strategic concerns of the Great Powers, the sponsors of the peace negotiations. Austria, fearing a victorious Serbia, wished to deny the Serbs access to the Adriatic and insisted upon the creation of an artificial state, Albania, athwart Serbia's path. Germany and Italy gave Austria support in the creation of Albania. The Russians drew back from war over an area so far from their strategic interests.

Having lost Albania, Serbia sought compensation at the expense of her Bulgarian ally in Macedonia. Bulgaria countered with a surprise attack on the combined Serbian and Greek forces on the night of June 29, but was soundly defeated. Seizing upon this quarrel among the victors, the Turks recaptured most of Thrace, while the Romanians attacked Bulgaria from the north.

This Second Balkan War intensified the instability of the entire region. Its conclusion in August 1913 by the Treaty of Bucharest was satisfying to the smaller Balkan states, but left the major powers very discontented. Between them Serbia and Greece acquired much of Macedonia, although the Turks kept strategic control over the Straits, so that Russia was still denied access to the sea. Romania gained much of Bulgaria's Black Sea coastline, while Bulgaria was now given only a narrow access to the Aegean, so the Bulgars cast about for new allies. Austria felt threatened, for Serbia was a united nation with two hundred thousand soldiers ready for mobilization. If Austria had to fight Russia, it would have to wage the war on two fronts.

Germany's support was now essential, which once again made Berlin the center of diplomacy. Further, because Austria had opposed Romania's attack on Bulgaria (despite a secret agreement with Romania, which had made her an adjunct to the Triple Alliance), Romania now moved into the Russian camp. Austria was thereby deprived of the huge Romanian army, 400,000 strong. By now the structure of alliances and the nature of military planning had closed off most freedom of maneuver for the major powers.

What were the military plans, and how did they promote a lockstep to destruction? Since 1905 Count von Schlieffen (1833–1913) committed the German government to a plan in case of war with France and Russia. This plan called for a rapid strike against France, achieving victory within six weeks, and then mobilizing the slower and more massive Russian forces. Germany could not fight a sustained war on two fronts. A German army would hold East Prussia without taking the offensive until France's defeat would permit transferring troops from the western to the eastern front. Then an assault upon St. Petersburg might begin.

In order to assure the quick, surgical defeat of France, Schlieffen also anticipated violation of Dutch and Belgian neutrality, for the chief sweep into France was to be through the flat lands of the Low Countries. It was known that British policy long had been to protect the neutrality of the Scheldt River estuary, the best continental point from which an invasion of the British Isles might take place. The Germans anticipated that the British would declare war, once German troops entered Holland. For this reason, the Germans wanted the march to be too rapid for an effective British naval or military response, and it had to follow exceptionally rapid mobilization.

There are three points to remember with respect to this plan. First, because its success hinged upon speed rather than surprise, Germany could not afford to pass through intermediate stages of mobilization. Ordinarily, partial mobilization would be the first step. It would help prepare the army for war and serve as a forceful diplomatic warning that the mobilizing nation meant business. Further, partial mobilization could be halted quickly; full mobilization could not. In short, by committing themselves to a plan of rapid and full mobilization, the Germans eliminated an important stage in military preparation, which could be used for a diplomatic cooling-off period.

Second, the German plan also dependend upon the cooperation of the Austrians, who would be required to put at least half of their force into the field against Russia. The Austrians would move on Warsaw, in order to block Russian entry into southern Germany. But the Austrians could do this only if they, too, were not engaged in a war on two fronts; that is, if they were not already committed to sending their army against Serbia. Thus, the Germans took a close interest in the developing crisis in Austro-Serbian relations.

Third, in 1911 the chief of the German general staff, Count Helmuth von Moltke (1848–1916), made modifications. The original plan anticipated that French troops might be drawn into an offensive across the Rhine, so that their flank would be exposed to the German right wing. This situation meant the temporary sacrifice of some German territory in order to draw France to its own destruction. Moltke chose a different course that hinged upon Holland's continued neutrality. He saw Dutch neutrality as essential because German supplies from neutral nations would arrive via this route. He also unreasonably hoped that Britain might not enter the war if only Belgium, and not Holland, were involved. However, in order to strike into France only through Belgium over the short border Germany shared with her, the Germans had to capture Liege immediately. This city controlled railway communication toward France, and the entire invading German army, expected to number 600,000, would have to pass through it. Germany could not afford to hesitate, once mobilization had begun. In concentrating all strategic attention upon the capture of Liege, Moltke removed the final possibility that mobilization might take place in escalating stages rather than all at once. Once mobilization began, war was certain.

Germany's decision to mobilize did not turn on France, however, but upon Russia. German and Austrian leaders feared the Russian forces above all others. Both Moltke and the Austrian chief of staff, Conrad von Hotzendorff, felt that the odds ran against them. Moltke did not really expect that Britain would remain out of the war. Hotzendorff anticipated defeat but wished Austria to go down fighting, and even Tirpitz recognized that British naval superiority made destroying the German fleet likely. Nonetheless, the German and Austrian leaders reasoned that the situation would grow worse rather than better as the Russian army and economy were strengthened, and that the odds were marginally more in favor of them in an early rather than a late war. Germany in particular deluded itself into thinking that a preventive war, fought before Russia had clearly achieved equality, might lead to victory or, at worst, stalemate. A desperate series of gambles in brinksmanship began.

Rapid mobilization was also the main plan of the French and the Russians. The French, uncertain as to whether the Germans would hold to the Schlieffen plan, expected to attack the Germans in Lorraine. This would expose the French, and they knew it, but they counted upon a rapid Russian offensive against Germany, which would force the Germans to transfer troops to the eastern front. If all this happened before the German invasion through Belgium was successful, however, Russia must begin mobilization in secret. Otherwise, it could not expect to mobilize over so wide an area with a relatively slow communications network in time to meet the German threat. Because at least one partner in each of the alliance systems was committed to complete mobilization, the others were trapped into a rigid timetable.

But there were still forces working toward peace. The naval race was over, for both Britain and Germany realized that Britain had attained an insurmountable superiority. Each nation had become the other's best customer, and business communities in both countries favored peace. Both nations had reached agreement on the Berlin-to-Baghdad railway. Further, Britain was preoccupied with the Irish home rule crisis. The French were also less anti-German than they had been. A new radical-socialist government, elected in May 1914, was opposed to the French three-year compulsory military service law. Many predicted that a radical, Joseph Caillaux (1862–1944), would soon form a new ministry, and he was known to be anti-Russian and well disposed toward Germany. Indeed, the British felt secure enough to send four of their battleships on a goodwill tour to Kiel in June, placing a portion of the Royal Navy in German hands as potential hostages.

### The War: Chance and History

When the war came, it arose over an expected issue, in an unexpected place. The machinery of mobilization took over from the slower, calming processes of diplomacy. Yet even so, had it not been for the personalities of three people, war might have been further postponed. The three people were the wife of the radical Caillaux, the German Chancellor Bethmann-Hollweg, and the Russian Foreign Minister Sergei Sazanov. People are, indeed, trapped by events, but people also make those events.

In France, the pro-German Caillaux and the socialist leader Jean Jaurès (1859–1914) had been in an excellent position to form a coalition government in order to displace the administration of René Viviani (1863–1925). Caillaux failed to achieve his goal, however, when his wife shot the editor of Paris's most prestigious newspaper, *Figaro*. Ostensibly, her violence resulted from press attacks upon Caillaux. Rocked by scandal, France was in no position to displace the precarious radical-socialist coalition already in power, a coalition that gravitated more strongly to Russia as the summer passed.

In the meantime, the match was lit to the Balkan powder keg. On June 28, 1914 in the Bosnian city of Sarajevo, the visiting Austrian Archduke Francis Ferdinand and his wife were assassinated by members of a terrorist society, the Black Hand. The chief of the intelligence division of the Serbian General Staff (the same man who earlier had been responsible

**Diplomatic Alignment Before 1914**

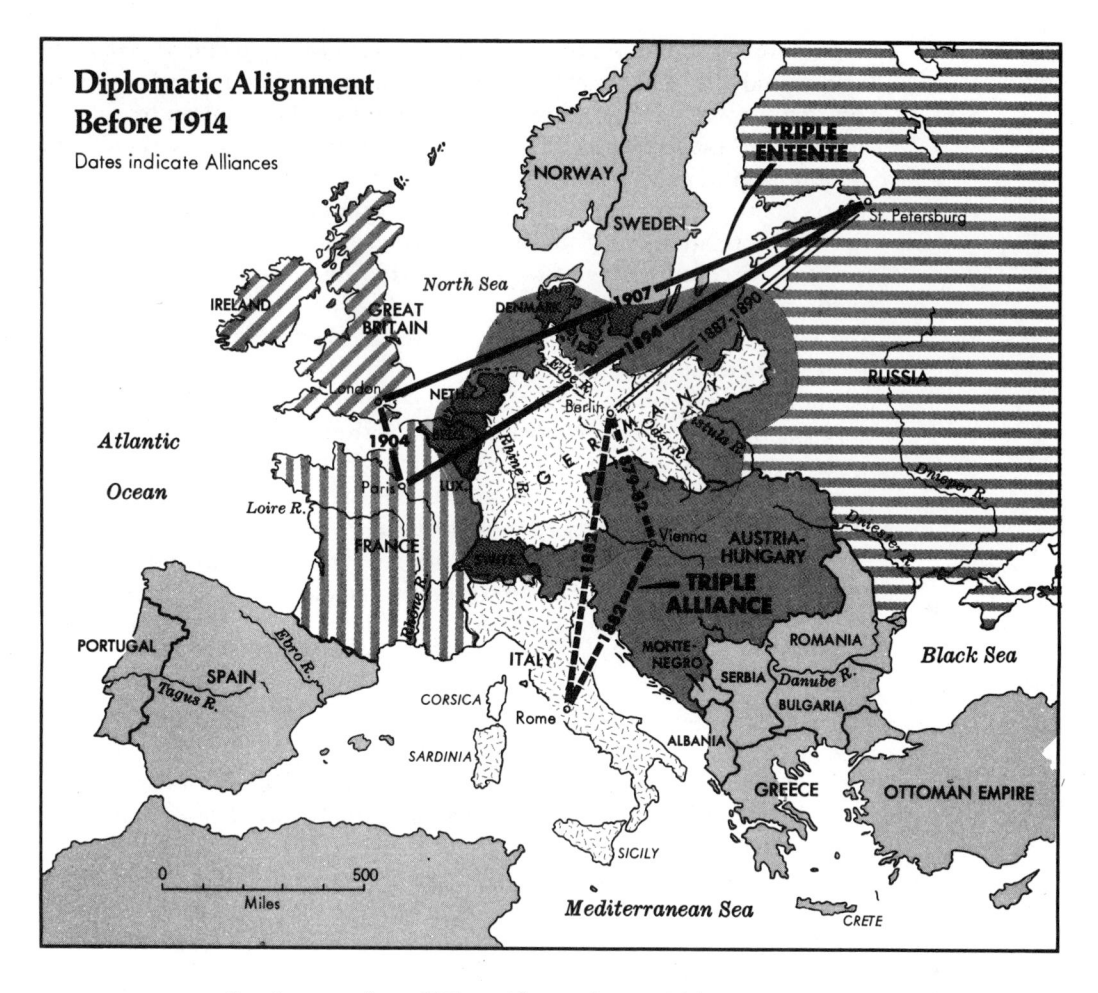

Dates indicate Alliances

for the murder of King Alexander and his queen) organized the plot, of which Serbian Prime Minister Pašić was aware.

Emperor Francis Joseph sent a representative to the Kaiser who, after consultation with Bethmann-Hollweg, gave Austria a virtually blank check of support in any action it chose to take against the Serbs. In doing so, Germany was gambling that if Austria moved boldly, Russia would hesitate. In any event, if Austria took no action in the face of so obvious a provocation, it would no longer have the respect of the other Great Powers and would be of little use to Germany in the game of power politics.

The Austrians sent an ultimatum to Belgrade on July 23. Their delay arose because of the need for consultations with Germany and with the less bellicose prime minister of Hungary, whose support was required. The ultimatum contained ten demands, deliberately and collectively unacceptable and intended to humiliate Serbia. They demanded a reply in forty-eight hours. Serbia ordered up her troops and then responded with conciliatory words, which appeared to accept the humiliation but in fact also rejected the substance of the specific demands. Especially repugnant was the requirement that Austrian officials be a part of future Serbian efforts to suppress the Black Hand and similar bodies. Austria broke diplomatic relations and moved to partial mobilization against Serbia and, less forcefully, against Italy. While Bethmann-Hollweg now counseled war, the Austrians, aware that mobilization would require another two weeks, sought postponement. However, they were unable to delay because of German pressure, and against the advice of the Austrian chief of staff, the government approved a declaration of war on July 28.

In the meantime, the Russians moved with unexpected speed. Urged on by France, Russia began mobilization on July 26, within hours of learning of the Austrian ultimatum to Serbia, and introduced an advanced stage of war readiness. All forts in Poland and western Russia were placed on a war footing. Harbors were mined, and soldiers were moved to frontier posts. Because the Russians kept these measures secret, they gained the necessary edge and later openly announced full mobilization. Also on July 26 the French recalled all officers on leave and then drew in their troops from north Africa. British overtures for mediation were ignored by Bethmann-Hollweg. Russian Foreign Minister Sazonov, unstable and unperceptive, failed to recognize Austria's fear of Russian mobilization. If Sazonov had trumpeted Russia's preparations for war instead of keeping them secret, they might have been a deterrent.

As soon as the Germans did learn of Russia's partial mobilization, they recognized that Austria had to fully mobilize, and that this would bring the row of dominoes falling. Moltke, aware of his precarious military position, cautioned peace on the same day that the British navy was ordered to its war station on Scapa Flow (off North Scotland). Grey now warned the German ambassador in London that Britain would probably intervene; and when Bethmann-Hollweg received word of this, he temporized. Moltke, on the other hand, appeared to reverse himself, for he had learned of the Russian tsar's proclamation on July 30 of general mobilization. In the face of apparently contradictory advice from Bethmann-Hollweg and Moltke, advice that even ran counter to that previously given, the Austrians acted upon their own counsel and mobilized. Germany sent an ultimatum to Russia, demanding a cessation of military measures within twelve hours. When no reply was received, they declared war on Russia (August 1), immediately throwing German troops toward Belgium. Germany sent ultimatums to Brussels and Paris, declared war on France on August 3, invaded Belgium the following day (captured Liege on August 7), and ignored a British counterultimatum demanding German withdrawal back across the Belgian frontier. Shortly before midnight on August 4, 1914, Britain declared war. Seldom has so intricate a lockstep fallen into place with such deathlike precision. Bethmann-Hollweg later remarked, "Once the dice were set rolling nothing could stop them." The world, at least as Europeans knew it, was at war. Ten million soldiers would die on the battlefields of Europe in the next four years.

## Who's Responsible?

After the war, Article 231 of the Treaty of Versailles charged Germany and her allies with the entire legal and moral responsibility for the outbreak of war. A long and bitter debate ensued. As tempers cooled and historians explored new sources of evidence, this simplistic search for a single scapegoat was much modified. Today many historians support England's F. H. Hinsley, a close student of the war, who has written:

> ... the question of culpability or even of degrees of culpability is an irrelevant question in this final period because events passed beyond men's control on 23 July, 1914, even if they had not passed beyond it earlier.
>
> It is, of course, still possible to say that theoretically a general war could have been avoided after 23 July if this or that government had acted otherwise than it did. But it was not practically possible after that date for any government to have acted otherwise than it did. If some government appears to have been more responsible than the others for the course of events after the ultimatum had been delivered, or if some government appears to have been more responsible for the course of events at some stage and another government most responsible at another stage, this is not because one or the other government was more instrumental than others in affecting the course of events. It is because the apparent instrumentality of the governments varies with their changing positions within a course of events over which all the governments lost control once one of them issued an ultimatum in a tense situation.*

## The Fronts

The war was essentially a European struggle that extended into the Middle East, Africa, and the Far East. Following Japanese and American entry into the war, it truly involved the world. Although North and South America as well as Asia had been involved in the Great War for Empire in the seventeenth and eighteenth centuries, for the first time fully independent nations and relatively independent technologies were drawn together in a single conflict. The modern world had never seen a war with

---

*F. H. Hinsley, *The Causes of the First World War* (Hull, England: The University of Hull, 1964), p. 8.

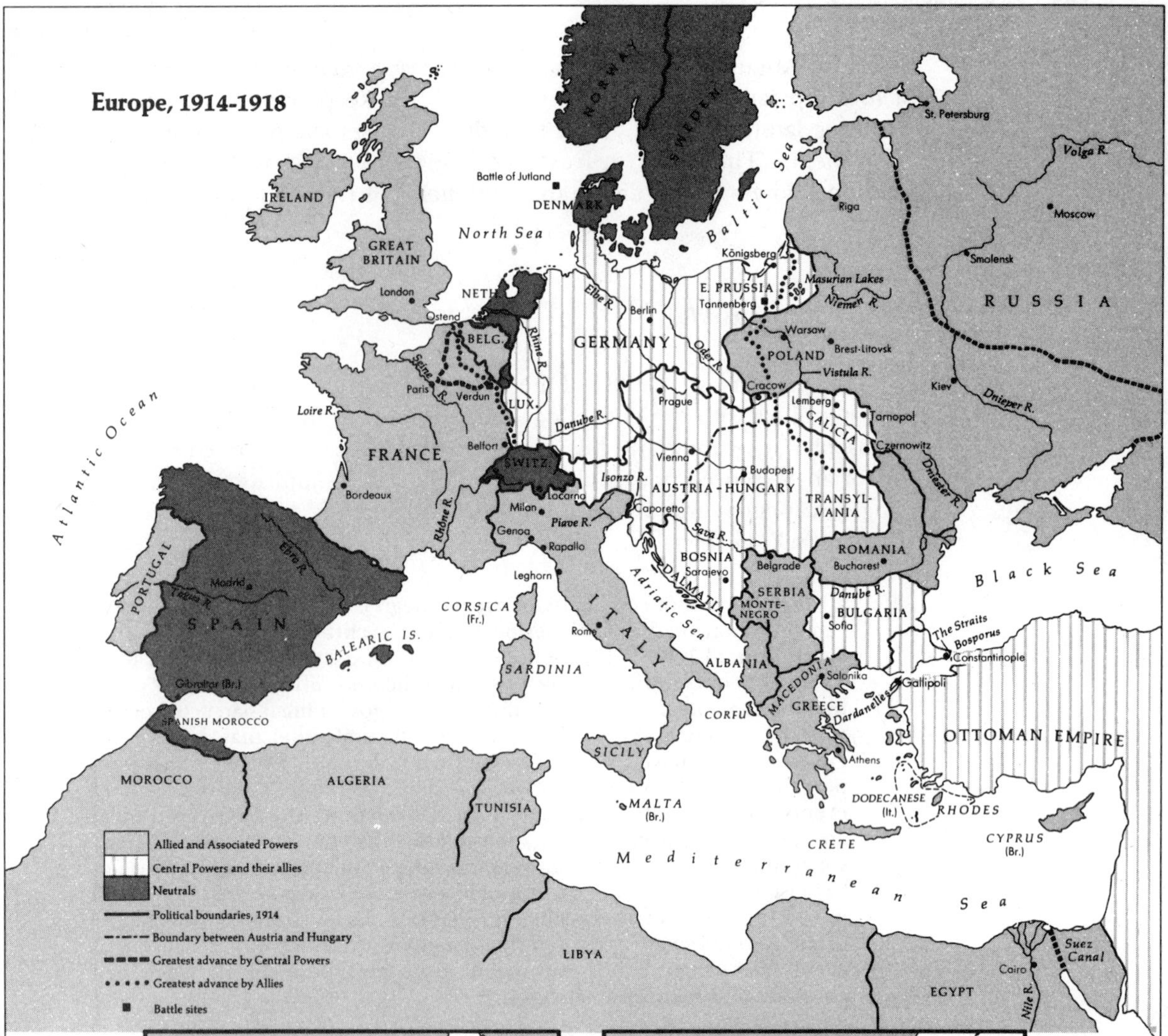
Europe, 1914-1918
NORWAY
SWEDEN
Baltic Sea
St. Petersburg
Volga R.
Battle of Jutland
DENMARK
IRELAND
Riga
Moscow
North Sea
GREAT BRITAIN
Königsberg
Smolensk
London
NETH.
E. PRUSSIA
Masurian Lakes
Tannenberg
Niemen R.
RUSSIA
Ostend
Elbe R.
Berlin
BELG.
Rhine R.
GERMANY
Warsaw
Brest-Litovsk
Seine R.
Oder R.
POLAND
Vistula R.
Paris
Verdun
Kiev
Atlantic Ocean
LUX.
Prague
Cracow
Dnieper R.
Loire R.
Lemberg
Tarnopol
Danube R.
GALICIA
Belfort
FRANCE
Vienna
Czernowitz
SWITZ.
Isonzo R.
Budapest
Dniester R.
Bordeaux
Locarno
AUSTRIA-HUNGARY
TRANSYLVANIA
Milan
Caporetto
Piave R.
Rhône R.
Sava R.
Genoa
Rapallo
ROMANIA
Ebro R.
BOSNIA
Belgrade
Bucharest
PORTUGAL
Madrid
Leghorn
Sarajevo
DALMATIA
Black Sea
Tagus R.
SERBIA
Danube R.
CORSICA (Fr.)
MONTENEGRO
BULGARIA
SPAIN
Sofia
The Straits
BALEARIC IS.
Rome
ITALY
Adriatic Sea
Bosporus
ALBANIA
Constantinople
SARDINIA
MACEDONIA
Salonika
Gallipoli
Gibraltar (Br.)
GREECE
Dardanelles
CORFU
SPANISH MOROCCO
OTTOMAN EMPIRE
SICILY
Athens
MOROCCO
ALGERIA
MALTA (Br.)
DODECANESE (It.)
RHODES
TUNISIA
CRETE
CYPRUS (Br.)
Allied and Associated Powers
Central Powers and their allies
Neutrals
Political boundaries, 1914
Boundary between Austria and Hungary
Greatest advance by Central Powers
Greatest advance by Allies
Battle sites
Mediterranean Sea
LIBYA
Suez Canal
Cairo
EGYPT
Nile R.

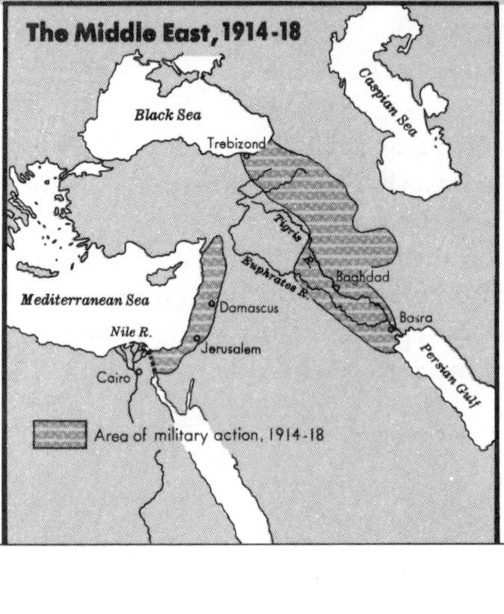
The Middle East, 1914-18
Black Sea
Caspian Sea
Trebizond
Tigris R.
Euphrates R.
Baghdad
Mediterranean Sea
Damascus
Basra
Nile R.
Jerusalem
Persian Gulf
Cairo
Area of military action, 1914-18

Asia and the Pacific, 1914-15
Tsingtau
JAPAN
CHINA
FORMOSA
Pacific Ocean
INDIA
Madras
PHILIPPINE IS.
PENANG I.
YAP
CAROLINE IS.
Rabaul
Indian Ocean
Battles and other military actions, 1914-15
AUSTRALIA

more far-reaching domestic repercussions and diplomatic results. The same was true of its impact upon technology and commerce, upon birth rates and settlement patterns, upon imperialism and nationalism. But the war remained, in terms of devastated land and broken lives, fundamentally a European-rooted conflict carried out essentially in four theatres:

1) On the western front, where Germany and France met;
2) On the eastern front, where Russia clashed with the Austro-Hungarian, German and Central Powers;
3) In the Balkans and at the eastern end of the Mediterranean;
4) On the seas.

## *In Europe*

The first popular response to war resulted in a wave of patriotic parades, violent attacks on enemy embassies, and unverified atrocity stories. The rape of neutral Belgium, so strategically important to Britain, was given particular attention by the British press. Reports that advancing German soldiers were cutting off the hands of Belgian babies so that they might never carry arms against the Kaiser (reports ultimately proven false) reflected all of the classic elements of the psychology of mass rumor. The public, including most of organized labor—which by Marxist theory was expected to be opposed to war—found pleasure in the end of the suspense.

Money interests were displeased, however, for the war abruptly ended speculation in the Near East and the lucrative Anglo-German trade. It also threatened the peace and stability upon which entrepreneurship feeds. Faced with a panic, the major stock markets (except Berlin's) closed. Vigorous action by David Lloyd George quickly had the banks of London open again, so he took a giant stride forward in public esteem. In both world wars the British were slow to find their natural leader. He emerged only at the most critical stage after a period of careful but dramatic preparation. Lloyd George displaced the ineffectual Prime Minister Herbert Asquith and his untidy wartime coalition government in December 1915. (In 1940 Winston Churchill replaced the unfortunate Neville Chamberlain. Both men understood the use of words in moving large groups to higher resolve.) Lloyd George and the British brilliantly exploited the report that Bethmann-Hollweg had called the treaty that assured Belgian neutrality merely "a scrap of paper" and that the kaiser had referred to the British Expeditionary Force in Europe as a "contemptible little army." The Force, calling themselves the Old Contemptibles, in time proved otherwise.

Although Major General Erich von Ludendorff (1865–1937) had occupied Liege, the French, under General Joseph Joffre (1852–1931), advanced upon the Ardennes forest, as the Germans had hoped. A military engineer whose experience lay mostly in the colonies, Joffre was far less able than the German leaders he faced, and the French were slow to recognize the nature of German technical superiority, especially in machine guns and rapid-fire artillery. The French were driven back almost at once, and on August 23, following the loss of 150,000 soldiers, they narrowly escaped from the German trap. On the same day the British stood off a German sweep at Mons, a few miles inside Belgium. Within three weeks of the opening of the war, the western front had settled into the form of warfare that became its norm, and after four years of war led to a German penetration and Allied counterpenetration of less than one hundred miles along the Franco-Belgian border.

Germany's desire to knock France out of the war quickly abated, as Moltke had feared, because of the realities of a war on two fronts. The advancing Russian army defeated the Germans inside East Prussia on August 19. Fearing that the flat terrain and the mobile Russian troops would combine to expose Germany itself, Moltke appointed General Paul von Hindenburg to take charge of the eastern front and transferred the victorious Ludendorff there as chief of staff. Moving swiftly, Hindenburg cut off one of the two advancing Russian armies at Tannenberg and rushing troops across Germany by rail, he captured 100,000 men. In the face of so overwhelming a defeat, the Russian commander committed suicide, and the Germans swept on another fifty miles to the Masurian lakes, where the second Russian army also was defeated.

Victory on the eastern front was bought at great cost to the Germans, however. In the west the French armies took the offensive on September 6. With British support, they halted the German advance across the Marne River and forced the Germans into retreat. A quick victory over France was now out of the question for the Germans, and Moltke foresaw a long war on two fronts, which might well end in stalemate. The new German Chief of Staff on the western front, Erich von Falkenhayn, hoping to rescue Moltke's strategy, sent troops racing for the sea, capturing all save a small portion of Belgium. But at Ypres, thirty miles short of Calais and the English Channel, a combined British and French force, fighting desperately to prevent the fall of the Channel ports, halted the German rush. The western front thereupon settled down into tedious, deadly trench warfare in which movement was measured in yards rather than miles.

With the western front bogged in the mire of a joint holding action, attention once again turned to the East, where the Austrians had fallen into the error the Germans feared. Having placed their major strength against Serbia, the Austrians were ill-prepared to do battle with the Russians, who struck deep into Galicia and, in the region of Lemberg, fought out one of the major engagements of the war from August 23 until the middle of September. Austria retreated across the Carpathian Mountains into Hungary, leaving the whole of Galicia open to Russia's southern army, which had exacted a toll of 250,000 casualties. During these same days, however, the German victories in East Prussia offset the Russian gains at Austria's expense.

In a short war, Germany had reason to expect a victory; in a long war, it did not. A long war would make it possible for British control of the seas slowly to strangle the Central Powers, cutting off the flow of arms, munitions, and food. A long war might well mean the entry of the United States on the side of the Allied Powers. A long war could mean that the Allies would develop new weapons to offset the initial German technological superiority. Germany's war strategy now changed, therefore, from an attempt to defeat France above Paris to trying to buy time for the German armies until new weapons, in particular the submarine, might be perfected and built in great quantity. The war thus moved into its scientific and technological phase; modern science would ultimately determine the victor.

Although the initial blockade was not a serious matter, Germany saw that it posed a long-term danger of the most serious kind. The Royal Navy had taken control of the seas, and a British cruiser victory off Heligoland had induced the Germans to keep their High Seas Fleet safely within the Baltic. In January 1915 a German squadron barely escaped the British at the Dogger Bank, and Admiral Tirpitz turned to the U-boat as the only means of offsetting such clear Allied superiority. On February 4 the kaiser proclaimed the waters around the British Isles to be a war zone where all shipping, neutral included, might be attacked without warning.

The U-boat was essentially a psychological weapon. Germany had no more than twenty-one at this time, and some were not in sound condition. Militarily the underwater vessels could not be expected to counterbalance British dominance in traditional sea warfare, but psychologically their use might persuade the British to lift at least a portion of their blockade. The gesture was a desperate one, therefore, and ill-advised, for the U-boat was to World War I what the atomic bomb was to World War II: a "secret" weapon, feared and hated by all nations, especially neutrals. Bethmann-Hollweg predicted that the use of U-boats would incense Americans, who were enjoying wartime prosperity from British trade, and that the United States might be driven to intervene in the war. Arguing that Germany would be branded a "mad dog" among nations, he at last convinced the kaiser to put an end to unrestricted U-boat warfare in August. This came too late, however, for 1,200 passengers (including 128 Americans) died when the *Lusitania* was sunk on May 5. American opinion now swung to a consistently anti-German position.

The problem of the U-boat remained, nonetheless, for the Germans were tempted to use it whenever victory on land eluded them. International law did not provide for undersea raiders, and the British exploited this fact. When Germany promised to observe neutral shipping rights within specially prescribed lanes, the Allied nations simply flew American flags on their own vessels. When the Allies extracted from the Germans the promise that no ship would be sunk without warning, they added armor-piercing deck guns to their cargo vessels; and when a submarine surfaced to issue the necessary warning, they sank it as as it rode on the surface of the water. If the Germans attacked a ship without warning, however, the propaganda loss might well offset the immediate gain. Because there were no clear rules for this kind of new warfare, international law always lagging behind military technology, each nation could declare the other wrong.

But the Germans did not feel compelled to return to U-boat warfare yet. During 1915 they sought to conquer Poland and help their uncooperative ally, Austria, defeat Serbia, so that Austrian troops could be released for the Russian front. Aided by excellent leadership and by a railway system that permitted rapid movement of troops from one front to another, the Germans remained in a potentially favorable position throughout the year. Other new inventions helped, most notably flame throwers, chlorine gas, and airplanes in which machine guns could fire past the propeller by synchronization. Chlorine gas did not become popular, and the British produced their own technological breakthrough by 1916, the tracked armored vehicle, which soon became the tank. The air battle was not waged over protection for ground troops or destruction of convoys and factories as in World War II, however, for aircraft were not yet sufficiently well developed or capable of the speeds and distances necessary to bring the war to the home front. Rather, the battle for air supremacy was fought largely over photography and the observation of artillery placements.

For the war was an artillery war. The French and British especially favored massive artillery barrages to destroy enemy trenches before sending troops "over the top" to kill those who remained. In fact, however, the artillery bombardments proved ineffective, for they were not precise enough to eliminate pinpoint targets, and they destroyed the roads, drainage ditches, and communications behind the area of bombardment so thoroughly that when Allied troops were able to move into the area, they found their own advance halted by flooding, which prevented their bringing supplies and horses or moving artillery forward to new positions. As minister of munitions from 1915, Lloyd George was able to assure full production of the necessary guns and shells, which had been in short supply on the western front earlier, but he could not change the Allied notion of laying waste to the land, which also laid waste to the Allied advance.

The single decisive area of battle in 1915 was on a new front: Turkey. Combat there was decisive by virtue of being indecisive. In November 1914, the Ottoman Empire, fearful of dismemberment by Russia, joined Germany. Having little respect for the Turks, who had been defeated so easily in the First Balkan War, Winston Churchill, the First Lord of the British Admiralty, recommended an offensive against Turkey in order to turn the German flank to the East. Although the First Sea Lord strongly opposed the plan, Churchill was able to persuade him to order the British Mediterranean fleet to force its way through the Dardanelles and capture Constantinople without aid from land forces. After a month-long naval bombardment of the Turkish fortresses on the Gallipoli peninsula, which controlled the Dardanelles, an Anglo-French squadron attempted to run the narrow strait, only to have three battleships sunk by mines and the fleet thrown back.

Committed now, the British could not abandon the area. In any event, political considerations were now taking temporary precidence over military because the Allies were in the midst of delicate negotiations with both Italy and Romania, and were trying to draw them into the war. Failure at Gallipoli would cool Italian ardor in particular. Asquith therefore persuaded the Secretary of State for War, Lord Kitchener, to put troops ashore on Gallipoli. British, Australian, and New Zealand troops were landed on April 25, and the French and Indians followed. The Turks, battling to protect their capital, held firm, while British leadership proved exceptionally inept. The Anzac troops and the Australian and New Zealand governments felt they had been sacrificed deliberately for political ends—Australian nationalism may be said to date from Gallipoli. A quarrel between Churchill and the First Sea Lord over naval support at Gallipoli erupted publicly in May, leading to the fall of the Liberal government. A coalition was formed, which included conservatives. Asquith remained as prime minister, and Churchill was expelled from the Cabinet. It was cold comfort that Italy did enter the war in May. The indecisiveness of the campaign led to a firm decision not to become further involved in the area.

Allied disillusionment was heightened by continuing German victories on the eastern front. In March 1915, when the Russians took the Austrian fortress city of Przemysl and 100,000 prisoners, Falkenhayn transferred troops from the western front. The German counterattack in May unrolled eastward without halt through Galicia, over Warsaw, north to Vilna, just short of Riga, past Brest-Litovsk. The Austrians, now cooperating with the German command, shared in the victories, in which over a million prisoners were taken. Falkenhayn drew back from plunging more deeply into Russia, however, for he wished to avoid Napoleon's mistake of losing communication with his power base. Germany had been favored by interior lines of defense and communication; but as the Russian army retreated across Poland, it scorched the earth so that advancing Germans could not live off it. This destruction created a mass flight of thousands of civilians who choked the roads and turned cities into centers of chaos. In September, therefore, Falkenhayn stopped.

Quickly sending an army to the Danube where Bulgaria had entered the war on the side of the Central Powers, Falkenhayn tried to stabilize the unsteady Austro-Serbian situation. In October, Austro-German and Bulgarian armies attacked Serbia on two sides. Despite an Anglo-French effort to support Serbia from Salonika, where they landed troops (contrary to Greek neutrality), the Serbs were defeated. The Anglo-French army was pinned down along the Greek frontier, the Italians had proved to be ineffective, and the Central Powers were again in a position to take the initiative in the West. In December, therefore, Falkenhayn turned his attention once more to the western front, where he planned to attack Verdun, one of the French anchor fortresses. He hoped to draw the French out into a battle where they would bleed to death in the face of the German artillery.

## The Home Front

Ultimately, perhaps the most important factor in the outcome of World War I was public opinion on the home front. If morale was high at home or if the true nature of events could be kept from the public, armies might bend but not break. If the home front, the center of strength, would not hold, neither could the military. Verdun was more important psychologically than militarily, and it marked the turning of the tide. Because the German public was not informed of Falkenhayn's strategy, which had to remain concealed if it were to work, the public assumed that Germany wanted to take Verdun. Just as television coverage of the 1961–1973 war in Vietnam made secret large-scale planning impossible, coverage by the flourishing popular press prohibited Falkenhayn's fictitious investment in Verdun, which forced him to actually try to capture what he did not want. Rather than being able to pull troops back from Verdun to let the French initially overrun German positions only to be pounded to pieces later, the Germans now felt compelled to close on the Meuse and seize the city itself. Here, beginning on February 21, the greatest single, most fruitless engagement of the war was fought.

The slaughter of Verdun only ended when it became irrelevant. In May the Austrians attacked the Italians and moved upon Verona. To relieve the Italians, the Russian southern army advanced against the Austrians; the Russians, seriously weakened in 1915, were once again a formidable force. They had defeated the Turks at Erzurum, received

Allied munitions via Vladivostok on the Pacific coast, and benefited from a temporarily stabilized political situation on the home front. As the refreshed Russian army advanced through Galicia, the Germans were forced to divert troops to aid even the Austrians, even though that weakened their own line on the Baltic.

The Russian advance petered out because they tried to fight sophisticated weaponry with flesh, but not before the Austrians drew back from further invasions of Italy and the French and British were able to halt the Germans at Verdun. The Russian army lost an additional million men. Russia was not a military force of consequence in World War I again, but she had relieved the intolerable German pressure on the western front.

The German failure to capture Verdun weakened resolve at home. On July 1 an Anglo-French attack began on the Somme, which threw untried British volunteers against the war's chief development in arms, the machine gun. The Maxim gun, as it was called, had been invented by an American-born Englishman, Sir Hiram Maxim. Because it used the recoil that resulted from the explosion of one cartridge to expel the empty chamber and reload the weapon, the machine gun could outfire any other weapon. The British had developed the gun to a high degree and were aware of the technological superiority that arose from such a weapon. As early as 1898 the English writer Hilaire Belloc could say, "Whatever happens, we have got the Maxim gun, and they have not." But the Germans improved upon it and trained their defending troops to use it with far greater skill and flexibility. The British commander, a hymn-singing man of great courage and little imagination, Sir Douglas Haig (1861–1928), chose to throw wave after wave against the unbreaking shore, and in a single day the British alone lost 55,000 men. Both sides had demonstrated that neither would collapse, nor could either advance.

### *Bringing America Into the War*

In the meantime the Germans had returned to using the U-boat. Public opinion was clamoring for full employment of all weapons that might bring victory and end the bloodshed. The German leadership saw that morale was declining and that the stalemate won on the western front might be lost at home if drastic action were not taken. In the eyes of the Germans, the English "hunger blockade," which struck at women and children as well as the fighting men, justified use of the submarines. Falkenhayn supported Tirpitz in returning to submarine warfare, and the Germans attempted a limited and tactical use of their weapon. This policy proved that partial offensives fail on all counts. They seldom achieve their objective, and public and international opinion suffers. Tirpitz resigned on March 4 when the kaiser once again accepted Bethmann-Hollweg's argument that unrestricted use of the raiders would bring the United States into the war. But a fatal clash was assured because U-boats were allowed to attack enemy merchant ships, which were armed with deck cannons. On March 25 a U-boat in the English Channel sank the *Sussex* with the loss of ninety lives, some American. An American note temporarily strengthened Bethmann-Hollweg's hand, and he was able to promise President Woodrow Wilson that U-boats would no longer attack without warning, and that they would ensure the safety of passengers and crews. Under the conditions of warfare, however, this promise was impossible to keep.

Still, America clearly wanted to remain aloof from the war. There were profits to be realized in trading with the warring nations. The great crisis of Europe struck many Americans as none of their business, and no side was seen to be without fault. While public opinion was generally anti-German in the United States, relations with Britain were also deteriorating. American business resented the British policy of blacklisting any company thought to be trading with the Central Powers. The British blockade brought up specters of the War of 1812 and of the American Civil War. Most important, an uprising in Ireland on Easter Sunday, 1916, which the British suppressed with great harshness, rekindled anti-British feeling in many quarters. Wilson did not want to see American lives lost in the trenches on the western front. In November 1916, he was reelected to a second term under a slogan that he did not support, but it emotionally summed up for most Americans their attitude toward the conflict: "He kept us out of war."

Wilson knew that he could not do so indefinitely, and he hoped to mediate between the European powers. Nobody in 1916 wished this mediation, however. Each side could still envision victory, although neither had recent gains. The Germans resorted to a harsh conscription of every male between seventeen and sixty for military or industrial service. Forced labor was drawn into German factories from Belgium. Women worked in steel mines and plants. The winter of 1916–1917 undermined German morale on a home front plagued by scarcity of consumer goods, heat, and light—coal having been allocated to essential wartime industries. Railways were choked with military traffic. A potato famine, caused by premature frost and lack of fertilization, reduced Germans to a diet of turnips. In both Germany and Austria will had weakened, and the civilians were trying to substitute scapegoats for the lack of foodstuffs; socialist groups were talking of revolution.

Conditions were only slightly less grim within the Allied nations. The Russian army was near mutiny, food and coal were scarce, and the railways were approaching collapse. The British had also turned to conscription in 1916, taking all men between eighteen and forty-one. Provided

Russia remained in the war, however, long-range projections now clearly favored the Allied powers.

Russia did not remain in the war. In March 1917, virtually without bloodshed, the Rusian Duma (parliament) established a provisional government; the Tsar abdicated. The first President, Prince George Lvov, was soon challenged; but his successor, Aleksandr Kerensky, temporarily appeared able to recharge Russian spirits. A disastrous Russian offensive in July ended in defeat; and the troops, joined by the peasants, turned increasingly to the demands for peace and land voiced by Lenin and Leon Trotsky (1879–1940). In November (October by the Russian calendar) Lenin's Bolshevik group displaced the Russian socialists and asked for a separate armistice with the Central Powers. In December, German and Russian leaders met at Brest-Litovsk. As talks proceeded, the Germans once again began transferring troops to the West, while the Bolshevik Red Guards forcefully dispersed the new constituent assembly, elected in November. Unable to go on, professing to want no territorial gains won by war, and hopeful of stirring revolution in Germany and eastern Europe, the Bolsheviks signed a crushing peace in March of 1918. Not only was Russia out of the war, but she was now apparently hostile to the Allies, in their eyes a German satellite as well as the subversive center for potential world revolution.

The loss of Russia was, in part, offset in 1917 by the entry of the United States into the war. Bethmann-Hollweg lost his battle against the U-boat. In the face of British and French determination not to negotiate a peace, and the expectation that the Russians would remain in the war, Germany desperately turned to unrestricted submarine warfare on January 31. Those who favored use of the U-boats argued that even if the United States entered the war, she could have little effect short of six months, and that by then Britain would be broken. Wilson responded by severing diplomatic relations with Germany on February 3. More American vessels were sunk in March, while British intelligence agents leaked the information (which they had obtained earlier) that the German foreign secretary had secretly offered an alliance to Mexico with the promise of giving her back her *irredenta* (lost territory) of Texas, New Mexico, and Arizona. On April 6, Congress declared war on Germany, slightly less than a month after the revolution began in Russia.

### The Collapse of the Powers

At first the German strategy appeared correct, for America's entry made little initial difference on the battlefield. Ludendorff had taken up a defensive position along the Hindenburg Line. On April 9 the British took the offensive in France at Arras, making use of paralyzing gas for the first time, and the Canadian Corps won a major victory for Commonwealth contingents at Vimy Ridge. The French attacked on April 16, under new leadership, but failed to break through the German lines. They sustained 100,000 casualties and lost nearly 200 tanks. Already bled white, France was near the breaking point, and mutinies ranged through the army; some units marched on Paris only to be turned back by the French cavalry.

Yet another effort to break the German lines came in July. Following an unprecedented bombardment, Britain's General Haig sent his army into the worst conditions of the war. Allied bombardment at Passchendaele destroyed the drainage system at Flanders, and the battlefield became a sea of mud. August's torrential rains stopped the exposed Allies, while the Germans fought from within concrete pillboxes. By November 250,000 British troops had been destroyed to little purpose, and British morale was plummeting. Food was scarce, labor was restive. On the Italian front an Austro-German army had broken through the lines at Caporetto, hurling the Italians back to the Piave River and taking more than a quarter-million prisoners in a battle which was later recalled to the world in Ernest Hemingway's *A Farewell to Arms.* Caporetto led to the fall of the French government and the rise of Georges Clemenceau (1841–1929). British arms brought victory against the Turks only on lesser fronts, for in March an Anglo-Indian army captured Baghdad and in December took Jerusalem.

The genuinely cheering news came from the sea, but not until after heavy losses. German predictions at first seemed correct, for in the first four months of 1917 well over two million tons of Allied shipping were sunk in the Atlantic. Only when Lloyd George ordered the Admiralty to provide convoys for merchant vessels were the losses halted. In the next six months nearly 1,500 ships safely reached Britain, with the loss of 10 convoy-protected vessels. This nullification of the German U-boat strength was achieved by the British with the assistance of American and French destroyer escorts, but the actual destruction of the submarines themselves fell almost entirely to the British navy. The Germans had been right on one count: American troops would be even more than six months in reaching Europe. They had been wrong on another count: the desperate gamble of unrestricted submarine warfare had failed to bring the Allies to their knees.

All nations knew that the war must end in 1918. Only the United States could go on for a long time. From America, Woodrow Wilson announced in the goals he set in a message to Congress, which were called the Fourteen Points:

1) Covenants of peace, openly arrived at;
2) Freedom of the seas in peace and war, except as modified by international action;
3) Removal of economic barriers between nations;
4) Reduction of armaments;
5) Impartial adjustment of territorial claims;
6) Evacuation of Russia;
7) Evacuation of Belgium;
8) Restoration of France and the return of Alsace-Lorraine;
9) Readjustment of the Italian frontiers;
10) Independent development for the nationalities of Austria-Hungary;
11) Reconstruction of the Balkan states along national lines, with access to the sea for Serbia;
12) Self-determination of peoples in the Ottoman Empire;
13) Independence for Poland, with an outlet to the sea; and
14) A general association of nations to provide mutual guarantees for the future.

In an additional statement in February he elevated the principle of self-determination of peoples to equality with the first five, more general, points. Wilson hoped these principles could become a basis for peace.

By now, however, following Russia's collapse, the Germans had transferred a million troops from the eastern front, and Ludendorff was prepared to launch a final offensive before the American army could arrive. After a stunning, short bombardment with gas shells, which did not damage the hard, spring earth, German troops moved to ground held by the British, north of Amiens. Five major assaults drove back the Entente. As the Royal Flying Corps attacked the long German transport columns from the air, the British retreated slowly in order. Sensing that the war was at its turning point, the Entente powers agreed for the first time to a unified command under French Marshall Ferdinand Foch (1851-1929). The American commander, General John J. Pershing (1860-1948), who had come to France in 1917 to prepare for the arrival of American troops, had insisted on a separate, integrated American army. The United States persistently refused to refer to itself as an Allied power, choosing instead to be an associated nation. In the face of the crisis, Pershing postponed the plan for an American army operating in its own sector and rushed the first American troops to the French lines in May.

As the German attack around Amiens ground to a halt, Ludendorff struck in Flanders. Haig, aware that a German breakthrough to the sea was possible, ordered his troops to fight and die with their backs to the wall, without giving ground. The British held. Ludendorff struck toward the French and broke through to the Marne. Americans relieved the French at Chateau-Thierry and Belleau Wood. Fresh, with new weapons and a sense of mission, with 300,000 men arriving monthly, they stopped the German offensive. Foch now counterattacked with 300 tanks and broke through Ludendorff's exposed flank. The Germans retreated from the Marne.

The Allied offensive, which began on July 18, did not stop until the armistice. On August 8, when Canadian and Australian troops broke through the German line at Amiens, Ludendorff knew that defeat was at hand. On September 15 the Allied army, long tied down at Salonika, took the offensive. On the 26th, American, British, and French troops launched an offensive between the Meuse River and the Argonne forest, with Sedan as their objective. On the 19th, the Bulgarians signed a separate armistice, and on that date the British stormed the Hindenburg Line. The Germans asked for an armistice on the basis of the Fourteen Points, but even Wilson declared that there could be no peace without unconditional surrender and abdication of the kaiser. The Germans fought on. Ludendorff was dismissed, and Austria asked for peace. On October 30, Turkey surrendered; on November 3, the Austrians signed an armistice for the Italian front. The German navy was in mutiny, German cities were in the upheaval of riots. On November 7 Kurt Eisner, a socialist, formed a government in Munich and declared the separate Republic of Bavaria. On the 9th the kaiser abdicated, then fled to Holland.

The armistice was signed on November 11. Its terms were made known a week before. Germany had to evacuate all conquered territory and all land west of the Rhine, and had to surrender most of its armies. Germany had to give up its U-boats and High Seas Fleet (although German sailors scuttled much of the latter at Scapa Flow before the British could take possession). German armies were to be withdrawn from a number of strategic locations, and much war material was to be surrendered at once. The Treaty of Brest-Litovsk was annulled.

The armistice was signed by German political leaders who had proclaimed a republic on the 9th, following the kaiser's abdication. The German Supreme Command was not party to the surrender. Later, Ludendorff declared that anti-German and especially socialist elements among political leaders at home had taken a victory from him that he might yet have won, giving rise to a German military insistence that they had been stabbed in the back. That the home front was in a state of panic was true, but clearly German troops could not have gone on fighting for long and had no hope of further victory.

The war was over. Peacemaking began.

### New Weapons, New Ways

The war had changed pre-1914 Europe to such an extent, had so altered the course of history, that no assembly of diplomats could do much beyond accepting the new facts. Millions lay dead or permanently

Progressively, mechanized transport had replaced animal transport in western armies in the nineteenth century, and yet a large proportion of German transport at the time of the Blitzkrieg upon Poland in 1939 was still animal. By 1942, when German and British troops met at *El Alamein,* on the Egyptian front, the tank had become totally dominant. *Source: Wide World Photos*

maimed. An entire generation had been wiped away. Russia had fallen to the dreaded communism while its specter gripped the fallen Germany. The old, ordered world of Edwardian England, *la belle époque,* was gone.

The war had shown the world the new instruments of destruction that modern technology could produce, and in the process had destroyed some comforting old assumptions about progress and the human's innate power to reason. For the first time in history, airplanes and dirigibles were used in combat, mostly for reconnaissance purposes, but also for air raids on enemy towns. The principle was established that it was as proper to strike at civilians as at military targets from the air. Poison gas was used for the first time, and by both sides. This particular weapon was also in its infancy, and hence of minor usefulness; the wind often blew the gas back into the attacker's own lines, but humans had shown themselves capable of using it. Soon gas masks were introduced, which showed that while the technology of war had changed, an older principle had not—for every weapon there is a countermeasure, which escalates the search for the ultimate weapon. What chemical warfare could not achieve, the Allies hoped a different invention of theirs would—the tank. Tanks first made their appearance against the Germans in 1916; the effect was devastating. Their monstrous appearance and power made even the most battle-hardened Germans take flight and retreat. But the British began tank warfare with insufficient reserves. When the Germans captured some of the new machines, they put their technical ingenuity to copying them, so that before long, the contest was between tank and tank, and not between tank and infantryman. Here, too, an old lesson was repeated—in time the enemy acquires the weapons one attempts to keep to oneself.

When a decision eluded the armies on the battlefield, both sides extended the war to civilian populations. The Allied war at sea was designed to blockade the Central Powers, to shut their armies off from overseas resources, and to starve their people. The Central Powers responded with a submarine war designed to sink Allied, and later neutral, shipping that carried needed supplies, and to counterblockade Britain. This was total war, with its concept of the "home front" and the "battle of production" that must accompany the battle in the trenches; labor had to do its duty as the soldiers did, the state itself was a garrison. This was no limited war, fought for limited and well-specified objectives by professional armies. This was a war in which everyone was involved, a war that called for a total effort, and in which production figures did indeed decide the ultimate outcome as much as any military offensive did.

If the concept of the home front was sometimes more of a slogan than a reality—not every worker made munitions, not every woman was trained as a nurse, not every child rolled bandages—the number of active participants in the war was huge. In the largest of his campaigns, Frederick the Great had not employed more than 30,000 soldiers; even Napoleon's armies—the largest Europe had seen—only numbered in the hundreds of thousands. But in their opening campaign of 1914 alone, the Germans sent seven armies into the field; the Allies countered with six. The average number of soldiers at any given time was twenty million; the total number between 1914 and 1918 was nearly sixty million.

And these armies and the home front labored to the accompaniment of a barrage of propaganda that was equally without parallel. The propaganda was as vague and as unrestrained as the eventual war aims themselves. If one was on the side of the Central Powers, one was fighting against Allied "strangulation" or "encirclement"; one was fighting against Britain, "The Land Without Music," for a superior culture, for Mozart and Beethoven. On the Allied side, one was fighting not because Britain wished to prevent the profound change in Europe's balance of power that a German victory (military or diplomatic) would have meant, or because France wanted to change the verdict of 1871. Instead, if the propagandists were to be believed, one was fighting for Western civilization against the *Boche* and the "Hun," against people out to "dominate the world" who along the way were shooting French nurses and bayoneting Belgian babies. Ultimately, one was fighting "the war to end all wars,"

**Territorial Settlements in Europe, 1919-1926**

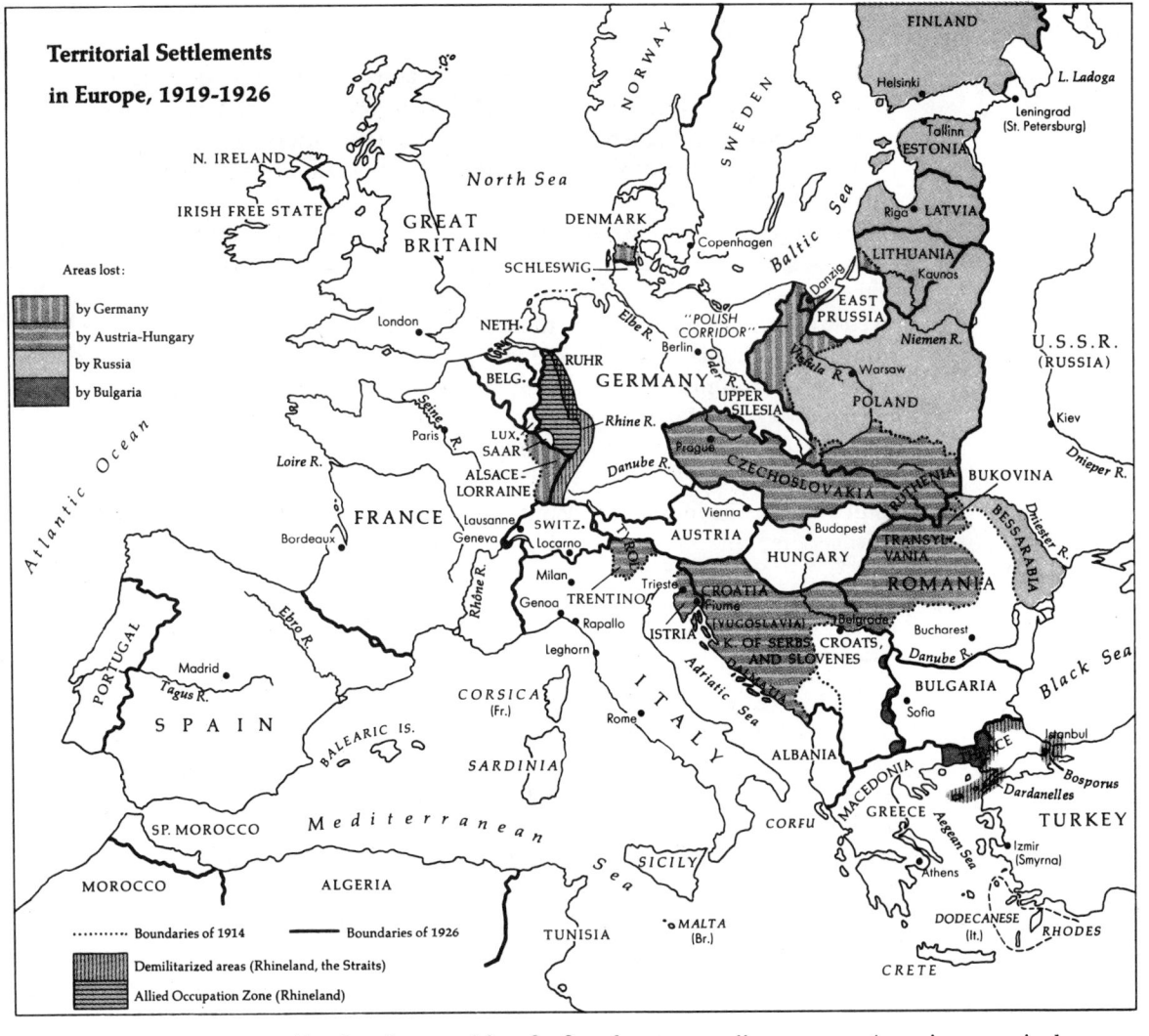

Areas lost:
- by Germany
- by Austria-Hungary
- by Russia
- by Bulgaria

······ Boundaries of 1914 ——— Boundaries of 1926

Demilitarized areas (Rhineland, the Straits)
Allied Occupation Zone (Rhineland)

to "make the world safe for democracy," as some Americans naively suggested.

The propaganda was so obvious that there was an occasional suspension of belief. The fighting troops, in particular, were freer from feelings of hate than some civilians. Still, certain passions had been roused that even the most generous peacemakers had to take into account. The tensions of the war, the sacrifices made, and the appeals of the propagandists led—before any peace conference could assemble—to revolution and the death of three empires. Russia lost more than tsarist rule. It also lost the Polish and Baltic nationalities, nearly one-third of its territory, being roughly reduced in 1918 to the borders of the sixteenth century Duchy of Muscovy. The Turkish empire was dismantled even more thoroughly. The Sultan was gone, and so were its Arab and its Balkan possessions. Only the Anatolian holdings remained. Austria experienced a similar fate. The centuries-old Hapsburg rule was ended, and every nationality except the Austro-German was breaking away.

Some of these losses were regained. Russia eventually recovered most of the territory it had surrendered as a result of losing the war. Turkey fought to obtain somewhat better borders than it got as a result of the war's outcome and the decisions of the peacemakers. But the casualties were permanent. These figures, too, were unprecedented, unequalled even by America's Civil War, the other mass war of modern times. The number of military and civilian dead between 1914 and 1918 came to ten million, the number of wounded to twenty million. France alone lost nearly 1,400,000 dead; Germany, 1,800,000. It was a frightful price to pay for a war that was "in the final analysis," as a British military historian put it fifty years later, "nothing more than a prolonged and expensive audit to prove that the industrial resources of one side were smaller than those of the other."

### The Peace

On January 18, 1919, the victors assembled in Paris to settle the terms of the peace. It was a doubly historic day. On January 18, forty-eight years earlier, the German empire which Bismarck had created was proclaimed. The Prussian troops were deep in France then, and the great ceremony had taken place in Versailles' Hall of Mirrors. Now the new victors met the Germans at Versailles once again.

The conditions agreed on in Paris were severe. The treaties that the new German government—not the one that saw itself responsible for the war—was made to accept at Versailles later that year deprived Germany of territory, money, power, and security. The Germans, as expected, were made to return Alsace-Lorraine to France. The French also meant to reclaim the coal-rich Saar region and parts of the Rhineland, but were opposed by Woodrow Wilson, who would not accept so flagrant a violation of his declared principle of national self-determination. They reached a compromise. The Left Bank of the Rhine would be demilitarized and the French would obtain special economic and administrative concessions in the Saar for a period of fifteen years, which would then be followed by a plebiscite.

While Germans complained about Versailles in the years to come, angered by the assumption that everyone held them responsible for the war, the treaty that the Austrians had to sign was a crueler one. Germany lost some territory, and continued as a nation; Austria-Hungary ceased to exist. The peace conference formalized the dissolution of the Hapsburg Empire, assigning some of its territory to Romania, Italy, and

Serbia, and establishing four new seccessor states—the republics of Austria, Hungary, Czechoslovakia, and a restored Poland. The last also received some German territory, so that it would have access to the Baltic.

An infinitely older order was also changed by the victors through the dismemberment of the Ottoman Empire. The Empire had begun to break apart during the war, and the Allies would not put it together again. However, a new mood did not permit overseas what it still did in Europe—outright annexation. Hence, former enemy territories, German as well as Turkish, were placed under the supervision of a new League of Nations, which then assigned these territories to the powers as mandates. In this way they would be prepared—according to the League's instructions—for eventual self-government. Thus Turkish Palestine, Iraq, and Transjordan became British, and Syria and Lebanon became French mandates. The former German colonies were mandated to Japan, France, Britain, Australia, New Zealand, and South Africa.

No such distinctions like those made between mandates and annexations applied to the matter of financial reparation. The Germans and their allies, said the peacemakers, had started the war and would have to pay for it. Their payments would have to be large enough to cover the damage suffered by the Allied population, and to meet the costs of "all pensions to military and naval victims of the war" and to their families. Because it would be impossible to estimate the amount involved with any degree of accuracy in 1919, the Germans were instructed to sign a blanket promise of payment; they would meet whatever bills the Allies ultimately presented, and meanwhile, they would offer an immediate payment of $5 billion in gold or cash. This effectively mortgaged the new German government's chances of creating a democracy in the Weimar Republic.

The Allies also wished to be secure against future German attack. To achieve such security, the peace treaties severely limited the war-making ability of the former enemy nations. The Central Powers could have no air force, no tanks, no heavy artillery, no battleships. The German army—potentially the most powerful—would have no general staff, and would be reduced to one hundred thousand soldiers. All of them had to enlist for a twelve-year period so that they could build up no reserves as they had been able to do when Napoleon attempted to limit Prussia's army to the size of a police force.

The Treaty of Versailles was not written in the spirit of forgiveness. But the Peace of Paris also contained one very new and different element. This was the embodiment of Wilson's idealistic vision in the League of Nations. The League was to be a permanent consultative system between the victors and the neutrals, which the defeated would join at some later date. It was divided into an Assembly, in which each member state had an equal vote, and a Council, in which special weight was given to the great powers. It also (like its successor organization, the United Nations), had a Permanent Secretariat with headquarters in Geneva, in neutral Switzerland.

The mission of the League was to settle disputes between nations equitably and peaceably. Discussion was to replace force. Reason, not war, would decide international issues. The hopes were high—too high, the critics charged. And the performance of the League in later years gave substance to their charge. Yet in 1919, despite the hatreds that remained, despite the exhaustion of Europe, and despite the failure of the United States to join its own creation, the way seemed open to rebuild Europe.

The Great War's impact on modern memory was ultimately negative, however. European states were broken and never truly recovered. The irrational in the human race seemed to many to have triumphed. Of the 6,211,427 from Britain and Ireland who had enlisted during the war, 744,702 were killed and 1,693,262 were wounded: Although it might behave as though it were a great power, Britain—and even more so France—were never again nations of the front rank. The short, intense age of Progress, of belief in inevitable Reason, was over. The horror and pain were juxtaposed against a mythic and now illusory ideal and found to be more powerful. As an English poet of the war, Herbert Read, wrote in his ironic attack on the vision of the heroic soldier, war was no longer splendid, no longer a great adventure:

> He cannot shriek,
> Bloody saliva
> dribbles down his shapeless jacket.
> I saw him stab
> and stab again
> a well-killed Boche.
> This is the happy warrior....

The only poetic thing in the British army, Read said, was the army helmet, for it looked like an iron mushroom. Thirty-five years later the mushroom again became a symbol of destruction.

# PART SIX

# The Years That Became Ours: 1919 to the 1980s

*The Peace? Oh, that was the part in between.* —John Mulgan, New Zealand novelist, 1939

## AN OVERVIEW

Throughout most of Europe after the war the great desire was to return to "normalcy," to reestablish a sound civilian society and a prosperous economy. Yet, wartime passions did not exhaust themselves that easily, especially not in Germany and France, the great continental opponents of the war. And in all nations, the human losses suffered were felt for years to come. Millions of young people had been killed, and often the best and most talented were missing. Considerably more officers than enlisted men had died—in Britain's case, the proportion was nearly three to one—so that it was perhaps not surprising that Europe suffered from a notable absence of leadership in the 1920s.

Economic recovery had to surmount not only the immediate physical destruction of the war, but some of its long-range consequences as well. All of the European belligerents had gone heavily into debt between 1914 and 1918; most of the overseas holdings of the Central Powers had been confiscated, while many of the British and French foreign investments had to be liquidated to pay for the war. Foreign trade was badly disrupted. Many of Europe's markets abroad had been taken over by the United States or, to a lesser extent, by Japan. The war's dislocations resulted in minor recessions in the early twenties, and in a major series of inflations. These ranged from some striking price increases in Great Britain to astronomic ones in Germany, where the price of a morning paper rose from 10 pfennigs in 1920, to 150,000 marks on September 1,

1923, to 25 million one month later and to eight billion on November 8, when the inflationary spiral was finally broken.

Against this background of spiraling inflation, political radicalization took place. Italy went fascist in 1922, and Russia remained communist. Both ideologies were imitated in other countries. Sizable fascist groups were organized in southeastern Europe, Germany, and France, and short-lived communist revolutions occurred in Hungary and the German state of Bavaria in 1919.

Despite these trends, the search for normalcy was on the whole a successful one. The bloody and uncompromising Bolshevik regimes in Hungary and Bavaria did not survive, and fascism was quelled outside of Italy. The general fashion ran toward democratic republics or constitutional monarchies, not totalitarianisms of the left or right. The new German republic's constitution, drafted at Weimar, was adopted by parliamentarians representing an overwhelming majority of Germany's voters, and in subsequent years the new state tried to fend off attempts by various groups—Nazi, monarchist, and communist—to undermine or destroy it. The government of the new Czechoslovak Republic worked well; the new Republic of Austria developed a partially successful two-party system; and democracy was safe in France, despite the rise of native fascists and a near twenty percent vote that went to the Communist Party. Parliament still ruled in Great Britain, although there was a modest shift to the left so that the two-party system now meant Conservative and Labour, not Conservative and Liberal. All in all, there was free speech in Europe; the rights of the individual appeared to be secure once more.

Despite all obstacles economic recovery was taking place. The French, who had suffered the most intensive damage of the war, led the way in rebuilding. Between 1919 and 1925, they constructed some eight hundred thousand new houses and farm buildings, more than had been destroyed during the course of the war, which was evidence of one of the greatest economic achievements of postwar Europe. And others followed fairly close behind. Even the British, suffering both from the war and from a more general economic exhaustion, saw their production rise again, though on a more modest scale. In 1929, eleven years after the war's end, most of Europe was better off than it had been in 1914.

A new vitality also entered Europe's intellectual life; there was "a festival of the survivors," as one of the Dada group called it. It was the period of Pablo Picasso and Bertold Brecht, of experimentation in the arts, drama, and the novel. These were years so exciting that America's most innovative writers—Ernest Hemingway and Henry Miller, Ezra Pound and T. S. Eliot—preferred life in Paris, Rome, and London, while Thomas Wolfe considered Germany his second home.

Yet it was, in all, a dangerous excitement and a fragile recovery. Nations continued to behave as though they were great powers when, in fact, they lacked the resources to provide leadership. An event that began in New York in 1929 showed how true it was.

## VI. 1 The Hidden Political Collapse of Europe

> *An intelligent victor will, whenever possible, present his demands to the vanquished in installments.* —Adolf Hitler, *Mein Kampf,* 1924 (?)

### From Depression to War

In October 1929, after a month of ominous fluctuations, but also after years of unprecedented boom, prices on the New York Stock Exchange suddenly collapsed. Within weeks, the stock market disaster had affected the rest of the economy. Production and sales fell, banks as well as brokerage houses closed their doors, and the first of a long series of unemployment notices went out. The United States was entering the gravest economic crisis of its history.

The great depression quickly spread to other countries. The American disaster was turning into what many observers called the World Economic Crisis. The first European nation to experience a spectacular crash along American lines was Austria, where in 1931, one of the country's largest banks, the *Credit Anstalt,* went into bankruptcy. That same year, Great Britain, the world's banker for over a century, abandoned the gold standard and saw its pound sterling devalued by some thirty percent. Europe, too, was facing its most serious and universal economic crisis since the coming of capitalism.

Why had it happened? There is no shortage of explanations. They included the technical—the excessive use of margin buying in stock market speculation—and the eccentric—the influence of sunspots on the stock index. They included the modern Marxist explanation—that wealth was too unevenly distributed, that too many workers and farmers were unable to buy the products that the new machines produced, which created a glut—and a more old-fashioned explanation—that the depression was merely a sharpened form of the very ancient phenomenon of the business cycle. The war produced major dislocations in Europe's economy, especially by driving Britain into bankruptcy and destroying the common market in southeastern Europe that the Hapsburg Empire had provided. Modern machinery displaced human labor and created unemployment, for while industrial production in the twenties consistently rose, industrial employment just as consistently fell. Most important, the pyramid of war debts, reparations, and short-term American loans to Germany had created a vacuum at Europe's center.

No one explanation, obviously, could account for the exact origins of the Great Depression. It was more likely that a combination of them was responsible, though neither historians nor economists ever quite agree in their precise analysis of that combination. There is far less disagreement, on the other hand, about the depression's results. These meant disaster, especially on a continent that was just recovering from the effects of the war.

Production plummeted. The countries most affected were those that had led in productivity and income—the United States, Germany, Great Britain, Belgium, Holland, and France. In 1929, the American gross national product had been $114 billion. In 1933, it was $54 billion. Europe was even worse off. According to one estimate, production in 1932 was not quite 40 percent of what it had been in 1929. Prices, personal income, and trade were also decreasing. Between 1929 and 1932, the volume of international trade shrank by two-thirds.

Two sets of figures rose. One was bankruptcies. In Germany, for instance, these nearly doubled between the last predepression and the first postdepression year. The other was unemployment. At the depression's lowest point, some sixteen million Americans were out of work—one out of three workers. British and German figures were similar. In 1932, six million German workers, out of a total population of sixty million, lost their jobs. But even these figures did not tell the entire story, for only those who applied for unemployment compensation were counted. Those too proud or too ignorant to ask were not included. In the second place, the figures did not include those who were put on part-time shifts. If both these sets of figures were taken into account, it would be reasonable to say that in 1932 hardly more than two-fifths of Germany's labor force was working an eight-hour day.

The intangibles, faith and hope, suffered, too. The depression followed too closely upon the war; public mood could scarcely be other than one of dejection. No European government managed to cope with events in any sort of imaginative way. The best ideas that occurred to them were to raise tariff barriers, which did not help, or to cut government spending by letting state employees work shorter hours for less pay, a measure that could not invigorate the economy.

Thus, in many European countries the thirties was a period of social demoralization and political radicalization. There was no organized movement of revolt, no mass party of radical right or radical left in the United States, Britain, or the Netherlands. But elsewhere the story was different. The Communist Party clearly profited from the depression. In

1930, in Germany's first postdepression national election, the communist vote went from 3.25 million to 4.59 million; in France, it rose by several hundred thousand. Yet there it stopped. Several reasons accounted for the failure of communism in these two countries. In this period Moscow was exercising a direct, and often clumsy, control over foreign communist parties, which hurt their national image and their electoral chances. Middle-class voters were unwilling to support the communists in any event; the sole exceptions were some intellectuals who were attracted both by the Marxist interpretation of history and by the chance it offered for political involvement. The Labor vote was split, as it had been for some time, between evolutionary democratic socialists, and the revolutionary communists; for the most part the bulk of the vote still went to the former. Further, there was an appealing new mass movement to the right of fascism.

In Italy an earlier economic crisis, the first great postwar depression of 1921, may have played a role in bringing Benito Mussolini to power. The introduction of universal suffrage at the end of the war produced a socialist party, which was frightening the right. In southeastern Europe and the Baltic states, authoritarian tendencies were greatly strengthened by the events of 1929; by 1934, only Finland and Czechoslovakia managed to maintain their democratic institutions. The struggles of the new nations in this inter-war period produced new leadership. Fascist movements in Western Europe in particular were a depression-connected phenomenon. In Spain, Belgium, France, and elsewhere, what had formerly been fringe groups turned into strong movements. Nowhere was this more true than in Germany and Austria.

After 1929 Germany's Nazis captured an audience they had never before been able to attract—many of the merchants who had gone bankrupt, workers who feared for their jobs and craved job security, farmers who could no longer make a living from the land, college students who faced the prospect of years of unemployment. In 1928, the last year of prosperity, Adolf Hitler's Nazi Party had 12 deputies in the Reichstag out of a total of 491. In 1930, the first postdepression election, the number rose to 107 of 577. In the summer of 1932, it reached 230 out of a total of 608.

At the end of that year, as economic conditions were improving slightly, the number of Nazi deputies decreased slightly to 196. The figures were similar for Austria, where the number of registered members of the Nazi Party rose from 7,000 to 100,000 between 1928 and 1930. The appeal of National Socialism to the workers was, in a period of depression, especially clear.

These were dangerous years, then. Where democracy was firmly anchored—as in France, Britain, or Holland—the old order survived. Where it was not, the extremists' chances had never been better.

### The Soviet Union: Communism

The one country without unemployment worries, according to official figures, was the Soviet Union. By the 1930s, communist rule in Russia was firmly established, though it had undergone a series of basic changes since seizing power. When tsarism collapsed in the spring of 1917, a liberal regime, led by Aleksandr Kerensky (1881-1970) followed. Kerensky's government could not cope with Russia's most urgent problems, for Russia was hungry, and what scant supplies there were went to the war front. The Russian peasants, sensing change, were more anxious than ever before to seize the land, which they felt had been withheld from them after Emancipation. And nearly all Russians wanted out of the war. When Kerensky would provide neither land reform nor an end to the war, Russia's small Communist Party offered "Bread, Land, and Peace"; this was dubious Marxism and good politics. With the aid of superior propaganda, organization, and boldness, the communists, who represented perhaps two percent of all Russians, seized control of the country in October 1917.

Assuming power and holding it were not the same thing. As we have seen, Lenin's government took Russia out of the war early in 1918. The war at home was not so easily ended. The various opponents of Bolshevik rule, from Social Revolutionaries to former tsarist generals, fought the new regime in a bitter civil war. The advantage seemed to be with the Whites (as the anti-Bolshevik forces were called) because they started with better military leadership—few tsarist officers were willing to fight on the Red side—and had the active support of the Western Allies, who both wished to keep Russia in the war and to see Bolshevism defeated. But then under the leadership of Leon Trotsky, the communists organized a Red Army, which for all its original improvisation became a powerful fighting force. By 1921, the Civil War was over and the Red Army in command.

Despite its uneasy hold over the country, the regime set out to construct a model Marxist society. All industry was nationalized, and money disappeared as the state took over the distribution as well as the production of goods. Committees of workers ran the factories, and a similar vast experiment was then extended to the land. The peasants were mobilized against the rich, and peasant committees administered the seized farms. The regime opened the tsarist secret archives, repudiated Russia's debts, separated church and state, let students run the schools, and introduced a vast new literacy program to the illiterate countryside. These were exciting years, but they ended in failure. Too much had been tried in too short a time. The workers did not know how to run the factories, no more than the peasant communes could induce the farmers whose land they had seized to produce food. By 1921 Russia faced starvation and was

**Russia in Revolution, 1917-1921**

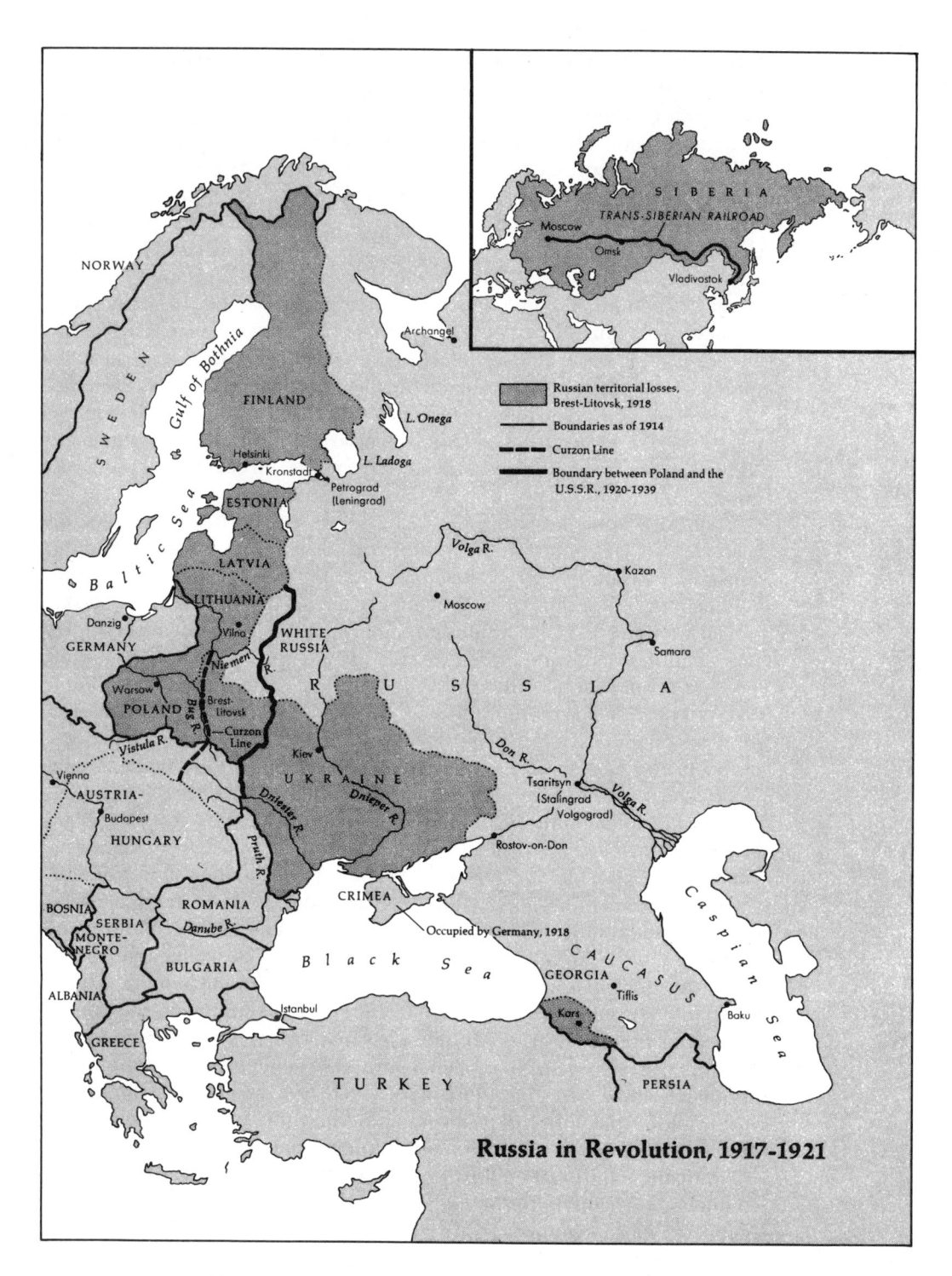

threatened with a degree of unrest. Even the secret police, which the communists had organized soon after their seizure of power, could not cope with this new situation.

Lenin now decided to change course. Under the New Economic Policy (NEP) proclaimed that year, he reintroduced a degree of capitalism to Russia. In industry, the state retained what Lenin called "the commanding heights," that is, the control of heavy industry, banking, transportation, and foreign trade, while small and even medium-scale private enterprise was permitted. The owner of a shop or factory might employ as many as twenty people and retain the profits. The same policy was applied to the land. The *kulak,* as the richer and more enterprising peasant was called, was encouraged to own or to rent land and to hire agricultural labor. Social and economic inequality was a fact of Russian life once more. While less than pure ideologically, the NEP made excellent sense pragmatically. During this period, which lasted until 1928, Russia made a great and badly needed economic recovery. The threat of starvation was gone.

Politically, however, these were troubled years. In 1924 Lenin died of a stroke; a fierce contest for succession broke out. The two leading contenders were Joseph Stalin (1879–1953), general secretary of the Communist Party, and Leon Trotsky, creator of the Red Army. Trotsky was an advocate of world revolution. There was no other way, he thought, that communism could be maintained in Russia. Stalin, on the other hand, felt that world revolution could wait, that "Socialism in One Country" was perfectly feasible. Although Trotsky was no stranger to political intrigue, Stalin proved the superior tactician; by 1929, Trotsky lost every party post he once held, and was banished to Siberia. This began a long exile that ended with his murder in Mexico City, in 1940.

Stalin terminated the NEP. In its place, he proclaimed a Five Year Plan in 1928, the first in a series. Its objectives were to collectivize and mechanize agriculture, and to industrialize the Soviet Union. When some of the *kulaks* resisted collectivization, Stalin declared war on them. He said in a 1929 speech that they were to be "liquidated as a class." How many of them were killed in the process, how many starved or died along the deportation routes, we can only estimate; the minimum number would seem to be five million. The land was turned into collective farms run by managing boards loyal to the Party, whose task it was to oversee the members' work and to turn over to the government a fixed amount of produce at fixed rates; the remainder would be distributed to the members according to the work performed. Because the system meant an end to the farming of tiny strips of land, it offered new efficiency. So did the government's organized effort to manufacture modern farm machinery and make it available to the collectives.

In the cities, an industrial Five Year Plan destroyed the capitalist class created by the NEP as thoroughly as the *kulaks* had been driven from the land. State planning, management, and ownership once more took the place of private enterprise. The industrialization of Russia was begun in earnest. The first Five Year Plan, as well as the succeeding Plans, achieved some impressive results. Steel mills and power plants went up all over Russia; production of chemicals, building materials, heavy machinery, and railroads was vastly increased. Between 1928 and 1940 Russia's urban population nearly doubled, growing from 18 percent to 33 percent. By the end of that period, too, Russia's industrial production was approaching that of the West, even though the Russian standard of living was infinitely lower. Russia concentrated on capital goods rather than on consumer items. Still, in the overall view, what had taken the West from the middle of the nineteenth to the beginning of the twentieth century to achieve, Russia had done in a dozen years.

Russia had done so at a heavy price. Part of the price was the abandonment of some basic Marxist tenets—equality and internationalism. As for the concept of equality, a new class of privileged Russians came into existence in the thirties. It included the managers of the factories and the collective farms, bureaucrats, and those artists and intellectuals who were willing to serve the new regime. Their monetary rewards as well as their social position made them a new elite, raising them far above the mass of ordinary Russians. As for the concept of internationalism, a distinct conservatism characterized the thirties. The stress was on Russia's history and traditions. Earlier experiments in easy divorce and progressive schools were slowly abandoned. The Communist International was changed from an assembly of equals into a Russian-directed institution. The worker had a fatherland once more, and it was Russia. Peter the Great became nearly as much of a hero as Engels, and when the Red Army created new medals they were named after tsarist generals. The high point of the new Russian nationalism came in World War II, when the *Internationale* was abandoned as the national anthem.

The price was the establishment of a governmental system as oppressive as tsarism had ever been. This was true despite the passage in 1936 of a Soviet Constitution, which on paper offered all the freedoms of a Western democratic state. Because only one party existed and that party controlled the state, and was controlled in turn by one man, Stalin, the Constitution's promises were empty. The regime had an utterly ruthless secret police at its disposal that in the mid-thirties conducted a series of show trials as well as a mass terror that were without precedent in the nineteenth-century Russia of the Romanovs. Starting in 1935, they arrested large numbers of leading communists, accused them of various crimes against state and party, and executed them. Among those killed in the purges were the men who had shared power with Stalin in the twenties, including every member of the Party's executive committee, the

*Politbureau,* except for Stalin and Trotsky. Among those shot were fifty of the seventy-one members of the slightly larger Central Committee of the Communist Party. Among those who vanished were Russia's leading generals and admirals, the prime ministers of all non-Russian Soviet Republics, and two successive heads of the secret police who had been in charge of earlier purges. The number of arrests, and of subsequent prison sentences, exiles, or executions of less prominent Russians ran into millions. The most recent historian of the great terror has estimated the figure at twelve million; the exact figure will never be known.

Stalin emerged from these years with vast new powers. He became more of a father figure than any Romanov Tsar since Peter, became leader, mentor, generalissimo. Avenues and factories were named after him, as were entire towns. A later communist regime in Russia called such idolatry the "cult of personality," and the term understates the case.

## The Rise of Fascism

The cult of personality also characterized Europe's fascist regimes of the thirties, although publicly they were communism's most bitter enemies. In Italy, Mussolini's fascism became less easygoing than it had been in the early twenties, had abolished the last vestiges of parliamentary rule, turned to active aggression abroad, and throughout it all, staged a *Duce* cult which, while theatrical, correctly indicated Mussolini's vast powers. In Portugal, Antonio de Salazar (1889–1970) ran the country's affairs as undisputed sole leader. In Spain, a civil war brought an authoritarian military regime to power that after an initial period in which power was shared by several generals, was led by 1938 by one man alone—Francisco Franco (1892–1975), chief of government, regent, generalissimo, supreme leader—the *Caudillo*. In the Baltic states, strong rightist prime ministers governed without the aid of parliaments. In southeastern Europe the fashion became royal dictatorships, although sometimes—as in Romania—one purpose of such autocratic rule was to keep more extreme right-wing forces from seizing the government. Indeed, all of the dictatorships of the 1930s arose with the excuse of preventing some form of extremism.

The most extreme kind of Fascism was found in Germany. It was the National Socialism, or Nazism for short, of Adolf Hitler (1889–1945). Unlike Stalin or Franco, Hitler came to power not by revolution, coup d'etat, or civil war, but by ostensibly legal means. On January 30, 1933, he was appointed Chancellor of Germany by the President of the Republic. He was the leader of what had been, for over a year, the country's strongest single party. And it no longer seemed possible to block his appointment. However, Hitler was forced to accept a majority of non-

Perhaps the most famous painting from the 1930s was the work of the Spanish artist Pablo Picasso, who depicted the horror of the bombing of an unarmed civilian population in his mural of *Guernica*. Source: *The Museum of Modern Art, New York*

Nazi, conservative ministers in his coalition cabinet, who might restrain him.

Within a matter of months, these men had either been removed or neutralized, and Hitler had transformed his chancellorship into a dictatorship. Germany was changed from a democratic republic into Hitler's concept of the state—a state was governed by the absolute authority of one leader. He had achieved this transformation by terror; concentration camps and strong-arm squads appeared early in his regime. He had achieved his position in part by an appeal to patriotism; he promised that if given the necessary authority, he would free Germany from the humiliations of Versailles. Fear of communism also contributed. He had achieved a dictatorship in part by an appeal to the country's deep instinct for order. He did not mean to end freedom, he said, but the confusion of the multi-party system and the inefficiency of parliamentary rule. And Hitler had achieved his position by tackling Germany's most pressing economic problem. When he took power, nearly six million Germans were still on unemployment relief; less than a year later, a million of them found work, and by 1936 there was nearly full employment in Germany.

Like the Russians, the Germans now had a government that might be accused by its opponents of violating most of the democratic decencies, but in reply, it could point to some solid achievements. Not only was economic prosperity returning; a number of the formerly unemployed were working on some spectacular programs. One was the *Autobahnen,* a set of super-highways whose construction Hitler was sponsoring. Another was the development by the government of a cheap car at a time when the automobile in Europe was still a privilege of the rich. Its original name was the Strength-Through-Joy car, after the Nazi Labor organiza-

*The automobile age* would free individuals and families to reach out into the countryside; the automobile would become the single most important symbol of modern industry; too many automobiles, and the pollution they brought, would also remind man that an improved technology does not invariably produce an improved life. *Source: E.P.A Documerica–Blair Pittman*

tion which arranged inexpensive vacations and other workers' benefits; in time it was renamed the people's car (or the *Volkswagen*).

Nor were material gains all. There was a feeling of community, a sense of belonging, that met the spiritual needs of many. The Nazis achieved this by intoxicating mass meetings, which resembled religious revivals more than prosaic political assemblies. They furthered this unity by providing their followers with uniforms and titles—in a country that had long been extraordinarily fond of both. Hitler was utterly serious about breaking out of the restrictions of Versailles, and as he did so—from the reoccupation of the Rhineland to the reintroduction of universal military service and rearmament—none of the victors of 1918 tried to stop him. In the foreign sector as in the domestic, Nazi triumph seemed to follow triumph.

David Lloyd George, British Prime Minister from 1916 to 1922, and the man who had done as much as any individual to defeat Imperial Germany in World War I, summed up the change in the Autumn of 1936:

> Whatever one may think of Hitler's methods—and they are certainly not those of a parliamentary country—there can be no doubt that he has

achieved a marvelous transformation in the spirit of the people, in their attitude toward each other, and in their social and economic outlook.... It is not the Germany that followed the war—broken, dejected, and bowed down with a sense of apprehension and impotence. It is now full of hope and confidence and a renewed sense of determination.... There is for the first time since the war a general sense of security. The people are more cheerful. There is a greater sense of general gaiety of spirit throughout the land. It is a happier Germany.

Hitler made no secret of his intention to govern with a strong hand. Many Germans had given him their vote for precisely that reason, for they were tired of parliamentary bickering and inaction in the face of crisis. But many had not voted for the *Führerstaat* that Hitler now instituted. Under it, all authority derived from the leader, all ultimate decisions were made by him. Those that were not were to be decided in his spirit—whether in politics or in the arts, whether in education or in law. As a lawyer, for instance, said in a speech to German judges in 1939:

In any decision you make, ask yourself, 'How would the Führer decide in my place?' In any decision that is your responsibility, ask yourself, 'Will it be in harmony with the National Socialist spirit of the German people?' If you do that, your conscience will rest on a firm, an iron foundation, and you will imbue your actions with the authority of the Third Reich, which derives from the unity of the National Socialist body politic with the eternal validity of the will of the *Führer,* Adolf Hitler.

Hitler's Third Reich proclaimed itself a total state, in which every activity was organized and made to serve Nazi aims.

The abundance of Nazi organizations created much duplication of effort. Behind a facade of a perfect, well-functioning order, there was much inefficiency. Yet one organization, at least, worked well enough: The apparatus of the political police. During the twelve years of Nazi rule, many acts of nonconformity and resistance took place. However, except for the churches, which retained some limited freedom of action due to Hitler's caution in this field, little organized public opposition to Nazism ever appeared. What worked chillingly well, too, was the implementation of that part of the Nazi program that was closest to Hitler's heart—the eradication of "the racially undesirable."

The first group of people to be systematically killed by the state were the mentally ill. Acting on nothing more than a brief written order signed by Hitler, an organization was established that between the fall of 1939 and the summer of 1941 rounded up, and then killed by starvation, infection, or gassing, about one hundred thousand patients from Germany's mental hospitals. When the program was abruptly halted, apparently because a German Catholic bishop was brave enough to protest from the pulpit, the staff's experiences were put to use on another, larger project—killing Jews in those parts of Europe that came under Hitler's control.

As a young man in Vienna, Hitler had absorbed both the ideas of pseudo-Darwinism and of anti-Semitism. They were ideas that guided him for the rest of his life. In his autobiographical *Mein Kampf (My Struggle)*, begun in 1924, he wrote:

> If one were to divide mankind into three species: the culture-creators, the culture-bearers, and the culture-destroyers, only the Aryan would be likely to fit the first definition. It is to him that we must trace the foundations and the walls of all that human beings have created. . . .
>
> The most powerful antipode to the Aryan is the Jew. . . . No, the Jew possessess no culture-creating ability whatever, since he does not, and never did, have that quality without which men cannot truly develop toward a higher order: idealism; therefore, his intellect will never act as a constructive force. . . .
>
> He is and remains the typical parasite, a sponger who, like a malign bacillus, spreads more and more as long as he will find some favorable feeding ground. And the consequences of his existence, too, resemble those of the parasite: where he appears, the host nation will sooner or later die.

Hence, the "host nation" must expunge the bacillus. These were not idle words. The philosophy of National Socialism was hazy and changeable; as a system it never possessed anything resembling the precise theoretical foundations or the rigorous ideological definitions of Marxism. But Hitler's racial views were immutable, as was his determination to act on them. By a series of measures begun in 1933, the German Jews were deprived of civil rights, were excluded from a long list of professions, and were forced to wear a yellow star of identification. After 1941, thousands were deported to the East—along with other European Jews under Nazi control—where they were either worked to death or exterminated. In this way six million European Jews died at Nazi hands.

The price of national happiness, then, was the creation of the Total State, and the eradication of those who were assigned no place in it. The price was war. The price was a mortgage on the future.

## VI. 2  The Second World War:
## An Era of Continuous War for Continuous Peace

*Since this century's beginning, a time of tempest has seemed to come upon the continents of the earth.* —Dwight D. Eisenhower, 1953

The 1920s seemed to be a decade of international reconciliation as well as one of domestic recovery. If old antipathies did not suddenly vanish, many leaders were determined to prevent the rise of conditions that would lead to another 1914. Their most notable efforts were embodied in two great documents. One was the Treaty of Locarno, signed in that Swiss town in 1925. In it, Germany, France, and Belgium agreed not to alter their mutual borders by force, and Britain and Italy agreed to act as guarantors, who would come to the aid of the aggrieved party should any violation of the Locarno promise occur. Because neither France nor Belgium desired any territorial changes, what Locarno meant was that Germany voluntarily accepted the new borders that had been imposed at Versailles. In return, the Western powers admitted Germany into the League of Nations a year later. The villain of the war became the associate at Geneva.

The other great document was the Kellogg-Briand Pact of 1928, named after the French foreign minister and the American Secretary of State, who were the first to sign it. Sixty-five states, including Soviet Russia and all the antagonists of the war, signed it. The treaty called for nothing less than the renunciation of war as a means of national policy. The lesson of 1914 seemed learned. No quarrel between nations was ever again to be resolved by killing and maiming millions. Yet Kellogg-Briand merely established a principle without providing any penalties against those who might violate it.

In the thirties, a dozen years after Versailles, the spirit of conciliation was broken. Force and arbitrary action became the fashion once more. The trend began not among the old European adversaries, but in the Far East.

### Origins

In 1931, Japan's technologically superior forces took advantage of a weaker China and invaded Manchuria, which set an example that caught on. Soon Europe's two fascist powers, Germany and Italy, engaged in a series of unilateral treaty violations and acts of aggression that ended in general war. In 1933, Hitler took Germany out of the League of Nations; two years later he abrogated those parts of the Versailles Treaty that limited Germany's military sovereignty. Germany was openly building a great new army and a formidable air force. In the spring of 1936, units of that new army moved into those parts of the Rhineland that were supposed to remain demilitarized under the terms of the peace settlement.

That same year, the three powers that intended to change the international status quo—Germany, Italy, and Japan—became treaty partners. Japan followed the occupation of Manchuria with an invasion of China proper. In 1935, Italy began its invasion of Africa's last independent monarchy, Abyssinia, and within a year completed its conquest. In Europe from 1936 to 1939, the Spanish Civil War caused both Italy and Germany to actively intervene on the nationalist side, and the Soviet Union to intervene, though on a smaller scale, on the side of the government. Then, in 1938, the initiative was Hitler's once more. That spring German troops occupied Austria, and the Nazis proclaimed the *Anschluss* (union) of Austria with Germany, which the victors of 1918 had expressly forbidden at Paris. To some this was a joyous sort of occupation; a majority of Austrians were said to have welcomed the Germans. Hitler's next move, however, did not come off as smoothly. In the fall of 1938, Hitler told the world that he intended to take radical action if the Czechoslovak Republic did not agree to the incorporation of its Sudeten region into Germany. The area's population of some three million German-speaking people, he said, was being terrorized by the Czechs, and he was ready to take them under his protection. In the end the crisis was resolved by a four-power conference—Germany, Italy, France and Britain—which convened at Munich. Hitler's demands were met. Unopposed, German troops moved into the Sudeten region. Within six months, two major areas in central Europe had been incorporated into Hitler's Reich.

Munich was the high point of Hitler's unbloody triumphs. It was also the low point in the Western powers' ability to deal with aggression. Yet Munich merely represented a difference in degree. From the first, the West had responded to the new mood of the thirties either with inaction or with covert encouragement of the aggressors.

The West had countered the Japanese invasion of Manchuria with nothing more than a League of Nations resolution condemning it. It had met Germany's illegal rearmament with the same kind of verbal disapproval and nothing else. During the Abyssinian war, the League did vote to impose economic sanctions against Italy, but it then implemented the sanction in so loose a fashion that Italy lacked no essential supplies. In the Spanish Civil War, the West responded to foreign intervention by pretending that none existed. In the Austrian annexation, it limited its

**Europe on the Eve of World War II, August 1939**

response to verbal protests. And in the Czech case, it helped to persuade the Czechs to cede the territory that Hitler demanded without resistance.

The West's motives were neither cowardly nor thoughtless; national memories of the previous war and its often pointless sacrifices were still strong; a second world war seemed like the worst of all conceivable disasters. It would exhaust Europe and leave the Soviet Union as the only power to profit. The West's leaders, especially the British Prime Minister,

Neville Chamberlain (1869–1940), felt that they could avoid war only if they met some of the legitimate desires of the restive nations. In any event, they were not ready for war and needed time to rearm. It seemed legitimate to some extent that Italy and Japan, both of them dynamic nations, should want to expand their power. It was also reasonable for Germany to want to both undo the wrongs of Versailles and to gather all Germans into one Reich. To many, appeasement seemed preferable to a new mass slaughter; better Munich than Verdun. Appeasement might have worked in the cases of Italy and Japan, whose aims were traditional and possibly negotiable. Only in the German case was it clear that appeasement truly failed.

The reason for this failure was that a chasm existed between Hitler's announced aims and his true ones. Hitler's actual purpose was not the correction of Versailles, of which he spoke publicly and often, nor even the protection of Germans living beyond the Reich's borders; it was the acquisition, by force if necessary, of large territories of Eastern Europe never before held by Germany, of *Lebensraum* or "room to grow in." "To demand the borders of 1914 is political nonsense of such degree and

One of the figures most responsible for the world as it is today was the German Chancellor, *Adolf Hitler*, here seen on his way to the Berlin Opera House with his chauffeur in March of 1939, in the week Hitler annihilated the state of Czechoslovakia. *Source: Wide World Photos*

consequence that it appears a crime," he had written in *Mein Kampf.* "The borders of 1914 meant nothing to the German nation.... We National Socialists, by contrast, must without wavering keep to our foreign policy aim, which is to secure the German nation the soil and space to which it is entitled on this earth."

The Western leaders, if they had in fact read *Mein Kampf,* hoped that this was a younger Hitler speaking, that the responsibilities of power had moderated his aims. Hitler, for his part, did what he could to confirm the West in that illusion. All he wished to do, he said in speech after speech, was to let the Wilsonian right of self-determination apply to Germans, too. "I want no Czechs in the Reich," he said at the height of the Sudeten crisis. But in truth he did; his earlier aims were unchanged. He still wished to expand eastward, and he wished to do so by war. He told his highest military leaders in 1937, Germany needed colonizing space in the East as much as ever, and "the only way of solving the German question is the way of force." The rest was tactics, "Circumstances have forced me to talk for decades about practically nothing but peace," he explained to a group of German newspaper editors in a confidential speech in 1938. "The reason that for years I talked about nothing but peace was that I had to."

In Hitler's eyes, Munich thus was not quite the triumph it appeared to the rest of the world. He did not just want the Sudeten area; he wanted to destroy the Czech state. In March 1939, after staging a series of "incidents," he blackmailed—by threatening to bomb Prague—the Czech president into asking for German protection, and under that pretext ordered German troops to invade Czechoslovakia. The Czechoslovak Republic created at Paris in 1919 ceased to exist. The Czech part was named Bohemia and Moravia and was attached to the Reich as a protectorate; the Slovak part was given nominal independence, though it obviously relied on Germany for its survival.

That was the end of appeasement. This step was too brutal and too sudden for even the most vocal advocates of that policy to accept. In April 1939, the British issued a public treaty guarantee for Poland, Hitler's next obvious victim. A German press campaign had started against Poland, which held some ethnically German territory, and which was unwilling to return Danzig—established at Versailles as a Free City—to Germany. France and Poland were already allied. The warnings were clear—a German attack on Poland would mean a European war.

As a result, Hitler wavered during the summer of 1939. While he wished to move against Poland, he did not want to provoke a general war. Hitler's mixture of fixed, irrational ideas combined with sound common sense and political genius misled his contemporaries. He was eager to unleash a war in the East that would enable the Germans to settle and rule while the Slavs would serve or be destroyed, but he was far from eager to start a world war that Germany might lose. In August, he thought he had an answer to his dilemma. Both Berlin and Moscow announced that Nazi Germany and Soviet Russia—mortal ideological enemies for years—had concluded a pact of friendship and nonaggression.

Hitler induced the Russians to sign the pact by the addition of secret provisions in which the Soviet Union was promised the eastern half of Poland, control over the Baltic states, and increased influence in the Balkans. Thus the Russians would regain what they lost after World War I. Hitler did not think the price too high, for he expected the pact to dissuade the British and French from intervening in the Polish war he was about to start—for with Russia either pro-German or at least neutral, how could the West aid Poland?

Thereupon, Hitler hurled the German army into Poland and by September 1, the two nations were at war. Half a week later, after frantic diplomatic activity designed to persuade the Germans to undo their action, Britain and France, to Hitler's surprise, honored their treaty obligations to Poland and declared war on Germany. Twenty-five years and one month after the opening of what now was seen to have been only the first World War, the second World War had begun. World War II was even longer and more destructive than its predecessor.

### The War

The war began, as it had in 1914, with a German plan. This time the plan worked. Hitler's generals had prepared for a lightning invasion, a *Blitzkrieg,* of Poland. Headed by mechanized divisions, and supported by overwhelming air power, the German divisions poured across the border. The Polish army was outgunned and outmanoeuvred. On September 17, the Russians insured a German victory by invading Poland from the east. On September 27, less than four weeks after the start of the invasion, Warsaw surrendered to the Germans.

This still left Britain and France in the war. But the Germans remained passive in the West for the time being; the winter of 1939 to 1940 was called "the phony war." Now that he had achieved his Polish victory, Hitler was hoping to make peace with the Western powers. While he did not mind the prospect of fighting the French, he had never really wanted to go to war against Britain. In his eyes, the British were ethnic kinfolk and Germany's natural allies. When his peace hopes proved illusory, however, he struck again, with great speed, precision, and complete surprise.

In April 1940, the Germans suddenly turned north and invaded Denmark and Norway. The Danes offered no resistance. The Norwegians did but were defeated in a matter of days. The Germans now had excellent bases for their air and submarine war against England.

A month later, German armies invaded Holland and Belgium, outflanking the formidable French defense works of the Maginot line. By the end of May German motorized troops were deep in northern France, racing first to the channel ports opposite Britain and then moving toward Paris. In mid-June, the French quit the battle, asking the Germans for an armistice, which was signed on June 22, 1940 at Compiègne, at the same spot and in the same railroad car where the armistice of November 11, 1918 had been signed. France had been defeated by Germany's superior military organization, poor French leadership, and poor French morale. More than half of France, including Paris, came under German occupation, and the unoccupied part—its temporary capital, the small resort town of Vichy—was governed by an authoritarian, collaborationist regime under an aged Marshall, Henri-Philippe Petain (1856–1951).

The British, threatened as they had not been since the days of Napoleon, changed political leadership. Neville Chamberlain, whose name seemed identified with appeasement, was replaced by Winston Churchill (1874–1965). There was no doubt about his resolve and ability to fight on. In the midst of French collapse, the British had also managed to withdraw most of their expeditionary force from the beaches around the French port of Dunkirk. Even more important, the British Royal Air Force was successfully meeting a determined effort by Germany to defeat them in the air. Nor had all the French surrendered to the Germans; from London, General Charles de Gaulle (1890–1970) organized a Free French force that rejected the armistice and continued resistance. It was his vision that "France overseas" could still liberate European France.

Hitler was poorly served by his Axis partner, Italy, giving rise to muted optimism in the Allied camp. In June 1940, Italy joined Germany in the attack on France; in October 1940, in his anxiety for some victories of his own, Mussolini began to invade Greece. The campaign went badly, and in the spring of 1941, Hitler was compelled to come to his partner's assistance. In so doing he had to move through Yugoslavia, where a pro-German Yugoslav government seemed ready to grant a right of passage to German troops. A coup overthrew that government in April 1941, and Hitler resorted to force. Once more he won, but it was a costly victory. He had extended the war far beyond his original intentions—he had wanted no Balkan front—and continuing partisan warfare in Yugoslavia would tie down many of his troops. His Yugoslav campaign delayed, by crucial months, another Eastern Campaign—one he had already planned. This was the war against Russia.

On December 18, 1940, Hitler issued a special order to his generals. Its essential sentence read, "The German armed forces must be prepared to crush Russia in a quick campaign (Operation Barbarossa) before the conclusion of the war with England." Two major reasons, one immediate, the other long-range, caused Hitler to turn on his treaty partner of 1939.

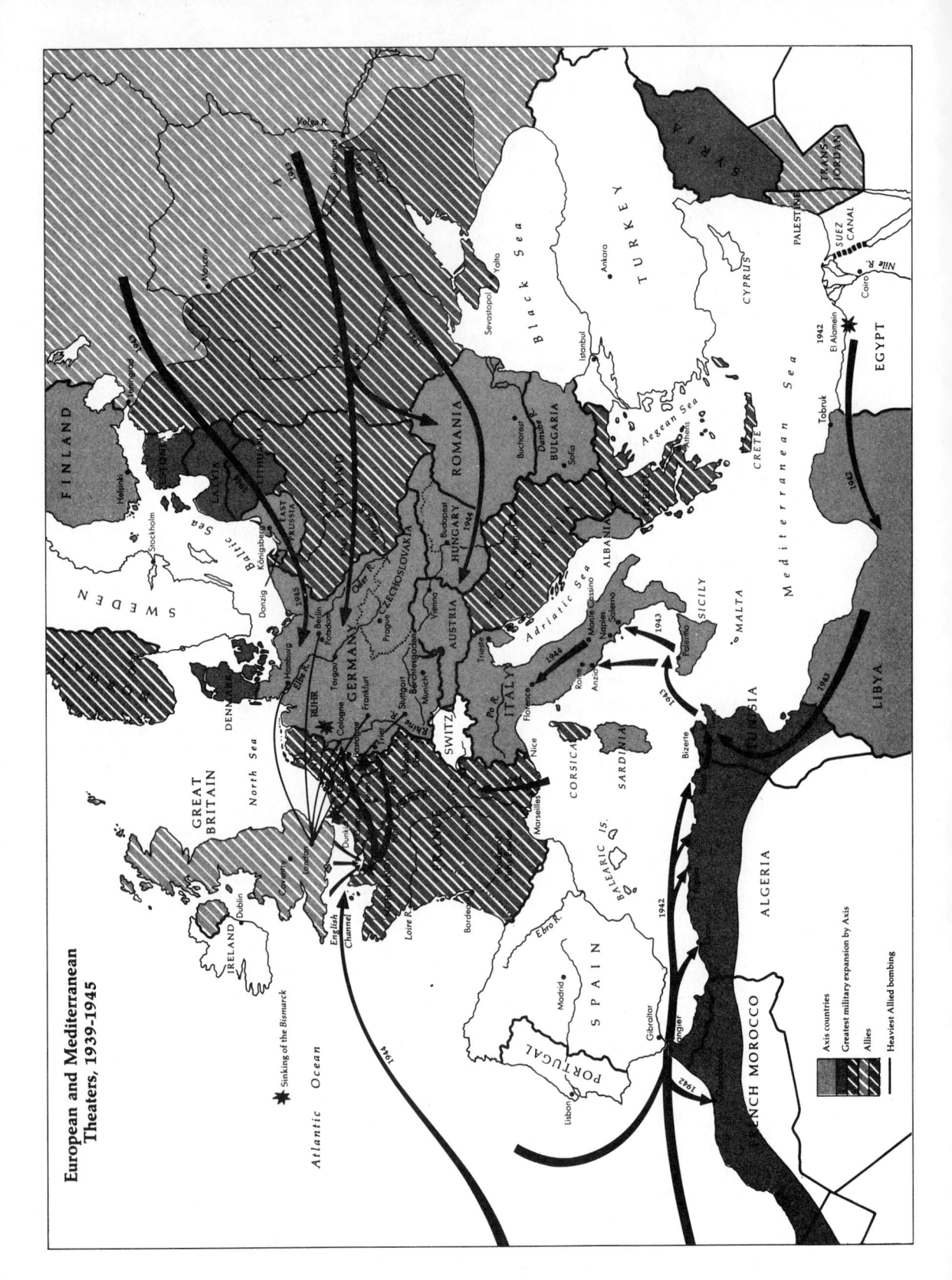

**European and Mediterranean Theaters, 1939-1945**

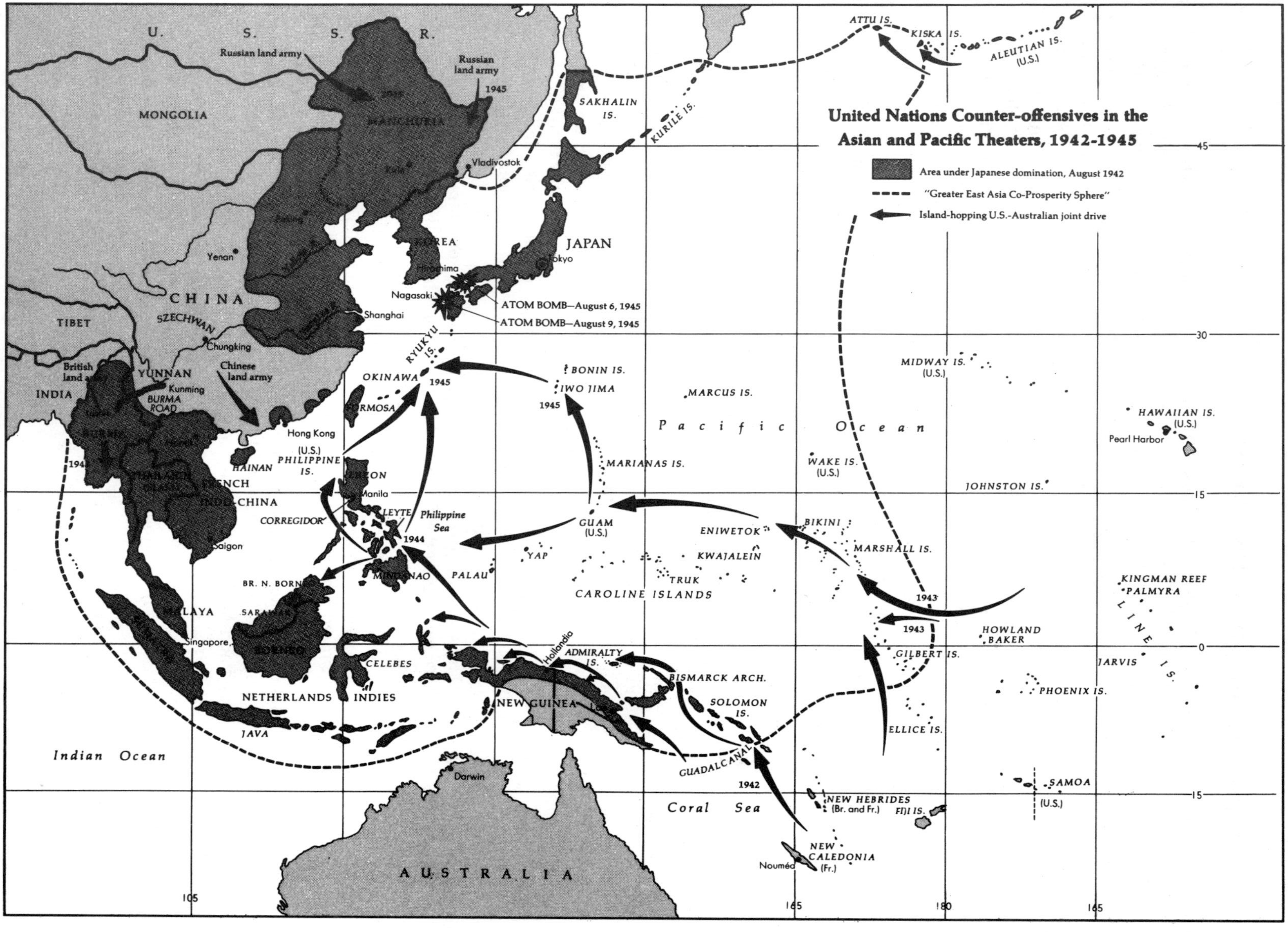
United Nations Counter-offensives in the Asian and Pacific Theaters, 1942-1945
Area under Japanese domination, August 1942
"Greater East Asia Co-Prosperity Sphere"
Island-hopping U.S.-Australian joint drive
U. S. S. R.
Russian land army
Russian land army
1945
MONGOLIA
MANCHURIA
SAKHALIN IS.
KURILE IS.
ATTU IS.
KISKA IS.
ALEUTIAN IS. (U.S.)
Vladivostok
KOREA
JAPAN
Tokyo
Hiroshima
Nagasaki
ATOM BOMB—August 6, 1945
ATOM BOMB—August 9, 1945
Yenan
CHINA
TIBET
SZECHWAN
Shanghai
Chungking
British land army
YUNNAN
Kunming
BURMA ROAD
INDIA
Chinese land army
RYUKYU IS.
OKINAWA
1945
FORMOSA
Hong Kong
(U.S.) PHILIPPINE IS.
HAINAN
FRENCH INDO-CHINA
LUZON
Manila
CORREGIDOR
LEYTE
Philippine Sea
1944
Saigon
MINDANAO
BR. N. BORNEO
SARAWAK
BORNEO
MALAYA
Singapore
CELEBES
NETHERLANDS INDIES
JAVA
Indian Ocean
BONIN IS.
IWO JIMA
1945
MARCUS IS.
Pacific Ocean
MARIANAS IS.
GUAM (U.S.)
YAP
PALAU
ENIWETOK
KWAJALEIN
TRUK
CAROLINE ISLANDS
BIKINI
MARSHALL IS.
MIDWAY IS. (U.S.)
WAKE IS. (U.S.)
JOHNSTON IS.
HAWAIIAN IS. (U.S.)
Pearl Harbor
KINGMAN REEF
PALMYRA
LINE IS.
HOWLAND
BAKER
JARVIS
1943
1943
GILBERT IS.
PHOENIX IS.
ELLICE IS.
SAMOA
(U.S.)
Hollandia
ADMIRALTY IS.
BISMARCK ARCH.
SOLOMON IS.
NEW GUINEA
GUADALCANAL
1942
Coral Sea
NEW HEBRIDES (Br. and Fr.)
FIJI IS.
NEW CALEDONIA (Fr.)
Nouméa
Darwin
AUSTRALIA
45
30
15
0
15
105
165
180
165

One was that the Russians were pressing too hard for concessions in the Balkans as well as in the Baltic states. The other was that Hitler had never abandoned his original aim of conquering space so that Germans could settle in the Soviet Union. "Fate itself," he wrote in *Mein Kampf*, "seems to give us a hint here. By surrendering Russia to Bolshevism, it robbed the Russian people of that intelligence which, in the past, created and safeguarded Russia's existence as a state. . . . The huge empire in the East is ready to collapse." As the campaign began, he said to his chief of military operations, "We only have to kick in the door, and the whole rotten structure will come tumbling down."

The structure tottered but did not fall. Attacking on a two thousand mile front on June 22, 1941, and aided by three new allies—Finland, Hungary, and Romania—the Germans were at the gates of Leningrad and within miles of Moscow by autumn. They had also conquered the Ukraine and taken hundreds of thousands of Soviet prisoners. And their Asian ally, Japan, while refraining from attacking the Soviet Union, was now actively intervening in the war.

The Japanese had been taking advantage of Hitler's victories for their own purposes. They drove deeper into the Chinese mainland and used the defeat of France to move into French Indochina. Then, on December 7, 1941, they attacked the power that had been most adamant in its opposition to Japanese expansion, the United States. Originally Hitler had not wanted America in the war. He had reacted to a considerable amount of American aid to Britain—from the supply of much essential war material to the transfer of fifty destroyers—with notable restraint, for he felt it was worth trying to keep America at least nominally neutral. But when the Japanese attack on Pearl Harbor came, Hitler was "delighted," and within a matter of days, both Germany and Italy joined Japan in declaring war on the United States.

The war was growing beyond the dictators' potential to control it. There was war in the Far East, in Russia, and in North Africa, where the Germans and Italians engaged in desert combat against the British. As in World War I, the larger the scale and the longer the action, the more the superiority in resources on the part of Britain and its empire, and of the United States, was bound to show. As in World War I, an intensive German effort to disrupt allied shipping by means of submarine warfare failed. And also like World War I, the Germans had not won their Russian campaign. As the winter of 1941 set in, they were stymied short of Leningrad and Moscow, the Russian government had not fallen, and Russia's industrial capacity was beginning to exert itself. Nor were the German's prepared for Russia's bitter winter. Their plans had called for a short war, to begin in the spring. The Yugoslav campaign had postponed that date by three months, and they now had to improvise a far longer campaign amid conditions that had defeated more than one invader before them.

Further, if Russia's mud and cold were not enough to check the Germans, their own occupation policy was.

In some areas of Russia, the Germans originally were accepted readily enough by the Russian population; in others, they were welcomed as liberators. Nazi attitudes soon changed that. No material concessions, Hitler's instructions went, were to be made to the Russians. They were Slavs, and thus "subhuman," and to be treated as such. As one of the Nazi leaders sent to govern occupied Russia told his officials, "We are a master nation which must consider that racially and biologically, the least German worker is a thousand times more valuable than the local population." The figures on Soviet prisoners of war tell the story and explain why even those Russians who had no love for communism soon saw no alternative except to fight the Germans with all the strength at their command. The total number of Russian prisoners taken by the Germans came to 5,160,000. Of that number, 1,981,000 are recorded to have died in German prisoner-of-war camps, mainly of starvation and exposure. Another 818,000 were released to civilian or military status—usually to serve, much against Hitler's wishes, as auxiliary troops in the German service. Sixty-seven thousand escaped. Another 1,241,000 were not officially accounted for or were exterminated—a Hitler order condemned active Communists to "special treatment," that is, to death at the hands of his secret police. The total number of those actually surviving as prisoners of war was 1,053,000, or 1 in 5.

In 1942 there was another German advance into Russia, while the Japanese did well in the Pacific. And while the Americans were beginning to check the Japanese, a great offensive in the summer of 1942 took the Germans to the oil-rich region of southeastern Russia. But then one of the fiercest of the war's battles, which lasted from December 1942 to January 1943, brought the first great German defeat at Stalingrad. Two hundred thousand German soldiers marched into Russian captivity. It was the beginning of the end for Hitler and his allies.

In the summer of 1943, Allied armies, after ejecting the Germans and Italians from North Africa, invaded Italy. In September the Italians surrendered. While the Italian campaign had not been the decisive success that some had hoped because the Germans continued to hold northern Italy, intensified partisan warfare—especially in Yugoslavia and France—further weakened the German hold on Europe. And on June 6, 1944, a major second front was launched against the Germans with the Western Allies' invasion of France. On August 25, Paris was liberated. Soviet armies, meanwhile, had expelled the Germans from Russia proper and were beginning to advance into Poland and the Balkans. As 1945 opened, the Allies had reached the borders of Germany.

Action on land was supported by a fierce air war, the main target being the enemy's industrial plants, as well as the civilian population. Many

With the testing of the *atomic bomb* at the Pacific atoll of Bikini in July, 1946 —a placename that would frivolously be given to the briefest of bathing suits —modern man came to recognize the symbolism of total destruction, the mushroom cloud. *Source: Wide World Photos*

German cities were turned into rubble, yet the Germans showed the same resilience under bombardment that the British had shown earlier. The Germans counterattacked in the Ardennes Forest of Belgium and, in the Battle of the Bulge, as the last great engagement of the European war was known, temporarily threatened to throw back the Allied advance.

But by the late spring of 1945, Germany's heartland was under assault from both West and East. American, British, and French forces had crossed the Rhine, and the Russians were advancing on Berlin. On April 28, 1945, American and Russian troops met at the river Elbe. Two days later, Hitler committed suicide in his Berlin bunker. One of his last mad acts had been to order the flooding of the city's subways, which would delay the Russians; the flooding drowned many thousands of Berliners who had taken refuge from the fighting in the subway stations. On May 7, Hitler's high command travelled to Rheims, in France, to sign the unconditional surrender that the Allies had demanded.

The European war was over. The end to the war in the Far East followed more rapidly than expected. Heavy American air attacks, which culminated in dropping two atomic bombs, the first on Hiroshima, brought the Japanese surrender in August 1945. The Pacific war was over as well.

The cost of World War II was even greater than that of World War I. The Russians alone lost seven million military dead; the Germans, half that number. (The United States, by contrast, lost 190,000.) The total military deaths exceeded fifteen million. Civilian deaths—resulting mostly from bombing and planned extermination—while impossible to tabulate with precision, equalled at least that number.

## VI. 3 The West Since 1945

> *Surely the task of statesmanship is more difficult today than ever before in history. . . . The distance between what we know and what we need to know appears to be greater than ever*—Walter Lippmann, American political commentator, in *A Preface to Politics*, 1913.

### *Pointing to the Future*

The shape of postwar Europe was determined during Allied summit conferences held during the war. The two most important conferences were those that took place at Yalta, in the Russian Crimea, in February 1945, and at Potsdam, Prussia's former capital, five months later. The Russians, whose troops by that time were advancing deep into Poland and southeastern Europe, were assured of controlling those areas in the future. The Russians made two counter-concessions: Russia, which had remained neutral toward Japan, agreed at Yalta to enter the war in the Far East within two months of the end of the war in Europe. This seemed a major concession to the West because the war against Japan appeared far from won. Indeed, Russia's promise seemed valuable enough for the West to offer an added inducement to Moscow—an agreement to let Russia recover the Far Eastern territories that it lost to Japan in the War of 1905. The second Russian concession was a promise to hold free elections to institute representative governments in the areas under the control of the Red Army. The Western leaders were sceptical about accepting Russian assurances but because neither they nor the nations they led were willing to remove the Russians by force from Poland, Hungary, Romania or Yugoslavia, it was difficult to conceive of any credible alternative.

Yalta and Potsdam also provided three major territorial changes in Europe, which affected the Soviet Union, Poland, and Germany. Russia could extend its borders westward into Poland and Germany by some two hundred miles. The new Russo-Polish border would follow the so-called

Curzon line, the frontier contemplated by the Allies after the First World War before the Poles added to their holdings by fighting the still weak Bolshevik forces. Thus Russia was allowed to keep the eastern half of Poland that had been assigned to it under the secret terms of the Nazi-Soviet Pact. Russia also was given part of German East Prussia, Königsberg—the ancient coronation city of Prussia's kings—which was renamed Kaliningrad. Poland was compensated for its losses to Russia by annexing German territory. The Polish border, like the Russian, moved some two hundred miles to the west, and the rivers Oder and Neisse formed the new border between Poland and Germany. Theoretically the area was placed under Polish administration only, pending the negotiation of a final peace settlement. Thus, up to seventeen million people were displaced in one of the largest mass migrations in history. But a generation has passed since the end of the war, and no such peace conference has been held. Yalta and Potsdam also provided for the division of Germany into four occupation zones. There were three at first—Russian, American, and British. A fourth was then added at the insistence of the West, and it was to be administered by the French. Germany had not only lost the war and more continental territory than it had in 1919, it had ceased to exist as a sovereign state.

The year 1945 also marked the nadir of geographical Europe's power. Its fate, symbolically enough, had largely been determined from outside the continent. Of the two superpowers that emerged during the war, the Soviet Union was only partly European, and the other, the United States, was three thousand miles away from Europe. The decisive votes were cast

*Joseph Stalin* was the leader of the Soviet Union in 1945. During World War II Russia had fought with the allied powers against Germany; shortly, Stalin would be perceived to be an enemy. *Source: Wide World Photos*

by Joseph Stalin, Franklin Delano Roosevelt, and after him by Harry S Truman, the next President of the United States.

The decline of Europe extended into the immediate postwar period. The continent seemed as incapable of defending itself against a possible Soviet attack as it was of affecting any true economic recovery without substantial American aid. "Does Europe Have a Future?" was the title of an American book that attracted attention, and negative answers, in 1946. But the decades since showed that such pessimism was ill-placed. As had happened time and again since the rise of ancient Greece, European civilization (of which America was very much a part, in many ways) reasserted itself.

True, much of Europe was in ruins at the end of the war. Europe's industrial capacity and its political power seemed gone. The whole continent, wrote an American historian, "was in a position in which the First World War had left Vienna ... a former world capital in danger of becoming a slum." Yet with the help of the United States, it did not. As soon as hostilities ceased, America sent millions of dollars in immediate (and piecemeal) aid to Europe, preventing the worst in starvation and disease, if not initiating any true recovery. But in 1947 the United States embarked on a systematic and long-range aid program to Europe, named after the Secretary of State, George Marshall (1880–1959). The Marshall Plan's motives were mixed, as is true of any political action. Simple humanitarian impulses united with the less sentimental desire of reestablishing American markets in Europe and saving the continent from communism by making it prosperous. (The offer of similar aid to the USSR and Eastern Europe thus seemed less than sincere.) Enlightened self-interest rather than pure philanthropy accounted for the Marshall Plan; even so, history had known few instances of self-interest quite so enlightened or so generous.

Nor had it known many that were as successful. Within a remarkably short period production revived, and by the early 1950s, it reached and exceeded prewar levels and has continued upward ever since. The continent where the Industrial Revolution had originated had not, after all, lost either its desire for material goods or its ability to manufacture and distribute them. The story of the Marshall Plan and of the subsequent spectacular recovery of Europe can be told in pages of statistics. It can be told, a quarter of a century later, in terms of problems created, of pollution, clogged highways, and of a spiritual disenchantment with technology, all by-products of a shared prosperity. Or it can be summed up by the recollections of an American economist and management consultant, Peter Drucker. In 1947, he frequently was asked to give a basic lecture entitled "Can Europe Survive?" Ten years later, his most popular lecture was "How to Meet the Threat of European Competition."

## The Cold War

Europe's recovery took place against a background of international frictions. The wartime alliance between the Western nations and Russia almost immediately gave way after 1945 to an active antagonism that became known as the Cold War. Europe was divided, largely along the military lines that prevailed at the end of the war, into communist and noncommunist spheres. Russian armies occupied eastern and central Europe as far as the Elbe River, this controlling the Balkans and splitting Germany in two. American, British, and French armies controlled much of Europe's western and southern half. These lines, which reflected the advances of the various armies in the closing phases of the war, by and large remained the same in the years that followed. What most alarmed the West was that, as in 1815, the Russians seemed anxious to extend their domination even further. Winston Churchill expressed the fears of many when in the spring of 1946 he said in a speech at Fulton, Missouri:

> From Stettin in the Baltic to Trieste in the Adriatic, an iron curtain has descended across the Continent.... Nobody knows what Soviet Russia and its Communist international organizations intend to do in the immediate future, or what are the limits, if any, to their expansive and proselytizing tendencies.... I do not believe that Soviet Russia desires war. What they desire is the fruits of war and the indefinite expansion of their power and doctrines.

The Russians were clearly not content with the kind of diplomatic influence they possessed in Eastern Europe. Instead, they were exercising

It was *Winston Churchill,* the British war-time leader who had fallen from office at the end of World War II, who most persistently warned the West against the danger to its security posed by Soviet Communism. Here he is seen addressing the members of the "Congress of Europe" as it met in The Hague in 1948. *Source: Wide World Photos*

a direct, often brutal, control over the internal affairs of what were, nominally at least, independent states. Thus, in just about every area where the Red Army was present, the promise of free elections that was made during the war was discarded, and communist governments were established that took their directives from Moscow. The eastern part of Germany, which in theory was merely occupied by the Russians, was in fact detached from the rest of the country and placed under communist rule. In Czechoslovakia, which had tried to steer a relatively independent course—it followed the Soviet Union in international affairs while it maintained a semblance of Western democratic procedure domestically—the Soviets supported a coup that replaced the country's old leadership with an uncompromising communist dictatorship in 1948.

After the crudely executed Czech coup, the West's policy was one of containment. While Russian rule over non-Russian areas could not be pushed back, at least for the time being, it could be kept from spreading. One of the first, and largest, steps toward this end was abandoning the idea of keeping Germany weak for years to come; instead, the West encouraged rapid German recovery. In 1947, as a means toward this end, the three Western zones of occupation were merged, and a year later a major currency reform was introduced, which set the stage for the country's economic revival. The Russian answer was to close off all land routes to the Western-occupied sectors of Berlin, the former capital. Although Berlin was surrounded by Russian-occupied territory, it was administered by all four powers. The West, thereupon organized an unprecedented airlift into their sectors of Berlin, supplying a city of over two million people entirely by airplane. It accompanied this technical feat by a counter-blockade of the Russian-occupied part of Germany. By the spring of 1949 the Russians lifted the blockade of Berlin. Yet other Berlin crises followed; here as elsewhere it was one of the characteristics of the Cold War that few issues were ever definitely settled.

The West also embarked on a large, overall policy in the pursuit of containment, a policy of clear warnings backed by the creation of military alliances. At Fulton, Churchill also had said:

> From what I have seen of our Russian friends and allies during the war, I am convinced that there is nothing they admire so much as strength, and there is nothing for which they have less respect than for weakness, especially military weakness.

The Western policy-makers took Churchill's advice. They would have to contain further Russian expansion. The first concrete application of containment was the Truman Doctrine of 1947. A communist takeover seemed to threaten Greece, the one country of southeastern Europe not under Soviet control. Nor did Turkey seem safe, whose access to the Dardanelles had long been the object of Russian ambitions. Yet the

British, who had traditionally tried to protect that part of the world from Russian expansion, were no longer able to do so. Even though impoverished by the war, they had embarked on an ambitious and expensive welfare state scheme at home. In this situation, the United States agreed to assume Britain's role. President Truman (1884-1972) declared that the United States was ready to halt any Soviet designs on Greece or Turkey, and Congress appropriated $400,000,000 for their defense, while authorizing the dispatch of American military advisors and equipment.

Following the Czech coup, America's involvement in the defense of Europe became even more intensive. In the spring of 1949 the United States, together with most of the noncommunist powers of Europe, formed the North Atlantic Treaty Organization. NATO's origins had been European. In the Treaty of Brussels, concluded a year earlier, Great Britain, France, and the three Benelux nations (Belgium, the Netherlands, and Luxembourg) had concluded a fifty-year alliance against outside aggression. In April 1949, the United States formally joined the Brussels powers, along with Canada, Iceland, Denmark, Norway, Portugal, and Italy. Later, Greece and Turkey joined these original contracting powers, and finally the Federal Republic of Germany (West Germany). An armed attack on one was to be considered an armed attack on all, and a multinational military organization was then established to coordinate the defense of the West. In many ways, NATO was more sound than substance. It had few divisions in the field; in terms of conventional military forces it was clearly inferior to the Russians for many years. Cooperation between the various allies was often tenuous; this was most dramatically shown when General Charles de Gaulle became president of France and forced NATO headquarters to move from Paris to Brussels. A Western diplomat said of NATO in its early days, "[NATO] is a pious lie, but fortunately the Russians have believed it."

If they did not, they certainly took America's nuclear backing of NATO seriously enough to do their utmost to catch up. In 1949, the Soviet Union broke America's nuclear monopoly by exploding its first atomic bomb. And in 1955, the Soviets organized the European states under their control into the Warsaw Pact, thus confronting the Western military alliance with its Eastern counterpart.

This division of Europe into Eastern and Western blocs, into hostile alliances and hostile ideological systems, long outlasted the immediate postwar period. Changing the status quo was simply too fraught with risks. The ceaseless development of modern weapons, from atomic bombs to hydrogen bombs to rockets to intercontinental ballistic missiles, had created a balance of terror by the mid-fifties that made any direct military confrontation between the superpowers awesome to contemplate. This new technological weaponry added a new element of danger to the most routine of diplomatic crises. But the principal influence of the new technology was restraint, even if it did allow the lines of 1945 to harden. Each side was capable of destroying the other several times over—a situation that everyone was sufficiently aware of to let caution prevail.

Thus the Russians yielded on the Berlin blockade, and on a number of subsequent crises, such as one over a communist-controlled Cuba. Thus, too, the West did nothing to support a number of uprisings that broke out in Eastern Europe against communist domination. The first of these occurred in East Germany in 1953, when there suddenly appeared the chance of greater freedom after Stalin's death in that year. The uprising was followed in 1956 by near revolutions in Poland and Hungary, the Berlin Wall in 1961, and later, in 1968, by an attempt to introduce a more liberal though a still communist regime in Czechoslovakia. Each of these efforts was defeated by armed Soviet intervention and greeted by inactivity on the part of the West. Eastern Europe remained in the Soviet sphere.

The exceptions were Yugoslavia and Albania. When Marshal Josip Broz Tito (1892–1980) broke with Stalin in 1948, the West sent Yugoslavia much material aid so that he could maintain his independence from the Soviet Union. But Yugoslavia was unusual. It was the one Balkan country that had liberated itself from the Germans, and that had no large Russian army stationed in its territory. It was fiercely independent, and plainly ready to fight the Soviet Union if need be. Its Dalmation coastline made it possible for the West to send supplies. Nonetheless, while not Stalinist, it was a communist state. Albania gravitated from Soviet to Chinese communism.

Yet there developed, cautiously in the sixties and more determinedly in the early seventies, a feeling that the Cold War was a matter of the past. In part this was because the West had achieved so many of its aims. The political and economic recovery of Europe had taken place, which ended Russian hopes of further continental expansion. In 1945, an American diplomat at Potsdam offered Stalin his congratulations on the Red Army's reaching Berlin. Stalin's response was, "Tsar Alexander got to Paris." After NATO, there were no more such Russian replies. Russia had not only been contained; it had been persuaded to withdraw from two areas. One was Iran, which Russian troops, bowing to Western pressures, evacuated in 1946; the other was Austria, which the Russians left in 1955, in return for a promise of neutrality and heavy reparations. But there was another, weightier reason why the Cold War was relegated to the past. This was the recognition of the futility of constant confrontation; there was at least a limited convergence of interests between East and West that made détente possible.

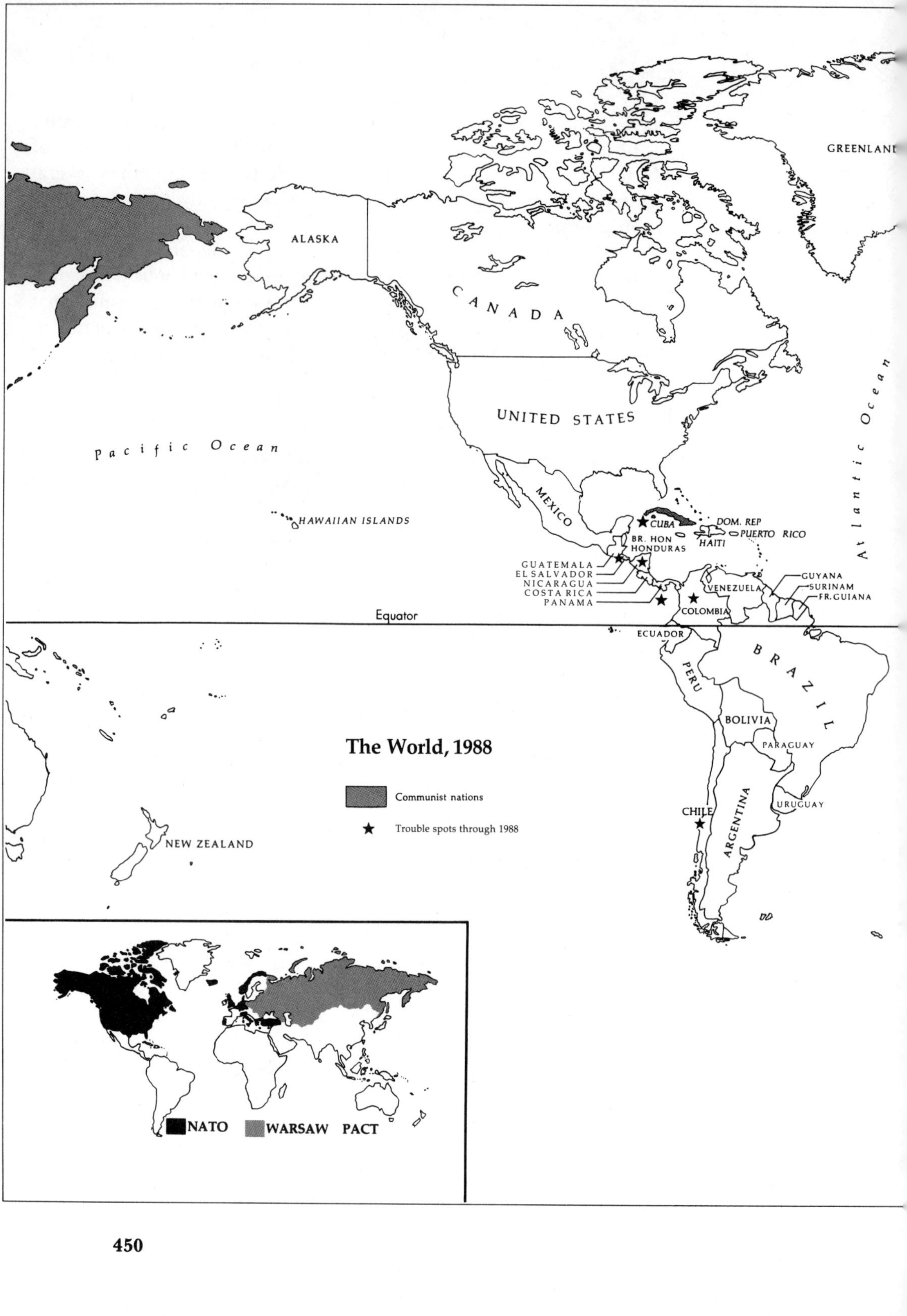
The World, 1988
Communist nations
Trouble spots through 1988
GREENLAND
ALASKA
CANADA
UNITED STATES
Pacific Ocean
Atlantic Ocean
MEXICO
HAWAIIAN ISLANDS
CUBA
DOM. REP
PUERTO RICO
HAITI
BR. HON
HONDURAS
GUATEMALA
EL SALVADOR
NICARAGUA
COSTA RICA
PANAMA
VENEZUELA
GUYANA
SURINAM
FR. GUIANA
COLOMBIA
Equator
ECUADOR
PERU
BRAZIL
BOLIVIA
PARAGUAY
URUGUAY
CHILE
ARGENTINA
NEW ZEALAND
NATO
WARSAW PACT

ICELAND
UNITED KINGDOM
EIRE
NORWAY
SWEDEN
FINLAND
DEN.
NETH.
BEL.
L.
E. GER.
POLAND
W. GER.
CZECH.
FRANCE
AUST.
HUN.
SW.
ROM.
YUG.
BUL.
ITALY
ALB.
SPAIN
PORTUGAL
GREECE
TURKEY
U.S.S.R.
MONGOLIA
CHINA
N. KOREA
S. KOREA
JAPAN
KASHMIR
TIBET
BHUTAN
NEPAL
MOROCCO
IFNI
TUNISIA
LEBANON
ISRAEL
SYRIA
IRAQ
JORDAN
IRAN
AFGHAN
PAKISTAN
INDIA
BANGLA-DESH
BURMA
TAIWAN
ALGERIA
LIBYA
EGYPT
SAUDI ARABIA
OMAN
MAURITANIA
MALI
NIGER
CHAD
SUDAN
YEMEN
SOUTHERN YEMEN
N. VIETNAM
THAI.
CAM.
S. VIETNAM
PHILIPPINE IS.
SENEGAL
GAMBIA
BURKINA FASSO
GUINEA
NIGERIA
DJIBOUTI
ETHIOPIA
SIERRA LEONE
LIBERIA
IVORY COAST
GHANA
TOGO
DAHOMEY
CENTRAL AFRICAN REPUBLIC
CAM.
EQ. GUINEA
GABON
REP. OF CONGO
CABINDA
UGANDA
RWANDA
KENYA
SOMALI REPUBLIC
SRI LANKA
MALAYSIA
NEW GUINEA
WEST IRIAN
ZAIRE
BURUNDI
TANZANIA
MALAWI
DIEGO GARCIA
Indian Ocean
INDONESIA
PAPUA
ANGOLA
ZAMBIA
MOZAM-BIQUE
MADAGASCAR
MAURITIUS
RHOD.
SOUTH WEST AFRICA
BOTS-WANA
SWAZILAND
LESOTHO
REPUBLIC OF SOUTH AFRICA
AUSTRALIA

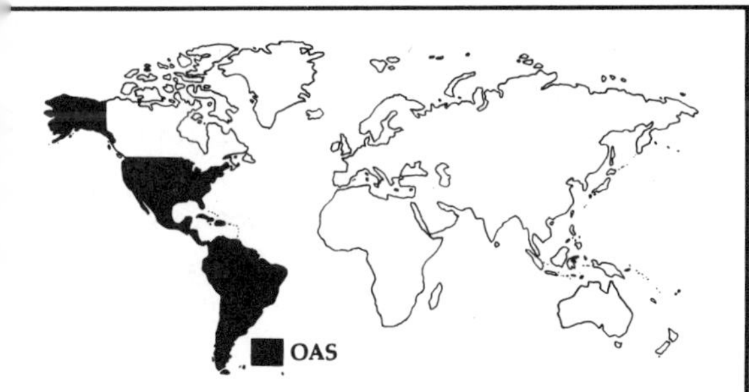
OAS

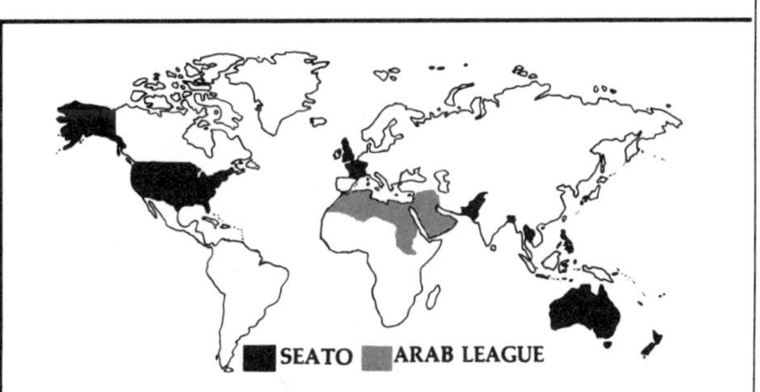
SEATO
ARAB LEAGUE

*International Organizations*

One organization that was expected to help resolve Cold War tensions proved to be a disappointment even to its most fervent well-wishers. This was the United Nations. The idea for a new international organization to replace the League of Nations had first been discussed between the Allies during their wartime conferences; its formal charter was written and adopted in 1945 in San Francisco. The organization's initial membership was relatively small; it contained only the victors of World War II. Over the years the membership grew, and included nearly all the nations of the world except neutral Switzerland. In purpose and organization the UN closely resembled its predecessor. Like the League, its stated function never was to serve as a world government. Instead, its aim was to maintain peace and develop closer ties among its members. Like the League, too, the UN was organized into a General Assembly and a Security Council and was provided with a Permanent Secretariat. It was also given supervision over a number of specialized, functional international agencies, from an International Labor Organization to an International Finance Corporation, from an Educational, Scientific, and Cultural Organization to a Universal Postal Union. In the General Assembly, which was free to discuss any issue of international interest, all members were equal, with one vote for each.

In the Security Council, they were not. Here there were five permanent members—China, France, Great Britain, the USSR, and the United States—plus six others elected for two-year terms each by the Assembly. All votes in the Security Council, which was given the final decision over major matters affecting international order, had to be unanimous. What this has meant is that any one of the major powers could—and frequently would—veto any decision it had cause to dislike.

But the power of the veto has been only one among several reasons for the UN's lack of determining influence. There has also been the fact that a substantial part of its transactions have been public, so that the UN has tended to be a propaganda forum rather than a place where the essentially quiet and private business of effective diplomacy might be carried out. Its membership has grown to such proportions—over a hundred and thirty nations joined by the 1970s—that concerted actions became nearly impossible. And from the very beginning, it lacked an army or a police force to oversee its decisions. The result has been that where it did decide to intervene as in Korea, Palestine, or the Congo, it had to borrow an army from designated member nations, who were then tempted to pursue their national goals rather than UN policies.

Not that the UN's record, any more than the League's, has been only a series of failures. Some of its specialized agencies have done admirable work. The World Health Organization has helped to prevent cholera epidemics. The Food and Agricultural Organization has done yeoman service in increasing agricultural production in India; the International Bank for Reconstruction and Development has expended funds to aid nations in industrializing. The United Nations acted to neutralize potential sources of trouble by dispatching its borrowed forces—especially in the Middle East and the Congo. Beyond that, it may have decreased the risk of accidental wars by providing a permanent forum for the discussion of international affairs and by helping for the first time to shape world opinion. Even some of the public vituperation exchanged may have had its therapeutic value. "Better jaw jaw than war war" was Churchill's summary.

Equally important was what Europe accomplished independently of the UN, especially by its establishment of a Common Market. Its beginnings go back to 1952, to the creation of a European Coal and Steel Community between France, Germany, Italy, and the Benelux countries. More than one person deserved the credit for it. The idea was a Frenchman's, Jean Monnet (1888–1979); its implementation would have been impossible without the enthusiastic support it received from Germany's Chancellor Konrad Adenauer (1876–1967), or from Belgium's Foreign Minister Paul-Henri Spaak (1899–1972). There was the need, dictated by a sense of realism, to let Germany revive without allowing it to dominate the continent economically. There was the wish on the part of German and French leaders to make a new beginning, to put an end to the automatic Franco-German hostility of the past. The Marshall Plan demonstrated the benefits to be derived from international cooperation.

Two new yet old principles reappeared in Europe. One was the partial surrender of national sovereignty, the other was the acceptance of planning on an inter-European scale. And while some of the Coal and Steel Community's specific decisions caused obvious hardships, the Community was so successful that in 1957 it took the next step. Under the Treaty of Rome it extended the coal and steel pact to all industry and trade. Starting in 1958, a European Economic Community was established. Gradually all existing barriers to trade were abolished in the Common Market area. The target date was 1970, by which time all legal obstacles to the free flow of industry and commerce were to be removed—whether customs duties, import quotas, cartel agreements, or restrictions to the free flow of labor and capital between the member nations. The Community also agreed to abolish all economic barriers between them and to adopt a common tariff against the rest of the world. Thus the Common Market has to some extent been a discriminatory organization.

In the European Community's initial years, Great Britain—having a special relationship with its empire and commonwealth, and fearing both continental economic competition and the possibility of continental political union—attempted to oppose it. The British did so by forming a more loosely grouped counter-organization, the European Free Trade Area (or EFTA), comprising Britain, Denmark, Norway, Sweden, Switzerland, Austria, and Portugal. When Britain then tried to reverse its policy and join the Common Market, its admission was blocked by France. But by the early seventies that opposition gave way to cooperation, and Britain, Denmark, and Ireland joined the Common Market.

Despite the difficulties and dislocations that common planning and the abolition of protective tariffs meant for individual industries, especially for agriculture, the rate of economic growth provided under the Community was spectacular. For years that growth rate consistently outpaced the United States and provided a degree of prosperity to the ordinary European that was without precedent. While that prosperity was due to the individual performance of the member nations and might have occurred even without existence of the Common Market, the Community did add an essential element to the creation of Europe's new wealth. This was the recognition of the need for mass production, and hence for mass consumption and mass distribution. In a small country such as Belgium, mass production did not pay because there could be only limited consumption; but with goods, labor, and capital moving freely in an area as large as the Common Market, modern technology could be used to its greatest advantage.

The Renaissance of Europe since 1945 has included a new awareness of its past. This European awareness has not obliterated national distinctions. The political, constitutional, and socioeconomic approaches of the various European nations have shown considerable variety. Thus after the war, the British opted for the welfare state, and in so decisive a fashion that Conservative as well as Labour governments were obliged to maintain it for nearly forty years, until Prime Minister Margaret Thatcher (1925– ), who was elected in 1979, reversed the trend. West Germany, on the other hand, under Christian Democratic leadership, opted for a predominantly free enterprise system—though one that offered extensive state social services—and was so successful that the socialists, when they came to power, preferred abandoning Marx to abandoning the market economy. England continued as a loose constitutional monarchy, while West Germany, following the defeat of Nazism, established a parliamentary democracy. And France, after de Gaulle assumed power in 1958, largely patterned its government after the American presidential system. Italy returned to its pre-Mussolini addiction to frequent governmental crises, while Holland continued its tendency of political stability. Thus for all the Common Market's common shelter, the economic development of its members was by no means equal. As the seventies opened, the French

GNP, for instance, exceeded Italy's by some 60 percent, and Great Britain's by 30 percent. As one Frenchman wrote, "Great Britain declines in an orderly fashion, France advances in confusion." Yet for all these differences, a new European spirit prevailed. The two old enemies, Germany and France, were, however tentatively, on the same side, their armies to a considerable extent integrated into NATO. War between them had become as unlikely as war between the United States and Canada. One of Napoleon's judgments moved from the realm of rhetoric to that of reality: "Europe is but one province of the world. When we make war, we make civil war."

By the 1980s, then, Europe was on the verge of becoming a genuine third force. With generally healthy economies and stable social systems, with currencies that were prevailingly strong in relation to the American dollar (the currency that had dominated postwar markets), and with political systems that tended to move toward the center, Europeans had fully recovered from most of the scars of World War II. This recovery had taken two generations or more, and the memory of the Holocaust had left deep emotional trauma in several societies. Separatist movements, most notably in Northern Ireland and in Spain, contributed a fear of intermittent violence to the United Kingdom and the Iberian peninsula. But on the whole Europe was, as a bloc, ready to play a major role once again.

Most strikingly, however, Europeans could no longer think of themselves or their history as isolated, separate from the rest of the world. Western historians who attempted to write about "Western civilization" after 1945 found themselves constantly having to bring Asia, Africa, and Latin America into their accounts. General histories of the world since 1945 devoted three-quarters of their space to non-Western developments. While there were still highly distinct characteristics that, taken collectively, defined a sense of Western civilization, these characteristics were being modified rapidly. Much of the traditional life of east Asia had become "Western" in its reliance on high technology, and while traditional modes of social organization remained dominant in the Near East and Africa, there too daily life was changing under the impact of the new technology. Europeans and North Americans, in turn, were being transformed by a heavy influx of immigration from the non-Western world—by non-Western languages, social customs, diet and leisure activities, and much else.

If the nations of western Europe had changed rapidly during the forty years after World War II, those of eastern Europe had changed far less. Nonetheless, they were changing, and in the 1980s dramatic shifts in the Warsaw Bloc nations and in the Soviet Union itself gave rise to the hope of lessened tensions in the Western world. Substantial economic and some political liberalization in Hungary, the creation of a sustained opposition in Poland based on the trade union movement and known as Solidarity, and the slow emergence of Bulgaria and even Albania from behind their barriers spoke of greater trade and of some exchange of ideas.

Most dramatically, the Soviet Union appeared to be on the verge of significant change. By the mid-eighties a clear trend toward polycentrism—that is, toward the emergence of separate power centers in both the eastern European satellite states and in some of the ethnically diverse Soviet socialist republics—had combined with economic problems and a destructive interventionist war in Afghanistan to force the Soviet leadership to reexamine its priorities. The choice of a tough, Westernized, much younger leader, Mikhail Gorbachev (1931– ), as party leader in 1985 ushered in a period of *glasnost,* or greater openness, largely within Soviet society itself but to some extent also with the West. Modest dissent, some public demonstrations against government policies, and more economic freedom were the initial domestic products, while on the international scene the Soviet Union and the United States moved toward the signing of an arms limitation treaty.

Issues of poverty, oppression, and Marxism remained basic in many parts of the world, of course. Repetitive small-scale wars in Central America, the continued dominance of Marxist regimes in Cuba and of right-wing militarist regimes in Chile, and growing unrest in Mexico, where population growth had gone far beyond the capacity of the economy and of social services to cope, promised continued instability in the Western Hemisphere. These islands of insecurity, by-products of the age of imperialism, were likely to remain in the headlines for years to come.

## The End of Empires

The existence of a new European mood had not meant that problems affecting both individual states and the continent as a whole had vanished. Two problems in particular tested the ability of governments to survive. One was decolonization, the other a certain revival of political extremism. The fifties through the early sixties was a period that saw a radical reversal of the previous century's imperialist expansion. One after another, the colonized territories tried to establish their independence from European control. From Guinea to Somalia, from Morocco to India, the flags of France, Britain, Italy, Holland, Belgium, and Portugal came down. In their places were hoisted the newly designed flags of the newly sovereign states. By the mid-eighties, no substantial area was under colonial rule, although the racially discriminatory regime prevailed in the Republic of South Africa.

In the final analysis imperialism has been more a cluster of attitudes than an economic or political policy. The recipient of the good and ill that imperialism brought, whether Bantu, Apache, Maori, or Malay, became one of "the wretched of the earth," a person who knew that life's fundamental decisions were being made somewhere else by people who might or might not understand his or her needs, frustrations, and desires, by a people alien, self-imposed, and white. Thus racism became inextricably mixed with the imperial experience, until Britishers forgot that the epithet "Wog" (Westernized Oriental Gentleman) was a dirty word, one of the many in the vocabulary of imperialism.

This was an expanding vocabulary, which was able to accommodate terms of racial opprobrium and encompassed the outright appropriation of native lands to crown, federal government, or company, while speaking of the protection of native rights. Imperialists had been a paradoxical people, for that which they practiced was a paradox: Imperialism brought immense benefits to millions, equally immense burdens to yet other millions; the experience of imperialism to those who controlled and to those who were controlled was a mixed one. One cannot yet speak of a "balance sheet of imperialism," for this implies that Western standards may continue to be used to pass judgment upon a 500-year experience. It is as though one might award a point system to the colonial power that built good roads, provided education, sanitation, and peaceful frontiers, and at the same time massacred innocent women and children. But if it is patently unfair for the imperialists' heirs to judge the fruits of their fathers at this time, it is equally unfair for the victims to report their sole patrimony as victimization.

Not until the imperial revolution has played out the century can one suggest—and then only upon standards other than those we use now—what the fundamental influence of imperialism has been. The words, the rhetoric, and the thought processes of imperialism have become the heritage of us all—black, white, European, North American, and African—who attempt to understand the intricacies of the human experience. Imperialism was a state of mind. As he lay dying, England's King George V asked, among his final words, "How is the Empire?" Our answer may well be quite unlike that of the prime minister who replied to his king, "All's well, sir, with the Empire."

One development that resulted from the abandonment of empire was the creation of the state of Israel, physically in the Near East and in many ways of the Eastern culture, and yet in other important ways a projection of European culture abroad. Some saw Israel as a settlement nation to be compared to Australia or South Africa; others saw it as a return to the ancient Jewish homeland. The Arab states saw it as an intrusion into Arab and Islamic society, while Britain saw it as the natural inheritor of the Palestine that had passed to Britain as a mandated territory after World War I.

Indeed, one reason Britain was prepared to relinquish control in Palestine was because of the tension between the newly arriving Jews and the Arabs, who had been there for centuries. To the former, Palestine was to become a National Home. It would restore the Jews to their ancestral lands and remove them from the status of perpetual sojourners in others' nations, a condition made all the more undesirable in the light of Hitler's Germany and the Soviet *pogroms*. In World War I, Britain promised to support the idea of a National Home, and the gas chambers of World War II reinforced the promise. Thus Britain withdrew in 1948, and the United Nations accepted an independent Palestine, which was divided into two states. The Arabs refused to accept this division, but most non-Arab nations accorded Palestine recognition, and it began to carve out a place for itself with vigor, dedication, and intelligence. In three wars, the most dramatic being the Six-Day War of June 1967, Israel either soundly defeated Arab armies or successfully held them at bay, which extended the area of Israeli control. This at once added to Israel's security by making the enemy more distant, and decreased Israel's security by increasing the enemy's rage. In the context of Cold War politics, Israel became dependent on the aid of the United States, the Western anchor of European civilization, while the Arab states became clients of the Soviet Union, the anchor in the east. Thus Israel became a symbol of the potential for further civil war in Western society, as well as the focus of strife between Western and non-Western nations. The issue was not one of decolonization, and yet it had arisen from the age of imperialism.

Tensions within third world societies, and between the West and the non-West, were seized upon by diverse groups intent on disrupting the order of things to achieve often specific goals. Many of these goals sprang from the residue of the age of imperialism. In Northern Ireland Protestant and Catholic battled for dominance, equal rights, independence, or some form of merger with the Republic of Ireland in a vastly complex civil war. Throughout the Near and Middle East, ethnic and religious clashes arose from and contributed to world-wide tensions. In south Asia, both India and Sri Lanka were riven by similar clashes, and in India Sikh extremists demanding a separate state assassinated that nation's long-serving prime minister, Indira Gandhi (1917–1984), bringing to office her son, Rajiv, who—having been born in 1944—became one of the first genuinely postwar leaders of a major nation. In South Africa, continued racial repression, and in remote corners of the Pacific Ocean continued colonialism, led to repetitive violence.

Thus the world was faced for the first time with a new threat: random

No artist better captured the sense of psychic insecurity that gripped the Western world after World War II than the English painter *Francis Bacon,* whose ghostly and decomposing faces precisely spoke to the fears of the time: all that had seemed clear was now open to question, the past haunting both present and future. *Source: The Museum of Modern Art, New York*

terrorism. Terrorists would and could strike at virtually any target in the name of their cause, which might range from Basque separatism to revenge for Turkish massacres of Armenians after World War I. International air traffic, cruise ships, even the Olympic Games became targets for terrorists. In response, governments felt compelled to restrict in various ways freedom of international movement and often freedom of movement within their own borders. Many years earlier a philosopher had called the twentiety century the "age of anxiety," and now the truth of this judgment was brought home to the average citizen.

By the end of the decade of the eighties there were few colonies left. One, the Falkland Islands, had been the focus of a short, intense war between Great Britain, which possessed the south Atlantic colony, and Argentina, which called the islands Las Malvinas and claimed them. This war, in 1982, served to remind Western nations that even colonial remnants might foment wars and that the age of imperialism was not yet quite over.

One significant development stemmed from issues that were both colonial in origin and far more ancient: the Iranian revolution of 1979. Iran, which occupies the ancient land of Persia, had never formally been annexed by any European power, but it had effectively been dominated by the British, French, and to a lesser extent Germans and prerevolutionary Russians. In 1953 the British, French, and Americans worked behind the scenes in Iran to effect the overthrow of a nationalist premier, and thereafter the nation was under the authoritarian if economically progressive rule of the Pahlavi dynasty. The shah of Iran sought to move too fast in economic and social reforms, angering the fundamentalist Islamic leaders, while he did not move fast enough on the political front to prevent the rise of a radical underground opposition. In a bloody revolution from the right, the shah was sent into exile and a religious leader, the Ayatollah Khomeini (1901– ) became the effective head of state. Thereafter Iran proved to be a destabilizing factor throughout the Middle East and most particularly in its long war with Iraq and through complex interventions in an increasingly chaotic Lebanon.

Still, one vast area that once had felt itself to be manipulated by colonial or imperial policies had emerged onto the world scene in leadership roles: mainland China, known as the People's Republic, with a Communist government, and the new Japan, democratized and intensely committed to free enterprise. The latter, in particular, dominated a developing society of the Pacific Rim, which was being changed in dramatic ways through the application of technology and often of technologies in which the Japanese were the world's leading manufacturers. To a considerable extent Westernized, Japan was, by the 1980s, one of the world's great economic powers.

### Time of Danger, Time of Challenge

The first two decades after World War II were also a time when Europe suffered from ideology-fatigue; too much demonstrable harm had come from a commitment to what philosopher Eric Hoffer has called the attitude of "the true believer." The trend was away from hard and fast political programs and absolute demands. Instead, the major parties of both the right and the left were willing to exchange dogma for pragmatism, and the center became the direction toward which both were moving. In the late sixties, some dramatic changes took place as student rebellions erupted from Paris to Belgrade, and revolutionary Marxism, in forms that ranged from Stalinist to Maoist to Trotskyist to Castro's in Cuba, excited a certain appeal again.

Yet both decolonization and reradicalization can now be seen in perspective. What is perhaps most notable about the former is how unviolently it was achieved in many instances. Where there was extensive fighting—as in Algeria, Indochina, Kenya, or Portuguese Africa—it was in regions with substantial numbers of British, French, or Portuguese settlers (over a million French *colons* in the case of Algeria) who were reluctant to abandon their homes, their property, and what had become their country as well. Where there were no, or few, such settlers—as in Ghana, Nigeria, Libya, or Jamaica—independence usually was achieved with next to no European resistance. In any event, in a more subtle form much European influence remained. There were pervasive social and cultural influences because nineteenth-century Africa as well as much of Asia had been divided into areas where either French or English was the lingua franca of the many, and the literary language of the few. Nor did Europe's economic influence cease because many of the new states quickly discovered that they were poor and in need of the kind of economic and technical development that required outside aid.

As for the new radicalism, it largely remained restricted to an academic minority. To the parents' generation, it was not only the best Germany, but also the best France, Holland, or Belgium that they remembered, at least until the rise of international terrorism. Thus the riots that looked so menacing on television were not followed by the emergence of either radical Marxist or fascist parties that attracted a mass following, despite inroads in Italy. The lessons of the recent past were too obvious; one could not break with that past and its lessons. The vast majority of Europeans were not ready to exchange the existing state of affairs—despite all its imperfections, despite a polluted Rhine, smog over Paris, and unequal access to education in England—for the pursuit of abstract utopias.

That the mood might change again was true. "History," British historian A. J. P. Taylor has reminded us, "is a great school of skepticism." Yet even to the skeptic, if one considered its age and its record of previous illnesses, Europe again looked in good health, its civilizations ready to play their role in the future. And for the first time, the civilizations of Africa, Asia, and most particularly, those that were oil-rich were going to help shape that future. By the mid-1970s, one was forced to think in terms of the relevance of World, rather than European, history.

This was true on all fronts, political, economic, social, and intellectual. Indeed, the awareness was perhaps best signaled in the religious sphere, where the rise of fundamentalist Islam and, in North America, fundamentalist Christianity threatened the bedrock of the secular nation state to which, since the nineteenth century, individuals increasingly had been expected to give their primary loyalties. Organized religions often sought to reach out beyond their own sectarian concerns or to find dramatic expressions for their awareness of world-wide needs. One dramatic indication came from the Roman Catholic church, which in 1978 chose as pope the first non-Italian in 450 years, a Pole, Karol Wojtyla (1920– ), who as John Paul II would travel on a world-wide basis, speaking out on a wide range of social issues.

## Emergence of Social Issues

In truth, social issues dominated the world's concerns by the late 1980s, creating anxieties of a kind, and deep threats to an individual's sense of security, not felt since the Middle Ages. There was the clear threat of population growth as the world-wide birth rate soared. Many nations turned, sometimes oppressively, to methods of artificial birth control. Other societies found birth control religiously offensive, and yet others saw the "revenge of the cradles" as a way of overtaking a rival or throwing off an oppressor. Some nations were doubling their populations within a generation. In some states half the population was below the age of 21, intensifying generational conflict, economic dislocation, and political strife. Other nations—the United States for example—were nearly at a steady state, although a vast flood of immigration could upset population balances. Shifts in demography, in the relative ranking within a society of different ethnic communities, and in age or gender distribution had profound effects on jobs, housing, and politics.

In much of the West the 1970s and 1980s also saw fundamental changes in the role of women. Increasingly, women demanded, and gained, full access to economic and political rights that originally had been reserved to men. As more and more women entered the work force, became more highly educated, or competed as equals in the political arena or on the playing field, the nature of the family and of marriage—the custom by which the family was assured of stability (and by which property was divided)—underwent profound stress. As more and more children were born outside marriage, state support systems that were geared to the assumption of the nuclear family as the primary unit of society had, in turn, to be altered. This produced deep political divisions in most Western societies, for often the required changes related to strongly held moral views.

Perhaps no two issues more divided Western societies in terms of moral views than abortion and gay rights. Abortion—the artificial termination of pregnancy—deeply offended many of religious persuasion, while the denial of abortion equally offended those who, whether religious or not in their private convictions, did not feel that the state had the right to regulate a woman's body or intervene in the private and sexual affairs of individuals. Some societies in western Europe, notably Britain, the Low Countries, and Scandinavia, moved to positions that were close to abortion on demand and left the decision almost entirely to the individuals concerned, usually the woman; other societies experienced prolonged domestic strife over abortion itself and over whether the state, a church, or other family members should play a role in abortion decisions. This was especially so in nations whose people were predominantly Roman Catholic and in the United States.

The issue of gay rights received little major public attention in much of the West until the rise of a disease, acquired immune deficiency syndrome (AIDS), that posed daunting medical and social problems. With no known cure, highly contagious, almost always leading to death, and highly visible among public personages, especially in the world of entertainment, AIDS threatened to be the greatest scourge since the Black Death of the Middle Ages. Initially AIDS was seen as being endemic to the homosexual population and as transmitted either through sexual contact or through the use of infected needles by users of illegal drugs, so that the attack on AIDS was essentially one of enforcing anti-drug and anti-gay laws. But as gays successfully fought the latter laws as an aspect of the wider drive in the West for full civil liberties, and as medical evidence increasingly supported the view that AIDS could be spread through heterosexual activity, the public and belatedly political leadership throughout the West—and to a lesser extent in Africa and Latin America—realized that a major new threat to individuals' sense of security was at hand.

Drugs, and the illegal abuse of controlled substances, also posed for most nations of the West a major new threat in the 1980s. More and more people appeared to be using drugs and under their influence to be performing their jobs badly or turning to crime to obtain the money to purchase yet more drugs. As drug-related crime rates soared, as work forces and athletic teams and political leaders were discovered to be deeply influenced by drug use or to be involved in the trafficking of drugs, the West found itself faced with yet another seemingly intractable issue: How does a government assure its people maximum freedom while protecting them from the abuses of that freedom that many people appear willing, even eager, to practice, notwithstanding responsibilities to their family or church or nation?

Problems such as these, which in an earlier century might have been contained within a single society, quickly became world-wide, for by the 1980s it was no longer possible to quarantine ideas, social practices, or expectations. Transportation and communication had been revolutionized. Humanity had explored outer space, had plumbed the greatest depths of the oceans, had ascended the highest mountains. A single aircraft could remain aloft for days and could circumnavigate the world in a matter of hours. The military forces of the United States and the Soviet Union could deliver destruction against each other in a matter of minutes, while other nations—Britain, France, Israel, China, and others that did not officially admit so—possessed nuclear weaponry and vast destructive capacity. Bullet trains in Japan and their equivalent in France could carry passengers at speeds far in excess of a hundred miles an hour. Networks of paved highways covered South Africa or India to an extent not thought possible only decades before. By satellite, telecommunications were virtually instant to many corners of the globe.

This meant, of course, that modern life represented a paradox: Almost certainly there had never been a time when so many people enjoyed so high a standard of living. Life was better for the great majority of people than ever before. Yet, because of instant communication, far more people were aware of the great risks of the world in which they lived. For more, the sense of daily security—of knowing where the next meal would come from—was far higher, and the sense of long-range insecurity was also far higher than ever before.

As the world became smaller, there was good news as well as bad. The ongoing technological revolution was transforming the nature of education, the work place, the uses of leisure time, and health. Diseases that had ravaged past generations—tuberculosis, polio, smallpox—were either eradicated or were under control. Bodies of information that might have been restricted to a small, ruling elite were, through computerized libraries, information retrieval systems, and extensive computer networking, now known to vast numbers. The computer itself, together with the microchip, had taken the drudgery out of many manufacturing processes and had freed individuals to be more productive, to spend more time at leisure or with friends and family. To live in a technological world required more education than ever before, and in schools and universities around the world individuals were seeking that education. World-wide literacy rates were increasing, and with literacy came the sense that individuals could do something about their own lives, could to at least some extent influence the environment in which they lived.

The environmental movement, though expressed unevenly in different societies, had also experienced some triumphs and, more important, had successfully alerted political leaders in many nations to their essential interconnectedness environmentally. The world had polluted itself with acid rain, nuclear fallout, vast and growing waste deposits, depleted forests, and severely damaged rivers. But technology promised, if there were a political and economic will to reverse this trend, that reversal was possible, especially if problems were approached on an international scale. If leaders would talk to each other, they might bring under control the forces promoting pollution.

They might even be able to talk to each other outside the captive castle of their single language. More and more the citizens of the world were bilingual. Once the lingua franca of the known world in the West had been Latin. For generations it had been French. In the twentieth century the language of commerce and technology, and thus to a good extent the language of education, had become English. Much of western Europe could converse together in English. The next likely step, as world-wide patterns of immigration changed, would be toward bilingualism in those societies that had resolutely remained unilingual. Just as computers were forcing individuals to move beyond literacy to numeracy, to the ability to not only read but to work with abstract numbers, so too would the demographic trends of the world be likely to promote an awareness of the need to communicate, and thus to understand each other, in two or more languages.

Knowledge had freed some of humankind to be contemporaries and partners with those who make the future. Many, ignorant or oblivious to the past and the way in which it shaped their lives, would continue to be victims. But there would always be those who knew that to understand the past, and to know themselves, was to prepare for the future.

History is now.

# Epilogue

Epilogue

> *After such knowledge, what forgiveness? Think now*
> *History has many cunning passages, contrived corridors*
> *And issues, deceives with whispering ambitions*
> *Guides us by vanities. Think now....*—T. S. Eliot, 1920

"The trouble with History," someone once said, "is that it never tells us the Truth." Of course it doesn't. Rather, it shows us there are no simple truths. Even the theme used to weave the various strands of this book together—people's continued search for both the reality and the sense of security—is but a single theme among many hundreds that might have been chosen. Further, it is a theme, many could argue, that is at once too simple because it is so obvious, and too complex because it is capable of so many different interpretations. As a theme for understanding people, not all will find it equally useful, equally convincing, or equally true. Contained within the theme of the search for security, of looking to the past for answers, are a number of moral ambiguities that any person who seeks self-knowledge must investigate. This account might best close, then, with ten questions, each intended as a means both for interrogating the past and for examining the self.

*Moral ambiguity 1:* Can one write history for a predetermined group? Is there something that may be called German history? American history? Black history? Women's history? Is history that is organized around groups such as these acceptable, or is history that is organized in terms of the national identity simply one means of heightening nationalism? Is history that is organized around ethnic identity a means of instilling pride or of separating one group from another?

*Moral ambiguity 2:* Should historians bring God into their story? If God exists, surely the omission would mean deleting the single most important link in all cause and effect sequences? If God does not exist, should one say so? Does it matter to history whether or not God exists, provided that people believe God to exist?

*Moral ambiguity 3:* Do people's compulsion to differentiate themselves from others help or hinder the development of humankind? Does the belief in being a Chosen people, for example, give a people vigor? Do we not all make assumptions of a similar sort—that we are wiser, stronger, better by virtue of coming from a particular school, gang, state, church, nation? That because we are under (or over) a certain age, we are wiser? Do such self-judgments, when accepted by large groups, comprise a danger to society? Or do such judgments cement society?

*Moral ambiguity 4:* Is there not a danger that scholarship, history, or the

The great Norwegian painter Edvard Munch sought to capture mankind in all of its anxieties, insecurities, and traumas. In 1895 he created a series of lithographs, all versions of the present picture, usually entitled "The Scream." The sense of alienation, of self-fear, of dread that Nature cannot be controlled as rational man once hoped, even Munch's awareness of the presence of sexual tension, are well shown in this complex, yet simple, clash of colors and figures. Few artists have spoken so well for the modern world and its discontents.
*Source: Collection, The Museum of Modern Art.*

books we read, have a predetermined cause in mind? Is it possible to organize knowledge in any meaningful pattern without having a predetermined conclusion? For whom must the pattern be meaningful?

*Moral ambiguity 5:* Should we not stand by our own people? Is this acceptable to an American in 1941? a Frenchman in 1789? an Afrikaaner in 1988? What is meant by "our own people"—a nationality? a class? an ethnic group? Where does loyalty lie?

*Moral ambiguity 6:* Is there not a special risk in departing from facts to engage in theory? Has it not been theory that has often led humans to destroy each other? Yet has it not also been theory that has made it possible for humans to prosper, grow, and realize new opportunities? What is the gap between theory and practice?

*Moral ambiguity 7:* What if a theory we now despise proves to be right? What do we mean by "right"? Is there ever just reason to prevent human beings from pursuing any theory?

*Moral ambiguity 8:* So what is "relevant"? Who has the right to decide? Historians? Politicians? Ourselves?

*Moral ambiguity 9:* Is not the law meant to be relevant? Do we not praise

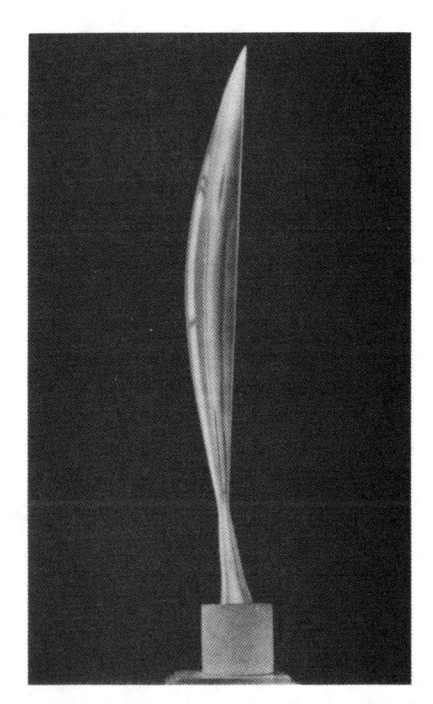

*Constantine Brancusi,* a Romanian sculptor, sought to remind man of his freedom, that he could still soar, as he worked with forms "as palpable as a globed fruit," forms which virtually asked to be touched rather than hidden away in a museum, as here with his "Bird in Space." *Source: The Museum of Modern Art, New York*

it for doing for us what we wish, protecting us, providing for a more organized society? Yet what if the law is mad? May one resist the law? Who determines that it is mad? Or irrelevant? Is one person's relevance another's madness?

*Moral ambiguity 10:* Do we mislead ourselves by language? Do the words we, or our writers, our teachers, our politicians, or our advertisers choose lead us to conclusions through their own emotional weight, rather than through their logical meanings? Is history capable of being known? How best might we know it, express it, explain it?

At the outset, we asserted that history is not a body of data to be memorized, it is a set of arguments to be debated. But to be effective in society, we must also conclude for ourselves, not merely continue the debate. "Now this is not the end. It is not even the beginning of the end. But it is, perhaps, the end of the beginning" wrote Winston Churchill in 1942, summing up the place of all that has gone before, the past that is prologue to the future that is already upon us as we read these words.

# When You Want To Read More

Every year over a thousand new titles in history are published in the United States alone. Obviously no one person can read all of these books, much less work their way backwards through the many thousands already published or the many other thousands published each year in Europe and elsewhere. When reading history, one should select books because they will broaden one's knowledge about subjects of direct concern to one's major interests, because they are particularly important, or simply because they are attractive and well-written. This is especially so for the non-professional reader who cannot be expected, even if deeply interested in the French Revolution, to read even the fifty books which appeared in the last year on this subject. The lists that follow, then, are meant to be genuinely helpful to the reader. They are not a bibliography of the books consulted while writing the present volume, for that bibliography would, in a sense, extend over many hundreds of titles and many years of reading. Rather, the titles listed below are chosen because those who have found this book helpful, enjoyable, or challenging will find the additional titles show the same characteristics. Many excellent books have been omitted, of course, as have significant works of a revisionist nature, or books which are largely meant for an audience of specialized scholars, simply because they are, in fact, unreadable. The most accessible edition is cited, and unless needed to clarify the major title, lengthy sub-titles generally have been omitted. No book not in English translation has been included.

## Broad-ranging books that help one to think about fundamental problems

J. R. L. Anderson. *The Ulysses Factor: The Exploring Instinct in Man.* New York, 1970.

Philippe Ariès. *Western Attitudes toward Death.* Baltimore, 1974.

T. S. R. Boase. *Death in the Middle Ages: Mortality, Judgment and Remembrance.* New York, 1972.

Norman Cohn. *The Pursuit of the Millennium.* London, 1970.

Alfred W. Crosby. *Ecological Imperialism: The Biological Expansion of Europe, 900 to 1900.* Cambridge, 1986.

Georges Duby and Paul Veyne, eds. *A History of Private Life.* 2 vols. Cambridge, Mass., 1987–1988.

Henry Kamen. *The Rise of Toleration.* New York, 1967.

Joseph and Barrie Klaits. *Animals and Man in Historical Perspective.* New York, 1974.

A. L. Kroeber. *An Anthropologist Looks at History.* Berkeley, 1963.

Allan J. Lichtman and Valerie French. *Historians and the Living Past.* Arlington Heights, Ill., 1978.

Francis L. Loewenheim, et al. *The Historian and the Diplomat.* New York, 1967.

Richard D. Mandell. *Sport: A Cultural History.* New York, 1984.

William H. McNeill. *Plagues and Peoples.* New York, 1977.

William H. McNeill. *The Rise of the West: A History of the Human Community.* Chicago, 1963.

H. J. Muller. *The Uses of the Past.* New York, 1954.

C. V. Wedgewood. *The Sense of the Past: Truth and Opinion.* New York, 1967.

E. A. Wrigley. *Population and History.* New York, 1969.


## Books on the nature of History

Marc Bloch. *The Historian's Craft.* New York, 1953.

Edward Hallett Carr. *What Is History?* New York, 1965.

G. Kitson Clark. *The Critical Historian.* New York, 1967.

L. P. Curtis, Jr. *The Historian's Workshop.* New York, 1970.

G. R. Elton. *Political History: Principles and Practice.* New York, 1970.

David Hackett Fischer. *Historians' Fallacies: Toward a Logic of Historical Thought.* New York, 1970.

John A. Garraty. *The Nature of Biography.* New York, 1957.

Peter Gay. *Style in History.* New York, 1974.

E. H. Gombrich. *In Search of Cultural History.* Oxford, 1969.

J. H. Hexter. *Doing History*. Bloomington, Indiana, 1971.
H. Stuart Hughes. *History as Art and as Science*. New York, 1964.
George Kubler. *The Shape of Time*. New Haven, 1962.
Bruce Mazlish. *Psychoanalysis and History*. Englewood Cliffs, N.J., 1963.
Ved Mehta. *Fly and the Fly-Bottle*. London, 1963.
Matthew Melko. *The Nature of Civilizations*. Boston, 1969.
A. L. Rowse. *The Use of History*. London, 1946.
Robert Allen Skotheim. *The Historian and the Climate of Opinion*. Reading, Mass., 1969.
Page Smith. *The Historian and History*. New York, 1964.
Pardon E. Tillinghast. *The Specious Past: Historians and Others*. Reading, Mass., 1972.
Robin W. Winks. *The Historian as Detective*. New York, 1969.

# The Earliest Beginnings

W. F. Albright. *From the Stone Age to Christianity*. New York, 1959.
C. W. Ceram. *Gods, Graves and Scholars: The Story of Archaeology*. New York, 1954.
V. Gordon Childe. *What Happened in History*. London, 1942.
P. E. Cleaton. *Lost Languages*. New York, 1962.
Glyn Daniel. *The Idea of Prehistory*. London, 1962.
I. E. S. Edwards. *The Pyramids of Egypt*. London, 1947.
L. Finkelstein. *The Jews: Their History, Culture and Religion*, 2 vols. New York, 1970.
Henri Frankfurt. *The Birth of Civilization in the Near East*. New York, 1968.
Oliver R. Gurney. *The Hittites*. Baltimore, 1972.
William W. Hallo and William Kelly Simpson. *The Ancient Near East*. New York, 1971.
Tom B. Jones. *Paths to the Ancient Past*. New York, 1967.
S. N. Kramer. *History Begins at Sumer*. Garden City, New York, 1959.
J. Lassoe. *People of Ancient Assyria*. New York, 1963.
Alexander Marshack. *The Roots of Civilization*. New York, 1972.
Joan Oates. *Babylon*. London, 1979.
H. M. Orlinsky. *Ancient Israel*, 2nd ed. Ithaca, N.Y., 1960.
Stuart Piggott. *Approach to Archaeology*. New York, 1959.
*Reader's Digest Atlas of the Bible*. New York, 1981.
Chester G. Starr. *Early Man: Prehistory and the Civilizations of the Ancient Near East*. New York, 1973.
Bruce Trigger. *Beyond History: The Methods of Prehistory*. New York, 1968.

## Mediterranean Antiquity

### Greece

H. C. Baldry. *Greek Literature for the Modern Reader*. New York, 1951.

John Boardman, Jasper Griffin, Oswyn Murray, eds. *The Oxford History of the Classical World*. Oxford, 1986.

C. M. Bowra. *The Greek Experience*. New York, 1961.

R. M. Cook. *The Greeks until Alexander*. New York, 1962.

Francis M. Cornford. *Before and After Socrates*. Cambridge, n.d.

J. K. Davies. *Democracy and Classical Greece*. New York, 1978.

W. G. de Burgh. *The Legacy of the Ancient World*, 2 vols. London, 1947.

Moses I. Finley. *The Ancient Greeks*. New York, 1977.

Edith Hamilton. *The Greek Way to Western Civilization*. New York, 1942.

Homer. *The Iliad*.

Homer. *The Odyssey*.

A. H. M. Jones. *Athenian Democracy*. New York, 1969.

H. D. Kitto. *The Greeks*. Baltimore, 1964.

Gilbert Murray. *Five Stages of Greek Religion*. Garden City, N.Y., 1955.

Milton C. Nahm. *Selections from Early Greek Philosophy*. New York, 1947.

W. W. Tarn. *Alexander the Great*. Cambridge, 1956.

A. E. Taylor. *Aristotle*. New York, 1955.

A. E. Taylor. *Socrates*. New York, 1956.

Thucydides. *The History of the Peloponnesian War*.

Arnold J. Toynbee. *Greek Civilization and Character*. New York, 1953.

A. G. Woodhead. *The Greeks in the West*. New York, 1962.

### Rome

Thomas W. Africa. *Rome of the Caesars*. New York, 1965.

E. Badian. *Roman Imperialism in the Late Republic*. London, 1971.

R. H. Barrow. *The Romans*. London, 1955.

R. Bloch. *The Etruscans*. New York, 1969.

R. Bloch. *The Origins of Rome*. New York, 1960.

M. P. Charlesworth. *The Roman Empire*. New York, 1951.

Martin Clarke. *The Roman Mind*. Cambridge, Mass., 1956.

F. R. Cowell. *Cicero and the Roman Republic*. London, 1956.

Glyn Daniel. *The Art of the Romans*. London, 1965.

Michael Grant. *From Alexander to Cleopatra*. New York, 1982.

Keith Hopkins. *Conquerors and Slaves*. Cambridge, 1981.

A. H. M. Jones. *The Later Roman Empire*, 4 vols. New York, 1964.
Ramsay Macmullen. *Constantine*. New York, 1969.
Ramsay Macmullen. *Soldier and Civilian in the Late Roman Empire*. Cambridge, Mass., 1963.
Harold Mattingly. *Roman Imperial Civilization*. London, 1957.
Fergus Millar. *The Emperor in the Roman World*. Ithaca, 1977.
Stewart Perowne. *Hadrian*. New York, 1960.
Frank Tenney. *Life and Literature in the Roman Republic*. Berkeley, 1956.

### *Judaism and Christianity*
Roland Bainton. *Early Christianity*. Princeton, 1960.
Peter Brown. *Augustine of Hippo*. Berkeley, 1967.
C. N. Cochrane. *Christianity and Classical Culture*. New York, 1944.
Jean Danielou. *The Theology of Jewish Christianity*. London, 1964.
Christopher Dawson. *Religion and the Rise of Western Culture*. New York, 1977.
John Ferguson. *The Religions of the Roman Empire*. London, 1970.
W. H. C. Frend. *Martyrdom and Persecution in the Early Church*. Grand Rapids, 1981.
Erwin R. Goodenough. *The Church in the Roman Empire*. New York, 1970.
Michael Grant. *The Jews in the Roman World*. New York, 1973.
A. H. M. Jones. *Constantine and the Conversion of Europe*. New York, 1948.
Kenneth Scott Latourette. *History of Christianity*. New York, 1975.
A. R. Lewis. *Emerging Medieval Europe*. New York, 1967.
Sigmund Mowinckel. *He that Cometh*. London, 1956.
A. D. Nock. *St. Paul*. Oxford, 1955.
H. B. Parkes. *Gods and Men: The Origins of Western Culture*. New York, 1959.
Jaroslav Pelikan. *Jesus through the Centuries*. New Haven, 1985.
Edward M. Peters. *Monks, Bishops, and Pagans*. Philadelphia, 1975.
Steven Runciman. *Byzantine Civilization*. New York, 1956.
Spyros Vryonis. *Byzantium and Europe*. New York, 1967.
J. M. Wallace-Hadrill. *The Barbarian West*. London, 1952.

## Traditional Europe

### *Early Middle Ages*
The Venerable Bede. *The History of the English Church and People*.
Marc Bloch. *Feudal Society*, 2 vols. Chicago, 1961–64.

Robert Brentano. *The Early Middle Ages*. New York, 1964.

R. W. Chambers. *Beowulf*. 3rd ed., Cambridge, 1959.

Alfons Dopsch. *The Economic and Social Foundations of European Civilization*. New York, 1969.

Eleanor Duckett. *The Wandering Saints of the Early Middle Ages*. New York, 1959.

Jean Dunrabin. *France in the Making, 843–1180*. Oxford, 1985.

Lina Eckenstein. *Women Under Monasticism*. New York, 1963.

F. L. Ganshof. *Feudalism*. London, 1952.

Denys Hay. *Europe: The Emergence of an Idea*. Edinburgh, 1968.

Richard Hodges and David Whitehouse. *Mohammed, Charlemagne, and the Origins of Europe*. London, 1984.

Gwyn Jones. *A History of the Vikings*. New York, 1968.

W. P. Ker. *The Dark Ages*. London, 1955.

Robert S. Lopez. *The Birth of Europe*. New York, 1967.

Otto J. Maenchen-Helfer. *The World of the Huns*. Berkeley, 1973.

Joseph F. O'Callaghan. *A History of Medieval Spain*. Ithaca, 1975.

Sidney Painter. *The Rise of the Feudal Monarchies*. Ithaca, N.Y., 1951.

James B. Ross and Mary Martin McLaughlin, eds. *The Portable Medieval Reader*. New York, 1949.

Doris M. Stenton. *English Society in the Early Middle Ages*. London, 1952.

Frank M. Stenton. *Anglo-Saxon England*. London, 1977.

Joseph F. Strayer. *Feudalism*. Princeton, 1965.

E. A. Thompson. *The Early Germans*. Oxford, 1965.

Dorothy Whitlock. *The Beginnings of English Society*. London, 1952.

### East and West

Peter Brown. *The Cult of the Saints*. Chicago, 1982.

Deno Geanakoplos. *Byzantine East and Latin West: Two Worlds of Christendom in Middle Ages and Renaissance*. New York, 1966.

H. A. R. Gibb. *Mohammedanism: An Historical Survey*. New York, 1953.

Alfred Guillaume. *Islam*. London, 1956.

Oleg Grabar. *Islamic Art*. New Haven, 1972.

Philip K. Hitti. *The Arabs: A Short History*. Princeton, 1943.

J. M. Hussey. *Church and Learning in the Byzantine Empire, 867–1185*. Oxford, 1937.

Halil Inalcik. *The Ottoman Empire*. New York, 1973.

R. J. H. Jenkins. *Byzantium: The Imperial Centuries*. New York, 1967.

Muhsin Mahdi. *Ibn Khaldûn's Philosophy of History*. Chicago, 1964.

Roy P. Mottahedeh. *Loyalty and Leadership in Early Islamic Society*. Princeton, 1980.

Henri Pirenne. *Mohammed and Charlemagne*. London, 1939.

Fazler Rahman. *Islam.* London, 1979.
David Talbot Rice. *The Art of Byzantium,* 1959.

## High Middle Ages

Henry Adams. *Mont-Saint-Michel and Chartres,* reprint ed. Boston, 1959.
H. L. Adelson. *Medieval Commerce.* Princeton, 1962.
Frederick B. Artz. *The Mind of the Middle Ages.* New York, 1954.
John W. Baldwin. *The Scholastic Culture of the Middle Ages, 1000–1300.* Lexington, Mass., 1971.
Geoffrey Barraclough. *The Origins of Modern Germany,* 2nd ed. Oxford, 1957.
Christopher Brooke. *The Twelfth Century Renaissance.* London, 1969.
Helen Maude Cam. *England before Elizabeth,* 2nd ed. New York, 1952.
G. G. Coulton. *Medieval Panorama.* New York, 1955.
Maurice De Wulf. *Philosophy and Civilization in the Middle Ages.* New York, 1953.
David C. Douglas. *William the Conqueror.* Berkeley, 1964.
Georges Duby. *The Three Orders: Feudal Society Imagined.* Chicago, 1980.
Etienne Gilson. *Héloise and Abélard.* Ann Arbor, Mich., 1960.
C. H. Haskins. *The Renaissance of the Twelfth Century.* New York, 1957.
C. H. Haskins. *The Rise of the Universities.* New York, 1923.
David Herlihy. *The Social History of Italy and Western Europe, 700–1500.* London, 1980.
C. Warren Hollister. *Medieval Europe.* New York, 1982.
Johan Huizinga. *The Waning of the Middle Ages.* New York, 1954.
Dom David Knowles. *The Evolution of Medieval Thought.* New York, 1962.
Robert Lopez. *The Commercial Revolution of the Middle Ages.* Cambridge, 1976.
John B. Morrall. *Political Thought in Medieval Times.* New York, 1972.
J. H. Mundy and P. Riesenberg. *The Medieval Town.* Princeton, 1938.
John J. Norwich. *A History of Venice.* New York, 1982.
Sidney Painter. *French Chivalry.* Ithaca, N.Y., 1957.
Erwin Panofsky. *Gothic Architecture and Scholasticism.* New York, 1957.
Edward Peters. *Witchcraft in Europe.* Philadelphia, 1972.
Henri Pirenne. *Economic and Social History of Medieval Europe.* New York, 1937.
A. L. Poole. *From Domesday to Magna Carta.* Oxford, 1951.
Eileen Power. *Medieval People.* New York, 1924.
F. M. Powicke. *The Thirteenth Century, 1216–1307.* Oxford, 1953.
Steven Runciman. *The Sicilian Vespers: A History of the Mediterranean World in the Later Thirteenth Century.* Cambridge, 1958.
Kenneth M. Setton. *History of the Crusades,* 2 vols. Madison, Wisc., 1969.
R. W. Southern. *The Making of the Middle Ages.* New Haven, 1953.
R. W. Southern. *Western Society and the Church in the Middle Ages.* London, 1970.

H. O. Taylor. *The Medieval Mind,* 2 vols. Cambridge, Mass., 1949.
Brian Tierney. *The Crisis of Church and State, 1050–1300.* Englewood Cliffs, N.J., 1964.
Walter Ullmann. *The Growth of Papal Government in the Middle Ages.* New York, 1968.
Walter Ullmann. *A History of Political Thought in the Middle Ages.* London, 1965.
Lynn White, Jr. *Medieval Technology and Social Change.* New York, 1962.


## Europe, 1300–1700

Angus Armitage. *The World of Copernicus.* New York, 1947.
Roland Bainton. *Here I Stand: A Life of Martin Luther.* New York, 1955.
Franklin L. Baumer. *Modern European Thought.* New York, 1977.
H. Benesch. *The Art of the Renaissance in Northern Europe.* Cambridge, Mass., 1945.
S. T. Bindoff. *Tudor England.* London, 1950.
Marie Boas. *The Scientific Renaissance, 1450–1630.* New York, 1961.
Fernand Braudel. *Capitalism and Material Life, 1400–1800.* New York, 1974.
Fernand Braudel. *The Mediterranean and the Mediterranean World in the Age of Philip II.* 2 vols. New York, 1972–73.
Jacob Burckhardt. *The Civilization of the Renaissance in Italy.* London, 1950.
Herbert Butterfield. *The Origins of Modern Science, 1300–1800,* revised ed. New York, 1957.
Owen Chadwick. *The Reformation.* Baltimore, 1964.
Edward P. Cheyney. *The Dawn of a New Era, 1250–1453.* New York, 1936.
Sir George Clark. *Early Modern Europe.* London, 1957.
A. C. Crombie. *Medieval and Early Modern Science.* Cambridge, Mass., 1963.
R. T. Davies. *The Golden Century of Spain.* New York, 1967.
Ludwig Dehio. *The Precarious Balance: Four Centuries of the European Power Struggle.* New York, 1962.
A. G. Dickens. *The English Reformation,* revised ed. Boston, 1967.
A. G. Dickens. *Reformation and Society in Sixteenth Century Europe.* London, 1966.
John H. Elliott. *Europe Divided, 1559–1598.* New York, 1968.
John H. Elliott. *Imperial Spain, 1496–1716.* London, 1963.
Geoffrey R. Elton. *Reformation Europe, 1517–1559.* New York, 1968.
Michael T. Florinsky. *Russia: A History and Interpretation,* 2 vols. New York, 1966.
Carl J. Friedrich. *The Age of the Baroque, 1610–1660.* New York, 1952.
Pieter Geyl. *The Netherlands in the Seventeenth Century,* 2 vols. New York, 1961–64.
Myron P. Gilmore. *The World of Humanism.* New York, 1952.
J. R. Hale. *Renaissance Europe: Individual and Society, 1480–1520.* Berkeley, 1978.
E. Harris Harbison. *The Age of Reformation.* Ithaca, N.Y., 1955.

Denys Hay. *Europe in the Fourteenth and Fifteenth Centuries.* New York, 1966.
Denys Hay. *The Italian Renaissance in Its Historical Background.* Cambridge, 1977.
Hajo Holborn. *A History of Modern Germany, II, The Reformation.* New York, 1959.
Beresford J. Kidd. *The Counter-Reformation.* Westport, Conn., 1980.
Raymond F. Kierstead. *State and Society in Seventeenth Century France.* New York, 1975.
Paul Oskar Kristeller. *Renaissance Thought.* 2 vols. New York, 1961.
Frederick C. Lane. *Venice: A Maritime Republic.* Baltimore, 1973.
Garrett Mattingly. *The Armada.* Boston, 1959.
Garrett Mattingly. *Renaissance Diplomacy.* Boston, 1955.
Charles H. McIlwain. *Growth of Political Thought in the West.* New York, 1932.
May McKisack. *The Fourteenth Century.* Oxford, 1959.
E. William Monter. *Calvin's Geneva.* Melbourne, Fla., 1975.
George L. Mosse. *Calvinism: Authoritarian or Democratic?* New York, 1957.
John E. Neale. *The Age of Catherine de Medici.* London, 1943.
John E. Neale. *Queen Elizabeth I.* London, 1957.
Marvin R. O'Connell. *The Counter Reformation, 1559–1610.* New York, 1974.
John H. Plumb. *The Italian Renaissance.* New York, 1965.
Nancy Roelker. *The Paris of Henry of Navarre.* Cambridge, Mass., 1958.
George Sarton. *Six Wings: Men of Science in the Renaissance.* Bloomington, Indiana, 1956.
J. J. Scarisbrick. *Henry VIII.* Berkeley, 1968.
Geoffrey Scott. *The Architecture of Humanism.* Garden City, N.Y., 1954.
W. J. Stankiewicz. *Politics and Religion in Seventeenth Century France.* Berkeley, 1960.
Lynn Thorndike. *Science and Thought in the Fifteenth Century.* New York, 1929.
Brian Tierney. *Foundations of the Conciliar Theory.* Cambridge, 1955.
E. M. W. Tillyard. *The Elizabethan World Picture.* London, 1961.
C. V. Wedgwood. *The Thirty Years' War.* London, 1938.

# The New World in the Making

### *The Expansion of Europe, 1500–1800*
Henri Baudet. *Paradise on Earth: Some Thoughts on European Images of Non-European Man.* New Haven, 1965.
Geoffrey Blainey. *The Causes of War.* New York, 1973.
Charles R. Boxer. *The Dutch Seaborne Empire, 1600–1800.* London, 1965.

Charles R. Boxer. *The Portuguese Seaborne Empire, 1415–1825*. New York, 1969.

John Bartlet Brebner. *The Explorers of North America, 1492–1806*. Garden City, N.Y., 1955.

Carlos M. Cipolla. *European Culture and Overseas Expansion*. London, 1970.

Norman Daniel. *Islam, Europe and Empire*. Edinburgh, 1966.

Basil Davidson. *The African Slave Trade*. Boston, 1981.

Bailey W. Diffie. *Prelude to Empire: Portugal Overseas before Henry the Navigator*. Lincoln, Neb., 1960.

Walter L. Dorn. *Competition for Empire, 1740–1763*. New York, 1963.

John H. Elliott. *The Old World and the New, 1492–1650*. Cambridge, 1970.

J. R. Hale. *Renaissance Exploration*. London, 1968.

E. J. Hobsbawm. *Industry and Empire*. London, 1969.

Johan H. Huizinga. *Dutch Civilisation in the 17th Century*. London, 1968.

Francis Jennings. *The Invasion of America*. New York, 1976.

Henri Labouret. *Africa before the White Man*. New York, 1963.

Donald F. Lach. *India in the Eyes of Europe: The Sixteenth Century*. Chicago, 1968.

Joseph R. Levenson. *European Expansion and the Counter-Example of Asia, 1300–1600*. Englewood Cliffs, N.J., 1967.

Samuel Eliot Morison. *Christopher Columbus, Mariner*. New York, 1956.

K. M. Panikkar. *Asia and Western Dominance*. London, 1959.

John Parker. *Discovery: Developing Views of the Earth*. New York, 1972.

John H. Parry. *The Age of Reconnaissance*. New York, 1964.

John H. Parry. *The Spanish Seaborne Empire*. London, 1966.

Stanley J. and Barbara H. Stein. *Colonial Heritage of Latin America*. London, 1970.

The Travels of Marco Polo.

Marcel Trudel. *The Beginnings of New France, 1524–1663*. Toronto, 1973.

Robin W. Winks. *The Age of Imperialism*. Englewood Cliffs, N.J., 1969.

Louis B. Wright. *Cultural Life of the American Colonies, 1607–1763*. New York, 1957.

## *The Age of Revolution, 1688–1815*

Robert Anchor. *The Enlightenment Tradition*. Berkeley, 1979.

Carl Becker. *The Heavenly City of the Eighteenth Century Philosophers*. New Haven, 1932.

Paul H. Beik. *The French Revolution*. New York, 1970.

Jerome Blum. *Lord and Peasant in Russia from the Ninth to the Nineteenth Century*. Princeton, 1961.

Geoffrey Bruun. *Europe and the French Imperium, 1799–1814*. New York, 1938.

E. A. Burtt. *The Metaphysical Foundations of Modern Physical Science*. Garden City, N.Y., 1954.

Ernst Cassirer. *The Philosophy of the Enlightenment.* Boston, 1955.

Alfred Cobban. *In Search of Humanity: The Role of the Enlightenment in Modern History.* New York, 1960.

William Doyle. *Origins of the French Revolution.* Oxford, 1980.

Sidney B. Fay and Klaus Epstein. *The Rise of Brandenburg-Prussia to 1786.* New York, 1964.

Franklin Ford. *Robe and Sword: The Regrouping of the French Aristocracy after Louis XIV.* Cambridge, Mass., 1953.

Peter Gay. *The Enlightenment,* 2 vols. New York, 1974.

Leo Gershoy. *From Despotism to Revolution, 1763–1789.* New York, 1944.

Pieter Geyl. *Napoleon: For and Against.* New Haven, 1949.

Ralph W. Greenlaw. *The Economic Origins of the French Revolution.* Boston, 1958.

A. L. Guérard. *Napoleon I.* New York, 1956.

Paul Hazard. *European Thought in the Eighteenth Century.* New Haven, 1954.

Richard Herr. *The Eighteenth-Century Revolution in Spain.* Princeton, 1958.

Vincent J. Knapp. *Europe in the Era of Social Transformation: 1700–Present.* Englewood Cliffs, N.J., 1976.

Peter Laslett. *The World We Have Lost.* New York, 1971.

Frank Manuel. *The Age of Reason.* Ithaca, N.Y., 1951.

Edmund S. Morgan. *The Birth of the Republic, 1763–89.* Chicago, 1956.

Sir Lewis Namier. *England in the Age of the American Revolution.* London, 1961.

Robert R. Palmer. *The Age of the Democratic Revolution,* 2 vols. Princeton, 1959–64.

Jack H. Plumb. *England in the Eighteenth Century.* London, 1950.

Sidney Pollard. *The Idea of Progress.* New York, 1968.

Marc Raeff. *Catherine the Great.* New York, 1972.

George Rudé. *The Crowd in History.* New York, 1964.

George Rudé. *Revolutionary Europe, 1783–1815.* Cleveland, 1964.

William H. Sewell. *Work and Revolution in France.* Cambridge, 1980.

B. H. Summer. *Peter the Great and the Ottoman Empire.* Oxford, 1949.

J. L. Talmon. *The Origins of Totalitarian Democracy.* New York, 1961.

J. M. Thompson. *Robespierre and the French Revolution.* New York, 1953.

### *Industry and Commerce*

T. S. Ashton. *The Industrial Revolution, 1760–1830.* London, 1948.

Asa Briggs. *The Age of Improvement.* New York, 1962.

Rondo Cameron. *France and the Economic Development of Europe.* Princeton, 1966.

Carlo Cipolla. *The Emergence of Industrial Societies.* London, 1973.

Elie Halévy. *The Growth of Philosophic Radicalism.* Boston, 1972.

Robert Heilbroner. *The Worldly Philosophers.* New York, 1953.

William O. Henderson. *The Industrialization of Europe.* London, 1969.

David S. Landes. *The Unbound Prometheus: Technological Change and Industrial Development in Western Europe from 1750 to the Present.* London, 1969.

Alan S. Milward and S. B. Saul. *The Development of the Economies of Continental Europe.* Cambridge, Mass., 1977.

John U. Nef. *War and Human Progress.* Chicago, 1950.

Sidney Pollard. *Peaceful Conquest: The Industrialization of Europe.* Oxford, 1981.

Philip A. M. Taylor. *The Industrial Revolution in Britain.* Boston, 1958.

Edward P. Thompson. *The Making of the English Working Class.* London, 1963.

A. P. Usher. *A History of Mechanical Inventions.* Cambridge, 1954.

## The Nineteenth Century

M. S. Anderson. *The Ascendancy of Europe, 1815–1914.* London, 1972.

Frederick B. Artz. *Reaction and Revolution, 1815–1832.* New York, 1932.

Shlomo Avineri. *The Social and Political Thought of Karl Marx.* Cambridge, 1970.

Jacques Barzun. *Romanticism and the Modern Ego.* Boston, 1943.

Isaiah Berlin. *The Hedgehog and the Fox.* London, 1953.

James H. Billington. *The Icon and the Axe.* New York, 1970.

Robert C. Binkley. *Realism and Nationalism, 1852–1871.* New York, 1935.

Asa Briggs. *Victorian People.* Chicago, 1955.

C. E. Carrington. *The British Overseas.* Cambridge, 1968.

David Caute. *The Left in Europe since 1789.* New York, 1966.

G. Kitson Clark. *The Making of Victorian England.* Cambridge, Mass., 1962.

Alfred Cobban. *A History of Modern France, II, 1799–1871.* London, 1961.

Maurice Cowling. *Mill and Liberalism.* Cambridge, 1963.

Gordon A. Craig. *Germany, 1866–1945.* New York, 1978.

Philip D. Curtin. *The Atlantic Slave Trade.* Madison, Wisc., 1969.

Charles Delzell. *The Unification of Italy.* New York, 1964.

David K. Fieldhouse. *The Colonial Empires.* London, 1966.

David K. Fieldhouse. *Economics and Empire, 1830–1914.* London, 1973.

Geoffrey Finlayson. *Decade of Reform: England in the Eighteen Thirties.* New York, 1970.

Peter Gay. *The Bourgeois Experience: Victoria to Freud.* Oxford, 1984.

Heinz Gollwitzer. *Europe in the Age of Imperialism, 1880–1914.* New York, 1969.

Brison D. Gooch. *The Reign of Napoleon III.* Chicago, 1969.

Theodore S. Hamerow. *Restoration, Revolution, Reaction: Economics and Politics in Germany, 1815–1871.* Princeton, 1958.

Carlton J. H. Hayes. *A Generation of Materialism, 1871–1900.* New York, 1941.

Gertrude Himmelfarb. *Darwin and the Darwinian Revolution.* New York, 1968.
Hajo Holborn. *A History of Modern Germany, III.* New York, 1969.
Walter E. Houghton. *The Victorian Frame of Mind, 1830–1870.* New Haven, 1957.
William Irvine. *Apes, Angels, and Victorians: The Story of Darwin, Huxley, and Evolution.* New York, 1955.
Barbara Jelavich. *The Hapsburg Empire in European Affairs, 1814–1918.* Chicago, 1969.
James Joll. *The Anarchists.* Cambridge, Mass., 1980.
Elie Kedourie. *Nationalism.* New York, 1961.
V. G. Kiernan. *Marxism and Imperialism.* New York, 1974.
Russell Kirk. *The Conservative Mind: Burke to Santayana.* Chicago, 1953.
Henry A. Kissinger. *A World Restored: Metternich, Castlereagh and the Problem of Peace, 1812–1822.* Boston, 1957.
Melvin Kranzberg. *1848: A Turning Point?* Boston, 1959.
Leonard Krieger. *The German Idea of Freedom.* Boston, 1957.
Shirley R. Letwin. *The Pursuit of Certainty.* Cambridge, 1965.
Arthur O. Lovejoy. *Essays in the History of Ideas.* Baltimore, 1948.
David McLellan. *Karl Marx.* New York, 1976.
James Morris. *Pax Britannica.* New York, 1968.
Sir Lewis Namier. *Basic Factors in Nineteenth-Century European History.* London, 1953.
Ronald Pearsall. *The Worm in the Bud: The World of Victorian Sexuality.* London, 1971.
Morse Peckham. *Beyond the Tragic Vision: The Quest for Identity in the Nineteenth Century.* New York, 1962.
Otto Pflanze. *Bismarck and the Development of Germany.* Princeton, 1963.
Joachim Remak. *The Origins of World War I, 1871–1914.* New York, 1967.
Nicholas V. Riasanovsky. *A History of Russia.* New York, 1984.
Norman Rich. *The Age of Nationalism and Reform, 1850–1890.* New York, 1970.
Patrick Richardson. *Empire and Slavery.* London, 1968.
George Rudé. *Debate on Europe, 1815–1850.* New York, 1972.
Carl E. Schorske. *Fin-de-Siècle Vienna: Politics and Culture.* New York, 1981.
L. C. B. Seaman. *From Vienna to Versailles.* New York, 1963.
Hugh Seton-Watson. *The Decline of Imperial Russia, 1855–1914.* New York, 1952.
Boyd C. Shafer. *Nationalism: Myth and Reality.* New York, 1955.
Walter M. Simon. *European Positivism in the Nineteenth Century.* Ithaca, N.Y., 1963.
Walter M. Simon. *French Liberalism, 1789–1848.* New York, 1972.
Denis Mack Smith. *Cavour and Garibaldi, 1860.* Cambridge, 1954.
Louis L. Snyder. *The Idea of Racialism.* Princeton, 1962.
Raymond J. Sontag. *Germany and England: Background of Conflict, 1848–1894.* New York, 1938.

Fritz Stern. *Gold and Iron: Bismarck, Bleichroder, and the Building of the German Empire*. New York, 1979.
A. J. P. Taylor. *Bismarck: The Man and the Statesman*. New York, 1967.
A. P. Thornton. *Doctrines of Imperialism*. New York, 1965.
Frank Miller Turner. *Between Science and Religion*. New Haven, 1974.
Eugen Weber. *France, Fin de Siècle*. Cambridge, Mass., 1986.
Arnold Whitridge. *Men in Crisis: The Revolutions of 1848*. New York, 1949.
Eric Williams. *Capitalism and Slavery*. Chapel Hill, N.C., 1944.
Roger L. Williams. *The World of Napoleon III*. New York, 1962.
Edmund Wilson. *To the Finland Station*. New York, 1940.
Robin W. Winks. *British Imperialism*. New York, 1963.
Edward A. Wrigley. *Industrial Growth and Population Change*. Cambridge, 1961.
G. M. Young. *Victorian England*. Garden City, N.Y., 1954.

## The Twentieth Century

Robert Anchor. *The Modern Western Experience*. Englewood Cliffs, N.J., 1978.
Hannah Arendt. *The Origins of Totalitarianism*. New York, 1958.
Raymond Aron. *The Century of Total War*. Boston, 1955.
Geoffrey Barraclough. *An Introduction to Contemporary History*. New York, 1984.
C. E. Black. *Dynamics of Modernization*. Boston, n.d.
C. E. Black. *The Eastern World since 1945*. New York, n.d.
Zbigniew Brzesinski. *The Soviet Bloc*. Cambridge, Mass., 1967.
Alan Bullock. *Hitler: A Study in Tyrrany*. New York, 1953.
Peter Calvocoressi. *World Politics since 1945*. London, 1968.
Edward Hallett Carr. *The Twenty Years' Crisis, 1919–1939*. New York, 1946.
Alfred Cobban. *A History of Modern France, III, 1871–1962*. Baltimore, 1965.
Maurice Cowling. *The Impact of Hitler*. Chicago, 1977.
George Dangerfield. *The Damnable Question: A Study in Anglo-Irish Relations*. Boston, 1976.
George Dangerfield. *The Strange Death of Liberal England, 1910–1914*. New York, 1935.
Robert V. Daniels. *Red October*. New York, 1967.
Edward Mead Earle. *Modern France: Problems of the Third and Fourth Republics*. Princeton, 1951.
Keith Eubank. *The Origins of World War II*. New York, 1969.
Herbert Feis. *Churchill, Roosevelt, Stalin*. Princeton, 1967.
Fritz Fischer. *Germany's Aims in the First World War*. London, 1967.

Charles A. Fisher. *The Reality of Place.* London, 1965.
Paul Fussell. *The Great War and Modern Memory.* Oxford, 1975.
Hans W. Gatzke. *European Diplomacy Between Two Wars, 1919–1939.* New York, 1972.
Peter Gay and R. K. Webb. *Modern Europe.* New York, 1973.
Peter Gay. *Weimar Culture.* New York, 1968.
Felix Gilbert. *The End of the European Era, 1890 to the Present.* New York, 1970.
Theodore M. Greene. *Liberalism, Its Theory and Practice.* Austin, 1957.
Stanley Hoffmann, et al. *In Search of France.* Cambridge, Mass., 1963.
Hajo Holborn. *The Political Collapse of Europe.* New York, 1951.
Robert A. Huttenback. *Racism and Empire.* Ithaca, N.Y., 1976.
Gabriel Jackson. *The Spanish Republic and the Civil War, 1931–1939.* Princeton, 1965.
Robert Rhodes James. *The British Revolution, 1880–1939.* New York, 1977.
Erich Kahler. *The Germans.* Princeton, 1974.
Paul Kennedy. *The Rise and Fall of the Great Powers.* New York, 1987.
V. G. Kiernan. *The Lords of Human Kind.* London, 1969.
Eugen Kogon. *The Theory and Practice of Hell.* London, 1950.
Lawrence Lafore. *The Long Fuse.* Philadelphia, 1965.
Walter Laqueur. *Europe since Hitler: The Rebirth of Europe.* New York, 1982.
Ivo J. Lederer. *The Versailles Settlement.* Boston, 1960.
Dwight E. Lee. *The Outbreak of the First World War,* revised ed. Boston, 1963.
William Roger Louis. *The Origins of the Second World War: A. J. P. Taylor and His Critics.* New York, 1972.
Evan Luard. *A History of the United Nations.* London, 1982.
Charles S. Maier. *The Origins of the Cold War and Contemporary Europe.* New York, 1978.
Charles S. Maier. *Recasting Bourgeois Europe: Stabilization in France, Italy, and Germany in the Decade after World War I.* Princeton, 1975.
Arthur J. Marder. *The Anatomy of British Sea Power.* New York, 1940.
Philip Mason. *Patterns of Dominance.* London, 1970.
Ernst Nolte. *Three Faces of Fascism.* New York, 1966.
Stanley G. Payne. *The Spanish Revolution.* New York, 1970.
Michael M. Postan. *An Economic History of Western Europe, 1945–1964.* London, 1966.
Joachim Remak. *Serajevo: The Story of Political Murder.* New York, 1959.
Henry L. Roberts. *Russia and America.* New York, 1956.
Esmonde M. Robertson. *The Origins of the Second World War.* London, 1971.
Bernard Semmel. *Imperialism and Social Reform.* Garden City, N.Y., 1960.
John L. Snell. *The Nazi Revolution.* Boston, 1959.
Raymond J. Sontag. *A Broken World, 1919–1939.* New York, 1971.

Peter N. Stearns. *European Society in Upheaval*. New York, 1967.
A. J. P. Taylor. *The Struggle for Mastery in Europe, 1848–1918*. Oxford, 1954.
Hugh Thomas. *The Spanish Civil War*. New York, 1961.
Hugh Thomas. *The Cuban Revolution*. London, 1986.
Christopher Thorne. *The Approach of War, 1938–39*. London, 1967.
Donald Treadgold. *Twentieth-Century Russia*. Chicago, 1959.
Barbara Tuchman. *The Guns of August*. New York, 1962.
Henry A. Turner, Jr. *Reappraisals of Fascism*. New York, 1975.
T. E. Vadney. *The World since 1945*. New York, 1987.
Morton G. White. *The Age of Analysis: Twentieth-Century Philosophers*. New York, n.d.
Chester Wilmot. *The Struggle for Europe*. London, 1952.
Henry R. Winkler. *Twentieth-Century Britain*. New York, 1976.
Bertram D. Wolfe. *Three Who Made a Revolution*. Boston, 1948.
Gordon Wright. *The Ordeal of Total War, 1939–1945*. New York, 1968.

# Index

Abbasids, 117
abortion, 463
absolutism, 223
Abyssinia, 432
acculturation, 145
Acre, 174
Acropolis, 64
Adams, John, 220
Adenauer, Konrad, 453
Aegean civilization, 41
*Aeneid*, 98
Aeschylus, 65, 68
Africa
   Boer War in, 380–381
   exploration of, 209
   imperialism in, 345–346, 363, 375–376
Afrikaans, 219
Agadir, Morocco, 387
*agathos*, 53
Age of Discovery, 179, 180, 191–194
   mercantilism in, 202–205
   science and technology in, 205–207
*agora*, 13
agriculture
   beginnings of, 17–20
   commercial, 168
   in early Europe, 140, 150, 151–153
   in eighteenth century, 233

agriculture *(cont.)*:
   in Nile Valley, 23
   in nineteenth century, 335
   in Tigris-Euphrates Valleys, 20
   in traditional Europe, 167–169
Ahriman, 39
Ahura Mazda, 39
AIDS, 463
aircraft, in World War I, 400, 409
Akhenaton, 33
Albania, 389, 449
Albuquerque, Alfonso de, 212
Alexander II, 327, 328, 330
Alexander III, 331
Alexander the Great, 50, 70–71
Alexandria, 74, 77–78, 79
Alexius, 161
Algeciras conference, 383
*Alice in Wonderland* (Carroll), 340
alienation, 276
Allah, 115
Al-Mamun, 132
alphabet, Cyrillic, 129
Alsace-Lorraine, 294, 295, 378, 412
Amenhotep IV, 33
American Revolution, 204, 243, 254
Amsterdam, 200, 218
*Anabasis (The March of Up-Country)*, 70

493

## INDEX

anarchism, 329–330
Anatolia, 78, 148
Anglican Church, 216
Anglo-American War, 365
Anglo-French wars, 223–225
annexation, 349, 351
Antarctic, 226
Antioch, 74, 105
Antiochus IV, 80
anti-Semitism, 324–327, 430
   *See also* Jews
Antony, Mark, 90
apostles, 100
Aquinas, St. Thomas, 178, 194
Arabs, 114–118, 147, 211–212, 457–458
   cultural traditions, 130–134
Aramaic, 33, 39, 75
Archbishop of Canterbury, 114
Ardashir, 51, 104
*arete*, 53
Argentina, 349, 374, 460
aristocracy
   in ancient Greece, 53–54, 56
   in eighteenth century, 233
   in Europe, 189
   in French Revolution, 245, 246
   Industrial Revolution and, 235
   in medieval Europe, 143–144
   Roman, 85–86, 88
   in traditional England, 170
*aristoi*, 42, 53
Aristotle, 68
Armada, 216–217
armistice, 408
art
   Byzantine, 128–129
   Dutch, 217
   French, 314–315
artillery, 400
arts
   in Austria-Hungary, 321
   in medieval Europe, 163
   in post-World War I Europe, 418
   in Renaissance, 179–180
Asquith, Herbert, 397, 401
Assyria, 35, 38
astronomy, 206
Asturias, 142
Atahualpa, 211
Athens, 49, 55–60, 61, 63, 78
   decline of, 68–70
   Golden Age of, 63–68

atomic bomb, 442, 448
Augsburg, Peace of, 184
Augustine, 125
Augustus (Octavian), 90, 93–94, 97
Aulard, Alphonse, 238
Aurelian, 105
Aurelius, Marcus, 94, 103
*Ausgleich*, 323–324
Australia, 348, 356, 357, 368, 401
Austria, 175, 256, 259, 289, 290, 293–294, 319–327, 419
   Nazism in, 421
   in World War I, 378–379, 385–386, 389–391, 392–394, 398–399, 400, 401–402, 403, 404, 408, 412
   in World War II, 432
Austria-Hungary, 384–386, 389, 412
Austro-Hungarian empire, 319–327
autarchy, 53, 197
*Autobhanen*, 427
autocracy, Russian, 327–331
automobile, 307, 427–428
Avars, 111, 112, 128, 143
Averroes, 131
Avignon, 172
Aztecs, 210

Babylon, 71
Bacon, Francis, 227, 459
Bactria, 51
Bagehot, Walter, 286
Baghdad, 117–118, 132–134
Bakunin, Mikhail, 271, 329–330
balance of power, 344–345
Balboa, Vasco Nunez de, 210
Balkan League, 388–392
Balkans, 378–379, 384–386
Ballot Act of 1872, 315–316
bankers, 200
barbarians, 83, 84, 107, 108–111, 125, 145
barbarism, 12–13, 30–31, 36
Basil II, 147
Battle of Hastings, 146
Battle of the Bulge, 442
Bedouins, 107
Belgium, 261–262, 351, 394, 397, 398, 437, 442
Bell, Alexander Graham, 306
Belloc, Hilaire, 403
*Beowulf*, 13, 42
Berbers, 131, 147
Berlin, Isaiah, 5

Berlin airlift, 447
Bernstein, Eduard, 335
Bertillon, Alphonse, 313
Bethmann-Hollweg, Theobald von, 386, 387, 392, 393, 394, 395, 399, 403–404
Bible, 100, 182, 188–189
biology, 282
birth control, 306, 462
birth rate, 233
bishoprics, 156
Bismarck, Otto von, 292–298, 321, 378–379
Black Death, 168
Black Hand, 392
blacks, 339
   *See also* racism
Blanc, Louis, 275
Boccaccio, Giovanni, 176
Boer War, 380–381
Bohemia, 221
Bolsheviks, 330, 405, 422
Boniface VIII, 163, 182
*Book of the Courtier*, 177
borrowing, 200
Bosnia-Hercegovina, 386
Bossuet, Jacques, 223
Botticelli, Sandro, 179
Boulainvilliers, Comte de, 339
Boulanger, Georges, 312
Brancusi, Constantine, 471
Brazil, 214
Brentano, Clemens, 339
Briand, Aristide, 314
British. *See* England; Great Britain
British Empire, 342–344, 360–364, 376
   *See also* Great Britain, imperialism
bronze, 19
Brunelleschi, Filippo, 179
Brutus, 89
Budapest, 320
*Buddenbrooks* (Mann), 299
Buffon, Leclerc, 339
Bulgaria, 386, 389, 402
Bulgars, 128
bullion, 202
Bulow, Bernhard von, 382–383
burghers, 208
Burgundy, 170
Burke, Edmund, 257, 361
Byzantine Empire, 111–114, 127–128, 128–130, 147, 149, 161, 162, 175
Byzantium, 52, 111

Cabada, 348
Cabet, Etienne, 275
Cabot, John, 215
Caesar, Augustus (Octavian), 90, 93–94, 97
Caesar, Julius, 89, 92
Caillaux, Joseph, 392
calculus, 206
caliphate, 132
Calvin, Jean, 185–186
Calvinism, 186
camera, 307
Camoes, Luis Vaz de, 214
Canaan, 32
Canaanites, 33, 36
Canada, 204–205, 224, 270, 364–368
Canal Zone, 373
*Candide* (Voltaire), 232
Canute, 146
Cape Colony, 380–381
Cape of Good Hope, 219
Capetian dynasty, 162
capitalism, 190
   early, 196–202, 234
   imperialism and, 337
   Industrial Revolution and, 234–235
   laissez-faire, 202, 267, 343
   Lenin's view of, 337–338
   Marxian view of, 280–281
Caprivi, Georg Leo von, 379
Caracalla, 98
Carcassone, 139
cardinals, college of, 158
Caribbean colonies, 342–343
Carlsbad Decrees, 259
Carnegie, Andrew, 285, 287
Carolingian kings, 143
Carroll, Lewis, 340
Carthage, 83, 87, 95
Carthaginian civilization, 76, 87
cartography, 193
Casa de Contratacion, 213
Cassius, 89
Castiglione, Baldassare de, 177
Catherine of Aragon, 184, 215
Catholic Church, 182, 187
   in France, 314
   Germany and, 294–297
   in Italy, 291–292
   in Spain, 208
   *See also* papacy; religion
cause, proximate, 189

cavalry, 150–151
Cavour, Camillo di, 288–289
Celts, 95–96
Cervantes, Miguel de, 180
Ceylon, 364
Chamberlain, Joseph, 379
Chamberlain, Neville, 434, 437
Champlain, Samuel de, 364
Champollion, Jean-Jacques, 27
change, 258–259
  technological, 305–308
  *See also* progress
Charlemagne, 143–144
Charles I, 227
Charles V, 183, 214
Charles X, 261
child labor, 274
Children's Crusade, 162
China, 372, 432, 460
  contact with Roman Empire, 102
  trade with, 76
chivalry, 166
chlorine gas, 400, 409
Christendom, 157, 158, 160, 175, 194–195
Christianity
  in Age of Discovery, 212–213
  beginnings of, 100–102
  in Byzantine Empire, 112, 113–114
  in early Europe, 156–159
  European expansionism and, 194–195
  Gregorian, 136–138
  growth of, in Europe, 135–138
  in medieval Europe, 160
  in Middle Ages, 126
  Reformation and, 181–190
  in Renaissance, 176
  in Roman Empire, 105–106, 107–108
  in traditional Europe, 174
Christian Socialist Party, 326
Churchill, Winston, 401, 437, 446, 447, 472
Church of England, 184, 215
Church of Holy Wisdom, 128
Cicero, 92
cinema, 307
Cistercian movement, 152, 157
cities
  in ancient Greece, 44
  earliest, 20
  in Hellenistic civilization, 74, 78–79
  Industrial Revolution and, 234
  in medieval Europe, 164

Cities *(cont.):*
  in Roman Empire, 97–98
  *See also* urbanization; specific cities
citizenship, 171
city-states, Greek, 49, 63–65, 68–69
civilizations
  boundaries of, 12
  contact between, 14, 21, 28, 30–31, 75–76, 193
  expansion of earliest, 26
  features of, 12–15
  Mediterranean, 30–32
class. *See* social class
class struggle, 278–279
Cleisthenes, 56
Clemenceau, Georges, 406
Cleopatra, 90
Clermont, 160
Cleveland, Grover, 370
client states, Roman, 87
climatic change, effect on early civilizations, 24–26
Climatic Optimum, 25
Clive, Robert, 225
cloth making, 198
Clovis, 111, 142
Cluny, 155
coal production, 341
codex, 102
Coen, Jan Pieterszoon, 218
Colbert, J. B., 205
Cold War, 446–449
colonies, 193, 204, 212–213, 219–221, 225, 243, 308, 342–345, 375–376
  Canada as example, 364–368
  economic gains from, 343, 350–353
  New Zealand as example, 355–359
  responses to administrators, 353–359
  trusteeship and, 361–364
  U.S., 373
  *See also* imperialism
Columbus, Christopher, 209–210
Combes, Emile, 314
commercial revolution, 197
commodities, in early world trade, 200
Commodus, 103
Common Market, 453–454
Communards, 311
communes, 273–274
communications
  modern, 464
  in nineteenth century, 305

communications *(cont.)*:
  technology for, 306–307
Communism, 262, 277, 281, 420–421
  in Soviet Union, 422–426
*Communist Manifesto* (Marx and Engels), 276
companies, limited-liability, 199
competition, 204
computer, 464
Congress of Vienna, 342, 344
conquerors, 30
conquistadors, 210–211
conservatism
  British, 316–317
  Burkean, 257–259
  imperialism and, 361
  nationalism and, 270
  nineteenth-century, 267–268, 271
Considerant, Victor, 275
Constantine, 106
Constantinople, 51, 106, 110, 111, 112, 117, 127, 128–129, 161, 162, 175, 178
consuls, Roman, 85, 86
continuity, change and, 12
Cook, James, 226
cooling cycles, 25
Copernicus, Nicholas, 206
copper tools, 19
Cordoba, Spain, 132
Corn Laws, 342, 343
Cortes, Hernando, 210
cosmology, 206
cosmopolitanism, 129
Council of Constance, 172
Council of the Indies, 212
Council of Trent, 187
Crassus, Marcus Licimius, 89
creation, views of, 283–284
Crete, 28–29, 31
crime, in medieval Europe, 165
Crimean War, 289, 311, 327
Croats, 385
Cromwell, Oliver, 227
Crusades, 159–162, 174
Cuba, 370–372
cultures, effects of imperialism on, 353–359, 360
Cunard, Samuel, 308
Cyrillic alphabet, 129
Cyrus the Great, 36, 61
Czechoslovakia, 432, 433, 435, 447–448

da Gama, Christopher, 209
da Gama, Vasco, 209, 211
Daimler, Gottlieb, 307
Damascus, 117
Dante, 167
Dardanelles, 401
Darius I, 61
Darius II, 70
Darwin, Charles, 282–284, 285
Darwinism, 284–287, 340
David, Jacques Louis, 247
David, King, 37
da Vinci, Leonardo, 179
Declaration of Rights of Man and the Citizen, 246
*Decline of the West, The* (Spengler), 310
decolonization, 456–460, 461
*decurions*, 97
de Gaulle, Charles, 437, 448
Deism, 228
Delcasse, Theophile, 314
Delacroix, Eugene, 237
democracy, 238, 246, 249
  Athenian, 57
  in colonies, 363
  Greek, 65
democratic revolution, 253
*demos*, 42
*denarius*, 134
Denmark, 293, 436
Depression, 419–421
Descartes, Rene, 227
*Descent of Man* (Darwin), 283
despots, enlightened, 232
determinism, economic, 277–278
devaluation, 201
*Devotio Moderna*, 174
dialectical materialism, 278, 281
Dias, Bartholomeu, 209
Dickens, Charles, 340
Diderot, Denis, 229
Diet at Worms, 183
*Digenis Akritas*, 130
Diocletian, 105
*Discourse on Method* (Descartes), 227
discovery, nature of, 193
*Discus Thrower*, 58
Disraeli, Benjamin, 315, 317, 343
*Divine Comedy* (Dante), 167
Divine Right of Kings, 223
division of labor
  in early agricultural communities, 19, 20

division of labor *(cont.):*
  in temple-cities, 20
Donatello, 179
*Don Quixote* (Cervantes), 180
Drake, Sir Francis, 216
drama, Greek, 59
*Dreadnought,* 384
Dreyfus, Alfred, 313–314
Drucker, Peter, 445
drugs, 463–464
duchies, 154, 155
*Duma,* 331
Dupleix, Joseph, 225
Durham Report, 365–366
Dutch colonies, 350
Dutch culture, 217–218

East India Company, 201, 205
East Indies, 209
ecclesiastical councils, 108
ecclesiastical laws, 158
economic determinism, 277–278
economic regulations, 202–205
economics
  classical, 279–281
  in Hellenistic civilization, 74, 75
  of international trade, 344
  laissez-faire, 202, 267, 343
  Marxian, 276–279, 280–281
  Marxist-Leninist, 338
  mercantilism and, 202–205
  in Roman Empire, 97
  in traditional Europe, 168
economic systems, 196–202
Edict of Nantes, 222
Edison, Thomas A., 306–307
education
  in early Europe, 157–158
  during Enlightenment, 232
  in English colonies, 219
  in Hellenistic civilizations, 72
  in traditional Europe, 172
Edward III, 169
Egypt
  ancient, 31, 32, 33
  earliest civilization, 23–24
  Hellenism in, 50, 51
  imperialism in, 346
  Ptolemaic, 72, 77–78
  Upper, 81
Einstein, Albert, 299, 315

Eisner, Kurt, 408
electricity, 306–307
Elgin, Lord, 366
El Greco, 213
Elizabethan Age, 180
Elizabeth I, 188, 216
emirs, 134
empires. *See* imperialism; specific empires
Engels, Friedrich, 262, 276–277
engine, internal combustion, 307
England
  in Age of Exploration, 215–216
  Anglo-Saxon, 141–142
  Catholic Church in, 114
  Christianity in, 138
  Church in, 184
  colonization by, 219–221
  economic system in, 202–205
  Enlightenment in, 232–233
  Industrial Revolution in, 232–233, 234–236
  mercantilism in, 202–205
  monarchies in, 169–171, 208, 215–216
  parliamentary government in, 227
  population growth in, 233
  Protestant, 216
  during Reformation, 184
  trading system of, 198
  wars with France, 223–225
  war with Spain, 216–217
  *See also* Great Britain
*English in Ireland in the Eighteenth Century, The* (Froude), 286–287
English language, 180, 465
Enlightenment, 191, 228–232
  ideas of government in, 244–245
Entente Cordiale, 383
entrepreneurs, 197–198, 234
environmental movement, 465
*ephebeia,* 72
Epicurus, 93
Epirus, 87
*Epistles,* 100
equestrians, Roman, 88, 90
Erasmus, 177–178, 180
Erasmus of Rotterdam, 177
*Essay Concerning Human Understanding* (Locke), 227
Essenes, 81, 99
Ethiopia, 209
Etruria, 83, 84, 86

Etruscans, 76, 83, 85
eugenics, 285–286, 340
Euripedes, 68
Europe
  Age of Discovery in, 191–194
  Church in, 172–174
  Cold War and, 446–449
  Common Market in, 453–454
  Communism in, 420–421
  conservativism in, 257–260
  defense of, 447–449
  demographic change in, 167–169
  Depression in, 419–421
  development of independent nations in, 175
  economic system in, 196–202
  fascism in, 426–430
  Germanic, 134–135, 138–139
  growth of Christianity in, 135–138
  imperialism of, 341–364, 374–377
  industrialization in, 334–335
  liberalism in, 266–268
  Marxism in, 276–279
  in Middle Ages, 123–135, 140–146, 148–163
  modern, 190–191, 454–455, 460–462
  modernization in, 232–234
  nationalism in, 254–256, 268–271, 288–300
  nineteenth-century, 310–327, 333–340
  population boom in, 334–335
  post-World War I, 417–418
  post-World War II, 443–455
  racism in, 338–340
  Reformation in, 181–190
  Renaissance in, 175–181
  revolutions in, 260
  rise of monarchies in, 169–172
  socialism in, 272–275
  statism in, 244
  territorial expansion of, 190–196
  trade in eighteenth century, 243
  urbanization in, 164–165
  in World War I, 377–414
  *See also* individual countries
European Economic Community, 453–454
European Free Trade Area (EFTA), 454
evolution, 282–284
evolutionary socialism, 336
exploration, 190, 194, 195–196, 209–215, 220, 226

Ezra, 38

"factory," 197
Falkenhayn, Erich von, 398, 401, 402, 403
Falkland Islands, 460
family
  in eighteenth century, 233
  modern, 462
famine, 168
Faraday, Michael, 306
farming. *See* agriculture
fascism, 418, 426–430
  in Europe, 421
*Fathers and Sons* (Turgenev), 329
Fatimid dynasty, 132
Ferdinand, 208
Ferdinand, Archduke, 392
Ferdinand of Styria, 221
Ferdinand VII, 260
Ferry, Jules, 344
feudalism, 144, 207–208
Feuerbach, Ludwig, 277–278
fitness (for survival), 282–283, 285–286
Five Ordinances, 261
Flavians, 94
Florence, 179
Foch, Ferdinand, 407
Ford, Henry, 307
Fourier, Charles, 273–274
Fourteen Points, 406–407
France
  alliance with Italy (1858), 289
  colonies of, 346, 349, 350
  economy of, 454–455
  Enlightenment in, 228–232, 245
  factors contributing to Revolution, 236–242
  industrialization of, 315
  late nineteenth-century, 310–315, 344
  medieval, 154–155, 162
  mercantilism in, 205
  monarchies in, 169–171, 208, 222–223
  in Morocco, 382–383, 387–388
  nationalism in, 269
  in nineteenth century, 261, 262–263
  post-World War I, 418
  during Reformation, 188
  during Revolution, 245–249
  Third Republic, 311–315
  wars with England, 223–225
  war with Prussia, 294

France *(cont.)*:
  in World War I, 381, 383, 390, 392, 394, 397–398, 400, 402, 406–408
  in World War II, 436, 437, 441, 442
France, Anatole, 308
Franco, Francisco, 426
Franco-Prussian War, 311
Franks, 111, 117, 135, 140, 142, 143–145
freedoms, basic, 267
free enterprise, 202, 267
free love, 274
free speech, 265–266
free trade, 202, 267, 341, 342, 343
French and Indian War, 224
French Canadians, 366, 367
French Century, 222
French Republic, 311–312
French Revolution, 236–242, 245–249
  significance of, 253–254
Freud, Sigmund, 336
Frobisher, Martin, 195
Fronde, 223
Froude, James Anthony, 286–287
Fuggers, 197, 198
Fulton, Robert, 308
fundamentalists, 283–284

Galatians, 96
Galileo, 206
Gallipoli, 401
Galt, Alexander T., 366
Galton, Francis, 340
Gandhi, Indira, 458
Gandhi, Mohandas, 360
*Gargantua and Pantagruel* (Rabelais), 180
Garibaldi, Giuseppe, 290
Gaul, 89, 104, 139, 143
Gauls, 95–96
Gay, Peter, 266
gay rights, 463
Geneva, Switzerland, 185–186
*German Catechism*, 269, 270
Germanic Europe, 134–135, 138–139
Germanic peoples, 104, 107, 109, 126
German Social Democrats, 297–298
Germany
  colonies of, 346, 350
  conservatism in, 295–296
  industrialization in, 298–299, 382
  Industrial Revolution in, 235–236
  inflation in, 417–418

Germany *(cont.)*:
  kings in, 154
  late nineteenth-century, 336–337
  medieval, 154
  nationalism in, 269, 270
  nationalism of, 292–300
  Nazis in, 421, 426–430
  post-World War I, 417–418
  post-World War II, 444, 447
  racism in, 339
  Reformation in, 182–184
  revolutions in, 262
  social security measures in, 268
  in Thirty Years' War, 221–222
  unification of, 294, 296
  in World War I, 378–379, 382–388, 390–414
  in World War II, 431–442
Ghana, 364
*Gilgamesh*, 22
Giotto, 179
Gladstone, William Ewart, 315, 318
*glasnost*, 456
Gobineau, Joseph Arthur de, 339
Godfrey of Lorraine, 161
gods, Greek, 57
Goethe, Johann Wolfgang von, 257
Golden Horn, 128, 129
Gorbachev, Mikhail, 456
gospels, 100
Gothic architecture, 159
Goths, 104, 107, 108–109
government
  liberal view of, 266–267
  parliamentary, 227
  role of, 244–245
Goya, Francisco, 248, 300
Gracchus, Gaius, 88
Gracchus, Tiberius, 88
Great Britain
  in Boer War, 380–381
  in Canada, 364–368
  Depression in, 419, 420
  formation of, 317
  imperialism of, 342–344, 350–351, 355–359, 360–368
  industrialization in, 341
  late ninteenth-century, 315–319
  in New Zealand, 361–364
  in nineteenth century, 255–256
  post-World War I, 417–418

Great Britain *(cont.)*:
  post-World War II, 454
  Reform Act, 263
  in World War I, 383, 384, 387, 392, 394–395, 397–401, 403, 404, 406–408, 410, 414
  in World War II, 436–437, 442
  *See also* England
Greece, 448
  in Balkan War, 389
  break from Turkish empire, 260–261
  in Byzantine Empire, 130
Greece, ancient, 53–54
  aristocracy in, 53–54, 56
  cities in, 43
  city-states, 49–50, 53–70
  code of honor in, 53
  Golden Age of, 61–71
  Hellenistic, 50–51, 72–77
  heroic period, 40–45
  homosexuality in, 60
  households in, 40, 53
  migration from, 43–44
  military in, 54
  *polis*, 56–59, 63–68, 69
  religion in, 57
  Roman intervention in, 87
  urbanization of, 53–54
  women in, 59–60
Greek gods, 43
Gregory, 125
Gregory I, 114, 136
Gregory VII, 158
Grey, Sir Edward, 383, 387, 394
Grotius, Hugo, 203, 222
Grove, William R., 306
*Grundrisse* (Marx), 276
Guam, 371, 373
guilds, 199–200
gunboats, 342
Gutenberg, John, 180
gutta-percha, 307
gymnasium, 72

Hadrian, 103
Hagia Sophia, 128
Haig, Sir Douglas, 403, 406, 407
Halifax, 220
*Hamlet* (Shakespeare), 180
Hammurabi, 22
Han China, 102, 108
Hannibal, 87
Hanseatic League, 215
Hapsburgs, 183, 214, 222, 255, 256, 319
Harun al-Rashid, 132
Hasidim, 80
Hatshepsut, 24
Hawaii, 226, 369–370
Hazlitt, William, 340
Hebrews, 32–33, 36–39
hedonism, 93
Hegel, G. W. F., 270, 278
Heine, Heinrich, 276
heliocentrism, 206
Hellenic League, 70
Hellenism, 50–51, 84, 85
  in Byzantine period, 130
  Christianized, 111
  Roman attitudes toward, 91
  Romanized, 52
Hellenistic civilization, 72–82
Hellenization, 72
*helots*, 53
Henry, The Navigator, 209
Henry II, 162
Henry III, 157
Henry IV of Navarre, 188, 222
Henry VII, 208
Henry VIII, 184, 185, 215
Heraclius I, 112
heredity, 340
heresy, 165
Herodotus, 68
heroic Greece, 40–45
Herzl, Theodor, 314, 325
Hesiod, 54
*hetarae*, 60
Hindenburg, Paul von, 398
Hinsely, F. H., 395
historiography, French Revolution and, 236–242
history
  moral ambiguities in, 469–472
  relevance of, 1–8
Hitler, Adolf, 327, 426–430, 432–437, 440–442
Hittite Empire, 30, 31, 32, 35
Hobbes, Thomas, 223
Hobson, John A., 344
Hoffer, Eric, 460
Hofmannsthal, Hugo von, 320, 321
Holbein, Hans, 177, 185

holidays, national, 269–270
Holland, 203, 216, 217–219, 437
Holmes, Oliver Wendell, Jr., 266
Holocaust, 430, 458
Holstein, 293
Holy Roman Empire, 162, 183, 214, 222
Holy See, 295
home front, 410
Homer, 13, 42, 43, 57
Home Rule, Irish, 317–319
hominids, 17
homosexuality, 463
  in ancient Greece, 60
*Homo Univesale*, 178
*honestiores*, 97
*hoplites*, 57
horse collar, 151
Hotzendorf, Conrad von, 391
Huguenots, 222
humanism, 177–178, 180
humanitarianism, 347
humanities, 93
human nature, 246, 257
humans, evolution of, 16, 17
*humiliores*, 97
Hundred Years' War, 169, 170, 171
Hungary, 145, 323, 385
  See also Austria-Hungary
Huns, 108
hunting and gathering, 17
Hus, John, 221
Huxley, Thomas, 283, 340
Hyksos, 23, 30, 31

Iberia, 208
Ibsen, Henrik, 308
Ice Age, 25
icons, 113, 125, 129
Ikhnaton, 33, 34
Illyria, 105
imperialism, 226, 342–344
  British, 316, 350–351, 355–359, 360–368
  capitalism and, 337–338
  cost of, 350–351
  effects of, 359–360, 457
  end of, 456–460
  motivations for, 345–350, 376
  "new," 374–377
  reactions to, 353–359
  trusteeship and, 361–364

imperialism *(cont.)*:
  types of, 354
  U.S., 368–374
*Imperialism: A Study* (Hobson), 344
Incas, 211
India, 350, 360, 362–363, 458
  French versus English in, 224–225
  trade with, 76, 211
Indian Ocean, 76
Indians, American, 369
individualism, 228, 244, 246, 264–266, 267
indulgences, 182
industrialism, in Germany, 298–299
industrialization, 234–235, 305, 334–335, 341
Industrial Revolution, 207, 232, 234–236
Indus Valley, 25
infallibility, papal, 295
inflation, 190, 200, 201, 417–418
Inquisition, 208
*Institutes of the Christian Religion* (Calvin), 185, 186
insurance, 337
intellectual revolution, 206–207
interest rates, 200
international cooperation, 333–334
International Court of Arbitration, 334
International Institute of Public Health, 334
International Labor Office, 333–334
international organizations, 448, 452–455
invention, 236, 305–308
Iran, 460
  See also Persia
Iraq, 132
Ireland, 138, 216, 319, 458
Irish Free State, 319
Irish Home Rule, 317–319
iron, 34–35
Iron Age, 35
Isabella, 208
Islam, 52, 115, 118
  in Middle Ages, 126
  during Renaissance, 178
  rituals of, 131
Islamic culture, 130–134, 147
Isocrates, 70
Israel, 457–458
  legendary history of, 36–39
Israelites, 36–37

Istanbul, 178
Italy, 381
   colonies of, 356, 350
   fascism in, 426
   Greek cities in, 83–84
   Lombard, 141, 142
   in medieval period, 162
   nationalism in, 270
   Renaissance in, 176, 179
   revolution in, 260, 262
   unification of, 290
   in World War I, 388, 401, 402, 406
   in World War II, 432, 434, 437, 441

Jameson, L. S., 380
Jamestown, 220
Japan, 369, 374, 381–382, 460
   in World War II, 431, 432, 439, 441, 442, 440
Jaures, Jean, 392
Jeroboam II, 38
Jerome, 124, 125
Jerusalem, 161, 162
Jesuits, 187, 259, 295
Jesus of Nazareth, 100
*Jewish State* (Herzl), 314
Jews, 259
   ancient, 38–39
   in Austria-Hungary, 324–327
   conversion to Christianity, 276
   in Hellenistic period, 78–82
   homeland for, 458
   in medieval period, 161, 162
   Nazi persecution of, 430
   professions of, 324–325
   in Roman Empire, 99, 103
   *See also* Hebrews; Judaism
jihad, 131
Joffre, Joseph, 397–398
John (king of England), 170
John Paul II, 462
Jonson, Ben, 180
Joseph, Franz, 323, 392
Josiah, 38
Judah, 38
Judaism, 36, 38–39, 99, 100, 102
Jugurtha, 88
Justinian, 111, 112

*Kapital, Das* (Marx), 276
Kellogg-Briand Pact, 431

Kepler, John, 206
Kerensky, Aleksandr, 405, 422
Keynes, John Maynard, 334, 338
Khomeini, Ayatollah, 460
Kidd, Benjamin, 340
kings
   divine right of, 223
   in Hellenistic civilizations, 76–77
   Roman, 85
kingship, 158–159, 162–163, 169–172
Kino, Eusebio, 213
Kipling, Rudyard, 348
Kitchener, Lord, 401
Kleist, Heinrich von, 269, 270
knights, 165–166
Knossos, 28–29
Knox, John, 186
*koine*, 74
Koran, 115, 178
Kropotkin, Prince, 330
Kruger, Paul, 380
*Kulturkampf*, 295

labor
   in early capitalism, 198, 199
   manual, 15
   organized, 267–268, 335
   *See also* work; workers
labor theory of value, 279
Labour Party, 317
Lambton, "Radical Jack," 365–366
land management, 152, 153
language, 180
   Aramaic, 75
   in Byzantine Empire, 129, 130
   English, 180, 465
   Greek, 74, 75, 79
   Latin, 91
   in modern world, 465
   racism and, 339
La Salle, Sieur de, 220
Latin, 91, 92
Latin America, U.S. in, 373–374
Latin Empire, 162
Latium, 76
law
   British, 361
   international, 203, 222
   in medieval period, 158, 165
   Roman, 98
League of Corinth, 70

League of Nations, 413–414, 452
Lefebvre, Georges, 242
legal institutions, 165
leisure ethic, 64
lending, 200
Lenin, V. I., 308, 337, 405, 422, 424
Leo I, 135
Leo III, 129, 142
Leo IX, 157
Leo X, 182
Levant, 31, 33, 39, 161
*Leviathan* (Hobbes), 223
liberalism
 British, 316–318
 nineteenth-century, 264–268, 271
Lib-Imps, 383
Lima, 211
lingua franca, 461, 465
literacy, 464
literature
 French, 314
 Latin, 92–93
 nineteenth-century, 308
 Renaissance, 177–178, 180
 *See also* specific works
Little Englanders, 343
Liverpool, 234
Livingston, Robert R., 308
Livy, 92, 98
Lloyd George, David, 316–317, 387, 397, 400, 406, 428
Locke, John, 226–227, 229, 244
logic, study of, 157
Lombards, 111, 141
lords, medieval, 153–155
Louis IV, 344
Louis Napoleon, 263, 263, 264, 310–311
Louis Philippe, 261, 262
Louis the Pious, 144
Louis XI, 208
Louis XIII, 222
Louis XIV, 223
Louis XVI, 245, 246
Louis XVIII, 261
loyalty, territorial, 11
Lucretius, 92, 93
Ludendorff, Erich von, 397, 398, 405, 407–408
Lueger, Karl, 325–326, 327
*Lusitania*, 399
Luther, Martin, 181–184
Lutheranism, 184, 186

Lvov, George, 405
Lyceum, 68
Lycurgus, 54

Macao, 212
Maccabees, 80
Macedon, 50
Macedonia, 70, 78, 389
Machiavelli, Nicolo, 178
machine gun, 403
Mackenzie, William Lyon, 365
Mackinder, Halford John, 383
Magyars, 145, 323, 385
*Maine*, 370–371
Malacca, 209, 218, 219, 343
Malay, 376
Malaya, 307
Malthus, 279–280
Manchester school, 343
Manifest Destiny, 368
Manila Bay, 370, 371
Mann, Thomas, 299
Manual I, 214
manufacture, 198, 199
 domestic, 198, 234
Manzikert, 148
Maoris, 196, 355–359
maps, creation of, 193
Marconi, Guglielmo, 306
Marius, Gaius, 88–89
marriage
 in ancient Greece, 59–60
 in eighteenth century, 233
 modern, 462
Marsden, Samuel, 355
Marshall, George, 445
Marshall Plan, 445
Martel, Charles, 117, 142–143
Marx, Karl, 262, 275, 276–279, 308
Marxism, 276–279
 revisionist, 335–336
 Russian, 330
Marxist-Leninism, 337–338
Marxists, 238–230
Massachusetts, 219
materialism, dialectical, 278, 281
mathematics, 206
Mauritius, 343
Mauthausen, Austria, 6
Maxim gun, 403
Maximilian, 311
Mazarin, Cardinal, 223

Mazzini, Guiseppi, 320
Mboya, Tom, 363
McKinley, William, 371, 372
Mecca, 114, 115
Medici, Catherine de, 188
Medicis, 197
Medina, 114
*Mein Kampf* (Hitler), 430, 435, 440
meliorism, 303
Menes-Narmer, 23
Mensheviks, 330
mercantilism, 202–205, 213, 342, 343
   in British colonies, 220–221
   Dutch, 218–219
mercenary soldiers, 69, 70
merchant class, 199–201
merchant marine, 203, 218
Mercia, 142
Mesopotamia, 20–22, 24, 26, 35, 61, 71
   in Hellenistic period, 78
*mestizo*, 210
metals, precious, 200, 202, 213
Methodist church, 347
*metics*, 59
Metternich, Prince von, 259
Mexico, 210, 212, 213, 311, 374
Michelangelo, 180
Michelet, Jules, 238
Middle Ages
   750–950, 127–147
   950–1300, 147–164
middle class, 235, 249, 254, 271, 279
Middle East. *See* specific civilizations, countries
migration, 255
   of ancient Greeks, 43–44
   invasion and, 31–32
Miletus, 61
*Milion*, 129
military
   in ancient Greece, 69–70
   Roman, 87–88, 98
   social class and, 201
military state, Sparta as, 54–55
Mill, John Stuart, 264–267
milling, 151
Miltiades, 61
mining, 200, 207
   in early Europe, 156
Minoan Crete, 29
*mir*, 328, 332
missiles, 304

missionaries, 213, 347
*mission civilitrice*, 349
Mississippi River, 220
mobility
   in ancient Near East, 83
   in Hellenistic civilization, 72
   social, 172
modern history, 253
modernity, 191
modernization, 226–227, 228, 232, 242, 305, 360, 362
modern world, 190–191
Mogul Empire, 224
Mohammed, 115
Moltke, Helmut von, 378, 391, 394, 398
Mommsen, Theodore, 299
monarchies, European, 169–172, 183–184, 208
monasticism, 136–137, 145, 152, 156–157, 183
money, 130, 134, 200–201, 202, 334
Monnet, Jean, 453
Monophysites, 112
monopolies, 201, 205, 218, 337–338
Monroe Doctrine, 370, 373
Montaigne, Michel de, 180
Montcalm, Marquis de, 224
Montezuma, 210
Mont St. Michel, 159
More, Sir Thomas, 195
Morocco, 382–383, 386, 387–388
Morse, Samuel F. B., 306
Moses, 32–33
Moslems, 111, 115–118, 131–132
   Crusades against, 160–161
motion pictures, 307
Munch, Edvard, 470
Munich, 432
Muscovy, 175
Mussolini, Benito, 292, 345, 421, 426, 437
Mycenae, 31–32, 34

Nabatea, 114
Napoleon Bonaparte, 247, 248–249, 269
Napoleon, Louis, 263, 264
Napoleon III, 289, 290, 294, 310–311
Narbonne, 96
nationalism, 207–208, 254, 320, 360
   in Europe, 171
   German, 292–300
   Irish, 318
   Italian, 288–292

nationalism *(cont.):*
    in nineteenth-century Europe, 268–271
    racism and, 339
*National Life* (Pearson), 340
National Socialism. *See* Nazis
national sovereignty, 254
natives, imperialism and, 347–348, 356–359, 361–362, 369, 376, 457
NATO, 448–449
naturalism, 179
natural selection, 282–283
naval stores, 200
Nazis, 421, 426–430
Nebuchadnezzar, 38
Nehemiah, 38
Nehru, Jawaharlal, 360
Neolithic agricultural revolution, 17
Netherlands, 216
    *See also* Holland
Newcomen, Thomas, 207
New England colonies, 219–220
New France, 204–205, 364, 367
New Harmony, Indiana, 275
New Lanark, Scotland, 274–275
New Spain, 212–213
New Testament, 100
Newton, Isaac, 206
New World, 194, 209, 212, 219
New Zealand, 355–359, 401
Nicholas II, 331
Nietzsche, Friedrich, 207, 308
nihilists, 329
Nile Valley, 23
Nobel Prize, 299, 325
nobility, in modern Europe, 201
nomads, 83
Normandy, 155
Normans, 146
North Africa, 440
North Atlantic Treaty Organization (NATO), 448–449
Northumbria, 142
Norway, 436
Nova Scotia, 205
Numidia, 88

Octavian (Augustus), 90, 93–94, 97
October Manifesto, 331
*Odyssey*, 13
*oikos*, 40, 53
*oikumene*, 71
Old Testament, 32, 38, 79, 80

Olympic games, 57
*On Liberty*, (Mill), 264–265
*On the Nature of Things* (Lucretius), 92
*On the Revolutions of the Heavenly Orbs* (Copernicus), 206
Open Door Policy, 372–373
Optimates, 88, 89
*Opus Dei*, 15
oral tradition, Greek, 42
Orangement, 319
oratory, 91
*Origin of Species* (Darwin), 282–283
Ostrogoths, 109
Ottoman Empire, 378, 385–386, 401, 413
Ottoman Turks, 117, 174–175
Ovid, 92
Owen, Robert, 274–275
Owen, Robert Dale, 275

Pacific, U.S. in, 369–370, 371–372
painting, 179–180
Palacky, Frantisek, 320–321
Palestine
    ancient, 33, 36–39
    in Hellenistic period, 75, 78–82
    modern, 458
    under Roman Empire, 99
Palmyra, 105, 114
Panama Canal, 373
Pankhurst, Emmeline, 316
*Panther*, 387
papacy, 135, 136, 138, 142, 157, 158, 160, 163, 172–174, 182, 187, 188, 292, 294–295, 462
papal infallibility, 295
Papal states, 173, 259, 289, 290, 291–292
Papineau, Louis-Joseph, 365
Paris Commune, 311
Parliament, House of, 265
parliamentary government, 227
Parnell, Charles, 318
*pars occidentalis*, 105
*pars orientalis*, 105
Parthian Empire, 51, 81, 104
parties, political
    Austrian, 326–327
    British, 315–319
    French, 312
Pasic, Nikola, 385, 393
pastoralists, 18
patricians, 85
patron, 123

Pax Romana, 97, 102
Peace of Augsburg, 214
Peace of Paris, 224, 225
Peace of Westphalia, 222
Pearson, Karl, 340
peasants, 201, 271
   in early Europe, 152
   French, 236–238, 246
   Russian, 328–329, 332, 422
Peasants' War, 153
Pelopennesus, 30, 31
Peloponnesian War, 49, 63
Pepin, 143
perfectibility, 228
Pericles, 65
*perioeci*, 55
Perry, Matthew C., 369
Pershing, John J., 407
Persia, 39, 108
   in Hellenistic period, 75, 76, 78, 83
   Sasanid, 51, 52, 112
Persian Empire, 50, 52, 61–63, 69, 70, 125
Persian War, 45
Peru, 211
Petain, Henri-Philippe, 437
Peter I, 385
Peter the Great, 329
Petrarch, 176
phalanx, 273–274
Pharaohs, 23–24, 77
Pharisees, 81
Philip II, 214, 215, 216
Philip IV, 163
Philip of Macedon, 50, 70
Philippines, 370, 371, 372
Philistines, 36–37
philosophers, Greek, 57–58, 66–68
*philosophes*, 228–229, 232
philosophy
   in the Enlightenment, 228–229
   Greek, 57–58, 66–68
   Islamic, 131
   in Renaissance, 178
   Roman, 91–92, 93
   in seventeenth century, 226–227
photography, 307
*Physics and Politics* (Bagehot), 286
Picasso, Pablo, 427
Piedmont (Italy), 288–289
Pisistratus, 56
Pius VII, 259
Pius IX, 296

Pizarro, Francisco, 211
plague, 168, 233
Plato, 67–68
Platt, Orville H., 372
plebians, 85–86
Plekhanov, George, 330
plow, 19, 140
Plymouth, 220
poetry, 40–41, 92
Poincare, Raymond, 388
poison gas, 400, 409
Poland, 255, 262, 400, 401–402, 413, 435–436, 443–444, 456
Polignac, Prince of, 261
*polis*, 56–59, 63–68, 69, 72, 77
*politeuma*, 79
Pompey (Gnaeus Pompeius), 89
Pontus, 89
Populares, 88
population
   boom in Europe, 334–335
   in eighteenth century, 233
   Malthusian theory of, 279–280
   in modern world, 462
   in traditional Europe, 168
Populists, Russian, 329
Portugal, 208–215, 426
   monarchy in, 214
   versus Holland, 218
*potentiores*, 104
Potsdam conference, 443
power, balance of, 344–345
power, electrical, 306–307
predation, 16, 17
preparation, doctrine of, 362–364, 368
presidios, 213
price revolution, 200
primacy, 7
*Prince, The*, (Machiavelli), 178
*Principia Mathematica* (Newton), 206
*Principles of Ethics* (Spencer), 285
*Principles of Population* (Malthus), 279
printing, 180, 200, 305
profit motive, 199
progress, 191, 232, 333, 340
proletariat, 279
   dictatorship of, 281
promiscuity, 274
propaganda, World War I, 410–411
Protestantism, 182–188
Prussia, 256, 293–296, 311
Ptolemaic Egypt, 72, 77–78

Ptolemy, 78
public speaking, 91
Puerto Rico, 371
Punic Wars, 87
Puritans, 219–220
pyramids, 23

Quebec Act, 364–365

Rabelais, Francois, 180
racism, 214, 286, 325, 338–340
    imperialism and, 348, 359, 362–363, 457
radicalism, 461
railroads, 235, 236, 308
    electrical, 306
Ranke, Leopold von, 299
rationalists, 228–229
reactionism, 259–260
Read, Herbert, 414
*Realpolitik*, 272, 292, 292
reason, 226–227, 228–229, 232
recency, 7
Red Army, 422, 447
*Reflections on the Revolution* (Burke), 257, 258
Reform Act of 1832, 263
Reform Act of 1867, 315
Reformation, 176, 181–190
refrigeration, 308
Reichstag, 297, 299
Religion, 119
    in Age of Discovery, 194–195, 212–213
    in ancient Greece, 43
    in Byzantine Empire, 112, 113–114
    Darwinism and, 283–284
    in early Europe, 135–138, 156–159
    Greek, 57
    industrial revolution and, 234
    liberalism and, 266–267
    in medieval period, 125, 126, 148, 163
    modern, 462
    Reformation and, 181–190
    in Roman Empire, 99, 105–106, 107–108
    science versus, 206–207
    in traditional Europe, 166–167, 172–174
    *See also* specific religions
Rembrandt, 217

Renaissance, 149, 175–181
Renan, Ernest, 287
Republic, French, 247, 311–312
republican government, 247
revolutions, 260–264
    *See also* American Revolution; French Revolution
rhetoric, 91
Rhine-Danube frontier, 96, 104
Rhodes, 78
Rhodes, Cecil, 350, 380
Rhodesia, 348
Ricardo, David, 280
Richelieu, Cardinal, 222–223
rights, 246, 267
    natural, 244
Robespierre, Maximillien, 247
*robot*, 201
Roca, Julio, 374
Rockefeller, John D., 285
Rodin, Auguste, 229
Rolfe, John, 220
Rollo, 155
Roman Church, 113–114
Roman Empire, 51–52, 84–85, 90, 93–99
    contact with China, 102
    decline of, 103–111
    duration of, 125
    economic system in, 97, 103, 105, 106
    influence on European Renaissance, 175–176
    military in, 98, 106, 107
    political system in, 98–99
    religion in, 99, 100–102, 105–106, 107–108
    social classes in, 97, 104
    stability in, 98
Romania, 389–390
Roman law, 98
Romanticism, 269
Rome
    government in, 88–90
    intellectual life in, 91–93
    military power of, 87–88
    origins of, 85
    social structure in, 85–86, 90–91
Romulus and Remus, 86
Roosevelt, Theodore, 287, 373
Rosetta stone, 27
Rouen, France, 198

Rousseau, Jean-Jacques, 244
Royal Commission, 203
rubber, 307
Rubicon, 89
Rule of St. Benedict, 137
Russia, 175, 205, 255, 382
   imperialism of, 374
   industrialization of, 331–332, 425
   in Mediterranean, 378–379
   post-World War I, 422–426
   revolution in, 260, 405
   tsarist, 327–332
   in World War I, 386, 388–389, 390, 394, 398–399, 401, 402–403, 404, 405, 411
   in World War II, 437, 440–442
   *See also* Soviet Union
Russian Social Democratic Party, 330
Russification, 374
Russo-Japanese War, 331, 374

Saba, 114
Sadducees, 81, 99
saint-critics, 167
Saint-Simon, Count of, 275
Saladin, 162
Salamis, 61
Salazar, Antonio de, 426
Salisbury, Lord, 353
Samson, 36, 37
Sarajevo, 392
Sargon of Akkad, 22
Sasanid Empire, 51, 52
Sasanid monarchy, 104, 107, 112
Sasanids, 83, 125
Saul, 37
savagery, 12–13
Saxony, 154
Sazanov, Sergei, 392, 394
Scandinavia, 145, 156
Schlieffen, Count von, 390
Schnitzler, Arthur, 321
Schonerer, George von, 325–326, 327
Schubert, Franz, 321
science
   in Age of Discovery, 205–207
   nineteenth-century, 305–309
   in the Enlightenment, 228
scientific method, 196, 226, 227
Scriptures, 79, 181, 182
sculpture, 179

Sea Peoples, 33–34
sea power, 225, 343, 384, 399–400, 403–404, 406
sea travel, 196–197
secularism, 163
security
   golden age of, 337–338
   search for, 5, 7, 16
Selden, John, 203
Seleucids, 77, 78, 80
self-definition, 11
self-government, 254
Seljuk Turks, 147, 148, 161
Septaguint, 79
Serbia, 260, 385, 389–390, 393–394, 402
Serbs, 385–386, 389
serfdom, 144
   in Russia, 327–330
Servetus, Michael, 186
Seven Years' War, 224, 225
Severus, Septimus, 103
sexuality
   in ancient Greece, 60
   religion and, 183
Shakespeare, William, 180
*shari'a*, 131
Shaw, George Bernard, 308
shipbuilding, 308
Sieyes, Emanual-Joseph, 245
Singapore, 343
Sistine Chapel, 180
Slater, Samuel, 235
slavery, 327, 338–339, 347
   in ancient Greece, 40, 42, 59
   in early Europe, 143
Slavic peoples, 128, 129
Slavophiles, 329
Slavs, 112
Smith, Adam, 202, 267, 279, 343
social class
   British, 317
   capitalism and, 199, 201
   in early Europe, 143–144
   in eighteenth-century Europe, 233–234
   Industrial Revolution and, 235
   in Roman Empire, 97, 104
   *See also* aristocracy; middle class; peasants
*Social Contract, The* (Rousseau), 244
Social Darwinism, 284–287

Social Democratic Party, 326, 335–336
Social Democrats, German, 297–298
*Social Evolution* (Kidd), 340
socialism, 272–275, 310, 335
　evolutionary, 336
　German, 297–298
　Marxian, 276–279, 281
*Social Statics* (Spencer), 284
society
　boundaries of, 12
　as contract, 258
　origins of, 18
Socrates, 66–67, 69, 92
*solidus*, 130
Solomon, 37
Solon, 56
*Song of Roland*, 126
sophists, 66
Sophocles, 65, 68
sorcery, 195
South Africa, 381
South America, exploration of, 209
Soviet Bloc, 455–456
Soviet Union, 256
　Cold War and, 446–449
　industrialization in, 425
　modern, 455–456
　pact with Nazi Germany, 436
　post-World War II, 443–444
　in World War II, 440–442
　between world wars, 422–426
　*See also* Russia
Spaak, Paul-Henri, 453
Spain
　exploration and colonization by, 208–215
　Franco's, 426
　medieval, 142
　monarchy in, 208, 214
　Moslem, 131
　Reformation in, 187
　revolution in, 260
　war with England, 216–217
　war with U.S., 371
Spanish Armada, 216–217
Spanish Civil War, 432
Spanish Inquisition, 208
Sparta, 49, 54–55, 63, 69
specialization, 305
Spencer, Herbert, 283, 284–285
Spengler, Oswald, 310
Spice Islands, 209

*Spirit of the Age*, 340
St. Antony the Coenobite, 137
St. Augustine, 125, 137
St. Basil, 137
St. Benedict, 15, 137
St. Jerome, 124
St. John Cassian, 137
St. John of Damascus, 135–136
St. Paul, 100
St. Peter's Basilica, 180
Stalin, Joseph, 424–426, 444, 449
state
　Hegel's view of, 270
　liberal view of, 267
　purpose of, 244–245, 257–258
state governments, European, 190
statism, 171, 189, 194, 248
　mercantilism and, 205
　modern, 221–222, 223
status, 235
　*See also* aristocracy; social class
Statute of Treason, 165
steam engine, 207, 236, 308
steamship, 308
steel, 34
steel production, 341
Stephen, Sir James, 362
Stephenson, George, 236, 308
stewardship, 361
stirrup, 150
stock market crash, 419
stoicism, 93
Stolypin, Peter, 332
*Struggle for Existence in Human Society* (Huxley), 340
student rebellion, 259
submarines. *See* U-boat
subsistence, 280
Suez Canal, 308, 345
suffrage, British, 315–316
suffragettes, 316
Suleiman the Magnificent, 214
Sulla, Lucius, 89
Sumerians, 21–22
*Summa Theologica* (Aquinas), 178
supply and demand, 280
surplus value, 279, 280
survival of the fittest, 282–283
*Sussex*, 404
Switzerland, 269–270
　Reformation in, 185–186
*Syllabus of Errors*, 295

Syria, 132

Taine, Hippolyte, 238
Talmud, 80
tanks, 409–410
tariffs, protective, 199, 202, 268, 316, 344
Tasman, Abel Janszoon, 355
taxation, 201
Taylor, A. J. P., 461
technology, 19
   in Age of Discovery, 205–207
   in early Europe, 151
   German, 298–299
   industrial, 234
   Industrial Revolution and, 236
   modern, 464
   nineteenth-century, 305–308, 335
telegraph, 306
   wireless, 306, 307
telephone, 306
Temple-cities, 20–22
Tennis Court Oath, 245
Tenochtitlan, 210
territories. *See* imperialism
terrorism, 222, 458–459
Tesla, Nikola, 306
Tetzel, 182
Thales of Miletus, 57
Thatcher, Margaret, 454
Thebes, 69
*themistes*, 44
Themistocles, 61
Theodora, 111
Theodore, 114
Theognis, 54
theology, 178, 181–187, 228
   *See also* religion
Thermopoylae, 61
*thes*, 42
thesis-antithesis-synthesis, 278
Thiers, Adolphe, 311–312
*Thinker, The* (Rodin), 229
Third Estate, 245
Third Reich, 429
Third Republic, 311–315
Thirty-Nine Articles, 216
Thirty Years' War, 221–222
Thomson, William, 306
Thrace, 389
Three Emperors League, 379
Thucydides, 68
Thutmose I, 24

Tiberius Gracchus, 88
Tigris-Euphrates Valleys, 36
   development of cities in, 20
time perception
   industrialization and, 234
   Victorian, 340
Timgad, 96
Tirpitz, Alfred von, 382, 384, 388, 399, 403
Titian, 179
Tito, Josip Broz, 449
Tocqueville, Alexis de, 238, 267, 303
tool making, 17
Torah, 38, 79
torture, 165
totalitarianism, 244–245
trade, 197
   in Age of Discovery, 211–212
   in Age of Exploration, 215
   in ancient Greece, 43
   balance of, 202
   Dutch, 218
   in eighteenth century, 243
   free, 202, 267, 341, 342, 343
   imperialism and, 342–343
   overseas, 198
   primitive, 20
   West Indies route, 204
   world, 341–342, 372–373
tragedy, Greek, 59
Trajan, 94–95, 103
transatlantic cables, 306
transportation, nineteenth-century, 307–308
Transvaal, 380–381
treason, 165
Treaty of Locarno, 431
Treaty of Paris (1898), 371
Treaty of San Stefano, 378
Treaty of Tordesillas, 212
Treaty of Versailles, 395, 412–414
Treitschke, Heinrich von, 287
Trevithick, Richard, 308
tribunes, Roman, 86, 88
Triple Alliance, 379, 384
Triple Entente, 384
Tripoli, 388
Trotsky, Leon, 405, 422, 424
Truman, Harry S., 445, 448
Truman Doctrine, 447–448
trusteeship, 361–362
tsars, 327–332

## 512 INDEX

Tudors, 208
Turgenev, Ivan, 329
Turkey, 148, 386, 388–389, 401, 406, 408, 411, 448
Turks, 147, 148, 161, 174–175
Twain, Mark, 308
Twelve Tables, 85

U.S.S.R.. *See* Soviet Union
U-boat, 399–400, 403–404, 405, 406
Ulster, Ireland, 318–319
Umayyads, 117
unemployment, during Depression, 420
Union of South Africa, 381
United Kingdom. *See* Great Britain
United Nations, 452–453
United Netherlands Chartered East India Company, 218
United States
  in Cold War, 447–449
  Great Depression in, 419–420
  imperialism of, 346, 368–374
  Industrial Revolution in, 235
  post-World War II, 445
  statehood in, 369
  territories of, 369
  wars and, 256
  war with Spain, 371
  in World War I, 403–405, 406–408, 413
  in World War II, 440, 442
Upper Egypt, 81
Urban II, 160, 161
urbanization, 164, 234, 335
  and Industrial Revolution, 234
  in traditional Europe, 168–169
Utopia, 195
Utopians, 273–275, 281

Valentinian, 106
Valla, Lorenzo, 176
Vandals, 109
van Eyck, Jan, 179
Varthema, Ludovico, 196
Vatican, 292
Verdun, 138, 402
Vespucci, 209
Via Domitia, 96
Victor Emmanuel I, 259–260
Victor Emmanuel II, 289, 290
Victoria (Queen), 316, 342
Victorian Compromise, 316–317
Victorians, 340

Vienna, 175, 320, 321, 323
Vikings, 145
Virchow, Rudolf, 295
Virgil, 92, 98
Visigoths, 142
Viviani, Rene, 392
Volkswagen, 427–428
Voltaire, 229, 232, 244
voting, 266, 315–316
Vulgate, 124

wages, 199, 280
Wakefield, Edward Gibbon, 355–356
war
  Bismarck's conception of, 294
  humane methods of, 222
  justification for, 287
  in nineteenth century, 333
  total, 410
  *See also* specific wars
warlord protectors, 153–155
Warsaw Pact, 448
Washington, George, 225, 226
watermill, 151
Watlings Island, 209
Watt, James, 207, 236, 308
*Wealth of Nations* (Smith), 202, 343
weapons
  modern, 448
  in World War I, 400, 409–410
welfare, social, 164
welfare socialism, 338
welfare state, 316
*Weltpolitik*, 378, 382
Wesleyan Methodists, 347
Wessex, 142, 154
West, Rebecca, 3
"Western" civilization, 455
West Germany, 454
West Indies trade, 204
Whitby Abbey, 166
White Man's burden, 348
Whitney, Eli, 236
Wilhelm, Kaiser, 387, 408
William I, 294
William II, 298–299
William III, 223–224
William the Conqueror, 146
Wilson, Woodrow, 404, 405, 406–407, 412
windmill, 151
Windthorst, Ludwig, 295

witchcraft, 195
Witte, Sergei, 331
Wog, 457
Wolfe, James, 224
women
  in Greek society, 59–60
  role of, 462
women's suffrage, 316
work
  in ancient Greece, 64
  attitudes toward, 15
  *See also* labor
workers
  in early capitalism, 198, 199, 234
  Marxian view of, 280–281
  in view of Utopians, 273–275
World Economic Crisis, 419–421
World War I, 256, 377–414
  casualties of, 412
  factors leading to, 377–392
  fronts in, 395–402, 405–408
  U.S. in, 403–405, 406–408, 413

World War II, 431–443
  casualties of, 442–443
  fronts of, 436–442
  origins of, 431–436
Worms Diet at, 183

Xenophon, 70
Xerxes I, 61

Yahweh, 33, 38
Yalta conference, 443
Yugoslavia, 437, 449

*Zeitgeist*, 340
Zenobia, 105
Zionism, 314, 325
Zola, Emile, 308
Zoroastrianism, 39–40
Zurich, Switzerland, 185
Zweig, Stefan, 336–337
Zwingli, Ulrich, 185